*The Civil War and
Yadkin County, North Carolina*

THE CIVIL WAR AND YADKIN COUNTY, NORTH CAROLINA

——— *A HISTORY* ———

*with Contemporary Photographs and Letters;
New Evidence Regarding Home Guard Activity
and the Shootout at the Bond School House;
a Roster of Militia Officers;
the Names of Yadkin Men at Appomattox;
and 1200 Confederate Army and Navy Service
Records with Parents, Vital Dates,
and Place of Burial for Most*

by FRANCES H. CASSTEVENS

McFarland & Company, Inc., Publishers
Jefferson, North Carolina, and London

Dedicated to the people of Yadkin County
so that they will never forget their heritage

The present work is a reprint of the illustrated case bound edition of The Civil War and Yadkin County, North Carolina, *first published in 1997 by McFarland.*

LIBRARY OF CONGRESS CATALOGUING-IN-PUBLICATION DATA

Casstevens, Frances Harding.
The Civil War and Yadkin County, North Carolina : a history : with contemporary photographs and letters / by Frances H. Casstevens.
p.   cm.
"New evidence regarding home guard activity and the shootout at the Bond School House; a roster of militia officers; the names of Yadkin men at Appomattox; and 1200 Confederate Army and Navy service records with parents, vital dates, and place of burial for most."

Includes bibliographical references and index.

ISBN-13: 978-0-7864-2444-3
softcover : 50# alkaline paper ∞

1. Yadkin County (N.C.)—History.
2. North Carolina—History—Civil War, 1861–1865.
3. Soldiers—North Carolina—Yadkin County—Registers.
4. Sailors—North Carolina—Yadkin County—Registers.
5. Yadkin County (N.C.)—Genealogy.
6. Registers of births, etc.—North Carolina—Yadkin County.
I. Title.
F262.Y19C37   2005
973.7'09756'66—dc21
97-18931

British Library cataloguing data are available

©1997 Frances H. Casstevens. All rights reserved

No part of this book, specifically including the index, may be reproduced or transmitted in any form or by any means, electronic or mechanical, including photocopying or recording, or by any information storage and retrieval system, without permission in writing from the publisher.

Cover photograph: Captain Reuben E. Wilson, "Yadkin Gray Eagles,"
later Company A, 1st Battalion Sharpshooters
(courtesy of Lucille Hauser Miller and Greensboro Historical Museum)

Manufactured in the United States of America

*McFarland & Company, Inc., Publishers
Box 611, Jefferson, North Carolina 28640
www.mcfarlandpub.com*

Table of Contents

Acknowledgments	vi
Preface	1
Introduction	5
1 The Influences of Geography, Politics, Economics and Religion on War Sentiment in Yadkin County	9
2 Yadkin Men on the Battlefield	27
3 On the Home Front: Civilian Life	61
4 "Conditions Are Deplorable in Yadkin": Militia and Home Guard Activity	71
5 The Counter Rebellion—The Bond School House Affair	85
6 The Yankee Invasion—Stoneman's Raid	97
7 The Aftermath—Results of the War on Life in Yadkin County	105
Epilogue	125
Appendices	
A. Civil War Letters and Documents Relating to the Bond School House Affair	127
B. Yadkin Men Present at Appomattox, April 9, 1865	155
C. Rank Above Private Achieved by Yadkin Confederate Soldiers	157
D. Confederate Units in Which Yadkin Men Served	160
E. Officers of Yadkin Militia, 75th Regiment, 18th Brigade	162
F. Yadkin Veterans and Widows Who Drew Pensions, 1900–1910	165
G. Exemptions from Yadkin Home Guard Duty	176
H. Yadkin Men in the Confederate Military, 1861–1865	179
Bibliography	287
Index of Names	293

Acknowledgments

I WISH TO THANK all who provided information about their Civil War ancestors with me; without them this book could not have been written. I could not possibly list all those who have shared their family stories, photographs of Civil War ancestors, and copies of their service records. I have been encouraged by so many people, and I extend my sincere appreciation to each and every one of them.

My gratitude extends to the Yadkin County Public Library and the Yadkin County Historical and Genealogical Society, Inc., for their assistance in making reference material available.

Original material housed at the University of North Carolina–Chapel Hill, Duke University, and the North Carolina Department of Archives and History has been invaluable. Special thanks go to Louis H. Manarin and Weymouth T. Jordan, editors of *North Carolina Troops 1861–1865: A Roster*. The Forsyth County Public Library in Winston-Salem has provided access to much resource material, such as the *Official Records of the War of the Rebellion*, and old newspapers such as the Salem *People's Press*, which they have available on microfilm.

I am especially grateful to Allen Speer who rekindled my interest in the Civil War and inspired me to get my own book finished, as well as to Victor Seiders, a Civil War enthusiast. Stephen Bradley's and Gerald Wilson Cook's works on the North Carolina Militia proved most helpful. Both Lewis Brumfield and Alice Brumfield were helpful in this endeavor. Andrew Mackie assisted in many ways.

Cheryl L. Martin and Gary D. Reeder of Trinity, North Carolina, kindly supplied numerous names of Yadkin County soldiers, service records, and personal information.

Tim Casstevens, my son, who shares my interest in the Civil War, helped make possible several trips to Civil War battlefields. He also assisted in proofreading and making helpful comments which have added to the overall usefulness of this work.

Bertha Hemric McKinney and Studio One did an excellent job of reproducing some of the old photographs used in the book. I appreciate the drawing of the Confederate flag by Selinda Blackwell and that of the flag presented to the Yadkin Gray Eagles, drawn by my daughter, Caren Casstevens.

The names of others who sent information appear at the beginning of Appendix H, and in the Bibliography.

Preface

I HAVE COMPILED this book because I love my county, my state, and my country. I am a historian and a genealogist—the two disciplines are really inseparable. This book is not so much a history of the Civil War as a portrait of the political, religious, socio-economic, and genealogical history of the people of Yadkin County, North Carolina, who lived through some of the worst years in the history of our nation. To the scholarly historical and genealogical research, I have added the oral history and traditions of Yadkin County.

My interest in the American Civil War began when I read *Gone with the Wind* as a child. I then began reading everything I could find on the conflict, and I wrote a short story about a soldier returning home from the war in a high school English class. We were taught very little about the Civil War or any other military history in public school, but college provided the opportunity for me to really delve into Civil War history. While in graduate school at the University of North Carolina at Greensboro I chose the "Military Career of Brigadier Thomas Lanier Clingman" as my master's thesis.

By 1981, when the Yadkin County Historical and Genealogical Society, Inc., began collecting material for the *Heritage of Yadkin County, North Carolina,* information regarding the Civil War years began to surface. Several people submitted letters written by relatives who served in the Confederate Army. The late Hilton Jones submitted the names of the participants at the Bond School House affair, a "shootout" between the local militia and several deserters and draft dodgers in 1863. Other undocumented stories regarding Home Guard activity began to surface and were published in the *Heritage* volume. These stories stimulated interest in the Bond School House affair and in what actually happened in Yadkin County during the war. Documentation is often unavailable, but recently some letters have been located that shed more light on the Bond School House affair, as well as Home Guard activities during the war years.

Several years later, I began compiling a list of the Yadkin County men who served in the Confederate States Army. The only existing list was that of the late William E. Rutledge, Jr., published in 1961 in his book *An Illustrated History of Yadkin County, 1850–1965,* but it was inaccurate and incomplete. Rutledge used the sources available at the time, but this was before the North Carolina Division of Archives and History began its still ongoing project entitled *North Carolina Troops 1861–1865: A Roster*. By the time I started my list, several volumes of *North Carolina Troops* had been published. I also used earlier regimental histories, such as Walter Clark's *Histories of the Several Regiments* and Moore's *Roster of North Carolina Troops* to determine which regiments contained Yadkin County men. These names and other data were put into a computer database, and could be sorted by last name, regiment and company, place of burial, or date of death. As much additional personal information as possible was added about each individual soldier. This information was obtained from personal correspondence, queries published in the *Journal of the Yadkin County Historical Society*, county records, census records, family histories and genealogies, tombstone inscriptions, and oral tradition.

This preliminary list was published in the *Journal of the Yadkin County Historical and Genealogical Society* over several issues in 1992 and 1993 and resulted in the submission of additional names of Confederate soldiers. To date, the list is composed of the names of nearly 1,200 men (with the possible exception of a few duplicate names, which cannot be corrected due to lack of information about members of the Home Guard and Militia).

Then I decided I wanted more than just a list of names. I wanted to include background information on the soldiers and their families back home. I wanted not only to document events but to understand why they happened. Research into primary and secondary accounts, and of a number of letters written during the war years filled in some of the gaps. This book is the result.

Throughout this book I have tried to describe a number of events witnessed by Yadkin County people, in order to add to our understanding of those times. The first chapter describes Yadkin County as it was before the war began in 1861. The second chapter focuses on the early enthusiasm, the formation of Yadkin County regiments, and events in the daily lives of soldiers on the battlefront. The next chapter describes the war years and the hardships endured by the folks at home. The activities of the Home Guard and Militia and the problem of rounding up deserters is the focus of a chapter. Another chapter examines the Bond School House affair with the help of new information on that tragic event. Stoneman's Raid through Yadkin County is described in a separate chapter. The final chapter deals with some of the long-term effects of the war on Yadkin County and its people.

Countless books already have been written on the Civil War, so I have not rehashed the causes of the war or given detailed accounts of battles. Instead, I have included a list of the major battles in which Yadkin men were involved and concentrated more on individual lives.

A number of unpublished letters from soldiers and their families mentioned in the text are reprinted in full in Appendix A. The original spelling gives one a sense of how the words were pronounced, but it makes reading difficult, so most of the letters have been presented with modernized spelling.

Correspondence from the Adjutant General's papers to the local Militia units and the Home Guard helped clarify some conflicting accounts, since both organizations have been blamed, perhaps unfairly, for various acts committed in the county. Documents relating to the Bond School "shootout" are also presented in Appendix A.

Appendix B lists most Yadkin men who were present at the surrender at Appomattox Court House on April 9, 1865. Appendix C is a list of the names of officers in various regiments, those who obtained a rank above private in the Confederate military service and in the State Militia and Home Guard.

While there were some companies that were comprised almost entirely of Yadkin County men, Yadkinians also served in other North Carolina regiments, and regiments from other states. A list of those is found in Appendix D.

Appendix E lists the officers of the 75th Regiment, 18th Brigade, North Carolina Militia. The names of privates have not been preserved. Other names appeared in Stephen Bradley's *North Carolina Home Guard Examinations 1863–1864*. Those veterans or their widows who were drawing Confederate pensions from 1900 to 1910 are listed in Appendix F. Those Yadkin County men who were examined for a medical exemption from Home Guard duty appear in Appendix G.

The last section, Appendix H, is an alphabetical list of the nearly 1,200 men and boys known to have served in the Confederate States Army, the Confederate States Navy, the North Carolina Militia, and the Home Guard units of Yadkin County, together with the name of the company and regiment in which they served. Service-related information from the 13 published volumes of *North Carolina Troops 1861–1865: A Roster* is included here. Personal information, such as dates of birth, marriage, death, place of burial, parentage, names of wives and children, is also included if available. The text also includes some short biographical sketches about life after the war for some of those mentioned in earlier chapters.

I have excluded those Yadkin men who originally joined the Union Army. Those men who left Yadkin County before 1850 are not included, although I have mentioned Brigadier General Thomas Lanier Clingman, who often returned to Yadkin County to visit his family, and who lived here while recovering from wounds received in Virginia in August of 1864.

Nothing in this book is intended to call undue attention upon the acts of any one person before, during or after the Civil War, nor is this work intended to glorify any one person or act. I have merely tried to include everything that is known at the present about one particular time in the history of Yadkin County, a time that many have chosen to forget. It was written so that some of the facts about Yadkin County people during the Civil War will not become "lost" again. This information has been very difficult to uncover, but the story that information tells is both too tragic and too grand ever to be forgotten.

Introduction

In MANY PARTS of the South, time is still measured by what happened before "the War" and what happened after "the War." The "War" was the American Civil War, which was fought from the spring of 1861 through the middle of 1865. This war goes by many names: the American Civil War, the War of the Rebellion, the War for Secession, the War for Southern Rights, the War Between the States, the Late Unpleasantness, the War of Northern Aggression, Mr. Lincoln's War, and others. It has been called the first "modern" war. The impact of this particular war on our culture and our way of life was so great that it has taken more than a century for us to come to grips with that event and with the part our ancestors played in it. Even today, the Civil War stirs emotions in the hearts of many.

Rather than letting the Civil War become lost in the mists of time, many people seem determined to learn the truth and to explore every aspect of the times, the people, and the events. A movement toward "re-enacting" the war is sweeping the country. Everywhere there are men and boys dressed in the garb of Civil War soldiers, carrying and firing rifles and guns, riding horses and marching in parades, in an attempt to make history come alive. The wives and the children of the re-enactors are also taking part. Chapters of the Sons of Confederate Veterans are increasing in number. Television movies and feature films such as "Gettysburg" are watched with interest by Northerners and Southerners alike.

In the closing years of the 20th century, the vast amount of information available about the Civil War is proliferated through the use of computers and the "Information Superhighway"—the Internet. A large number of contemporary letters and diaries are being published. Almost daily, a new book on the Civil War based on these sources becomes available. We have tools that earlier generations never dreamed about—census records (published or on microfilm), military pay vouchers, a list of North Carolina's troops meticulously compiled from official records by the North Carolina Department of Archives and History, cemetery listings, artifacts from battlefields, guided tours of battlefields, books with pictures of North Carolina's soldiers, and television documentaries about the war, individual generals, and battles. This information, together with the number of re-enactments across the country, gives us some feeling for the horrors of battle, and the trials and tribulations of soldiers and their families.

Yet, nothing of any substance has been published about Yadkin County during in the Civil War. In the closing years of the 20th century, we want to know. Those who could have answered our questions are dead, and the stories they could have told died with them.

That part of the past that connected Yadkin County to the events of the Civil War has been repressed, suppressed, and distorted until it is in danger of being entirely forgotten. While practically every courthouse lawn in the South has had its Confederate memorial in the form of a statue, a cannon, or some other reminder of the conflict, Yadkin County had no such monument until 1987. Finally, the Veterans of Foreign Wars erected a marker on the north side of the courthouse that listed the names of all who had died in all wars in which Americans had been involved. Until recently, we in Yadkin County preferred to think that the American Civil War had passed us by. Only a few stories have been handed down of the hardships and privation, or of an ancestor who died on the battlefield. An example is Edna Bray Reece, who was born near the turn of the century. Mrs. Reece's grandfather, T. R. Minish, was a corporal in Company H, 54th Regiment. She wrote: "There was little in the old homeplace to indicate that [her grandfather] had ever been to war. There was his sword hanging on a nail in the little, upstairs parlor bedroom."[1] In my own family, a sword and a rifle hung in my father's law office. My father could tell me only that those items belonged to his father's older brother who was killed in the war. The story of Yadkin County soldiers and their families during the years between 1861 and 1865 was unwritten and untold.

Most people today are unaware of the role their ancestors played during the War Between the States. Earlier generations, who might have heard family stories, perhaps thought them best forgotten, and did not pass them along. Family genealogies seldom mention an ancestor's Civil War service. Out of the hundreds of family histories in the *Heritage of Yadkin County*, only a few mention Civil War service or events of the period. Yet, that era is always close to the surface. When people are asked what they have heard about their ancestor and the Civil War, many will come up with some anecdote about a relative who took part (or hid out) during the war.

For the most part, however, it seems that a "conspiracy of silence" about Yadkin County and the Civil War prevails. Why this "conspiracy of silence" in Yadkin County? Many families may harbor secrets that are best forgotten. Others don't know and don't care anything about their family history. The reasons may be simple or complex.

A hatred for the military and county officials was generated by such events as the shootout at the Bond School, the "murder" of deserters from the Confederate Army, and the rounding up of draftees. There may be "skeletons in the closet" that many would like to keep hidden. It may be no coincidence that the names of the Home Guard have not been preserved, nor the names of those they killed in "the line of duty." Perhaps these records were destroyed because the men involved in some of the Home Guard activities did not want to be remembered for those actions. In 1965, a hundred years after the final surrender, when William E. Rutledge, Jr., wrote an account of the shootout at the Bond School House in his *An Illustrated History of Yadkin County, North Carolina*, he chose to delete the names of the participants in that affair in order to avoid any possible embarrassment to the children and relatives of those involved.

I believe that tragedy of one kind or another touched everyone during the Civil War. There were losses in practically every family. The county was divided in its loyalties and hatred for the other side developed. When the war ended, perhaps in the interest of harmony, everyone may have avoided discussion of the war and related events. This silence may have been necessary in order for the grieving to end and the healing process to begin. The war years may simply have been too horrible to talk about. Many were probably too busy trying to eke out a living and rebuild their lives; they did not have time to dwell on the past.

Many Yadkin men deserted from the Confederate Army and some were courtmartialed. A few Yadkin men were executed for desertion. This was information that may not have been passed on to later generations. Many soldiers came home with or without leave to plant their crops. Most often they returned to duty, but deserted again when it was time to bring in the harvest. Some men who were granted "wheat furloughs" never returned to their companies when their leave was up, but hid out for the remainder of the war. Many of the deserters and draft dodgers owned no slaves, and had no one to care for their families and farms while they were away fighting for "the Cause." If one studies the individual cases, a pattern emerges—many deserted, returned to duty, deserted again, returned to duty, and eventually were either wounded, killed, went over to the enemy, or hid out at home. Likewise, many stayed and fought the entire time until they were killed or captured. Those who were captured were imprisoned a few months, then released to return to duty. Many were captured more than once. Casualties from battle and disease were frequent. Some men were wounded more than once, in one or more battles and still survived the war.

The Confederate soldiers who went over to the enemy after being captured perhaps thought it would be better to die in battle than to die in prison. These men were termed "Galvanized Yankees" and were distrusted by both sides. When the "Galvanized Yankees" returned to Yadkin County after the war, there was, probably, animosity toward them. Others left the county, joined the Yankees and fought against their friends, neighbors, and even brothers. Some returned, others did not.

On the other side of the coin, there were many Yadkin soldiers and their families who wholeheartedly supported the Confederacy and its cause. The Choplin family sent five sons and one son-in-law to fight for the Confederacy; only two returned.[2] Others wished to serve the cause but were not allowed to because they were either too old, too young, or too disabled. Several Yadkin County Confederates were with General Robert E. Lee when he surrendered to General U. S. Grant at Appomattox Court House on April 9, 1865 (see Appendix B).

After the war, some returning veterans probably talked about the battles. For many, it may have been too painful. A few remained "unreconstructed" the rest of their lives (see Chapter 7). The wounds and suffering the soldiers endured left visible scars; the hardships and humiliation of defeat or of being confined in Yankee prisons left invisible emotional scars.

With the defeat of the South and the enforcement of the Reconstruction policies, to brag about the bravery of one's ancestors while fighting for the Confederacy would not have been acceptable conversation. Ancestors who lived through the war because they deserted or went over to the enemy (as some did) would not have been talked about either, especially if neighbors and friends had relatives who had died on the battlefield, in the hospitals, or in the Northern prisons. At the same time, outside of Yadkin County, ex-officers who had served on both sides during the war soon began publishing their memoirs and, by the turn of the century, a wealth of information had been published.

One of the major effects of the war was that Yadkin County became a Republican county. Yet, perhaps because the Republican Party's formation was rooted in the events of the Civil War and the Reconstruction years, no one, not even the party's leaders, knows just when the Republican Party was established in Yadkin County.

Over 135 years after the first shots were fired at Fort Sumter in Charleston Harbor, questions are just being asked about the role ancestors played during the war. Were they pro–Confederacy or pro–Union? How did they cope with the death of a husband, brother or son? Which battles was great-grandfather in? Was he killed in battle? Or did he desert? Is he buried near his home or on some far-away battlefield? Is there a tombstone to mark his grave? How did his family manage during and after the war?

To answer some of these questions, I have tried to portray the past as an artist would by adding color to illuminate the shadows. I have included almost everything I have learned about this era to present a different perspective and to provide answers to some of the mysteries. It is my duty and my privilege to share what little I know, in hope that our heritage may be preserved. However, the deeper one delves into the past, the more questions arise.

In 1911, Claude Nicholson wrote a memorial tribute to Harriet Maynard Baity, and said that "A land without memories is a land without history." He described Yadkin County as "preeminently a land of memories—a land rich in history, rich in legends and lays that tell of the memories of long-vanished days. Every citizen of old Yadkin, in fact, every North Carolinian should know this history. Every mother should be able to teach it to her children, the glorious history of Yadkin's sons and daughters."[3]

To our detriment, we have not followed his advice.

Notes

1. Edna Bray Reece, "The T. R. Minish Family Warp and Weft," in Frances H. Casstevens, ed., *Heritage of Yadkin County, North Carolina* (Winston-Salem, N.C.: Hunter Publishing Company, 1981), pp. 508–509.

2. Curtis D. Choplin (compl.), *An American Tragedy: The Robert Choplin Family in the Civil War 1861–1865*, privately published, 1995.

3. Claude Nicholson, "Yadkin County's Centenarian" (Yadkinville, N.C.: *The Ripple*, 1911), courtesy of Thad Baity, Yadkinville, N.C.

1

The Influences of Geography, Politics, Economics and Religion on War Sentiment in Yadkin County

THE AMERICAN CIVIL WAR is unique in our national experience. Yet, some think of it as the second American Revolution. During the American Revolution, the 13 colonies fought against the British. In the America Civil War, the 13 Southern states fought the United States of America. The participants in both wars fought among themselves. The roots of divided sentiments during the American Civil War run deep into the history of our nation. The right to hold and voice opposing opinions is one of the basic tenets of the Constitution and the Bill of Rights. America was founded because of religious dissent.

The Civil War was far more devastating than anything that had happened in America up until that time. The Civil War devastated the South's economy. A generation of its finest young men either lost their lives or were physically or mentally incapacitated. The war had lasting effects on education, economics, religion, and politics for the South, the state of North Carolina and, particularly, Yadkin County. To understand the effects, one needs to contrast pre-war society against post-war society.

Like the nation, North Carolina was divided in sentiment, and that division was principally by regions. The coastal counties, the piedmont counties, and the mountain counties had differences in social structure, economics, religion, and politics. Basically, the coast represented the wealthy, plantation-owner class, the piedmont was and is noted for its thrifty, hard-working German settlers, such as the Moravians, while in the mountains were and are people living in isolated pockets of closely-related families. Yadkin County lies in the piedmont section, but has many similarities with the mountain counties.

Historical Background

Yadkin County is situated on the western edge of what is called the "Piedmont" section of North Carolina. It has rich river bottom land bordering the Yadkin River on the north and eastern borders of the county. Westward, the land changes to gently rolling hills, which culminate in the Brushy Mountains, like stepping-stones nestled at the foot of the Blue Ridge Mountains. Pilot Mountain to the northeast (across the Yadkin River in Stokes County) and the Saurtown Mountains provided distinctive landmarks which guided the pioneers on their journey to the Yadkin Valley. The land is dissected by small branches and larger creeks that flow eastward to join the Yadkin River on its way south to the Atlantic Ocean. Timbered ridges crisscross the county, and the earliest roads followed those ridges.

When the land owned by Lord Granville and his heirs that is now Yadkin County became available for purchase, settlers flocked into the area. Morgan Bryan, Squire and Daniel Boone, Abraham Creson, George Forbush, and several others arrived here by about 1748. These early pioneers traveled down the Great Philadelphia Wagon Road to cross the Yadkin River at the Shallow Ford. At this time, the area was part of Anson County.

The fertile land furnished everything the pioneers needed to live. There were abundant fish and game. Tall forest pine supplied the wood needed for hearth and home. Those who settled Yadkin County were a diverse group, coming from Pennsylvania, Virginia, South Carolina, Connecticut, Maryland, and Delaware. Their immigrant ancestors hailed from England, Ireland, Scotland, Germany, Switzerland, France, Sweden, Holland, and the countries of Africa. Their religious beliefs were as varied, ranging from Catholic to the several Protestant beliefs that were prevalent during the 18th century—Methodist, Baptist, Presbyterian, Quaker, Moravian, and Lutheran.

In politics, economics, philosophy, and lifestyles, Yadkin County was closer to the mountain people, who were opposed to the war, than to the coastal or even to other parts of the Piedmont area of the state. Other differences existed between the plantation class of the "low country," and the "yeoman upcountry" farmers: differences over taxation, internal improvements, election of officials, property qualifications for voting and officeholding.[1] These differences had been building since colonial times, and had erupted in the Regulators' War before the American Revolution. Abraham Creson, one of Yadkin County's earliest settlers, had been involved the Regulators' Movement, a clash between the people and governmental authorities. It was a rebellion against abuses in local government. It was also a clash between those who lived in eastern North Carolina and those who lived in the western counties.[2]

In matters of religion, the Yadkin Valley was closer to the mountain and western Piedmont counties than the coastal counties. The Moravians settled nearby, but they did not establish churches in Yadkin County, although their ministers did visit in some of the German-speaking homes. The back country was visited by the early circuit-riding Methodist preachers, such as Bishop Francis Asbury and Jesse Lee, who inspired the establishment of Methodist churches (Mt. Sinai, Asbury, Center, Jonesville). The Baptists established the Shallow Ford Baptist Church in the mid–1760s, and it was soon followed by Murphy's Church in the South Deep Creek and Petty's Meeting House at Hamptonville. Quakers from Randolph, Guilford, and Chatham counties established Deep Creek Friends and Hunting Creek Friends in the late 1800s.[3] The issue of slavery divided the churches. The Methodist Church split into northern and southern branches, as did the Baptists.

By the 1860s, there had been people in the land "beyond the Yadkin" for approximately 120 years. Some lived there only briefly; others stayed and worked to build communities and towns, operated stores and industries, built and attended churches and schools. Some of the men had served in the French and Indian War, the Regulators' War, and the American Revolutionary War; others had served in the War of 1812, and some had taken part in the Mexican War.

As the population increased, additional counties were formed. In 1750, Rowan County was formed from Anson, and in 1770 Surry was taken from Rowan. Likewise, Stokes, Forsyth and Wilkes counties were formed from what had once been Rowan. Political differences motivated the formation of Yadkin County. After an election to poll public opinion, an act of the North Carolina General Assembly in 1850 separated Yadkin County from the southern part of Surry County, that part lying south of the Yadkin River. The river served as the boundary on the north side and part of the east. The western and southern boundaries are indistinct.[4]

Pre-War Society

Changes began with the formation of the new county of Yadkin. A new county seat was established in the center of the county and named Wilson. Later, the name was changed to Yadkinville. The new town soon attracted settlers and businesses away from some of the older settlements of Huntsville, Hamptonville, and Jonesville. County officials were elected, a county seat chosen, and a courthouse and jail constructed. The period between 1850 and 1860 was one of growth, prosperity, and peace.

The dominant social evolution of the people of North Carolina by 1860 tended toward the "landlocked, isolated, divided, uneducated, backward." There was great emphasis on "sectionalism" and a preoccupation with local affairs which grew "out of the basic geographical conditions that kept the various parts of the state more isolated from each other than from neighboring states." The people also tended to be conservative, individualistic, superstitious, and prone to "physical combat or the duel to settle disputes." The state was divided by "social stratification, or a division of population into coastal and economic classes."[5] These characteristics, however, may not accurately describe Yadkin County people as they were in 1860.

Pre–Civil War society in the county was patterned like the shape of a pyramid. At the top were a few large landowners, such as Tyre Glenn, Joseph Bitting, the Conrads, the Poindexters, the Williams, and the Puryears along the Yadkin River, and these large "plantations" consisting of thousands of acres were farmed by slaves. The majority in the middle of the social scale were the small farmers with their wives and children and few, if any, slaves. At the bottom were the "day laborers" and "domestics" who did not own land but worked for hire for others, and often lived in the household of their employers. There were a few free people of color—black and Indian—and people of mixed ancestry. At the very bottom were the slaves, who had nothing, had no civil rights, and could not leave the land without the permission of their owners.

There was a class of professional people—doctors, lawyers, teachers, preachers, and county officials—who owned and operated farms in addition to their professional work.

The small towns were established before and shortly after 1800. Those existing in 1860 were Boonville, Huntsville, Hamptonville, Jonesville, and Yadkinville. Most of the population lived in the country in small communities a few miles apart, each having a church, a one-room school, and perhaps a store and a mill. The people in the communities knew their neighbors, and usually were related either by blood, marriage, or both. It was a close-knit society.

When Yadkin County was formed from Surry in 1850, it had a population of 9,808 (8,664 whites, 86 free persons of color, and 1,058 slaves). The number of persons owning slaves was 134, according to the 1851 Yadkin County Tax List. These 134 slave owners listed a total of 510 "black polls," which may refer only to black males over the age of 21. The Huntsville district had the most slave owners (25), with the Baltimore district being second with 22 slave owners. The East Bend and Quaker Meeting House districts both had 17 persons who owned slaves. The fewest slave owners were in Knobs Township, where there were only two. Slave ownership was not restricted to males. Nineteen of the total 134 who listed slaves for tax purposes in 1851 were women.[6]

By 1860, according to the Federal Census of Yadkin County, there were 1,436 slaves in the county (692 male and 744 female), a slave population less than 10 percent of the total population. The same was true of all the mountain counties and the Piedmont county of Randolph. Piedmont counties immediately surrounding Yadkin County had slave populations that varied from 10 to 33.4 percent. Only the coastal counties had slave populations of 50 percent or greater of the total population.[7] There were slave traders operating in the county who made vast fortunes dealing in human bondage. One of the slave auction sites was under a large oak tree between the home of T. C. Hauser and Dr. H. C. Wilson, who owned the Wildwood Plantation.

Mrs. Elizabeth Reece Burrus, born near Boonville on November 25, 1843, the youngest of ten children of John and Elizabeth Crutchfield Reece, recalled life in Yadkin County when she was a child in the antebellum period:

> I can recall when neighbors visited a great deal. When I was a little girl, mother had about two or three visiting days a week. She always carried me with her. On the other days we had visitors at home. I have heard her tell about having a visitor in the spring before the beans and potatoes had come, and the salads had given out. She spoke of having nothing to boil. The lady said, "Law, Betsy, just go out and get a mess of narrow dock. Don't you have it?" Mother replied, "Just lots of it, but I didn't think it was good unless mixed with other salads." Both went out and picked some narrow dock [a variety of coarse weeds of the buckwheat family], and cooked it with a piece of meat. Mother said it was as good as any salad she had ever tasted. In those days the visitors helped do the work just as if they were at home.
>
> Cooking was not such a burden then as it is of late years. There was no extra cooking done for company. They ate just what the family was to have for that day. People could have wheat bread and store coffee only twice a week, so if company happened to drop in on those days, they got wheat bread and coffee. For supper the meal was of corn bread and milk, or mush and milk. Pint cups were used for the milk, half-pints for the children. The children also used pewter plates and dishes altogether—so as to keep the other kind from being broken. We also had our little tin cups. Oh, how I wanted a nice plate and glass tumbler like the others, but my mother would say, "When you children get large enough not to break things, you may have the other kind."

In those days everything was very inconvenient. When people needed salt, they had to go on a several days' trip for it. Neighbors would go together with several teams over into Virginia to a salt lake. It was usually necessary to go 20 or 25 miles to the mill. In some sections there were tub mills that would grind corn.

Calico was 25 cents a yard, and everything was in like proportion. But the goods then were very much better than now. A new store dress would last a year, and a nice pair of store shoes, two or three years. People wore home-made dresses and home-made shoes. Any woman, who was anything much, had a silk dress, but it would last many years. In the summer all children went to church and everywhere else bare-footed. For everyday wear, many people wore dresses woven of flax at home. Tablecloths and towels were made of flax cloth. Every man had a flax patch and a cotton patch; all did so in time of the war of '61. In the fall of the year it was so delightful to see the cotton when it was opening. I was certainly delighted to pick it. To pull flax when it was ready was the grandest pastime there was—just to have 8 or 10 in the patch pulling [was a lot of fun].

When a couple married, they built a small log house, made a table and some bedsteads. They would bore holes in a log in one part of the house, put in long pegs and nail undressed plank on the pegs for the table. They made the bedstead on the same plan by nailing a plank to posts in the house. The planks for the floor and ceiling also had to be undressed, for there were no saw mills in those days. Neither was such a thing thought of as a well; everyone built springs at the foot of the hill.

People were more healthy then than now. There were no doctors. [Doctors were plentiful, but some people could not afford to or would not use them.] People made their own medicine out of roots and herbs. If anyone in the family got sick they sent for some old lady in the neighborhood who understood how to fix up different kinds of herb medicines. There was a lot of game in those days. Father said it was not uncommon to go out and kill a deer before breakfast, that the country was full of deer, foxes, squirrels, rabbits, and opossums. There was no end of them.[8]

The typical Yadkin County farmhouse before the 1860s was similar to that of John Martin's, built in 1834. It was a five-room, story-and-a-half log house, with five glass windows. Cooking was done on an open hearth fire in a building separate from the main house. Nearby were a spring, a springhouse, a garden and an orchard. There were shrubs and flowers in the yard, as well as trees to shade the house. On the typical farm, there would also be walnut and pear trees near the house. Outbuildings included a barn, a smokehouse, a corn crib, and perhaps an icehouse.[9] Some farmers also operated a blacksmith shop or a gristmill which families in the community patronized.

The Yadkin County family farm was practically self-sufficient. Few items (other than salt, lead for bullets, writing paper, laudanum, stamps) had to be purchased. Most everything else that was needed was either grown on the farm or made from the raw materials available. In large gardens the farmers grew Irish potatoes, sweet potatoes, cabbage, onions, and other vegetables. Surplus fruit could always be turned into cider or brandy. Corn was grown for bread and to feed the hogs. Clothes were woven from flax or wool, and shoes were made from tanned leather. Tables, chairs, and beds were made from the abundant forest wood. Tobacco was grown for chewing or "dipping," and "corn licker" was made for sipping. Households were large and included not only immediate family members, but also grandparents and younger relatives, who were often employed as laborers or serving girls. The household might include "bound" children who were apprenticed to learn a trade, such as blacksmithing or leather working.

Reps Martin (born January 13, 1836) and Nancy Elizabeth Poindexter Martin, like most families, bought only coffee and a few other items. For sweetening, they generally used cane syrup and honey. They cured their own meat and caught fish in the river. They dried and stored fruits and vegetables for the winter. The women wove all the cloth for clothing and bed linens. They attended log rollings, corn huskings, quilting bees, and barn raisings. Most such gatherings were followed by music and dancing to the "Virginia Reel," but the Reps Martin family did not believe in dancing or drinking and did not participate in those kinds of activities.[10] Horse races were popular, and fortunes were won or lost in a single day. There were "race paths" at Huntsville, East Bend, and other sections of the county.

Religion

The influence of religion played a major part in whether Yadkin citizens were pro- or anti-war. Quakers did not believe in slavery, nor did they believe in killing. For the Quakers, peace testimony meant that they should stand up for their beliefs.

Early in the history of Yadkin County, even when it was a part of Surry County (from 1770 until 1850), there were a number of Quaker (Friends) churches. In the middle of the county, Quaker Deep Creek Friends Church was established as a preparatory meeting by 1784. The church already had a meeting house by 1789, and was officially established as a Friends Meeting by 1793.[11] Swan Creek Baptist Church was originally founded as a Quaker Church before 1797.[12] Hunting Creek Friends Church, near Hamptonville and Windsor's Cross Roads, was established in 1799 or 1801. Abandoned in 1828, the church became active again in 1843.[13] Forbush Friends Church was also established around 1845.[14] These churches were influential in creating an atmosphere in the county that was both anti-slavery and anti-war. Members of Friends churches could be "disowned" for holding slaves, as was the case with the widow Obedience Hutchens Harding, who, after the death of her husband, was thrown out of the Deep Creek Quaker Church in the early 1800s for "owning slaves" she had inherited under the provisions of her husband William Harding's will, the final distribution of which was approved at the August 1800 term of Surry County court.[15] The Quakers had strict rules. A man or woman could also be disowned for "marrying out," which referred to the practice of Quakers marrying non–Quakers.

Methodists and Baptists had also been active in establishing churches in the county: a Methodist Church at Jonesville was founded between 1794 and 1810, and a Baptist Church was founded near the Shallowford in 1769.[16] Mt. Sinai Methodist Church, established about 1808, south of Huntsville, had an upstairs gallery where slaves could sit when they attended services. Other churches established in the late 18th century were

Center Methodist, 1796; and Flat Rock Baptist Church, before 1783. The Yadkin Baptist Association, established by 1786, included the Yadkin churches.[17]

According to Lefler and Newsome:

> Early in the nineteenth century the churches tended to be critical of slavery, but gradually they [with the exception of the Quaker church] shifted to strong defense of the institution and worked for the amelioration of the lot of the slave. The issue of slavery split the Methodist Church into Northern and Southern branches in 1844, and the Baptist churches in 1845. On slavery as well as other social, economic, and moral problems, the churches generally championed the prevailing local attitude.
>
> It would be difficult to overestimate the influence of the churches upon the religious, moral, and social life of antebellum North Carolina. Thousands of people looked to their Protestant ministers as mentors in temporal as well as in spiritual affairs.[18]

Ministers of the gospel in Yadkin County in 1860 were: John Hughes, L. D. Swaim, Thomas Howell, William G. Brown (Baptist); Andrew Thomson, Wesley A. Roby, and J. F. Kerns (Methodist, Episcopal); Isaac Davis and Denson A. Poindexter (probably Baptist); and Silas Livermore, born in Massachusetts (missionary).

Mrs. Elizabeth Reece Burrus, who was a child at this time, described the churches around Boonville where she lived:

> There were only a few churches and these were a long way apart. In some sections stands were built in the groves; in others, arbors were erected. People who lived near enough walked in the summer. They went barefoot until they got near the preaching place, then they stopped and put on their shoes and socks.... There were few denominations in this section. The Baptists were the leading belief; there were Methodists and some few Friends, but very few. The Reece family are Baptists. I remember a meeting house called the old Reece meeting-house. It was built long before I was born [1843], and I am 73 years old.[19]

Churches and brush arbors were attended by large numbers of people, especially during the camp meetings and revivals. When a person died, he was buried soon after, and months later, whenever a preacher was available, a funeral service was held. Basil Armstrong Thomasson, who lived near Hamptonville, wrote in his diary of attending many camp meetings, church services, and memorial services in the 1850s. He noted on February 15, 1854, that "Old Mrs. Willard died, age 104 or 105." Six months later, on August 13, 1854, her funeral was preached.[20]

Education

Education outside the home began in the 1790s with the establishment of schools at some of the churches, such as Flat Rock Baptist and Deep Creek Friends. The

Jonesville Male and Female Academy attracted students from all across the South. The Jonesville Academy was chartered by the State in 1818. By 1861, the Academy advertised that it could furnish competent and experienced teachers, a library, and large buildings well-furnished with apparatus, for a monthly tuition of $6 to $7. The East Bend Academy was flourishing as early as 1854.[21] Dr. John H. Kinyoun was "proprietor" of the East Bend Academy in 1856, and by 1859, the school had 250 students, from as far away as Texas.[22]

In 1839, the first state public school law was passed. It appropriated $40 per year to any area that would provide a building and another $20 in local taxes. Districts were formed and log schools were built. By 1853, Yadkin had 42 districts, with 31 schools. Total enrollment was 1,593. The school term ran from three to four months. The teachers in the county were paid a monthly salary of $10–$15.[23]

In 1859, the number of school districts had increased to 49, and each had a three-man committee to oversee the hiring and firing of the teachers and to make other decisions regarding their particular school.[24]

Mrs. Elizabeth Reece Burrus recalled:

> In those days there was no chance of much schooling. There were only one or two months of schooling in the winter and the schools were so far apart that a good many children couldn't go at all. If they could get a teacher who could read, write, and sort of teach arithmetic, he was thought to be a good scholar; if he should know geography and grammar, he was a most excellent one.[25]

The schools offered a chance of employment for females, and the first female teacher was licensed in Yadkin County in 1856. In the 1860 census, several women list their occupations as "teacher." Just as the public school system was getting started, the war intervened. By 1862, although there were 70 schools with a total enrollment of 1,274 males and 817 females, the school term had been reduced to three months and four days. The total number of eligible children was 3,690, so only about two-thirds were attending school.[26]

But even this meager start had provided some of the lower classes of the population with the rudiments of education. The upper class families, such as the Conrads, the Williams, the Puryears, the Clingmans, the Glenns, the Speers, and the Hardings sent their young men (and women) for higher education at colleges and universities, such the University of North Carolina at Chapel Hill, Union Institute, or Trinity College, or for legal training under Judge Richmond Pearson. Girls, such as Ruth Harding and Annice Speer, attended the academies at East Bend or Jonesville, or the Salem Academy, before entering Greensboro Female College.

Sidney Francis Conrad, born in 1846, first attended the neighborhood free school, starting at age 6. He then attended the private school of Jackson Blackwood in Charlotte, then high school in East Bend, then the Moravian Boys School in Salem, Sheek Military Academy at Madison, and Baldwin High School in Bethania (all before he entered the Confederate Army at age 17).[27]

Whatever education these young men and women acquired was to be invaluable. When the boys entered the Confederate Army, the ability to read, write and count often meant being promoted to the rank of an officer of a company or regiment. Women who could write provided great emotional support by their letters to their men in the service of the Confederacy far from home.

Economics

Economically, Yadkin County had a few large plantations which were maintained by large numbers of slaves. Most farms were small, about 160 acres or less, and could be managed with the help of a wife and several children. The 1851 Yadkin County Tax List shows clearly the pattern of land ownership. For example, in Douthit's District (the Hamptonville area), the largest landowner was James Howard with 639 acres, valued at $795; the smallest was Thomas Blackman with 20 acres valued at $30. In the Huntsville District, which incorporated the Yadkin River bottom land, the largest landowners were Joseph Williams with 3,000 acres; second was H. C. Tapscott with 1,123; Elisha Chin with 636; and William Harding with 600 acres. The acreage of most farms ranged from 50 to 400 acres.[28]

Commerce was mainly carried on in the town and community stores where items that could not be made could be bought. The account books of the T. C. Hauser store in Yadkinville show that in 1855 some of the customers bought hats, wearing apparel, as well as cloth, red cotton cloth, silk, ribbons, pins, spools of thread, and buttons with which to make clothing. Luxury items purchased were silk handkerchiefs and combs. Food items that could not be grown here were purchased, such as pepper, cinnamon, and coffee. Sometimes tobacco (probably chewing or plug tobacco), eggs and sacks of corn were bought. Other household items available included rugs, knives and forks, and tumblers. Washing products included borax, starch, indigo, and cakes of soap. Other chemicals and minerals bought were copperas (used in making inks and pigments), nitric acid (used in making explosives and dyes), and lead (for making bullets). Farming and building tools were available: shovels, pitchforks, whetstones, awls, claw hammers, nails, screws, shingles, and wooden handles. Leather goods were available at the store in addition to shoes and boots, such as saddles, horse traces, and bridle belts. Laudanum (an opium derivative) was often purchased for a variety of ailments and pain. For entertainment, one could buy a fiddle, a fiddle bow, and individual fiddle strings. The most expensive item sold in the store was a fiddle (one at $6, another at $4). The second most expensive item was shoes, which ranged in price from $2 a pair down to $1.25. Another "luxury" item was a set of knives and forks, which sold for $1.50.[29]

The 1850s saw a boom in the fortunes of some of the prominent families in the county. Some of the finest, most durable houses were built in the period 1850–1860, such as the Dalton-Hunt House (built by Sarah Byrd Dalton at Huntsville), Glenwood (the home of Tyre Glenn at Enon), the Foote-Laugenhour house at Footville (built by Henry Foote), Judge Richmond Pearson's home on the Yadkin River, the Jeremiah Glen house near Smithtown, the Gray-Hartman house built in 1860 by Joseph Gray, and the house of Nathan Long at Longtown.[30] These and many more large homes were evidence of an improving economy. Alongside these mansions were numerous small shacks and log cabins which housed the slaves.

Property values in Yadkin County in 1860 were: real property, $1,162,636; personal

$2,261,356, for a total of $3,423,992.[31] The 1860 Yadkin County tax list shows a total acreage of 213,387 (valued at $971,263) and 187 town lots (valued at $37,264). A total of 1,640 persons listed their taxes. Of those, 1,493 were male and 147 female. There were 1,634 households, and 172 houses were unoccupied, for a total of 1,804 dwelling houses.

In 1860, Yadkin County had a total of 38 businesses classified as industries. The 1860 Census of Manufacturers lists: carriage factories 2; flour/meal 4; iron, iron bar, etc. 1; leather 4; liquors, distilled 22; lumber, sawed 3; tin, copper & sheet iron 1; tobacco, manufactured 1.

Yet, basically, Yadkin County was still a rural county, with only a few small, family-owned businesses, such as flour and grist mills, tanneries, distilleries, a tobacco factory, a few stores, and several ferries that carried travelers across the river. But business was increasing: 15 men listed their occupation as "miller" in 1850; the number of millers had increased to 25 by 1860, and 4 millwrights were constructing milling machinery for an occupation.

By 1860, Yadkinville had a "tobacconist," L. D. Kelly, who had moved from Huntsville to Yadkinville when the new town was established. At East Bend there were four more tobacconists: J. W. Nance, J. F. Brown, W. D. Kelly, and J. G. Nicholson.[32] The tobacco manufacturing industry would see its peak in the years after the war and before the turn of the century. In 1860, the milling of flour and meal was the second largest industry in the state, and tobacco manufacturing was third.[33]

There were craftsmen for every need, such as tinsmiths, blacksmiths, shoemakers, tanners, saddlers, hatters, coopers, blacksmiths, carpenters, cabinetmakers, chairmakers, painters, plasterers, carriage makers, brick and stone masons, weavers, tailors, and a potter.

There were a number of "white-collar" professions listed by persons enumerated in the 1860 Yadkin County census. Male teachers were Neil Bohannon, Martin Caudle, Sidney Choplin, J. C. Brown, John M. Folk, A. A. Anderson, John C. Kelly, John W. Allgood, Theodore Griffin, W. H. Brandon, William C. Carter, Wiley W. Johnson, Joseph W. Johnson, Richard G. Green, M. C. Mires, John C. Holder, W. L. Van Eaton, James A. Martin, John D. Johnson, and Jesse Tulbert. Female teachers were Elen Roby, Mary E. Potts, Sarah J. Carington, Mary M. Crumel, Mary E. Davis, and Betty Anglon.

Physicians were numerous: Lewis York, C. L. Cook, R. W. Woodruff, Evan Benbow, John H. Kinyoun, George M. D. Kimbro, H. C. Wilson, John Hampton, Martin L. Cranfill, D. S. Cockerham, Thomas Long, and B. B. Benham. John A. Mock practiced dentistry in Jonesville. Attorneys were John Hampton, Miles M. Cowles, R. M. Armfield, and Joseph Dobson.

County, state, and federal governments provided a number of jobs. The elected and appointed officials in 1860 were: sheriff: William Long; deputy sheriffs: Windford Myers, E. C. Roughton, H. G. Hampton, Wiley Felts; clerk of court: William A. Joyce; Supreme Court clerk: James M. Dodge; constables: John Taylor, George Nicks, George Holcomb, Samuel C. Welch; county trustee: N. G. Howell; county surveyor: Joseph L. R. Naylor; mail carriers: Alvia H. Johnson and Charles Russell; manager of the poor house: Peter Friddle

Richmond M. Pearson was one of the judges of the North Carolina Supreme Court. J. F. Salmons was a "collecting officer" for federal tax on whiskey manufactured. There were also stagecoach drivers and ferry operators, hotel and tavern keepers.

Merchants were N. B. Dozier and Richard Critchfield (Boonville), R. C. Poindexter (East Bend), Neil Bohannon (Huntsville), T. S. Martin, T. C. Hauser, and John H. Ball (Yadkinville), Andrew C. Cowles (Hamptonville), William B. Madison (Zion), J. M. Johnson and A. N. Tomlin (Jonesville). These stores provided jobs for clerks, such as J. M. Hampton, W. A. Dickens, L. M. Cornelius, W. S. Williams, and J. W. Berk. A. H. Thomasson ran a hotel in Yadkinville, and Dr. B. B. Benham owned a hotel in Jonesville.

Although Yadkin County had a very small slave population, there were several slave "traders": Larkin Lynch, Peter W. Welfare, Horace C. Davis, and Joseph A. Bitting were located in Huntsville; E. B. Hampton in Jonesville; and J. M. Myers in Boonville. Others traded in slaves, but were not listed as such, because it was not their main occupation.

A small number of persons engaged in the mining and the production of iron: Stephen Hobson and J. J. Jones, a 45-year-old miner who had been born in Greenland. This industry provided other jobs, such as colliers and hammermen, as well as blacksmiths. However, the majority of Yadkin County men listed their occupations as farmers or farm laborers.[34]

Thus, in 1860, Yadkin County was growing and had the potential for an educated population with opportunities to enter occupations and careers off the farm.

Politics

When trying to understand a people and their beliefs, political preference may be a good indicator. North Carolina voted "Federalists" in the first election in 1789. The Federalist Party, led by Alexander Hamilton, was supported by the New England financial, commercial and industrial classes. Thomas Jefferson and his supporters, known as the "Republicans" (but referred to as the "Democratic-Republicans") believed in an agrarian economy and a weak central government, with the distribution of power spread among the several states. Early in the 19th century, the South was the core of this Republican Party, "but it [also] drew support from agrarian interests, mechanics, and poor people throughout the Union."[35] They were united in their opposition to Hamilton's policies. However, while the Federal government was Federalist, from 1801 to 1815, in North Carolina (with the exception of Benjamin Williams, 1817-18), all of the governors were Republicans.[36]

The Republicans gained strength in North Carolina in 1800, but the election of 1824 split the Republican party into two factions—the National Republicans, led by John Adams and Henry Clay, and the Democratic-Republicans, led by Andrew Jackson and supported in the South and West. John Quincy Adams was elected president in 1824; then Andrew Jackson served from 1829 until 1837.[37] Dissatisfaction with Jackson's policies led to the formation of the Whig Party. The North Carolina Whig Party was formally organized in 1835 and its strongest support was in the western part of the state and on the coast. That support was understandable because the Whigs favored internal improvements, a national bank, protective tariffs, and policies that would help economic development in the inaccessible mountain counties and the coastal cities, which were becoming more trade-oriented.[38]

After 1835 there was bitter rivalry "between the North Carolina Whigs and Democrats in both state and national politics." The Whig Party was even stronger in the western counties than in the east, with such leaders as Willie P. Mangum, John M. Morehead, David L. Swaim, William A. Graham, George E. Badger, James Graham, Thomas L. Clingman, and Zebulon B. Vance, all from western counties.[39] The party leaders favored public schools, internal improvements, sound banks and currency. In 1840, the Whigs were at the height of their power and prevailed in the national elections of 1840, 1844, and 1848. Ironically, the demise of the national Whig Party came when the party failed to take steps against the extension of slavery into the territories. In 1852, Winfield Scott, the last Whig candidate for president, was defeated by Franklin Pierce, the Democratic Party candidate, who was followed by Democrat James Buchanan in 1856. It was at this point that the Republican Party was born (a new party, unrelated to the old Republican Party of Jefferson).[40]

About the time of the demise of the Whig Party, a couple of Yadkin County Whigs, R. F. Armfield and W. A. Joyce, planned to publish a Whig newspaper. Word of the paper was spread. In 1854, a former Yadkin native, Henry P. Clingman, living in Independence County, Arkansas, wrote to a friend in Yadkin, saying that he probably could not get many there (in Arkansas) to subscribe to the paper, because there were "25 democrats to one Whig."[41]

Many Yadkinians were Whig supporters who later supported the Republican Party. Judge Richmond Pearson's sentiments would later carry over as opposition to the Confederate States conscription laws. The Whig and later the Republican Party in the South fared better in the counties with few slaves. The ratio of slaves to whites in Yadkin County was 1:10, a smaller proportion of the population than in some surrounding counties, such as Iredell (4:10), or Mecklenburg (5:8).[42] While Yadkin County had a number of slaves, these were primarily in the hands of a few wealthy plantation owners who lived along the Yadkin River.

Although the Republican Party was not in control of Yadkin County until after the war, there was much to attract Yadkin County residents to it even before the war. Those who opposed slavery, supported a strong central government, and favored internal improvements that could be brought about with Federal money flocked to the Republic Party. Outside the South, between 1854 and 1856 the Republican Party grew in strength. It attracted northern Whigs, "Free-Soilers," "Know-Nothings" and farmers who had been Democrats.

In 1860, the Republican Party nominated Abraham Lincoln, but he was not on the ballot in North Carolina. Still, voters in 1860 were split along sectional lines. The Democrats had their roots in the old Democratic-Republican Party, whose power base came from the small farmers, traders, artisans, as well as plantation owners. Many in Yadkin County were Democrats, and the first sheriff elected in the county in 1852 was Democrat George Holcomb.[43]

In the presidential election of 1860,[44] Yadkin townships voted as follows:

	John Bell (Constitutional Union)	John C. Breckenridge (Southern Democrat)	Stephen A. Douglas (Northern Democrat)
Mt. Nebo	45	117	0
Jonesville	138	46	5
East Bend	94	87	0
Huntsville	38	75	3
Hamptonville	264	47	2
Yadkinville	163	173	12
Total	742	545	22

A vote for John Bell of the Constitutional Union Party was interpreted as a pro–Union vote. Even after the 1860 election, sentiment in Yadkin County continued to be pro–Union. A Hamptonville resident wrote the pro–Union Whig newspaper, the *Fayetteville Observer*, on December 28, 1860:

> We are unanimous for the Union as it is. Some difference of opinion as to the guarantees we ought to insist upon. If there is cause for disunion now, it has existed for 8 years. But as the question is now placed upon us it ought to be settled now and forever; but let reason and forbearance prevail.[45]

North Carolina was hesitant to leave the Union and join the Confederacy. An election was held on February 28, 1861, in the 86 counties that existed in 1861 to send representatives to a convention to consider secession. Of those elected, 42 were secessionists, 28 were conditional unionists, and 50 were unconditional unionists. However, since the people of North Carolina, whether pro-secession or anti-secession, were afraid the convention would vote to secede, they voted against it 47,322 to 46,672. The convention, "which might have been controlled by unionists," never met.[46] In Yadkin County, the vote was 1,490 against the convention and only 34 for the convention.[47]

Sentiments were divided in the spring of 1861. Several leading Yadkin County citizens complained to Governor John W. Ellis in a letter dated April 22, 1861, that:

> Col. Caleb Bohannan, in command of the regiment in Yadkin Co. is a Lincoln man, at least it would seem so from his conduct. Presuming upon his authority as Col. he has called out one of the Companies in the Co. & in making speeches to them, he has declared that no man ought to support the S. Conf. but if Lincoln made a "call for volunteers he hoped to see them come forward," that every secessionist ought to be hung, and that if guns were fired in honor of the capture of Sumter, he would mob those who did it, and actually tried to induce others to join him for that purpose.

The men who signed that letter were H. C. Wilson, T. C. Hauser, J. A. Bitting, T. S. Martin, W. W. Long, T. Long, and J. P. Clingman, some of the richest and most influential men in the county. Five of them were Huntsville area slave owners; slave owners H. C. Wilson and T. C. Hauser lived near Yadkinville. Even before the state left the Union, these men favored secession. They were so concerned about having a Lincoln supporter in charge of militia that they asked the governor to take the command of the regiment away from Capt. Bohannon.[48]

President Abraham Lincoln's call for 75,000 volunteers to put down the "rebellion" after the Confederates took Fort Sumter, and the subsequent federal blockade of Southern ports, tipped the scales, and North Carolina, along with formerly hesitant Southern states, no longer hesitated. In North Carolina another election was set for and held on May 13, 1861, to choose delegates to the North Carolina State Convention which was to vote on whether North Carolina should secede or not.[49]

Before this convention met, a notice appeared in the *People's Press* on April 26, 1861, which announced an important meeting in Yadkin County to elect a delegate to Congress. At this time, Yadkin was still part of the 6th Congressional District:

> THE MEETING AT YADKINVILLE.—We have received the proceedings of a meeting of the citizens of Yadkin County, held in the Court-House at Yadkinville, on the 19th inst., for the purpose of appointing delegates to the District Convention, to be held at Yadkinville, on the 27th inst. As the proceedings of said meeting could possibly only appear in our columns one day previous to the meeting of the Convention, and as our columns are very much crowded we omit the proceedings.
>
> Let delegates from all portions of the District attend the Convention, as business of importance will be transacted; even should no candidate for Congress be nominated.[50]

The next week, the same paper reported:

> THE CONVENTION AT YADKINVILLE.—We learn that at the District Convention held at Yadkinville, last Saturday, the nomination for Congress was tendered to Gen. Leach, which under existing circumstances, he declined.
>
> The citizens of Yadkin and Surry, we learn, are fully aroused to the importance of the times, and they are raising men and money for the defence of Southern homes and Southern fire-sides.[51]

A delegate to that 6th District Meeting, which was held in Yadkinville, took exception to an earlier press report:

> Messrs. Editors.—I see, in a recent issue of your paper, the statement that the Convention of the 6th Congressional District, which assembled in Yadkinville on the 27th ult., tendered to General Leach a nomination as a candidate for a seat in the United States Congress, and that the General, being present, promptly declined it! This statement does great injustice to the delegates composing that Convention. They were not the men to desire to send a delegate to Abraham Lincoln's Congress—to a Capitol filled with hostile bayonets, and ruffian soldiers, collected for the subjugation of the South. And I speak what I know when I say, had a nomination been seriously attempted, a majority of the delegates composing that Convention would have withdrawn

with scorn and indignation. No nomination was made, no proposition to nominate was even voted upon.

By publishing this you will do justice to a body of honorable men, and oblige one who was

A DELEGATE.[52]

Another general election to send delegates to the state convention in Raleigh was held and this time Yadkin County voted overwhelmingly (806 votes) to send R. F. Armfield (the Whig candidate). Dr. H. C. Wilson (the Democrat candidate) received 288 votes. (The *People's Press* reported that Armfield defeated Dr. Wilson by some 500 votes.[53]) The state convention met on May 20, 1861, and an ordinance introduced by Burton Craig declared "that the union now subsisting between the state of North Carolina and the other states, under the title of 'The United States of America,' is hereby dissolved, and that the state of North Carolina is in full possession and exercise of all those rights of sovereignty which belong and appertain to a free and independent state." The same day, the convention ratified the Provisional Constitution of the Confederate States of America.[54]

Once North Carolina joined the Confederacy, delegates to the Provisional Congress of the Confederate States were elected on June 20, 1861. From Yadkin, R. C. Puryear was the delegate. His election, and the delegates from other districts were reported in the local papers.[55]

Confederate Flag (courtesy of Selinda Blackwell).

Thus, after the state convention, Yadkin County somewhat reluctantly found itself a part of the Confederate States of America and at war with the rest of the country.

Notes

1. Daniel W. Crofts, *Reluctant Confederates* (Chapel Hill: University of North Carolina Press, 1989) p. 44.

2. Frances H. Casstevens, "Abraham Creson and the War of Regulation," *Journal of the Yadkin County Historical Society* V (September 1986):4–8.

3. The Rev. David B. Witt, "Flat Rock Baptist Church," in *Heritage of Yadkin County*, pp. 226–227; Mildred Matthews, "Deep Creek Friends Church," in *Heritage of Yadkin County*, pp. 199–201.

4. *Public Laws of North Carolina, 1850–51*, Chapter 40, p. 100.

5. Hugh Lefler and Albert Ray Newsome, *The History of a Southern State: North Carolina*, 3rd ed. (Chapel Hill: University of North Carolina Press, 1973), p. 419.

6. Yadkin County Tax List, 1851, Yadkin County Tax Collector's Office, Yadkinville, N.C.
7. Crofts, p. 41; Frances H. Castevens, "Ante-Bellum Slavery in Yadkin County," *Journal of the Yadkin County Historical & Genealogical Society* V (June 1986): 11–12.
8. Elizabeth Reece Burrus, "Customs of the Early Days," *Journal of the Yadkin County Historical & Genealogical Society* VI (June 1987): 12–13.
9. Winnie Ward Hobson, "John and Jane Kerr Martin Family," in *Heritage of Yadkin County*, pp. 490–491.
10. *Ibid.*, p. 491.
11. Mildred Matthews, "Deep Creek Friends Meeting," in *Heritage of Yadkin County*, p. 199.
12. Frances H. Casstevens," Swan Creek Baptist Church (Independent)," in *Heritage of Yadkin County*, p. 235.
13. Mildred Matthews, "Hunting Creek Friends Church," in *Heritage of Yadkin County*, p. 201.
14. Mildred Matthews, "Forbush Friends Church," in *Heritage of Yadkin County*, p. 200.
15. William Wade Hinshaw, *Encyclopedia of American Quaker Genealogy*, vol. I (1936, rpt. Baltimore: Genealogical Publishing Co., 1969); Frances H. Casstevens, "The Ancestry of William Harding of Surry (Yadkin) County," in *Heritage of Yadkin County*, p. 382.
16. Morgan Edwards, *Materials Toward a History of the Baptist in the Province of North Carolina*, vol. VI. Reprinted in *North Carolina Historical Review* VII (March 1930): 388.
17. Rilla W. Fletcher, "Center United Methodist Church," in *Heritage of Yadkin County*, pp. 205–206; Ruth Harding, "Huntsville Methodist Church (Formerly Mt. Sinai)," in *Heritage of Yadkin County*, p. 207; David B. Witt, "Flat Rock Baptist Church," in *Heritage of Yadkin County*, pp. 225–227; James Albert Hutchens, "Forbush Baptist Church," in *Heritage of Yadkin County*, pp. 227–228.
18. Lefler and Newsome, p. 419.
19. Burrus, p. 13.
20. Basil Armstrong Thomasson, "Book of Remembrance," vol. 1, August 23, 1853–July 4, 1857. Typescript, by Jean Harris Thomasson, 1980.
21. Fred C. Hobson, "Education in Yadkin County, in *Heritage of Yadkin County*, pp. 246–247.
22. Julia Harris O'Daniel and Laura Conrad Patton, *Kinfolk of Jacob Conrad*, privately published, 1970, p. 157
23. *Ibid.*, 242–243.
24. "1859 Yadkin County Committees for School Districts," *Journal of the Yadkin County Historical & Genealogical Society* VI (September 1987): 21–24.
25. Burrus, p. 13.
26. Hobson, pp. 245–246.
27. O'Daniel and Harris, p. 338.
28. Yadkin County Tax List, 1851, Tax Collector's Office, Yadkin County Court House, Yadkinville, N.C. Also reprinted in the *Journal of the Yadkin County Historical Society* IV (March 1985): 17–19; *Journal* V (September 1986): 19–21.
29. "Old Store Account Books," *Journal of the Yadkin County Historical & Genealogical Society* XI (September 1992): 23–24. This article lists the names of some of the customers of the T. C. Hauser Store from March 19 to August 2, 1855, and was extracted from the original account books, which are in the possession of the Charles Bruce Davis Museum of Art, History, and Science, Inc., Yadkinville, N.C.
30. Lewis Brumfield, ed., *Historical Architecture of Yadkin County, North Carolina*. Winston-Salem, N.C.: Winston Printing Co., 1987.
31. *Eighth Census of the United States—1860: Statistics* (Washington, D.C.: U.S. Government Printing Office, 1866), p. 309.
32. *Population Schedules of the Eighth Census of the United States*. National Archives Microfilm Publication, Microcopy No. 653, Roll 919, North Carolina, vol. 17, 501–945, Yadkin and Yancey Counties, Department of Archives and History, Raleigh, North Carolina (hereinafter cited as 1860 Yadkin Census).

33. Lefler and Newsome, p. 398.
34. 1860 Yadkin County Census; *Heritage of Yadkin County*, pp. 154–155.
35. Lefler and Newsome, p. 287.
36. *Ibid.*, p. 301.
37. *Ibid.*, pp. 340–44.
38. *Ibid.*, pp. 344–345.
39. *Ibid.*, p. 345.
40. Frances H. Casstevens, "The Republican Party in Yadkin County," in *Heritage of Yadkin County*, pp. 184–185; Blum, p. 845.
41. H. P. Clingman to Joe, June 15, 1854. Southern Historical Collection, University of North Carolina, Chapel Hill, N.C., S. H. Steelman Papers, #4074. Armfield and Joyce refer to Yadkin County Attorney R. F. Armfield and W. A. Joyce.
42. *Eighth Census of the United States, 1860: Statistics.*
43. Stephen W. Comer, "The Democratic Party in Yadkin County," in *Heritage of Yadkin County*, pp. 182–183.
44. Election Returns of Yadkin County, North Carolina, State Department of Archives and History, Raleigh, N.C.
45. James H. Boykin, *North Carolina in 1861* (New York: Bookman Associates, 1961), p. 137.
46. Lefler and Newsome, p. 449.
47. Election Returns of Yadkin County, North Carolina, State Department of Archives and History, Raleigh, North Carolina..
48. Noble J. Tolbert, ed., *The Papers of John Willis Ellis*, vol. II, 1860–1861 (Raleigh, N.C.: State Dept. of Archives and History, 1964), pp. 662–663.
49. Lefler and Newsome, p. 450.
50. Salem, N.C., *People's Press*, April 26, 1861.
51. *Ibid.*, May 3, 1861.
52. *Ibid.*, April 26, 1861.
53. *Ibid.*
54. Lefler and Newsome, p. 451.
55. Salem, N.C., *People's Press*, June 21, 1861.

2

Yadkin Men on the Battlefield

WHETHER THE PEOPLE of Yadkin County wanted to go to war or not, their destiny was out of their control. National events had a great bearing on the events that took place in North Carolina and in Yadkin County. Below is a correlation of events that occurred outside the county and state and the resulting actions taken by the state and the county. Some of these events will be dealt with in detail in subsequent chapters. The events at the Bond School House were certainly related to the enforcement of Confederate conscription laws, and Lincoln's Emancipation Proclamation, which took effect January 1, 1863.

Event Outside Yadkin County

Lincoln elected president in Nov. 1860. Seven states secede.

Lincoln inaugurated March 1861. Ft. Sumter, S.C., fired on 4-12-1861, and war is declared.

Lincoln calls for 75,000 troops on 4-15-1861 to put down "rebellion."

Virginia secedes on 4-17-1861, followed by other states.
North Carolina calls another convention and votes to secede on 5-20-1861.

Battle of First Manassas, 7-21-1861 (Confederate victory).

Event Inside Yadkin County

Yadkin County votes for Bell in the presidential election.

Yadkin votes against electing delegates the convention on secession on 2-28-1861.

Yadkin votes to elect delegates to the convention on 5-13-1861. N.C. convention votes to secede 5-20-1861.

Flag presented to Yadkin Gray Eagles on 6-21-1861.
Several Yadkin companies formed and many volunteers enlist.

Yadkin boys are at Battle of First Manassas in July.
Much food sent from Yadkin to men of Co. F, 28th Reg. July–Aug. 1861, and other companies

Event Outside Yadkin County	Event Inside Yadkin County
Battle of Shiloh 4/6–7/1862 (Union victory).	Many Yadkin County men enlist during this period. Yadkin Gray Eagles formed.
Confederate Conscription Act 4-16-1862.	Anguish of Yadkin families over relatives captured at Hanover Courthouse, and heavy casualties at Sharpsburg.
Hanover Court House 5-27-1862 (Union victory).	
Second Manassas, 8-29-1862 (Confederate victory).	Many Yadkin men begin hiding out to avoid conscription.
Battle of Sharpsburg 9-17-1862.	Shortages of food, inflation, hoarding, cause hardships on families at home.
Emancipation Proclamation 9-22-1862 issued by Lincoln.	
Battle of Fredericksburg 12-13-1862 (Confederate victory).	
Battle of Gettysburg 7/1–3/1863 Union victory).	Bond School House shootout 2-12-1863.
Vicksburg surrenders, 7-1-1863.	Judge Pearson issues writ of habeas corpus to release men arrested after the incident.
New York Draft Riots 7/13–17/1863.	Home Guard established, summer 1863.
Battles of Chattanooga 11/23–25/1863 (Union victory).	General Hoke and 21st N.C. Reg. sent to Yadkin and other counties to round up deserters, 9-11-1863.
Battle of Ream's Station, 8/24-25/1864.	Mob storms Yadkin jail, July 1864. Large number of men leave county to join Federals in Tennessee. Some caught and jailed. Many deserters/conscripts caught, some killed by Home Guard.
Sherman's March through Georgia, Nov.–Dec. 1864.	
Sherman in N.C., 2/1–3/23/1865.	Stoneman's men destroy property in Jonesville, Hamptonville, and Huntsville. Home Guard attempts to stop Yankees at Shallow Ford, 4-11-1865.
Stoneman's Raid, March–Apr., 1865, through N.C. mountains and Piedmont.	
Lee surrenders at Appomattox 4-9-1865. Johnston surrenders to Schofield in N.C. 4-26-1865, and the war ends.	Many Yadkin men present at surrender return home.
Last Confederate Army surrenders, 6-23-1865.	Jesse Dobbins returns home, gets troops from Salisbury to quash warrants against him and others.

Once North Carolina joined the Confederacy, it sent the most men to fight in the war and, as a result, had the most casualties. Of the 125,000 troops North Carolina furnished the Confederacy, 111,000 were volunteers and about 19,000 were conscripts. These men were organized into 72 regiments, plus 10,000 reserves in eight regiments, and 4,000 homeguards.[1]

There were 41,000 deaths among North Carolina troops. In the Battle of Gettysburg, Pennsylvania, the 26th North Carolina lost 714 out of 800 men (86 percent) the highest regimental loss during the war on either side.[2] One-fourth of the total casualties at Gettysburg were North Carolinians. Overall, North Carolina lost at least 19,673 men killed in battle, and 20,602 died from disease, for a total of 40,275, the highest of any of the Southern states.³ North Carolinians are proud to claim that we were "First at Bethel, farthest at Gettysburg, and last at Appomattox." The same can be said of Yadkin County men. There were Yadkin men at the first victory of the war at Big Bethel, Virginia, on June 10, 1861, at the surrender at Appomattox on April 9, 1865, and at many of the engagements in between.⁴

North Carolina also had the largest number of desertions (23,694). At the beginning of the war absenteeism was about 21 percent, but by December of 1864 the number absent from service had risen to 51 percent.⁵ Perhaps one of the reasons for desertion was the fact that the majority of the people of North Carolina were poor, hardworking, non-slaveholding farmers, tenant farmers, and hired farm laborers, and they had no one to farm the land in their absence.

The population of North Carolina was 992,622 in 1860. The population of Yadkin County at that time was 10,714 (about 1 percent of the state total).⁶ Only 27.7 percent of North Carolina families owned any slaves and only 133 families in the entire state owned more than 100 slaves. Even among the planter class, only 6 percent of them owned more than 20 slaves. Five percent (34,658 slaveholders only, not spouses or children) of the population owned an average of 9.6 percent slaves.⁷

While the deep South was staunchly pro-secession, the upper Southern states, including North Carolina, were hesitant to join the Confederacy. Many people in Yadkin County, and in other counties of the mountains and Piedmont, resisted the war effort of the Confederate government.⁸ This "southern Unionism" has been explored by Daniel W. Crofts in *Reluctant Confederates*."⁹ William R. Trotter has examined antiwar sentiment and activities. He states that some 9,000 North Carolinians rejected the Confederacy entirely and crossed the Blue Ridge Mountains to join the U. S. Army for a variety of reasons.¹⁰ Some were staunchly pro–Union. They owned no slaves and they were opposed to leaving the Union to protect the rights of those who did. Many, like the Quakers, were against war for any reason.

Others tried to avoid the draft by hiring substitutes or by hiding out. Some of those who had enlisted or who were drafted deserted because they were needed at home. As the economic pinch of the war increased, the numbers of deserters or men absent without leave increased considerably.

Yadkin County Companies Are Formed

Many in Yadkin County were staunchly pro–Confederate and pro-war. Even before North Carolina had voted to leave the Union, Yadkin boys began to form their own companies, such as the "Yadkin Gray Eagles." These young men eagerly marched off to camps to drill and train. Brothers often joined the same companies, as did Samuel and Greenberry Harding, Edwin and John Hauser, the Holcomb brothers, and the Choplin brothers.

To get recruits, an enlistment bounty of $10 was offered, beginning on May 16, 1861, to be paid immediately after the recruit was declared fit to serve. The bounty increased over time, and by 1862 enlistment bounty was $50. By 1864 it had increased to $90, according to a Yadkin County soldier's letter.¹¹

The Yadkin County Courthouse grounds were used to muster troops. Several companies were formed there and men came to Yadkinville from surrounding counties to enlist. Other muster grounds were located at the southeast corner of the Rockford–Union Grove Church Road intersection, the corner of Highway 67 and the Flint Hill Road, and Lone Hickory Road at the intersection of Arnold Road.

Several companies comprised almost entirely of Yadkin County men were: 21st Regiment, Company B ("Yadkin Gray Eagles"), later changed to the 1st Battalion of Sharpshooters, Company A; 28th Regiment, Company F ("The Yadkin Boys"); 28th Regiment, Company I ("The Yadkin Stars"); 38th Regiment, Company B ("The Men of Yadkin"); 5th Regiment, Company A (Senior Reserves); and 70th Regiment, Company E (Millard's Battalion) Junior Reserves. Men from Yadkin County served in a number of North Carolina infantry, cavalry and artillery and in regiments from other states (see Appendix D for complete list).

On Monday, June 17, 1861, a group gathered at the courthouse in Yadkinville to send off to the war the "Yadkin Gray Eagles," the first company to be organized in Yadkin County. Some of the ladies from the county's wealthiest families had made a flag out of their silk dresses to present to the soldiers. Among those ladies present were Miss Louise M. Glen, Miss Mary Lilly Conelly, Miss Fannie Conelly, Miss Mary Elizabeth Glen, and Miss E. S. Conrad.

Miss Louise Glen's flag presentation speech was printed verbatim in the Salem, North Carolina, *People's Press*.

> Gentlemen of the Yadkin Gray Eagles:
> As representatives of the ladies of our County, we have come to present you this banner—an offering fresh from our hands, and one that will be accompanied by many heartfelt wishes for your success—you who go forth to battle for the maintenance of our rights. Our enemies have threatened to take from us our liberty that we hold dearer than life itself, and subject us to their hateful control. And even now they have invaded our soil—and are preparing to execute their threat. Who then can hesitate, when such may be our country's fate? Your mothers, wives, and sisters all bid you go, trusting to the God of Liberty and your own brave deeds to bring you off conquerors in the conflict. And may you return to your homes and firesides and enjoy once more the blessings of that freedom for which you have fought.
> Then take this, Capt. Conelly, and remember that wherever you may be, through whatever scenes you may pass, we will look to you as our defenders, and our prayers will be for success and protection for you and all those engaged in this glorious Cause. We give it to you pure and spotless, but when the war is over and you return home, how much more beautiful it will be when faded and worn from use in such work.
> The first in our midst to respond to your country's call, we feel secure that wherever the post of danger is, there our flag will wave o'er a brave and true band, who
> > Scorning the sordid lust of pelf
> > Will serve their country for herself.[12]

The flag which the ladies presented was a variation of the first Confederate flag, the "Stars and Bars." The Yadkin Gray Eagles' flag measured 51 inches by 41 inches. It

Sketch of the flag presented to the "Yadkin Gray Eagles" (courtesy Caren J. Casstevens).

had a 3-inch ruffle around the outside. On a blue field in the upper corner were 13 stars, each with a smaller star inside. There were three broad stripes: red, white, and red. Embroidered in gold on the front was "Yadkin Gray Eagles"; on the back was the motto, "We scorn the sordid lust of pelf and serve our country for herself."[13]

The captain, in receiving the flag, promised: "When this cruel war is over, Miss Lou, this flag untarnished shall be returned to you." This was the only company flag to be carried through 26 battles, from Manassas to Appomattox, but, as promised, it was returned to its donor, Louise Glen (then the wife of Joseph Williams). Her daughter, Mrs. Robert Daniels of Panther Creek,[14] kept the flag until she donated it to the North Carolina Department of Archives and History, Raleigh, North Carolina.

Most of those who enlisted gave their occupations as farmers or farm laborers at the time of enrollment.[15] Many joined voluntarily for one year in the first months of the war. Some of the more affluent hired substitutes to go in their stead. Alfred M. Haynes enlisted in Company B, 38th Regiment, on October 16, 1861, but was released after providing George C. Poplin as a substitute on February 1, 1862. William W. Rutledge served only four months (from October 16, 1861, to February 1, 1862) before being discharged after he provided a substitute. James Monroe Jones, who had been ill with typhoid fever but "believed the South was right in declaring war against the North," wanted to do his part. So he hired Henry Starling as a substitute to go in his place. He reportedly bought Starling a complete uniform and a rifle, and paid him $1,500.[16]

Yadkin County men also enlisted as "substitutes" for others who did not live in Yadkin County. Thomas Streeter Johnson enlisted at age 24 on May 3, 1862, as a substitute for David Lenard Deafled. David Anthony enlisted in Company H, 54th Regiment, as a substitute for James W. H. S. Daniel. Anderson E. Swiney agreed to go in place of Richard N. Tiddy. Thomas J. Cook enlisted for Joshua Spicer, and Thomas Kelly, age 52, enlisted as a substitute for James Patterson (who was a Yadkin man).[17]

Company F, 28th Regiment, known as "The Yadkin Boys," trained in East Bend on land adjoining Nancy Stimpson's back yard. Mrs. Irma Matthews Robertson's Uncle Bill used to watch the boys train. Mrs. Robertson believed the training grounds were behind the houses on the east side of the road going from East Bend School to Enon and to the south of Highway 67. Capt. John Hendricks Kinyoun, who was also a doctor, kept a notebook on the height of the men of Co. F, 28th Regiment. Beside the name of each man, Kinyoun listed the man's height. It is not known whether he measured them in their shoes or boots or barefooted, but some were remarkably tall for the 19th century. L. Choplin was listed as 6', 1½" tall; William H. Apperson was 6' 1", John O. Kelly was 5' 10", and William D. Kelly, 5' 11". Most were in the range of 5' 6" to 5' 11", with the shortest being 5' 5". The average height for the officers listed was 5' 9"; when the privates are included, the average increased to 5' 10". Kinyoun also noted in his notebook some facts about marching times: common time was 90 paces; quick time, 110 paces, and double quick step, 165 paces.[18]

The 54th Regiment began enrolling in Yadkinville. John Thomas Conrad and John H. Cornelius enlisted at "Camp Enon" (possibly this camp was near the present-day Enon community).[19] In addition to Yadkin County men, males came from all the surrounding counties to enlist at recruitment sites in Yadkin County. Yadkin men also joined outside the county in Forsyth, Davie, Davidson, Surry, and Wilkes counties. Many enlisted near Raleigh in Wake County. Other Yadkin boys, perhaps when visiting relatives in camp, such as at Petersburg, Virginia, joined regiments from other states there.

Ironically, several slaves actively participated in the war by going to war and serving as bodyguards for their masters. The North Carolina General Assembly amended the statutes regarding Confederate pensions and provided $200 per year "to such colored servants who went with their masters to the war and can prove their service to the satisfaction of the county and State pension boards."[20] Their devotion to their masters is to be commended, and their monetary compensation well deserved. The names of only a few are known: Alfred ("Teen") Blackburn, Dudley Glenn, and Peter Lomax Harris.[21] Harris is buried at the Presbyterian Church in Boonville beside his wife, who was a Carter.

The new recruits were given a grand send-off. On their way to camp at High Point, the "Yadkin Stars" passed through Salem, where they were entertained by the Salem Brass Band, and a speech by R. L. Patterson.[22] From there they went to camps in the eastern part of the state for training.

The South hoped to win the war quickly and then to be left alone to go its own way, but that was not to be. After a few victories early in the war, such as the rout of Federal troops at First Manassas (First Bull Run), yet to come were some of the most terrible battles the world had seen up until that time, and seldom since.

Army Life

The Confederate Army was organized along the same lines as the Union Army. Both used General William J. Hardee's book on military tactics, *Rifle and Light Infantry Tactics*.[23]

The organization at full strength was: Army (Robert E. Lee's) = 2 or 3 corps + cavalry (led by a general); Corps (A. P. Hill's) = 2 or 3 divisions (led by a lieutenant general); Division (Pender's) = 2 or 3 brigades (led by a major general); Brigade (Lane's) = 5 regiments (5,000 men, led by a brigadier general); Regiment (28th N.C.) = 10 companies (1,000 men, led by a brigadier general); and Company (Company I) = 100 men, led by a captain.

An army, such as the Army of Northern Virginia (commanded by General Robert E. Lee) was composed of corps, made up of divisions, composed of brigades. A brigade was run by a brigadier general and his staff, which included an assistant adjutant general, assistant inspector general, quartermaster, ordnance officer, and aide-de-camp. A regiment had a colonel, lieutenant colonel, major, adjutants, assistant quartermaster, assistant commissary of subsistence, surgeons, assistant surgeon, chaplain, ensign, sergeant majors, quartermaster sergeants, commissary sergeant, ordnance sergeant, and hospital stewards.

The company, the lowest unit in the military structure, was commanded by a captain, who was assisted by a 1st lieutenant, a 2nd lieutenant, and a 3rd lieutenant. The lowest ranking officers of the company were non-commissioned: 1st sergeant, 2nd sergeant, 3rd sergeant, 4th sergeant, 1st corporal, 2nd corporal, 3rd corporal, and 4th corporal. The rest of the men were privates.

Out of over a thousand Yadkin County men who served the Confederacy in some capacity, one of those men, John Kerr Connally, rose in rank to become a lieutenant colonel. Another became a colonel, William H. Asbury Speer. Attorney Robert F. Armfield was elected 1st lieutenant, then lieutenant colonel, and was transferred to become a member of the field and staff of the 38th Regiment.[24] (Armfield resigned his commission in January 1863 to become solicitor of the Sixth Judicial Circuit of North Carolina.) Reuben Wilson, senior captain of the 1st Battalion of Sharpshooters, was known as "major," in recognition of his battalion command.

Several men were regimental captains, such as Neil Bohannon, Captain of Co. I, 28th Regiment. James Free Brindle rose to the rank of sergeant in Co. I, 28th Regiment. Capt. John Hendricks Kinyoun resigned from his position in Co. F, 28th Regiment to become the assistant surgeon of the entire Confederate Army, and was assigned to the 66th Regiment, N.C. Infantry, C.S.A.[25]

Thomas Lanier Clingman, who was born and raised in Yadkin, became a brigadier general, although he was living in Asheville when he formed a company. (See Appendix C for list of ranks above that of private achieved by Yadkin men in the Confederate States Army.)

The individual soldier served either in the infantry, cavalry, or artillery. Infantrymen traveled on foot from place to place. Occasionally, troops were transported by rail, but this was the exception rather than the rule. Each foot soldier carried his own weapon, usually a rifled musket with a bayonet attached, ammunition, personal belongings, and food for several days. In order for a soldier to fire his rifle, nine steps were involved:

1. At the command "Load," the rifle butt was placed between the feet, and the right hand on the cartridge box; 2. "Handle Cartridge," he reached into the cartridge box, grasped the cartridge, and put it between his teeth; 3. "Tear Cartridge," the cartridge was torn open with the teeth and placed in front of and level with the muzzle of the gun; 4. "Charge Cartridge" required the pouring of powder into the barrel and the placing of a bullet into the barrel. The cartridge paper was dropped to the ground; 5. "Draw Rammer"—the ramrod was pulled out with the right hand, and the large end inserted just inside the rim of the gun barrel; 6. "Ram Cartridge"—Supporting the rammer with the left thumb and finger, the soldier reached up to the top of the rammer with his right hand and pushing it downward, rammed the cartridge to the bottom of the barrel; 7. "Return Rammer"—Procedures 5 and 6 were done in reverse to return the rammer to its original position; 8. "Prime"—The rifle was raised into firing position, and the hammer cocked to safety lock. A cap was retrieved from the cap box and placed on the nipple. The stock was grasped tightly with the right hand; 9. "Shoulder Arms"—Firing position was assumed until the commands to fire were given: "Ready, Aim, Fire."

At "Ready," the rifle was raised with the right hand, and grasped with the left hand between the middle and lower bands. The stock was gripped in the right hand. The barrel was elevated. At "Aim," those in the front rank raised rifles to the shoulder and leaned forward, taking aim at the target. The rear rank raised rifles and leaned forward, aiming over the right shoulder of the soldier directly in front. At "Fire," the trigger was pulled, and the gun fired. Firing position was held until another command was issued, such as "Load," "Shoulder Arms," "Fire-at-Will," or "Cease Firing."

Those in the cavalry traveled on horseback, and each carried a rifle, sabre, and pistol, in addition to personal belongings and equipment. The cavalry served as scouts, observing and reporting the movements of enemy troops. They also protected the flanks of the army, but in battle they sometimes dismounted and fought along with the infantrymen. Mounted, they could also raid and retreat rapidly.

The artillerymen carried no weapons. Each was part of a team which operated a single cannon. Special training was required, and each member of the team worked to move, load, aim, and fire the cannons. During the Civil War, there were basically four types of cannon. Howitzers and Napoleon guns of bronze had an effective firing range of about a mile. The Parrot Rifle was cast iron. The Three-Inch Ordnance Rifle was a very strong gun for its size and weight. Six horses were required to move cannons. Each cannon also had to have an ammunition wagon. The "caisson" was a wagon that carried two chests of ammunition; a "limber" carried only one chest. Cannons were usually placed in a group called a "battery." Each battery had its own guns, a traveling forge, caissons and other wagons which carried tents and supplies. Each gun crew was usually made up of about 15 men, who, when moving from place to place, rode on the ammunition chests, or rode the horses pulling the wagons, or walked beside the wagons.[26]

While many museums display the uniforms and accoutrements of colonels and generals, who usually owned several uniforms, the uniforms of the majority of the soldiers—the sergeants, corporals, and privates—are not so easily found. These men wore what they had, and that was generally the clothes that they farmed in, thus the great variety of styles and colors of clothing worn by members of the Confederate Army. Some, such as Alfred May of the 61st N.C., wore a handmade "grayish-blue shell jacket" and "Union-issue sky blue trousers," which may have come from a dead or captured soldier.[27] His socks, if he had any, would have been knitted by his wife or mother back home. When William H. Asbury Speer's calico shirts wore out, he wrote his mother to have two shirts made, "colored so they will not show dirt."[28] Some Southern soldiers wore clothing that had been dyed the "butternut" color by using dye from walnuts or other natural dyes.

Shoes and boots, so essential to the foot soldier, soon wore out, and unless received from home or picked up somewhere on the battlefield from a dead soldier, the soldier may have gone barefooted, in summer and in winter. Early in the war, shoes had been obtained from back home. R. S. Folger, acting adjutant of the 28th Regiment, North Carolina Troops, wrote a "letter to the editor," which was published in the Salem *People's Press* on March 27, 1863, expressing his thanks for the many donations his regiment had received from home. He especially noted that Co. I, 28th Regiment (an almost entirely Yadkin County regiment), had received "fifty pairs of shoes, gotten up by Miss Lou, Laura and Joe Grays, and Miss Lucy Hamlin, of Huntsville, Yadkin County." He referred to these ladies as "ministering angels," and that their donations would "inspire the bosoms of all true patriots, and nerve their arms to deeds of noble daring."[29]

Hats were an essential item of clothing and the common soldier wore anything from a broad-brimmed felt hat to a gray forage cap with a band or a pompom on the crown in the color of his branch of the service (light blue for infantry; red for artillery; yellow for cavalry).

In his pocket, the average foot soldier might have a clay pipe for smoking, and a twist of tobacco. Other precious belongings were carried rolled up in a blanket that was worn across his shoulders. He might carry a small Bible in his pocket in which there was a letter from home, together with a picture of a loved one. Before a battle, he would write he name on a piece of paper and attach it to his clothing, so that if killed, his body could be identified.[30]

Officers wore woolen uniforms year round, and all soldiers wore cotton flannel underwear, during both summer and winter. Brigadier General Thomas Lanier Clingman wrote home to his mother about having some "drawers made." Mrs. Jane Clingman replied to his request, but gave specific washing instructions:

> I can make two pair out of the new flannel and I think get two more by piecing up the old ones, which we will do as soon as we can. I am certain that your flannel is injured by washing. It should not be put in very hot water or boiled at all, and [washed in] moderately warm water with soap and rinsed in warm soap suds, which will keep it soft and free from shrinking. At least, you can direct your washer to do so.[31]

The soldier's equipment was a mixture of "military goods from a variety of sources." He may have carried a rifle made in Fayetteville or an Enfield rifle musket imported from England, with a bayonet attached, and with it a ramrod (either metal or of hickory) for packing a bullet and a small amount of powder. The powder was carried in a small metal flask. The rifle's sling might be Federal issue (captured in battle), as well as a cartridge box and metal (or wooden) canteen, both hung on his shoulder by a leather strap. He might also carry a Colt .44 revolver. He would wear a holster for his pistol and a leather belt with a buckle with the letters "CSA." He would carry a tin box for percussion caps, a bullet mold, a knife, and perhaps a sword, picked up on the battlefield from a dead officer.

Daily Life of the Soldiers

It took some time for the former farm boys to adjust to army life. After a glorious send-off by the folks back home, as they marched in the heat of summer in their wool uniforms, they had little idea of how miserable they would be having to stand picket duty on a cold and snowy night far away from home. Homesick and lonely, most of these men did not endure the hardships of war for money (although some probably did enlist just for the enlistment money). Pay was always minimal, even for officers. As the war progressed and inflation became rampant, a soldier's wages were not sufficient to provide for his family. When Frederick Long enlisted in Company I, 28th Regiment, his pay as a 2nd lieutenant was $80 per month, according to information provided by Rich Long, "a first cousin, four times removed."

Company F, 28th Regiment, left Yadkin County in the fall of 1861, traveled to Salem and then on to Wilmington. John Thomas Conrad wrote:

> Camp near Wilmington, N.C. Oct. 15, 1861.
> We are getting along finely, drilling four hours every day. I guess we will get some old flint and steel muskets tomorrow, but it is only for the purpose of learning maneuvers of arms, and they will be replaced by new ones, as soon as they can be had. I have not been on duty since I have been here though I am expecting to be officer of the Guard ever[y] day.[32]

Much of the time while the regiments were near Wilmington was devoted to drilling. John Thomas Conrad wrote home on November 21, 1861:

> The Col is drilling us only once a day now, though we have company drill every morning and battalion in the evening.... I wish you could see us drill, it is one of the most imposing and grand scenes ever you beheld, the guns and bayonets glittering in the sun and the whole battalion marching off at the same step in one solid column; I think we are improving rapidly and in a short time will be able to compete with any regiment on a drill.[33]

The 28th Regiment was sent to Virginia, about 75 miles north of Richmond. John Thomas Conrad remarked that "Gordonsville is a small village about the size of Huntsville, but where two Rail Roads cross." He thought the country was very beautiful, "though I dont think the land is any better than it is in Old Yadkin."[34] Later, at the Rapidan River in Orange County, he remarked that the Rapidan "reminds me very much of our dear old mill hill."[35]

The problems of troop movement increased with the number of battles and the number of men involved, and the subsequent destruction of roads and rails. "Transportation is almost out of the question up in this country and it can't be had when we leave the Rail Road.... Excepting the cavalry, the majority of the men traveled on foot, and they learned to travel light. John Thomas Conrad wrote that he had kept his "two blankets and what clothing I could conveniently carry in a Knap Sack which consists of two over shirts 1 checked shirt, 1 pr. drawers 1 pr. pants and over coat."[36]

Whenever the men got a chance to stop and sit down, they would write home. Letters from soldiers were cherished items and were often kept inside the family Bible. Not as many letters from the wives and relatives back home to the soldiers have survived. Many were probably lost when the soldiers had to pack up and move on short notice, or when the soldiers were killed and buried with the letters inside their pockets. Although both the soldiers and their families wrote each other frequently, many letters were never received at their intended destinations.

Soldiers were always anxious for news from home, just as those at home were for news from the battlefields. Calvin Holcomb speculates about the reason he has not had any letters from home: "I have not had a letter from home in some time. I don't know the reason, but guess the Rail Road being cut is the reason."[37] John Thomas Conrad wrote from the camp of the 1st N.C. Cavalry near "Balfield," Virginia, on January 20, 1865: "I don't know whether letters from here go through or not but hope they do and hope you receive mine regularly, for I know you and Johnnie are ever anxious to hear from me often, though I fear the mails are so deranged that you seldom hear from me."[38]

To conserve paper (because it cost "$2 per quire"), often two letters would be written on one page, the first written horizontal in the normal method, the other written vertically across the original letter. A picture of one such letter can be seen in *Kinfolk of Jacob Conrad*.[39] Other times, two persons would use the same letter, with the second author adding his comments at the bottom, such as the letter from J. W. Wall (Appendix A).

Colonel William H. Asbury Speer wrote of a religious revival that occurred among the troops; almost every one of them had joined the church.[40] John Thomas Conrad notes that "Our new Chaplain, the Rev. Mr. Kenedy from Charlotte is preaching now and I must go and hear him.... I hope he will be of service and benefit to the regiment."[41] Conrad wrote home that "I did not lose my bible as I carry it in my pocket all the time and read it every day. I have commenced at the beginning and intend to read through."[42]

Feeding an army was a problem, especially in the days before refrigeration. At times there was plenty to eat, other times food was scarce. The soldiers sometimes received food from the folks back home. Capt. John Hendricks Kinyoun, Company F, 28th North Carolina Regiment, recorded, in a period of less than a month (July 19–August 17), the items received from home, including beans, potatoes, squash, beets, onions, radishes, cabbages, cucumbers, pickles, chickens, mutton, pork, bacon, loaves of bread, "oven-light" biscuits, sugar cakes, custards fruit pies, sugar, honey, molasses, and staples, such as cornmeal, milk, and vinegar. They also sent cider, whiskey, cordial, and brandy, and "a good lot of dry wood...."[43]

Horses, in addition to being the chief mode of transportation, could also be a source of food. Alexander Steelman, who served in a Virginia cavalry unit, told his grandchildren that when food was scarce, they had to eat "horse meat."[44] Horses were frequent casualties of the war, and those that survived had to be attended to, even before the needs of the men. Colonel W. H. A. Speer paid $400 for a "strong & fine horse." He sold his previous horse for what he had paid for him, even though "He was a sorry horse ... they are very scarce & high."[45]

The duties of the cavalry men were double—they not only had to care for themselves, but had to take care of their horses, too. Cavalry soldiers had to always be sure their horses had enough to eat. Ebenezer Parks, son of Dempsey and Nancy Parks, who joined the 54th North Carolina as a Ranger, recalled that as the war continued, he had "only one worn-out blanket for his bedroll and many times woke up covered in snow." Parks recalled having to feed his horse first and the men were often so poorly supplied that they had to eat "slobbered corn," grain that had dropped from the horse's feed and lay on the ground, too thinly for the horse to find.[46] When the troops were on the move, it was "frequently midnight before we would lie down to sleep as we had to cook rations every night, and we had so few cooking utensils along with us,"[47] wrote John Thomas Conrad.

Alvis Tobias Davis joined the 5th North Carolina Cavalry when he was 17. A notation in the company muster rolls for July and August 1864 on Davis' record states "No horse since 15 July, 1864." Davis picked up some fodder one day for his horse by mistake from a pile that belonged to someone else. The officer in charge while Davis' regular commander was away made him walk and lead his horse. When Davis' regular commander, Benjamin Franklin Ward, returned, he said to him: "Bob White, mount that horse," and Davis didn't have to walk any more. (Davis was nicknamed "Bob White" because he could imitate a quail.[48])

The cavalry did offer some advantages in that they rode instead of walked everywhere the army moved, but the men on horseback did not always escape enemy fire just because they could move around quickly.

Between battles, the soldiers were often bored. To pass the time, they played cards or chess, whittled, cleaned their guns, repaired clothing, cooked their own food, rested their weary bones, and read their Bibles. There was usually someone in camp who could play a musical instrument to entertain himself and his companions.

Music was an important part of military life. "Musician" was a designated position in most regiments, and was usually an older man or very young man who played a drum, a fife or a bugle. Some of these instruments were used in rallying troops, or to help the men keep time when marching. Some regiments even had regimental bands, and a number of songs were composed about various companies or regiments. A soldier might also have a Jew's harp, a harmonica, a guitar, a banjo or a fiddle, which they played in camp. Thousands of songs were written during this period. The words to a song written about the 28th North Carolina Regiment, sung to the tune of "Dixie," are below.

"28th Regiment, N.C.V."

Words to a song, sung to tune of Dixie Land, brought home from the war by Isaac Columbus Poindexter, Sergeant, Co. F, 28th Regiment, N.C. Infantry

Away down South in the Land of Cotton
Times of peace are not forgotten,
Look away, look away, look away, Dixie Land.

Though the clouds of war hang o'er,
We soon shall see its storm no more,
Look away, look away, look away, Dixie Land.

Chorus:
Then shout "Hurrah for Dixie"
   Hurrah! Hurrah!
In Dixie Land we'll take our stand
To live and die for Dixie,
   Hurrah! Hurrah!
We'll live and die for Dixie.

'Tis true their ships our ports blockade,
And cruel feet our soil invade;
But when the Twenty-Eight gets there
The scamps will run in wild despair.

When "Norman" brings his boys to scurry
The Yankees better move in a hurry
The "Invincibles," if well equipped
And led by "Edwards," can't be whipped.

The Yankee rogues would better pack,
When the "Stanly Hunters" find their track.
When "Lowe" shall bid his "Farmers" fire
His foes will reap destruction dire.

As "Barringer" leads on his "Grays,"
Full many a Yankee'll end his days.
When "Kinyoun" comes with his "Yadkin Boys,"
He'll put an end to the Yankees' joys.

And "Martin's Guards of Independence"
Have fame in store for their descendents.
And "Wright" with his "Cleveland Regulators,"
Will send dismay to Yankee [torn]

And "Speer" with his brilliant "Yadkin Stars,"
Will die in defence of the *Stars and Bars*,
While the "Stanly Guards," by "Moody" led,
Will be the Yankees' special dread.

The Twenty-Eighth is organized
With "Reeves" and "Lowe," both highly prized.
If "Lane" will only be their Colonel,
Then their glory'll be eternal.

There were at least three songs written about the 21st North Carolina Regiment: "21st Regiment Quickstep," "Col. Kirkland's March," and "Col. Hoke's March." (These songs have been preserved on three cassette tapes by Fayetteville, North Carolina, modern-day "The Regiment Band of the 11th N.C. Troops.") Other songs, popular with the troops on both sides, are well known even today, such as "Lorena," "Dixie," "My Old Kentucky Home," "Home, Sweet Home," "Swannee River," "Listen to the Mockingbird," "The Yellow Rose of Texas," and "The Battle Hymn of the Republic."

Jesse Franklin Williams, of the Army of Tennessee, was in Georgia and Tennessee during most of 1864. He described having to march for 33 days, and said his "feat [sic] is very sore. At this time we have fard [fared] tolable well on this march...."[49] He says in another letter from camp about 30 miles from Chattanooga, Tennessee, that he has "got a pair of shoes ... and there is lots of the men barefoot." His unit had not been fighting but had been tearing up railroad tracks. He tells of how his brother John is within 30 miles, but he can't get to see him, and relays Cousin Thomas' "best respects" to the family and friends. He also mentions that "Cousin James got a transfur to the calvry [sic] and left our brigade."[50] Most of his letters are filled with longing to be home with his wife and small children, and with advice to his wife about how to manage the livestock and crops.

The weather added to the soldiers' misery. In a letter to a friend, written from the winter quarters of the 21st Regiment at Camp Martin near Manassas, Virginia, Reuben E. Wilson of Company B, 21st Regiment, described the terrible conditions of army life:

> I have been here one week it has rained, snowed, and hailed nearly all the time, and this mud is over our boots, and it is ten inches deep in mud.... We are now in our winter quarters, our little houses are built of logs, sticks, chimneys dirt floors chinck[ed]. We have no beds, and we are fixed up as good as could be.

The last time I went on picket guard, I tracked up a Coon and killed him. We were out there three days and nights, and it snowed all the time. What little we did sleep was on the ground, and it was very cold. We are not allowed to have any fire on picket duty.[51]

Especially during the winter months, the roads were in terrible condition. Colonel W. H. A. Speer wrote from Camp Gregg in February of 1863, "The roads are amost impassable. We have built a corduroy road from here to the depot to haul provisions on."[52] Even during the coldest months, the men lived in tents. The soldiers added "chimmineys" to the tents, in order to have a fire and to keep warm.[53] The tents were designed to shelter two persons. A North Carolina textile mill probably produced this tent material; those used by Southern troops were hand-stitched and had wooden buttons instead of the metal buttons used on Federal tents. Very few of these tents still exist, but the North Carolina Museum of History has recently acquired one, which once belonged to Orderly Sergeant Alfred May, who served in the 61st Regiment of Clingman's Brigade.[54]

The soldiers wrote home about the terrible conditions and how they wished they were back home. J. W. Wall of Company D, 21st Regiment, wrote to his cousin R. S. Phillips on December 20, 1863: "You wrote you had no brandy to drink. This Sunday is very cold and I have nothing to drink but cold water."[55] To his wife and children he wrote: "I want to know how the stock is getting along this cold weather. I want to know if the babe can talk yet or not, and all about the children."[56] Wall later died at Orange Court House of unknown causes.

Battles and Casualties

Who would have thought that the names of quiet, peaceful towns and cities would take on new meanings because of the war, names now synonymous with carnage, bloodshed, death and suffering. Pristine forests and golden fields were forever stained by the blood that was shed there in the great battles that pitted North against South. Places such as Cold Harbor, Charleston, Atlanta, Fair Oaks, Fredericksburg, Chancellorsville, Malvern Hill, Petersburg, Shiloh, Seven Pines, Spotsylvania, Vicksburg, and Appomattox had formerly been picturesque towns and villages surrounded by stately plantation homes. These places suffered heavy damage and destruction as the armies battled back and forth over them. Mountains and valleys, such as Kennesaw Mountain, Lookout Mountain, Missionary Ridge, Little Round Top, and the Shenandoah Valley of Virginia, still bear the scars of those powerful armies and their incessant bombardment. The once clear and sparkling streams ran red with the blood of the dead and dying. Even non–Civil War buffs have heard of the carnage at Gettysburg and the burning of Atlanta. White-columned mansions and unpainted log cabins were burned and pillaged alike; towns and cities were devastated; roads, railroads, and bridges were destroyed as they were trampled by the opposing Union and Confederate armies. The people, both black and white, fled from the path of these destructive forces.

Many battles are still referred to by two or more names. The South usually refers to a battle by the name of the nearest town, whereas the North refers to the same battle by the name of the nearest stream (Manassas = Bull Run). Many names were so similar as to bring on confusion. There is Pittsburgh, Pennsylvania, and Pittsburgh Landing, Tennessee, near where the battle of Shiloh took place. Seminary Ridge is to the south and west of Gettysburg and Cemetery Hill runs south of the town.

Of all the battles that were fought during the Civil War, the most famous, those that had the greatest impact on the war, or that caused the greatest casualties, were: First Bull Run, Shiloh, Seven Pines, Seven Days, Second Bull Run, Antietam (Sharpsburg), Fredericksburg, Stones River, Chancellorsville, Gettysburg, Chicamauga, Chattanooga, the Wilderness, Spotsylvania, Atlanta, Franklin, Nashville, and Five Forks. Below is a sampling of the number of troops involved and the casualties in some of the major battles. An asterisk indicates the victor.[57]

Battle	Killed	Wounded	Captured	Total Involved
1st Manassas (Bull Run), VA				
7/23/1861				
*Confederate	387	1,582	13	32,500
Union	460	1,124	1,312	35,000
2nd Manassas (Bull Run), VA				
8/29/1861				
*Confederate	1,553	7,812	109	54,000
Union	1,747	8,452	4,263	63,000
Sharpsburg (Antietam), MD				
9/17/1862				
Confederate	1,512	7,816	1,844	45,000
*Union	2,107	9,549	753	87,000
Fredericksburg, VA				
12/13/1862				
*Confederate	608	4,116	653	78,000
Union	1,284	9,600	1,769	116,683
Chancellorsville, VA				
5/1–4/1863				
*Confederate	1,649	9,106	1,708	60,000
Union	1,606	9,762	5,919	130,000
Gettysburg, PA				
7/2–3/1863				
Confederate	3,500	18,000	6,500	77,518
*Union	3,155	14,529	5,365	93,500
The Wilderness, VA				
5/5–6/1864				
Confederate	(8,000–11,000 estimate)			61,000 (est.)
Union	2,246	12,037	3,383	118,000
(results inconclusive)				

Battle	Killed	Wounded	Captured	Total Involved
Spotsylvania, VA *5/8–19/1864*				
Confederate	(10,000 estimate)			50,000
Union	2,725	13,416	2,258	100,000
(tactical draw)				

Major Battles Involving Yadkin Men

The following list of battles in which Yadkin County men were either wounded, killed, or captured was compiled from individual service records. It is not a complete listing of all the battles every Yadkin soldiers participated in, but it does serve to show that Yadkin men were in most of the major battles.

1st Manassas, VA	Fussell's Mill, VA	Mine Run, VA
2nd Manassas, VA	Frayser's Farm, VA	New Bern, NC
Amelia Court House, VA	Fredericksburg, VA	Orange Court House, VA
Atlanta, GA	Gaine's Mill, VA	Ox Hill, VA
Bentonville, NC	Gettysburg, PA	Petersburg, VA
Bermuda Hundred, VA	Globe Tavern, VA	Plymouth, NC
Bethesda Church, VA	Good Allis Tavern, VA	Rappahannock Station, VA
Burkesville, VA	Gravel Hill, VA	
Bond School House, NC	Hanover Court House, VA	Ream's Station, VA
Charleston, SC	Harpers Ferry, VA	Richmond, VA
Cedar Creek, VA	Hatcher's Run, VA	Riddell's Shop, VA
Cedar Mountain, VA	Hazel River, VA	Sayler's Creek, VA
Chancellorsville, VA	Horse Shoe, VA	Seven Days (VA)
Chickamauga, GA	Jarratt's Station, VA	Sharpsburg, MD
Chattanooga, TN	Jericho Mills, VA	Shepherdstown, WV
Cold Harbor, VA	Jones Farm, VA	South Anna Bridge, VA
Culpeper, VA	Kinston, NC	Spotsylvania, VA
Deep Bottom, VA	Madison Court House, VA	Vicksburg, MI
Drewery's Bluff, VA		Weldon Railroad, VA
Farmville, VA	Malvern Hill, VA	Wilderness, VA
Five Forks, VA	Manchester, VA	Wilmington, NC
Fort Fisher, NC	Mechanicsville, VA	Winchester, VA

A number of Yadkin men fought under the Confederacy's best generals. Andrew Jackson Bovender, Green Bovender, Abe Murphy and Cam Brown were all in Stonewall Jackson's army. Green Bovender was later killed at Richmond and Abe Murphy died near Richmond.[58] (See Appendix A for letters.)

Seven Days' Battles

The Seven Days' Battles, a series of battles near Richmond, Virginia, from June 25 to July 1, 1862, resulted in heavy casualties among the troops, including Yadkin County men. John Thomas Conrad of Company F, 28th Regiment, wrote home of these battles:

> I have no estimates of the loss of men either side but thousands of friends are mourning the loss of some dear one who has fallen in the late series of battles before Richmond, and I felt that I never can be thankful enough to my heavenly father for shielding me in the hour of danger.... Our loss in the late battles in the Regiment is 19 killed, 130 wounded, and 26 missing. That of my company 2 killed, T. R. Hicks and G. M. Danner, 14 wounded, myself and Trulove slightly; Lee Cornelius, J. C. Brown, J. H. Poindexter, S. D. Creson, R. H. Hutchens, A. E. Head, John Tacket all slightly; H. C. Baker, Robt. Choplin, John T. Sprinkle and Allen Womack, severely; 2 missing Coston Kittle and Joseph Choplin.[59]

Conrad sums up army life: "We have all had a hard, hard time, living nearly all the time on half rations and making some hard marches, but they have all borne their sufferings manfully, flattering themselves that with the help of God we have gained a Great victory over our enemies."[60] Those conditions were made even worse by the sights and smells of the battlefield after a major engagement. After a visit to the Fredericksburg battlefield in January of 1863, John Thomas Conrad wrote: "Yesterday, Dr. Kinyoun, Maj. Speer, Neal, Jimmy and myself visited the battlefield at Fredericksburg.... We could not see much as it has been a month since the battle, except dead horses and half buried Yankees, pieces of shell etc. and etc." [61]

Isaac Columbus Poindexter was in the heaviest fighting in some of the worst battles of the war. Poindexter first saw action in the Seven Days' Battles (June 25–July 1, 1862). After Harpers Ferry was taken, he participated in A. P. Hill's famous 17-mile march to Sharpsburg to assist Lee's army. In August, he was admitted to Chimborazo Hospital in Richmond with the common malady that debilitated many of the soldiers—chronic diarrhea. He recovered in time to take part in the battle of Fredericksburg (December 13, 1862).[62]

Hardships increased as the war continued. Abner S. Haire wrote his wife, Ellan P. Haire, on May 26, 1862: "We had to march about Sixty miles with out anything to eat. Scearcly [sic] any thing to eat for about 5 days. The Yankees was after us and we had to go it nite and day. The yankees is bomshelling us now at this time."[63] Haire was a private in Company B, 38th Regiment, North Carolina Troops. After being wounded at Mechanicsville, Virginia, on June 27, 1862, he was taken to a hospital in Richmond where he died of wounds on June 29, 1862.

Chancellorsville

After the battle of Chancellorsville on May 7, 1863, W. H. A. Speer wrote home to his father that he had survived:

> ... safe and sound from one of the most terrific fights ... that the world ever witnessed.... We left camp 9 days ago today. We went to Fredericksburg that

John Thomas Conrad (1838–1913), 1st Lieutenant, Company F, 28th Regiment, North Carolina Troops (courtesy Charles Conrad).

day and formed line of battle. We stayed there till Friday morning till day break … at which time we took up march for Chancellorsville. We were under the fire of the enemy all day Friday and fighting also Friday night. Saturday morning we left by day under Gen. [Thomas J. "Stonewall"] Jackson and went around the enemy's flank, traveling 20 miles. Attacked them in their rear about two hours by sun and drove them four miles by dark—we continued to fight till 3 o'clock Sunday morning. We had a hard fight for two hours Saturday night from 1 o'clock till 3, where I got slightly wounded on the knee…. But Sunday was the bloodiest day of this war! We had 40,000 men engaged and the enemy 120,000 nearly all day…. O father, the scene was awful.[64]

He goes on to describe the number of terrible casualties at Chancellorsville in which some regiments lost half of their officers and men. "Our loss in killed and wounded foots up about 10,000. The enemies, from their statements, over 20,000 killed and wounded. We have over 10,000 of their men prisoners."

Even for a hardened soldier, Speer was disturbed by the knowledge that the "Yankee hospital caught on fire and burnt up some 500 of their wounded and 10 or 15 of ours, and the woods caught on fire from shells and burnt up hundreds of their dead and wounded and some of ours."[65]

Isaac C. Poindexter participated in Stonewall Jackson's flank attack on Federal General Hooker at Chancellorsville (May 1–4, 1863). At the Battle of the Wilderness (May 5–6, 1864), he was taken prisoner and spent the next 10 months in Elmira Prison in New York. After his release in March 1865, Poindexter rejoined his company during the siege of Richmond.[66]

Although the casualties at Chancellorsville were high, it is considered one of Lee's most brilliantly fought battles, and a Confederate victory against vastly superior numbers of Federal troops. Private Thomas Dinkins of Company B, 38th North Carolina Regiment, and a Yadkin County man, was nominated for the "Badge of Distinction" for gallantry at Chancellorsville, Virginia, in the fighting between May 1–4, 1863.[67]

Fredericksburg

Milas Mason described the horrors he had witnessed, stating that it was "an awful sight to see the men slaughtered up in such a manner and such a destruction of clothing, blankets, knapsacks and guns."[68] Mason, a Davie County resident who enlisted in

Northampton County, in Company G, 5th Regiment, wrote to his uncle, William Gabard of Yadkin County, after the battle of Fredericksburg, on May 12, 1863:

> Dear uncle, that I am tired of this war you may be sure. Oh how I long to be at my home, sweet home, where I have enjoyed so much satisfaction, but my trust is ever in the Lord. He has been pleased to hear and answer our prayers in days that have passed and gone, and I hope He will hear and answer us again that we may be permitted to return safe home again.... We were in line of battle and marching under the roaring of cannon and muskets and fighting 7 days in succession. I was in 2 engagements, one on Saturday evening and one on Sunday, and some days we were behind breastworks and the yankees throwing bombshells and grapeshot at us and some times they would burst right over us and some times wound and kill some.[69]

As the war began in earnest and news of the casualties was reported, the glamour of war soon disappeared, and the horror became evident. Even when not wounded in battle, countless men became deathly ill from diseases such as typhoid, tuberculosis, measles, and syphilis. Infectious diseases, mainly dysentery and respiratory inflammations, were responsible for the most deaths. Even minor wounds could prove fatal because sterilization techniques were unheard of, and there were no antibiotics. Amputation was the only means to combat sepsis (hospital gangrene). Although medical knowledge and treatment were primitive, the Confederate Medical Corps established hospitals in and around Richmond, in addition to the field hospitals set up temporarily on the battlefield. Later in the war, hospitals were established in North Carolina at Charlotte, New Bern, Washington, and Wilmington. When those became overcrowded, "wayside hospitals" were set up along the main roads of travel, such as near Asheville, Greensboro, Raleigh, and Wilmington. These hospitals provided "comfortable beds, warm fires, suitable provisions, proper dressings for wounds, and with medications." North Carolina also set up a Soldiers' Home, where men on leave might stay while on furlough. Early in the war, a laboratory was set up at Lincolnton to manufacture drugs from indigenous plants. The North Carolina Medical Department also furnished "artificial limbs" for its soldiers.[70]

After the larger battles, it was sometimes days before the dead were buried and the wounded treated. Lorenzo Dow Whitaker enlisted when he was only 17 as a private in the Yadkin Gray Eagles.[71] At the Battle of Second Manassas on August 28, 1862, Whitaker "had his left eye shot out," and his knee was severely damaged as well. According to family tradition, he "laid under a tree, nursing himself, for 3 days" until he was found by the medical staff and treatment was begun. He was transferred to Wayside Hospital in Richmond, and then transferred to Hospital #4 in Richmond. On October 13, 1862, he received a 60-day furlough. By January, Whitaker had returned to his regiment, and there he remained, with only a brief furlough in the spring of 1864, until the war's end in April 1865.[72]

Gettysburg

Colonel W. H. A. Speer thought he had seen the worst fighting imaginable, but the worst was yet to come. Only a month later, July 1–3, 1863, Speer and the 28th Regiment were on that terrible field of death and destruction forever burned into the hearts of Southerners—Gettysburg.

Confederate cannon on Seminary Ridge, Gettysburg Battlefield, Gettysburg, PA, positioned along the line from where the North Carolina Troops began their charge on July 3, 1863 (courtesy Tim Casstevens).

Our grand army made its way into Pa. across the Blue Ridge to Gettysburg PA where we met the enemy on the 1st of July and had a battle on the 2nd and 3rd—the most terrific battles the world ever seen or human beings even engaged in. I will now try to describe it to you. On the 2nd and 3rd days of July there were 275 pieces of cannon engaged on our side and over 500 on the Yankee.... Added to the engagement was some 80 or 100,000 infantry. I was with our Regt. and Brigade in it all. I went into the fight on the 3rd with 326 men with guns and could only muster next day 100 men. After some of the slight wounded coming back and two or three stragglers, I have 118 men in the Regt—the balance are killed, wounded or missing.... We made a charge to take their stronghold and could not hold our position but had to fall back and left our wounded and killed on that part of the ground in the hands of the enemy.

Speer mentioned some of the Yadkin men who were with him at Gettysburg:

Jones Holcomb, Jonas MaCokey were killed dead. A shell exploded in the line as we were charging, killing them both dead, wounding 3 others and knocking me down. Sgt. Cast and Buchanan supposed killed, Sgt. Hendricks wounded through the legs and in the hands of the enemy. John G. Holcomb—thigh and hand left at our hospital in the Yankee hands. J. G. Danner mortal, since dead. E. H. Reece severe and [we] left D. C. Hall.... J. G.

The North Carolina Monument, Gettysburg Battlefield, Gettysburg, PA.

Reynolds in the Yankee lines wounded. Sgt. S[imon] Bohanon slight, H. H. Snow, severe. M. Carter severe, N. C. Dozier slight. Berry [Greenberry] Harding struck 3 times slight. C. V. Hutchens, S. N. Johnson, both slight. All these are inside of our own lines. Capt. Apperson took in 24 men and only came [out] with 4 unhurt. Gen. Lowe out, Marler in Yankee hands. Capt. Lovell's company—every man in it was struck.[73]

The North Carolina Troops, including the 28th Regiment, as part of Lane's Brigade, Pender-Wilcox's Division, A. P. Hill's (formerly Jackson's) 2nd Corps, Army of Northern Virginia, were part of the assault on Cemetery Ridge. A visit to Gettysburg will make clear, as no book or movie can, the futility of "Pickett's charge"—a charge over an open field for a mile into the very jaws of hell. Speer testified: "We charged a battery one mile off and pass[ed] over a very level piece of ground all the way with 70 pieces of cannon throwing all sorts of missiles into our ranks. We had two columns cut down and destroyed."[74] Isaac Columbus Poindexter was one of the last to withdraw from Pickett's charge.[75] General Trimble reportedly said that his division (including Lane's Brigade) was the last to fall back from Pickett's charge, and that "they did so in good order."[76]

The pain, the suffering, the dying, and the acts of courage at Gettysburg can never be fully known. What is known has been pieced together from stories told by the survivors, from letters, and diaries, and from sometimes unexpected sources. In a newspaper account in February of 1904 at the time of the death of Colonel John Kerr Connally,[77] a close friend, the Rev. A. A. Tyson, recalled that he was with Connally on the first day's fighting at Gettysburg on July 1. Colonel Connally led his 55th North Carolina Regiment in the charge of Union General Reynolds' position west of the town. Tyson described the scene:

> The color-bearers were shot down one after another and Col. Connally himself seized the flag and bore it on. He was shot twice and fell with a shattered arm. I took Col. Connally to the field hospital and when the army returned [to Virginia] I volunteered to remain with him. I went to Federal General Smyth, of Indiana, and told him my colonel was in the hospital and he and his surgeon called there.

Connally's left arm was badly shattered and had to be amputated. He was captured after the Battle of Gettysburg at Cashtown, Pennsylvania, and was imprisoned for eight months, until exchanged.

While some had entered the war in May of 1861, others did not enter the conflict until they came of age after the fighting had been going on for some time. Such was the case of Bloom V. Holcomb, who enlisted at age 19 in 1863 in Company I, of the 28th Regiment, North Carolina Troops. His initiation came at Gettysburg with Lane's Brigade of Wilcox's Division. After the Confederates left Pennsylvania, he spent the winter with his regiment at Liberty Mills. In the spring of 1864, Holcomb took part in the fighting at Wilderness and Spotsylvania Court House.[78]

Battles Near Petersburg, VA

Bloom Holcomb was wounded in the battle at Cold Harbor. After recovering, he returned to duty in the trenches at Petersburg in the summer of 1864. There, he saw the heavy casualties created by the "Crater," an explosion caused when Federal troops tried to tunnel under the Confederate lines. The tunnel was filled with dynamite and when detonated, created an enormous hole. The Federals almost broke the Confederate line, but many of the Federal troops were trapped in the Crater, and killed by Confederate gunfire. When Petersburg was evacuated, Holcomb was in the retreat to Appomattox. He was captured in the fighting at Saylor's Creek on April 6, 1865. Taken as a prisoner to Fort Delaware, Delaware, he was confined until June 20, 1865.[79]

After being wounded in the fighting near the Globe Tavern just outside of Petersburg, Virginia, Brigadier General Thomas L. Clingman was taken to the field hospital for removal of a bullet in his leg. He put his pistol under his pillow just before being given chloroform, and told the surgeon, "If I wake up and find my leg cut off I'll be dammed if I don't shoot the man who did it." Luckily for the surgeon, it was not necessary to amputate Clingman's leg.[80]

Two battles were fought at Ream's Station, one on June 29, 1864, and another on August 24-25, 1864. Both were Confederate victories, but in the second one several Yadkin County men serving in Company I, 28th North Carolina Regiment, were killed, among them Col. William H. A. Asbury Speer, and Samuel Speer Harding. General Robert E. Lee described the battle:

> Headquarters A. N. V., Aug 26, 1864. Hon J A Seddon—Gen A P Hill attacked the enemy in his entrenchments at Ream's Station yesterday evening

& on the second assault carried his whole entire line. Cooks & McRae's NC Brigades under Heth's & Lane's N C Brigade & Wilcox's Division under Connor with Pegram's Artillery composed the assaulting column. One line of breastworks was carried by the cavalry under Hampton with great gallantry which contributed largely to our success. Seven stands of colours, 2000 prisoners, & nine pieces of Artillery are in our possession. Loss of the enemy in killed & wounded is reported heavy, ours relatively small. Our profound gratitude is due to the Giver of all victories & our thanks to the brave men & officers engaged.

[Signed] R E Lee, General[81]

Thomas G. Scott, of Company I, 28th Regiment, North Carolina Troops, wrote on August 27, 1864, from Petersburg, Virginia, of the death of a friend and fellow officer, Sergeant Samuel Speer Harding, to Harding's father who lived in Huntsville, North Carolina:

I sit myself to inform you of the late fighting. Your son Sammy was killed the twenty-fifth of this month. I am sorry to inform you of the fighting. But I felt hit was my duty to write to you about Sergeant S. S. Harding. I am sorry to tell you of his death. He was shot through the hip. He did not live long after he was shot. I did not get to see him after he was killed.... I will keep Sammy's things till you come after them if I can, for he was a good friend of mine.[82]

Scott also reported the death of Colonel William H. Asbury Speer: "I will tell you that Col. Speer was shot through the head. He will die if he all ready ain't dead now. I was sorry to loose my Col. and Sergeant."[83]

Even if the soldiers survived the battles, diseases such as typhoid fever, diarrhea, measles, rheumatism, colds, bronchitis and pneumonia were debilitating and often fatal, as documented in troop rosters, regimental histories, pension applications, letters and diaries. Local papers carried news of the deaths of area soldiers. The death of Private William A. Conrad of the Yadkin Gray Eagles in a military hospital in January 1862 was reported in the *People's Press* on January 31, 1862. The death of 18-year-old Private Lewis A. Williams on December 8, 1861, from measles at Wilmington was reported.[84] Private Roby Pendry enlisted at age 21, on August 13, 1861, and died at Wilmington on February 4, 1862, of "measles."[85] Typhoid fever killed many soldiers, including Wiley Pilcher, who died at Wilmington of "fever."[86] Long lists of battle casualties were published in the papers.

Capt. Thomas V. Apperson of East Bend kept a muster roll of Company F, 28th Regiment. The muster roll carried a brief record of the men. During a two-month period, 18 men were absent without leave or had deserted, seven were prisoners of war, four had been killed in action, and six had been wounded. Four were recorded as missing in action, and an additional nine were sick and in the hospital.[87]

At times, the cavalry were required to dismount and fight alongside the infantry. However, the fighting could be just as devastating to mounted soldiers as those of the infantry fighting on the front lines. Thomas Franklin Holcomb "was knocked from his horse by a passing shell."[88] Under the heavy artillery firing at Upperville, many Yadkin County men were killed or injured while serving in Company H, 63rd Regiment, North Carolina Cavalry. A shell killed the company's captain, William H. Booe, and the same shell wounded Henry Miller and killed his horse. Other casualties in that battle were the regimental Colonel Peter G. Evans, mortally wounded; W. H. Hobson, wounded three times, captured, and his horse killed; Thomas Bracken, wounded, captured, horse killed; Cope Wynn, wounded, captured, horse killed; John Kerr, Henry Jones, Henry Wood, Henry Minor and David Todd were killed and their horses either killed or wounded. Ellis Lakey and F. A. Beaty were wounded, captured, and their horses killed. F. A. Arnold, J. D. Hodges, and Joseph Brandon (a Yadkin man) had their horses wounded. Major John M. Galloway reported that the long list of casualties and added "if any one thinks it is merely fun to ride at the head of a charging cavalry column let him read this list and think over it."[89]

Prisoners

The exchange of prisoners was common during the Civil War. This was initiated by an informal agreement between the commanders of the armies after a particular battle. The practice was "codified by a cartel" between the United States and the Confederate States in July of 1862. Because so many of the captured Confederates returned to battle after being released from capture, the cartel was suspended by the United States in May of 1863, but individual commanders still continued to arrange paroles. Again the Federal government stopped the practice in early 1864, and paroles and exchanges were resumed only after the Confederates agreed to treat captured white and black troops equally. There were specific sites designated as exchange points: City Point, Virginia, on the east coast, and Vicksburg in the west. Equal ranks were exchanged equally, or the equivalent—one colonel equaled 15 privates. If one side still had prisoners left and the other side had none, the excess prisoners were to be released on "parole." A parole meant that the former prisoner was prohibited from taking up arms again, until he was formally exchanged. Parole camps were established where paroled soldiers stayed until they were formally exchanged. Sometimes, a parolee was allowed, after taking an oath, to return home until exchanged.[90]

Many of the Southern boys taken prisoner by the Federal troops were sent to Point Lookout, Maryland. Isaac Columbus Poindexter brought home from the war a detailed map of the hospital and military prison at Point Lookout.[91] When Richmond fell on April 3, Poindexter was captured in the hospital, having been sent there for a lymph gland disorder. He was confined at Point Lookout, Maryland, and held until he was released, after taking the Oath of Allegiance on July 25, 1865.[92]

A great number of Yadkin County men were captured in the Battle at Hanover Court House, in May of 1862, including some of "The Yadkin Boys," Company F, 28th North Carolina, as described in the diary of Captain William H. Asbury Speer of that company.[93]

> We were now almost starved to death, not having had anything to eat in 36 hours. [We] slept one night in the rain without any tents, marched and fought

all day, [were] taken prisoner, slept on the cold, wet ground, then marched 18 miles over some of the worst road in the world, without anything to eat.[94]

After his capture, Speer was confined during the summer of 1862 at Governor's Island in New York Harbor and on Johnson's Island in Lake Erie. Officers were kept in separate prisons from most of the privates (which is noted in Col. Speer's diary).[95]

Zacharia Melton became separated from his unit during a battle. Upon hearing soldiers approaching, he climbed a tree to see whether they were friend or foe. They were Yankees, but they passed him by without detecting him. Zacharia was so happy that he laughed out loud. The Yankees heard him, returned, and shot him, then took him prisoner.[96]

Few prisoners escaped, but there were exceptions. Sidney Francis Conrad, who had just joined the Confederacy at age 17 when the draft was extended, had just arrived at Camp Vance near Morganton. Shortly thereafter, he and all others at the camp were captured in Kirk's Raid. He put his "wits to work and escaped with a few others." Later, when he had been paroled and started home to the Yadkin River area, he encountered Stoneman's men, and was "in their hands twice, but managed to escape, and bushwacked them into a final farewell shot of twelve buckshots."[97]

James Henry Shore was drafted when he was 16 years old. He walked to Camp Fisher near Salisbury, where he and other young men were trained. Because guns and ammunition were in short supply, they trained with "wooden guns." After a short time, he and other young solders were ordered to East Tennessee to join the corps of General Longstreet. After a skirmish, Captain Conrad of their unit would not retreat, so Shore and a few other Confederate soldiers forced their captain to hide in a ravine. They piled brush on him to avoid his being captured. Shore and many others were captured, and the Yankees marched their captives to Strawberry Plains, Tennessee. The march lasted a day and night. They walked for about five hours, then rested for two. Arriving at the railroad, the Confederate captives were put in cattle cars and sent to Camp Douglas, near Chicago, Illinois. Here, Shore and thousands of other Southern boys were kept for two years, until the war was over. Life in a Yankee prison was hard, but worse in some prisons than in others. To pass the time, the men played checkers, cribbage, and card games. At Camp Douglas, the Confederate prisoners were furnished only a bare minimum of food. Clothing was scarce, and the buildings were cold. Many died from diseases, malnutrition, and the cold. While captured Southerners in other prisons were sometimes allowed mail from home, there was no mail to or from the South at Camp Douglas. The wooden barracks in which Shore and other prisoners lived were about three feet off the ground, with sheeting that came down to the ground. Once, some of the prisoners decided to dig a tunnel from the barracks to outside the prison fence. They dug at night with sticks and rocks, and piled the dirt underneath the barracks. Finally, the tunnel extended beyond the prison fence, and many of the prisoners escaped, but not Shore.[98]

Especially when men were in prison, they wanted and needed to hear the news from home. J. L. Holcomb, in Davids Island Prison, in a New York harbor, wrote his folks: "Write me if you please address to—Davids Island, NY, just put a Confederate stamp on and leave it open and it will come."[99]

Desertion and Punishment

Many of the men just couldn't take the demands of war, so they deserted. The typical service record, which is repeated over and over, reads much like that of Private Alfred W. Martin, who "resided in Yadkin County where he enlisted at age 21, August 13, 1861. Deserted on August 5, 1862."[100] Others, who had enlisted early in the war, were captured, exchanged, returned to duty, deserted, and returned to duty again, to be captured and held till the end or near the end of the war. Such was the case with Private Ellis Long, who at age 20 lived in Yadkin County at the time of enlistment on August 13, 1861. Long was captured at Fredericksburg, Virginia, on December 13, 1862. He was then exchanged on or about December 17, 1862. He remained with the army until he deserted on July 23, 1863. He then returned to duty on an unspecified date, and was reported present for duty from September 1864, through February 1865. He was then captured near Petersburg, Virginia, on April 2, 1865, and confined at Fort Delaware. Long was released on June 19, 1865, after taking the Oath of Allegiance to the United States of America.[101]

Nancy Reece Holt told the story of a Quaker from Hunting Creek Friends Church who was forced to fight. He refused to carry a gun, so they strapped it on to his back during a battle. All through the battle, even though men were falling dead all around the Quaker lad, not a single bullet touched him. To avoid capture, he lay down on the ground and pretended to be dead. After the enemy had passed, he got up, took off the rifle, and walked back to Yadkin County.

Deserters, when initially captured, were kept in the guard house for a number of days. As desertions increased and the troop numbers diminished, some of the deserters were executed to set an example and to prevent others from deserting. The 44th North Carolina Regiment executed a number of men for desertion.

One Yadkin man, Milton F. Willard, son of Jonathan and Kesiah Willard, left camp with two others and was caught and returned to Petersburg, where he was imprisoned, tried, and sentenced to die. Milton had enlisted along with J. H. Willard on July 30, 1864, but Milton deserted on August 17, 1864. Although he returned to duty on August 30, he was tried and "shot for desertion" on September 30, 1864.[102] In a letter to his wife, he described his months in prison before his execution:

> I have not heard a thing from you since I left home. But I heard that a letter came to camp, but I never saw it. Jonathan Brown, Eli Brown, the three of us, left the camp near Petersburg 16th of August and got in about 18 miles of Farmerville, VA. Was taken up by the Georgia cavalrymen and sent back to the guardhouse. Have been here ever since. A mighty miserable place it is. We get about half enought to eat and not a peach nor apple can be had here without money and I have had none of that. We get nothing here but meat and bread, sometimes a mess of peas or rice, but mighty seldom. Eli Brown came here. We have to lie on the ground and not a thing over us. And our hands are tied fast together. We are as lousy as a hound and cannot scratch ourselves. I tell you we have seen sights for the last three months if anybody ever did. The nights are very cold here. I lay very cold every night. But my trials last in this world but short and I hope I may find rest in Heaven

for my soul. I have been under guard about a month and was waiting to know my doom before I wrote you a letter.

His sister, Clarisy Willard, wrote the commanding officer Horace Eddleman, begging for mercy, but her letter was too late. Milton had already been executed. He did, however, promise to mark the burial site so that if she came for his body, she could locate it. At the time of his death, Milton F. Willard was no more than 36 years old, and he left a widow and three small children. His Bible and three of his letters were preserved by his oldest daughter, Nancy Willard, who related the sad story when she was 74 years old (born 1852).[103]

Many of the soldiers enlisted in one company and then were listed as deserters, while actually they had joined another regiment or another company, such as George W. Minesh, who enlisted as a private at age 17 on October 16, 1861, in Company B, 38th Regiment. He was reported to have deserted about November 6, 1861. Actually, he enlisted the next spring on March 17, 1862, in Company H, 54th Regiment, but was discharged from that company on July 2, 1862, because he was underage.[104] James Washington Reaves enlisted at age 19 on March 8, 1862. He stuck it out through most of the war, but near the end he was reported AWOL (absent without leave) on February 8, 1865.[105]

As desertions increased and troops numbers decreased, members of the military were often sent back to their states to try and bring back deserters. "Capt. Clark of this Regt. [28th N.C.T.] is detailed to come home after deserters & those who are liable to conscript. If he comes to Yadkin, I hope he will call and see you. He is a nice man, a Christian man, unassuming," wrote Col. W. H. A. Speer in August of 1863.[106]

These are just a few examples, but these same service records are repeated over and over again. There were heroes and there were cowards, and there were men who were both and men who were neither. There were men who stayed just as long as they could take it, and then headed home when their concerns about their family grew too strong. Most did what they thought they had to do.

The Lighter Side of Army Life

The reports from the army camps were not all gloom and doom, however. As in any situation, there were lighter moments. Calvin M. Holcomb, of Company I, 28th Regiment, told his folks back home in a letter dated February 19, 1862, at Wilmington, that he had had the opportunity to visit the "Sea" and pick up some seashells. Another bright ray was the box of apples that had arrived from home. He sold the apples to his buddies in the regiment and decided that if he had about "five bushels" he could make some money.[107] Reubin Wilson reported that while on picket duty, he had "tracked up a Coon and killed him. Wilson, however, wished he was home so he could "take a fox hunt."[108]

The soldiers on the battlefield still retained some measure of influence on events. They were allowed to vote. An election was held on July 28, 1864, to elect a governor for the State of North Carolina for the next two years. The men of Company A, 1st Battalion Sharpshooters, voted unanimously for Zebulon B. Vance, the incumbent. The vote was 49 for Vance, and none for Holden, the peace candidate.[109]

The War Ends

Being able to vote in state elections did little to end the war. Eventually, those who had earlier hoped for a Confederate victory became pessimistic. In a letter to home written on January 20, 1865, John Thomas Conrad predicted:

> I think unless we do better than we have been doing and the war lasts much longer, that the war will be transferred to the soil of North Carolina in the Spring and perhaps sooner, if Sherman is not stopped in his headlong career in Georgia, but I hope Longstreet will find himself strong enough to compete with him and ware him out. It seems that everything is working against us.[110]

Finally, the war ended on April 9, 1865—a few days shy of four years since it began on April 12, 1861. General Robert E. Lee, to avoid further useless bloodshed, surrendered to Union General U. S. Grant in the McLean House at Appomattox Court House, Virginia. Ironically, the Wilmer McLean family had moved to Appomattox after their home near the battlefield at Manassas, Virginia, had been damaged. The McLeans witnessed the beginning and the ending of the war.

With all the deaths from battle wounds and disease, quite a number of Yadkin County men were at the surrendering of Lee's remaining 28,000 troops at Appomattox.[111] Of the 1,826 men who had served in the 28th Regiment, North Carolina Troops (of which Company I and Company F contained mostly Yadkin men), 230 men were present at the surrender and were paroled on April 12, 1865.[112] The 28th Regiment had participated in some of the major battles of the war: Fredericksburg (December 1862); Chancellorsville (May 1863); Gettysburg (July 1–3, 1863); Spotsylvania Court House (May 1864); Second Battle of Cold Harbor (June 1864); and Petersburg (September 1864).[113] There were also quite a few men there from Co. A, 1st Battalion North Carolina Sharpshooters, of which the "Yadkin Gray Eagles" was a part, and other regiments which contained Yadkin County men (see Appendix B).

Service-Related Statistics on Yadkin Soldiers*

Service in Home Guard Only	50	Missing in action	
Service in the Militia Only	79	(presumed dead)	6
Service in the Confederate States Army	1057	TOTAL YADKIN MEN IN SOME KIND OF SERVICE	
Service in the Confederate States Navy	2	Men with battle-related Deaths	89
Total	1188	Men with Battlefield Wounds**	296
		Total Casualties	385
Battle-related Deaths			
Died in battle	60	Other deaths	
Died of wounds	23	Died at home	10

Died (unknown reason)	36	Executed (for desertion)	4
Died in hospitals	29	Total Other Deaths	182
Died of disease	93		
Died in prison	8	TOTAL KNOWN DEATHS	271
Killed by Home Guard	2+	CAPTURED (at least once)	276

*Figures do not include Militia or Home Guard **Some wounded more than once, only one wound recorded here.
Primary Source: Manarin & Jordan's North Carolina Troops 1861–1865

Of the 125,000 enlisted men from North Carolina, Yadkin County sent its fair share. Assuming that the majority of the adult male population of Yadkin County (1,542) had voted on February 23, 1861, to send delegates to a state convention to consider secession, at least 78 percent of those Yadkin County men (approximately 1,200 men) served in the Confederate Army, the State Militia, Home Guard, and or the Junior and Senior Reserves. (Again, these figures are incomplete, especially for the Militia and Home Guard.) Approximately 12 percent of the total county population of 10,714 had actively participated in some form of military organization. Another way of looking at the figures is from the 1860 Census of Population. In 1860 there were 1,634 households in Yadkin County. If 1,200 men served in some capacity, that is approximately 73 percent of the households. Of course, in some households, there was more than one member of the family in the service of the Confederate Army. In other families, the eligible males avoided conscription or joined the Union Army. Overall, practically every family in Yadkin County had one or more of the male members of the household in some form of military service from 1861 to 1865.

These numbers are significant, especially when one considers that Yadkin County was known for its anti-war sentiment, and that it was a county in which there were few slaves (which is why some say the war was fought), and a large number of anti-war Quakers and anti-war Methodists. While some of these men were drafted and may have gone to the battle front unwillingly, a large number volunteered their services, survived, and remained until the end of the war. Many were supported by their families but just as many had families opposed to the war. Families were divided. Often brothers fought on opposing sides.

Many of the soldiers deserted, one or more times, but returned to duty. However, many did not. The final notation in the service records of 212 who were at one time thought to be deserters shows that 4 were dropped for being absent or AWOL, 144 were listed as having deserted, 38 were AWOL, 23 had joined the enemy, 1 remained at home after furlough, and 2 were under arrest or being court-martialed.

Those who deserted or fought for the Union should not be condemned, for they too fought and acted on their convictions. It was altogether a different time, and a very different set of circumstances from what we face today. Let us hope we learn from their experiences.

Notes

1. Lefler and Newsome, p. 456.
2. Walter J. Loehr, M.D., "Civil War Medicine in North Carolina," *North Carolina Medical Journal* 43 (February 1982): 120.
3. Lefler and Newsome, p. 457.
4. *Ibid.*, p. 457.
5. Clement Eaton, *A History of the Southern Confederacy* (New York: Macmillan, 1972), p. 271.
6. Lefler and Newsome, p. 391; 1860 Yadkin County Census.
7. Lefler and Newsome, pp. 420–421, 715; J. C. G. Kennedy, *Agriculture in the United States in 1860* (Washington, D.C.: Government Printing Office, 1864).
8. William R. Trotter, *The Civil War in North Carolina. Bushwhackers: The Mountains* (Winston-Salem, N.C.: John F. Blair, Publisher, 1988), pp. 33–45.
9. Crofts, p. xxii.
10. Trotter, p. 43.
11. Mark Mayo Boatner, *Civil War Dictionary* (New York: McKay, 1988), p. 74; J. D. Holcomb to brother, July 26, 1863, in *Heritage of Yadkin County*, p. 144.
12. Salem, N.C., *People's Press,* 21 June 1861, on microfilm at the Winston-Salem, North Carolina, Pubic Library. Miss Lou Glenn was the daughter of plantation owner Tyre Glenn. Capt. Conelly is Captain John Kerr Connally, related to the ladies present. He lived at Panther Creek with the Williams family.
13. Charles Mathis, "Flag Made of Women's Dresses Represented Yadkin in Civil War," *Yadkin Ripple,* 7 January 1982.
14. "Reuben E. Wilson" *Confederate Veteran* VI (May 1898): 222.
15. Louis H. Manarin and Weymouth T. Jordan, Jr., eds., *North Carolina Troops 1861–1865: A Roster* (Raleigh, N.C.: Department of Archives and History, 1993), vol. X, pp. 25, 28; 1860 Yadkin County Census. Hereinafter cited as N.C. Troops.
16. C. Hilton Jones, "History of James Monroe Jones Family," in *Heritage of Yadkin County,* p. 444.
17. See the several volumes of N.C. Troops. Volume and page are given in the Appendix H.
18. Alice Kinyoun Houts, "Presents for the Yadkin Boys," *Journal of North Carolina Genealogy* IX (1963): 1131–1135; also reprinted in *Heritage of Yadkin County,* p. 142.
19. *N.C. Troops,* vol. VIII, p. 174.
20. *Public Laws of North Carolina, 1927,* Chapter 96.
21. Russell Scott Koonts, "Black North Carolina Confederate Pensioners," *The North Carolina Genealogical Society Journal* (November 1995): 343–352.
22. Salem, N.C., *People's Press,* 24 May 1861.
23. Eaton, p. 121.
24. *N.C. Troops,* vol. X, p. 20.
25. Houts, p. 1131.
26. U. S. Department of Interior, National Park Service.
27. North Carolina Museum of History, *The Corner Stone* III, no. 3 (December 1995): 1, 3–4.
28. Speer, Allen P., ed., *Voices from Cemetery Hill: The Civil War Diary, Reports, and Letters of Colonel William Henry Asbury Speer (1861–1864)* (Johnson City, Tenn.: The Overthemountain Press, 1997), Colonel William H. A. Speer to father and mother, August 14, 1863, p. 112.
29. R. S. Folger, "Letter to the Editor," Salem, North Carolina *People's Press,* March 27, 1863, reprinted in "The Forsyth County Genealogical Society Newsletter," December 1995. Miss Lucy Hamlin was the daughter of Jim Hamlin, who was later Sheriff of Yadkin County. The Grays mentioned are the family of Joseph Gray who built and lived in the Gray-Hartman house in Huntsville, before moving to Rockford. The Folgers, Hamlins, Grays were related by blood and marriage.

30. Pictures and descriptions of the clothing and equipment of both Federal and Confederate soldiers are pictured in John MacDonald, *Great Battles of the Civil War* (New York: Macmillan, 1988), pp. 14–15.
31. Mrs. Jane Clingman to Gen. Thomas L. Clingman, August 1, 1864, copy courtesy of the late Bruce Jarratt, reproduced in *Heritage of Yadkin County*, p. 142.
32. O'Daniel and Patton, p. 285.
33. *Ibid.*, pp. 290–291.
34. *Ibid.*, pp. 295–296.
35. *Ibid.*, p. 297.
36. *Ibid.*, p. 298.
37. Calvin Holcomb to brother, July 7, 1864, in *Heritage of Yadkin County*, p. 144.
38. O'Daniel and Patton, p. 323.
39. *Ibid.*, pp. 306–307.
40. Colonel William H. A. Speer to father and mother, April 28, 1863, in *Voices from Cemetery Hill*, p. 97.
41. O'Daniel and Patton, p. 321.
42. *Ibid.*, p. 304.
43. Hoots, pp. 1113–1135. Also reprinted in *Heritage of Yadkin County*, p. 142.
44. Lucy S. Shumate, "The H. J. Steelman Family," *Heritage of Yadkin County*, p. 630.
45. Colonel W. H. A. Speer to father, April 1, 1863, in Speer, *Voices from Cemetery Hill*, p. 93.
46. Information from descendant Cheryl Martin, Trinity, N.C.
47. O'Daniel and Patton, p. 319.
48. Margaret Miller Conrad and Mrs. Richard Maxwell Conrad, "Alvis Tobias Davis," in *Heritage of Yadkin County*, pp. 335–336.
49. Letter from Jesse Franklin Williams, on the bank of the big Tennessee River, to wife, Sarah Louzania Patterson Williams, dated October 31, 1864, original in possession of Mrs. Sarah Augusta D. Phillips, Mt. Airy, N.C., cited by permission.
50. Letter from Jesse Franklin Williams to J. A., dated October 16, 1864, original in possession of Mrs. Sarah Augusta Davis Phillips, Mt. Airy, N.C., cited with permission.
51. Letter from Reuben Wilson to Alvis Pilcher, in *Heritage of Yadkin County*, p. 143.
52. Colonel William H. A. Speer to mother, February 20, 1863, in Speer, *Voices from Cemetery Hill*, p. 89.
53. Letter from John William Wall to wife, Agnes Tate Wall, dated December 20, 1863, private possession of Virgie Wooten Mathis.
54. *The Corner Stone* III, no. 3 (December 1995): 3–4.
55. J. W. Wall to R. S. Philips, December 20, 1863, cited with permission from Richard Andrew Mathis, Macon, Georgia, great-great-grandson of J. W. Wall.
56. *Ibid.*
57. McDonald, *Great Battles of the Civil War*.
58. Letter from John Bovender to Albert Poindexter, August 25, 1862, and letter from Richard Poindexter to Catherine Bovender Poindexter, November 8, 1863, both courtesy of Patricia L. Caldwell.
59. O'Daniel and Patton, pp. 310–311.
60. *Ibid.*
61. *Ibid.*, p. 322.
62. *N.C. Troops*, vol. VIII, pp. 181–182; additional details furnished by Randall G. Poindexter, Boonville, N.C.
63. Abner S. Haire to Ellan P. Haire, May 28, 1862, *Heritage of Yadkin County*, p. 143.
64. Colonel William H. A. Speer to father and mother, May 7, 1863, in *Voices from Cemetery Hill*, pp. 98–99.
65. *Ibid*, p. 100.
66. *N.C. Troops*, vol. VIII, pp. 181–182; additional details furnished by Randall G. Poindexter, Boonville, N.C.

67. *N.C. Troops*, vol. X, p. 24.

68. Letter from Milas Mason to William Gabard, original in family Bible of Mattie May Reavis, Yadkinville, N.C., a typed copy of which was furnished by Cliff Gabard, Anaheim, Calif., reproduced in *Journal of the Yadkin County Historical & Genealogical Society* XIII (December 1994): 9–10.

69. *Ibid.*

70. Loehr, pp. 120–121.

71. The Yadkin Gray Eagles was attached to the 11th Regiment, North Carolina Volunteers. This regiment became the 21st Regiment, North Carolina Troops, in November 1861. In April of 1862, companies B and E were taken out of the 21st to become Company A and Company B, 1st Battalion of North Carolina Sharpshooters.

72. Frances H. Casstevens, "Lorenzo Dow Whitaker, of Company B, 21st Regiment, CSA," *Journal of the Yadkin County Historical Society* XII (September 1993): 12–14.

73. Colonel William H. A. Speer to mother and father, July 10, 1863, in *Voices from Cemetery Hill*, pp. 105–109.

74. *Ibid*, p. 109.

75. *N.C. Troops*, vol. VIII, pp. 181–182; additional details furnished by Randall G. Poindexter, Boonville, N.C.

76. Glen Tucker, *High Tide at Gettysburg* (Bobbs-Merrill, 1958, rpt. New York: Smithmark Publishers, 1995), p. 372.

77. "Colonel J. K. Connally Joins His Comrades of Gettysburg," Asheville, N.C., *Citizen-Times*, 2 February 1904.

78. Clement A. Evans, ed., *Confederate Military History* (Atlanta: Confederate Publishing Co., 1899), vol. V, "North Carolina," by D. H. Hill, p. 546.

79. *Ibid.*

80. A[ugustus] H[enry] J[arratt], "General Thomas L. Clingman," *University of North Carolina Magazine*, New Series XVIII (April 1901): 169.

81. Catherine Devereaux Edmondston, *The Diary of a Secesh Lady: Catherine Devereaux Edmondston 1860–1866*, Beth G. Crabtree and James W. Patton, eds. (Raleigh, N.C.: Department of Cultural Resources, 1979), p. 609.

82. Letter from T. G. Scott to William Harding, August 27, 1864, in private possession of Frances H. Casstevens, Yadkinville, N.C.

83. *Ibid.*

84. Salem, N.C., *People's Press,* January 4, 1862, and January 31, 1862.

85. *N.C. Troops*, vol. VIII, 213.

86. *N.C. Troops*, vol. VIII, 216.

87. Copy of the troops roster kept by Capt. Peter Apperson in possession of a descendant, Dewey Bowman, Sr., of East Bend, N.C.

88. John D. Holcomb, Jr., "John D. Holcomb, Sr. and Family," in *Heritage of Yadkin County*, p. 416.

89. Walter Clark, ed. *Histories of the Several Regiments and Battalions from North Carolina in the Great War 1861–1865* (Raleigh: E. M. Uzzell, 1901), vol. III, p. 587.

90. Mark Boatner Boatner III, *The Civil War Dictionary*, rev. ed. (New York: Vintage Books, 1991), pp. 619–620.

91. Description taken from map of hospital and military prison at Point Lookout, courtesy of Randall G. Poindexter, Boonville, N.C.

92. *N.C. Troops*, vol. VIII, pp. 181–182; additional details furnished by Randall G. Poindexter, Boonville, N.C.

93. Diary of Colonel William H. A. Speer, May 1862, in *Voices from Cemetery Hill*, p. 58.

94. *Ibid.*, p. 60.

95. *Ibid.*, p. 65.

96. Mrs. Nancy Lumley, Winston-Salem, N.C., a descendant of Zachariah Melton.

97. O'Daniel and Harris, pp. 338–339.

98. Egbert L. Davis, "The James Henry Shore Family," in *Heritage of Yadkin County*, pp. 588–599.

99. J. L. Holcomb, July 26, 1863, in *Heritage of Yadkin County*, p. 144.

100. *N.C. Troops*, vol. VIII, p. 215.

101. *N.C. Troops*, vol. VIII, 214.

102. *N.C. Troops*, vol. X, p. 76.

103. Harvey Dinkins, "Aunt Nancy Willard, Yadkin County, Recalls Troubled Days of Civil War," Greensboro, N.C., *Daily News*, October 4, 1925.

104. *N.C. Troops*, vol. XIII, p. 324, and vol. X, p. 27.

105. *N.C. Troops*, vol. VIII, p. 216.

106. Colonel William H. A. Speer to father and mother, August 14, 1863, in Speer, *Voices from Cemetery Hill*, p. 110.

107. C. M. Holcomb to brother Bloom Holcomb, February 19, 1862, in *Heritage of Yadkin County*, p. 143

108. Reuben Wilson to Alvis Pilcher, in *Heritage of Yadkin County*, p. 143.

109. Original list of voters and votes cast in The Special Collections Library, Duke University, Durham, N.C.

110. O'Daniel and Patton, 324.

111. R. A. Brock, *The Appomattox Roster* (New York: Antequarian Press, 1962).

112. *N.C. Troops*, vol. VIII, p. 110.

113. *N.C. Troops*, vol. VIII, pp. 99–110.

3

On the Home Front: Civilian Life

NORTH CAROLINA was hesitant to leave the Union, but once that decision was made, it had a tremendous effect on civilian life all over the state. Initially there was great excitement about the war and a feeling that the Confederacy could beat the enemy in one battle or, at least, within a very short time. At the beginning, the young men joined eagerly. The folks at home had high expectations that the war would be won quickly and the boys would be coming home soon. But those hopes soon faded as the days stretched into weeks, the weeks into months, and the months into years. There was always that fear that the war would never end, or that their loved ones would be killed in battle before it did end. As the war progressed, fear became the prevailing emotion among the people at home: fear of being taken into the army, fear of loved ones leaving, fear of being invaded by Yankees, fear of slave uprisings, fear of being robbed by deserters.

It soon became a stressful time for all. There was little the homefolk could do except worry about their loved ones so far away from home. They tried to help out by writing letters, and sending clothing and food to the boys in Gray, which was not a problem in the first year of the war. Richard C. Puryear, plantation-slave owner, served in the Confederate Congress. He assisted the war effort by sending food from his plantation. In the first days of the war, he sent the Guilford Grays, stationed at Fort Macon, "two boxes of provisions, one bag of flour, one bag of meal, and one box of eggs."[1]

Quaker men were eventually allowed to pay a monetary fine in order to be exempt, and some left the state. A few, who had not been Quakers originally, joined the Society of Friends to avoid military service. N. H. Vestal, John Vestal, Bond Vestal, Henry Stallings and Joshua Steelman were reported to have joined the Friends.[2] Some of the plantation owners who owned large numbers of slaves got exemptions, such as Joseph Bitting, who was "detailed to look after the families of soldiers and provide for their comfort."[3] Government officials could also be exempt. Barnet C. Myers, a slave owner, remained at home during those years, and, as clerk of the Reece's Church (later Boonville Baptist Church), he was active in various relief and missionary activities among the soldiers and their families. Myers was a justice of the peace, which probably explained his exemption from military duty.[4] What other area churches and organizations (such as the Masons) were doing to assist needy families during the war years has not been documented.

John Norman, a blacksmith born in 1812, remained home. One day, a Confederate general stopped by his shop to get his horse shod. While Norman was making the horseshoes, the general fell asleep. Norman, who always had a sense of humor, decided to play a trick on the general. He shouted, "The enemy is coming," which woke the general and brought him to his feet. They exchanged a few more jokes, and the general was on his way, with no hard feelings.[5]

Yadkin County families were bothered by rumor (as well as the truth) of their loved ones being killed or wounded. John Joseph Conrad had been very concerned about his youngest, John Thomas. John Joseph had been told by a man named "Headspeth" that John Thomas Conrad, of Company F, 28th Regiment, had been killed in the fighting at Hanover Court House. Headspeth (Hudspeth) also brought news that "most all of our noble boys had been taken prisoners or killed...." The elder Conrad was relieved when he learned the truth—that his son was alive.[6]

As the war wore on, reality set in. The women, children, old men, and disabled men were left at home to carry on the many tasks of survival. Frequently, the man of the house and several of the older sons enlisted or were drafted. Problems developed that most people could not cope with, such as inflation. A pound of bacon that had cost $.33 in 1862, was $7.50 by 1865. The price of flour rose during the same period from $18 per barrel to $500. Corn increased from $1.10 to $30 a bushel near the end of the war.[7] The blockade prevented imported goods from getting to those who wanted them and could afford them. There were food shortages because of hoarding. In Salisbury a group of 50 to 75 women stormed the train depot in search of flour which they believed had been stored there by a speculator. Ladies in Greensboro also attempted to seize flour.[8] Yadkin County women experienced shortages and inflation also. John Bovender wrote his son-in-law, Albert Poindexter, on August 25, 1862, reporting that "corn is selling at 2 dollars a bushell, wheat 3.25 cents, rye 2 dollars, butter and cheese 20 cents per pound, Brandy 5 dollars per gallon, milk cows 30 to 40 dollars and other things in proportion."[9] (See Appendix A.)

Even by late 1862, some people were refusing to accept Confederate currency in payment of debts. John H. Kinyoun wrote to the governor that on his return from Richmond where he worked as a surgeon in the hospital there, he had tried to pay off his debts, but two individuals had "absolutely refused to take the confederate money...." Kinyoun saw that action as a blow "at our Cause and Country...." He begged the governor to put a stop to this "distructive policy."[10]

The women looked after their children, livestock, and crops. Tremendous efforts went into the growing and harvesting of flax and cotton, which were necessary in order to make clothing. The soldiers' families worked hard to raise enough food for themselves and to send to their loved ones on the battlefield.[11] The "chores" were numerous and endless, and some were not easy without the help of a man, such as hog killing, plowing, planting, and clearing new land. The women and young girls spun and wove cloth, carded wool, made candles, knitted, gathered and stored fruits and vegetables. Every family had a root cellar for preserving foods. If they could write, the families back home wrote letters to their loved ones, or else got someone who could to do it for them.

Sometimes it was the children of the family, with only a few months of schooling, who were the only literate members of the family.

Little can be actually documented about what Yadkin County women did to survive during the war. One exception is Harriet Maynard Baity, who lived to be 101 years old and passed on some of her experiences. Harriet was born on June 30, 1810. She married Pleasant Baity on January 28, 1830; her husband did not serve in the war because he was disabled. Harriet still "worked, labored and toiled to keep the wolf from the door. Many were the days she followed the plow from the rising to the setting of the sun. Many were the nights she wove and spun by the tallow candle in order that none might suffer from the cold, even those in the ranks of battle."[12]

With no indoor plumbing facilities, water had to be carried from the spring to the house for cooking and bathing. There were usually babies and young children to feed and care for.

Wood had to be to chopped and split, to keep the fires going. To help provide the wood needed for heat and cooking, one Yadkin county woman wrote to her husband in the 21st Regiment that she had held a "chopping," which provided plenty of wood.[13] Neighbors had to help neighbors. There is also a story, related by the late Mrs. Irma Matthews Robertson, teacher and writer of local history and genealogy, of the ice storm that broke so many branches from the trees that all the women had to do was go into the forests and gather the wood they needed.[14]

There were not many jobs outside of the home in which women could work and earn money. There were a few cotton mills, however, which employed women during the war years, such as the Richard Gwyn cotton mill in Elkin. The academy at Jonesville also employed female teachers. Many young girls worked outside their own homes as serving girls or "domestic servants" for the weathier families.

The women cared for the sick and wounded soldiers who sometimes came home to recuperate. They also found time to attend church, and to help other soldiers' families who were in need.[15] Many of the soldiers died of typhoid fever, and those at home were not immune either. Other diseases, now almost unheard of, were often fatal to nineteenth century families. These included diphtheria, whooping cough, smallpox, and tuberculosis. Malnutrition and poor eating habits led to scurvy and rickets. Many of the county doctors were in the military tending to the wounded soldiers. There was often only an old "granny woman" to call on when illnesses occurred, who "doctored" the patient with a mixture of roots and herbs. At difficult births, women such as Eliza Lineberry Bowman (the author's great-grandmother) of the Smithtown–East Bend area were sent for. Several women gave their occupations as "accoucheur" (meaning "one who assists in childbirth") in the Yadkin County census of 1860 and 1870.

Frequently, families lived in isolated areas, deep in the woods, and at some distance from the traveled roads and neighbors. When a crisis arose, there was no telephone with which to call for help, and no local fire department. When a fire started in the kitchen of Dr. John H. Kinyoun, it spread quickly and the dwelling house, dining hall, and kitchen were all burned, but most of the furniture was saved. His sister, Lettitia, who was sick in bed with typhoid fever at the time, had to be moved to the home of a neighbor, Joseph Marler.[16] Disaster followed disaster, and only a few weeks later, and Dr. Kinyoun was far away, caring for wounded soldiers as a member of the 28th Regiment, North Carolina Troops.

There is no doubt that the war caused hardships among the families of Yadkin County. All classes suffered. One Yadkin County woman, Sarah Louzania Patterson Williams, wrote on January 1, 1865, to her husband, Jesse Franklin Williams, serving in the Confederate army:

> I have no cattle but the two milk cows and one small yearling and I do not know how many hogs for they have gone perfectly wild and I do not know if the sheep are all alive or not. I have had them tended to so good as I could. The dogs were among my sheep last summer and killed two of them, the old bell one and the one that always held his head to one side.... I have been trying to get my hogs to fatten but I fear I shall not. I expect the sows have young pigs or will soon if I don't get them I shall have no meat of my own.[17]

In addition to the burden of running the farm and caring for the children, the loneliness sometimes became too much to bear. After four years of war, Mrs. Williams was at a very low point. Early in 1865, she wrote her husband, "there is plenty of deserters," and that she personally knew of 31 deserters near her home, and that "there are deserters here to night." She wrote her husband, "Franklin, I dreamed of you last night. I thought you certainly had come home." She added, "Franklin, why don't you come home. I know you have had chances to had got away before now. If you was here you could live independent."[18] She was implying that if he were home, he would not be bothered by the Home Guard.

Many women were faced with the problem of their husband hiding out nearby while trying to avoid being conscripted. This meant that while he was in hiding he had to be furnished food and other necessities. If he hid near the house, he could slip in at night to eat and see his family. However, there was the fear and stress on the family that the Home Guard might come at any moment in search of the missing conscript.

Thefts of food and other valuables were frequently committed by deserters or those hiding out to avoid the conscription laws. The people at home in Yadkin County feared they were in personal danger from deserters. One deserter, whose name is not known, reportedly stole so much that the people were as afraid of him as they were of the Yankees. Mrs. Robertson was told that a deserter once came to her grandfather's house and took a gun off the wall while her grandmother was in the house. She was left with only an ax and a butcher knife with which to defend herself, her children, and her home. The event so frightened her that, unless Grandpa was there, she slept with the ax and the knife by her bed until the war was over. The deserter came back and stole a little wooden box which contained some trinkets that Grandma cherished. Grandma's trinkets and beads were eventually found in the woods, but the little wooden box was never located. Later, the deserter was arrested. Because he made threats and tried to take the officer's guns, one of the arresting officers shot and killed the deserter somewhere between Mrs. Robertson's grandfather's home and East Bend at a place called "Indian Heaps."[19]

Deserters and "bushwhackers" hid out in some unusual places. A Yadkin woman told Mrs. Robertson that when a certain man thought someone was looking to take him away to the army he hid under a brush pile.[20] Creek banks and caves offered hiding places for some. One man dug a cave close to a creek and lived in it for about four years, until the war was over.[21] The late Hobert Vanhoy told a story of one of his ancestors who hid in a cave on a creek bank whose entrance could only be gained by diving under the water of the creek. There is a cave located on the west side of Highway 601, only a few miles from Deep Creek Friends Church where, according to legend, men hid out during the Civil War to avoid being conscripted. Robert Mackie, who lived near Yadkinville, reportedly hid out in a cave near his home during the war. Mackie was 35 years old, according to the 1860 Yadkin County census.

Area newspapers printed lists of deserters from the Confederate Army. The *Carolina Watchman*, a Salisbury paper, listed on August 18, 1862, the names of 26 men who had deserted from the 42nd Regiment. Two of them were Yadkin County men: B. F. Tucker and William Henry Wilson, of Company D, 42nd Regiment.[22]

Some of those who went absent without leave (AWOL) from the army did not hide out in their home counties but went to states under Federal control, such as Tennessee, or the Northern states. Moses P. Nicholson sent his family ahead by train and boat to Coatsville, Indiana. Then he and his brother went AWOL and traveled across the mountains on foot. The lived on water and huckleberries for several days. After the war was over, however, Nicholson returned to Yadkin County and purchased land near Flint Hill in 1879.[23]

Others left during the war (or soon after), never to return to Yadkin County. Quite a few Union supporters and draft dodgers fled the country. M. F. Farrington, while living in Westfield, Hamilton County, Indiana, wrote on August 28, 1864, to Jesse and William Dobbins, and described how he and 136 Yadkin "fellers" left Yadkin County on July 11, 1863. Along with Farrington were Sandy Vestal and John M. Martin. The group become divided, but 48 of the men made it to Indiana.[24] (For more on what happened to those who fled Yadkin County, see chapters 5 and 6.)

Yadkin County people read the area newspapers for accounts of battles and lists of casualties. News, accurate and inaccurate, of battles filtered back from the battle lines to the home folk rather quickly. Brigadier General Thomas Lanier Clingman's mother wrote from her plantation near the Shallow Ford of the Yadkin: "It is rumored here today that Gov. Vance was shot a few days ago ... somewhere near Greenville, but I hope there is no truth in it. Also a passenger in the stage today says that Grant has undermined and blown up a portion of our breastworks near Petersburg. I have been in fear of that for some time, ever since I have heard of his digging so much."[25]

All of these problems were compounded when Stoneman's men swept through the area, burning, looting, and carrying off livestock and valuables in early April 1865. Martha Doub Logan recalled hearing her grandmother Davis tell of how they buried their silver and money in the "wash house."

The women of Yadkin County did not confine their activities to sending food and clothing to their loved ones. They used every means available to try to get them released from the military. Elizabeth Chamberlain of Hamptonville wrote Governor Vance that her husband, L. L. Chamberlain, "has been forced from me to the army while he is deseased [diseased] in different ways, and I have understood that he was not allowed to stop to be examined but was sent right to the army and has to stay there diseased and afflicted." She describes her situation as that of a "poor woman and 1 child," and says she has neither "father nor brother to assist" her. She begs Vance to answer her letter, but warns him not to "put your name on the back for fear that I never git it." Vance passed the letter on to his secretary, and asked the secretary to reply that the governor did not have the power to release her husband and to explain the reasons why.[26]

Others did not sit idly by but acted with courage and daring. A story has been handed down in the Royall family of Nancy Vanhoy, the mother of Isaac Royall, who owned a considerable amount of land (believed to have stretched from the Pinnix graveyard through Marler and past the Lydall plant). Vanhoy is credited with not only selling part of her land to help the Confederacy, but riding horseback to warn Confederate soldiers.

The relatives back home frequently visited the army camp sites with items from home. William Harding, with two sons in Company I, 28th Regiment, made several trips to Virginia. On August 30, 1862, he was in Lynchburg, as reported by John Thomas Conrad, there recuperating in a private home.[27]

While many of the soldiers are buried in unmarked battlefield graves, several were brought back to Yadkin County for burial. Embalming was practiced during the Civil War. If someone notified the family quickly enough of the death of a relative, they could employ an embalmer and seal the body in a lead coffin for transportation home. After the Battle of Ream's Station, near Petersburg, Virginia, William Harding made another trip to Virginia. He was accompanied by his youngest son, 9-year-old Thomas Renny. Their task was to bring back the body of Samuel Speer Harding, who had been killed in the fighting on August 25, 1864. It is believed that Samuel Speer Harding was brought home in a lead coffin on a wagon and buried in the Speer-Harding cemetery near Yadkinville.[28]

Not all bodies were brought in lead coffins. Some were brought in canvas "body bags" or woven "body baskets." The sons of Robert Alexander and Charlotte Martin Pettitt Poindexter, Thomas C. M. Poindexter and William George Poindexter, were brought home by family members in a wagon. "It took 2 days to make the trip home to near East Bend. These 2 were buried by candlelight as the bodies were so decomposed."[29] Mrs. Irma Matthews Robertson's grandfather told her of a local family who had a soldier in the Confederate Army. They learned that he was either sick or wounded and that he was not so far from home. The soldier's wife and her father decided to go to see him, but when they arrived he was already dead. They decided to bring him home in the wagon for burial. The weather was hot and they had to "fight buzzards all the way home."[30]

For numerous reasons, most families did not have the means nor the opportunity to have their loved ones embalmed, and thousands remain buried in unmarked battlefield graves, not in the family cemeteries. But there are exceptions. James Dallas Conrad, of the 28th Regiment, was wounded at Gettysburg, and died three months later on September 16, 1863. His father, John Joseph Conrad, took a wagon and went to Gettysburg to pick up his son's body. The body was put in a box and covered with sawdust.[31]

County Government

With the coming of war, county government had to make changes. As early as June 1861, a special court of the justices of the peace, at which 22 were present, was held to double the state and county tax for the year 1861 on all objects of taxation "which increase shall be applied by to the equip[ment] of the volunteers now raised and to be raised in said county and providing for their families." The tax was not to be "collected out of the effects of any man or the head of any family who has volunteered or any

The old Yadkin County Courthouse, circa 1900. It was built by the author's great-grandfather, William White, who served in the militia. Note that the fence around the structure kept out the "hogs and cattle" (courtesy Anne Speer Riley and Studio One).

volunteer before the collection of the same." T. C. Hauser, Isaac Jarratt, J. A. Williams, Aquilla Speer and Josiah Cowles were appointed to a committee to receive the tax and "pay out the same." William A. Roby was appointed to purchase "corn, wheat, flour, bacon, pork" and other provisions for the families of soldiers and other needy persons, in place of J. A. Bitting.[32] (Bitting's biographical sketch mentions that he took care of the families of the soldiers.[33]) Salt, a necessary commodity, was a matter of great concern. Isaac Jarratt was ordered to write the governor about the salt agent for the state giving wagoners part of the salt intended for the county in payment for hauling the salt.[34]

Thirty-one justices were present for court in October 1863 when it was ordered that the salt agent, S. H. Bohanon, be "required in distributing the salt in said county, just to supply the families of soldiers and indigent families in said county, and the balance if any, to be distributed among such as receive Confederate money."[35] The agent was ordered to go to Raleigh and to get permission to have "conscripts" go to Saltville, Virginia, to haul salt back to the county.

The county paid the poll tax for soldiers on active duty. On January 6, 1863, a court order empowered the county trustee to pay to W. W. Long, sheriff of Yadkin County, "the amount of poll taxes, both county and state, out of any money in his hands" owed for the year 1860 for those Yadkin County men who were serving in the Confederate armed forces. One list gave the names of the soldiers (except Capt. Speer's and Cook's companies) and the other lists men from those excepted from the first list—Company I, 28th Regiment, and Company B, 38th. The poll tax was $1.75 and payment was one of the qualifications for voting. Perhaps the reason was to enable the soldiers on the battlefield to vote by absentee ballot for them.

Some aspects of county government remained largely unchanged, although somewhat diminished, during the war years. Marriage licenses were obtained, and marriages performed. A number of solders married while on furlough (see individual soldier listings in Appendix H). People died and estates were probated. Deeds and mortgage-deeds were made and recorded.[36] Elections were held, but with fewer voting than before the war years. Prices continued to rise and shortages of goods occurred, but the county government could do nothing about those things.

It was not an easy time for anyone, either at home or on the battlefield. But, things would get worse before they got any better.

Notes

1. Salem, N.C., *People's Press*, Friday, May 24, 1861.
2. Letter from J. M. Martin to Jesse and William Dobbins, October 2, 1864, Jesse Dobbins Papers, in Speer, *Voices from Cemetery Hill*, p. 207.
3. R. D. W. Connor, *History of North Carolina: North Carolina Biographies*, vol. IV (Chicago: Lewis Publishing Company, 1919), p. 66.
4. Thomas D. Hamm, "Barnet C. Myers," in *Heritage of Yadkin County*, p. 519.
5. Virginia N. Woodruff and Betty N. Kennedy, "The James Harrison Norman Family," in *Heritage of Yadkin County*, p. 525.
6. O'Daniel and Patton, pp. 90–91.
7. J. G. DeRoulhac Hamilton, *Reconstruction in North Carolina* (1914, rpt., Gloucester, Mass.: Peter Smith, 1964), p. 77.
8. W. Buck Yearns and John G. Barrett, *North Carolina: Civil War Documents* (Chapel Hill: University of North Carolina Press, 1980), pp. 219–211, 262–263.
9. Letter from John Bovender to Albert Poindexter, August 25, 1862, courtesy of Patricia L. Caldwell.
10. John H. Kinyoun to Governor Zebulon B. Vance, in Frontis W. Johnston, ed., *The Papers of Zebulon Baird Vance*, vol. I, 1843–1862 (Raleigh, N.C.: State Department of Archives and History), 1963, p. 291.
11. Houts, pp. 1133–1135.
12. Nicholson, "Yadkin County's Centenarian," courtesy of Thad Baity.
13. Letter from J. W. Wall to wife and children, from near Orange Court House, Virginia, December 20, 1863, courtesy of Richard Andrew Mathis, Macon, Georgia. See Appendix A for copy of entire letter.
14. Personal conversation with Mrs. Irma Matthews Robertson.
15. Lefler and Newsome, p. 463.
16. Salem, N.C., *People's Press*, April 5, 1861.
17. Letter from Sarah Louzania Patterson Williams to husband, Jesse Franklin Williams, dated January 1, 1865, courtesy of Mrs. Sarah Augusta Davis Phillips.
18. *Ibid.*
19. Irma Matthews Robertson, "Stories About Yadkin County During the Civil War," *Journal of the Yadkin County Historical & Genealogical Society* IX (June 1990): 21.
20. *Ibid.*
21. *Ibid.*
22. List of deserters from the 42nd Regiment, N.C.S.T., Salisbury, N.C., *Carolina Watchman*, August 18, 1862, from microfilm in the North Carolina Room, Winston-Salem Public Library, Winston-Salem, N.C.

23. Mary Eliza Nicholson, "History as Gathered on Anderson and Grace Nicholson Families," in *Heritage of Yadkin County*, p. 524.

24. Letter from M. F. Farrington and Iredell Warden to Jesse and William Dobbins, August 28, 1864, in *Journal of the Yadkin County Historical Society* IV (December 1986): 14; *Martin Family News* II (July 1, 1986).

25. Jane Poindexter Clingman to Gen. Thomas L. Clingman, August 1, 1864, *Heritage of Yadkin County*, p. 142.

26. Elizabeth Chamberlain to Governor Zebulon Vance, November 21, 1862. Johnston, Frontis W., ed., *The Papers of Zebulon Baird Vance*, vol. II, 1843–1862 (Raleigh, N.C.: State Department of Archives and History, 1963), pp. 380–381.

27. O'Daniel and Patton, p. 312.

28. Family tradition, related to the author by her cousin, Felix Harding, age 84 in 1995, as told to him by his grandfather, Greenberry Harding, brother of Samuel Speer Harding, and who was in the same company and regiment, Company I, 28th Regiment, North Carolina Troops.

29. Information from Miss Eugenia Poindexter, of East Bend, N.C. Thomas C. M. Poindexter, Company F, 28th Regiment, died July 10, 1862, of typhoid fever in a hospital in Richmond, Virginia. William George Poindexter died at Gettysburg on July 3, 1863, of battle wounds. They may not have been brought home at the same time, or the second body could have been another relative or friend.

30. *Journal of the Yadkin County Historical Society* IX (June 1990): 21.

31. Family tradition, related to me by a Conrad descendant, Mr. Charles Conrad (age 75), March 12, 1996.

32. Yadkin County Court Minutes 1851–1838, 2 vols. North Carolina State Archives, Microfilm reel No. C. 105.300.01.

33. Connor, Vol. IV, p. 66

34. Yadkin County Court Minutes, 1851–1868.

35. *Ibid.*

36. Records of Yadkin County in Clerk of Superior Court's Office and Register of Deeds' Office, Court House, Yadkinville, N.C.

4

"Conditions Are Deplorable in Yadkin": Militia and Home Guard Activity

THE STATE MILITIA had been organized since colonial times. However, the fear of slave uprisings stimulated a reactivation of the local militia system in the mid–1850s. The 1st North Carolina Division that fought and won the battle at Bethel, Virginia, on June 10, 1861, was a unit of volunteer militia. Laws were soon enacted to revitalize the militia. After the Civil War began, the State Militia was reorganized and received their orders from the adjutant general of North Carolina, who had the power to control the quartermaster, the paymaster general, and the chief of ordnance for both the Militia and the North Carolina troops.

There was much activity throughout the state involving both the Militia and the Home Guard, although very little has been published about the activities of either group. While the orders from the existing correspondence from the state's adjutant general show one side of the coin, the reports made by the Militia and the Home Guard to their superiors, if found, might tell a different story. This is a vastly unexplored area in the annals of Civil War history. Simply to say that there was quite a lot of activity in Yadkin County concerning efforts by the Militia and Home Guard is an understatement.

According to the correspondence of the adjutant general, there were at least two militia companies operating in Yadkin County during the war: the 75th Regiment, under the command of Col. Andrew C. Cowles at Hamptonville; and the 92nd Regiment at Jonesville, one of whose officers was Lt. Col. James A. Hague. In April of 1861, Col. Caleb Bohannan was in command of a militia regiment in Yadkin County.[1] On April 15, 1862, Colonel Andrew C. Cowles of Hamptonville, commander of the 75th Regiment, 18th Brigade of North Carolina Militia, was ordered to purchase "rifles & double barrel shotguns" for the "detail militia" of his regiment.[2]

When the Home Guard was formed, the 9th Battalion, commanded by Col. N. G. Hunt of Panther Creek in Little Yadkin Township, operated in the county. The 9th Battalion had fewer than 10 companies, and was not a full battalion. There is no complete list of those who served in either the Militia or the Home Guard during the

Civil War years. (See Appendix E for a list of Militia officers. Some additional men who served in these units can be found in the individual listings in Appendix H.) Many Militia officers eventually enlisted in the regular army or were conscripted. However, those officers could avoid regular army duty if they met certain criteria. "All *commissioned* officers of the Militia are exempt from the Conscript Act, *provided* they were elected prior to the 8th July [1862]."[3]

To keep the Confederate Army operational after the volunteer enlistment times expired, the Confederate Congress saw the need to pass a "conscription" law on April 16, 1862, which decreed that all men between 18 and 35 years were to serve for a period of three years. The age limit was raised in September to 45, and by February of 1864, men aged 17 to 50 came under the conscription law.[4] Militia was used not only to enforce the Conscription Act but to round up Confederate Army deserters.

Some deserters were determined not to be captured and many hid out in the mountains, swearing "they would die at home before they would be forced off...."[5] As early as November 6, 1862, Col. A. C. Cowles was ordered by the adjutant general to bring in "B. A. Phillips, B. S. Cozzens, G. W. Shipwash, Wm. Norman, J. S. Colvard, Milton Murrah, S. D. Cresson, S. F. Marler, G. W. Shepherd, W. A. Speer, L. W. Hall, James W. Tackett, J. F. Flinn," all deserters from the 28th Regiment.[6] There is documentation that a large number of deserters were captured. Lt. Col. William A. Joyce, second in command of the Yadkin County Militia, received word that 15 conscripts from Yadkin County who had deserted from the 44th Reg. N.C. Troops were "now in the County going at-large and that no attempt has been made by any militia officer to arrest them." Joyce was reminded that Governor Vance had issued specific orders regarding the arrest of deserters and was told that "if these deserters are not immediately arrested and sent to Camp at this place, measures will be taken to punish the Commanding Officer of the Militia of Yadkin County for neglect of duty...."[7]

The members of the Militia were subject to punishment themselves if they did not obey orders to bring in deserters and conscripts. Sometimes, Militia officers listened to their conscience instead of obeying orders. Someone reported that Lt. Lester [Jester] of the Fall Creek Company, a part of Cowles' Militia regiment, had "kept concealed two deserters from the 54th Reg. N.C. Troops, nearly all the last summer."[8] Lt. O. A. Lineberry of Jonesville, a Militia officer, was reminded that "when Militia men fail to obey orders to arrest conscripts, and deserters, they should be arrested and placed in jail till a Court Martial can be ordered to try them."[9] The Militia was expected to feed the conscripts and deserters that they had arrested, and they were authorized to "purchase provisions, taking care not to purchase any more than is actually necessary." The Militia members were to be paid for the time spent in capturing and transporting deserters to one of the military encampments.[10]

Many of those known to have been in the Militia, the Home Guard, or both, were community leaders and active in their local churches, such as Benjamin A. Phillips and Lafayette Dee Shugart. Shugart, a member of the Militia and the Home Guard, was described as "being kind and understand[ing] but at the same time very persistent and very firm in the execution of his duties in the Home Guard." Shugart is believed to have been a member of the Militia who was ordered to the Bond School House in February of 1863 to arrest conscripts hiding there.[11] The conscripts had taken refuge from the cold in the school house near Quaker Deep Creek Church. When the Militia arrived, firing began on both sides, and four men were killed. (Chapter 5 has more information on this event.) Militia officer Lieutenant Colonel W. A. Joyce wrote Governor Vance after the affair at the Bond School urging that a reward be offered for those "four bad and dangerous men to insure their apprehension." Joyce believed that it would "deter others from resisting the execution of the law." He informed the governor: "We have arrested and sent out of the county within the three months past over 100 men, and yet we have a considerable number left." Joyce requested a detachment of 40 to 50 men be sent to Yadkin because the county Militia had "scarcely any arms or ammunition."[12]

Home Guard Is Formed

Governor Zebulon Vance ordered the Militia to arrest Confederate deserters, but those orders were overruled by Judge Richmond Pearson, thereby making the conscription laws illegal. In order to override Pearson's decision, the North Carolina General Assembly gave the governor specific powers to arrest deserters, and created the "Guard for Home Defense" (Home Guard). Pearson then ruled that the Home Guard did not have the authority, overruling Vance again, so the General Assembly gave Vance "full legal authority to employ the Home Guard for this purpose,"[13] in order to bypass the judge's ruling. The formation of the Home Guard was authorized by General Orders No. 1, which gave Governor Vance the authority to command the Home Guard. The military establishment and state officials continued to feud with Judge Pearson over enforcement of the conscript laws, as evident in the adjutant general's letter to Liles:

> The decision of Judge Pearson is not considered law. The case has been made up to be brought before the Supreme Court, until their decision is known, the orders heretofore issued from this office in regard to the apprehension of deserters and conscripts should be executed.[14]

Usually, the Home Guard troops worked in groups. However, William Alexander Conrad, a member of the Home Guard, attempted to catch some deserters on his own, and paid with his life. Conrad lived on the east side of the Yadkin River in the Conrad house that overlooks the river near the Conrad Ferry site. On a Sunday morning in July of 1864, he was attending church services at Brookstown Methodist Church when he learned that three "deserters" were heading toward Glenn's Ferry, owned by Tyre Glenn who lived nearby at the "Glenwood," one of the finest antebellum homes in the county. He rushed to the river to head them off, but found the men already crossing the river in a small boat. One of them shot Conrad, and the wound proved fatal. He died several months later. Years after the war, it was learned that the men were Union soldiers who had escaped from prison and were on their way to Ohio.[15]

Although the North Carolina Militia is incorrectly thought to have been replaced by the "Home Guard" through legislation enacted on July 3, 1863, both groups continued to operate, either separately or in conjunction. Activities conducted by one group are often attributed to the other, e.g., the soldiers at the Bond School House were thought to be members of the "Home Guard," when, in fact, the Home Guard was not formed until five months later. The situation was even further confused because members of the

William Alexander Conrad, a member of the Home Guard, was killed at Glenn's Ferry in 1864 while attempting to stop some escaped prisoners (courtesy Charles Conrad).

Militia were also subject to Home Guard duty. Many men in the Militia did not want to accept commissions in the Home Guard, but the Home Guard orders took precedence over those of the Militia. After the formation of the Home Guard, the job of rounding up deserters fell under their domain. The Militia's duties concerning conscripts and deserters "were not forbidden by changed rules, but the hunting up of deserters [was] put under the direction of the Commander of the Home Guard instead of the Commander of the Militia." However, there was still some overlap. Militia members were also sometimes members of the Home Guard. "The members of the militia being members of the Home Guard must obey the orders of the H. G. Commander in every respect."[16]

While on active duty, the Home Guard members were entitled to be paid for rations. By 1864, $1 was the daily allowance for those who furnished their own rations, but those who could not, were supposed to be provided rations.[17] The reluctance on the part of Militia men to serve in the Home Guard may have been part of a power struggle—a question of "who's in charge." Or there may have been other underlying reasons. The adjutant general of North Carolina stated the Home Guard's position in a letter to Major E. R. Liles of the 39th Battalion, Home Guard, on October 26, 1863:

> In reply [to your letter] I have to state that we cannot force officers to accept commissions in the Home Guards. The vacancies of those who decline must be filled by election. If the company refuse to elect, recommend a proper person for the position and he will be commissioned.
>
> When officers refuse or fail to obey orders, they should be tried by a General Court Martial to be ordered from this office. The Commanders of the Militia have nothing to do with members of the Home Guard, except the Militia Officers when off duty. No order of theirs [the Militia] can keep the Militia Officer away from his duty in the Home Guard.[18]

Perhaps some members of the Militia joined the regular Confederate Army on this account, and thus were exempt from Home Guard service. However, when they were discharged from their military duty or resigned (in the case of officers), they were then subject to Home Guard duty. Those men who became ineligible or too disabled to render service in the Confederate States Army were still liable for Home Guard duty, as were all men from 18 to 50. There were a few legal exemptions. These exemptions were physicians, millers, postmasters and mail carriers, Militia officers, a deputy sheriff in each county if there was no tax collector, one editor to each newspaper, college professors and teachers, and those who had a proven disability. Special boards were set up oversee examinations of men by physicians to rule on exemption from Home Guard duty. After an examination, many were exempted entirely, approved for light duty, or given deferments. A list of Yadkin County men who were examined at Yadkinville on Tuesday, November 1, 1864,[19] is reproduced in Appendix G.

Letters from the adjutant general to various Militia units further clarified certain occupations that were exempt from service in the Militia, the Home Guard, and the regular Army. "Those persons who may have been teachers but who were not at the time of the enrollment are subject to the Conscript Act.... Those tanners who are detailed are exempt."[20] Jesse and Benjamin Mackie worked in their father's (Robert Mackie's) tanyard making leather goods for the Confederate Army, and were exempt from military service.[21] A few men avoided going to the army by hauling salt from Saltville, Virginia. Others were exempt to work in the iron mining and foundry works of Stephen Hobson.[22]

Capturing Deserters and Draft Dodgers

After the Home Guard was formed, the job of rounding up deserters and conscripts fell under its domain. With the backing of the General Assembly and Governor Vance, the Home Guard may have become overzealous in its efforts to capture deserters and bring in conscripts for military duty. In attempting to arrest those persons, an undetermined number of men were killed by the Home Guard. A few surviving family stories testify to these killings. Some of these stories may be true. There was much activity in hunting down and arresting deserters on the part of the Home Guard (as well as regular army troops stationed in the state) because it was their job to do so. In looking over the individual soldier service records, quite a few soldiers reportedly "died at home, cause of death not reported." Could some of these men have been deserters who were killed by the Home Guard? Or were these men reported "dead" to stop the Home Guard from searching for them?

Three deaths can be verified. J. M. Martin, who had recently left Yadkin County and was then in New Providence, Iowa, conveyed the news from back home to William and Jesse Dobbins who were with the Federal troops in Tennessee.[23] Martin stated that three men had recently been killed in Yadkin County by the Home Guard: Ray Lakey, Solomon Green, and Elexander Blewbaker [Alexander Brewbaker].[24]

Ray Lakey's death occurred in the Forbush community when the Home Guard visited his home. Lakey, a young boy at the time, witnessed the soldiers coming down the road. The boy was frightened and hid in the barn. After a few minutes, he decided to leave the barn and hide in the woods. As he started to run across an open field, the Home Guard saw him and shot him in the back. He is buried in the family cemetery on the farm where he was killed. (According to another account, one of the Lakeys of the Baltimore area was hiding out when the Home Guard, attempting to capture him, "shot his buttons off" and killed him instead.[25] This may be the same Lakey, or another man.)

Mrs. Mary Lou Howell Foster told the story of Elexander (Alexander) Brewbaker of Huntsville, a private in Company I, 28th Regiment. A Huntsville girl, Miss Mary Chapman, loved "El" Brewbaker (a nickname for Alexander), and when he came home on a furlough, she begged him not to return to the war. While he was attending a cornhusking, the Home Guard found him and "hung" him. He was interred in the Mt. Sinai Methodist Church cemetery in an "unmarked grave." Miss Chapman never married, and left her property to one of the younger Brewbaker boys because he looked so much like her beloved.[26]

Other accounts are undocumented family stories. One of the Phillips boys, coming home from the army after being properly discharged, was shot at by the Home Guard, who thought he was a deserter.[27]

While in the Confederate Army, John Danner worried about his family at home. Every chance he got, he came home to cut wood, plow fields, plant crops, and do the necessary chores around the farm. Each time, the Home Guard captured him and returned him to the army. The third time he was captured, the Home Guard members tied him to a stake and shot him.[28]

"Bushwhacker" technically refers to a sniper, or a guerrilla-type fighter who, from the cover of bushes or trees, attacks or shoots at passing soldiers.[29] Those who had been drafted but were not yet in the military were called "conscripts." A conscript who refused to enter the army and who lived or hid out in the woods came to be called a bushwhacker. Generally, in family-related tales, the term bushwhacker is synonymous with conscript, one who avoided being drafted into the Confederate Army.

The late Prather Eddleman was 91 years old when he told the story of a bushwhacker, Tom Eddleman (the father of Samuel Eddleman). Tom hid out in the loft of his log house which stood where the Frank "Teeter" Eddleman house now stands on Speer Bridge Road between Old and New Highway 421. Prather told how the Home Guard came searching for Tom Eddleman. They entered the house and noticed cracks between the ceiling boards of the loft where Tom was hiding. They proceeded to run their bayonets up through the cracks all along the ceiling. One bayonet stabbed Tom in the side, but he made no noise. After the Home Guard left, he came down out of the loft bleeding. His sister cleaned and dressed his wound.[30] Prather Eddleman also told of another bushwhacker being shot while hiding in a thicket near where Forbush Baptist Church now stands. This man's name was Norman, a deserter from the army who was caught and shot on the spot.[31]

"Bridge" Dave Shore had built a mill and a large rock dam on Harmon Creek about 1850. In March of 1863, his son Frederick came home from the Confederate Army without leave to visit sick family members. His presence in Yadkin County was reported to the Home Guard and they visited Shore's mill and demanded that Frederick and some other local boys, who were believed hiding in the mill, be turned over to them, or they would burn the mill. Shore refused, saying the boys were not in the mill. The mill was burned, never to be rebuilt, but the boys were not found. Later, Frederick Shore returned to his regiment and was killed at Gettysburg in July of that same year.[32] Another relative, Anderson Shore, and his friend John Harville were killed by the Home Guard near the "Green Pond." They were buried in the Harville Cemetery, according to some of the Shore descendants.

In that same area there is the story of "Haney's Rock," where, reportedly, a man whose occupation was shoemaker hid out to avoid being conscripted. Attempts to document this story turned up "Findley Mahathey, 25, shoemaker" in the 1860 Yadkin County census. Mahathey may or may not be the person who hid out at "Haney's Rock" on South Deep Creek, but "Haney" may be a corruption of his name.

A Huntsville area soldier came home from the war for a time to make shoes for his children. The Home Guard came by to arrest him for desertion, and they asked his children where he was. They told the Home Guard that "He's in Goose Heaven making shoes." The Home Guard presumed he was dead, when in actuality he was making the children's shoes in a gully called "Goose Heaven." The shoemaker-soldier later returned to his unit, after finishing the shoes.[33]

William T. Dobbins was surprised one night when he was awakened to find armed "Rebel" guards standing around his bed. He was ordered to get out of bed and accompany them to town. As he wrote in his diary, "they took me like a thief or a murderer when I was innocent." He was put in the Yadkin County jail the next morning around daylight. He escaped when the jailer opened the door to let out some ladies who had been visiting their husbands.[34] William T. Dobbins was the brother of Jesse Dobbins, and they were to be involved shortly in the infamous "shootout" at the Bond School House (see Chapter 5).

Occasionally, the Home Guard arrested someone who was exempt from military or Home Guard duty, as was the case with R. W. Warden. On June 14, 1863, Col. A. C. Cowles of the 75th Regiment, N.C. Militia, was ordered to arrest Warden, a deserter from the 21st Regiment, N.C. Troops, who had reportedly returned to Yadkin County.[35] Almost a year later, on March 24, 1864, Major J. C. Gilmer, the commander of a militia regiment in Surry County, was ordered to release the same R. W. Warden, who was on detail as a salt manufacturer, and who had been arrested on a visit to his father "for the benefit of his health, with a pass from the Provost Marshall at Wythville."[36]

Undoubtedly, with all those in hiding, the Home Guard was kept busy, and their activities were not popular. In order to get back at the Home Guard, a group of boys took action. Some members of the Home Guard were sleeping in an abandoned house in the southern part of the county near the Iredell County line. The boys, led by Henry Groce, crept up to the house and, through an open window, saw the Home Guard's guns all stacked inside. They slipped into the house and stole the guns.[37]

The enlistment bounties and laws regarding the punishment of deserters were designed to alleviate the problems of desertion, but they did not. Opposition to the draft laws mounted, and the authorities tried to quiet the voices of opposition to the Confederacy and its policies. John Bovender wrote in the summer of 1862: "The Law got Caner [Elkanah Willard] bound over to the Superior Court for speaking in favor of the Union" [38] (see Appendix A). As early as March 1862, it was necessary to send troops into Chatham County to arrest deserters. On every side it was said that extreme disloyalty existed in Davidson, Forsyth, Randolph, Moore, and Guilford counties. Large numbers of deserters collected in this central region, knowing that the Quakers living there opposed the war. In Yadkin and Wilkes the disaffected men threatened to interfere with upcoming elections, making it necessary for Captain D. G. McRae, enrolling officer in Wilkes, to ask for arms and men "to arrest the large number of deserters and conscripts sulking about...." Farther west in Madison County, Major General E. Kirby Smith had troops to deal with the large number of deserters.[39]

Drafting or conscripting men into the Confederate Army seemed only to increase the number of deserters. In Cherokee County, a large number of deserters "had assumed a sort of military occupation, taking a town," and in Wilkes County, "they had organized, drilling regularly, and were intrenched in a camp to the number of 500." Reports indicated that there were 300 or 400 organized deserters in Randolph County and also a large number in the counties of Catawba, Yadkin, and Iredell.[40] Some of the soldiers on the battlefield, such as Col. W. H. A. Speer, thought the South could win the war if all those that had deserted were brought back, and the people at home shared what they had with others so that the wives and families of the soldiers would be taken care of.[41]

In neighboring Forsyth County, the Salem *People's Press* reported in September 1864 that "57 deserters, recusant conscripts, and men whose furlough had recently expired, were returned to duty—some coming in voluntarily and others were arrested.... Upwards of 300 deserters and recusant conscripts have been taken and have surrendered under the Proclamation of Gov. Vance, in Randolph and adjoining counties of Chatham, Moore, and Montgomery."[42] The problem was not confined to Yadkin County.

North Carolina Supreme Court Chief Justice Richmond Pearson did not believe that the Confederate conscription laws were constitutional, and he championed individual rights and "the sanctity of contract under the common law." When Confederate authorities arrested Jackson Caudle under the Conscription Law, Pearson was called, and he ordered Caudle released on a writ of habeas corpus. Caudle had been working for three years at an iron forge, an industry vital to the Confederate cause. Pearson issued writs for other men arrested under the Conscription Law on several occasions.[43]

By 1864 the military manpower shortage was critical, so bringing in conscripts became the main activity of the Home Guard. Even old Isaac Jarratt, plantation owner and slave trader who had served in the War of 1812, was now a captain of the Home Guard. He was ordered on June 13, 1864, to "order every man between the ages of 17 & 59 in the Districts which compose your command to appear at Yadkinville on the 6th day of July for Examination & Enrollment." Jarratt was also ordered to enroll and "order to appear" on the 9th of the month, "every male Free Negro between the ages of 18 & 50."[44] According to the 1860 Yadkin County census, there were over 100 free Negroes in Yadkin County. This order extending the age limit for Home Guard service, and the order to include free Negroes, may have contributed to further criminal acts and mob violence.

Events seemed to climax during the hot summer months. By July of 1864, anarchy reigned in Yadkin. Conditions were so volatile that a company of the 68th Regiment, N.C. Troops, was ordered to assist the Yadkin County Home Guard in protecting "the polls in districts threatened by deserters."[45] In addition, the reserves in Davie, Yadkin and Wilkes counties were ordered out, and Major Harbin of the Davie County Home Guard was authorized to use up to 25 mounted men, "if they furnish their own horses."[46] The involvement of the military was requested by local officials, and Major J. R. McLean, stationed at Camp Vance near Morganton, described the events in a letter to Judge Pearson dated August 4, 1864.[47]

The Jail Break

A breakout at the county jail had occurred in late June or early July of 1864, when 33 men stormed the jail at night and demanded the keys from the jailer. Among those in the mob was Elkanah Willard, a brother of those indicted in the Bond School killing, who had been arrested in 1862 for his Union sentiments. At the time of the jail break, there were only three prisoners: William Willard, Harrison [Horace] Allgood, and a man named Reed.[48]

Military personnel outside the county were contacted. Major McLean, commander at Camp Vance near Morganton, became involved in Yadkin County affairs. McLean sent troops to arrest Dr. M. L. Cranfill for "aiding and assisting." This was about the same time the county jail in Yadkinville was "forcibly entered by a mob and the prisoners, three of whom, at least, were awaiting trial for murder, were released, and allowed to go at large." In an August 4, 1864, letter, he stated that the events were a matter of "Common Fame," and had occurred "some few weeks ago." Shortly after the jailbreak, a mob descended on the town of Yadkinville and took the "arms and ammunition belonging to the Home Guard." McLean sent his troops after the men. The "jailbreakers, escaped murderers, deserters from the army, recusant conscripts ... escaped Yankee prisoners, and a few disloyal persons," and about "forty or fifty, including two of the escaped prisoners," and "the man who took the keys from the jailer" were caught in Watauga County near the Tennessee border and brought back to Camp Vance.[49]

The escaped prisoners joined a large body of men who were trying to flee the county to avoid being conscripted. Major McLean had arrested Dr. M. L. Cranfill in Yadkin County for helping men to escape and leave the county. Although martial law had never been formally declared in North Carolina during the war years, the military, because of the conscript laws, frequently arrested civilians. This led to a conflict between military authority and civil law, championed by Judge Pearson. Pearson summoned McLean to appear before him to testify why he had arrested Dr. Cranfill. Cranfill stated in a petition to Judge Pearson for a writ of habeas corpus that he had done nothing and was exempt from the draft because he was a medical doctor[50] (see Appendix A). Later, while in custody, Cranfill confessed to having knowledge about the flight of a number of persons attempting to avoid the draft. McLean stated that conditions were "deplorable" in Yadkin County, and that the "prominent and law-abiding citizens" distrust the power of the civil authorities to protect "their persons and property," and that there was a "strong desire for military interferences and arrests." McLean did send Cranfill to Pearson, but he (McLean) declined to appear before Pearson, citing poor health and an inability to leave his post at Camp Vance. He suggested that solicitor R. F. Armfield and Joseph Dobson, "who had counselled the detention of Adams and others for offences similar" to that which M. L. Cranfill was charged, appear before the judge in his stead.[51]

The situation in Yadkin County was becoming critical. Col. N. G. Hunt, of the 9th Battalion, Home Guard, wrote the adjutant general that there were "numerous" deserters in Yadkin County. Hunt was ordered to capture or destroy "these disturbers of the public peace." Maj. A. A. Harbin, commander of the 3rd Battalion Home Guard in Davie County, was ordered to assist Hunt. Ammunition was to be supplied, but there were no "arms to spare."[52] The adjutant general ordered two Davie County Home Guard battalions to Yadkinville and unite with the 9th Battalion, under the command of Major

Hunt to scout for deserters in Yadkin County.[53] The adjutant general also ordered 6,000 pounds of bacon to be sent to Yadkin County's commissary, but regretted that the state had no tents to send.[54] The adjutant general made it quite clear as to what actions the Home Guard should take: "The state of things in Yadkin, as represented by Maj. Hunt, require that vigorous and prompt measures be adopted to correct them."[55]

North Carolina was threatened both from within and without. In October of 1863, when the coast was again threatened, General Order No. 24 was issued by the adjutant general's department. This order instructed commanding officers of the Home Guard in the counties of Surry, Yadkin, Rowan, Cabarrus, Mecklenburg, Lincoln, Gaston, and Cleveland, and all counties east of these, to assemble the men under their commands without delay. Once gathered, the men were to be divided into three classes (determined by lot or draft) which rotated duty shifts unless all units of men were required for the defense of the state. The battalion officers were ordered to arm and equip the men who were then to report to General Collett Leventhorp in Goldsboro to be organized into regiments.[56]

The problem of desertion and draft dodging continued, but by February 20, 1865, the adjutant general stated in a letter to R. F. Armfield of Yadkinville that there were no troops available that could be sent to Yadkin County to put down deserters.[57] The Home Guard and the Militia had more important duties that pertained to defending the state from enemy troops. In January of 1865, when coastal North Carolina was invaded by Federal General William T. Sherman's troops, orders were issued to the Home Guard of Yadkin and other Piedmont counties to go to Goldsboro and report to Brigadier General C. Leventhorp.[58] Thus, when Union General Stoneman's men were approaching Yadkin County from the east, only remnants of the Militia and Home Guard were available to dig trenches and set up breastworks on the west bank of the Yadkin River at Shallowford. Their attempt to stop the Yankees failed, and they fled when the Yankees crossed the Yadkin River.[59] (See Chapter 6 for more on Stoneman's Raid.)

The alleged killing by the local Home Guard of other local men, whether factual, fictitious, accidental or deliberate, caused resentment and bitterness among the people of Yadkin County. However, the Home Guard was acting under direct orders from the adjutant general of North Carolina in enforcing the laws of the state. Other Home Guard units from surrounding counties and regular Confederate troops were also present in the county at various times, and some of the deaths may have been carried out by these outside units. When deserters were captured, they were generally returned to their units, or tried by a military court, and sentenced to imprisonment for a time, then released. A few deserters were tried in a military court, sentenced to die, and were executed. Two such executions were Milton F. Willard and John Harrison by the 44th N.C. Regiment near Petersburg. (See Appendix A for Harrison's letters.)

It would seem that as desperately as the Confederacy needed men for the Army, the Home Guard would have tried to capture deserters and conscripts rather than kill them. Yet, deaths undoubtedly did occur as the Home Guard hunted down their neighbors and friends to arrest them for desertion or draft dodging. Perhaps they operated on the philosophy that a dead Union sympathizer was better than a reluctant Confederate; or, perhaps, after giving the man a chance to give himself up and go voluntarily, he ran or pulled out a gun, or did something else that caused the Home Guard to kill him.

These and other war-related deaths were endured in silence by many families. As a result, some families may have harbored a seething hatred for the Confederacy and all it stood for. The facts about a father's death (if it occurred as a result of his being hunted down for desertion or draft dodging) may have been kept from his children, and even from his grandchildren, or his death may have been used to instill hatred against the Confederacy. From the tales that are just now beginning to surface, it is evident that there was much violence in Yadkin County, which, perhaps, was more terrifying to the people living there than the guns of the Yankees in faraway Virginia. Could there have been so many killings that even those who previously supported the Confederacy became pro–Union in sentiment? Was this legalized "murder" one reason, and perhaps the primary reason, that Yadkin County became Republican immediately after the war and has remained so for 130 years? Because the Home Guard was under the direct order of North Carolina Governor Vance, Yadkin County could have purposely distanced itself from the state by voting Republican from the time of the party's formation shortly after the end of the war to the time of this writing.

Notes

1. Gerald Wilson Cook, *The Last Tarheel Militia 1861–1865*, privately published, 1987, p. 17.
2. Cook, p. 22; Stephen E. Bradley, Jr. (abst.), *North Carolina Confederate Militia and Home Guard Records*, vol. I (privately published, 1995), p. 50; Microfilm #AG 44, North Carolina Department of Archives and History, Raleigh, N.C.
3. Adjutant General's *State Militia Letter Book*, p. 161, dated July 31, 1862, cited in Cook, p. 24; Microfilm #AG44, North Carolina State Department of Archives and History, Raleigh, N.C.
4. Boatner, p. 172.
5. Barrett, p. 185.
6. Adjutant General to Col. A. C. Cowles, November 6, 1862, cited in Cook, p. 28.
7. Adjutant General to Lt. Col. Wm. A. Joyce, December 9, 1862, cited in Cook, p. 29.
8. Adjutant General to Col. A. C. Cowles, January 28, 1863, cited in Cook, p. 33.
9. Adjutant General to Lt. O. A. Lineberry, January 29, 1863, cited in Cook, p. 34.
10. Cook, p. 26.
11. Hazel Shugart Wall and Dorothy S. Shugart, "Lafayette D. and Elizabeth Woodhouse Shugart," in *Heritage of Yadkin County*, p. 594.
12. William A. Joyce to Governor Vance, February 16, 1863. *O. R.*, series I, vol. 18, Chapter XXX, pp. 880–881.
13. Cook, p. 18.
14. *Ibid.*
15. O'Daniel and Harris, p. 131.
16. Adjutant General to Lt. J. M. Marshall, Mt. Airy, July 28, 1864, cited in Cook, p. 49.
17. Adjutant General to Major N. G. Hunt, 9th Battalion Home Guard, Panther Creek, July 27, 1864, cited in Bradley, vol. III, p. 58.
18. Adjutant General to Maj. E. R. Liles, 39th Batt. H.G., Lilesville, October 26, 1863, cited in Cook, *The Last Tarheel Militia*, p. 64.
19. Stephen E. Bradley, Jr., *North Carolina Confederate Home Guard Examinations 1863–1864* (Keysville, Va.: privately published, 1993), p. ii.
20. Adjutant General to Captain John B. Pugh, October 2nd, 1862, cited in Cook, pp. 26–27.
21. Information from Andrew Mackie, a descendant.

22. Frances H. Casstevens, "Mining from 1770 On," in *Heritage of Yadkin County*, p. 89.

23. C. Hilton Jones, "Yadkin County During the Civil War," in *Heritage of Yadkin County*, pp. 144–145; Letter from J. M. Martin to William and Jesse Dobbins, October 2, 1864, Jesse Dobbins Papers, in Speer, *Voices from Cemetery Hill*, pp. 207–208.

24. J. M. Martin of New Providence, Iowa, to William and Jesse Dobbins, October 2, 1864, Jesse Dobbins Papers, in Speer, *Voices from Cemetery Hill*, p. 207.

25. Information told by an aunt to Edith Garner Sharpless, of Yadkinville, N.C.

26. "Interview with Mary Lou Howell Foster, July 29, 1991," *Journal of the Yadkin County Historical & Genealogical Society* X (September 1991): 16; conversation with Sue Brewbaker Royall, March 2, 1996.

27. Information told by an aunt to Edith Garner Sharpless, of Yadkinville, N.C.

28. *Ibid.*

29. Boatner, p. 109.

30. "Bushwackers During the Civil War: A Story About Yadkin County Men as Told by Prayther Eddleman (age 91) to Ernest Groce, March, 1988," in *Journal of the Yadkin County Historical Society* VII (June 1988): 10.

31. *Ibid.*

32. Jones, in *Heritage of Yadkin County*, pp. 145–146.

33. This account was related by Anne Clingman White, of Yadkinville, N.C., on March 9, 1995, to Frances H. Casstevens. The soldier who lived near the Wyo community was an ancestor of Anne's husband, David White.

34. Diary of William T. Dobbins, in Speer, *Voices from Cemetery Hill*, p. 215.

35. Ajdutant General to Col. A. C. Cowles, 75th Regiment NCM, Hamptonville, N.C., June 14, 1863, cited in Bradley, vol. I, p. 61.

36. Adjutant General to Maj. J. C. Gilmer, commander of Home Guard, Mt. Airy, N.C., cited in Bradley, vol. III, p. 41.

37. Jones, in *Heritage of Yadkin County*, pp. 145–146.

38. Letter from John Bovender to Albert Poindexter, August 25, 1862, courtesy of Patricia L. Caldwell.

39. Barrett, p. 184.

40. *Ibid.*, p. 186.

41. Letter from Col. William H. A. Speer to father and mother, Feb. 18, 1864, in Speer, *Voices from Cemetery Hill*, p. 121.

42. Salem *People's Press* 29 September 1864, reprinted in *The Forsyth County Genealogical Society Newsletter*, November 1995.

43. James Albert Hutchens, "Richmond Mumford Pearson," *Heritage of Yadkin County*, pp. 177–180.

44. David H. Ray to Capt. I. C. Jarratt, June 13, 1864, in *Heritage of Yadkin County*, p. 146, courtesy of the late Bruce Jarratt.

45. Adjutant General to Maj. N. C. Hunt, 9th Battalion Home Guard, Panther Creek, cited in Bradley, vol. III, p. 58.

46. Adjutant General to Major A. A. Harbin, 3rd Battalion Home Guard, Mocksville, August 26, 1864, cited in Bradley, vol. III, p. 845.

47. Letter from Major J. R. McLean to Judge Richmond M. Pearson, dated August 4, 1864, in Richmond M. Pearson Collection, Duke University, Durham, N.C., cited with permission.

48. Letter from J. M. Martin to Jesse and William Dobbins, October 2, 1864, in Speer, *Voices from Cemetery Hill*, p. 208.

49. McLean to Pearson, August 4, 1864, Richmond M. Pearson Collection, Duke University, Durham, N.C., cited with permission.

50. Jessie Casey, Petition of M. L. Cranfil to the Hon. R. M. Pearson, July 1, 1864, Pearson Collection, Duke University, Durham, N.C., cited with permission.

51. *Ibid.*

52. Adjutant General to Maj. N. G. Hunt, Panther Creek, July 16, 1864, cited in Bradley, vol. II, p. 54.

53. Special Order 78, cited in Bradley, vol. II, p. 43.

54. Adjutant General to Major A. A. Harbin, 3rd Battalion Home Guard, Yadkinville, September 6, 1864, cited in Bradley, vol. III, p. 70.

55. Adjutant General to Major A. A. Harbin, 3rd Battalion Home Guard, Mocksville, cited in Bradley, vol. II, p. 54.

56. "Minutes, May 16–August 11, 1861, Executive Department. General and Special Orders, August 18, 1863–April 11, 1865," pp. 478–479, Adjutant General's Department Papers, North Carolina Department of Archives and History.

57. Adjutant General to R. F. Armfield, Yadkinville, February 20, 1865, cited in Bradley, vol. III, p. 120.

58. Special Order 6, cited in Bradley, vol. II, pp. 60–61.

59. Thomas C. Phillips, Sr., "Dr. Wm. M. Phillips," *Heritage of Yadkin County*, p. 541. See also telegrams and other official records in the section on Stoneman's Raid.

5

The Counter Rebellion— The Bond School House Affair

THE BOND SCHOOL HOUSE affair came about because some Yadkin County men were hiding out to avoid conscription in the Confederate Army, and had planned to leave the county. Attorney R. F. Armfield wrote Governor Zebulon Vance:

> When the time came for them to go, perhaps nearly one hundred in this county took to the woods, lying out day and night to avoid arrest, and although the militia officers have exerted themselves with great zeal, yet these skulkers have always had many more active friends than they need, and could always get timely information of enemy movement to arrest them and so avoided it.[1]

As battle casualties mounted, and more men deserted from the battle lines, enforcement of the conscription laws became necessary to replenish the military forces of the Confederacy. To add to the problems facing the South, President Lincoln's Emancipation Proclamation went into effect on January 1, 1863. This proclamation, which freed the slaves in the states that were in "rebellion" against the United States (only the Southern states) had far-reaching effects. It put the war in the category of a crusade against slavery conducted by the North against the South, and gained support for the North.

Lincoln's proclamation may have precipitated an event on February 12, 1863, at the Bond School House, which shook the people of Yadkin County and stained the reputations of many with the blood that was shed that day. The truth of that event, which cannot even be classified as a skirmish, has long been suppressed, and the subsequent interference with the due process of the law left an indelible mark on Yadkin County and its people. That event was the death of two members of the Militia (James West and John Williams) who were attempting to arrest a group of escaped prisoners, deserters and conscripts who were hiding out in the Bond School House. Two of the draft dodgers (or conscripts), Eck Algood and Solomon Hinshaw, were also killed and at least one, Benjamin Willard, was wounded.

Someone reportedly passed the school, saw the conscripts there, and reported their presence to the authorities in Yadkinville. Gathering a group of men, James West led a group of militia out of Yadkinville the long way around, probably to not come close to the homes of Jesse Dobbins, one of the leaders, or his father, Jacob Dobbins. Jacob Dobbins' house was a short distance north of Jesse's, about halfway between Jesse's house and the Bond School. There may have been a road connecting these two homes with the school and Deep Creek Friends Church. At that time, there were at least three roads leading from Yadkinville to the Deep Creek Friends Church area: Rockford Road (present-day Country Club Road); the old Yadkinville-to-Boonville Road which ran past Shugart's Mill, part of which is now named Shugart's Mill Road; and a road east of Yadkinville which ran from Shugartown north to Rockford. A road off the Rockford Road ran by Dobbins' Mill Pond and came out on the Rockford Road again right at Jesse Dobbins' house.

"Capt." James P. West (1821–Feb. 12, 1863) was killed in the shootout at the Bond School House (courtesy Gladys West Haynes).

Although the exact number of militia at the Bond School is unknown, the likely members present included James West and John Williams (both killed), Richmond Murphy Gabard (known to have been there), and at least 10 others. Boonville historian C. Hilton Jones, now deceased, believed there were only 15 members of the militia at the school. Jones compiled a list of the names of the men who were present, and named four—Billy Williams, Leonard Kelly, Deck Reece, and Lafayette D. Shugart—who are not mentioned in other accounts. He also stated that there were supposedly eight more "whose names have been lost."[2]

The late Gerald Wilson Cook, in *The Last Tarheel Militia*, stated that it was the Militia that was involved at the Bond School, *not* the Home Guard. He believed that Billy [William Sanford] Williams, who was a captain in the Militia and therefore the highest ranking officer at the scene, would have been in charge. Second Lieutenant Leonard Kelly and 1st. Lieutenant Richmond Murphy Gabard (both of Yadkinville), were the other two commissioned officers. The rest, including James West and John Williams (the two Militia members who were killed), were probably privates in the Militia.[3]

The Militia probably took the old Yadkinville-Boonville Road, and turned right (crossing present-day U. S. Highway 601, about one-half mile past what is now "Jim's Grill"). This would have taken them near the Daniel Vestal home, where they reportedly stopped. There, the lady of the house had a premonition of what was going to happen to James West. When West told the Vestals his purpose of arresting the men hiding out in the school, Mrs. Vestal replied: "Yes, and thee will get thy head shot off thy shoulders too."[4]

The school (named after John Bond, a Quaker who lived nearby) was situated in a field just south of the Deep Creek Quaker Church. It was February 12, 1863. Snow had fallen and it was cold. The conscripts had taken refuge in the school and were planning to cross the mountains to Union lines. In the school were Jesse Dobbins, William Dobbins, John ("Jackson") Douglas, Jr., Anderson Douglas, Hugh Sprinkle, William Willard, Benjamin Willard, Leander Willard, Enoch Brown, Horace Allgood, Thomas Adams, James Wooten, Robert E. Hutchens, Solomon Hinshaw, and Eck Allgood (the latter two were killed in the fight). Even though the "draft dodgers" kept a lookout for the approach of the Militia, they were surprised and, reportedly, fired upon by the Militia. Those inside the school returned fire, and four men (West and Williams, and Sol Hinshaw and Eck Allgood) were dead in the next few minutes. Several were wounded, including conscripts Enoch Brown and Benjamin Willard.

Not only do accounts of the event differ, but even the number of the Militia at the school varies from 12 to 56, and the number of the conscripts ranges from 16 to 50. Legal documents and contemporary letters provide the facts about the Bond School House affair.

On February 16, four days after the event, William A. Joyce, Lt. Col. of the Yadkin County Militia, wrote of the event to Governor Zebulon B. Vance that things had reached "a critical stage," and that 20 to 30 "conscripts had lodged themselves in a Yadkin County school house," where they had "fought a pitched battle with a small squad of militia, each side suffering a few casualties."[5] A week after the event, attorney R. F. Armfield wrote what was probably a more accurate account to Governor Vance:

> Last Thursday, 12 of the militia officers came on 16 of these desperadoes in a school house about 4 miles from this town, armed, fortified, and ready for the fight. The firing immediately commenced, which side fired first in not positively certain, but from the best information I can get I believe it was those in the school-house. They finally fled, leaving 2 of their number dead and carrying off 2 wounded, after killing 2 of the officers. In the schoolhouse were found cartridges of the most deadly and murderous quality, made of home-made powder (one of the men known to have been among them has been engaged in making powder). Four of the conscripts who were in the fight have since come in and surrendered and are now in jail here, but the leaders and the most guilty of them are still at large; and the section of the country in which they lurk is so disloyal (I grieve to say it), and the people so readily conceal the murderers and convey intelligence to them that it will be exceedingly difficult to find them, even if they do not draw together a larger force than they have yet had and again give battle to the sheriff and his posse. But my principal object in writing this letter is to ask you what we shall do with those four murderers we have and the others if we get them? Suppose we try them for murder, do you not believe that our supreme court will decide the conscription act unconstitutional and thus leave these men justified in resisting its execution? I believe they will, and tremble to think of the consequences of such a blow upon the cause of our independence. It would demoralize our army in the field and bring the first horrors of civil war to our own doors and then perhaps subjugation to the enemy, which no honorable

man ought to want to survive.... I hope you know I am conservative and for the rights of the citizens and the States, but for my country always, and for independence at all hazards.[6]

Those two documents were all the information that was available until someone using the name "Col. Ham" wrote a letter to the editor of the *Yadkin Ripple* in 1906, 43 years after the shooting.[7] "Col. Ham's" letter was probably based on the account by A. A. Willard, a nephew of the participants. Only a condensed version of Willard's account has ever been made available to anyone outside the Willard family. The "Col. Ham" letter was located and copied by Lewis Brumfield in 1984 while going through some old issues of the *Yadkin Ripple*. (See Appendix A for the "Col. Ham" letter.)

In 1965, William E. Rutledge, Jr., wrote an account of the fighting at the Bond School House in his book *An Illustrated History of Yadkin County*, but out of respect for those still living (or their close relatives) omitted the names of the "bushwhackers." A condensed version by Tom Willard of the account written by A. A. Willard appeared in the *Yadkin Ripple* on November 19, 1992. It has taken over 130 years for more information to surface.

At long last, copies of the warrant and the indictment, which were thought destroyed, have now been found (see Appendix A). The names of the "conscripts" can now be documented. Still unknown are the names of all of the Militia who were at the scene, but the list of witnesses who were summoned is more than likely a list of those who witnessed the killings and, thus, include the names of some, if not all, of the Militia.

The warrant, dated February 16, 1863, the day after the incident, indicted Hugh Sprinkle, Jesse Dobbins, William Dobbins, Benjamin Willard, John Douglas, Jr., Anderson Douglas, Sanford Douglas, Lee Willard, William Willard, Horace Allgood, Thomas Adams, Enoch Brown, Robert Hutchens, and James Wooten for the murder of James West and John Williams, an act done "with malice aforethought." By February 16, 1863, John Douglas, Jr., Anderson Douglas, Sanford Douglas and Hugh Sprinkle were "committed to jail," but the others, including the Dobbins brothers and the Willard brothers, had fled the county.[8] Judge Richmond Pearson was petitioned to get the Douglases and Sprinkle released on a writ of habeas corpus, but when they were brought before him, he had each post a $250 bond until a trial could be held.[9]

An indictment by the grand jury, presented to the Superior Court of Law, fall term, 1863, gave more details. The indictment does not mention the death of John Williams, but describes, in 19th century legal terminology, how the deed was done.

> ...with a leaden bullet aforesaid, by them out of the Rifle gun aforesaid, by the force of the powder aforesaid so shot, discharged and sent forth, the said James West in and upon the left side of the head of him the said James West, close to the left eye of him the said James West, then and there feloniously, wilfully and with their malice aforethought did strike, shoot, penetrate and wound, giving the said James West then and there with the said leaden bullet so by them as foresaid, shot discharged and sent forth out of the rifle gun aforesaid in and upon the said James West by the force of the powder aforesaid one mortal wound of the breadth of one inch and the depth of six inches

of which said mortal wound the said James West then and there instantly died, ... [and those prevously named in the indictment did] kill and murder against the peace and dignity of the state.

The indictment focuses on Jesse Dobbins as the person, who "with a certain Rifle-gun made of iron and steel, of the value of one dollar then and there charged and loaded with powder and one leaden bullet of no value" shot James West on the left side of his head close to the his left eye. West was mortally wounded by the bullet which penetrated "one inch and of the depth of six inches," and he died instantly. A "true bill" was found "against all the parties," signed by solicitor R. F. Armfield, and Isaac Jarratt, foreman of the jury.

Witnesses who testified before the grand jury were: A. C. Cowles, Isaac Long, Sr., H. C. Cowles, A. D Gentry, J. C. Fleming, R. M. Gabard, J. S. Haynes, A. W. Blackburn, W. A. Joyce, William S. Arnold, E. C. Roughton, Wm. Reynolds, W. W. Long, John Bovender, Hugh Brown, and Wm. Adams.[10] Most of these witnesses were members of a Yadkin County regiment of North Carolina Militia. A. C. Cowles was colonel and head of the Yadkin regiment, and William A. Joyce was second in command. A. D Gentry and John Bovender were captains, and Richmond M. Gabard was 1st lieutenant. Gabard is known to have been at the school. These 16, plus the two who were killed, may be all of the Militia who were involved in the incident.

The incident raised legal problems as to whether the conscripts were under the jurisdiction of the military or civil authorities. Judge Richmond Pearson issued writs of habeas corpus for the release of the three Douglas brothers and Hugh Sprinkle, who gave themselves up. On May 27, 1863, Joseph Dobson wrote the adjutant general requesting advice about the disposition of the four men who were arrested after the encounter. The adjutant general replied: "...men bound over to answer a criminal charge [murder] can not be lawfully arrested as conscripts or deserters, unless by consent of the district attorney...."[11] The adjutant general wrote to Thomas W. Lindsey a month later on June 24, 1863, saying that orders had been issued to arrest the Douglas boys and Hugh Sprinkle. He also assured Lindsey that "There is no power to suspend the Habeas Corpus act." He advised him to respect the decision handed down by judges and "the rights of all persons who are not liable to the Conscript act."[12]

Mrs. Ruby F. Hinshaw told a slightly different, and somewhat incorrect, version. She wrote a letter to the editor of the *Winston-Salem Journal* to correct Arlene Edwards' article about the fight at Quaker Deep Creek School House. Mrs. Hinshaw stated that Sol Hinshaw (her grandfather) and a Mr. Algood, "father of the late Lum Algood," were the two Union sympathizers who had been killed.

> My father, the late Will Hinshaw, told me the story many times. He was only 10 months old and did not recall the incident, but Jesse Dobbins, a union sympathizer and Murfe Gabard [Richmond Murphy Gabard], the home guard who survived the battle, told him of the incident many times.
>
> Sol Hinshaw was the first man killed. They meant to kill Jesse Dobbins because he had threatened the home guard, but he slid down under a bench and escaped. The Willard boys did most of the shooting. Murfe Gabard stood behind a tree and saw them shoot Jim West. Bark was flying in his face

and a bullet went through his hat. Milton Willard, grandfather of the late Will R. Willard, was captured in Virginia and tied to the stake and shot. The majority of the Willard boys were never captured. Murfe Gabard was [the] grandfather of Homer Gabard of Yadkinville, and Annie and Early Caudle of Boonville. Mr. Jesse Dobbins has many descendants in and around Yadkinville.[13]

The men hiding in the Bond School House were not all dodging the conscription law. Horace Allgood was a deserter from the Confederate Army. William T. Dobbins, having been arrested and taken to Yadkinville by "Rebel" guards, escaped from the Yadkin County jail a few days later. He had been hiding out before taking refuge in the Bond School with his brother and the others.[14] The men hiding in the school when the shooting occurred were not all pacifists, and they were not all Quakers, although many did join the Quaker Church later. Roscoe Willard, a descendant of one of the Willards involved, said, when asked if his ancestors were members of the Deep Creek Quakers Church, that his ancestors were members of nearby Mt. Pleasant Methodist Church. Some of those in the school later served in the Confederate Army. Anderson Douglas fought and was wounded in the service of the Confederacy. His arm had to be amputated from a wound he received at Ream's Station, Virginia. Hugh Sprinkle served in Co. C, 30th Regiment, N.C. Troops. Some served in the Union Army (Jesse Dobbins and William T. Dobbins). John (Jackson) Douglas was shot by the Home Guard in the arm, and because of this disability, he escaped further military service. Sandford Douglas remained in hiding after the Bond School House fight.[15]

Several of the 16 men known to have been in the school were brothers. Some of these brothers did not live in the North Deep Creek neighborhood, although most did. Brothers Jesse and William Dobbins lived just south of the school. The three Willards, Benjamin, Lee (Leander), and William, were the sons of Allen and Nancy Willard, who lived in the neighborhood of the Bond School. The three Douglases (John, Jr., Anderson, and Sanford) were from the Yadkinville area. The two Allgood boys (Horace and Eck) and Hugh Sprinkle lived near South Deep Creek Baptist Church. Thomas Adams, Enoch Brown, and James Wooten probably lived closer to Forbush Friends or East Bend. Elkanah Willard, another of the Willard brothers, was not at the school. Milton F. Willard was executed at Petersburg, Virginia, but he is not mentioned as having been in the Bond School when the trouble occurred there, except in the article written many years later by Ruby Hinshaw. He may simply have been a deserter who kept deserting until he was tried and executed. (See his letters and the article by his daughter, Nancy Willard, in Appendix A.)

Some view Jesse Dobbins as a folk hero who was wrongly accused of a murder he did not commit. Others see him as a villain, a traitor, and a murderer. The truth probably lies somewhere in between. Jesse Dobbins wrote an account of the event some time after the war had ended.[16] His brother, William T. Dobbins, also wrote an account, which agreed with Jesse's, but with additional information about William being arrested by the Home Guard before February 12. He had been taken to jail, but he escaped and hid out in the woods until joining the group in the Bond School.[17]

Jesse Dobbins' "diary" gave the date of the incident as February 5, instead of the official date of February 12. Dobbins also told how he had been hauling salt out of

The Anderson Douglas home stood until recently, located just south of Yadkinville. Douglas was arrested in connection with the Bond School House affair, but later served in Company F, 28th Regiment, North Carolina Troops (courtesy Lucille Hauser Miller).

Virginia until he was conscripted. He learned that the officials were after him, and he hid out from about January 20, 1863, until the first of February, when it snowed. Then, he and about 15 others took refuge in the school. Dobbins describes being attacked by the enemy (referring to the Yadkin County militia), then he and several others escaped and made their way to Kentucky.[18] Dobbins told of his flight to join the Federal forces and escape the "filthy Rebs." He had to travel nearly 500 miles during the dead of winter, with the weather so cold that his clothes often froze to his body. Dobbins also attributed the death of his brother, William, to the "cold that he got when going out."[19] However, William did not die until sometime in the fall of 1864, more than a year later.

After leaving Yadkin County, Jesse Dobbins and the others traveled across the Blue Ridge Mountains, and through Tennessee to Kentucky—almost 500 miles in very cold weather. He had enlisted in the 4th Ohio Battery and then transferred to the 1st Tennessee Battery. Letters from Dobbins to his family indicate that three others who were sought in connection with the Bond School House affair—Thomas Adams, James Caswell Wooten, and Robert E. Hutchens—also fled to Kentucky with him and his brother, William.[20] Adams was with William Dobbins when he made and signed his will shortly before his death. That will was probated in Yadkin County in 1867, with Jonathan Wagoner and Thomas Adams attesting to Dobbins' signature. Jesse Dobbins was named executor.[21]

Although Jesse Dobbins was unwilling to fight for the Confederacy, he was willing to join the Union Army. He wrote in his post-war account that he "was willing to join the United States army for the purpose of fighting for the Libertys of my Dear country that is more preshus than gold…. The rebs say that I am a traitor to my country. Why tis this, because I am for a majority a ruling and for keeping the power in the people."²² According to his service record in the National Archives, Jesse Dobbins enlisted on February 27, 1863, at Lexington, Kentucky, for a period of three years. He was 34 years old, had dark hair and eyes, and was 5 feet, 10 inches tall. Most of the next two years was spent in Tennessee in Company B, 1st Regiment, Tennessee State Artillery. From July to September of 1864, he was listed as absent, sick in Fort Hospital, Cumberland Gap, Tennessee. From January to February of 1865 he was listed as sick in the hospital at Cumberland Gap. By June of 1865, Dobbins was on duty as a wagon master. Most of this is stated in his federal pension application, dated July 3, 1883, and filed with the Adjutant General's Office of the U. S. War Department.

Jesse Dobbins, who was involved in the Bond School House affair, fled the county and joined the Union Army. He later returned to Yadkin County where he farmed and ran a grist mill (courtesy Yadkin County Historical & Genealogical Society).

After the war, Jesse Dobbins returned to Yadkin County. According to an account by Abram A. Willard, nephew of some of the participants in the affair:

> He [Jesse] rode to Yadkinville during court, while his friends were greeting him with a warm hand clasp, the High Sheriff stepped forward, grasped him by the arm, and said, "Consider yourself under arrest." "What is the charge against me?" Dobbins asked.
>
> "Murder," said the sheriff. Dobbins's sudden movement of his person surprised the Sheriff and, freeing himself, he stepped back saying, "Sheriff, I have no ill feelings and bear no malice against you, and there has been enough men killed, but before I will submit to arrest under the charge of murder when I was fighting in self-defense, there will be more killed." So saying, he backed off and jumped astride a horse hitched nearby and rode in haste to Salisbury sixty miles away where a regiment of Union soldiers entrenched. Dobbins returned with them the next day. The soldiers surrounded the court house.

Dobbins, the colonel, and three soldiers entered the clerk's office. There were several men present at the time. The colonel, after looking around, asked, "Which one of you gentlemen is the clerk of this court here?"

The clerk answered, "I am. What can I do for you?"

"What the hell is going on here?" the colonel asked. "Don't you know the war is over? You can get your damned old records and burn them."

The clerk quickly gathered up the records and started to lay them on the fire. The colonel commanded him to stop and said, "It might be well for future reference not to burn the records. You can cancel the charge of murder and all other charges if any against the conscripts."[23]

Neither Jesse Dobbins nor any of the others mentioned in the warrant and the indictment were ever tried for the death of Captain James West. The Douglases and Hugh Sprinkle were jailed in Yadkin County, but they were never tried for the crime. Jesse Dobbins did return to Yadkin County accompanied by Federal troops, who, under the martial law in effect at that time, ordered the warrant be quashed. A trunk found by descendants of Jesse Dobbins not only contained Jesse's and William's diaries, but many family letters written during the Civil War years, and all of the warrants that were issued against Dobbins and the other conscripts who were indicted for the murder of West and Williams. How Jesse Dobbins got those warrants is still another unanswered question, but he may have obtained them when he came back to Yadkinville with the Federal troops at his side.

Even with the new evidence contained in letters to Jesse Dobbins and the diaries of Jesse and William, the shootout at the Bond School House remains a mysterious episode. Because the affair was suppressed, the rumors persisted and the facts were modified. The person or persons who actually shot and killed James West and Williams may never be known, but it has been said that Benjamin Willard fired the shot that killed James West. Which of the Militia killed the two conscripts, Eck Willard and Solomon Hinshaw? Did the conscripts fire in "self-defense," because they, like Judge Pearson, believed the conscript laws illegal? Who was the person who reportedly passed by the school, saw the men, and reported their whereabouts to the officials in Yadkinville? Has the blame been misplaced in the Bond School House affair? We probably will never know the answers to all these questions.

Were the members of the Militia negligent in firing into a building at random, without giving the men a chance to give themselves up? Did they give the men inside a chance to surrender? Could bloodshed have been avoided? Did the Militia fire first, or were they fired upon? No written accounts by any member of the Militia have been found to tell their side of the story.

None of those at the Bond School House, conscripts or Militia, were entirely innocent or blameless. For whatever reason the conscripts were hiding out in the school, whether they were wanted as conscripts or had deserted or did not believe in fighting, those men were lawbreakers. Attempting to avoid the draft, escaping from jail, or deserting from the army were all crimes. Their acts contributed to the deaths of four men—two of the Militia and two of the conscripts. The Militia might have been less quick to fire into the school, and they could have tried harder to capture the men without bloodshed. The whole affair has been surrounded in a veil of secrecy. However, because a trial was never held, the guilt or innocence of the men indicted for the deaths was never proven in a court of law.

What we know of this tragic event is based on half-truths, rumors, gossip, secondhand and biased accounts, and possibly even lies, from supporters of one side or the other. Perhaps much hatred, suffering, shame and disgrace could have been avoided if the truth had been told. The events at the Bond School serve as an example of the lengths to which men will go for what they believe in. The deadly deeds done in Yadkin County at the Bond School are but a microcosm of the American Civil War, a war which resulted from a combination of uncompromising and conflicting ideals and men who dared to act upon their convictions.

Other Incidents

Some of the conscripts who had been at the Bond School were captured more than a year later as they attempted to cross the mountains. This was probably shortly after U.S. Col. George W. Kirk's raid on Camp Vance near Morganton on June 28, 1864. Kirk led a raid out of east Tennessee, which resulted in the capture of about 240 junior reserves who were training at Camp Vance. The camp commander was away, and the camp was under the command of Lieutenant W. Bullock.[24]

The events in the summer of 1864 concerning those who were attempting to flee the county are as follows: First, a large group of men was planning to leave the county. They were assisted and encouraged in their plans by Dr. M. L. Cranfill and Alex Johnson. By July 1, 1864, Cranfill had been arrested by Major J. R. McLean in connection with assisting a large group to leave the county. Kirk's raid on Camp Vance probably took place while Major McLean was in Yadkin County making arrests.

Those being held in the Yadkin County jail were rescued in a "break out," led by Elkanah Willard. The jail was "forcibly entered by a mob and the prisoners, three of whom, at least, were awaiting trial for murder, were released and allowed to go at large." Then, shortly thereafter, another mob entered the town "and the arms and ammunition belonging to the Home Guard forcibly seized and carried off." After the guns had been stolen, McLean states that about 150 men left the county to join the enemy and "enlist (some of them at all events) in the Federal Army."[25] Thereafter, the jail was not considered safe, as described by Major J. R. McLean in a letter (see Appendix A) to Judge Richmond Pearson.

After this jailbreak and the theft of the weapons, a large group (136 according to M. F. Farrington in a letter to Jesse and Williams Dobbins) left Yadkin County on July 11, 1864. The group, led by Alexander Johnson and James Reedy (Reed?) attempted to get to Tennessee, and to make their presence less noticeable, they split into two parties. The group got scattered, and only 48 made it to Indiana. Those included Sandy Vestal, John M. Martin, I. A. Warden, M. F. Farrington, and others. The other group was captured attempting to cross at Birch Mountain, and were held at Camp Vance.[26] The Willard boys were in that group, as were Enoch Brown and Horace Allgood, and probably Elkanah Willard, who had assisted in the jailbreak.[27] It is believed that Romulus Vestal was also among those who were captured while fleeing Yadkin in the summer of 1864.[28] An R. S. (probably Romulus) Vestal enlisted at Camp Vance on July 6, 1864, and he deserted shortly thereafter.[29] Kirk's raid probably took place while Major McLean was in Yadkin making arrests. Enoch Brown and the Willard boys soon escaped from Camp Vance, but were recaptured. The Yadkin County officials did not know what to do with the prisoners at Camp Vance, but they did not believe that they should be brought back to the Yadkin County jail because "Our jail is entirely unsafe, to say nothing of the danger of their being rescued by their friends as heretofore."[30] The Willard boys were sent to the Forsyth County jail, where their sister helped them escape.[31] Elkanah Willard was put in the Morganton jail. He also escaped and made his way home.[32]

Warrants for their arrest on charges of murder were issued and the state Militia was called in.[33] According to A. A. Willard, when news of Elkanah Willard's escape reached the authorities, they ordered the Militia to go to Winston, take the other Willard boys from the jail, and "shoot or hang them." When they reached the Winston jail, the troops found that the Willard boys had already escaped.[34]

Major McLean wrote Judge Pearson in August, describing the jailbreak and noting that the escaped prisoners and about 40 or 50 others were "arrested in Watauga County, near the Tennessee line, bought to this Camp and delivered" to him. Among those being held at Camp Vance were L. L. Chamberlain, A. A. Lindsay, Thomas Johnson, and Wilburn Wright. A man named Adams had been arrested earlier because he had been "induced by others to take a false step, of which he seems to have repented, as he, voluntarily, turned back," McLean noted. McLean defended the previous month's arrest of Dr. M. L. Cranfill because he believed it was a "military necessity," and described Cranfill as a "dangerous man, able and disposed to interfere with, and render negatory, efforts and plans on foot to arrest a band of deserters and recusant conscripts, known still to infest and disgrace the County of Yadkin."[35]

The number of deserters and conscripts hiding out continued to grow; they banded together in groups in various counties. On August 24, 1864, orders were issued to the 1st, 3rd, 9th, 17th, 21st, 39th, 43rd, 54th, 63rd, 66th, 68th, and 79th battalions of the Home Guard to "capture or destroy the deserters from the Confederate States Army who are represented as banded together in the Counties of Johnston, Union, Wilkes, and Yadkin," and were reported to have committed robbery, murder and other "depredations on the peaceful citizens."[36] How many men hid out and how many left to join the Union Army is a subject for future research.

Notes

1. Barrett, p. 185.
2. C. Hilton Jones, "Yadkin County During the Civil War," in *Heritage of Yadkin County*, p. 145.
3. Cook, pp. 55, 181–182.
4. Col. Ham, "Reminiscences of 43 Years Ago," *The Yadkin Ripple*, February 14, 1906.
5. Barrett, pp. 185–186.
6. O. R., series I, vol. 18, pp. 886–887; Yearns and Barrett, p. 108.
7. Col. Ham, "Reminiscences of 43 Years Ago," *The Yadkin Ripple*, February 14, 1906.
8. Copy of warrant reprinted in *Journal of the Yadkin County Historical & Genealogical Society* VI (March 1987): 5–6.
9. Writ of habeas corpus issued by Judge Ricmond Pearson, typed copy courtesy of Allen P. Speer.

10. Indictment is reprinted in the *Journal of the Yadkin County Historical & Genealogical Society* VI (June 1987): 4–6.

11. Adjutant General to Joseph Dobson, Esq., Yadkinville, May 27, 1863, cited in Bradley, Vol. I, p. 84.

12. Bradley, vol. I, p. 93.

13. Ruby F. Hinshaw, "History Made Clear," Letter to the Editor, *Winston-Salem Journal*, July 24, 1970.

14. Diary of William T. Dobbins, in Speer, *Voices from Cemetery Hill*, p. 215.

15. Col. Ham letter; J. M. Martin to Jesse and William Dobbins, October 2, 1864, in Speer, *Voices from Cemetery Hill*, p. 207.

16. Arlene Edwards, "Early Civil War Days When Yadkin Had Draft Trouble," Winston-Salem, N.C., *Journal & Sentinel*, July 12, 1970.

17. Diary of Jesse Dobbins and diary of William Dobbins, in Speer, *Voices from Cemetery Hill*, p. 215.

18. Diary of Jesse Dobbins, in Speer, *Voices from Cemetery Hill*, pp. 212–213.

19. Edwards, "Early Civil War Days When Yadkin Had Draft Trouble," *Winston-Salem Journal*, July 12, 1970.

20. *Ibid.*

21. Yadkin County Court Minutes, 1851–1868, microfilm.

22. Diary of Jesse Dobbins, in Speer, *Voices from Cemetery Hill*, pp. 210–214.

23. A. A. Willard, "The Bond Schoolhouse Fight," condensed by Tom Willard, ed. (typewritten).

24. Barrett, pp. 234–235.

25. Maj. J. R. McLean to the Hon. R. M. Pearson, Pearson Papers, August 4, 1864, Duke University, Durham, N.C., cited with permission.

26. Letter from M. F. Farrington to William and Jesse Dobbins, August 28, 1864, *Martin Family News* II (July 1, 1986); *Journal of the Yadkin County Historical Society* V (December 1986): 14; A. A. Willard account.

27. Letter from W. A. Joyce to Major J. R. McLean, July 30, 1864, Richmond M. Pearson Collection, Duke University, Durham, N.C., cited with permission.

28. J. M. Martin to Jesse and William Dobbins, October 2, 1864, in Speer, *Voices from Cemetery Hill*, p. 207.

29. *N.C. Troops*, vol. X, p. 19.

30. W. A. Joyce to Maj. J. R. McLean, July 30, 1864, Pearson Papers, Duke University.

31. A. A. Willard's account.

32. *Ibid.*

33. *Ibid.*

34. *Ibid.*

35. Maj. J. R. McLean to the Hon. R. M. Pearson, August 4, 1864, Pearson Papers, August 4, 1864, Duke University, Durham, North Carolina.

36. Bradley, vol. II, Militia Letter Book 1864–1865 and Home Guard Orders, p. 43.

6

The Yankee Invasion— Stoneman's Raid

THROUGHOUT THE PIEDMONT and western North Carolina stand a number of state historical marker signs that indicate U.S. Major General George H. Stoneman and his men passed that way in 1856, similar to the one which stands just across the Yadkin River in Forsyth County, on the Shallowford Road.

> STONEMAN'S RAID
> On a raid through Western North Carolina Gen.
> Stoneman's U. S. Cavalry fought a skirmish with
> Southern troops at Shallow Ford, April 11, 1865.[1]

While the Confederate and Union armies were fighting across Virginia, Tennessee, Georgia, and many other states, Yadkin County remained untouched by enemy forces until Stoneman and his men arrived in early April of 1865. Stoneman, a protégé of General George B. McClellan, had had little success as a Federal officer until near the closing of the war. While in Georgia with Sherman, Stoneman attempted to free Federal prisoners held in the Confederate prison at Andersonville. His force was badly beaten by a Confederate cavalry, and Stoneman was captured. After the capture of Atlanta, Stoneman was sent to Tennessee to serve under General Schofield. Stoneman was about to set off on a raid in southwestern Virginia when orders were received by Schofield to relieve Stoneman of his command. However, Schofield withheld the order and had Stoneman reinstated after the Virginia raid succeeded. This gave Stoneman confidence to invade North Carolina.

As the commander of the district of east Tennessee, Stoneman led a Union cavalry force of 6,000 across the mountains into North Carolina. Stoneman's principal objective was to destroy Confederate property, especially the railroads. They were to avoid battle whenever possible. The force moved rapidly, as only a cavalry can do. There were one ambulance and four ammunition wagons, plus four pieces of artillery. The division was divided into three brigades: the 8th, 9th, and 13th Tennessee, the 15th Pennsylvania, the 10th and 11th Michigan, the 11th and 12th Kentucky, and the 12th Ohio. Many

Tennessee regiments were composed of North Carolinians who had fled west to avoid serving in the Confederate Army. The division commander was Brigadier General Alvan C. Gillem. He and many of his men were "home Yankees" who "had suffered depredations from their Confederate neighbors and now were determined to wring out some measure of revenge." This brought frequent conflict between Gillem and Stoneman. The Tennessee regiments lacked discipline, but Stoneman's other regiments were fine, well-behaved troops.

The raid began at Morristown, Tennessee, on March 23, 1865. Moving eastward, they entered Watauga County on March 28 and were soon in Boone. Gillem burned the jail and all the Watauga County records. In Boone, Stoneman divided his forces. Stoneman and one brigade moved east through Deep Gap toward Wilkesboro, a route that followed present-day U. S. Highway 421. Gillem and the other two brigades followed present-day U. S. Highway 321 to Patterson and Happy Valley. Both forces reunited at Wilkesboro. The next day, Colonel Palmer took his brigade across to the north side of the Yadkin River. After a heavy rain, the river rose, and Palmer could not rejoin the rest of the force, including Gillem and Stoneman on the south side of the river at Jonesville.[2]

General J. F. Hoke sent a telegram from Salisbury describing Stoneman's advance on Jonesville: "Lieutenant-Colonel G. C. Stowe reports Stoneman's advance at Jonesville, Yadkin County, last night in two (2) columns, one on each side of the river. Force from six to eight thousand (8000); six (6) piece artillery."[3]

Separated by the Yadkin River, the divided force continued eastward, one on the north side of the river and the other on the south. Palmer arrived in Elkin on April 1 and found a cotton mill and 60 at work there. The girls apparently welcomed the troops. The mayor of Elkin, a member of the Masonic Lodge, reportedly met Union General Palmer at the outskirts of Elkin and asked that Palmer spare the town. Palmer, also a Mason, complied. After receiving orders by flag signals from Stoneman across the river on a bluff, Palmer moved on down the north side of the river toward Rockford.[4]

While Elkin remained untouched, Gillem's troops did considerable damage across the Yadkin River at Jonesville. They devastated the Jonesville Academy, breaking chandeliers and school equipment.[5] This force continued eastward on the south side of the Yadkin River within Yadkin County until they could ford the river at Rockford on April 2. They then moved north through Dobson and Mount Airy, and recrossed the Blue Ridge Mountains at Fancy Gap. Arriving in Hillsville, Virginia, on April 3, they burned bridges and destroyed the railroad track.[6]

Sometime near the end of the war, Yankee soldiers came to the home of Catherine Shugart Reece, who lived near Charity Baptist Church (east of Boonville). They may have been a detachment of Stoneman's men on their way to ford the river at Rockford to rejoin their forces. Mrs. Reece, a widow with several small children, had only an old mule with which to eke out a living. She saw a cloud of dust as the Union soldiers approached. She ordered her children to lock the door of the house, and she went to the barn, taking along a broadaxe. She stationed herself at the barn door, and when the Yankees approached, she told them, "Kill me, if you want to, that's the only way you'll get my mule." She added, "And if any of you comes any closer, I'll kill you with this broadaxe." The soldier in charge took her seriously, and ordered his men to leave her and her mule alone.[7]

Some of Stoneman's men may also have passed Huntsville on March 31 going east toward Salem. On April 1, 1865, General P. G. T. Beauregard in High Point telegraphed Brigadier General Featherstone at Salisbury: "Enemy reported yesterday evening about Huntsville, moving towards Salem and Winston. Push up troops rapidly as possible, and look out for him on way to Greensboro."[8]

And at 9:45 P.M., Beauregard telegraphed General Robert E. Lee in Petersburg, Virginia, as well as General J. E. Johnston at Smithfield:

> Have just returned from Salisbury. Not now threatened by enemy. Reported to be about Huntsville yesterday evening, apparently moving on Greensboro, where I have ordered troops from Salisbury. Danville will probably be next point aimed at. Are there any troops there?[9]

While in Virginia, Stoneman learned that General Robert E. Lee had abandoned Richmond and was retreating westward. Lee hoped to join other Confederate forces in southwestern Virginia, but Stoneman's cavalry being in that region had a "profound effect on the events that led to Lee's surrender at Appomattox." Had the Confederate Army been able to reach the mountains of Virginia and North Carolina, they could have possibly carried on the war for some time.

Returning to North Carolina, Stoneman's men camped at Danbury in Stokes County on April 9. He sent out detachments to destroy communications. One detachment of Palmer's brigade narrowly missed capturing Jefferson Davis and the whole Confederate government as they fled south by rail, passing through Danville, Virginia, and Greensboro, North Carolina, on their way south.

On April 10, Stoneman left Germanton with the second and third brigades, under the command of Brig. Gen. Simeon Brown and Col. John Miller, and rode through Bethania on to Shallow Ford near the Yadkin River. At Bethania, they reportedly "ate everything they could find, and moved on to the Shallow Ford, on the Yadkin west of Winston." On April 11, the Confederate Home Guard at the ford was taken by surprise about dawn; after putting up some resistance, the guard fled, "leaving behind a hundred new muskets."[10] This story about the "hundred new muskets" is somewhat questionable, but someone digging for relics at Shallow Ford in recent years found an 1863 Colt musket buried under 18 inches of soil. Another gun was found shortly after the Yankees crossed by some of the slaves from Cooleemee Plantation in neighboring Davie County who came upon the skirmish site.[11]

Dr. William M. Phillips, who was 14 years old at the time of Stoneman's Raid, told about accompanying a group of county Militia (Home Guard) to Shallow Ford. They dug ditches and set up breastworks along the west side of the river where they thought the Union troops would cross. However, Stoneman's men crossed a few miles below the breastworks (possible in the vicinity of the Joseph Bitting place) and then moved northward up the west bank toward the breastwork site. When the Militia heard that the Yankees had already crossed the river, they dispersed to their homes.[12]

A Mrs. Billings, a long-time resident of the West Bend community, had heard that Stoneman's men passed the Black plantation two times, the second time quite near the end of the war. This would tend to support the telegrams sent by Beauregard on April 1 to Featherstone. They looted and stole everything they could find. Two rifles that had been brought home with the Black brothers, who had died while serving in a Georgia cavalry unit in 1864, were heated in a fire and then the barrels wrapped around a tree. The Black family had attempted to hide its horses and cattle by putting them in a large cave near the Yadkin River.[13]

After crossing the river, the Yankees moved through the village of Huntsville and burned the "Red Store." According to local tradition, they continued "looting and burning and taking the stock of all the slaveholders."[14] They also visited the plantation of Joseph Bitting, a slave owner who lived on a ridge south of the "Dalton-Hunt House," east of Farmington Road. Here they killed, captured, or ran off cattle and other stock. A courier quickly spread the news at Salisbury of a "small force of Yankees entering that place [Huntsville] yesterday morning at 6 o'clock."[15] Reports also reached General Beauregard at his Greensboro headquarters, that while camped near Shallow Ford on the west bank of the Yadkin River, the Yankees captured the "mail-rider," but he was released.[16]

There was much looting by Stoneman's men in the Huntsville area. Two Yankees appeared at the William Harding home on the Georgia Road (now the Wyo Road). One of the daughters sought the help of her brother Greenberry, who had been wounded and disabled while serving in Co. I, 28th Regiment, N.C. Troops. Greenberry was plowing some distance away, but he "cut the horse traces" and ran to the house. He fired his pistol and, according to family tradition, killed one of the Union soldiers. The other "hightailed" it back across the river.[17]

Some of Stoneman's men reportedly camped at the home of Dr. John Pattillo Clingman on Spillman Road, just a couple of miles south of Huntsville. In the house was Mrs. Clingman, who had just had a baby. Her husband and their 14-year-old son, John Jarratt Clingman, were away at war. Another child, a little 6-year-old boy, went outside to where the soldiers were camped in the front yard, and begged them not to burn the house and to spare the lives of his mother and the new baby. The soldiers complied, and the house is still standing.[18]

Stoneman's men left the Clingman house and continued south to Farmington and Mocksville. Because some of the Home Guard had fired at Stoneman's men, the Federals wanted to burn Mocksville, but Stoneman forbade it.[19] The Federal troops then moved on to Salisbury, where they hoped to find and release prisoners being held in the Confederate prison there. However, the Union troops found that all the Yankee captives at the now-empty Salisbury prison had been moved in February. At the depot, they did find a great stockpile of food and military stores, which were burned along with government buildings, stores and factories.[20]

From Salisbury, Stoneman's men moved to Statesville, then to Lenoir. Stoneman himself, with a few men to guard his prisoners, returned into Tennessee. Palmer continued to raid toward Charlotte, while Gillem and his two brigades moved on to Asheville.[21]

A detachment of Stoneman's men may have moved through the Hamptonville and Buck Shoals area in the western part of Yadkin County, and destroyed property and burned the mill at Buck Shoals.[22] Bertie Madison recalled a story told by her grandfather, Charles Andrew Madison, born November 10, 1857. Charles Madison recalled that when he was just a small boy, the Yankees came through the Buck Shoals area, "burning barns and taking whatever they wanted." He recalled that one Yankee soldier got sick and the others left him. Madison's father, William Braxton Madison, operated a

The William Harding (later Isaac Brown) House, off Speer Bridge Road, birthplace of Sgt. Greenberry Patterson Harding and Sgt. Samuel Speer Harding, of Company I, 28th Regiment.

store with John Madison. Bertie did not know whether the store had been looted or burned during the raid.[23] However, Alfred "Teen" Blackburn, who served as a bodyguard for his master, Augustus Blackburn, verified these actions. He could remember seeing Stoneman's men when they came to Hamptonville, "riding three abreast and burning everything along the way."[24]

During Stoneman's Raid or just after the war, a detachment of troops marched into Yadkinville by the Thomas J. Phillips place, which is on the eastern edge of the present town. William M. Phillips, a young boy at the time, recalled that when his family heard the Yankees were coming, they took all the livestock out of the barn and hid them in the woods. Phillips, who later became a doctor, remembered watching from a window as the soldiers marched by his home. A soldier approached the house and asked if there were any guns in the house and, if so, to hand them over. Phillips handed a gun, barrel first, to the soldier, and was told to turn the gun the other way. When he did not comply, the soldier took the gun anyway.[25]

Some of the acts attributed to Stoneman's men may have occurred later under Federal occupation during the "Reconstruction" years of 1865 to 1868. Acts of vandalism, theft, burning and looting may have been caused by deserters or stragglers from either the Union or Confederate armies. But the terror these acts inspired remains as part of folklore, sometimes undocumented but grounded in fact, though perhaps time has distorted the sequence of events.

General William T. Sherman devastated Georgia and South Carolina before turning his troops toward North Carolina. Everything General Joseph E. Johnston could muster, including the junior reserves, was not enough to defeat Sherman at Kinston, Averasboro, and Bentonville on March 19–21.[26] After that battle, Johnston moved his troops to Smithfield where he waited for the several thousand men in the Army of Tennessee coming up from Georgia, but they arrived with no guns. While he waited, news came that Richmond had fallen. When they heard that Lee had actually surrendered, some of Confederate troops did not believe it.[27]

The war was over for most when General Robert E. Lee signed the surrender of the Army of Virginia in a meeting with U.S. General Grant in the McLean house at Appomattox Court House, Virginia, on April 9, 1865. A number of Yadkin County men were there (see Appendix B). James Alexander Shugart of Company A, 1st Battalion North Carolina Sharpshooters, recalled "leaning against a fence" as a man rode by carrying the white flag toward the enemy lines. Shugart had just returned to his outfit from a foraging detail. He described abandoned equipment, dying horses, and discouraged, wounded soldiers straggling back to rejoin their outfits.[28]

Brigadier General Clingman was in Yadkin County recovering from wounds when he learned of Lee's surrender. He mounted his horse, and with "a colored servant," went to join Gen. Joseph E. Johnston at Smithfield.[29] He pleaded with Johnston to give him a command of the rear guard and to fight to the finish. Clingman then made his most famous speech:

Brigadier General Thomas L. Clingman in a photo taken after the war (courtesy Anne Clingman White).

> Sir, much has been said about dying in the last ditch. You have left with you here thirty thousand of as brave men as the sun ever shone upon. Let us take our stand here and fight the two armies of Grant and Sherman to the end, and thus show to the world how far we can surpass the Thermopylae of the Greeks.[30]

General Johnston reportedly replied: "General, if all the men were like you I would; but many of them are young and many have families to provide for and I cannot sacrifice them uselessly."[31] Other sources say that Johnston simply replied to Clingman: "I am not in the Thermopylae business."[32]

In between the surrenders of Lee and Johnston, President Abraham Lincoln was assassinated at Ford's Theatre on April 14. A few days later, Johnston surrendered to U.S. General J. M. Schofield in an agreement dated April 26, 1865, at the James Bennett house three miles west of Durham. Johnston and Sherman could never agree on the terms of surrender, but the problem was resolved by letting Johnston surrender to Schofield. This way, Johnston managed to get better terms than Lee had received. The majority of Johnston's men were to be provided transportation, and each Confederate brigade or group was allowed to "keep one-seventh of their arms until they reached their respective state capitals." Both officers and enlisted men were to be allowed to keep their private property and their horses. He also obtained enough rations for his men for ten days. The troops were to be mustered out at Greensboro where the supplies were deposited, then the men were to be paroled and freed to return to their homes.[33]

It was a sad day for the South, but a day that most people had hoped for on both sides of the conflict, and a return to peace.

Notes

1. Division of Archives and History, *Guide to North Carolina Historical Highway Markers*, 7th ed. (Raleigh, N.C.: Department of Cultural Resources, Division of Archives and History, 1979), p. 117.

2. Victor Seiders, "Stoneman's Raid—The Civil War Comes to Yadkin County," *Journal of the Yadkin County Historical Society Journal* XIV (March 1995): 8–10; Barrett, p. 484; Trotter, pp. 259–261.

3. Alfred Roman, *The Military Operation of General Beauregard*, vol. II (New York: Harper & Sons, 1884), p. 660.

4. Trotter, p. 259.

5. Ruby Bray Canipe, *Early Elkin-Jonesville History and Genealogy* (Jonesville, N.C.: Tarheel Graphics, 1981), p. 61.

6. Barrett, p. 353.

7. Family tradition, related by Dorothy Shugart McLeod, of Yadkinville, N.C., age 84, on February 10, 1995.

8. Roman, p. 660.

9. *Ibid.*

10. Ina Woestemeyer Van Noppen, *Stoneman's Last Raid*, 2nd ed. (Raleigh: State University Press, 1961), p. 47; *Official Records*, series 1, XLIX, part I, p. 333.

11. Personal conversation with Rick Manning, March 1996.

12. Thomas C. Phillips, "Dr. Wm. M. Phillips," in *Heritage of Yadkin County*, p. 541.

13. Personal conversation between Mrs. Billings and her granddaughter's husband, Julius Perdue, of Pfafftown, N.C.

14. Emma Long, "Both Gaiety and Gloom Mark Early Days," in William E. Rutledge, ed., *An Illustrated History of Yadkin County* (Yadkinville, N.C.: privately published, 1965) p. 26.

15. Salisbury, *Daily Carolina Watchman*, April 12, 1865.

16. Van Noppen, p. 62.

17. Personal conversation with Felix Harding, Winston-Salem, N.C., 1995.

18. Information from Anne Clingman White, granddaughter of John Jarratt Clingman, and great-granddaughter of Dr. John Pattillo Clingman, March 1996.

19. Barrett, p. 356, footnote.

20. Barrett, pp. 357–359.

21. *Ibid.*, p. 363.

22. Gerald Wilson Cook, "Some Family Stories About the Madisons of Yadkin County," *Journal of the Yadkin County Historical Society* XIV (December 1995): 15.

23. *Ibid.*

24. Margaret Cowles Bell Gough, "Teen Blackburn—Indestructible," in *Heritage of Yadkin County*, p. 22.

25. Phillips, in *Heritage of Yadkin County*, p. 541.

26. Barrett, pp. 318–349; Lefler and Newsome, pp. 459–460.

27. Barrett, pp. 368–369, 372.

28. Dorothy McLeod, "James Alexander and Martha Frances Reece Shugart," in *Heritage of Yadkin County*, p. 595.

29. Jane P. Kerr, "General Thomas Clingman," *The Trinity Archive* XII, no. 6 (March 1899): 393.

30. Burgwyn, "Clingman's Brigade," p. 449; and Clingman, "Charlotte Speech," in Clingman, *Selections from the Speeches and Writings of Honorable Thomas L. Clingman of North Carolina with Additions and Explanatory Notes,* 2nd ed. (Raleigh, N.C.: John Nichols, Book and Job Printer, 1878), p. 112.

31. Kerr, p. 394.

32. Glenn Tucker, "For Want of a Scribe," *North Carolina Historical Review* XLIII (April 1966): 180.

33. Lefler and Newsome, p. 458; Bennett, pp. 388–389.

7

The Aftermath—
Results of the War
on Life in Yadkin County

AFTER THE SURRENDERS at Appomattox and Greensboro, the weary soldiers headed home, usually on foot. Edwin Lafayette Transou, of Boonville, who had been standing in rank when Lee surrendered, walked home by way of Wilkesboro. He traveled a "rambling way, around the foot of the Blue Ridge Mountains, fearing to travel any main road on account of meeting Yankee soldiers going home."[1] The soldiers straggled home to Yadkin County, a land not physically damaged to any extent, but neglected and destitute financially. They came home penniless, ragged, dirty, sick, and usually barefoot. Large pots of soup were put alongside the road by the home folks for the hungry soldiers to eat.

John Wesley Choplin was luckier than some. He walked home from Greensboro at the end of the war. On his back he carried a 100-pound bag of flour, a gold breast pin for his daughter, and shoes for each of his children. When he reached home, his wife called the three children and made bread, the first wheat bread they had had since the last of the 1861 crop had been eaten. The family had not been able to afford new shoes.[2] One of the Brandon boys who had served in the cavalry rode his horse home and hitched him to the plow, a favorite family tale in the Brandon and Hudspeth families.

Of the soldiers who returned from the war, most were not only scarred physically but emotionally as well. They had witnessed death firsthand. Their brothers, friends and comrades had fallen, sometimes right beside them, on the battlefield. The cries of the wounded would ring in their ears forever. Many of the Yadkin boys had been captured more than once, and had to endure the hardships and humiliation in Yankee prisons for weeks, months, and even years before being released. Some had even witnessed General Robert E. Lee at the surrender, an emotional time for men on both sides of the conflict. The physical and mental capacities of the men were stressed to the limit. Many had left home as boys eager to fight, but returned as broken old men. Some soldiers never regained their health or physical strength. Others, miraculously, lived long lives, which they attributed to the hardships they had been exposed to early in life during the war years.

Society

There were many changes in the social structure. Major adjustments had to be made to a society that was no longer slave-based. The abolition of slavery greatly diminished the workforce, already made smaller by the absence of those killed or wounded in the war. No one knew what to do with the former slaves, or how they should be cared for. Gradually, a system of sharecropping evolved.

The people of a defeated South started rebuilding their lives, either with their loved ones or without them. The people of Yadkin County worked from sunup till sundown trying to scratch out a living from the red Yadkin County clay. They plowed, planted, and harvested what they could. They hunted for rabbit and possum, raccoon, and deer, and fished the river, ponds, and streams. Gradually, they covered the log cabins with siding, added windows, and porches with white columns. They went to church and prayed. Somehow, they managed to feed and clothe their children and, by being ultra-conservative, the farmers—both men and women—managed to make it from year to year, sometimes with very little, if any, cash left over. To get what they needed from the store, they traded eggs and butter for calico and candy. And they hoped that the next year would be better. The constant battle for survival probably helped heal the heartbreak of many families, which resulted from knowing that their husbands, fathers, sons, and brothers had given their lives and lay in an unmarked grave somewhere on a faraway battlefield, whether for a cause they supported or because they loved their county, their state, and the Southern way of life. Others remained bitter the rest of their lives because loved ones had been taken from them to fight in a war they did not support. Some of the women, like Elizabeth Ashby Speer, mother of Colonel William Henry Asbury Speer, remained bitter for a long time. In August of 1867, three years after the Colonel's death, she wrote her brother:

> In my last letter to you I told of my bereavement, my oldest Son Asbury was killed in the Rebel Army, he was Col. in the 28 North Carolina Regiment, he was killed at Reems Station. My poor heart bleeds when I think of my poor child being murdered. It was not better than murder to make men go to the army and get killed. He lived four days after he was wounded, a piece of shell struck him in the head and broke his skull. He was in his sense all the time and said to those that stood by, he should soon be where there was no war, that he had given his body to his country and his soul to God. If that be true he is better off than to be here in this troublesome world.[3]

There were many widows after the war, and few eligible bachelors. Some widows remarried, others did not. Mrs. Irma Robertson told of a Confederate soldier who took so long in getting home that his wife thought him dead and was planning to remarry. Luckily, her husband arrived home just before the wedding. Frequently, brides in these postwar marriages were older than grooms.[4] Black couples, former slaves who had not been allowed to marry, applied for marriage licenses. Stephen Conrad (listed as "colored") married Millie Glenn ("colored") on December 25, 1865. There were several more marriages for black couples in 1865 and 1866, and the number increased in subsequent years.[5]

The 1870 Federal census revealed a decrease in population (10,697 as compared to 10,714 in 1860). Many families sold their land and left the county for Midwest and Western states and territories. Some of the large plantations were sold for taxes and broken up into smaller pieces. By 1880, the population had increased considerably to 12,420, a trend that continued in subsequent census records.[6]

The black population declined after the war, and many left their masters to make their fortunes as free persons. They migrated to the cities and to the Northern states, and many suffered great hardships being homeless, penniless, and jobless. Those who remained in Yadkin County established black communities near the former plantations along the Yadkin River, such as at Huntsville, Jonesville, and Barney Hill. These communities grew around a church, school, and neighborhood store. The Freedman's Bureau was created by the U.S. Congress on March 3, 1865, to help blacks find jobs, establish churches and schools, and to assist the freed slaves with other problems. Many blacks became sharecroppers, working on the same land they had farmed as slaves, and some became landowners.

Politics and Local Government

When the war ended, chaos began. Union General Schofield had been placed in charge of North Carolina, and Federal troops were used to maintain order. He organized a police force in every county. Local "squires" were appointed and committees set up in every district to prevent looting and robbing and other acts of violence. President Johnson appointed William W. Holden governor of North Carolina, and Holden then appointed justices to administer the amnesty oaths, to hold county court and to appoint sheriffs and clerks of court. Holden also had the power to appoint magistrates and mayors and town commissioners. He tried to fill all those positions with former Union men or Union sympathizers. Taking an oath of allegiance to the United States became a prerequisite for practicing a profession or operating a business. Even before marriages were performed, both parties had to take the oath. Former Confederate soldiers and Confederate government officials could not vote or hold office until they had signed the oath, and some even had to receive special presidential pardons.[7] For several years, the entire state of North Carolina was under military rule. It was not until the Constitution of 1868 was adopted that North Carolina was readmitted to the Union and martial law was ended, three years after the war's end.

The Republican Party in North Carolina was officially organized in Raleigh on March 27, 1867. Delegates, both black and white, attended from 56 out of the 86 North Carolina counties in existence at the time. One of the leaders of the new party was Calvin Cowles, of the Hamptonville Cowles family, who had married Governor Holden's daughter. The new party was composed of Southern whites called "scalawags," Northerners who came South after the war, called "carpetbaggers," and the recently freed slaves.[8] The Republican Party was then organized in every county.[9]

Although eventually the state became Democratic, once the Republican Party was established it became the dominant party in Yadkin County. Credited with the establishment of the party in Yadkin County are W. W. Patterson, Wiley F. Shore, Jesse Dobbins, and Dr. Evan Benbow.[10] William Spillman, who owned and operated one of the leading river-bottom farms near Enon, was also one of the leaders of the Republican Party in Yadkin.[11]

State and county government was improved by the new state constitution of 1868. The Constitution of 1868 abolished slavery, provided for universal suffrage for men (not women) of both races, eliminated all property and religious qualifications for voting and office holding, set up popular elections for state and county officials, abolished the county court system, and established a county commissioner form of government based on townships. In addition, it set up a board of charities and public welfare and a uniform system of public schools. New state offices were created, those of the lieutenant governor, auditor, superintendent of public works, and superintendent of public instruction. The governor's term in office was extended to four years, and the name of the House of Commons was changed to the House of Representatives.[12]

A new voter registration was held from April 21 to April 23, 1868, and the people went to the polls and approved in the new Constitution and selected new state officials. The new government then ratified the Fourteenth Amendment to the U.S. Constitution and sent two Republicans to Congress.[13]

County officials for 1867-68 were: J. A. Hampton, county attorney; J. G. Marler, clerk of court; S. T. Speer (who had been sheriff during the war), clerk of Superior Court; E. C. Roughton, chairman of the County Court; A. H. Thompson (Thomasson), clerk and magistrate in Equity Court; T. L. Tulbert, register of deeds; E. C. Roughton, sheriff; and W. W. Patterson, surveyor. A special court was composed of A. C. Cowles, J. Williams, Sr., and John D. Holcomb.[14]

The county officials for 1869 reflect Republican Party domination: clerk of Superior Court—James A. Martin; coroner—William H. Brannon; register of deeds—Thomas L. Tulbert; sheriff—George Nicks; surveyor—Isaac Vestal; solicitor of 11th District—Virgil S. Lusk; treasurer—Benjamin Mackie; commissioners—W. W. Patterson, A. S. Jones, John W. Algood, Harrison Felts, and Aquilla Speer.[15]

In July of 1868, three years after the war had ended, the Yadkin County commissioners were busy restoring local government. County officers were sworn in on July 23. A new "blank docket book" was ordered to be purchased for Superior Court and county commissioner minutes. Roads and bridges, which had been neglected during the war, were ordered repaired. J. S. Jarvis and Isaac Jarratt were to repair the Jarratt Bridge, and J. W. Algood and David Shores were to repair Thompson's Bridge. Those who had been in charge of repairing the roads were ordered to report to the next board meeting. Allowances were made for paupers ($2 per month was the usual amount). The commissioners decided to sell part of the "poor house plantation." T. L. Tulbert was authorized to purchase "beds and bed blankets" for the jail, and make repairs to the building.

Jurors were chosen for the 1868 fall term of Superior Court, and each juror was to be paid $1.50 per day for court attendance. E. Spaugh, the Forsyth County jailor, submitted a claim to the county commissioners for keeping some of the men involved in the Bond School House affair. Spaugh claimed that Yadkin owed him $195.20 for the keeping in the Forsyth County jail of William Willard, Benjamin Willard, Lee Willard, and Enoch Brown. That claim and another for keeping David M. Reece were both disallowed.[16]

On December 23, 1868, J. N. Vestal, county surveyor, was authorized by the commissioners to lay off the county into nine townships: Buck Shoals, Knobs, Deep Creek,

Boonville, Liberty, Fall Creek, Forbush, East Bend, and Little Yadkin.[17] These township divisions lasted until the latter part of the twentieth century, with the exception of Little Yadkin, part of which was sold in 1911 to Forsyth County.[18] The remainder of Little Yadkin township was sold in 1927, and both parcels were annexed to Forsyth County.[19]

Looking to the future, the commissioners requested that meetings be held in the various communities to determine sentiment about the county taking $40,000 in "stock in the Yadkin Valley diversion of the North Western North Carolina Railroad." An election was held on the first Tuesday in August of 1869, with the final count 1,007 for and 178 against. The total number of registered voters in 1869 was 1,753.[20] However, this and other attempts to get a railroad in the county never materialized, an important factor in the economic growth (or lack of) in Yadkin County.

An act of the North Carolina legislature in 1875 created and chartered the Yadkin Bridge and Turnpike Authority. A bridge was to be constructed between Glenn's Ferry and Huntsville. Members of the commission from Yadkin County were John G. Marler and Dr. Leander G. Hunt.[21] In 1876, at a Republican meeting, W. W. Patterson, chairman of the Yadkin County Republican Party, and B. R. Brown, secretary, Thomas Haynes and Aquilla Speer were sent as delegates to the state convention.[22] Nicholas Williams of Little Yadkin, one of the planter class who remained with the Democrats after the war, was up before the Democratic state convention as a nominee for secretary of state.[23]

Religion

A number of new churches were organized in the county after the war. The religious revival undergone by the soldiers on the battlefield[24] carried over when the men returned home. Branson's *North Carolina Business Directory for 1867/1868* lists 19 churches: 8 Baptist, 10 Methodist, and 1 Christian Church in Yadkin County. Richard Poindexter was pastor of the "Yadkinville Christian Church."[25] This may have become the Church of Christ at Mt. Nebo, of which Richard Poindexter was also the first minister.[26] Some families changed their religious affiliation, such as that of William Evan Casstevens, who became a Quaker after he returned from the war.

Methodist churches proliferated. Baltimore Methodist Church was organized in 1866-1867 as a Methodist Protestant church. Boonville Methodist Church is first mentioned in 1871 in the church records. By 1888, the old Mt. Sinai Methodist Church was abandoned, and a new Huntsville Methodist Episcopal Church, South, was built off the Farmington Road close to town. What later became Mitchell's Chapel Methodist Church was founded in 1869 by some preachers from "across the mountains" who held a revival in a brush arbor near the Brindle graveyard. New Home Methodist Episcopal Church, near the older Prospect Methodist Church, was organized in 1867. Union Hill Methodist Church, near East Bend, was founded in 1875 or 1876. Fall Creek Baptist Church was established in 1875 and Forbush Baptist Church in 1876. Friendship Baptist was organized May 15, 1870. Oak Grove Baptist was established soon after the war in a brush arbor.[27] In 1867-1868, there were Masonic lodges at Yadkinville, Jonesville, and East Bend.[28] The Freedman's Bureau helped blacks establish the First Presbyterian Church at Boonville in 1872, which is still an active church.[29] Other black churches were established at Yadkinville in 1875, Huntsville in 1883 (now Tabernacle United Church of Christ), Enon, East Bend, and Jonesville.

Education

The late Fred C. Hobson, former Yadkin County school superintendent, wrote: "For some fifteen to twenty years after the Civil War, the public schools lost much of the progress that had been made. There was total economic prostration at both the state and county levels. From 1865 to 1871, public education became almost extinct." A few subscription schools and the academies provided the only educational opportunities.[30] The school system suffered a tremendous setback, and became practically nonexistent until about 1890. Little is known of the schools of the period, but Edna Bray Reece claims that a whole generation of Yadkin County children grew up illiterate.

Although the Quaker churches maintained their schools after the Civil War ended, Mrs. Irma Matthews Robertson was told there were no schools in the East Bend area. So, one mother began teaching her own children. Neighbors heard about her teaching and asked if she would teach their children. The mother, knowing they didn't have the money to pay, agreed to teach, provided she had the privilege of whipping the children if they didn't mind or would not study. The mother-teacher "nearly wore the children's clothes out whipping them, but they learned." Mrs. Jennie Bryant Foster (age 90) said that her father, William Riley Bryant, had enlisted at age 17 and had not received much formal education before war. After the war ended he returned to school, somewhere near Swaim's Knob Baptist Church, and received enough education to become a Methodist preacher.

Freedman's Bureau sent teams of missionaries to set up schools for freed slaves. One such school was the Hyatt Academy, which was located north of Boonville Presbyterian Church.

Economics

The postwar economy was devastated. Some men were heavily in debt, and their homes were sold to pay debts. Confederate money was worthless. The slaveowners, who had thousands of dollars tied up in slaves, were hit hard. Shortly before the war ended, Henry Perry, who lived near Smithtown, sold his farm and accepted Confederate currency in payment. After the deal was done, he learned that the war had ended, and he had sold his farm for nothing.[31]

Even though most food was raised or grown on the farm, much work was involved in manually plowing, planting and harvesting crops.

Eighteen sixty-seven was not a good crop year. Mrs. Elizabeth Speer wrote her brother:

> Crop cant be half crops, let the season be as it will, there is hundreds that will not make bread and many will not make seed owing to the wet in the spring and the drought in the summer. There was not a good wheat crop.

Corn and wheat is very high [and] there is not much to sell.... Bacon is scarce, not much to sell.... The hog cholera is raging in this country, as [a] great many have lost all they have got and they can't get any [hogs] to fatten.[32]

Even though times were hard and the weather uncooperative, there was still abundant game and fish to be found in the county. Yet many suffered, especially the freed slaves who fared the worst. Shirley Glenn Matthews related the story of her grandmother, a former slave, eating blackberry leaves to stay alive.

The use of tobacco had become popular during the war, and a tobacco manufacturing industry grew in the county. Before the war there had been a factory at Jonesville, started by Richard Gwyn and later run by William H. Reeves.[33] In 1870, tobacco factories were operated by Dr. Henry Clinton Wilson in Yadkinville, by George W. Burrus in Jonesville, and by Joseph A. Bitting at Huntsville.[34] The 1872 *Branson's North Carolina Business Directory* lists the W. H. Reeves factory at Jonesville, and the factories of P. A. Miller and Martin & Glenn at East Bend.[35] The factory of the Shugart brothers—James, Alexander and Isaac—operated at Boonville between 1870 and 1880 in a two-story log building sold in 1880 to the mercantile firm of Myers and Jones.[36] By 1881-82, 17 tobacco factories were operating in Yadkin, situated in every town and community.[37] These factories, employing both men and women, made and sold plug tobacco throughout the South. Other small industries were tanneries, grist and flour mills, and whiskey distilleries.[38] Nine grist mills were in operation in 1867-68: James Armstrong's at Jonesville; three at East Bend (Tyre Glenn's and J. Glen's, and Joyners, which was owned by William and R. Martin). Two mills were being operated in Yadkinville, those of G. A. Holcomb and T. C. Hauser; two at Hamptonville, Neil's and Rinehart's; and Carter and Wooten's (probably in the Fall Creek or Baltimore community).[39]

Frequently the small tobacco factory was operated in combination with a general store. The store owner took tobacco in as payment on accounts. He later turned the cured tobacco into tobacco products, such as plug tobacco or snuff, which he then sold in his own store or shipped to dealers in other sections of the country.[40] In 1867-68, the store of Fleming & Reece operated at Mt. Nebo; John E. Gough at Hamptonville; Nicholas Horn & Co., R. C. Poindexter, and D. A. Martin & Co. at East Bend; W. H. Reeves at Jonesville (known to have also been involved in the tobacco factory business); Martin & Roberts at Huntsville; Marler & Wilson and Nicholson & Gough at Yadkinville.[41]

The number of merchants increased to 12 by 1872, per the *North Carolina Business Directory* for that year, with a total of four merchants in Yadkinville.

Pensioners

It took several years for the state to get back on its feet financially. It was 1889 before the State of North Carolina enacted a law (Chapter 193, Laws of 1889), that allowed Confederate veterans or their widows to draw a pension. A pension board was set up in each county and to qualify for a pension, the veteran (or his widow) had to file a petition, and to swear that he did not own "over $2,000 in property." The pension laws were modified in 1907 (Chapter 674, Laws of 1907), and ratified on March 8, 1909, to state that a widow must have been "married to said soldier or sailor before the first day of January, 1868, and that she is now a widow, and has been for twelve months immediately preceding the Application for Pension a *bona fide* resident of North Carolina; that she holds no office under the United States, or under any State or county, from which she is receiving the sum of three hundred dollars as fees or as salary annually; that she is not worth in her own right, or in the right of her late husband, property as its assessed value for taxation to the amount of five hundred dollars ($500), nor has she disposed of property of such value by gift or voluntary conveyance since the 11th of March, 1885." The pension had to be approved by the county pension board. W. L. Woodhouse, J. A. Hoots, and J. H. James served on the Yadkin Pension Board.

In 1910, Woodhouse and E. L. Transou, pension board members, signed a letter testifying that Lucy Davis, then living in Boone County, Arkansas, was the widow of Martin Davis, who was "an honorable soldier in the Confederate Army," to substantiate Mrs. Davis's pension claim that was filed in Arkansas.[42]

The Yadkin County pension list for 1900 contains the names of 35 veterans and 30 widows, and by 1902, 79 veterans and 50 widows were receiving pensions.

A number of Yadkin County "pensioners" were not residents of the county before the war. Just why these veterans (or their widows) were receiving pensions in Yadkin County is unknown. Possibly they had moved here because there was housing and land available. The 1860 Yadkin County census shows a number of vacant dwellings. With families migrating out of the county after the war to western states, there may have been sales of property to persons whose homes had been destroyed in other areas.

The company and regiment of the veterans stated on the pension lists cannot always be verified. Granted, widows of soldiers may not have known their husband's company or regiment, only that they had served. It is also possible that the rolls containing the names of some veterans who applied for and received pensions were lost or destroyed. Many soldiers transferred from one regiment to another, and the regiment given may have been the last, not the first, in which he enlisted. Regimental numbers also changed when the North Carolina Troops were reorganized in 1862. "There was one system for numbering all regiments and a separate numbering system for the artillery and for the cavalry. Thus the 1st Cavalry Regiment was also the 9th Regiment State Troops." Initially, units were classified into "Volunteers" and "State Troops." To add to the confusion, the State Troops "kept their designations and the 1st through the 13th Volunteers were renumbered as the 11th through the 23rd State Troops." As the war progressed and regimental ranks were diminished, what was left was often combined with other regiments, companies, or battalions. Some of the Home Guard units, created in 1863, were officially organized into regiments and called up for active duty near the end of the war. There were also the junior reserves and senior reserves. These were also eventually given a regular regimental number.[43]

The military service records of men (or their widows) who applied for and received pensions were apparently not available or not consulted, but were based on statements of financial situation and testimony of persons who knew the petitioners. Others, who fared badly during the war, never applied for a pension, either because they did not qualify or simply as a matter of principle.

Anderson Douglas (one of the "conscripts" arrested in connection with the Bond School House affair) was noted to have an "arm off above elbow," and L[orenzo] D[ow]

Whitaker, of Chestnut Ridge (Center), had "lost an eye."[44] W. F. Cloer, of Company E, 49th Regiment, was drawing a Confederate pension in 1901, and was listed as "helpless from burns."[45]

Annie West, the widow of "Capt." James West, killed at the Bond School House shootout, began drawing a Confederate pension in 1902. Hers was the only pension granted to a widow of a member of the "Home Guard."[46] This designation was incorrect, since West was killed February 12, 1863, and the Home Guard was not established until July 3, 1863. Elizabeth Chamberlain, who had written Governor Vance to get her husband released from the army, was drawing a Confederate pension in 1900 as the widow of L. L. Chamberlain, who had died of "disease."[47]

Isaac Jarratt, who had fought in the War of 1812, was too old during the Civil War to be anything but a magistrate and a captain of the Home Guard. At age 81, he applied to the Department of the Interior, Pension Office, Washington, D.C. for a pension based on his War of 1812 service. However, because of holding even that minor office in the Confederacy, he was denied his Federal pension.[48]

The amount of the pensions was small, no more than $100 to $200 per year, but it helped ease the financial burden. Union pensioners drew larger amounts. Several Yadkin men or their widows drew Federal pensions. Sarah C. Dobbins, the widow of Jesse Dobbins, drew $8 per month beginning on September 3, 1890. She drew an additional $2 per month for each of her three children who were under 16 years of age.[49]

Postwar Careers

Captain Reuben E. Wilson remained bitter to the end of his life. With a shattered arm and the loss of a leg, Wilson remained unreconciled. He moved to Augusta, Georgia, and opened a business that lasted 12 to 15 years. His health began to fail and he returned to Winston-Salem to live with his sister, Mrs. L. P. Bitting. The rest of his life after the war, he never wore anything but his Confederate uniform.[50] In addition to his wounds, Wilson had other reasons to be bitter. In the hospital after having his leg amputated on April 2, he was arrested and later paroled on April 29. Ten days later he was again arrested and taken to Libby Prison and charged with shooting deserters who were attempting to leave Lee's army during the winter of 1864-65. The 1st Battalion Sharpshooters had been ordered to guard the fords along the Dan River to prevent desertion. Wilson was taken to Raleigh and imprisoned and was held until December 20, when he was acquitted. After Wilson's release, there remained only two former Confederates in Federal prisons: Jefferson Davis, the former president of the Confederate States of America, and John Gee, commander of the prison at Salisbury.[51]

Many of those who were able returned to work at what they had been doing before the war. Others embarked on new careers. T. C. Hauser sent his son, John Henry, on a trip to California. He sailed around Cape Horn shortly after the war. A photograph of him in San Jose, California, made in 1868, survives. He was back in Yadkinville by 1871, at which time he married Flora Ann Transou, the daughter of Ephraim Transou. Flora had traveled with her family to Texas just before the Civil War, but returned to North Carolina. When T. C. Hauser died in 1887, son John Henry bought the old mill on

Captain Reuben E. Wilson (1840–1907) as he looked after the war. Note the crutches he holds because his leg was amputated during the war (courtesy Lucille Hauser Miller).

Swisher Branch from his sister, which she had inherited from her father, and he ran the mill until he died in 1930.⁵²

Benjamin A. Phillips had been a constable of the Baltimore District in 1858, but resigned to take a job as an overseer of the Larkin Lynch plantation. During the war, he was wounded while serving in Company F, 28th Regiment N.C. Troops, and had to have his right arm amputated. He also received a serious injury to his left arm. "One Arm Ben," as he was called afterward, returned to the Baltimore community to take an active part in the Baltimore Methodist Church and community. He bought land and farmed with the help of his widowed sister, Elizabeth. Four years after the war, he married Dicy Ann Hurt, and they were the parents of five children.⁵³

Thomas R. Harding, who, according to family tradition, served in the Home Guard when only a boy of 10, went to work in his brother's store in Huntsville. He saved enough money to enter medical school in Baltimore, Maryland. After graduating, he practiced medicine for a few years in Huntsville, then moved to Yadkinville, where he married the granddaughter of William White (Effie M. Kelly). Each of their eight children graduated from college and entered a public service profession (medicine, law, social work, teaching, engineering). Dr. Harding died in 1929.⁵⁴ His older sister, Ruth Harding Brewbaker, was appointed postmistress of the Huntsville Post Office on April 2, 1886.⁵⁵ Early in the twentieth century, some of the Harding children were still reciting the rhyme: "Davis rode a white horse, Lincoln rode a mule. Davis was a smart man, Lincoln was a fool."⁵⁶

Stanley Samuel May returned from the war in April and married a local girl, Nancy Melinda Gabard. He worked with his father building wagons and caskets. He attended the free schools, then taught school in Davie County and in the Boonville area. He was ordained a Baptist minister in 1875 and preached for the next 60 years. The Rev. May died of pneumonia after breaking his leg on October 1, 1936.⁵⁷

Brigadier General Thomas L. Clingman attempted to recoup his fortunes and in partnership with William O. Walton acquired 1,920 acres of land on Linville Mountain. He tried to generate interest in developing the mountain areas of North Carolina. He also published his speeches and writings in 1877 and again in 1878. He established the Clingman Tobacco Cure Company in Durham which processed tobacco into a cake as a cure for everything from "gout to pleurisy." He spoke at various colleges and universities and lectured before the Philosophical Society in Washington, D.C., in 1874 and in 1877. He often addressed the lack of recognition accorded North Carolina's Confederate troops. Eventually, his health declined and he died on November 3, 1897. Clingman is buried in Asheville's Riverside Cemetery.[58]

Some left the county to make a new start. When Dr. John H. Kinyoun returned to his home in Yadkin County after the war, "he found everything in a state of devastation." He decided to move to Johnson County, Missouri, where he enjoyed a thriving medical practice. He was the "only physician within a forty mile radius." So, he took his wife, the former Elizabeth Ann Conrad, and their two children to live in a log cabin near Centerview, Missouri. Kinyoun kept in touch with the folks back in Yadkin. He wrote to a Winston newspaper about a plague of grasshoppers in Missouri and Kansas in 1875.[59] Mrs. Kinyoun died in Missouri at age 42 of pneumonia. Dr. Kinyoun died of heart failure in 1903. Both are buried in Centerview Cemetery, Johnson County, Missouri.[60]

Theophilus C. Hauser (1810–1887), "a Southern planter" who operated a store and mill. The first court held in the new county of Yadkin was in his store, just west of Yadkinville. He had two sons who served in the Confederate States Army (courtesy of Lucille Hauser Miller).

William H. Ball, as a private in Company B, 21st Regiment, was wounded at Second Manassas. After the war Ball moved to Granville, Delaware County, Indiana. In 1896 he wrote a letter to *The Yadkin Ripple*: "I have been absent from your town for 31 years.... I was raised in old Yadkin and that name sounds sweet to me. I joined the first company in the late war that went from Old Yadkin."[61]

Thomas B. Howell took his wife, Sarah Ann Hicks Howell, and their five children and left Yadkin County in October of 1868 for Kansas. They arrived there five years later, having made several extended stops along the way.[62]

Lt. Col. John Kerr Connally, an officer in the first company formed in Yadkinville, the "Yadkin Gray Eagles," moved to Texas after the war and practiced criminal law. Later, he moved to Virginia and was elected to the state senate from Richmond, being the youngest man elected to that body. He was in the state house in Richmond when it collapsed. Several men close to him were killed. He then moved to Asheville and established his home at "Fernihurst," where he devoted himself to the study of the Bible. He

Sarah Catherine Kimbrough Conrad (1839–1913), wife of John Thomas Conrad and daughter of Ormon and Sarah Taylor Kimbrough (courtesy Charles Conrad).

was preparing an analysis of the Bible which was nearly complete when he died. Shortly before his death he was awarded the Cross of Honor by the Zebulon Vance Camp, United Confederate Veterans for bravery on the first day's battle at Gettysburg. Connally led the regiment in the charge of Reynold's Brigade, and carried the flag after several of the regular color bearers were shot down. Connally himself seized the flag and bore it onward, and was shot twice in the process.[63]

James Henry Shore came home from the war and for the next two years helped his parents put their farm back together. Then, in 1867, he decided to "go west." Shore sold his only worldly possession, a fine buggy horse, and he and Nat Poindexter headed for California. They took a train to New York, then caught a ship to Panama, crossed the Isthmus of Panama by rail, and boarded another ship for California. Shore worked by splitting and hauling firewood all winter in San Francisco. In the spring of 1869, he went to the area around San Jose and began sharecropping with the owner of a large wheat farm. By 1872, he had several thousand dollars in the bank, owned his own farming equipment, wheat seed for the next year's planting, and a team of horses. He sold those and decided to return home, where he settled down, married his sweetheart, raised a family, and became a prosperous farmer. He expanded his acreage, and with the help of several tenant families, raised tobacco and corn as cash crops. He also had his own blacksmith shop.[64]

John Thomas Conrad and wife, Sarah Kimbrough Conrad, were the parents of eight children. In his later years, Conrad spent the winter months in Florida with son Alex and his family. During the tomato-picking season, he worked as timekeeper and payroll maker for a packing house at Little River. He died May 2, 1913, in Miami, and was returned for burial in the Kimbrough Graveyard, on Williams Road, in what is now Forsyth County. Wife Sarah had died four months earlier on January 25, 1913.[65]

Joseph Bitting went into the tobacco factory business at Huntsville for a few years. In 1870 he is listed as having capital of $2500, 5,000 pounds of tobacco valued at $5,500, and 4,000 pounds of tobacco products valued at $10,000. His product was divided between chewing tobacco (4,000 pounds) and smoking tobacco (1,000 pounds). His average workforce was four males, five females and six children.[66] Bitting then moved his tobacco factory to Georgia for a time, before transferring the his tobacco manufacturing business to Winston-Salem. He died at age 81.[67] His daughter Kate married Will Reynolds, and their home, "Tanglewood," is now a public recreational park on the east side of the Yadkin River.[68]

Some, who were old during the war, did not live long after. Broken financially and in spirit, they succumbed. William White, the old carpenter and builder of the first Yadkin County courthouse, died in 1867, heavily in debt. It was four years before his estate was finally settled. A petition filed in the 1871 spring term of Yadkin County court stated that the "late deceased William White was largely in debt and that all assets from personal and chattel property had been exhausted by sales and proceeds applied to payment of debts of deceased leaving a large balance of deceased's liabilities unpaid." The administrator, William L. White, received permission for a public auction of White's residence. Elizabeth I. Haynes purchased the house and 136 acres for $800.[69]

William White (1803–1867), contractor and builder of the first Yadkin County Courthouse. White died two years after the war, heavily in debt (courtesy Dorothy S. McLeod).

Age and illness took their toll. Tyre Glenn, who owned the large plantation known as "Glenwood," died in October of 1875 at age 75, "very suddenly of errysipilas [erysipelas] of the throat at his residence."[70] To make matters worse, the death of his son, Thomas Glenn, from consumption, was reported a year later. He was only about 24 years old.[71]

Jesse Virgil Dobbins, after joining the Union Army, returned to his home and went to work and prospered. He added a flour and saw mill to his grist mill at Dobbins' Mill Pond, just north of Yadkinville. Dobbins died at 53 of a heart attack at the mill on May 10, 1883. He left a widow and 11 children.[72] Some, however, said that Dobbins was murdered because of his part in the Bond School shootings. Dorothy Shugart McLeod remembers being told by her father that he was buried rather quickly without being embalmed, and that no autopsy or inquiry was held. The truth of the matter was that Dobbins died of a stroke. Just a month before his death, he applied for a pension based on disability, and was examined by a doctor. At that time, he stated that about December 24, 1864, he had "incurred nervous Rheumatism." The examining surgeon's certificate states that Dobbins was 52 years of age, weighed 175 pounds, and was 5 feet, 10 inches tall. The examination further revealed that:

> There is almost a total loss of grasp in the left hand, and inability to walk on left leg. The circulation in the affected limbs are impeded, causing said limbs to be colder than the opposite limb. The muscles are smaller in the diseased limbs than on the other side. He is unable to grasp any substance, and if so it falls from his hand. For the last five months, it seems as this man, is gradually losing the use of the effected limb. He still suffers from pain more regularly than he did several months age. This disability for obtaining a subsistence by manual labor is fully 3/4.

When Dobbins' widow applied for a Federal government pension, Dr. Allred wrote an affidavit describing Dobbins' physical disabilities. Dr. Allred had been treating Dobbins for a number of years. Allred graduated from Jefferson Medical College in Philadelphia in 1877, and when he practiced in Yadkin County, he had lived "within three miles of the said Jesse Dobbins" and was well acquainted with him, having been his family physician for five years.

> I well remember in 1878 in that fall Jesse Dobbins was confined to bed for 3 weeks with craussaus (?) pneumonia of left lung. After recovering [he] seemed in good health, until the fall of 1879, was confined to bed with Inflamatory Rheumatism; off & on through the winter, after he was able to get about, I detected that his Heart was incompetent to perform its duty, but seemed to give him no great trouble, until the following year, when he began suffering from Palpitation of heart; and gradually increased until his second attact [sic] of Pneumonia, which was in the year 1882, about November; after he commenced convalesing, I detected, a serious valve disease of the heart and remember telling him and the family he would not be able to do much more work and from that time on, the heart trouble continued until in March about 10th 1883, death came suddenly, while at his sawmill.

Allred stated that Jesse Dobbins suffered from "nervus rheumatism, and partial paralysis, manifesting itself in the left side, results of exposure." Dobbins had been given various drugs and medicine for his condition, including "quinine, iron dilute phos. acid, with flying blisters, and flannel clothing," with but "temporary results." Dr. Allred had examined Dobbins "about one week before his death, and found that he was rapidly losing the use of his left side." The doctor also stated that Dobbins died on March 10, 1883, "suddenly of paralysis of the brain." He "saw him immediately after the stroke."[73]

Jesse Dobbins is buried beside his wife, Sarah Catherine Dobbins, in the new part of the Deep Creek Friends cemetery, just yards from the Bond School House site. His tombstone has been vandalized and the lower portion is missing.

The Last Veterans

To help ease the pain of the war, many veterans gathered with others with whom they could talk freely and relive "old times." Organizations of United Confederate Veterans met frequently and in different parts of the state, as long as there were veterans alive. The first meeting of the Confederate Veterans was held in Richmond, Virginia, June 30–July 1, 1896. Three men from Winston-Salem attended that meeting, and they established a chapter named "The Henry Wyatt Camp" (reactivated in the 1930s as "The Captain M. W. Norfleet Camp #1249, Sons of the Confederate Veterans"). Samuel May attended one of the Confederate reunions at the Robert E. Lee Hotel in Winston-Salem in 1930. At age 95, he was the oldest active Confederate veteran in North Carolina. Colonel Reuben E. Wilson was a member of one of the Confederate Veterans organizations, as was Peter Apperson of East Bend. Not only white Confederate veterans joined veterans groups, but the former slaves who had served the Confederacy also had a veterans group. A small notebook found in the Alfred "Teen" Blackburn house contains the names of several African Americans who comprised a Confederate Veterans group.[74]

In 1929, John Henry Hauser, at age 82, attended a Confederate veterans reunion in Winston-Salem. He was interviewed by a *Sentinel* reporter. When asked if he had retired from active service, John Henry replied: "I should say not; I am running an old burr grist mill, located one and one half miles south of Yadkinville on the Mocksville road. We grind wheat and corn and the records show that my old mill has been in operation for 117 years."

Hauser declared, "I am still an old rebel—have never surrendered." Hauser, who had first enlisted at age 13, served out the war and returned uninjured. However, he was not at the surrender at Appomattox with the 1st Battalion of Sharpshooters. He was carried on the muster rolls only through December. He may have been on a detachment sent to guard fords or arrest deserters when the war ended, and simply walked home when it was over, but he never signed an Oath of Allegiance.[75]

Hauser also stated that out of the 100 men in his company, he knew of only two that were left—Lorenzo Dow Whitaker and himself. He did know of a few men still living who had served in other companies—the Rev. S. S. May, who was then 95; Henry Whitehead, who was living near Tobaccoville at age 93, and Henry Shore. Hauser proudly stated: "You know us fellows live longer than the average members of the present and former generations since the conflict between the states," because, he said, the soldiers "had to rough it."[76]

Lorenzo Dow Whitaker returned to Yadkin County and married his sweetheart, Lydia Gough, shortly before Christmas in 1866. After his first wife died, he married Margaret Adams. He had several children, and his descendants still live on Center Road, just west of Yadkinville.[77]

Most people think that Yadkin County's last Civil War veteran died in 1938. William F. Bryant died at his home near Jonesville on March 19, 1938, at the age of 96 years. He had served in Company H, 54th Regiment.[78] Actually, Alfred "Teen" Blackburn was the last. Blackburn, a slave who went to the war as a cook, bodyguard, and servant for his master, John Augustus Blackburn, served as a "body servant" in Company F, 21st Regiment N.C. Troops. He was the last North Carolina Confederate veteran

Left: *This photo of John Henry Hauser (1847–1930) was taken in San Jose, California, in 1868. Hauser served in Co. A, 1st Battalion Sharpshooter with his cousin Reuben E. Wilson.* Right: *Alfred "Teen" Blackburn, probably Yadkin's last Confederate veteran. He went with his master to the war, and later drew a Confederate pension for his services. He died December 15, 1951 (courtesy of Studio One).*

to receive a "Class B" pension for Confederate service.[79] Blackburn walked and carried the mail from Hamptonville to Jonesville, a distance of 10 miles, every day for 60 years. Later, he was given a 26-mile route between Hamptonville and Statesville. To make this route, he first bought a mule, then later a horse and buggy. Blackburn married Lucy Carson of Iredell County and they had ten children. With income from the mail route, he was able to educate his ten children. They became schoolteachers, principals, mail carriers, and one became a Washington, D.C., policeman.[80] Blackburn died on December 15, 1951, and is buried at Flat Rock Baptist Church, near Hamptonville.

An era ended with the death of Yadkin County's last Confederate soldier almost a hundred years after the Civil War began. For many, though, it is just beginning, because the truth is only now being revealed. Perhaps we, like some of our ancestors, will be able to emulate the philosophy of Sidney Francis Conrad (who became a Baptist preacher after the war): "Lee surrendered and I have never yet surrendered, but am reconciled to the results."[81]

Notes

1. Mary Transou Reece, "The Story of the Transou Family," *Heritage of Yadkin County*, p. 640.
2. Choplin, "Wesley Choplin," p. 3.
3. Elizabeth Ashby Speer to "Dear Brother," August 1867, *Journal of the Yadkin County Historical & Genealogical Society* VII (December 1988): 25; also in Speer, *Voices from Cemetery Hill*, p. 151.
4. Yadkin County Marriage Register, 1868–1872, Yadkin County Register of Deeds' Office, Yadkinville, N.C.
5. *Ibid.*
6. *Heritage of Yadkin County*, p. 7.
7. Hamilton, pp. 102–115.
8. Lefler and Newsome, p. 488.
9. Hamilton, pp. 240–241.
10. Irma Matthews Robertson, "The Dr. Evan Benbow Family," in *Heritage of Yadkin County*, p. 273.
11. Maude Davis Bunn, *Genealogy of the Marion-Davis Families* (Raleigh, N.C.: Edwards & Broughton, 1973), p. 53.
12. Lefler and Newsome, p. 490.
13. *Ibid.*, pp. 490–491.
14. Branson's *North Carolina Business Directory for 1867/1868* (Raleigh: Branson and Jones, Publishers, 1867), p. 116.
15. Branson's *North Carolina Business Directory for 1869* (Raleigh: J. A. Jones, Publisher, 1869), p. 170.
16. Wanda Carter Craaybeek, *Abstracts from the Minutes of Yadkin County, Board of Commissioner Meetings, 1868–1882 with Additional Abstracts Pertaining to Yadkin County*, privately published, 1990, pp. 14–27.
17. *Ibid.*
18. *Public Local Laws of North Carolina*, 1911, Chapter 588.
19. *Public Local Laws of North Carolina*, 1927, Chapter 490. See also David Leroy Corbett, *Formation of the North Carolina Counties*, 2nd ed. (Raleigh: N.C. Dept. of Archives and History, 1969).
20. Craaybeek, pp. 21–23, 26–27.
21. Winston-Salem, N.C., *Union Republican*, May 20, 1875.
22. *Ibid.*, July 13, 1876.
23. *Ibid.*, October 19, 1876.
24. Speer, *Voices from Cemetery Hill*, p. 151.
25. Branson's *North Carolina Business Directory for 1867/1868*, p. 117.
26. Mildred Matthews, "The Church of Christ," in *Heritage of Yadkin County*, p. 239.
27. *Heritage of Yadkin County*, pp. 199–240.
28. Branson's *North Carolina Business Directory for 1867/1868*, p. 147.
29. *Heritage of Yadkin County*, p. 238.
30. Hobson, in *Heritage of Yadkin County*, p. 246.
31. Nell Wilhelm Dinkins, "The Perry Story," *Heritage of Yadkin County*, p. 536.
32. Elizabeth Speer to A. Jackson Ashby, August 1867, original copy in private possession of Helen Ashby Shull, cited in Speer, *Voices from Cemetery Hill*, p. 151.
33. S. Carter Williams, *Yadkin County Record Book* (Yadkinville, N.C.: Williams Printing Co., 1939), p. 51.
34. U. S. Bureau of Census, "Schedule 4, Products of Industry, Yadkin County," *Tenth Census of North Carolina, Manufacturers Schedule*, pp. 1–4 (microfilm).
35. Branson's *The North Carolina Business Directory* (Raleigh: J. A. Jones, 1872), pp. 246–247.

36. Yadkin County, North Carolina, *Deed Book* 3, p. 366.

37. Oscar Hammerstein, "United States Tobacco Journal Directory, 1881–82," reproduced in Nannie May Tilley, *The Bright Tobacco Industry 1860–1925* (Chapel Hill: University of North Carolina Press, 1948), pp. 679–685.

38. Frances H. Casstevens, "19th Century Industry in Yadkin County," in *Heritage of Yadkin County*, pp. 86–87.

39. Branson's *North Carolina Business Directory for 1867/1868*, p. 117.

40. James Clark Robert, *The Tobacco Kingdom, Plantation, Market and Factory in Virginia and North Carolina 1800–1860* (Gloucester, Mass.: Peter Smith, 1965), pp. 175–176.

41. Branson's *North Carolina Business Directory for 1867/1868*, p. 117.

42. Letter from M. L. Woodhouse and E. L. Transou, members of the Pension Board of Yadkin County, to Any Pension Board in the State of Arkansas, copy courtesy of F. D. Fulkerson, Tulsa, Okla.

43. Stewart Sifakis, *Compendium of the Confederate Armies: North Carolina* (New York: Facts on File), p. 1.

44. Department of State Auditor, Pension Bureau, Confederate Pension Lists, 1900–1964. Microfilm Reels Nos. S.13.3 and S.13.4, N.C. State Archives, Raleigh, N.C.

45. *Ibid.*

46. *Ibid.*

47. *Ibid.*

48. Isaac Jarratt to Commissioner of Pensions, August 21, 1875, in *Heritage of Yadkin County*, p. 146; H. W. Atkinson to Isaac Jarratt, August 17, 1875, in *Heritage of Yadkin County*, p. 146.

49. Pension application of Sarah C. Dobbins, widow of Jesse Dobbins, filed in the United States Department of the Interior, Pension Office, Washington, D.C.

50. Lucille H. Miller and Sadie F. Wilson, "Reuben Everette Wilson," in *Heritage of Yadkin County*, pp. 663–664.

51. *N.C. Troops*, vol. III, p. 720.

52. Information from Victor Seiders and wife, Wanda Hauser Seiders (a descendant of John Henry Hauser), personal conversation, December 2, 1995.

53. Edith Garner Sharpless, "Benjamin A. Phillips," in *Heritage of Yadkin County*, p. 540.

54. Frances H. Casstevens, "Dr. Thomas Renny Harding Family," in *Heritage of Yadkin County*, pp. 385–387.

55. William E. Rutledge, *An Illustrated History of Yadkin County, North Carolina* (Yadkinville, N.C.: privately published, 1965), p. 30.

56. Personal conversation in 1995 with Helen Harding Bridges, age 84, who recalled singing the rhyme when she was a child.

57. Rutledge, pp. 169, 180.

58. Frances H. Casstevens, "The Military Career of Brigadier General Thomas Lanier Clingman" (Master's thesis, University of North Carolina at Greensboro, 1984), pp. 173–182.

59. Winston-Salem, N.C., *Union Republican*, June 17, 1875.

60. O'Daniel and Patton, p. 168.

61. William Ball, "Letter to the Editor," *The Yadkin Ripple*, in *Journal of the Yadkin County Historical Society* V (December 1986): 14.

62. Letter from Christine Jackson, dated July 9, 1993, in *Journal of the Yadkin County Historical & Genealogical Society* XIV (March 1995): 18.

63. "Colonel J. K. Connally Joins His Comrades of Gettysburg," Asheville, N.C., *Citizen Times*, February 3, 1904.

64. Davis, in *Heritage of Yadkin County*, pp. 589–590.

65. O'Daniel and Patton, p. 174.

66. *Ninth Census of 1870, Industry, North Carolina*, Schedule 4, Products of Industry, p. 4, microfilm reel # F.2.118N, University of North Carolina at Greensboro.

67. Connor, vol. IV, p. 66.

68. Rutledge, p. 27.

69. Register of Deeds, Yadkin County, N.C., Will Book 1, p. 47.
70. Winston-Salem, N.C., *Union Republican*, October 14, 1875.
71. *Ibid.*, March 2, 1876, and October 26, 1876.
72. Kathryn Dobbins Huggins, "Jesse Virgil and Sara Catharine (Mackie) Dobbins," in *Heritage of Yadkin County*, p. 349.
73. Physician's Affidavit, written and signed by Dr. E. W. Allred, a citizen of Surry County, N.C., 1888, in support of Pension Claim No. 308842, U. S. Government Pension Office, photocopy from original in the National Archives, Washington, D.C.
74. Notebook in possession of the Yadkin County Historical & Genealogical Society, Inc., Yadkinville, N.C, and is filed at the society's office in the Tulbert House, Yadkinville, N.C.
75. Information from Victor Seiders and wife, Wanda Hauser Seiders (a descendant of John Henry Hauser), personal conversation, December 2, 1995.
76. Lucille Miller and Sadie F. Wilson, "John Henry Hauser, Sr. and Family," in *Heritage of Yadkin County*, pp. 396–397.
77. Virginia "Bunny" J. Harvey, "Lorenzo Dow Whitaker, of Company B, 21st Regiment, C.S.A.," *Journal of the Yadkin County Historical & Genealogical Society* XII (September 1993): 12–15. For picture of Lorenzo Dow Whitaker and wife, Margaret Adams Whitaker, see cover of that issue.
78. Frances H. Casstevens, "Yadkin Units," in *Heritage of Yadkin County*, p. 140.
79. Information from Jeff Stepp, N. C. Confederate Burial Locator Project, Catawba, NC, personal communication on March 19, 1996.
80. Rutledge, p. 22; *Journal of the Yadkin County Historical Society* XI (March 1990): 23.; Marcellene Blackburn Lindsey and Wanda Carter Craaybeek, *People of Color of Yadkin County, North Carolina* (Yadkinville, N.C: Yadkin County Historical and Genealogical Society, Inc., 1992), pp. 110–116.
81. O'Daniel and Harris, p. 339.

Epilogue

IN THE LATE 1990s, Yadkin County is still a wonderful place in which to live. It is still rural and it is beautiful. Nestled near the foot of the Blue Ridge Mountains, the air is clean and the water is pure. But the face of Yadkin County is changing. There are many new homes, mobile home parks, schools, businesses, industries, and churches. Almost daily, the land is being cleared of forest to make room for new construction. Yet, in many ways, it remains distinct from its neighboring counties, and the people of Yadkin County want it that way. Although farming is still an important part of the economy of the county, it is no longer the principal source of income. Most of the population hold jobs outside the county in Winston-Salem, or other nearby cities, to which they commute daily in new cars over superhighways, and where they spend much of their income. After work, they return to the peace and quiet of their homes and communities in Yadkin County.

We are beginning to feel the stress of the environmental problems of the late twentieth century. There is a need for a county-wide water and sewer system, and when that comes, there will be more industry and greater economic and population growth. What the county will be 200 years after the American Civil War in 2065 is impossible to predict. One thing is certain: neither Yadkin County nor the rest of the country will ever be anything like it was on that day in April of 1861, when Confederate guns fired on Fort Sumter, or as it was four years later on another spring day when the guns were stacked at Appomattox.

Appendix A:
Civil War Letters and Documents Relating to the Bond School House Affair

The letters in this appendix are all formerly unpublished letters. Except for the J. F. Williams letter, modern-day spellings have been used, and end punctuation has been added for clarity. The original spellings have been retained in only a few instances to show how the words were pronounced (and are still pronounced in some areas of the state). The Williams letter is reproduced here as it was originally written because modernization would have changed almost every word. A major spelling difference was the use of the letter "c" for "k", as in "cil" for "kill."

Many other letters would have been included, if space concerns could have allowed for them. The book *Kinfolk of Jacob Conrad* by Julia Harris O'Daniel and Laura Conrad Patton (1970) is recommended for the original letters of John Thomas Conrad and other family members. Other Civil War–era letters in the *Heritage of Yadkin County, North Carolina,* are also referenced.

The documents relating to the Bond School House affair were originally published in the *Journal of the Yadkin County Historical & Genealogical Society* and are reprinted here for posterity. Some additional correspondence, included here in the appendix, was recently discovered in the Pearson Collection at Duke University, Durham, North Carolina, regarding the Yadkin County jailbreak. The public documents, the grand jury indictment, and the warrants in the murder of James West were long thought destroyed, and have been included here for posterity's sake.

Samuel Speer Harding to Father, William Harding[1]
[A four-page letter written on Confederate States of America stationery, by Samuel S. Harding serving as a member of Company I, 28th Regiment, North Carolina Troops]

1862
Wilmington, January 23rd

Dear Father I find my self seated to drop you few lines to inform you that I am better and I think that I will get well if nothing [else?] don't happen. Not that I think [it] will alth [?] though[?] [it] is required for me to take leave of my self and I think I will certainly do that. I was glad to hear from you all and to know that you was all well. The next week after N. Bohannon went home I went to Weldon me and six private to guard the brigs [prison or bridges?]. So we staid up there nine days and the last three days I was sick and I came back to Wilmington sick on Sunday and I have been very sick most of the time. The Doctor said that I had tifoid [typhoid] fever but as it happened it did not take much hold on me he fine [find?]. They broke it over me but you would not [know] me if you was to see me now. I don't think that I would way [weigh] more than 120 pounds. I think that I [have] fallen off, at least 40 pound. I received my box, and it had my keg of whiskey, but Neal Bohannon had [his] own things on the express, but we had to pay on them. I had to pay four dollars on my box. I have sold several gallons, and if I had a barrel [of] whiskey, I could sell the last bit of it at 50 cents a quart. We have some nuse [news] we heard the other day that there was a large quantity of vessels at Cape Hatteras, some that they was a hundred 20 [120], vessels. They have been a fine vessels on the coast but don't think that they is any danger of getting at Wilmington to a fite, no more danger, I don't believe, than in getting into one at home. I received my shirt that you sent me and was glad to get trunk, a good thing as it was and we all got own clothing. I got one pare [pair] of pants and, one shirt, and one pare of drawers, one pare of shoes, and one pare of socks and one over coat and drawed one good blanket that I wouldn't take ten dollars for it. You can tell Berry [Greenberry Harding, his brother] that I sent his coat home to him. I could of sold it for seven dollars, but I [thought] that I had better send it home. I am going to send you my blanket the first opportunity and want you take good care of it for me. I don't want you to make me any more things for I have got as many things as I want to and I don't want you [to send] me any more. I sent by Neal, twenty-five dollars, to Pap and he said that he paid it to Pap but you never said any[thing] about getting it, you can tell all of them, howdy[?] for me, you may look for me when you see me a coming. I have no nuse of any information to write to you must excuse my handwriting and spelling for I am quiet weak to day.

Samuel S. Harding

Thomas G. Scott to William Harding[2]
August 27, 1864

[Thomas G. Scott to William Harding of Yadkin County, N.C., August 27th, 1864, relayed the news of the death of William's son, Samuel Speer Harding, who was in Company I, 28th Reg., North Carolina Troops. After the war, Thomas Scott married Samuel Harding's sister, Alice Harding, and they had one child, Cora.]

Petersburg, Va.
August 27th, 1864

Dear Willie, I sit myself to inform you of the late fighting. Your son Sammy was killed the twenty-fifth of this month. I am sorry to inform you of the fighting. But I felt hit was my duty to write to you about Sergeant S. S. Harding. I am sorry to tell you of his death. He was shot through the hip. He did not live long after he was shot. I did not get to see him after he was killed. I was gone out with one of our men that was wounded and I did not get back till after dark. On the way, we was forced to fall back from the battlefield. If I had of known that he was killed, I would [have] stayed there all night. But what I would of buried him, but I will tell you that I got all of his things. One of our company got through and give them to me. I have his knapsack and I got his pocket book.... I will tell you that Col. [William H. Asbury] Speer was shot through the head. He will die if he all ready ain't dead now. I was sorry to loose my Col. and Sergeant. I will keep Sammy's things till you come after them if I can, for he was a good friend of mine.

T. G. Scott

Letter from John Bovender to Son-in-Law, Albert Poindexter[3]

N.C., Yadkin County, August 25th 1862

Dear Children I take my pen in hand to drop you a few lines to let you know that we are all well at present, hoping that these few lines will come safe to hand and find you all well and doing well. I can inform you that I received your letter which was a great satisfaction to hear from you. I have nothing worthy of your attention to write at present. Times is hard here and like to be harder. I will tell you something about the price of things here. Corn is selling at 2 dollars per bushel, wheat 3.25 cents, rye 2 dollars, bacon 35 cents per pound, butter and cheese 20 cents per pound, Brandy 5 dollars a gallon, milk cows 30 to 40 dollars and other things in proportion. I will tell you that George Bovender is dead. He went to the Army last fall and was taken sick and come home and lay some time. He died sometime in July. Biddy [Bovender] is married this summer to old Daniel Adams. I seen them today and they was all well. I can say what nobody else can say in this country. I have 2 son-in-laws both of one name [Daniel Adams]. One is the other's uncle. Father and Mother Thornton is both dead. They have been dead 3 years. Jackson Bovender has built him a mill at the saw mill. John Bovender is married to Jane Hutchens. I saw Nicklas Johnson yesterday and they was all well. Daniel Adams and his family was all well. Iredell Warden's family is well. Their daughter Elizabeth is dead and also their youngest son. Jackson's son John is in Jackson's Army at Gordonsville, VA. Green Bovender and Abe Murphy, Cam[?] Brown is all in Jackson's Army.

John Bovender's wife has no children. They have been married over 4 years. Matilda and family is well and the[y] have got Caner [Elkanah Willard] bound over to the Superior Court for speaking in favor of the Union. I don't hear from Nat Thornton and Catey. The last I heard from them they was in Alabama. I am still working in the shop just when I want to. I put up a wagon once in a while and shoot squirrels. There is lots of them here and if you want to get beat a shooting just come over some time and I will try you a round. I think I can beat you without specks [eyeglasses]. George Bovender has left his estate to his widow as long as she remains a widow. There is great distress about his leaving them. They are well fixt to live and has plenty to live on. I must draw my letter to a close and remain your well wishing father until death. This from John Bovender to Albert Poindexter.

Albert Poindexter to wife, Catherine Bovender Poindexter[4]

Oct. The 4, 1863
Chicamauga, Catucy[?] Co., Ga.

Dear companion

I seat my self this morning to try to inform you that I am tolerable well at present. I truly hope these few lines will find you all well. It has been a long time since I had a letter from home. The last letter I had got from home was dated Aug. The 2. It has been two months. I think the time long. I have written every chance I have had. I want to hear from home the worst I ever did. Times is hard here. Provisions is scarce here. Everything is eat out. I don't see how the people is to live hear. A man can't get a meals victuals no where in this country. Both armies has been through here and has destroyed everything through here. The Yankees is at Chattanooga and our forces is near there a fortifying. It is thought they will have a big fight at Chattanooga.

I would write some thing about the big fight that we had but I expect you have heard all about it and more too. I can't tell how many was killed and wounded but there was several thousand killed and wounded. Our regiments was detailed to gather up the guns. We picked up thirty-five or forty thousand guns. The dead men was strode all through the woods. Some places they lay thick on the ground. It was a awful sight to see such as I never want to see again. They all say it was the hardest fight that has ever been fought for the length of time. I must close for this time. I will write again as soon as I can. I want to come home the worst I ever did but there is no chance now. Nothing more only I remain yours truly until death. Write as soon as you can. The post master will know better how to direct a letter than I can tell you.

A. Poindexter

Albert Poindexter to wife, Catherine Bovender Poindexter[5]

Camp Chase, Ohio, Feb. The 14, 1864

Dear Companion,

I take my pen in hand to inform you that I am well at present. I truly hope these few lines will find their way to your hands and find you and the children well. I hant got any thing new to write. I ain't permitted to write but very little. The boys is all well that come in here with me. I have been a prisoner nearly four months. I have been in prison three months, the time seems long to me. I hope the time is not far distant when I will be releast. Write me soon for I am anxious to hear from home. Direct your letter to Albert Poindexter, Prisoner of War, Camp Chase, Prison No. 3, Mess 61. Farewell for this time.

A. Poindexter

Richard Poindexter to Sister-in-Law, Catherine Bovender Poindexter[6]

Mt. Nebo, Yadkin Co., NC
Nov. 8, 1863

Dear Sister, I seat myself to drop you a few lines to let you know that we are all well, hoping that these lines will find you all enjoying the same blessing. It has been a long time since I heard from you and I am very anxious to hear how you are getting along. I will tell you that I was over at Daniel Adams' yesterday and had took dinner with him and Bidd [Biddie Bovender Adams] is well and all of old Jack's folks are well so far as I know. And all of Iredell Warden's folks are well and all of "Cainer" [Elkanah] Willard's folks are well. Green [Green Bovender] got killed at Richmond and Abe Murphy, he died at Richmond or over there somewhere. I want you to write to me soon and let me know how you are getting along and where Albert [Poindexter] is and what he is doing. Direct your letter to Mount Nebo. ___ no more but yours truly.

Richard Poindexter

George Bovender is dead also.

John M. Harrison, Company B, 44th Regiment, to Wife, Margaret Harrison [7]

[Note: John M. Harrison enlisted at age 28 on November 28, 1862. He was court-martialed and shot on September 20, 1863, for "mutinous language." Undoubtedly, Harrison had deserted shortly after he enlisted, but was released and served on the battlefields with his company for eight months after January 1863. These letters do not indicate that he was pro-Union or that he was any different from most other soldiers in his desire for peace and to be able to return home to his wife and child.]

Goldsboro, NC
Jan. 23, 1863

Dear Wife
I embrace the kind opportunity to address you by letter to let you know that I am well at present, hoping these lines may find you enjoying the same thing. I have not been liberated since I was arrested on the way home. We were all taken to Richmond and to Fredericksburg then to Goldsboro, NC. We are now in the guard house at Goldsboro. I cannot tell when I shall get to come home but I hope it won't be too long. There is much talk about peace at this time. The general opinion is there will be peace made in about two months. I will send you some thread and a comb which I bought off the Yankees. Margaret, I want you to write to me as soon as you get this letter for I have not heard from you since I left home. I want you to write whether they have taken off any more conscripts since I left home. Tell my father-in-law that I expect to be at home this spring if nothing happens and I want him to field in enough corn ground for me and him both. Our fare is very hard. We do not get breakfast until about one o'clock and supper about dark—only two meals a day and not enough at that. I will close my letter for the present. You must write soon and let me know how you are getting along. Nothing more, but remain your affectionate husband until death.

J. M. Harris[on]

A. Documents re the Bond School House

Greenville
March 23, 1863

Dear Wife

I take the pleasure of dropping you a few lines this morning to let you know that I am not well. I am broke down by marching and I have been from place to place ever since the 7th of this month. I truly hope we will rest in a while and I hope when these few lines reach you they might find you and your child well and enjoying good health. I left the hospital [the] 5th of this month and on the 7th I had to start on a march. I would not grumble[?] if I could, but I don't have no chance and you may excuse me if I will write ever chance I can get.

When we left Goldsboro we went to Wilmington then to New Bern and we lay under the burst of shells all day which was shot at us from the Yankees. Hit was the 14th day of this month that we had to retreat from that place in great haste. About 40 of us was killed and wounded by this burst of shells that fell all around me, but thank God I was not hurt by none of them. I trust in Him to deliver me from shot at all times. I pray for peace both day and night for I want to come home and stay with you for I would give every thing I ever seen to be at home with you. I hope God will spare my life to meet with you again on earth. If not, on earth, I hope to meet you in heaven where there will be no parting there and no war. We started to Washington [North Carolina] and got scared and turned back and now I don't know where we will go from here. But I hope that we will go back to Goldsboro from here fir [for] I am tired of mud and water in this low land and I have went through water over my knees. I want you to write to me often and let me know how times is with you all. You can direct your letter to Goldsboro and I will get them. Direct your letters to Goldsboro in care of Capt. Lewis (?), 44th Reg., Co. B.

John M. Harrison to wife M. M. Harrison

[on back side]
I received your letter dated the 26th of January. That's all I have got from you yet. I hain't killed none yet, only the first week and that was at Petersburg.

John M. Harrison
to M. M. Harrison

N. C. Beauford County
April the 14th A.D. 1863

Dear Kind and Affectionate Wife

I set my self this morning through the mercy of the Lord to answer your kind letter dated the 30th of March, which gives me much satisfaction to hear your kind words once more in this life for you don't know how often I think of you and have often prayed for peace so I may come home and see you and nurse my little babe and live a good life and enjoy the liberty we once did. May the Lord help is my prayer. I will tell you something about where I am and what our poor [illegible]. We are in camp on the south side of Tar river below Washing[ton] at fort Yeates a fortifying the river to stop the gun boats.

And what we draw for one day's provisions I can set down and eat it at one little snack, and hardly have enough. We have been on a march ever since the ninth of the month and has not stopped since. We are all rough and dirty and lowly and I don't reckon I will get our clothes. I want you to write to me whether you got my letter I sent you with some pins and thread and a comb in it. Write soon and direct your letter to Greenville NC. If times gets no better I shall not write you but one more letter till [I] see you, so I must close by saying I remain loving husband until death. May the Lord help us in prayer, for Christ's sake. Yours truly

from John M. Harrison to M. M. Harrison

June 8, 1863
Fredericksburg, VA

Dear Companion

I set myself this morning to inform you that I am well at present and praying that these few lines will find you improving. [Illegible] I got here yesterday. We are lying here in line of battle in sight of the Yankees and we can see the Yankees and hear their drums. We are expecting a large fight at this place. You wrote me you wanted me to get a furlough and come home, but there is no [way][part of page torn away].

I want to see you and the babe the worst that I ever did in my life, and if I don't see you till I get a furlough, I won't know whether I shall see your or not but I [want] you to ask God in your prayers to keep me till I can come home again and see you again. [Illegible] for we fare a little better then we did when we was in N.C. We git a half pound of bacon a day, a one pound of crackers. I saw Alexander Mackie yesterday and he had started to the [torn].

You wrote that Jesse Dobbins and James Ooten [Wooten] was in the Army and you didn't write what regiment they was in [Dobbins and Wooten joined the Union Army after fleeing from the shootout at the Bond School] and I want you to write where they are at and I want you to write how all your folks is and what they are doing.

Margaret, I will send you a paper of needles that I paid one dollar for them. I want you to take care of your self and the child and if I never see you again on earth I hope that we will meet in heaven where there is no parting [part of page torn].

[In same letter was a note to his father, William Harrison, and mother.]

Dear Father and Mother, I take the opportunity to write you a few lines to let you know that I am well at present, hoping these few lines will find you well. I haven't time to write much this time, but I want you to write. Direct your letters to Richmond, VA, 44th NC Troops, Co. B, in care of Capt. Brown. Write me [rest of page torn away]

[from John M. Harrison to wife
Margaret Harrison]

June 24 A.D. 1863
Hanover Junction Va

Dear Wife

I take my pen in hand this evening to let you know that I am as well as common, truly hoping these few lines will find you in good health. I haven't had no letter from you in a long time. It seems that you have forgotten me but, not withstanding, I will write forever and would be much gratified to hear from you. We are Hanover Junction. We have stayed here for guarding. Would be glad to see you once more. I think it would be great pleasure, but I can't tell you when peace will be made. I want you to write in haste and write how the baby is getting along and tell father [William. M. Harrison] to write to me. I have no good news to write to you at this time. I believe you have written to me but I have not received them letters. The last time I wrote to you I sent some needles. Write whether you got them. Margaret, I have set 2 or 3 times to come home, but I did not get too, but if I ever get in N.C. again I will come home one day. Write me all of the important news. Please write soon. Send your letter to Hanover Junction, VA, Co. B, 44th Reg. NCT. My best love to you.

J. M. Harrison
to Margaret Harrison

August the 8th 1863
Camp Near Orange Court House

Kind and affectionate wife

With pleasure I seat my self this morning to answer your kind letter that reached my hands yesterday which give much satisfaction to hear from you one time more. This finds [illegible] me in common health and truly hoping these few lines may soon and safely reach your hands and find you enjoying good health. I have nothing of much importance to write at this time more than we are in Gen. Lee's main army and look for a big fight every day, but I trust to God will miss it.

I have had five letters from you and I will write every week or two. I want you to write in your next letter all about the times in that country. There is right smart said here about N.C. going in the Union as it be bout times for something to be done and the people ought to rally at home for peace on some terms. The officers held a [illegible] election yesterday but it was no fair one. The most of the people here is for peace and I think if they don't get it one way they will try for it another if times don't alter us to rationing[?]. We do tolerable well at this time so far as beef, bacon and bread stuff is concerned. You must write soon and get me all the news in that country. I hope through the mercy of divine Savior we will soon be permitted to see each other in peace. I want you to take care of your self and child and give my best respects to all inquiring friends. I hope the time is not far ahead when I can see you all so I must close by saying write soon. Yours are ever till death. Direct your letter to Richmond, Va. When this you see, remember me, though many miles apart we be from

John M. Harrison to Molly
[Margaret] Harrison

Milas Mason to William Gabard[8]

Camp near Fredericksburg VA
May 12, 1863

My Dear uncle and aunt and cousins one and all. I feel to thank God that I am yet alive and am in tolerable good health at present and I hope that when these few lines comes to your hands they may find you all well. I received a letter from Nella yesterday. She stated they were all well. She stated that you had been to see them. I was glad to hear that you had been to see them. She stated that you wanted me to write to you so I thought I would write you a letter today, but Dear uncle and aunt and cousins, I would rather be at your house today and talk with you all than to be here and have to write to you. Oh, that I could have been at old society last meeting day when you was there, but instead of that, I was a great distance off, but I hope and pray that the day may soon come when we may have peace and be permitted to return safe home to our Dear families again, for I tell you Dear uncle, that I am tired of this war you may be sure. Oh, how I long to be at my home sweet home where I have enjoyed so much satisfaction, but my trust is ever in the Lord. He has been pleased to hear and answer our prayers in days that have passed and gone, and I hope he will hear and answer us again that we may be permitted to return safe home again. Dear uncle and aunt, perhaps you have heard of the terrible battle that we have been in. We were in line of battle and marching and under the roaring of cannon and muskets and fighting 7 days in succession. I was in 2 engagements, one on Saturday evening and one on Sunday and some days we were behind breast works and the yankees throwing bombshells and grapeshot at us and sometime they would burst right over us and sometime wound some and kill some. From where we started in the fight on Saturday evening to where we stopped at night was about 2 or 3 miles that we run the yankees. I tell you, Dear uncle, that my trust was ever in the Lord to his will and prayed unto him as I went through the battle to be merciful unto us and I loaded and shot when I saw a chance for we had to go through fields and woods and thickets often. There was a great many killed and wounded on both sides but what I saw of the battleground, I think there was 4 or 5 yankees killed to one of our men, but there was often regiments that suffered a greater loss than ours did. We had a right smart wounded but not a great many killed, as I know of. There was not one of my mess wounded. Giles Horn was sick and was sent to the hospital the morning that we started to the fight, and the last account we had of him, he was at Richmond in the hospital. We have come back to our old camps again, but I don't know how long we will stay. Dear uncle, I have went through this battle safe and I do hope to the Lord that I may never be in another, for I tell you that it is an awful sight to see the men slaughtered up in such a manner and such a destruction of clothing, blankets, knapsacks and guns, I don't think that I would tell a false [hood] if I was to say that we got as much as 2 or 3 hundred wagon loads of guns, knapsacks and blankets, tent cloths, oilcloths, and other articles of various kinds that the yankees left in their flight for we run them from behind several breast works. It is said that we took some 10 or 15 thousand prisoners and they got some of our men, but I don't know how many. Both of the colonels of our regiment was wounded, and it is said that General [Thomas J. "Stonewall"] Jackson was wounded, and I understand today that he is dead and was carried by our camps today, but I can't say that it is a positive fact that he is dead, but I have heard it several times, but it is very certain that he was wounded in the left arm and some said that he was wounded in his right hand also. Dear uncle and aunt, I am sorry to state to you that Jacob Wagner was killed. He was shot on Saturday evening, which was the 2nd day of May, and he was taken to a house where they left the wounded, and he died Sunday morning, which was the 3rd of May. Giles Shives told me that he helped to bury him near a church and had a plank put up at his head with his name on it. He has left his family in a bad condition. I can't tell what will become of them, for I have done for them as long as I well can until I could be at home myself, but as it is—can I do for them more than to let her stay [illegible], but I hope her friends and relation will not let her suffer. I have been helping her better than twelve months and am willing to help her more if it is the Lord's will that I live to get safe home again and of Dear uncle and aunt and cousins one and all I earnestly ask an interest in your prayers that the good Lord will be pleased to grant me the privilege of soon returning safe home to my Dear little family and friends again and not only me but all the rest of the [soldiers? boys?] that are still alive and that we may soon have peace again. Dear [uncle, write] to me as soon as this letter comes to your hands. Direct your letter to Richmond, VA, Co. G, 5th Regiment, NC state troops in care of Captain Taylor. Put my name first and then say Richmond, VA, Co. G, 5 Regiment, NC state troops in care of Capt. Taylor. Fail not to write and tell Murphy [Richmond Murphy Gabard] and all the rest to write if he's at home. So no more, but I am your Nephew until Death.

Milas Mason

John William Wall to his wife, Agnes Tate Wall[9]
[John William Wall was in Company D, 21st Regiment, N.C. Troops]

Hanover Junction, December 2nd, 1863

Dear Wife, I embrace the present opportunity of writing you a few lines informing you that I am well at the time. Hoping when this comes to hand it may find you & all the children also well. I received your letter on the 25th of last month which gave me great satisfaction to hear from you. I was going to answer it much sooner than I did but we had to leave Raleigh last Sunday and go to Weldon. The next day we came to Petersburg & Richmond where we stayed overnight. Yesterday we came out here. I do not know how long we will stay here, but not long. I presume I understood that Mike Davis and Bob told it that me & John W. Beane had started to run away. Which is all an unrighteous & damnable lie. I saw some of the Yadkin boys, John Shores, Kral [Carl?] Williams at Camp Holmes and they said they wished [they] had a stayed with us. You wrote to me that you was fixing to come to High Point, but we were gone. I would have been very glad if you could have come. I drew one coat, a pair of pants & one shirt an a pair of drawers and a cap and I wish Beverly had that. I also received $50 of bounty money. I want to know how you are getting along getting wood and whether you have had a chopping or not. We took care of William Norman & Ellis' things. J. W. Beane sold their clothing and their blankets are in camp and it was left to us all whether to send them their money. I was in favor of sending it to Chandler Norman, but I don't know whether they will do so or not. I want to know how your hogs are getting along fattening. If they are getting anyways fat you had better kill them as corn is so scarce. You wrote to me that the children wanted to see me so bad. They don't [want] to see me any worse than I want to see them. I want you to take good care of everything if I never get back. I want you to have every thing your life time. I want you to write to me every week without fail and I will do the same. So I will come to close by remaining your affectionable husband till death. J. W. Wall

A word to Uncle Dick Philips
I am well at present and hope this may find you also well. I haven't time to write more now. I have to attend to my ammunition now, but I want you to write to me. Direct your letters to Hanover Junction, Va. in care of Cap. Barrow, Co. D, 21st Regiment, N.C. Troops.

[A letter from J. F. Spainhour written on bottom of Wall's letter]

A word to Sister Elizabeth
I am well except a cold and cough. I am not at all pleased with my situation, but I hope I can get along some how till I can better myself. I hope this may find you well and I want to know where Isaac is and how he is getting. I haven't time to or I would write more to you but I will write again hereafter if time long enough. I want you to write to me soon as you can.
Affectionately, your brother

J. F. Spainhour

To Elizabeth Carmical

John William Wall to his wife, Agnes Tate Wall
[John William Wall died near Orange Court House, Virginia, shortly after this letter was written.]

Camp of the 21st, N.C., right near Orange C. H. Va. December 20, 1863

Dear Wife & Children,
I will try to address you with a few lines to let you know that I have got better. I have had a very bad cold and chill and was right sick, but am better now. The doctor cured me for the pain in the side. I did not take no medicine. Hoping this may find you all well at home and getting along fine. I have wrote two letters home but have not received no answer yet. There was ten dollars in the one I wrote on the 10th of this month.
You wrote you had a chopping and got wood plenty. I was glad to hear it that the neighbors was so kind. The weather is very cold here. The ground is froze very hard. We have new tents and have built chimneys to them. When you write I want to know how the stock is getting along this cold weather. I want to know if the babe can talk yet or not, and all about the children. I have a cap for Beverly and Hilary. I will send by James Moore when [he] gets a furlough. I want you to send me a pair of yarn socks with him when he comes back. You may fix me up a box and send by Mr. Moore. He will get a furlough in about 18 days. Tell Capt. Kirk to send me some brandy. I want to know

how the Capt. is getting along anyhow. I would like to know how James Flinn is getting along and to do the best he can for me and himself and John Norman's people is getting an [?] for him to write to me.

I saw a letter yesterday evening stating that they had caught Michael Davis. Now a word to Elizabeth Michael [Carmichael?]. Her brother John F. Spainhour is very sick. The doctor says it is deep cold. I don't think he is any ways dangerous.

I want you to take good care of everything for things is so scarce, if I never get back, all is yours any how. I want James Flinn and Beverly to go a squirrel hunting and use my gun. I am afraid it will rust and ruin. I will send five post stamps in this letter. I will close by remaining your husband until death.

J. W. Wall

[On the bottom of this letter is one from Nathaniel K. Styers, who had written the above letter for J. W. Wall]

Aunt, as I wrote uncle William's letter for him, I will put a word to you and the children. I tell you I would like to be at East Bend this cold weather and get a drink of Mr. Kirk's brandy. I and Ed and Cousin James and Henry is well. I would like to be at your house today and get a good dinner like I did when we was stationed at East Bend, for we don't get much but flour and old beef here.

I will close my uninteresting letter by hoping to hear from you all soon.

Nathaniel K. Styers

Direct to Richmond, VA. Co. (D) 21st N. C. Reg. Hoke's Brigade

[The letter continues with more from J. W. Wall to Cousin R. S. Phillips]

Cousin R. S. Phillips
A word to you. I received your letter and read it with pleasure to hear you was all well. I returned my thanks to you for hauling wood for my folks till you are better paid.

We are one mile of the yankee picket line. I don't think there will [be] any fight this winter any more for the weather is too bad. They can't get about with the artillery. I am in hopes they will make peace before spring.

If you have any more oats to sell, I want you to let the old women have them, if you please. You wrote that they had Willie Myers in jail. I don't care if they keep him there, for it is nothing more than he deserves. I send howdy to Miss Nanny Philips. You wrote you had no brandy to drink. This Sunday is very cold, and I have nothing to drink but cold water.

So, I will close by asking you to write soon and give me all the news too.

J. W. Wall

Jesse Franklin Williams to wife, Sarah Louzania Patterson Williams[10]
[The original spelling of this letter has been retained, as it could be determined.]

February the 12 1864
Camp near Dalton, GA

Dear wife I take my pen in hand to rite you a fu lins. I am well at this time and hope these fu lines may fine you and my deare little babe well. I have had tolable good heth cins I got back to camp. I ced luis yestidda and he was well. I hant got much to rite to you fur I hant got any letter in a bout two weeks. I wont to her from you the worst. I [illegible] have cens I left thear. I wont to cum home mighty bad but it is a bad [illegible] now with thouth I just cum. So times is still here now but I dont noff how long that will be. if the wether stas good I expect that will be cum more before long. tha su old Johnson ces he is going to fite her. It ant worth his wile to fol back any farther. I have herd that NC was a bout to go back to the union. If it dus I am a cuming home or dy a trying. I wont you to rite cume and rite were it is or not. I wont you to tri to rase lots of chickings if you can. I hope I will git home and help you eat them and plant lots of unons. I have got to be a grate lover of them but I [can] eat any thing that coming [common] dog can. We git a plenty of corn bred and a little meat. We ar a makeing out tolabal well her now considon the times that cepe runing a way. I beleave this rigment will over half run away in the spring if times dont git better. Tel all of my foks and frens if I got any to rite to tha meet to wate for me for I have a bad cans to rite. I wall be glad to [get] a letter from any of them. You must rite. Cume and rite all of the nuse and rite of fen [often]. I hope I will git home and se you wonce more in this life and if I dont I hope we will meat in the world to cum. J. F. Williams.

**Indictment by the Yadkin County Grand Jury,
presented to the Superior Court of Law, Fall Term, 1863[11]**

State of North Carolina
Yadkin County
                                      Superior Court of Law
                                      Fall Term A.D. 1863

The Jurors for the state upon their oath present that Jesse Dobbins, William Dobbins, John Douglas Junior, Anderson Douglas, Sanford Douglas, Hugh Sprinkle, William Willard, Benjamin Willard, Lee Willard, Enoch Brown, Horace Allgood, Thomas Adams, James Wooten & Robert E. Hutchens, laborers, late of the County of Yadkin and State of North Carolina, not having the fear of God before their eyes, but being moved and seduced by the instigation of the devil, on the twelfth day of February in the year of our Lord one Thousand eight hundred and sixty-three, with force and arms at and in the County and State aforesaid, in and upon one James West, in the peace of God and the said State, then and there being, feloniously, wilfully and of their malice aforethought did make an assault; and that the said Jesse Dobbins, William Dobbins, John Douglas Junior, Anderson Douglas, Sanford Douglas, Hugh Sprinkle, William Willard, Benjamin Willard, Lee Willard, Enoch Brown, Horace Allgood, Thomas Adams, James Wooten, & Robert E. Hutchens with a certain Rifle-gun, made of iron and steel, of the value of one dollar, then and there charged and loaded with powder and one leaden bullet of no value, which said Rifle-gun, charged and loaded as aforesaid, the said Jesse Dobbins, William Dobbins, John Douglas Junior, Anderson Douglas, Sandford Douglas, Hugh Sprinkle, William Willard, Benjamin Willard, Lee

Willard, Enoch Brown, Horace Allgood, Thomas Adams, James Wooten, Robert E. Hutchens and each and every of them, then and there, in their right hands had and held, to, upon and against the said James West, then and there feloniously, wilfully and of their malice aforethought, did strike shoot and discharge, and the said Jesse Dobbins, William Dobbins, John Douglas Junior, Anderson Douglas, Sandford Douglas, Hugh Sprinkle, William Willard, Benjamin Willard, Lee Willard, Enoch Brown, Horace Allgood, Thomas Adams, James Wooten, Robert E. Hutchens and then and there with the leaden bullet aforesaid, by them out of the Rifle gun aforesaid, by the force of the powder aforesaid so shot, discharged and sent forth, the said James West in and upon the left side of the head of him the said James West, close to the left eye of him the said James West, then and there feloniously, wilfully and with their malice aforethought did strike, shoot, penetrate and wound, giving the said James West then and there with the said leaden bullet so by them as foresaid, shot discharged and sent forth out of the rifle gun aforesaid in and upon the said James West by the force of the powder aforesaid one mortal wound of the breadth of one inch and the depth of six inches of which said mortal wound the said James West then and there instantly died, and so the Jurors aforesaid upon their oath aforesaid do say that the said Jesse Dobbins, William Dobbins, John Douglas Junior, Anderson Douglas, Sandford Douglas, Hugh Sprinkle, William Willard, Benjamin Willard, Lee Willard, Enoch Brown, Horace Allgood, Thomas Adams, James Wooten, Robert E. Hutchens him the said James West in manner and form aforesaid feloniously wilfully, and of their malice aforethought, did kill and murder against the peace and dignity of the state.

And the Jurors aforesaid upon their oath aforesaid do further present, that afterwards to wit, on the day and year aforesaid, the said Jesse Dobbins of and in the County and State aforesaid, not having the fear of God before his eyes, but being moved and seduced by the instigation of the devil, with force and arms in and upon the said James West in the peace of God and of the said State then and there being, feloniously wilfully and of his malice aforethought did make an assault, and that the said Jesse Dobbins, with a certain Rifle-gun made of iron and then and there being, feloniously wilfully and of his malice aforethought did make an assault, and that the said Jesse Dobbins, with a certain Rifle-gun made of iron and steel, of the value of one dollar then and there charged and loaded with powder and one leaden bullet of no value which said rifle gun the said Jesse Dobbins then and there in both his hands had and held, to, upon and against the said James West, then and there, feloniously, wilfully and of his malice aforethought did strike, shoot and discharge, and the said Jesse Dobbins, then and there with the leaden bullet aforesaid out of the rifle gun aforesaid, shot, discharged and sent forth by the force of the powder aforesaid, the said James West in and upon the left side of the head of him the said James West close to the left eye of him, the said James West, then and there feloniously wilfully, and of his malice aforethought, did strike, shoot, penetrate and wound, giving to the said James West then and there with the said leaden bullet so by him shot, discharged and sent forth out of the rifle gun aforesaid by the force of the powder aforesaid in and upon the said James West one mortal wound of the breadth of one inch and of the depth of six inches, of which said mortal wound the said James West then and there instantly died, and that the said William Dobbins, John Douglas Junior, Anderson Douglas, Sanford Douglas, Hugh Sprinkle, William Willard, Benjamin Willard, Lee Willard, Enoch Brown, Horace Allgood, Thomas Adams, James

Wooten & Robert E. Hutchens then and there feloniously, wilfully and of their malice aforethought were present, aiding, abetting and assisting the said Jesse Dobbins the assault aforesaid, the stroke aforesaid and the mortal wound aforesaid to make, give and commit, and to do and commit the felony and murder aforesaid, and so the Jurors aforesaid upon their oath aforesaid do say that the said Jesse Dobbins, and the said William Dobbins, and the said John Douglas, Junior, and the said Anderson Douglas, and the said Sanford Douglas and the said Hugh Sprinkle and the said William Willard and the said Benjamin Willard, and the said Lee Willard, and the said Enoch Brown, and the said Horace Allgood and the said Thomas Adams, and the said James Wooten and the said Robert E. Hutchens him the said James West, in manner and form aforesaid feloniously, wilfully and of their malice aforethought, did kill and murder, aforesaid the peace and dignity of the State.

R. F. Armfield, Sol.

A true bill against all the parties.

    I Jarratt, Fourman [sic]

The witnesses were:

A. C. Cowles	W. W. Long+	John Bovender
H. C. Cowles	Hugh Brown+	Wm. Adams+
J. C. Fleming+	Isaac Long, Sr.+	Those marked thus +
J. S. Haynes+	A. D. Gentry+	sworn & sent
A. W. Blackburn	R. M. Gabard+	W. A. Joyce CSC
W. A. Joyce+	Wm. S. Arnold	
E. C. Roughton+	Wm. Reynolds+	

Warrant for Arrest of Bond School House Men[12]

The State of North Carolina
To any lawful officer to execute and return immediately.

    Whereas this Day personally appeared before me T. L. Tulbert, an acting Justice of the Peace in and for Yadkin County, Henry C. Cowles and maketh oath that Hugh Sprinkle, Jesse Dobbins, William Dobbins, Benjamin Willard, John Douglas Jr, Anderson Douglas, Sanford Douglas, Lee Willard, William Willard, Horace Allgood, Thomas Adams, Enoch Brown, Robert Hutchens, James Wooten did on this 13th [should read 12th] day of this instant kill and murder James West & John Williams, with malice aforethought, these are therefore to command you to arrest the said Hugh Sprinkle, Jesse Dobbins, William Dobbins, Benjamin Willard, John Douglas Jr., Anderson Douglas, Sanford Douglas, Lee Willard, William Willard, Horace Allgood, Thomas Adams, Enoch Brown, Robert Hutchens & James Wooten if to be found in your county, so that you have them before me or some other Justice of the Peace for said county, without delay to answer the charges aforesaid.

Given under my hand and seal, this the 13th day of February A.D. 1863

T. L. Tulbert, JP (seal)

[A notation on the back]

"Warrant Executed Feb 16th 1863 on John Douglas Jr, Anderson Douglas, Sanford Douglas & Hugh Sprinkle & committed to jail—the others not to be found by me."

S. T. Speer, Shff.

Jessie Casey to Judge R. M. Pearson, July 1, 1864[13]

[July 1, 1864]

To His Hon. R. M. Pearson,
The petition of M. L. Cranfill by his friend Jesse Casey

Humbly praying respectfully showeth that he is over thirty five years age, that he is by profession and occupation a physician, that for more than ten years last past he had been and is now regular and constantly engaged in the practice of his profession, and that not as a dentist, but in treating all manner of diseases. That he has been hitherto exempt from military service on account of his said profession. That as this morning he was arrested by a squad of soldiers from Camp Vance acting under orders from Major J. R. McLean, commandant of that post, who he is informed and believes, has issued special orders for him to be arrested and carried to Camp Vance. That he was arrested at a distance from any council, and asked his captors to allow him to see council, this was denied him and he was hurried off to camp without the opportunity of applying to council or any legal offices for redress and this compels him to apply through the affidavit of Jessie Casey to your Honor for the Writ of Habius Corpus. He further states that he has always acted as a legal citizen and that being exempt by law from military service his arrest and detention by the said Major J. R. McLean as aforesaid is without any covenant of law or just excuse whatsoever. He therefore prays your Hon. to issue the Writ of Habius Corpus to be directed to the said J. R. McLean commanding him to bring the body of your petitioner together with the cause of his detention before your Honor or some other judge of the Superior Court of Law, without delay, to the end that he may be restored to his liberty and your Petitioner as in duty bound will ever pray.

M. L. Cranfil
Jessie Casey

This day personally appeared before me A. H. Thomasson, acting justice of the peace in and for Yadkin County and North Carolina, Jessie Casey who maketh oath that the matters of fact set forth in the above petition are true of his own knowledge.

My
Jessie X Casey
mark

Sworn to and subscribed before me this 1st July 1864.

A. H. Thomasson (seal)

Yadkin Citizens to Major J. R. McLean at Camp Vance, July 30, 1864[14]

Yadkinville July 30, 1864

Maj J. R. McLean
Camp Vance
Major:

My attention has been called by Mrs. Speer to your letter of the 27th to her husband, the Sheriff. The Sheriff is absent and will be for a day or two and Mrs. Davis leaves here this morning for Camp Vance. I write to give you some information in regard to the 'Yadkin refugees' now in your custody.

Their are bills of indictment and capiases in the hands of the Sheriff against Wm, Lee and Ben Willard for the murder of James West & John Williams in the School House fight. Also against Enoch Brown and Hardee [Horace] Allgood who are said to have been captured with the Willards. These men are all conscripts and have been ordered into service and one of them, Allgood, is a deserter from the Army. It will not do to send them to the county to be imprisoned. Our jail is entirely unsafe, to say nothing of the danger of their being rescued by their friends as heretofore. Elkanah did assist in forcing the jail a few weeks ago as can be proven. He did not try to disguise himself.

A very important question is, what is to be done with the balance of these men who went off in that company with the Willards. It is worse than idle to send them to the army, better turn them loose here, because if sent to the army they will be certain to desert and will bring arms with them and perhaps induce others to desert. Doubtless, some better meaning men were persuaded off with them, but very few. If these men are not allowed to get back to this county, we are now in a fair way to clean it out. At least the prospect is better than it ever has been. If they come back we shall have terrible times. As to what should be done with the Willards I can only suggest that they be kept in some *very* safe place until some action is taken in the matter.

Very Truly
[signed] W. A. Joyce

I concur in the above. The Willards must not come back, and if they are sent to the army they will come.

[signed] Jos. Dobson

I concur fully in this letter.

[signed] R. F. Armfield

Major J. R. McLean to Hon. R. W. Pearson[15]

To Hon. R. W. Pearson
Chief Justice
Richmond Hill [Yadkin County, NC]
August 4, 1864

In obedience to the fiat of the Writ to me directed in the matter of M. L. Cranfill send herewith the body of the said Cranfill together with the cause of his arrest and detention. In the outset I desire briefly as possible to recite, but somewhat in detail, the causes, remote and immediate, which led to the arrest.

It is a matter of "Common Fame," and I presume, well known to your Honor that, some few weeks ago, the public jail of Yadkin County was forcibly entered by a mob and the prisoners, three of whom, at least, were awaiting trial for murder, were released, and allowed to go at large;—that, shortly after this the town of Yadkinville was entered by a mob composed, it is believed, of the same persons who broke the jail, and, possibly, of the escaped prisoners,—and the arms and ammunition belonging to the Home Guard forcibly seized and carried off;—that immediately thereafter a crowd of these jail-breakers, escaped murderers, deserters from the army, recusant conscripts (some of them known to have been lying out for two or three years and desperately bad men), escaped Yankee prisoners, and a few disloyal persons, over and under the military age, under the lead of one Alex. Johnson (charged with housebreaking and stealing in company with negro slaves in Davie County) about one hundred and fifty in number, left Yadkin County with the avowed purpose of going within the enemy's lines, and enlisting (some of them at all events) in the Federal Army.

Having been promptly informed of this movement, I dispatched troops to intercept them. About forty or fifty of them, including two of the escaped prisoners, the man who took the keys from the jailer etc., were arrested in Watauga County near the Tennessee line, brought to this Camp and delivered to me.

On examination of L. L. Chamberlin, A. A. Lindsay, Thos. Johnson & Wilburn Wright, who started to Tenn. with the party, & whom I send with this answer as witnesses for Your Honor to examine, I became satisfied that M. L. Cranfill knew that this exodus was in foot, knew the character of the persons engaged in it,—was guilty of aiding, assisting, and abetting deserters and recusant-conscripts in avoiding service in our army, and in going to the enemy,—and also, of assisting in the escape of felons charged with murder and other high crimes.

I, therefore, ordered his arrest for two reasons—: 1st as a 'military necessity' -, believing him to be a dangerous man, able and disposed to interfere with, and render negatory, efforts and plans on foot to arrest a band of deserters and recusant conscripts, known still to infest and disgrace the County of Yadkin.

2nd It was my purpose to turn him over, together with the witnesses to prove his guilt, whom I have under arrest, and all the information I had collected about him to the civil authorities for trial and punishment if guilty of Treason of any other crime.

To this end, before the Writ was served upon me, I had written Gen. V. Strong, C. S. Atty. giving information that I had such persons under arrest, and what I believed could be proven, and asking his advice as to what disposition should be made of them.

An early answer to this communication is expected.

I may add that another consideration has weight. I thought it probable that Dr. Cranfill as soon as he had an intimation that proceedings were about to begin against him, would do as he had advised others to do, namely, take French leave, and go to Tennessee.

I also invite your attention to enclosed copies of letters, written after it was known, by the writers, that orders for the arrest of Cranfill and others had been issued. They explain themselves: The one, signed by Shugarts, was written by Col. Armfield, *Solicitor* for the 6th Judicial Circuit, and was intended, I have no doubt, to embody his own views and convey them to me. It was the opinion of this distinguished lawyer, and sworn peace officer, that Adams should be arrested and detained.

Cranfill is just as guilty as Adams or more so, for he led and persuaded others, while Adams, being a man of much less intelligence, was probably induced by others to take a false step, of which he seems to have repented, as he, voluntarily, turned back. I was much gratified, that the course I had felt it my duty to pursue, met the approval of such eminent lawyers as Mr. *Solicitor* Armfield, and Mr. Dobson, and of so good a citizen as Col. Joyce, himself a judicial officer, and much more familiar with law than myself.

The other, by Col. W. A. Joyce ([Deputy] *Clerk* of the *Superior Court*), and endorsed by Mr. *Solicitor* Armfield and Mr. *Dobson*, shows the deplorable condition of things in the County of Yadkin,—the evident distrust, on the part of the most *prominent* and *law-abiding* citizens, of the power of the *civil* authorities to protect them in their person and property, and their strong desire for *military* interference and *arrests*.

In conclusion, I may say that I cannot, without disobedience of orders, leave my post, and am indeed too unwell to do so, in order to appear before you in person, nor have I had time or opportunity to employ counsel. I have however written *Solicitor* Armfield and Mr. Dobson, presuming they will gladly, appear for me, as they counseled the detention of Adams and others for offences similar to that of which Canfill [sic] is charged, and of which I honestly believe him to be guilty.

I enclose herewith notes of statements made by witnesses written down at the time of their examination before me.

All of which is respectfully submitted

J. R. McLean /s/]
Maj. Comdg.

P. S.

Since the above was written, I have had a conversation with Cranfill in which he admitted that he and his wife went to the spring, in the evening that the crowd assembled there for the purpose of going off, before sundown, that Alex. Johnson and others were there—that he talked with him but declined to say what conversation passed between them.

He also admitted that he saw Johnson and others after dark, not at the spring, but declined to say what passed between them, how many, or who were in the crowd.

These admissions were made after he had been distinctly informed that he need not say anything to criminate himself, nor answer any questions unless he chose to do so.

J. A. M./s/

M. F. Farrington and Iredell A. Warden to Jesse and William Dobbins[16]
August 28, 1864

Mr. Jesse Dobins Dear sir I take this opportunity of riteing you a few lines to let you no whar [sic] I am and how I am doing. I am well. I hope these few lines find you well. I am near Westfield Indiana. I am getting $1.25 per day for work. I left home the

11th of July last that was 136 of us Yadkin fellers Started together but we got scattered and only 48 of us got here. Sandy Vestle [Vestal], John M. Martin, I. A. Warden & others too tedious to mention Come out with us. R. S. Vestal and the Willard Boys and several others got lost from us and I suppose were caught and taken back. I saw your wife the day I started for here and the Children was well. Jane Sprinkle is Still living with them. I think she will make enuff to do her. She has Rented a part of the farm out and is tending a part herself. me and Jackson Bovender threshed with your mashion [machine]. Write soon as you get this letter. I am in Hamilton Countey near West fielde [sic] Indianna [sic]. I will close my few lines. This from Iredell A. Warden to William Dobins. Moffat Martin fetcht a letter from your Wife and he is gone to Iowa address at him Providence Harding County Iowa and he will send you the letter.

Newspaper Article Containing Two Letters from Milton F. Willard, 44th North Carolina Regiment, Shot for Desertion[17]

Aunt Nancy Willard, Yadkin County, Recalls Troubled Days of Civil War.
Her Father Shot for Being Union Sympathizer. "He Looked Mighty Cut Down."
By Harvey Dinkins

Guilford College. Oct. 3 [1925]—It has been said that still waters run deepest. This saying can be verified in actual life if one will take the trouble to visit "Aunt" Nancy Willard, who lives just off the Boone trail highway in the heart of Yadkin county. She lives in a little two-room cottage, all alone, but apparently happy. The 72 years of life weighs less heavily upon her than one would suspect, and when one learns more about her many experiences the wonder is much increased.

Her life is now taken up with the happenings of present day things and it is only by questioning, with a sympathetic interest, that she can be induced to tell of the things in her early childhood that, when they happened, threw a gloom over a whole generation and will be felt, no doubt, when many other generations have lived and died. She was eight years of age when the great civil war started and drew into its vortex father, uncles, cousins and associates.

North Carolina held a peculiar position during the war between the states. This is especially true of the central and western part of the state. There were men who were for the Union, whole heartedly. There were at the same time men who saw their duty in supporting the Confederacy. There are still men among us who can tell us what the call of duty meant in those troubled days. To obey its call meant to take life in hand and "carry on."

In those days a "bushwhacker" brought down upon himself the contempt of the ruling power and of those who supported it. But many a loyal Union man avoided conscription as long as it was in his power to do so. Then, too, there were thousands of those sincere people who felt that it was their duty to remain neutral and allow the conflict to decide itself, rather than to enlist and fight, brother against brother and friend against friend.

This was the state of affairs when the war governor of North Carolina is said to have sent word to President Lincoln, in response to his call for troops, that "he would not get a single soldier from North Carolina to help force the southern state back into the union."

But back against the foothills of the Blue Ridge mountains there were those who were loyal to the Union and desired to see it maintained. Of these, there were in Yadkin county the Willards, the Shores and others. As the war wore on and the enforcement of conscription became more severe, these people, the former of Irish descent and the latter of German stock, decided to push across the country and join the Federal army. Accordingly, it is related, a day was set for a general muster. When the date came there appeared a large number of men who were ready to make the attempt to cross the mountains to the nearest Federal force. There also came numerous neutral individuals who wished to enlist with the little army, and to be allowed to disband when they were safely through the lines. It was their intention to get work and return when the war ended.

Of the body of men who met, a company reported to be about 60 all told, started as an army unit across the mountains. It is with the one unfortunate member of the army that this article will deal. Local legend or tradition tells how the little army made splendid progress until it reached a point about four miles from the Tennessee state line. Here the party brushed against a detachment of Confederate troops and became hopelessly scattered. It is said that all of the party managed to reach the Federal lines except one, Milton F. Willard and possibly one or two others.

From his capture, we have a very vivid account of what befell Willard until he faced a court-martial at Petersburg, Virginia, a few weeks later. It will be recalled that at this time, which was some time in the month of July, 1864, the Federal forces were drawing tighter and tighter around Petersburg. It was a time when the weakening Confederate army was compelled to adopt severe means of keeping up morale, both at home and in the field. Anything that savored of disloyalty merited death. It was into a situation like this that Milton F. Willard, father of "Aunt" Nancy Willard, was brought as a suspicious prisoner.

It appears that at one time he attempted to escape and was apparently making fair headway toward home when he was captured and taken back. The account of this is given in the letters he wrote, which are printed below. This attempted escape was evidently the thing that had much to do with the severe penalty which the court-martial ordered upon him. His own letters written to his wife and oldest child, Nancy Willard, at home, will tell best the story of what he experienced during the remaining days following the capture.

It appears that he had no paper except his diary and Testament. A short letter, written in neat clear handwriting, with a lead pencil, was dated September 25, 1864, and ran as follows:

> Dear Wife: I have found out my doom and it is death I suppose. This is the last Sabbath I am ever to see on this earth, but I hope I am going where Sabbath will never end and I hope you and my dear children may meet me never more to part.
>
> Dear Wife, I don't want you to take on about me. I want to be remembered by you and all my friends and tell them that I was killed for nothing and for trying to get home to see you and help to raise my children. I want

to see you all mighty bad, but I never will without God delivers me out of my enemy's hands. My time is but short.

Another letter which was probably intended to be the last he should send home was more lengthy and was written on pages of his diary, which he had left beyond the date of his execution. At first were written the words, "All the days of my troubles in this world, 400 days, beginning April 28, 1863, ending September 30, 1864." Then started the letter that relates some of the experiences of his imprisonment.

> Dear Wife: I hope, by and through the blessing of God, you may live and raise your children in fear of the Lord. Teach them in the Quaker church for if I could be allowed to live I would join them, for they are the best of all saints.
>
> I want you to keep everything—(four words here were not legible). Don't have a sale and sell off your things. Keep everything you want to keep and sell everything you don't need. Get something to live on.
>
> I have not heard a thing from you since I left home. But I heard that a letter came to camp, but I never saw it. Jonathan Brown, Eli Brown, the three of us, left the camp near Petersburg 16th of August and got in about 18 miles of Farmerville, VA. Was taken up by the Georgia cavalrymen and sent back to the guardhouse. Have been here ever since. A mighty miserable place it is. We get about half enough to eat and not a peach nor apple can be had here without money and I have had none of that. We get nothing here but meal and bread, sometimes a mess of peas or rice, but mighty seldom. Eli Brown came here. We have to lie on the ground and not a thing over us. And our hands are tied fast together. We are as lousy as a hound and cannot scratch ourselves. I tell you we have seen sights for the last three months if anybody ever did. The nights are very cold here. I lay very cold every night. But my trials last in this world but short and I hope I may find rest in Heaven for my soul. I have been under guard about a month and was waiting to know my doom before I wrote you a letter.
>
> I tell you that here is no place for a poor man! (The words that followed had been censored but it was easy to make out the words, "Tell brother William never to come to this wicked war") I know nothing of brother Granville, but if you ever see him, tell him and every one of my friends to try to meet me in Heaven. Tell Dayton Shugart and William Adams and George Adams to never come here where they shoot North Carolinians for nothing. Dayton, I tell you to keep dark, if you want to live. Tell my poor mother farewell and try to meet me in Heaven. So nothing more at present. Only your affectionate—[words blurred out]—until death.

The Testament which he sent home with the letters bore on the fly leaf a letter to the oldest child, Nancy, who now has the Testament and letters. It is as follows:

> Nancy Willard: I want you to keep this book. Learn it and be a good child to your mother. I don't want you to forget me, my little girl and boys. I want

you to remember me and think I was killed for trying to get home to see you. Nathan and John, I want you to be good boys. So farewell. September 22, 1864, Milton F. Willard.

Inside the little morocco bound diary, against one of its covers, the doomed man had pasted a text taken from the Bible. He had evidently placed it there after he learned what his doom was to be. The words, "And when I had passed by and saw thee polluted in thine own blood, I said unto thee when thou wast in thy blood, Live; yea, I said unto thee when thou was in thy blood, Live," were a fitting remembrance for the condemned man to leave behind for the world to see the way his thoughts were drifting.

It was not for the unfortunate man to record the details of his own death. That heartless task was left to one who was a stranger.

The letter of an officer in charge, written three days after the execution tells the little that remains to be told of the final chapter in the unfortunate man's life. This letter was written in response to a communication sent by Miss Claresy Willard, the condemned man's sister. The note was written on note paper and is a fine bit of penmanship. It is dated at Petersburg, Virginia, October 15, 1864. It follows:

> Miss Claresy Willard, I received your letter bearing date of October 2nd requesting of me to try to do something for your brother, Milton, if he wasn't slain. I am sorry to say that he is shot. He was shot the twelfth of this month. If I could a done anything for him I would. I was mighty sorry to see him shot for he looked mighty cut down. But he said that he was prepared to die. You requested of me to put a board to his head so if you was to come after him so you would know him. Of course I will go with you to him. Anything that I can do I will if it will help you any way, although you are a stranger to me. Times is hard here and they are shooting lots of men.
>
> I hope that this unmerciful war will soon stop. I will close my remarks. Yours respectfully, Horace Eddleman, to Claresy Willard.

Thus ended another chapter in this queer volume which mortals have nicknamed Life.

All these memories and letters were written more than 60 years ago but the one to whom they meant most, of sorrow and disappointment, has kept them and is still carrying on. "Aunt" Nancy Willard perhaps never heard that appeal which has thrilled every truly patriotic American citizen: "It is rather for us to be here dedicated to the great task remaining before us, that from these honored dead we take increased devotion, to the cause for which they gave the last full measure of devotion; that we here highly resolve that these dead shall not have died in vain, that the nation under God, have a new birth of freedom, and that the government of the people, by the people and for the people shall not perish from the earth." But she heard the call of duty and as the years passed, she took care of her widowed mother. For nearly 40 years her mother was an invalid care at her hands and yet fell circumstances has not embittered her attitude toward the world. Today, when one goes to her little home they find here a cheerful and even witty person, and even though she doesn't know a single letter of the alphabet, she is no mean conversationalist. She is one of those rare, optimistic souls, whose cheery outlook on life is what makes life vastly more pleasant for all who know them.

Probate of William Dobbins' Will
Yadkin County, North Carolina
July 1867[18]

A paper writing proporting to be the last will and testament of Wm. L. Dobbins, dec'd is exhibited for probate in open court by Jesse Dobbins, the Executor herein named, whose execution whereof is proven by the oath of Thomas F. Adams a subscribing witness, thereto, who swears he saw the said William L. Dobbins execute the said paper writing, that he did all of his own accord, and was at the time of said writing of sound mind and memory, and that the said Thomas F. Adams, the other subscribing witness Jonathan Wagoner because and by agreement of and in the presence of the said William L. Dobbins. Therefore, it is considered by the court that the said paper writing and every part and parcel thereof is the last will and testament of the said William L. Dobbins, and the same is ordered to be recorded and filed and therefore the said Jesse Dobbins come forward and is duly qualified as Executor.

Reminiscences of 43 Years Ago

Just 43 years ago today, February 11, 1906, about sixteen conscripts had met at the Bond school house in Yadkin County, N.C., about one hundred yards south of where the Deep Creek quaker meeting house now stands, their place of rendezvous to consult and lay plans to cross the federal line. Among the number was James C. Wooten, Jesse Dobbins, William Dobbins, Horace Algood, Eck Algood, Robert Hutchens, Thomas Adams, Enoch Brown, Solomon Hinshaw, Jackson Douglas, Sandford Douglas, Anderson Douglas, William Willard, Hugh Sprinkle, Benjamin Willard and Leander D. Willard and if there was any others at that time, they are not remembered by the survivors of that memorable night and the vivid recollection of the heart renting scene that occurred next morning, February the 12th, 1863. During the night a skiff of snow had fallen, and the sun, on the morning of February the 12th, 1863, arose wrapped in a mantle of snow. But a gentle breeze commenced blowing from the north early in the morning, rolling away the dark and gloomy clouds, and the sun shone out in all of its beautiful splendor, casting a halo of peace and happiness on all around. The snow soon disappeared. But before the inmates of that house could give thanks to God, and rejoyce over the prospect of a beautiful springlike day, a horrible scene transpired that chilled the blood in their veins and for a moment stopped the beating of their hearts. The news was carried, by some treacherous and disloyal person, to James West, caption [sic] of the home guard, that the conscripts was congregated at the Deep Creek, or Bond school house. He in company with James Hanes, Henry Cowles, Jackson Shore, William Reynolds, John Williams, R. M. Gabard and about fifty others, hastened to the place, and while some of the conscripts were eating, and all listening attentively to Jackson Douglas, who had just arrived with a newspaper and was reading the news of war, so eager was they to hear, that they had forgotten to place out a guard, and without a moments warning, the report of a gun rang out long and Loud upon the clear morning breeze, and Solomon Hinshaw fell near the hearth with a bullet wound through his heart and died instantly without a groan, with a morsel of victual in his mouth, at the same time a volley of shots was fired through the spaces between the logs, it being a log house, but none taking effect except the shot that killed Hinshaw. Immediately James West appeared upon the door step, and with an oath demanded the surrender of all within, one conscript answered, I will surrender you d___ you, and leveled his gun, but just as he pulled the trigger, West pushed the gun up the contents almost cutting a joist in two over the door. Simultaneously the report of another gun, in the hands of another conscript rang out and James West sank upon the stone door step a lifeless, and headless form, almost all of his head being shot off. The conscripts were panic stricken, and they began to withdraw in disorder. Eck Algood being the first one to leave the house, was shot, and fell mortally wounded with five or six bullet holes through his body, at the same time Algood fell, John Williams, another home guard, was seen to place his hand over his heart, and was heard to exclaim O! God, I am shot. He died in a few minutes. Amidst the uproar and turmoil, a voice, cool and calm, in the house was heard to say, "boys don't run, stay and fight to the finish." But that voice was not obeyed; they withdrew in disorder leaving two of their number dead and dieing. The home guard fearing recruits to the conscript force also withdrew in haste and in disorder, leaving two of their number dead.

It has never been ascertained how many, if any, home guards were wounded in that battle. The wounded conscript was Enoch Brown, slightly wounded in left arm. Benjamin Willard wounded in left side and heel, Eck Algood, shot through the body. Before and after the firing had ceased at the school house, people from far and near hastened to the scene. Catharine Dobbins, who is now in very feeble health at her home about two and a half miles north of Yadkinville, N.C. And widow of the late Jessee Dobbins, knowing her husband was there, hastened to, and was the first one to appear upon the scene, the feelings of that noble hearted woman, as she stood and looked upon that dead form in the yard, and the headless form upon the door step, and that form still in death within, and as she heard a voice weak and feeble, nearby calling to her, can better be imagined than told. But her sad heart even in the hour of great trouble, was filled with great joy, when Algood, the wounded man, who was growing weaker every moment, from the loss of blood flowing from his wounds, told her that her husband had escaped unhurt. Kind and sympathetic friends carried the wounded man to Lydia Bond's, who lived at that time, where our friend and neighbor, Aquilla E. Shore now lives, where all earthly assitance possible was ministered unto him. But in great agony of pain he died the following day. Weeping friends carried the dead bodies to their respective homes, where they were prepared for burial.

This battle fanned the smoldering spirit of sectional strife into a flame, the conscripts was charged with murder. Warrants for their arrest [see copy of warrant also in Appendix A] was issued, the State Militia was called for, and was sent to assist in their capture. Jessee Dobbins, William Dobbins, Robert Hutchens and Thomas Adams, who remained near each other in their flight for freedom, started to, and in a short time succeeded in crossing the Federal line. They volunteered, but in about six months Robert Hutchens deserted, and in less than twelve months William Dobbins, died while in service at Cumberland Gap, Tennessee. James C. Wooten, Jessee Dobbins and Thomas Adams remained and fought for the reunion cause until Lee's surrender and the South acknowledged itself whipped, they were given an honorable discharge and returned to their homes in Yadkin County, N.C. where Jessee Dobbins made himself a useful and respected citizen until his death many years after the war. James C. Wooten, a lifelong friend of the writer, is in very feeble health, and is now living in about one quarter of a mile of the Deep Creek battle ground. The last known residence of Robert Hutchens was New Castle, Indiana, Henry county. The whereabouts of Thomas Adams is unknown to the writer.

In a short time after the battle, Jackson Douglas was shot and wounded in one arm, by the home guard, the wound causing his arm to forever dangle, a useless member, by his side until his death, which occurred several years after the close of the war, through that disability he escaped the war. Sandford Douglas, Anderson Douglas and Hugh Sprinkle, facing a worse fate if caught, surrendered and volunteered in a short time after joining the Southern army Sandford deserted, Anderson remained and fought for the Southern Confederacy until the end and the South subjugated. He was wounded at Ream[s] Station thirteen miles from Petersburg, Virginia. The wound was of such a nature that it necessitated the amputation of his right arm near the shoulder. He and Sandford are both living near Yadkinville. Horace Algood was successful in keeping himself secreted until peace was restored. He is now living in a pleasant and happy home near Yadkinville. Hugh Sprinkle fought until the end and is now living near Yadkinville.

Enoch Brown and the Willard boys made several unsuccessful attempts to cross the federal line. They in company with about five hundred others left Yadkin county, N.C., July the 10th 1864. Having for their leaders Alexander Johnson and James Reedy, who had from time to time been successful in piloting many conscripts across the line, two brothers of our highly esteemed friends the Editor of RIPPLE, was in that crowd, and neither of them ever lived to see their home again. As Johnson and Reedy thought best, they were divided into two companies and different routs chosen. Brown and the Willard boys going with Reedy, Johnson was successfuly in taking his men through. But at Rich Mountain, N.C. Reedy was surprised and fired upon by the Militia and home guard, killing many of his men, some took to the woods and made their escape. But only to be shot or captured. Among the number taken captives was Enoch Brown and the Willard boys, they were marched to Camp Vance, where they were held as prisoners. Brown and the Willard boys as fugitives from justice. In a very short time Brown and the Willard boys excaped, but was captured time and again and held for a time in many of the various jails of Northwestern, N.C., but no jail could hold them long at [a] time. The last place they broke jail was Winston, N.C. A sister of the Willard boys secreted an auger and a chisel upon her person, left her home in Yadkin county and went to Winston and after undergoing a rigid examination by the jailor, she was permitted to go up stairs to see her brothers. When she left the jail she left the augur and chisel with them. With the auger and chisel, they bored and cut out of the jail and made good their escape, and avoided being shot or hanged, as a detachment of state militia had been ordered there to take them out and hang or shoot them, and arrived the day after they escaped.

Soon after this the welcome word "peace" was heralded from Florida to California, and from the Atlantic to the Pacific Ocean. And they like thousands of others, at the close of the war, returned to their shattered homes penniless. All indictments against them was nole prosceivied [sic]. Enoch Brown and William Willard have been dead for years, Benjamin Willard is now living out on R.F.D. route 3, Yadkinville. Leander D. Willard is living near New Castle, Indiana, Henry county, and is highly respected by all who know him. R. M. Garbard [Gabard], a personal friend of the writer, is living at

A. Documents Re the Bond School House

Mt. Nebo Yadkin county, N.C. Henry Cowles, is and has been for years clerk of the federal court at Statesville, N.C., and so far as the writer knows he and Gabard are the only two home guards now living that took a part in the school house fight.

In proportion to the number engaged, that battle resulted in the greatest loss of life and the greatest number wounded of any battle fought during the late struggle between the north and the south. Eck Algood was buried in the Algood burying ground where the home for the unfortunate [county home] is now located in Yadkin county, N.C.

Solomon Hinshaw was buried at Deep Creek near where he was killed. John Williams was buried at the Williams burying ground near Spillman, N.C. James West was buried at Hamptonville, N.C.

The narrative would not be complete without adding the following. On their way to the school house the home guard passed by the home of Daniel Vestal, about one mile away. West, the captain, in conversation with Vestal and his wife, who were old time Quakers, remarked that a number of conscripts were at the Bond school house and that he was going out there and take ever D___ one of them prisoners. Mrs. Vestal answered, "Yes, and thee will get thee head shot off thy shoulders too." Whether or not the spirit of prophecy was upon Mrs. Vestal, we leave to the conjecture of the reader. But it is no less strange than true, it happened precisely as she foretold, and she always unto her death maintained the declaration that the horrible scene was revealed unto her before it occurred.

The facts we write about occurrred 41–43 years ago when a cruel war was raging and every mind and heart was filled with apprehension, and when men met their neighbors in deadly conflict. But now how changed the scene—peace contentment and happiness reigns, and every mind and heart is at ease, and men meet with their neighbors to worship a just and holy Jehovah, and where once the sound of the gun was heard, and the battle field strown with the dead, shouts of new born souls can be heard as they catch a glimpse of the blessed gospel light, that will light the world forever more.

COL. HAM[19]

Notes

1. Letter from Samuel Speer Harding to William Harding, dated January 3, 1862, in possession of Frances H. Casstevens, Yadkinville, N.C.
2. Letter from Thomas G. Scott to William Harding, dated August 27, 1864, in possession of Frances H. Casstevens, Yadkinville, N.C.
3. Letter from John Bovender, courtesy of Patricia L. Caldwell, Franklin, N.C.
4. Letter from Albert Poindexter, courtesy of Patricia L. Caldwell, Franklin, N.C.
5. *Ibid.*
6. Letter from Richard Poindexter, courtesy of Patricia L. Caldwell.
7. Letters from John M. Harrison, courtesy of Verne Harrison, Yadkinville, N.C.
8. Original letter from Milas Mason in possession of Mattie May Reavis, and reproduced here with her permission. She also has the William Gabard Bible in which the letter was found. A copy of the letter was furnished by Cliff Gabard, Anaheim, Calif. This letter has also been published in the *Journal of the Yadkin County Historical & Genealogical Society* XIII (December 1994): 9–10, and is used with permission.

A. Documents Re the Bond School House

9. Original letters from J. W. Wall, Company D, 21st Regiment, to wife Agnes, is in possession of Virgie Wooten Mathis, courtesy of a descendant, Richard Andrew Mathis, Macon, Ga.

10. Letter from Jesse F. Williams to wife Sarah Louzania Patterson Williams, courtesy of Mrs. Sarah Augusta D. Phillips, Mt. Airy, N.C., and used with her permission.

11. Indictment of the men involved in the shootout at the Bond School House was published in the *Journal of the Yadkin County Historical & Genealogical Society* VI (June 1987): 4–6, reprinted with permission.

12. Warrant for the men involved in the shootout at the Bond School House published in the *Journal of the Yadkin County Historical & Genealogical Society* VI (March 1987): 5–6, reprinted with permission.

13. Letter from Jessie Casey to Judge R. M. Pearson, dated July 1, 1864, Richmond Mumford Pearson Collection, Duke University, Durham, NC, reprinted with permission.

14. Letter from W. A. Joyce, Jos. Dobson, and R. F. Armfield to Maj. J. R. McLean, July 30, 1864, Richmond Mumford Pearson Collection, Duke University, Durham, N.C., reprinted with permission.

15. Letter from Maj. J. R. McLean to the Hon. R. W. Pearson, Richmond Mumford Pearson Collection, Duke University, Durham, N.C., reprinted with permission.

16. Letter from M. T. Farrington and Iredell A. Warden to Jesse and William Dobbins, August 28, 1864, published in *Journal of the Yadkin County Historical & Genealogical Society* V (December 1986): 14, reprinted with permission.

17. Harvey Dinkins, "Aunt Nancy Willard, Yadkin County, Recalls Troubled Days of Civil War," Greensboro, N.C., *Daily News*, October 4, 1925.

18. Probate of William Dobbins' Will, Yadkin County, N.C., Court Minutes 1851–1863, microfilm reel no. 1 C.106.3001, North Carolina Department of Archives and History.

19. The "Col. Ham" letter was transcribed from an old *Yadkin Ripple* published about 1906 by Lewis Brumfield on November 3, 1984. The whereabouts of this particular issue is unknown and it was among other missing issues and therefore was not saved on the microfilm which is available at the Yadkin County Public Library.

Appendix B:
Yadkin Men Present at Appomattox, April 9, 1865[1]

Name	Company/Regiment[2]
Anderson, Albert A.	Company B, 21st Regiment (Co. A, 1st Battallion)
Bell, Shadrack	Company I, 18th Regiment
Bran[n], John H.	Company B, 21st Regiment (Co. A, 1st Battalion)
Brooks, John	Company B, 21st Regiment (Co. A, 1st Battalion)
Brooks, S. J.	Company A, 1st Battalion Sharpshooters
Collins, David D.	Company B, 38th Regiment
Cook, Isom C.	Company A, 1st Battalion Sharpshooters
Crews, Ephraim W.	Company A, 1st Battalion Sharpshooters
Davis, Martin	Company A, 1st Battalion Sharpshooters
Farris, Archibald	Company A, 1st Battalion Sharpshooters
Haynes (Hanes), Thomas F.	Company I, 28th Regiment
Hobson, John W.	Company B, 21st Regiment (Co. A, 1st Battalion)
Hobson, Tyra C.	Company B, 28th Regiment
Hutchens, Isaac	Company I, 28th Regiment
Hutchens, Richard H.	Company F, 28th Regiment
Joyce, Abner R.	Company I, 28th Regiment
Lawrence, Lee	Company B, 21st Regiment (Co. A, 1st Battalion)
Martin, Morgan C. M.	Company B, 38th Regiment
Messick, George	Company H, 21st Regiment
Money, Howell	Company H, 54th Regiment
Newman, John P.	Company H, 54th Regiment
Nicholson, John P.	Company I(&K), 33rd Regiment
Osborne, David D.	Company B, 21st Regiment (Co. A, 1st Battalion)
Poindexter, Pleasant Henderson	Company I, 6th Regiment
Poplin, George C.	Company B, 38th Regiment
Reavis, Giles	Company A, 1st Battalion Sharpshooters

Reece, Evan H.	Company I, 28th Regiment
Riggsbee (Rigsby), Jobe	Company H, 54th Regiment
Scott, Thomas G.	Company I, 28th Regiment
Sheek, Miles C.	Company A, 1st Battalion Sharpshooters
Shermer, Perry A.	Company A, 1st Battalion Sharpshooters
Shugart, J. Alexander	Company A, 1st Battalion Sharpshooters
Smith, Jacob	Company H, 54th Regiment
Sprinkle, William R.	Company B, 38th Regiment
Swaim, Michael F.	Company H, 54th Regiment
Tanner, Thomas E.	Company A, 1st Battalion Sharpshooters
Todd, Leander A.	Company I, 28th Regiment
Veach, James L.	Company B, 38th Regiment
Waggoner, John W.	Company I, 28th Regiment
Webster, John	Company D, 14th Regiment
Wise, Henry A.	Company G, 4th Regiment
Woodruff, Richard W.	Company B, 21st Regiment (Co. A, 1st Battalion)

Notes

1. This list, which may not be complete, was compiled from Manarin and Jordan's *North Carolina Troops 1861–1865: A Roster*, from family histories published in the *Heritage of Yadkin County*, from R. A. Brock's *The Appomattox Roster*, and other sources.

2. Regiments are North Carolina Troops, unless otherwise specified.

Appendix C: Rank Above Private Achieved by Yadkin Confederate Soldiers[1]

Adams, Martin (Captain)
Allgood, John W. (Captain)
Anderson, Albert A. (Sergeant)
Angell, James A. (Corporal)
Apperson, John Alvis (Musician)
Apperson, Thomas V. (Captain)
Apperson, William H. (Ord. Sgt.)
Armfield, Robert (Lt. Colonel)
Armstrong, James C. (Captain)
Armsworthy, John W. (Sergeant)
Atwood, George W. (Corporal)
Atwood, William J. (Musician)
Baity, Francis A. (Corporal)
Barker, Larkin Jones (Hospital Steward)
Binkley, Peter (Captain)
Bohannon, Neal (Captain)
Bovender, John V. (Captain)
Brann, Henry T. (Corporal)
Brindle, James Free (Sergeant)
Brindle, Pleasant H. (Captain)
Brooks, John (Corporal)
Brown, James K. P. (Sergeant)
Brown, William S. (Captain)
Casey, Daniel C. (Sergeant)
Choplin, Joseph (Sergeant)
Clingman, Thomas L. (Brig. Gen.)
Cockerham, David (Corporal)
Cockerham, David S. (Captain)
Comer, James Q. (Captain)
Connally, John K. (Colonel)
Conrad, Sidney F. (Captain)
Conrad, W. Augustus (Corporal)
Cook, Columbus L. (Captain)
Cook, Thomas J. (Musician)
Cornelius, L. M. (Sergeant)
Cowles, Andrew C. (Colonel)
Cowles, William H. H. (Major)
Creson, Samuel D. (Corporal)
Crutchfield, Martin A. (Sergeant)
Davis, Daniel V. (Sergeant)
Davis, Thomas J. (Captain)
Denny, Emmitt (Sergeant)
Dickerson, Alphonso (Corporal)
Dozier, Smith W. (Corporal)
Duvall, Robert C. (Captain)
Eddleman, Horace (Corporal)
Farris, William D. (Sergeant)
Fleming, Samuel F. (Sergeant)
Fleming, Winston (Captain)

Fletcher, John F. (Corporal)
Gentry, Alfred D. (Captain)
Gentry, John W. (Corporal)
Gentry, William R. (Sergeant)
Grose [Groce], John (Sergeant)
Hampton, Alford (Corporal)
Hampton, John A. (Major)
Harding, Greenberry P. (Sergeant)
Harding, Samuel S. (Sergeant)
Hauser, Edwin T. (Sergeant)
Hobson, David F. (Corporal)
Hobson, J. D. (Corporal)
Hobson, John W. (Sergeant)
Holcomb, Bloom V. (Sergeant)
Holcomb, Calvin M. (Sergeant)
Holcomb, James N. (Musician)
Holder, John C. (Corporal)
Hunt, Leander G. (Hosp. Steward)
Hunt, Nathan G. (Major)
Jarratt, Isaac A. (Captain)
Jarratt, Isaac C. (Captain)
Jarvis, Enoch (Captain)
Jarvis, Willie L. (Corporal)
Johnson, Lewis W. (Corporal)
Jones, Jesse S. (Captain)
Joyce, William A. (Lt. Colonel)
Joyner, David W. (Corporal)
Kelly, John C. (Qtr. Master)
Kelly, Samuel L. (Corporal)
Kelly, William D. (Corporal)
Kimbrough, Lewis W. (Musician)
Kirk, Franklin W. (Captain)
Kittle [Kettle], Costin (Musician)
Kittle [Kettle], Eugene (Musician)
Lewis, William T. (Sergeant)
Lillington, Nicholas W. (Captain)
Lindsy, Thomas W. (Sergeant)
Logan, Richard M. (Sergeant)
Long, Daniel (Major)
Marler, James N. (Corporal)
Martin, John B. (Sergeant)
Martin, Reps (Sergeant)

Martin, Thomas A. (Corporal)
Martin, William L. (Sergeant)
May, Monroe (Sergeant)
McBride, J. L. (Corporal)
McBride, John G. (Sergeant)
Miller, Gaither W. (Corporal)
Minish, Thomas R. (Corporal)
Myers, Frederick A. (Sergeant)
Nance, Joseph W. (Corporal)
Naylor, Joseph R. (Cap-tain)
Pearson, John W. (Sergeant)
Poindexter, Albert (Blacksmith)
Poindexter, Isaac C. (Sergeant)
Poindexter, John A. H. (Sergeant)
Poindexter, Thomas C. M. (Sergeant)
Potts, John H. (Musician)
Riggsbee [Rigsby], Jobe (Sergeant)
Rose, Isaac W. (Musician)
Royal, John C. (Sergeant)
Royal, Willie D. (Musi-cian)
Shore[s], Alexander F. (Corporal)
Shore[s], J. W. (Corporal)
Shore[s], William C. (Sergeant)
Shugart, Isaac L. (Corporal)
Smith, Ephraim D. (Captain)
Smith, James T. (Corporal)
Speas, William H. (Corporal)
Speer, W. H. A. (Colonel)
Spillman, William (Colonel)
Sprinkle, Alexander (Musician)
Stowe, George C. (Captain)
Swaim, Little M. (Corporal)
Tesh, William A. (Corporal)
Transou, Edwin L. (Musician)
Tulbert, Joshua (Corporal)
Underwood, Henry (Musician)
Veach, James L. (Musi-cian)
Vestal, Daniel A. (Corporal)
Vestal, Miles J. (Sergeant)
Wheeling, George W. (Corporal)
Whitaker, Lorenzo D. (Sergeant)
Whitaker, William A. (Sergeant)

C. Rank Achieved

Williams, George D. (Sergeant)
Williams, Lewis A. (Corporal)
Williams, Williams S. (Captain)

Wilson, Reuben E. (Captain)
Wooten, Lewis W. (Corporal)

1. Compiled from Louis H. Manarin and Weymouth T. Jordan, eds. *North Carolina Troops 1861–1865: A Roster,* and Steven E. Bradley, Jr., ed. *North Carolina Confederate Militia: Officers Roster as Contained in the Adjutant-General's Offices Roster.*

Appendix D: Confederate Units in Which Yadkin Men Served

North Carolina Units

Artillery
1st Regiment, Co. H

Cavalry
1st Regiment, Cos. A, D, H
5th Regiment, Cos. D, H
5th Battalion, Co. D
6th Regiment, Cos. B, E
7th Regiment, Co. A
16th Battalion, Co. E
McRae's Battalion

Infantry
1st Regiment, Cos. A, B, C
1st Battalion Sharpshooters, Cos. A, B
2nd Battalion, Co. G
3rd Regiment, Cos. H, I
4th Regiment, Cos. B, C, G, H, I
6th Regiment, Cos. A, B, E, F, I
9th Battalion (Junior Reserves), Co. A
13th Regiment, Cos. C, F, G
18th Regiment, Cos. C, D, G, I, K
20th Regiment, Co. A
21st Regiment, Cos. A, B, C, D, F, G, H, I
23rd Regiment, Cos. C, D, F, G
24th Regiment, Co. B
25th Regiment
26th Regiment, Cos. A, C, E
27th Regiment, Co. B
28th Regiment, Cos. A, B, D, F, G, I
29th Regiment, Co. F
30th Regiment, Co. C
33rd Regiment, Cos. E, I
34th Regiment, Co. A
35th Regiment, Co. I
38th Regiment, F & S, Cos. A, F, G, H, K
42nd Regiment, Cos. B, D, E, F, G, K
44th Regiment, Cos. A, B, C, D, F, G, H, I
49th Regiment, Co. E
52nd Regiment, Cos. B, D, F, G, K
53rd Regiment, Co. E
54th Regiment, Cos. A, E, G, H
55th Regiment, Co. H
56th Regiment, Co. B
66th Regiment, Co. G
70th Regiment (Junior Reserves), Co. E
72nd Regiment (Junior Reserves), Co. C
74th Regiment (Senior Reserves), Cos. B, E, H
Branch-Lane Brigade
Clingman's Brigade

D. Confederate Regiments of Yadkin Men

Units of Other States

8th Regiment Georgia Cavalry, Co. D
39th Regiment Georgia Infantry, Co. I
6th Regiment Missouri Infantry
10th Regiment Virginia Cavalry, Co. B
37th Regiment Virginia Cavalry, Co. R
51st Regiment Virginia Infantry, Co. K
Virginia Horse Artillery, McGregor's Co.

Units of Mixed States

Army of Northern Virginia
Army of Tennessee
Confederate Navy
under Gen. P. G. T. Beauregard

Appendix E:
Officers of Yadkin Militia,
75th Regiment, 18th Brigade[1]

*These individuals resigned from the Militia and volunteered for duty in the regular Confederate military service.

Field and Staff

Name	Rank	Date Enlisted	Termination
Cowles, Andrew Carson	Colonel	4/15/1862	resigned
Joyce, William A.	Lt. Colonel	4/15/1862	
Long, Daniel, Jr.	Major	4/15/1862	
Hampton, John	Major/Surgeon	4/16/1862	
Benbow, Esau	Asst. Surgeon	4/16/1862	
Cowles, Henry C.	Adjutant	4/16/1862	
Steelman, Sanford	Asst. Com.	4/16/1862	
Jarratt, John C.	Asst. Quartermaster	4/22/1862	
Brown, William S.	Chaplain	4/16/1862	
York, Louis	Surgeon	4/16/1862	

Captains	Date Enlisted	District of County	Termination
Adams, Martin	2/8/1862	Deep Creek	volunteered*
Armstrong, James Clingman	2/8/1862	Swan Creek	
Binkley, Peter	3/10/1862	Baltimore	
Bovender, John V. B.	10/18/1862	Deep Creek	
Brindle, Pleasant Henderson	3/1/1862	Yadkinville	died
Cook, Joseph	2/8/1862	Buck Shoals	
Davis, Thomas J.	2/8/1862	North Boonville	
Fleming, Winston	3/20/1862	Fall Creek	
Gentry, Alfred	2/8/1862	Holly Springs	
Holcomb, Pleasant Henderson	2/8/1862	Hamptonville	
Jarvis, Enoch	2/8/1862	Chinquepin	

E. Yadkin Militia

Captains	Date Enlisted	District of County	Termination
Jones, Jesse Sanford	3/10/1862	Little Yadkin	
Kirk, Franklin Wesley	2/8/1862	Deep Creek	volunteered*
Naylor, Joseph R.	2/8/1862	Jonesville	resigned 1/30/1865
Reece, Thomas H.	2/8/1862	South Boonville	
Smith, Ephraim Davis	2/8/1862	Knobs	
Williams, William Sanford	2/8/1862	Huntsville	

1st Lieutenants	Date Enlisted	District	Termination
Barber, Charles	2/8/1862	Buck Shoals	
Brubaker, Thomas	3/10/1862	Huntsville	
Cartright, Louis J.	2/8/1862	South Boonville	
Danner, Francis	2/8/1862	Chinquepin	
Gabard, Richmond Murphy	3/10/1862	Yadkinville	
Hampton, Thomas D.	2/8/1862	Jonesville	volunteered*
Hobson, George Dick	3/10/1862	Baltimore	
Idol, Barnett Virgil	2/8/1862	Deep Creek	
Jester, Josiah	3/10/1862	Fall Creek	
Kimbrough, Nathaniel	3/10/1862	Little Yadkin	
Lineberry, Asbury O.	7/12/1862	Jonesville	
Long, William Dobson	2/8/1862	Hamptonville	
Reece, Joel D.	2/8/1862	North Boonville	
Salmons, Jesse Franklin	2/8/1862	Holly Springs	
Swaim, David	2/8/1862	Knobs	
Swaim, Ephraim David	2/8/1862	Knobs	

2nd Lieutenants	Date Enlisted	District	Termination
Adams, Columbus	4/5/1862	Fall Creek	
Adams, George	2/8/1862	Deep Creek	
Bagby, R. L.	7/12/1862	Jonesville	
Burgess, Robert	2/8/1862	Hamptonville	
Carter, Abel Duncan	2/8/1862	Knobs	
Cheek, John Vestal	2/8/1862	Yadkinville	
Cranfield, Thomas	2/8/1862	Chinquepin	
Davis, James	2/8/1862	South Boonville	
Dezern, Jesse Franklin	2/8/1862	East Bend	
Douglas, John Henry	2/8/1862	East Bend	
Farris, Cooly D.	2/8/1862	North Boonville	
Gough, Samuel	2/8/1862	Chinquepin	
Gough, John E.	unknown	Hamptonville?	resigned 3/8/1865
Haynes, Asbury	2/8/1862	Jonesville	volunteered*

2nd Lieutenants	Date Enlisted	District	Termination
Jester, James	3/10/1862	Fall Creek	
Jester, William Aaron	3/1/1862	Fall Creek	removed from district
Jones, Benjamin Franklin	3/10/1862	Huntsville	
Jones, Preston	3/1/1862	Little Yadkin	left county, vacated commission
Kelly, Leonard Davis	3/1/1862	Yadkinville	
Laugenhour, Andrew Lafayette	3/10/1862	Huntsville	
Lewis, Levi Branson	2/8/1862	Buck Shoals	
Marshall, Henry	2/8/1862	Jonesville	
Matthews, Bradley	2/8/1862	Swan Creek	
North, John	3/1/1862	Baltimore	
Pardue, Alison	2/8/1862	Holly Springs	
Phillips, John	3/1/1862	Baltimore	
Reece, Thomas	2/8/1862	North Boonville	
Rodwell, William H.	2/8/1862	Deep Creek	
Ross, Alexander	2/8/1862	Swan Creek	
Roughton, Elisha Clark	2/8/1862	Holly Springs	
Speer, James M.	2/8/1862	South Boonville	volunteered*
Swaim, Dabner Caldwell	2/8/1862	Knobs	
Tesh, Moses	3/1/1862	Little Yadkin	
Weatherman, George P.	2/8/1862	Hamptonville	
Windsor, Enos Lawson	2/8/1862	Buck Shoals	

Notes

1. Stephen E. Bradley, Jr., ed. *North Carolina Confederate Militia: Officers Roster as Contained in the Adjutant-General's Officers Roster* (Wilmington, N.C.: Broadfoot Publishing Co., 1992), pp. 204–206, reprinted with permission. Bradley's list was compared with that of Gerald W. Cook, *The Last Tarheel Militia 1861–1865*, privately published, 1987, and the above list is the combined result.

*Appendix F:
Yadkin Veterans and Widows
Who Drew Pensions,
1900–1910*

Soldier Name	Co./Reg.	Disability/Death	Post Office
Adams, Moses	H, 54th	died in service	Jonesville
Albea, J. R.	?	disease	Hamptonville
Angel, J. J.	B, 38th	killed	Tracadia
Anthony, James	B/?	disease	Hamptonville
Apperson, Wm. A.	F, 28th	disease	East Bend
Armstrong, John	D, 24th	wounds	Jonesville
Arnold, Thomas L.	H, 5th	wounds	Hamptonville
Atwood, Henry	A, 34th	wounds	Yadkinville
Atwood, J(I?). M.	B, 38th	wounds	Cross Roads Ch.
Azmon, B. B.	C, 26th	disease	Cross Roads Ch.
Baity, D. W.	F, 42nd	wounds	Cross Roads Ch.
Baity, P. H.	I, 28th	disease	Yadkinville
Barr, A. C.	I, 21st		Siloam
Bean, Alfred	F, 28th	wounds	Otis
Bell, W. W.	B, 38th		Hamptonville
Benge, John	I, 28th	disease	Jonesville
Blackman, John	B, 38th	killed	Conrad's
Blakley, Eli	F, 28th	disease	East Bend
Blakley, G. W.	F, 28th	wounds	East Bend
Bohanon, Neal	I, 28th	disease	Huntsville
Bovender, J. R.	F, 28th	wounds	Republic
Brandon, J. C. (H)?	H, 5th	wounds	Footville
Bray, D.	E, 42nd		Boonville
Brown, J. C.	E, 4th	disease	Marler
Burgess, J. M.	B, 1st Battalion	disease	Hamptonville
Campbell, A. F. (D)?	B, 42nd	disease	Buck Shoals
Casey, Thos. M.	I, 28th	wounds	Zion
Cass, Alfred	B, 42nd	disease	Buck Shoals
Cass, B. G.	B, 42nd	disease	Buck Shoals
Casstevens, John	H, 21		Hinshaw
Casstevens, Wm.	A, 28th	disease	Chestnut Ridge
Caudle, Jonathan J.	F, 37th	disease	Yadkinville
Caudle, W. S.	E, 70th	disease	Mt. Nebo
Chamberlin, L. L.	G, 13th	disease	Hamptonville
Cheek, Aaron	K, 52nd	wounds	Swan Creek
Choplin, W.	F, 28th	wounds	East Bend
Cloer, W. F.	E, 49th	helpless, burns	Garrett
Comer, J. Q.	I, 28th	disease	Hamptonville
Cook, Burt	G, 54th		Hamptonville
Cook, I. C.	A, 1st Battalion	wounds	Yadkinville
Cook, Pettis	F, 37th VA		Garrett
Cornelius, A. E.	F, 28th	disease	Cana
Cowles, John B.	H, 4th	wounds	Conrad's
Cranfill, Jonathan	G, 4th	wounds	Footville
Crater, R. W.	D, 63rd	disease	Gwyn
Cummings, W. W.	B, 38th	wounds	Buck Shoals
Davis, Henry A.	B, 38th		Boonville
Davis, L. C.	B, 28th	wounds	Conrad's
Davis, S. C.	G, 4th		Yadkinville
Davis, S.	E, 5th	disease	Siloam
Davis, Thos. W.	F, 28th	disease	Shore
Davis, Wm.	H, 10th	age	Yadkinville

F. Veterans and Widows Pensions

Pension Started	Pension Ended	Widow	Pension Received
		Grace	1902
		Nancy C.	1902–1907
		Kiziah	1902–1906
		Eliza	1902–1907
		Julia	1900–?
1900			
1900	1902—dropped		
1904			
1900			
1902	1908—dead		
1901			
1906			
		Jane	1904–1908
1901	1901		
		Atry	1908
1902			
		Lavinia	1900
1905			
1900			
		Elizabeth	1900
1900		R. F. Robertson	1908
1901			
		Eliza	1908
1905	1910—dead		
1902	1908—dead		
1902	1902—dead	Mary	1902
1900			
1901			
		Absela	1904–1906
1901	1904—dead		
1910			
1902			
		Elizabeth	1900
1900	1907—dead		
1900			
1901			
		Lucinda	1902
		Harriett	1902
1900			
		Nancy J.	1902–1904
1905			
1901			
1904			
1902			
1900			
		Mary	1902
1900	1910—dead		
1908			
		M. M.	1900
1906			

Soldier Name	Co./Reg.	Disability/Death	Post Office
Dinkins, John	B, 38th	disease	Conrad's
Dixon, Giles	A, 1st Battalion	age	Yadkinville
Douglas A.	B, 28th	lost arm	Yadkinville
Dudley, James	C, 26th	wounds	Yadkinville
Erwin, Samuel	A, 21st	disease	Mt. Nebo
Evans, I. C.	I, 28th	age	Boonville
Felts, H. T.	— —	— —	East Bend
Fortner, James	B, 44th	wounds	Conrad's
Freeman, William R.	A, 44th	disease	Jonesville
Gentry, J. V.	F, 37th		Brannon
Gentry, W. R.	I, 28th	disease	Yadkinville
Godfrey, T. N.	D, 5th Cavalry	disease	Marler
Gough, John	H, 63rd		
Gough, Martin F.	F, 28th	wounds	Boonville
Gross, C. L.	G, 44th	deranged	
Hall, D. C.	I, 28th	wounds	Hinshaw
Hall, L. W.	F, 28th	age	Siloam
Harbin, J. H.	E, 42nd	disease	Cana
Hare, Abner S.	B, 38th		Cross Roads Ch.
Harrell, Joseph	A, 42nd	disease	East Bend
Harvill, John	I, 28th	killed	Panther Creek
Haynes, James	B, 1st Battalion	disease	Footville
Haynes, Thomas F.	I, 28th	disease	Hamptonville
Haynes, W. L.	H, 54th	disease	Jonesville
Hendricks, C. G.	I, 28th	disease	Boonville
Henson, L.	C, 28th	disease	Longtown
Hinson, Fred	C, 5th	disease	Jonesville
Hobson, John P.	A, 54th	wounds	East Bend
Holcomb, P. H.	B, 38th	arrm off below elbow	Chestnut Ridge
Holcomb, Samuel	B, 1st Bat	disease	Chestnut Ridge
Holcomb, W. B.	F, 37th VA		
Holcomb, W. J.	G, 44th	disease	Jonesville
Holloman, Asa	H, 44th	debility	Swan Creek
Holloman, John	I, 3rd	wounds	Swan Creek
Horton, Amos	B, 1st Battalion		Buck Shoals
Hoots, John A.	D, 1st	age	Jennings
Hutchens, H.	F, 28th		East Bend
Hutchens, J. C.	A, 1st Battalion	disease	Yadkinville
Hutchens, William D.	F, 28th	killed	East Bend
Jefferson, Z. M.	I, 28th	disease	Boonville
Jenkins, John J.	H, 21st	disease	Jonesville
Jester, A. Z.	D, 42nd	wounds	Richmond Hill
Jester, Solomon	I, __	disease	Richmond Hill
Johnson, G. P.	A, __	disease	Buck Shoals
Johnson, Jeremiah C.	B, 1st Battalion	disease	Buck Shoals
Johnson, Jesse	A, 46th		Buck Shoals
Johnson, Neal	H, 21st	wounds	East Bend
Johnson, S. H.	A, __	disease	Buck Shoals
Johnson, W. A.	A, 21st	wounds	Buck Shoals
Joyce, Wm. A.	B, 2nd Batt.	wounds	East Bend
Joyner, John T.	F, 28th	disease	East Bend

F. Veterans and Widows Pensions   169

Pension Started	Pension Ended	Widow	Pension Received
1905	1908—dead	J. Dinkins	1908
1900			
1901			
		Jane	1900
1906			
1900			
1900	1908—dead	S. A.	1908
		Hannah	1900–1907
		Emaline	1908
1905			
		Jane	1906
1901			
		Nancy	1902
1900			
1906			
1908			
		Phoebe E. Williams	
1901	1904—dead		
		Temperance	1900
		Sarah	1902
1902	1910—dead		
1908			
		Elizabeth	1902
		Sarah J.	1900–1904
		Rena	1900–1906
1905			
1906	1907 ?		
1904			
		E. M.	1902
		Priscilla	1902–1906
	1904		
		Cynthia M. Warren	1904
1900	1907—dead		
1906			
		Lucy A. E.	1908
		Martha P.	1902–1906
		Mary	1900
1901			
1905			
1901			
1902	1902—dropped		
1902	1902—dropped; reinstated 1908		
		Nancy J.	1908
1901	1904—dropped		
1902			
1900	1901—dropped		
1900			
1902	1904—dead		

Soldier Name	Co./Reg.	Disability/Death	Post Office
Kettle, Eugene	F, 28th	disease	East Bend
Kiger, Lewis	G, 2nd Bat.		Huntsville
Kimmer, Henry	G, 66th	disease	Jonesville
King, I.	K, 54th	age	Yadkinville
Kinner, D. E.	C, 42nd	disease	Elkin
Lakey, Wm. D.	G, 21st		Siloam
Ladd, L. F.	B, 1st Bat.	disease	Buck Shoals
Ladd, Thomas	D, 44th		Buck Shoals
Leagans, Ananias	I, 28th	wounds	Cross Roads Church
Leeman, James	D, 52nd	killed	East Bend
Lindsay, Wade	F, 18th	wounds	Buck Shoals
Linville, J. F.	F, 42nd	wounds	Cross Roads Church
Logan, George	A, 54th	wounds	Conrad's
Logan, Richard	F, 28th	disease	East Bend
McCollum, John	F, 28th	disease	Martin
Macemore, Jno.	H, 21st	age	Jonesville
Macy, Wm. L.	I, 28th	disease	Yadkinville
Marler, H. F.	D, 18th Bat. VA	debility	East Bend
Martin, Gilbert	F, 28th	disease	East Bend
Martin, John H.	I, 28th	age	Benbow
Martin, W. L.	A, 9th	disease	Hamptonville
Mason, A. J.	G, 13th	old age	Yadkinville
Matthews, T. C.	F, 28th	wounds	Poindexter
Melton, Zach	I, 28th	disease	East Bend
Messick, George T.	H, 21st	wounds	Buck Shoals
Messick, J. L.	B, 52nd	disease	Buck Shoals
Mickles, Nichols	F, 28th	wounds	Poindexter
Miller, J. E.	E, 47th	disease	Farmington
Minnish, Thos. R	H, 54th	wounds	Jonesville
Money, B. J.	B, 38th	disease	Republic
Moulden, John K.	C, 42nd	died in service	Jonesville
Myers, A. C.	D, 42nd	wounds	Jonesville
Myers, Marshall C.	I, 66th		Buck Shoals
Newsom, Washington	G, 33rd	killed	Conrad's
Nichols, Martin S.	G, 13th	wounds	Branon
Nicholson, J. G.	F, 28th	disease	Jonesville
Norman, H. I.	F, 28th	disease	East Bend
Norman, Thos.	I, 28th	disease	Tracadia
Overby, A. M.	B, 21st	disease	Jonesville
Patterson, John	E, 56th	wounds	Forbush
Pendry, J. C.	A, 5th	disease	Chestnut Ridge
Pendry, John	B, 38th	disease	Yadkinville
Pendry, J. F.	B, 4th	disease	Chestnut Ridge
Poplin, Green	G, 54th	killed	Longtown
Privette, Abraham		disease	Zion
Pruette, Jacob	H, 28th	disease	Jonesville
Prunner, J. M.	K, 23rd	wounds	Jonesville
Rabin, Wm. S.	F, 42nd	killed	Cross Roads Church
Randleman, George W.	F, 6th	disease	East Bend
Reavis, Giles	A, 1st Battalion	disease	Yadkinville
Reece, A.	I, 28th	disease	Mt. Nebo
Reece, E. H.	I, 28th	disease	Boonville

F. Veterans and Widows Pensions   171

Pension Started	Pension Ended	Widow	Pension Received
1901	1910—dead		
		Mary Jane	1905–1908
1908			
1906			
1905			
		E. P. Flinn	1904
		Vicy	1902
		Sarah	1904
1900			
		Sarah	1900
		Eliza	1900
1900	1908—dead		
1900	1901—dropped		
		Martha D.	1900–1907
1905			
1910			
1906	1908—dead	Elizabeth	1908
1902			
		Betsy	1900
1901	1908—dead		
1902	1902—dropped		
1900	1910—dead		
1900			
1905			
1900	1902—dead		
1908			
1900	1906—dead		
		M. G.	1902
		Margaret	1902–1908
1900	1907—dead		
		Cynthia L.	1902
		Elizabeth	1900
1900			
1901	1902—dead		
1905			
1906			
1901			
1905	1905—marked off		
1908			
1901			
1906			
		Lucinda	1900
		Lucy	1900
1905	1906—dead		
1904			
		Martha	1902
1905			
1908			
		Elizabeth	1902
1910			

F. Veterans and Widows Pensions

Soldier Name	Co./Reg.	Disability/Death	Post Office
Reed, A. N.	B, 38th	age	Buck Shoals
Renegar, David	B, 38th	disease	Yadkinville
Richardson, John R.	I, 49th	age	Yadkinville
Ring, Enoch	B, 2nd Bat.	wounds	East Bend
Robbins, William D.	B, 1st Battalion		Buck Shoals
Rose, I. W.	I, 28th		Jonesville
Royal, John	B, 1st Battalion	disease	Yadkinville
Russell, P. S.	D, 42nd	age	Jennings
Rutledge, Wm.	E, 74th		Boonville
Seats, Nathaniel T.	A, 21st	disease	Cana
Shore, Daniel	H, 3rd	disease	Longtown
Shores, Isaac	B, 48th		Yadkinville
Shores, John C.	H, 21st	killed	Jonesville
Shores, M. G.	H, 54th	wounds	Jonesville
Shores, Nathan	B, 38th	wounds	Spillman
Sizemore, Abraham		disease	Marler
Sisk, H.		Disease	Charity
Slater, C. S.	G, 33rd	disease	Panther Creek
Smith, E. D.	H, 44th	wounds	Longtown
Smith, Pinkney	A, 4th	disease	Buck Shoals
Smith, T. A.	J, 28th	wounds	Hamptonville
Smith, W. T.	H, 54th	wounds	Jonesville
Snow, John C.	A, 11th	wounds	Panther Creek
Southard, M.	A, 24th	disease	Boonville
Sparks, James	D, 1st	disease	Jonesville
Spillman, M.D.	F, 28th	bad eyes	Yadkinville
Spillman, Thomas A.	A, 44th	disease	Spillman
Spillman, W. H.	F, 28th	debility	Shore
Sprinkle, James H.	I, 18th	killed	Forbush
Steel, Wm. D.	I, 6th	paralysis	East Bend
Steelman, Alex	A, 28th	disease	Boonville
Steelman, Jackson	H, 63rd	Disease	Footville
Stokes, James, Sr.	B, 38th	killed	Longtown
Swaim, Solomon	H, 54th		Boonville
Swaim, Virgil D.	G, 66th	disease	Swan Creek
Summers, Basil	A, 33rd	disease	Longtown
Talley, James E.	E, 54th	disease	Hamptonville
Taylor, Wm. Columbus	F, 28th	debility	East Bend
Vanhoy, Calvin	F, 29th	age	Marler
Vanhoy, John A.			Hamptonville
Vestal, James N.	D, 44th	disease	Boonville
Vestal, John B.	B, 38th	disease	Footville
Wagoner, Jacob W.	I, 28th	disease	Charity
Wall, John W.	D, 21st	disease	East Bend
Wallace, J. S.		Disease	Gwyn
Weatherman, Wm. R.	B, 1st Battalion	disease	Chestnut Ridge
Webb, Thomas P.	F, 28th	disease	East Bend
West, James	Home Guard	[killed]	Hamptonville
Whitaker, L. D.	B, 21st	wounds	Chestnut Ridge
Whitehead, Henry W.	I, 28th	disease	Chestnut Ridge

F. Veterans and Widows Pensions

Pension Started	Pension Ended	Widow	Pension Received
1910			
1901	1901—dead	Nancy	1902
1906	1907—taken off list		
1901	1906—reported out of county		
		Rebecca	1902
		Sarah E.	1908
		M. J.	1902–1906
1906			
		Mary M.	1904
1906			
		Elizabeth	1900–1908
		Catherine	1908
		Almeda	1900
1900	1904—dropped		
1900	1901—dead	Rhoda	1902
		Alley	1902
		Dicy	1900
1905			
1900	1904—dead		
1901	1904—dead	Cynthia	1905
1900			
1900	1902—dropped		
1900		Eliza	1908
		Ruth	1900
		Mary M.	1900
1906			
1901	1907—dead		
1905			
		Nancy S.	1900–1904
1904		Alley	1902
		Martha	1902
		Caroline	1900
		Lucinda	1902
		M. J.	1900
	1910—dead		
1902			
		Theresa D.	1902
		Susan	1900
1902			
1902	1902—dropped		
		Agnes	1900
1901	1905—dead		
1902			
		Annie	1902
1900			
1901	1902—dropped 1904—reinstated		

Soldier Name	Co./Regi.	Disability/Death	Post Office
Whitehead, John	A, 10th	debility	Chestnut Ridge
Wiles, Nathan	D, 21st	disease	Footville
Williams, E. A.	I, 18th	wounds	Richmond Hill
Willie, Wilburn	__. __ VA		Chestnut Ridge
Winfrey, W. H.	I, 6th	disease	East Bend
Wright, James Jacob W.	H, 54th		Boonville
Yarborough, William	C, 63rd	killed	Bean Shoals

Pension Started	Pension Ended	Widow	Pension Received
1902			
		Nancy J.	1902
1900			
		Elizabeth	1904
1905			
		Elizabeth	1902
		M. A.	1900

(From the Department of Archives and History, Raleigh, N.C., for the years 1900–1910 only. Department of State Auditor, Pension Bureau, Confederate Pension Lists, 1900–1964. 2 reels microfilm, reel No. S.13.3, Raleigh, North Carolina, Department of Archives and History, Raleigh, North Carolina.)

Appendix G: Exemptions from Yadkin Home Guard Duty

YADKIN COUNTY
Yadkinville, Nov 1st 1864 Tuesday
Major N. G. Hunt, Cmgd.

Name	Age	Reason	Name	Age	Reason
Adams, B.	37	old sore leg	Cooper, Jno.	47	cough, rheumatism
Adams, G.D.B.	29	disease of heart	Cornelius, A.E.	23	wound of ankle joint with deformity at Cedar Run
Algood, H.	25	ancylosis left elbow			
Allred, J.C.	37	hemorrhoids			
Arnold, W.S.	47	urinary calculi	Comer, A.W.	44	old scrofulous cicatrices
Athen, F.	27	enlarged testes	Cranfield, E.	48	cough with debility
Baker, A.C.	48	imperfect vision	Cranfield, W.F.	39	ancylosis ankle joint
Barber, B.B.	33	scrotal hernia	Crawford, E.	34	dislocated knee joints
Beason, A.	48	scrofulous, feeble	Davis, A.	40	disease of heart
Boles, E.	24	epilepsy	Davis, Josiah	45	asthma
Bolling, A.M.	24	hemorrhoids, deafness	Davis, S.C.	30	wounded in leg at Chancellorsville
Bolling, Jno. C.	31	deafness			
Bryant, S.	20	disease of heart	Davis, W.T.	45	disease of heart, general debility
Cartwright, S.J.	31	bronchial			
Casey, W.R.	22	phthisical w/hemorrhage	Demcy, J.M.	21	epilepsy
Castevens, M.	46	general infirmity	Douglas, J.T.	18	anemia
Caudle, Henderson	20	injury to thigh, gunshot wound	Dull, Jno.	28	mental incapacity, discharge
			Eldridge, W.	20	general debility
Caudle, M.A.	33	epilepsy	Farrington, H.H.	24	scrotal hernia
Claywell, J.W.	36	enlarged leg			
Colvard, B.	33	gunshot right forearm, at H[anover] C[ourt] house	Felts, J.E.	28	disease of heart
			Fiddler, A.	40	deformity of chest
			Fletcher, J.F.	22	double inguinal hernia, pulmophthisis
Cook, B.	26	deformity right foot			

G. Exemptions from Duty

Name	Age	Reason
Flinn, W.C.	37	phthisical
Gadd, D.W.	28	foot deformity, lame
Gibbs, Wm.	44	large hernia, disease of heart
Griffith, T.J.R.	38	dyspepsia, debility
Hall, T.R.	35	dislocated knee, discharge
Hall, Zeb	49	ulcer of leg, discharge
Hauser, E.T.	24	hemorrhage of lungs, discharge
Henshaw, J.	37	physical/mental disability
Hooper, P.F. (Surry county man)	46	hemorrhoids
Hoots, E.	28	phthisical, feeble
Hoots, W.A.	23	phthisical
Hoots, W.F.	31	piles with hemorrhage
Howard, W.M.	40	general debility
Howel, T.	23	epilepsy, loss of eye, discharge
Hutchins, J.S.	25	breast complaint
Jones, Jno. A.	30	scrofulous, back complaint
Kelly, J.C.	46	general debility
Kettle, Eugene	32	dyspepsia, disability
Leonard, Hardy	49	rheumatism, discharge
Lewis, A.	38	bronchitis, piles
Logan, J.	41	ascitis
Long, J.F.	19	febro cortiteginous tumor of thigh
Long, W.W.	38	obesity
Macey, H.C.	20	shortened right leg, very lame
Mackey, John	42	disease of heart, discharge
Mackey, R.W.	41	general infirmity, very feeble, discharge
Martin, D.A.	28	disease of heart
Matthews, A	41	affection of kidneys
Matthews, Alex	36	general debility
Matthews, F.P.	26	injury to ankle joint from old injury
Matthews, Wm.	36	phthisical
Matthews, Wm. R	33	dislocated hip joint, discharge
May, Saml.	49	general debility
Maynard, Horace	45	injury to left leg/thigh
Messick, J.B.	38	asthma
Miller, F.	47	atrophy both legs
Miller, P.A.	22	shortened left leg from coxalgia
Moore, D. M.	34	chronic asthma, severe, discharge
Morgan, H.	46	disease of lung, quite feeble
Mortin, W.C.	27	deformity of sternum
Myers, B.C.	40	rheumatism, left arm & shoulder
Myers, J. H	38	ascitis, dropsical, discharge
Nicholson, H.A.	28	scrofulous sore leg
Nicholson, W.S.	43	organic heart disease, hydrothorax, discharge
Norman, J.A.	25	phthisical, feeble
Pardue, Thos.	43	urinary calculi, discharge
Pass, E.H.	38	hemorrhoids
Pettyjohn, Richard	30	myopia
Phillips, W.A.	25	general debility
Plowman, J.	23	paralysis left arm
Poindexter, G.Z.	29	disease of heart/stomach
Poindexter, J.A.	25	disease of heart
Poindexter, R.C.	42	lame from injury to right hip joint, discharge
Reavis, A.H.	40	?
Reavis, A.M.	40	hairless, infirm
Reavis, Geo.	44	division of tendon, Achilles from cut
Reavis, Jno. H.	48	fracture thigh, collar one, etc.
Reavis, Wm.	44	chronic arthritic rheumatism
Reavis, J.E.	37	haemaplysis
Reavis, Charles	43	disease of heart, discharge
Rose, E.	34	inflammation of spine, lumbago
Seagraves, Jno.	27	excessive deafness
Shore, Henry	29	hernia
Shore, Isaac	46	fistula in ano
Shore, Jas.	39	chronic arctic rheumatism of extremities
Sizemore, A.	32	abdominal cyst, discharge
Sizemore, Jno.	36	phthisical, very infirm
Spear, A.S.	43	general debility
Spear, S.B.	41	chronic affection of leg
Steelman, Joseph	22	fistula in ano, disease of testicle, discharge
Steelman, Wm. Sr.	36	disposed to apoplexy

Name	Age	Reason	Name	Age	Reason
Stephens, M.	31	varicose veins	Wells, Jas.	48	asthma
Stimpson, T.B.	50	asthma & piles	Williams, J.M.	39	disease of heart
Swim, Wm.	39	rheumatism	Williams, J_	24	___, discharge
Tacket, Thomas	22	deformity right foot	Williams, Kennedy	40	non compos mentis, discharge
Tate, J.	35	dyspepsia, feeble			
Triplett, Alfred	21	disease of heart			
Tucker, Henry	47	double inguinal hernia	Zachery, R.G.	40	bronchitis with debility, piles
Wagoner, M.M.	37	hemorrhoids			
Warren, Jas.	35	rheumatism			

(From Stephen E. Bradley, Jr., ed. North Carolina Home Guard Examinations 1863-1864. *Privately published, 1993.)*

Appendix H: Yadkin Men in the Confederate Military, 1861–1865

Service information was obtained from Louis H. Manarin and Weymouth T. Jordan, eds., *North Carolina Troops 1861–1865: A Roster* (Raleigh: Division of Archives and History) 13+ vols., 1961–; Walter C. Clark, ed., *Histories of the Several Regiments and Battalions from North Carolina in the Great War, 1861–1865* (Raleigh and Goldsboro: State of North Carolina) 5 volumes, 1901; and John W. Moore, ed., *Roster of North Carolina Troops in the War Between the States* (Raleigh: State of North Carolina), 4 volumes, 1882. Volume and page have been cited in each entry of the following list. Only military ranks above private have been listed.

Information on the Militia and Home Guard was obtained from Stephen E. Bradley, Jr., *North Carolina Confederate Militia: Officers Roster* (Wilmington, N.C.: Broadfoot Publishing Co., 1992); Stephen E. Bradley, Jr., *North Carolina Confederate Militia and Home Guard Records* (3 vols., privately published, 1995) and Gerald W. Cook, *The Last Tarheel Militia: 1861-1865* (privately published, 1987).

Also included for each name, when known, are date of birth and death, marriage, parentage, and place of burial. The personal data was obtained from many sources, including the 1850, 1860, and 1870 Federal censuses of Yadkin County. Although the complete 1850 Surry County census covers what is now both Surry and Yadkin, only the "Southern Division"—the area south of the Yadkin River, now in Yadkin County—was used. The earlier a person is found after birth on the census, the more accurate the age, so the 1850 census was used whenever possible (these are cited as 1850 Surry, and 1860 Yadkin in the following material). The Yadkin County Marriage Register, the *Heritage of Yadkin County* (1981), and William E. Rutledge's *An Illustrated History of Yadkin County, 1850–1965* (1965 ed.) was also consulted. Other sources are Carl Hoots' *Cemeteries of Yadkin County, North Carolina* (1985) and a number of family histories, plus information submitted by descendants and published in the Yadkin County Historical & Genealogical Society's journal. Personal data has been included only when identity was certain.

Because some family names are very common, and many of the families are related, the given names are repeated frequently, making it almost impossible to determine direct lineage. For those with unusual names, determining lineage was much easier, as it was for surnames used by only one or two households in the county. To accurately identify each man is a nearly impossible task.

This is not a complete list of all Yadkin County men who served in some capacity during the Civil War. Men who initially joined the U.S. Army are not listed, although those who went over to the Union after being in the Confederate States Army are noted. In many instances, the place of residence of the soldier was not given, only the county in which he enlisted. There is also the problem of some men serving in more than one company. Duplications are inevitably present, especially when only initials were used.

Key to Abbreviations

bur. = buried
Co. = county
e. = enlisted
ch. = children
Ch. = Church
Cem. = cemetery
d. = died
dau. = daughter
m. = married
NC = North Carolina
s. = son
trans. = transferred
VA = Virginia

"Bovender" = "Bovender Genealogy," by Frances H. Casstevens, unpublished manuscript
Heritage = *Heritage of Yadkin County, North Carolina*, 1981
Hoots = Carl Hoots, *Cemeteries of Yadkin County, North Carolina*, 1985
NCT = *North Carolina Troops 1861-1865: A Roster*
"Poindexter" = "The Poindexter Family," by Frances H. Casstevens, unpublished manuscript

Rutledge = William E. Rutledge, Jr., *An Illustrated History of Yadkin County*, 1965 ed.
YCMR = Yadkin County Marriage Register
YCDC = Yadkin County Death Certificates
YCHGSJ = *Yadkin County Historical & Genealogical Society Journal*

Personal Sources

Weymoth Allgood, Yadkinville, NC; Clyde Bavender, Boonville, NC; Neish Brown, Eastlands, TX; Jody Watts Chadduck, Bodfish, CA; Wanda Craaybeek, Boonville, NC; Esther N. Clifton, Ft. Wayne, IN; Mary Haynes Dalton, Lewisville, NC; Nina Long Groce, Yadkinville, NC; Katherine Williams Hege, Yadkinville, NC; Cheryl L. Martin, Trinity, NC; Carol J. Adams Mehring, Golden, CO; Anne Whitaker McCracken, Chesterfield, VA; Douglas Reed Niemeyer, Beacon, NY; Helen M. Reynolds, Berlin, CT; Edith Phillips Sharpless, Yadkinville, NC; Sidney Seats, Lewisville, NC; Eunice Vestal, Huntington Beach, CA; Melvin C. Weatherman, Houston, TX 77080; Laura Ann Hoots Winslow, Chantilly, VA 22021; Polly Wood, Yadkinville, NC

Information as available is given in this order: name, company or regiment, rank, birth and death dates, place of burial (all churches and cemeteries are in Yadkin County, North Carolina, unless otherwise noted), short biography.

ADAMS, ALEXANDER G.; CO. K, 18TH REG.
Alexander G. Adams lived in Yadkin Co., at Camp Holmes on 7-25-1864. Present until he deserted to the enemy about 12-1-1864, and took the Oath of Allegiance on 12-2-1864 (NCT X, 413). Alex Adams, s. of Jonathan and Nancy Adams, m. Elizabeth Vanhoy, dau. of Abram and Jane Vanhoy, on 9-22-1867 (YCMR).

ADAMS, BENJAMIN F.; CO. F, 28TH REG.
Benjamin F. Adams was captured near Gettysburg July 1-5, 1863. Confined to Davids Island, NY harbor. Paroled and trans. to City Point, VA, where he was exchanged 9-16-1863. Returned to duty. Captured again near Pickett's Farm, VA, about 7-21-1864. Confined to Point Lookout MD, until released 10-18-1864 after joining the U. S. Army. He was assigned to Co. D, 4th Reg., U. S. Volunteer Infantry

(NCT VIII, 175). B. F. Adams m. Nancy Jane Williams on 3-14-1867 (YCMR).

ADAMS, BRYANT; CO. B, 21ST REG. (1826–?).
Bryant Adams e. in Yadkin Co. 5-12-1862. He was present or accounted for until 1-1-1862, when discharged. Reason not stated (NCT VI, 551). In 1860, Bryant (Briant) Adams, age 34, was living with wife, Elizabeth, and ch.: Martha C., age 11; William W. (age 6), and Elisabeth (age 3).

ADAMS, COLUMBUS; 75TH REG., 18TH BRIG. MILITIA.

ADAMS, ELAM J.; CO. F, 28TH REG.
Elam J. Adams was captured near Petersburg, VA 4-1-1865, then confined at Point Lookout, MD, until released 6-22-1865, after taking the Oath of Allegiance (NCT VIII, 175). E. J. Adams m. Sabra A. Reece on 3-3-1867 in Yadkin Co. E. J. Adams, s. of Jesse and Rebecca, m. Lucy Salena Reece, dau. of Wiley and Almeda Reece on 11-19-1875 (YCMR).

ADAMS, GABRIEL; CO. G, 44TH REG. (04/24/1833–?).
Gabriel Adams e. at Camp Holmes near Raleigh. He was present until he was captured at the South Anna Bridge, VA, 6-26-1863. Paroled at Ft. Monroe, VA 6-29-1863. He then returned to duty before 10-14-1863, when he was captured on that date at Bristoe Station, VA, and confined at the Old Capitol Prison, Washington, DC. Released from there 3-14-1864, after taking the Oath of Allegiance (NCT X, 455). Gabriel m. Malinda (Matilda?) Shore on 6-24-1858 in Yadkin Co. (YCMR). In 1860, Gabriel and Malinda (Matilda) had two ch. living in their household: Sarah A. (age 1), and Henry R. (age 8). After the war, Gabriel Adams did not return to North Carolina but moved to Pennsylvania, Ohio, and then settled in Monroeville, Indiana in 1865. He m. Mary Ellen Chapman and had 10 ch. He may have been the s. of Jonathan and ___ Morefield Adams (Mehring; YCHGSJ XIII [June] 1994, p. 15).

ADAMS, GEORGE; 75TH REG., 18TH BRIG. MILITIA.

ADAMS, HARVEY J.; CO. B, 38TH REG. (?–11/22/1862).
Harvey J. Adams e. in Yadkin Co., age 30, on 4-19-1862. He was counted as present until he d. in a Richmond, VA, hospital on 11-22-1862 of "variola" (NCT X, 21).

ADAMS, MARTIN; 75TH REG., 18TH BRIG. MILITIA (1816–?).
Martin Adams e. in Wake Co. on 9-4-1862 in Co. A, 1st Battalion NC Sharpshooters. Present through Dec. 1864. He was assigned "light duty at Richmond, Virginia" from Aug. 31 to Dec. 31, 1864. Medical Director's Records indicate he was stationed at the C. S Barracks until admitted to Howard's Grove Hospital, Richmond, VA, on 3-26-1865 with "variola" (NCT III, 70). Martin Adams, age 36, a wagoner, was living with wife Matilda (age 33), and ch., Catharine, Sally, John, and William when the 1850 Surry Co. Census was taken (1850 Surry). All the children were in school.

ADAMS, MOSES; CO. H, 54TH REG. (09/16/1820–07/02/1862; Mitchel's Chapel Meth.).
Moses Adams, a Yadkin Co. farmer, e. at age 41 on 3-17-1862. He d. in a hospital at Camp Vance prior to 7-2-1862. The cause of his death was not reported (NCT XIII, 319) Moses m. Gracey Wagoner, b. 3-30-1821, bur. at Fall Creek Baptist Church, (YCHGSJ XIV [2], 23-24; Hoots). According to family tradition related by Edna Bray Reece (*Heritage* p. 316), Moses Adams became sick while serving in the Confederate Army, and officials sent him home. On the way he became so ill he was unable to travel any further. He took temporary shelter in a school house, and soon d. He was bur. in the Brindle Graveyard (now Mitchel's Chapel Methodist Church). Children of Moses and Gracey Adams were (per 1860 Yadkin) Zachariah F, Mary Ann Elizabeth, David S. (and also Jane) (YCHGSJ XIV [2], 23-24).

ADAMS, SAMUEL; CO. H, 21ST REG.
Samuel Adams, a Yadkin resident, e. in Wake Co. on 11-1-1863. Present till he deserted on 6-10-1864. Took Oath of Allegiance at Louisville, KY, on 8-10-1864 (NCT VI, 601). Samuel Adams m. Martha E. Farrington on 3-5-1857 in Yadkin Co. (YCMR).

ADAMS, STEPHEN H.; CO. B, 38TH REG. (1838–?).
Stephen H. Adams lived in Yadkin Co., e. 4-24-1862, age 24. Present from 1862 until captured at Gettysburg, PA, 7/1-3/1863. Confined at Ft. Delaware, DE, until released 6-19-1865, after taking the Oath of Allegiance (NCT X, 21).

ADAMS, WILLIAM C.; CO. G, 44TH REG. (?–11/01/1864).
William C. Adams lived in Yadkin Co., e. in Wayne Co.. Present until captured at South Anna Bridge, VA, 6-26-1863. Paroled at Ft. Monroe, Va, 6-29-1863, and returned to duty before 1-1-1864. Hospitalized at Danville, VA, ca. 5-18-1864 with gunshot wound of knee. Place and date of wound not reported. Returned to duty before 8-25-1864, when he was wounded near Ream's Station, VA. Died in Richmond, VA, hospital on 11-1-1864. Cause of death not reported (NCT X, 455).

ALGOOD, JOHN; CO. G, 38TH REG.
John Algood e. at Camp Holmes on 6-30-1864. He deserted on 8-5-1864 (NCT X, 68). He may have been the s. of William and Sally Algood (1850 Surry).

ALLGOOD, HENRY P.; CO. H, 10TH REG. (1ST ARTILLERY) (06/06/1839–?).

Henry P. Allgood e. in Wake Co., at age 23, on 2-10-1863. He was discharged at Goldsboro, NC, 3-14-1863 because of ancylosis of the left elbow (NCT I, 126). Henry P. Allgood was the s. of Robert and Elizabeth Shore Allgood. He m. Elizabeth Atwood on 9-13-1866 in Yadkin Co. He may be bur. in either the Allgood family cemetery, Courtney Baptist Church cemetery, or Deep Creek Baptist Church cemetery, but no tombstone has been located (per Allgood).

ALLGOOD, JOHN W.; HOME GUARD
(06/09/1834–03/08/1871; Courtney Bapt. Church).

John William Allgood was also the s. of Henry Robert and Elizabeth Shore Allgood (1850 Surry). A teacher before the war, he served in the Home Guard during the war. John W. Allgood m. Mary Jane Baity on 3-6-1859 in Yadkin Co. (1860 Yadkin). He m. Gabard second.

ANDERSON, ALBERT A.; CO. B, 21ST REG. SERGEANT MAJOR (09/28/1842–?; Davie Co., NC).

Albert A. Anderson e. in Yadkin Co. where he was living and teaching school on 5-12-1861. Mustered in as Sergeant. Present until wounded at the First Battle of Manassas, VA, about 7-20-1862. He returned to duty before 11-1-1861. Present until he trans. to Co. A, 1st Battalion Sharpshooter on 4-16-1862 (NCT VI, 552). He trans. to the Field and Staff of this battalion when appointed sergeant major about 4-28-1862. Transferred back to Co. A, 1st Battalion with a rank of private and was detailed as acting sergeant major. Present through Dec. 1864, and paroled at Appomattox Court House, VA, on 4-9-1865 (NCT III, 70). (Anderson was a Davie Co. native who was teaching school in Yadkin Co. when the war began. He was known as "Uncle Ab," and as part of Stonewall Jackson's "foot cavalry," he was in some of the major battles of the war. He lived a long life after the war "endearing himself in the hearts of many friends, the family and the community." "Three Andersons of Calahaln Who Wore the Gray," by Mark Whitman in *Cooleemee History Loom*, no. 20, summer 1995, p. 8). Albert A. Anderson m. in Yadkin Co., M. Fannie Poindexter on 10-22-1865. Children were: Dr. Robert Poindexter Anderson (a dentist); Jennie Anderson; Ethel Anderson; Dr. Richard Benjamin (also a dentist); and Agnes Anderson, m. Iva C. Shugart on 7-8-1901 (YCMR; "Poindexter," 111).

ANGELL, DANIEL DAVIS; CO. B, 38TH REG. (03/04/1848–04/23/1937; Flat Rock Bapt.).

NC Pension records indicate that Daniel D. Angell served in this company (NCT X, 21). The s. of John Jefferson and Keziah Davis Angel, Daniel m. Susan Evelyn Reece, dau. of Alec and L. A. Reece, on 3-27-1870. She was b. 2-11-1848, d. 1-18-1921. They are bur. at Flat Rock Baptist Church. Children were: Laura Levada, Mira Maleter, Lettishia, Martha Francis, Monrovie Jones, Kisiah Emma, and Luca Monroe (per Winslow).

ANGELL, G. P.; CO. B, 38TH REG. (1844–?).

G. P. Angell, a Yadkin resident, e. at age 19 on 6-26-1863. Present until captured at Spotsylvania Court House, VA, 5-21-1864. Confined at Point Lookout, MD, 5-30-1864. Paroled from there about 3-14-1865, and trans. to Boulware's Wharf, James River, VA, where he was received on 3-16-1865 for exchange (NCT X, 21).

ANGELL, JAMES A.; CO. B, 38TH REG. (1842–?).

Born in Yadkin Co., resided there as a farmer before enlisting at age 19 on 10-16-1861. Mustered as a private, promoted to corporal Sept–Dec. 1863. Present until captured at Spotsylvania Court House, VA, on 5-21-1864. Confined at Point Lookout, MD, 5-30-1864. Paroled from there about 3-14-1865, and trans. to Boulware's Wharf, James River, VA, where he received on 3-16-1865 for exchange (NCT X, 21). James A. Angell, the s. of John and Keziah Angell, m. Josephine Reece, dau. of L. D. and Martha Reece, on 1-29-1873 (YCMR).

ANGELL, JOHN J.; CO. B, 38TH REG. (08/08/1850–03/05/1902).

John J. Angel, e. at age 51 on 4-19-1862. Reported AWOL July–Aug. 1862. Returned to duty. Reported AWOL again on 10-20-1862 through Dec. 1862. Transferred to Richmond, VA on 2-21-1863. He rejoined his company on 4-1-1863, and was present or accounted for until 9-24-1864, when he was again reported AWOL (NCT X, 21).

ANGELL, WILLIAM W.; CO. B, 38TH REG. (1840–09/13/1862).

William W. Angell, a Yadkin Co. farmer, e. on 10-16-1862 at age 22. Present until he d. in Richmond, VA, hospital on 9-13-1862 of "typhoid fever" (NCT X, 21).

ANTHONY, DAVID; CO. H, 54TH REG. (ca. 1820–?).

David Anthony e. at age 42 as a substitute for James W. H. S. Daniel. He was present in June 1862, but deserted 12-5-1862. Returned to duty on 9-23-1863. Captured at Rappahannock Station, VA, on 11-17-1863. Confined at Point Lookout, MD. He was paroled on 2-3-1865 and trans. for exchange. Reported in Richmond, VA, hospital about 2-7-1865 (NCT XIII, 319).

APPERSON, JOHN ALVIS; CO. F, 28TH REG. (07/27/1844–?).

John Alvis Apperson, a Yadkin resident, e. at age 18 on 2-1-1863. Mustered in as private and promoted to musician prior to 1-1-1865. Present or accounted for through Feb. 1865 (NCT VIII, 175). John Alvis C. Apperson, b. ca. 1844, was the s. of Thomas and Luvitha Apperson and was living in their household in 1850, along with brothers Peter A., and Thomas V. (*Heritage*, 267; 1850 Surry).

APPERSON, PETER ALEXANDER; CO. F, 28TH REG. 1ST SERG. (02/13/1842–02/09/1935; Macedonia Meth.,Yadkin Co., NC).
Peter A. Apperson e. at age 20 on 6-18-1861. Mustered in as private, promoted to sergeant Jan.-June 1862. Wounded near Richmond, VA, 6-25/7-1-1862. Returned to duty before 9-1-1862, when he was wounded again in the finger and or back at Ox Hill, VA. Returned to duty and was promoted to 1st sergeant on 12-1-1862. Wounded again in the right shoulder and captured at Gettysburg, PA, during the fighting 7/1-3/1863. Hospitalized at Davids Island, NY Harbor. Paroled and trans. to City Point, VA, where he was received for exchange on 9-16-1863. Returned to duty, but reported absent sick Sept–Dec. 1864. Returned to duty Jan.–Feb. 1865. Captured again near Petersburg, VA, 4-2-1865. Confined at Point Lookout, MD, until released 6-22-1865, after taking the Oath of Allegiance (NCT VIII, 175). Peter A. Apperson, s. of Thomas and Luvitha Vest Apperson (Epperson), m. Laura A. Miller, dau. of William Miller, on 5-4-1879, and they had one son, Henry Turner Apperson (b. 7-15-1880) (*Heritage*, 267; YCMR).

APPERSON, THOMAS VEST; CO. F, 28TH REG. (1838–?).
Thomas Vest Apperson, one of the officers of Company F, 28th Reg., e. at age 23. Appointed 1st lieutenant 6-18-1861, and elected captain on 4-12-1862. Wounded in the left leg and captured at Hanover Court House, VA, on 5-27-1862. Hospitalized at Portsmouth Grove, RI, 7-7-1862. Transferred to Ft. Monroe, VA, 9-17-1862. Paroled and transferred to Aiken's Landing, James River, VA, about 9-23-1862, for exchange. Exchanged at Aiken's Landing on 11-10-1862. Returned to duty before January 1863. Resigned 1-16-1865 for reasons of ill health and in order to serve in the cavalry (NCT VIII, 174). Thomas Apperson m. Angeletta ___. He was the s. of Thomas Apperson (Epperson) and wife Luvitha Vest Apperson, and brother of Peter Alexander and John Alvis Apperson, who also served.

APPERSON, WILLIAM HENRY; CO. F, 28TH REG. ORDNANCE SERGEANT (10/13/1826–02/20/1862; Kirk-Apperson Cem. [tombstone]).
William Henry Apperson e. at age 35 on 6-18-1862. Mustered in as Corporal, promoted to ordnance sergeant on 10-9-1861. Hospitalized at Wilmington about 2-15-1862 with typhoid fever and d. about 2-19-1862 (NCT VIII, 175). There is a tombstone for him in the Kirk-Apperson Cemetery, east of Macedonia Methodist Church on the old Tom Allen place. William Henry Apperson was the s. of Thomas and Luvitha Vest Apperson (Epperson) (1850 Surry).

ARMFIELD, ROBERT F.; CO. B, 38TH REG. (1829–1898).
A Yadkin Co. attorney, Robert F. Armfield studied law under Chief Justice Richmond Pearson (Brumfield, *Chief Justice Pearson and His Students*, 1992, p. 26). In 1855, Armfield was the first Master of the Yadkin Masonic Lodge, and was on the examining committee for the Jonesville Academy in 1859. Armfield was elected 1st lieutenant on 10-16-1861, and was present with this regiment until elected lieutenant colonel on 4-18-1862 and trans. to the Field and Staff of the regiment (NCT X, 20). After the war, he was appointed a Superior Court judge (Rutledge, p. 54; photograph on this page also).

ARMSTRONG, COLUMBUS F.; CO. B, 38TH REG. (1829–?; ?Swan Creek Bapt.).
Columbus F. Armstrong was a Yadkin Co. farmer before enlisting in Yadkin Co. at age 32 on 10-16-1861. Present until wounded in the arm near Mechanicsville, VA, about 6-16-1862. Reported AWOL July-Aug. 1862, and 10-1-1862 through. Dec. 1862. Discharged 3-31-1863, because of wounds received at Mechanicsville (NCT X, 21). C. F. Armstrong m. in Yadkin Co. on 10-23-1852 Rachael M. Gross. After his discharge from the CSA, he probably served in Co. A, 9th Battalion, Home Guard. He is probably the s. of Wesley and Mary Armstrong (1850 Surry).

ARMSTRONG, JAMES CLINGMAN; 75TH REG., 18TH BRIG. MILITIA.
James Clingman Armstrong served in the militia (75th Reg, 18th Brig.)

ARMSTRONG, JULIUS C.; CO. H, 54TH REG. (1832–?).
Julius C. Armstrong was 28 years old in 1860 (1860 Yadkin). He was reported present through April 1863, but deserted on 7-28-1863. Returned to duty on 10-1-1863. Present through Dec. 1863 and through Oct. 1864. He survived the war and NC Pension records indicate he was wounded in the shoulder by a piece of shell at Cedar Run or Fisher's Hill, VA, on 8-4-1864 (NCT XIII, 319). Julius Armstrong m. Mary Alon (Allen?) on 1-12-1858 in Yadkin Co.

ARMSTRONG, MEREDETH T(F?).; CO. I, 28TH REG. (1821–?).
Meredith Armstrong e. at age 40 on 8-13-1861. In 1860, he was living in Yadkin Co. with wife, Ann and 7 ch. He was captured at Hanover Court House, Va, on 5-17-1862. Confined at Ft. Columbus, NY Harbor, until exchanged at Aiken's Landing, James River, VA, 8-5-1862. Wounded in the thigh at the Battle of Second Manassas, VA, on 8/27–30/1862. He was discharged about 11-21-1862, under the provisions of the Conscription Act. He is probably the same person as "M. F. Armstrong" listed as a member of Co. E, 70th Reg. (Reserves) (NCT VIII, 207). Meredith Armstrong, age 27, and wife Anna, age 25, with ch., Moses (age 2) and Henry C. (age 1) (1850 Yadkin Co.).

ARMSWORTHY, JOHN WESLEY; CO. H, 54TH REG. (1829–02/01/1864).
John Wesley Armsworthy resided in Yadkin Co., where he e. at age 32. The 1860 Yadkin Census shows that he was m. and had three ch. (wife Edney J., age 24; ch.: Levi B., Elly F., and Henry). Armsworthy mustered in as a private. Reported AWOL in June 1862. Returned to duty before 1-1-1863, and present through April 1863. Captured at Fredericksburg, VA, on 5-4-1863. Confined at the Old Capitol Prison, Washington, DC. Transferred to Ft. Delaware, DE, 5-7-1863. Paroled and trans. to City Point, VA, on 5-12-1863 for exchange. Returned to duty on 5-27-1863, and promoted to Sergeant before 9-1-1863. Wounded in the right arm and captured at Rappahannock Station, VA, 11-7-1863. Hospitalized in Washington, DC, where he d. about 2-1-1864 of "pyemia" (NCT XIII, 319). John W. Armsworthy was the s. of John and Susannah Armsworthy. His father was b. in MD, his mother in VA (1850 Surry).

ARNOLD, JACOB; CO. B, 21ST REG.
Jacob Arnold e. on 5-12-1861. He was present through Oct. 1861. Later e. "at camp in Virginia" on 11-1-1863 in Company A, 1st Batt., NC Sharpshooters, e. "in camp" and present through Dec. 1864 (NCT III, 70; VI, 552)

ARNOLD, THOMAS LEE; CO. H, 63RD REG. (5TH CAVALRY) (02/07/1842–07/21/1918; Flat Rock Bapt.).
Thomas Lee Arnold e. on 9-1-1862 at age 20. He mustered in as private and was appointed Bugler Nov.–Dec. 1863. Present through Feb. 1865 (NCT II, 430). He was wounded at the Good Allis Tavern, VA. Thomas Lee Arnold was the s. of William Smith Arnold and Adaline Johnson Dickerson Arnold. He was m. on 11-2-1864 in Yadkin Co. to Caroline Mahala Gough, b. 2-27-1849, d. 1-23-1934. (*Heritage*, 269–270). Thomas Lee and Caroline were the parents of 11 ch.

ARNOLD, WILLIAM SMITH; CO. A, 9TH BAT. SERGEANT (10/20/1819–07/03/1906; Flat Rock Bapt., Yadkin Co., NC).
William Smith Arnold, age 41 in 1860, m. Adaline Johnson Dickerson. He was the s. of Daniel and Sarah Hardesty Arnold. William Smith and Adaline Dickerson Arnold were the parents of Thomas Lee Arnold. He was a 1st Sergeant in Co. A, 9th Battalion (Militia). William Smith Arnold's second wife was Martha Evans. He drove the stage between Hamptonville and Salem and was also an apprenticed veterinarian, Justice of the Peace, government store keeper, and farmer. The Arnold homeplace is on Four Mile Road near Hamptonville (*Heritage*, 270).

ASHLEY, BURGESS H.; CO. I, 28TH REG. (1821–?).
Burgess Ashley e. at age 40 on 8-13-1861. Deserted on 6-18-1863. Returned to duty on 12-13-1864. Deserted again on 1-1-1865 (NCT VIII, 207). Ashley is listed as Howell B. Ashley, age 37, a carpenter in the 1860 Yadkin Co. Census, living with wife Susannah, age 35, sons John (age 15) and Peter (age 12, and dau. Mary J. (age 4). He e. in Yadkin Co. at age 40 on 8-13-1863. Ashley deserted on 6-18-1863, but returned to duty on 12-13-1864. Deserted again on 1-11-1865 (NCT VIII, 207).

ASMON/AZMAN, B. B.; CO. C, 26TH REG. (1846–1908).
B. B. Asmon(Azman) e. at age 17 at Camp Holmes on 10-17-1863. He was discharged on 4-20-1864 because of debility at age 18 (NCT VII, 495). He lived to receive a pension in Yadkin Co. 1902–1908, when he was marked "dead" on the pension rolls.

ATWOOD, GEORGE W.; CO. I, 28TH REG. CORPORAL (?–06/27/1862).
George W. Atwood e. in Yadkin Co. at age 18 on 8-13-1861. Mustered in as private and promoted to corporal on 4-12-1862. He was killed at Gaine's Mill, VA, 6-27-1862 (NCT VIII, 207).

ATWOOD, HENRY; CO. A, 34TH REG. (1835–?).
Henry Atwood, a shoemaker, e. in Ashe Co., at age 27, on 8-10-1862. Present through April 1862. Wounded, reported absent wounded 8-6-1862. Reported AWOL but returned to duty 3-3-1863. Wounded in right hand at Chancellorsville on 5-3-1863, and returned to duty Nov.–Dec. 1863, and was present through Oct. 1864 (NCT IX, 255). He was b. in Yadkin Co., but his family had removed to Ashe Co. (NCT XI, 255). He drew a pension in Yadkin Co. after the war.

ATWOOD, ISAAC M.; CO. B, 38TH REG. (1846–04/15/1905; Deep Creek Bapt.).
Isaac M. Atwood was 14 in 1860 (1860 Yadkin), the s. of William J. Atwood, a well digger, and wife, Rebecca Wishon Atwood. Isaac was present or accounted for until wounded in the left arm at Mechanicsville, VA, 6-26-1862. Reported AWOL July–Aug. 1862 and Oct. 1862. Reported absent-sick Nov.–Dec. 1862. Returned to duty and was present until captured near Petersburg, VA, 4-2-1865. Confined at Hart's Island, NY Harbor, until released 6-21-1865 after taking the Oath of Allegiance (NCT X, 22).

ATWOOD, JESSE C.; CO. I, 28TH REG. (1843–03/06/1864).
Jesse C. Atwood e. at age 19 in March of 1862, and served until he d. in a Richmond, VA, hospital on 3-6-1864 of "febris typhoides" (typhoid fever) (NCT VIII, 207).

ATWOOD, WILLIAM J.; CO. B, 38TH REG. MUSICIAN (1811–?).
William J. Atwood, a well digger by occupation, was living in Yadkin Co. when he e. at age 50. Mustered in as a private, promoted to musician before 4-1-1862. Reduced in rank to private on 7-1-1862.

Reported AWOL 8-2-1862. Company rolls indicate he d. on an unknown date. However, the Roll of Honor states he was discharged on 9-27-1862 (NCT X, 22). William J. Atwood, s. of James and Margaret Atwood, m. first in 1832 in Surry Co., Rebecca Wishon. His second marriage was to Nancy Speer, dau. of Sarah Speer, on 2-10-1870 (YCMR). Children, all by first wife were: George W., b. 1837; Cynthia M., b. 1839; Barbara E., b. 1841; Isaac M., b. 1845; Margaret J., b. 1850; William, b. 1851; and Joseph Columbus, b. 1854 (Delfa Wright Ellis, *Ancestry of William Henry Wright and wife Polly Ann Royal and Their Descendants*, San Jose, CA: Alpine Systems, 1991, p. 259.

AXUM, SAMUEL I.; CO. A, 28TH REG. (1836–08/05/1862).
Born in Yadkin Co., but resided in Surry, Axum e. at age 26 on 3-18-1862. Present until he was captured at Hanover Court House, VA, on 5-27-1862, and confined at Ft. Columbus, NY Harbor. Exchanged at Aiken's Landing, James River, VA. He d. at "home" in Surry Co. on 2-12-1862. Cause of death not given (NCT VIII, 114).

BAGBY, R[ICHARD]. L.; 75TH REG., 18TH BRIG. MILITIA 2ND LIEUTENANT (ca. 1843–?).
Richard L. Bagby, age 19, the s. of Abner and Lucinda Bagby, served in the militia. He m. on 10-17-1865 in Yadkin Co. Martha Jane Lindsay (YCMR; *Heritage*, 270).

BAGGERLY, JEREMIAH [JERRY] E.; CO. I, 28TH REG. (1836–07/28/1863).
J. E. Baggerly, age 26, a "saddler" was living with his wife Martha Johnson (m. on 12-21-1853) and son, John W. in Yadkin Co. in 1860. He e. at age 27 on 8-13-1861. He was discharged on 10-17-1861 because of a "scrotal hernia in both sides" (NCT VIII, 208). He then e. in Wake Co. on 9-20-1862 in Co. I, 18th Reg. Jeremiah was present or accounted for until captured at Gettysburg, PA, July 2–3, 1863. Baggerly was hospitalized at Ft. Delaware, DE, until trans. to hospital at Chester, PA, 7-28-1863, where he d. of "chronic diarrhoea" 7-28-1863. His body was removed to Pittsville National Cemetery, Philadelphia, PA, for burial (NCT VI, 401; *Confederate Veteran* XIX, 1911, 572–573). The son, John W. Baggerly (Beggerly) m. Tabitha Wallace on 12-25-1898 (YCMR).

BAITY, D[AVID]. H.; CO. B, 21ST REG. (1840–?).
D. H. Baity e. at age 21 on 5-12-1861. He was present until he trans. to Co. A, 1st Battalion Sharpshooters on 4-26-1862. David H. Baity, age 19, was living with wife Polly J., and a male infant when counted in the 1860 Yadkin Co. census. His occupation was "mechanic." Another David H. Baity, age 18, was living with William D. Baity, Jr. (NCT VI, 552; 1860 Yadkin).

BAITY, DAVID W.; CO. F, 42ND REG. (03/06/1834–02/09/1920; Courtney Baptist Ch.).
David W. Baity e. in Rowan Co. at age 28 on 12-2-1862. He deserted on 3-13-1863 (NCT X, 250). David W. Baity is bur. at Courtney Baptist Church (Hoots, 66). (Note: a David Washington Baity e. in Wayne Co. on 10-1-1864 in Co. A, 21st Reg. He was present until wounded and captured at Cedar Creek, VA, 10-19-1864. He d. in Rockbridge Co., VA, about 12-25-1864 of wounds and or "erysipelas." He is probably a Yadkin resident and related to the Baity boys who were also in Co. A, 21st Reg., and may possibly be the same as David W. Baity of Co. F, 42nd Reg.) David W. Baity m. on 2-2-1859 Polly Cranfill (YCMR).

BAITY, FRANCIS A.; CO. H, 63RD REG. (5TH CAVALRY) (09/21/1830–05/21/1904; Courtney Bapt.).
F. A. Baity e. at age 32 on 7-14-1862 in Davie Co. Mustered in as corporal. Reported wounded and taken prisoner on June 21 at Upperville, VA, according to the May–June muster rolls. No Federal Provost Marshal records were found relating to his capture or release. Present or accounted for until admitted to a Richmond, VA, hospital with a gunshot wound in the right hip on 9-22-1863. He was furloughed for 60 days on 9-30-1863. Present through Dec. 1864 (NCT II, 430). Francis A. Baity m. in Yadkin Co. on 3-20-1854 Eliza Cranfill.

BAITY, GEORGE W.; CO. F, 42ND REG. (10/04/1831–07/15/1900; Courtney Bapt. Ch.).
George W. Baity e. in Davie Co. and was present through Oct. 1864. He was paroled at Mocksville on 6-3-1865 (NCT X, 250; Hoots, 65). George W. Baity m. in Yadkin Co. on 6-18-1852 Elizabeth Jane Baity.

BAITY, JOHN P. H.; CO. F, 42ND REG. (09/28/1839–01/16/1912; Courtney Bapt. Yadkin Co., NC).
John P. H. Baity's full name is probably John Pleasant Henderson Baity. In 1860, at age 20, he was living in his mother Catherine Baity's household together with several brothers and sisters. He e. at Petersburg at age 23 on 10-31-1862, and was present through Oct. 1864 (NCT X, 250). He is bur. at Courtney Baptist Church, Yadkin Co. (Hoots, 65).

BAITY, PLEASANT H.; CO. I, 28TH REG. (07/10/1844–02/14/1928; Courtney Bapt. Ch.).
Pleasant H. Baity, age 16, the s. of William D. Baity, Sr., and wife, Christina, was listed as living with his parents (1860 Yadkin). Pleasant e. on 3-8-1862 at age 18. He was wounded at Gettysburg, PA, July 1-3-1863. Returned to duty and was present Sept. 1864 through Feb. 1865. wife, Polly L. Baity, b. 10-18-1842, d. 10-21-1894, is bur. at Courtney Bapt. Church (NCT VIII, 307).

BAITY, W. D., JR.; CO. A, 21ST REG. (07/19/1829–02/06/1894).

William D. Baity, Jr., e. in Yadkin Co. on 10-1-1863 and was present or accounted for until he deserted on 12-18-1863 (NCT VI, 542). William D. Baity m. on Yadkin Co. on 9-13-1860 Sarah A. Sprinkle (YCMR).

BAITY, W. H.; CO. A, 21ST REG. (1833–?).
He may be the "H. W. Baity," age 27, listed in the 1860 census. He e. on 10-1-1863 and was present until he deserted 12-28-1863 (NCT VI, 542; 1860 Yadkin).

BAITY, WILLIAM D., SR.; CO. A, 21ST REG. (1821–?).
William D. Baity, Sr., age 39 was living with wife, Christina, and ch.: William W. (age 18), Pleasant H. (age 16), Columbus W (10), James M. (5), and Mary L. (2) in Yadkin Co. in 1860. He e. in Yadkin Co. on 10-1-1863. Present until captured at or near Hatcher's Run, VA, 2/5-6/1865. Confined at Point Lookout, MD, until released on 6-23-1865, after taking the Oath of Allegiance (NCT VI, 542).

BAITY, WILLIAM W.; CO. I, 28TH REG. (1842–12/08/1862).
The s. of William D. Baity, William W., age 18, was living with his parents in Yadkin Co. in 1860. He e. 8-13-1861, age 20, and d. of fever at Winchester, VA, on 12-8-1862 (NCT VIII, 208).

BAKER, H[ENRY]. C[ALVIN].; CO. F, 28TH REG. (1846–?).
H. C. Baker, age 14, was living in the John C. Kelly household in Yadkin Co. in 1860, and was a student. He e. as a "substitute" on 4-12-1862, and was wounded in the right leg at Gaines' Mill, VA, on 6-27-1862. His right leg was amputated. He was discharged 2-19-1863 (NCT VIII, 175; 1860 Yadkin).

BALL, JOHN H.; CO. A, 9TH REG. (1ST CAVALRY) (1839–?).
John H. Ball, a Yadkin Co. resident, e. in Ashe Co. at age 22 on 5-18-1861. He was present through Dec. 1864 (NCT II, 11).

BALL, JOHN R.; CO. H, 54TH REG.
John R. Ball e. on 8-29-1862. He was present through October 1864. He served as a teamster during part of the war (NCT XIII, 319).

BALL, WILLIAM H.; CO. B, 21ST REG. (1842–?).
William H. Ball, an 18-year-old laborer, was living in the household of Moses Groce, when the 1860 Yadkin Co. census was taken. He e. on 5-12-1861, and was present until he trans. to Co. A, 1st Battalion Sharpshooters on 4-26-1862. He was wounded at Second Manassas, VA, 8-28-1862. Detailed for light duty from Dec. 1863. He retired to the Invalid Corps on 7-8-1864 (NCT III, 70). After the war, Ball moved to Granville, IN. In 1896, a letter he wrote was published in the *Yadkin Ripple*: "... I have been absent from your town for 31 years.... I was raised in old Yadkin and that name sounds sweet to me. I joined the first company in the late war that went from Old Yadkin. I was wounded in the Second Bull Run battle in 1862. In August I got a 60 days furlough and came home. At the expiration of the 60 days, I returned to my company and was with the Company until July '64 when I was retired at Wilson, N.C. I am now in Indiana, Delaware Co." (NCT VI, 552).

BARBER, ANDREW J.; CO. H, 54TH REG.
Andrew J. Barber e. prior to 10-31-1864. He was captured at Ft. Steadman on 3-25-1865, and confined at Point Lookout, MD. He took the Oath of Allegiance on 6-23-1865, and was hospitalized at Point Lookout on 6-26-1865. He was released on 7-9-1865 (NCT XIII, 319). Andrew Barber may be the s. of Matthew and Mary M. Barber, and was listed as age 5 in 1850 (1850 Surry).

BARKER, LARKIN JONES; CO. I, 28TH REG. HOSP. STEWARD (11/13/1842–11/25/1897; Jonesville Cem., Jonesville, NC).
Larkin Barker mustered in as sergeant; promoted to Hospital Steward Mar. 1863–Oct. 1864, then trans. to Field and Staff of this regiment. Wife Mary E., b. 2-15-1850, d. 11-28-1930, and is also bur. at Jonesville Cemetery, Jonesville, NC (NCT VIII, 208). His tombstone indicates he was a doctor.

BARR, JOHN W.; CO. D, 21ST REG. (1821–?).
John W. Barr, a Yadkin resident, e. in Forsyth Co., at age 42, on 9-20-1863. Present through Oct. 1864. Reported AWOL through Feb. 1865 (NCT VI, 565).

BARRON, J. N.; CO. K, 38TH REG.
J. N. Barron lived in Yadkin Co. He e. at Camp Holmes on 7-30-1864 (NCT X, 95).

BATES, NEILLY; CO. A, 54TH REG. (1839–02/03/1863).
Neilly Bates, age 23, e. 5-3-1862. He was hospitalized in Richmond, VA, 12-7-1862 with typhoid fever, and d. there 2-3-1863 of "pneumonia" (NCT XIII, 250).

BEAN, ALFRED MONROE; CO. F, 28TH REG. (11/13/1832–1902; Union Hill Meth.).
Alfred Bean, age 25, was living with wife Anna and ch. Henry J (age 2) and Julia C (age 1) near East Bend in 1860. He e. at Camp Green, VA, on 2-18-1863. Deserted 6-5-1863. NC pension records indicate he was wounded in May 1863. (NCT VIII, 175). Alfred was the brother of Dollie Bean, wife of Ebenezer Nathan Parks. During the battle of Chancellorsville in May 1863, Alfred was wounded in the left lung by a mini ball that remained in his lung the rest of his life. He was wounded so seriously that he was granted a pension. Alfred's brother, Wiley, also served, and may have "deserted" in order to help his brother get home (per Cheryl Martin). The Bean brothers were sons of William and Katherine Bean.

BEAN, H. T.; CO. F, 28TH REG.
NC pension records indicate he served in this company (NCT VIII, 175). This may be Henry T. Bean, s. of Alfred and Anna, who m. E. J. Spillman on 1-23-1881 (YCMR).

BEAN, WILEY J.; CO. F, 28TH REG. (1840–06/24/1865).
Wiley Bean e. at Camp Gregg, VA, at age 23 on 2-18-1863. He deserted 6-5-1863, but returned to duty 9-15-1864. Captured in a hospital at Richmond, VA, 4-3-1865, Wiley was trans. to New Port News, VA, 4-23-1865. He d. at Newport News 5-8-1865 or 6-24-1865 of "chronic diarrhea" (NCT VIII, 175). Wiley may have deserted to help his brother, Alfred Monroe Bean, who had been seriously wounded, to get home, since "Wiley disappeared from the rolls on the same day as Alfred...." Alfred Monroe, Wiley, Barbara Monday, Sarah, Lunday, Emanuel, and Dollie (wife of Ebenezer Nathan Parks) were the ch. of William and Katherine Bean of the East Bend area. (NCT VIII, 175; Cheryl Martin).

BELL, DAVID L.; CO. I, 18TH REG. (1835–12/13/1862).
David L. Bell was 25 in 1860, a carpenter, the s. of Robert W. and Elizabeth Bell of Buck Shoals, Yadkin Co., NC. He reportedly came home from the war (probably on a furlough) so dirty that no one in the family, not even his wife, Mary Jacks Bell recognized him (per family story told by Carrie Gentry Dobbins, Boonville, NC to Cheryl L. Martin, Trinity, NC). David e. in Wake Co. at age 24 on 9-10-1862. He was present until killed in the battle of Fredericksburg, VA, on 12-13-1862 (NCT VI, 401). David and Mary Jacks Bell were the parents of Harriett (b. 1860); Virginia Ann (b. 10-1-1861), and David Lee Bell (b. Jan. 1863). His wife Mary d. before 1870, and the children were split up, with grandfather Martin Jacks of Eagle Mills Township, Iredell Co., taking Louiza. Harriett and David stayed with uncle A. W. Bell and grandparents Robert and Elizabeth Bell (David L. Bell Estate Papers; Mary Jacks Bell estate papers, and Guardian Papers, Yadkin Co., NC).

BELL, N. R.; CO. F, 13TH REG. (?–04/15/1864).
N. R. Bell e. at Camp Vance on 1-25-1864. He was present until he d. in a hospital at Gordonsville, VA. Cause of death not reported (NCT V, 337). This may be Noah Bell, s. of Cranberry Bell of Hamptonville area.

BELL, SHADRACK; CO. I, 18TH REG. (01/30/1839–06/26/1902; Flat Rock Bapt.).
Shadrack Bell was 20 in 1860 (1860 Yadkin), and worked as a carpenter. His wife, Ellen J. Burgis Bell, was 22, and they had an infant daughter. They were m. on 9-14-1858(6?) in Yadkin Co. He m. second, Alice L. Wiseman (b. 12-1-1867, d. 7-16-1935) on 9-30-1888 (YCMR). He was the s. of Cranberry and Margaret Bell, and was living with them and his siblings in 1850 (1850 Surry). He was a first cousin to David L. Bell. The Bell boys joined Co. I, 18th Reg. on 9-10-1862, along with another cousin, Roland H. Whitlock. Shadrack e. in Wake Co. at age 26 on 9-10-1862 and was present until wounded in the right lung at Fredericksburg, VA 12-13-1862. He returned to duty Mar.–Apr 1863 and was present or accounted for until paroled at Appomattox Court House, VA, on 4-9-1865. Shadrack and Alice are bur. at Flat Rock Baptist Church, Hamptonville. His second wife applied for a widow's pension at age 61 and was living at 837 Lockland Ave., Winston-Salem, NC (NCT VI, 401; Confederate Pension Records, Widow's Pension of Alice Bell, NC State Archives; Hoots, 139).

BELL, WALTER WARREN; CAPT. H. P. ALLEN'S COMPANY (10/15/1845–10/03/1896; Zion Bapt., Iredell Co., NC).
Willie Warren bell was the brother of David L. Bell. Capt. H. P. Allen's Company was one of the Partisan Ranger companies which operated throughout the war. He was the s. of Robert W. and Elizabeth Johnson Bell. He m. Beatrice ("Atry") M. Johnson. Her widow's pension application and the marker on his grave at Zion Bapt. Church, Iredell Co., state that he was a member of "Capt. Allen's Company" (per Cheryl Martin).

BENBOW, CHARLES; 75TH REG., 18TH BRIG. MILITIA 1ST LIEUTENANT (1833–?).
This is probably Charles Benbow, b. 1833, the s. of Thomas and Ann Mendenhall Benbow. Ann Mendenhall Benbow as a physician and a Quaker minister. The 75th Reg. 18th Brigade was a State Militia regiment. He is listed in the 1850 Surry Census as living with his parents and sister Hannah. Charles m. Elizabeth G. Bell on 9-18-1859 in Yadkin Co. After the war and after the death of Ann, Thomas Benbow took his family to Indiana, except Evan who remained in East Bend, Yadkin Co., and practiced medicine for many years. Dr. Evan Benbow was one of the founders of the Republican Party in Yadkin Co. (*Heritage*, 273–74; Hoots, 101).

BENBOW, ESAU; 75TH REG., 18TH BRIG. MILITIA.
Unidentified, unless this is a misreading of "Evan" Benbow.

BENGE, JOHN; CO. I, 28TH REG. (12/01/1845–01/05/1918; Fall Creek Bapt.).
John Benge resided in Yadkin Co. and was a farmer before enlisting at age 20 on 8-13-1861. He was discharged 5-1-1862 because of "epilepsy" (NCT VIII, 208). He lived to draw a Confederate Pension for several years. A John H. Benge m. Elizabeth Benge on 4-5-1862 (YCMR).

BENGE, NATHAN; CO. I, 28TH REG. (1843–01/05/1865).
Nathan Benge, a Yadkin farmer e. at age 18 on 8-13-1861. He was captured at Spotsylvania Court House,

VA, 5-12-1864. Confined at Point Lookout, MD, before being trans. to Elmira, NY, on 8-8-1864. He was paroled at Elmira and trans. to Venus Point, Savannah River, GA, where he was received 11-15-1864 for exchange. He d. at home 1-5-1865, cause of death not reported (NCT VIII, 208).

BENGE, URIAH D.; CO. B, 21ST REG.
Uriah D. Benge e. on 5-12-1861 and was present until he trans. to Co. A, 1st Bat. N.C. Sharpshooters on 4-26-1862. He was wounded at the Battle of Second Manassas, VA, 8-28-1862. Discharged 8-24-1864 because of "epilepsy of weekly occurrence from childhood." (NCT III, 70; VI, 552).

BENHAM, CALVIN C.; CO. A, 9TH REG. (1ST CAVALRY) (12/23/1835–01/29/1879; Jonesville Cem., Jonesville, NC).
Calvin C. Benham was the s. of Dr. Bilson B. Benham and wife, Elizabeth A. Cowles Benham, a noted Jonesville physician. Calvin e. at age 24 on 6-8-1861. He was captured at Gettysburg, PA, on 7-3-1863, and confined at Point Lookout, MD. Paroled at Cox's Wharf, VA, about 2-20-1865 (NCT II, 11; Rutledge, 42).

BINKLEY, JOHN W.; CO. F, 28TH REG. (12/18/1830–06/20/1912; Joppa Cem., Mocksville, NC).
John W. Binkley e. in Yadkin Co., age 25, on 6-18-1861. He was captured near Petersburg, VA, 4-2-1865, and confined at Point Lookout, MD, until released on 6-23-1865, after taking the Oath of Allegiance (NCT VIII, 175). John W. Binkley m. first on 10-3-1856 in Yadkin Co. Nancy J. Sprinkle. He m. second on 10-3-1865 Nancy Tate (YCMR).

BINKLEY, PETER; 75TH REG., 18TH BRIG. MILITIA (09/06/1829–08/31/1908; Baltimore Meth. Ch.).
Peter Binkley, b. ca 1830, was the s. of John and Sarah Binkley. His father was dead by 1850, and he and his mother and brothers and sisters lived near the Tyre Glenn plantation in the Enon community (1850 Surry). By 1860, Peter was living with wife Henrietta C. (age 25) and ch. Ellen (age 8), Columbus H. (6), Permelia C. (4), and Richard H. (1).

BLACK, JOHN H.; CO. D, 8TH REG., GEORGIA CAV. (04/23/1846–10/06/1864; Black Fam. Cem., Forsyth Co., NC).
John Howard Black e. with his brother in the Georgia cavalry at Weldon, NC. Both are bur. in the Black Family Cemetery, West Bend, Little Yadkin Township, now Forsyth Co., NC (per Mary Haynes Dalton, 9000 Shallow Ford Rd., Lewisville, NC 27023). John H. Black was the s. of Gabriel and Susannah Black (1850 Surry).

BLACK, MARMADUKE W.; CO. D, 8TH REG., GEORGIA CAV. (12/20/1844–07/09/1864; Black Fam. Cem., Forsyth Co., NC).
Marmaduke W. Black e. at Weldon, NC, in Co. D, 8th Reg., Georgia Cavalry. He d. of ascites. His brother, John Howard Black, e. in the same company. They were the s. of Gabriel and Susannah Black (1850 Surry). Both are bur. in the Black Family Cemetery in the West Bend Community, near Lewisville, NC (per Mary Haynes Dalton).

BLACKBURN, ALFRED TEEN; CO. F, 21ST REG. (04/26/1847–12/15/1951; Pleasant Hill Bapt. Iredell Co., NC).
Alfred Teen Blackburn went with his master, Lt. John Blackburn to the war as a bodyguard, cook, and helper. He received a Class B pension from the State of North Carolina, and was the last surviving Class B pensioner. Alfred Teen Blackburn is not listed in N.C. Troops in Co. F, 21st Regiment. However, an article about Alfred Teen Blackburn in Rutledge's, *An Illustrated History of Yadkin Co.*, pages 21–22, says that Alfred Blackburn was given by his master, W. H. H. Cowles, to his son-in-law, Augustus W. Blackburn, and that Alfred went with his master the year the Civil War broke out to Manassas and Bull Run as a cook, bodyguard, and helper. The date of Alfred's birth is also questionable, varying from 104 to 110 years of age at the time of his death (Rutledge, p. 21). To date, Alfred's service record has not been documented. There is, however, listed in Co. B, 38th Regiment a slave named Wiley Blackburn, who joined the company on 7-29-1862 as a "body servant." A Capt. Augustin Blackburn (later 2nd lieutenant) in that company was probably Wiley's master. Wiley was also credited with being a carrier of food to the Home Guard and to the women and children when their husbands were away in the Army (NCT X, 20). Wiley and Alfred were brothers, and they m. sisters. Wiley m. Caroline Carson, and Alfred m. Lucy Carson.

BLACKMAN, JOHN; CO. B, 38TH REG. (1835–06/26/1862).
John Blackman was a shoemaker before enlisting in Yadkin Co. at age 26 on 10-16-1861. He was present until killed at Mechanicsville, VA, 6-26-1862 (NCT X, 22). He is probably the s. of Thomas and Sarah Blackman and was listed as 14 years of age in the 1850 Surry). John Blackmon m. Viny Longbottom on 1-20-1855 in Yadkin Co. (YCMR).

BLAKELY, ELI Y. [D?]; CO. F, 28TH REG. (05/02/1844–03/30/1930; New Home Meth. Ch.).
Eli Y. Blakely, the s. of Temple and Jane Stewart Blakely (*Heritage*, 275), was residing in Yadkin Co. when he e. on 11-1-1863. He was reported AWOL Sept.–Oct. 1864, but returned to duty Nov.–Dec. 1864. He was captured near Petersburg, VA 4-2-1865. Confined at Hart's Island, NY Harbor, until released 6-17-1865, after taking the Oath of Allegiance (NCT VIII, 175). Eli m. on 10-12-1866 Nancy Stewart (YCMR; Hoots, 255).

BLAKELY, GEORGE WASHINGTON; CO. F, 28TH REG. (1838–1923; Prospect Meth. Ch.).

George W. Blakely was b. ca. 1838, the s. of Temple and Jane Stewart Blakely. George was residing in Yadkin Co. when he e. at age 22 on 6-18-1861. He retired on 2-18-1865, reason not reported, but pension records and family tradition say that he was "wounded at Reams' Station in 1862" (NCT VIII, 175). George m. Sarah S. Matthews on 3-14-1865 (YCMR). Mrs. Irma Matthews who knew him and his children, said he lost part of one of his hands. George and "Sookie" had four ch. who lived to adulthood: Henry, William, Mitty, and Paul. George Washington Blakley was still receiving a pension in 1910, and d. in 1923. Henry and William moved to Lee or Moore Co. about 1911 (*Heritage*, 275).

BOHANNON, NEAL; CO. I, 28TH REG. CAPTAIN (1830–06/20/1863; Martin/Miller Cem.).
Neal Bohannon m. on 3-9-1856 in Yadkin Co. Elizabeth A. Martin. He e. at age 31 on 8-13-1861, mustering in as sergeant, promoted to 1st sergeant on 10-8-1861. Appointed 1st lieutenant 4-12-1862. Captured at Hanover Court House, VA, 5-27-1862. Confined at Fort Monroe, VA, and Ft. Columbus, NY Harbor. Exchanged and promoted to captain on 11-1-1862. Died in VA about 6-20-1863 of typhoid fever. "He war a brave and good officer" (NCT VIII, 207) His wife, Elizabeth A. ("Mandy") Martin, b. 1-30-1838, d. 3-6-1901, is bur. at Bear Creek Bapt. Church cemetery, Davie Co., NC ("Poindexter").

BOHANNON, SIMON S.; CO. I, 28TH REG. CAPTAIN (01/20/1835–03/18/1910; Boonville Bapt. Ch.).
Simon S. Bohannon e. at age 26 on 8-13-1861. He mustered in as sergeant and was appointed 2nd lieutenant on 4-12-1862. Promoted to 1st lieutenant on 11-1-1862, and to captain on 6-10-1863. Wounded at Gettysburg, PA, July 1-3-1863. Returned to duty and captured again at Spotsylvania Court House, VA, about 5-12-1864. Confined at Ft. Delaware, DE. Transferred to Hilton Head Island, SC, and then trans. back to Ft. Delaware where he arrived on 3-12-1865. Released 6-16-1865 after taking the Oath of Allegiance (NCT VIII, 207). Simon S. Bohannon m. on 9-14-1865 Jane Jenkins.

BOON, JAMES A.; CO. B, 38TH REG. (1839–07/10/1862).
James A. Boone was a Yadkin farmer before enlisting at age 22 on 10-16-1861. He was present until wounded at Mechanicsville, VA, on 6-26-1862. Hospitalized at Richmond, VA, he d. 7-10-1862 of wounds (NCT X, 22).

BOONE, T. G.; CO. C, 44TH REG. (1839–?).
T. G. Boone, a Yadkin resident, e. at age 23 on 10-22-1862. Deserted on 11-24-1862 (NCT X, 419).

BOVENDER, GENERAL GREENE; CO. F, 28TH REG. (06/05/1834–05/05/1863).
G. G. Bovender e. at age 30 on 3-31-1862. He was wounded at Chancellorsville, VA, May 2–3, 1863, and d. 5-5-1863 at Richmond, VA, of wounds (NCT VIII, 175). He was the s. of John Bovender and Rachel Brown Bovender. General Greene (who is probably named after the Revolutionary General Nathanael Greene) m. second Nancy J. (Colvard) Vestal on 5-12-1858 in Yadkin Co., NC. After his death, she m. John A. Davis on 11-24-1865. General Greene Bovender was the uncle of John R. Bovender, b. 1847. General Greene and Nancy J. Bovender had two ch., both of whom d. in infancy: William A. Joyce Bovender, b. 12-23-1859, d. 7-26-1861, and General Virgil Green Bovender, Jr., b. 9-12-1862, d. at age six months ("Bovender"; Patterson Family Bible record; Clyde A. Bavender; *Heritage*, 276–277).

BOVENDER, GEORGE W[ASHINGTON].; CO. F, 28TH REG. (1824–06/27/1862).
George Washington Bovender, b. ca. 1824, was the s. of John and Rachel Brown Bovender. He m. Rachel Lyons, b. ca. 1825. George's will is recorded in Yadkin Co., Book 1, p. 81, Office of the Clerk of Court, Yadkin Co., NC. They had 10 ch.: Mary Ann E., William C., Matilda Jane, Amitta, Robert Ellis, Harriette, James R., Laura F., Rachel Luzania, and Biddy Bovender ("Bovender"). He was the brother of General Greene Bovender and the uncle of John R. Bovender. George W. Bovender e. at age 37 on 6-18-1861. He d. "at home" on or about 6-27-1862, cause not reported (NCT VIII, 175; *Heritage*, 278).

BOVENDER, JOHN R.; CO. F, 28TH REG. (1847–?).
John R. Bovender, the s. of Andrew Jackson and Anna Bovender, m. on 1-31-1866 in Yadkin Co., Frances Reece. John R. e. at age 16 on 6-18-1861. He deserted 9-13-1862, but returned to duty before 12-31-1862. Reported present Sept. 1864–Feb. 1865. He was wounded in the right thigh at or near Amelia Court House, VA, 4-5-1865. Reported in a Danville, VA, hospital 4-6-1865. NC pension records indicate he survived the war (NCT VIII, 175–176).

BOVENDER, JOHN V.; 75TH REG., 18TH BRIG. MILITIA (05/16/1843–08/04/1920; Union Cross Friends).
John V. Bovender, b. 5-16-1838 (or 1843), d. 8-4-1920. He m. on 3-3-1858 Jane Hutchens, b. 8-1-1838, d. 12-17-1960 (YCDC; "Bovender"; YCMR).

BRAN(N), HENRY T.; CO. F, 28TH REG. CORPORAL (05/14/1843–12/28/1931; Enon Bapt. Ch.).
Henry T. Bran resided in Yadkin Co. where he e. at age 18 on 6-18-1861. Mustered in as private and promoted to corporal on 11-1-1864. Captured near Petersburg, VA, 4-2-1865. Confined at Point Lookout, MD, until released 6-23-1865, after taking the Oath of Allegiance (NCT VIII, 176). H. T. Brann, s. of Thomas and Paulina Brann, m. Rebecca J. Hendrix on 9-3-1868, dau. of Bradley Hendrix.

BRAN(N), HOWARD; CO. D, 8TH REG., GEORGIA CAV.
Howard Bran e. at Greensboro in 1862 and was present until 10-16-1864. No record of birth/death, but he was probably a resident of Little Yadkin Township before the war (per Mary Haynes Dalton and Sidney Seats, both of Lewisville, NC).

BRAN(N), JOHN H.; CO. B, 21ST REG.
John H. Bran(n) was living in Yadkin Co. in 1860. He first e. in Co. B, 21st Reg. at age 24 on 5-12-1861. Present until he trans. to Co. A, 1st Bat. Sharpshooters on 4-26-1862 (NCT III, 71; VI, 552). He was detailed as a teamster for the battalion through Dec. 1864. Paroled at Appomattox Court House, VA, 4-9-1865 (NCT VI, 552).

BRAN(N), JOHN M.; CO. F, 28TH REG. (1839–12/29/1861).
John M. Bran lived in Yadkin Co. where he e. at age 22 on 6-18-1861. He d. in a hospital at Wilmington, NC, on 12-29-1861. Cause of death not reported (NCT VIII, 176).

BRAN(N), WILLIAM D.; CO. B, 21ST REG. (1833–?).
William D. Bran(n) e. in Yadkin Co. age 28 on 5-12-1861. Present until he trans. to Co. A, 1st Bat. N.C. Sharpshooters on 4-26-1862. Present or accounted for through Dec. 1864 (NCT III, 71; VI, 552)

BRANDON, JOSEPH C.; CO. H, 63RD REG. (5TH CAVALRY) (06/17/1833–06/14/1906; South Oak Ridge Bapt.).
Joseph C. Brandon and his brothers, Joshua and William Alexander, e. 7-10-1862, at age 29, in Davie Co. in Booe's Partisan Rangers, which became Co. H, 63rd Reg. (5th Reg. NC Cavalry)(NCT II, 431). Joseph, the s. of Thomas and Rachel Brandon, m. in 1854 Rosa (Rosey) A. Reavis (b. 9-4-1835, d. 10-17-1910) on 4-13-1854 (YCMR; Brumfield, *The Brandon, Hudspeth, Reavis and Steelman Book*, 1991, 37–42; 1850 Surry).

BRANDON, JOSHUA HOWELL; CO. H, 63RD REG. (5TH CAVALRY) (01/26/1836–01/26/1921).
Although a Yadkin Co. resident, Joshua Howell Brandon e. in a predominantly Davie Co. regiment at age 25 on 7-10-1862, along with his two brothers, and joined Col. William E. Booe's Partisan Rangers (NCT II, 431; Brumfield, *The Brandon, Hudspeth, Reavis and Steelman Book*, 1991, pp. 37–42). Joshua H. Brandon, s. of Thomas and Rachel Brandon, m. Emmie Ellen Johnson on 2-5-1867 in Yadkin Co. (YCMR). According to descendants, Joshua ("Josh") Howell Brandon was the private valet of General Robert E. Lee, and his main duty during the war was caring for Lee's horse, Traveler (information from Polly Wood, Yadkinville, NC; 1850 Surry). His home is featured in Brumfield, ed., *Historical Architecture of Yadkin Co.*, 1987.

BRANDON, WILLIAM ALEXANDER; CO. H, 63RD REG. (5TH CAVALRY) (1841–03/23/1896; South Oak Ridge Bapt.).
William Alexander Brandon, age 21, e. in July 1862, along with his brothers, Joseph C. Brandon and Joshua Howell Brandon. William Alexander was captured at Hanover Court House, VA, and confined at Point Lookout, MD, then Elmira, NY, before being exchanged at Boulware's Wharf, James River, VA (NCT II, 431). William Alexander, the s. of Thomas and Rachel Brandon, m. Nancy Caroline Steelman on 12-23-1866/7(?), dau. of George and Nancy Riding Steelman. This couple had 12 ch. A picture of William Alexander Brandon in his Confederate uniform is reproduced in *Heritage of Yadkin Co.* (YCMR; *Heritage*, 693).

BRANNON, JAMES M.; CO. G, 44TH REG. (1836–04/10/1864).
James M. Brannon e. at Camp Holmes, at age 26 on 11-18-1862. He was present until he deserted on 6-10-1862. Returned to duty before 1-1-1864. Died in a Richmond, VA, hospital about 4-10-1864 of "chronic diarrhoea" (NCT X, 456). James M. Brannhan (Brannon) m. Sarah C. Rinehart on 3-12-1860 (YCMR).

BREWBAKER, ALEXANDER; CO. I, 28TH REG. (1841–?; Mt. Sinai Meth., Huntsville, NC?).
Alexander Brewbaker, b. ca. 1840, was the s. of Isaac (a blacksmith) and Elizabeth Dixon Brewbaker (*Heritage*, 288). He e. at age 21 on 3-8-1862, and was listed as deserted on 4-5-1863 (NCT VIII, 208). Family tradition holds that he came home to see his sweetheart, Miss Mary Chapman, and was killed as a deserter by the Home Guard. He is probably bur. at Mt. Sinai Methodist Church Cemetery, Huntsville, NC, with the majority of his family (killed before Oct. 2, 1864, per letter from J. M. Martin to Jesse Dobbins; see Appendix A).

BREWBAKER, GARRET H.; CO. A, 21ST REG. (1834–1915; Mt. Sinai Meth., Huntsville, NC.).
Garret H. Brewbaker e. in Yadkin Co. on 10-1-1863 and was present until he deserted on 12-8-1864 (NCT VI, 542). Garret, b. ca. 1834, was the s. of Jacob (whose occupation was "potter") and Cynthia A. Brewbaker, of Huntsville. His father, Jacob, was a potter. He m. Eliza Jane Davis 2-17-1856 (YCMR).

BREWBAKER, THOMAS; 75TH REG., 18TH BRIG. MILITIA (07/17/1837–12/11/1913; Mt. Sinai Meth.).
Thomas Brewbaker served in the Militia. He was the s. of Isaac and Elizabeth ("Betsy") Dixon Brewbaker. Like his father, Thomas operated a blacksmith shop in Huntsville. Thomas m. Ruth Harding (born 10-23-1841, d. 01-14-1929). She was appointed Postmistress at Huntsville April 2, 1886, and served until the post office was abolished on January 31, 1907 (per

Sue Brewbaker Royal). Ruth was the dau. of William and Jane Speer Harding, also a Huntsville family (*Heritage*, 288).

BREWBAKER, WASHINGTON; CO. I, 28TH REG. (1828–?).
Washington Brewbaker e. at age 34 in Yadkin Co. on 3-8-1862, and deserted on 8-5-1862 (NCT VIII, 208). Washington m. Susan Hill on 9-11-1853 in Yadkin Co. (YCMR). He was the s. of Isaac and Elizabeth Dixon Brewbaker (*Heritage*, 288). According to an announcement in the *Carolina Watchman*, Washington Brewbaker m. on 9-4-1851 Martha Stipe.

BREWBAKER (BRUBAKER), RICHARD P.; CO. B, 38TH REG. (1836–?).
Richard P. Brewbaker was a blacksmith before enlisting in Yadkin Co. at age 25 on 10-16-1861. He deserted about 10-25-1861. He later served as a private in Co. B, 10th Reg. VA Cavalry (NCT X, 22). He was the s. of Isaac and Elizabeth Brewbaker, of Huntsville, NC, and was b. about 1836. Isaac was also a blacksmith, an occupation plied by the Brewbakers until the mid twentieth century. His brother, Alexander, also served (*Heritage*, 288).

BRINDLE (BRENDLE), JAMES FREE; CO. I, 28TH REG. CORPORAL (ca. 1838–?).
James Free Brindle was the s. of William and Nancy Brindle, and was living in their household in 1850 (1850 Surry; *Heritage*, 289). James e. in Yadkin Co. at age 23 on 8-13-1861. He mustered in as private, promoted to corporal 6-11-1862. Promoted to sergeant March 1863–Oct. 1864. Captured near Petersburg, VA, 4-2-1865. Confined at Ft. Delaware, DE, until released on 6-19-1865, after taking the Oath of Allegiance (NCT VII, 208).

BRINDLE, MARK; CO. I, 28TH REG. (01/31/1842–05/02/1929; Chester Cem., Union, Iowa).
Mark Brindle, a Yadkin resident, was a farmer before enlisting at age 18 on 8-13-1861. He was wounded in the arm, thigh, and finger at the Battle of Second Manassas, VA, 8-27-30-1862. He returned to duty 3-6-1863. Captured near Petersburg, VA, 4-2-1865, he was confined at Hart's Island, NY Harbor, until 6-18-1865, after taking the Oath of Allegiance (NCT VIII, 208). He was the s. of John and Elizabeth Huff Brindle He m. on 12-24-1872 Mary Frances Faris, dau. of Nicholas and Sarah W. Stone Faris, of near Steamboat Rock, Iowa. They had several ch. His second wife was Sarah Clemons, and they lived in Marshall Co. Iowa (*Heritage*, 289).

BRINDLE, PLEASANT HENDERSON; 75TH REG., 18TH BRIG. MILITIA (1836–?).
P. H. Brindle, s. of William and Nancy Brindle, was living in his father's household in Yadkin Co. in 1850. His age was 14, making his birth date around 1836 (1850 Surry).

BROOKS, JOEL; CO. C, 21ST REG. (1827–?).
Joel Brooks, a Yadkin Co. blacksmith, e. in Surry Co. on 10-1-1863. He was present until captured at Sayler's Creek, VA, on 4-6-1865. He was confined at Newport News, VA, until released on 6-27-1865, after taking the Oath (NCT VI, 556).

BROOKS, JOHN; CO. B, 21ST REG. CORPORAL.
Brooks e. in Yadkin Co. on 5-12-1862. Mustered in as private and promoted to corporal before 4-26-1862, when he trans. to Co. A, 1st Battalion NC Sharpshooters on 4-26-1821 as a corporal. Wounded near Fredericksburg, VA, 5-4-1863. Present through Dec. 1864. Admitted to Petersburg, VA, hospital on 1-8-1865 with wound but returned to duty on 2-22-1865. Paroled at Appomattox Court House, VA 4-9-1865 (NCT III, 71; VI, 552). John Brooks m. Luella J. Messick on 12-29-1865 (YCMR).

BROOKS, S. D.; CO. B, 21ST REG.
Records of Co. A, 1st Battalion NC Sharpshooter indicate he trans. from this company. However, company records do not indicate that he served in Co. B, 21st Reg (NCT VI, 552). Present on muster rolls of Co. A, 1st Battalion through Dec. 1864. (NCT III, 71; VI, 552).

BROOKS, S. J.; CO. A, 1ST BAT. SHARPSHOOTERS.
Brooks e. "in camp in Virginia" on 6-15-1863. Present through Dec. 1864. Paroled at Appomattox Court House, VA, 4-9-1865 (NCT III, 71).

BROWN, A. J.; CO. B, 38TH REG.
A. J. Brown e. in Yadkin Co. on 11-25-1863, present until he deserted on 4-11-1864 (NCT X, 22).

BROWN, B. F.; CO. B, 38TH REG.
B. F. Brown e. in Yadkin Co. on 11-25-1863 and deserted on 4-11-1864 (NCT X, 22).

BROWN, ENOCH F.; CO. G, 44TH REG.
(09/05/1838–03/02/1915; Boonville Bapt., Boonville, NC).
Enoch Brown e. at Camp Holmes, NC, and was present until he was captured at the South Anna Bridge, VA, on 6-26-1863. Paroled at Ft. Monroe, VA, 6-29-1863. Returned to duty and was captured at Bristoe Station on 10-14-1863. Confined at the Old Capitol Prison, Washington, DC, until released on 3-15-1864 after taking the Oath of Allegiance (NCT X, 456). Enoch F. Brown m. Caroline Holloway on 9-11-1859 (YCMR).

BROWN, G. W.; CO. B, 21ST REG. (02/15/1847–11/12/1914; Mitchell's Chapel Meth.).
G. W. Brown e. in Yadkin Co. on 5-12-1861, present until discharged on 2-2-1862 (NCT VI, 542). He e. in Co. A, 1st Battalion Sharpshooters in Lenoir Co. on 7-21-1864 and was present or accounted for on company rolls through Dec. 1864 (NCT III, 71). This may be the George W. Brown, s. of Jacob and

Elizabeth Brown, m. Lucinda Wagoner, dau. of William and Fanny Wagoner, on 9-14-1868 (YCMR).

BROWN, GEORGE W.; CO. G, 44TH REG. (1841–?).
George W. Brown was a Yadkin farmer before enlisting at Camp Holmes at age 21 on 11-28-1862. He was present until he deserted on 5-1-1863. Returned to duty Apr.–May 1864. Captured near Cold Harbor, VA, about 5-30-1864. Confined at Point Lookout, MD 6-8-1864 until released on 6-22-1864, after joining the U.S. Army. He was assigned to Co. E, 1st Reg. U.S. Volunteer Infantry (NCT X, 456). This may be the George W. Brown m. first Priscilla Chappel on 10-22-1858 and second Katherine Osborn on 4-28-1867 (YCMR).

BROWN, HAMPTON B.; CO. B, 38TH REG. 1ST SERGEANT (1825–?).
Hampton Brown, b. in Stokes Co., resided in Yadkin Co., where he worked as a tanner before enlisting at age 37 on 4-19-1862. Mustered in as private, promoted to 1st sergeant before 7-1-1862. Present until wounded in the thigh at Mechanicsville, VA, on 6-26-1862. Returned to duty Sept.–Oct. 1862. Wounded near Fredericksburg, VA, on 12-13-1862. Returned to duty Jan.–Feb. 1863. Captured at Gettysburg, PA, about 7-5-1863, after he was left behind to help attend the wounded. Confined at Davids Island, NY Harbor. Paroled there on 8-24-1863, and trans. to City Point, VA, where he was received on 8-28-1863 for exchange. Reported absent on detached service during Sept.–Dec. 1863. Discharged on 2-14-1864 because of "contractions & loss of use of left hand from abscess" (NCT X, 22).

BROWN, HENRY G.; CO. B, 38TH REG. (1843–?).
Henry G. Brown, a Yadkin resident, e. there at age 18 on 9-1-1862. Present until captured near Hagerstown, NY, on 7-2-1863, and sent to Baltimore, MD. Confined at Elmira prison in New York on 8-18-1864. Paroled at Elmira on 10-11-1864. Received at Venus Point, Savannah River, GA, on 11-15-1864 for exchange. Returned to duty and captured again near Petersburg, VA, on 4-2-1865. Confined at Hart's Island, NY Harbor, on 4-7-1865 and relased on 6-18-1865, after taking the Oath of Allegiance (NCT X, 22).

BROWN, JACKSON; CO. H, 54TH REG. (1830–?).
Jackson Brown resided in Yadkin where he e. on 8-29-1862. Deserted on 12-5-1862, but returned to duty Mar.–Apr. 1863. Deserted again near Fredericksburg, VA, about 5-11-1863 (NCT XIII, 320). Jackson Brown was 20 years old in 1850 (1850 Surry), and he was living with wife Lovice and s. William G.

BROWN, JACOB; CO. H, 54TH REG.
Jacob Brown e. at Port Royal, VA, 3-1-1863. He was in the same company as Jack and John Brown, both Yadkin Co. residents. Therefore, it is assumed that Jacob was also a Yadkin Co. boy. He deserted near Culpepper Court House about 7-12-1863, but returned to duty 10-15-1863 (NCT XIII, 320).

BROWN, JAMES A.; CO. A, 21ST REG. (?–01/27/1864).
A Yadkin Co. resident, the date and place of James A. Brown's enlistment was not reported. He d. 1-27-1864, place and cause of death not reported (NCT VI, 542).

BROWN, JAMES K. P.; CO. F, 28TH REG. SERGEANT (1845–?).
James K. P. Brown was a Yadkin Co. farmer before enlisting there at age 16 on 6-18-1861. He mustered in as a private and was promoted to corporal on 5-11-1863. Promoted to sergeant before 11-1-1864. Captured near Petersburg, VA, 4-2-1865. Confined at Point Lookout, MD, until released after taking the Oath on 6-23-1865 (NCT VIII, 176).

BROWN, JERRY HENDERSON; CO. E, 53RD REG. (1843–?).
Jerry Henderson Brown e. at age 19 on 3-27-1862, and was present through June 1863. Reported AWOL on 7-1-1863, but returned to duty 10-25-1863. Listed as under arrest Nov.–Dec. 1863. Returned to duty Jan.–Feb. 1864. Captured at Spotsylvania Court House, VA, on 5-19-1864. Confined at Point Lookout, MD, 5-25-1864, then at Elmira, NY on 7-3-1864. Paroled from Elmira on 10-11-1864, and sent to Venus Point, Savannah River, GA, on 11-15-1864. He survived the war (NCT XIII, 110–111).

BROWN, JESSE F.; CO. F, 28TH REG. (1843–08/08/1862).
Jesse F. Brown, Yadkin resident, e. at age 18 on 6-18-1861. He d. in a Richmond, VA hospital on 8-8-1862 of "fever typhoid & parotitis" (NCT VIII, 176).

BROWN, JOHN; ?
John Brown, b. ca. 1841 in Yadkin Co., NC, s. of Joel and Elizabeth Brown and brother to Thomas Brown (who served in Co. A, 1st Battalion Sharpshooters) is believed to have been killed at Manassas Junction, VA. Whether he was killed at the first or second battle is unknown, as is his company and regiment (information from Neish E. Brown, *History of Texas*, Chicago: The Lewis Publishing Co., 1896, pp. 627–267).

BROWN, JOHN; CO. H, 54TH REG. (1826–?).
John Brown, b. in Yadkin Co., e. there on 3-17-1862 at age 36. He was discharged before 7-2-1862, because he was overage (NCT XIII, 320).

BROWN, JOHN B.; CO. B, 21ST REG.
John B. Brown e. in Yadkin Co. on 5-12-1861. Present until he trans. to Co. A, 1st Battalion NC Sharpshooters on 4-16-1861 (NCT VI, 552).

BROWN, JOHN C.; CO. F, 28TH REG. SERGEANT (1833–11/25/1863).
John C. Brown was living in Yadkin Co. when he e. at age 29 on 4-4-1862. Mustered in as private, promoted to sergeant before 5-1-1862. He was captured in unspecified battle Aug.-Sept. 1862. Received at Aiken's Landing, James River, VA, on 9-27-1862 for exchange. Returned to duty before 1-1-1863. Captured at Gettysburg, PA, 7-3-1863. Confined at Point Lookout, MD, 10-15-1863. Hospitalized at Point Lookout on 11-17-1863 with smallpox and d. 11-25-1863 (NCT VIII, 176).

BROWN, JOSHUA; CO. A, 9TH BAT. HOME GUARD.

BROWN, M. G.; CO. G, 44TH REG. (1842–02/26/1864).
M. G. Brown e. at age 20 at Camp Holmes near Raleigh on 11-3-1862. Reported AWOL 6-8-1863. Returned to duty Dec. 1863. D. at Gordonsville, VA on 2-26-1864 of "pneumonia" (NCT X, 456).

BROWN, ROBERT W.; CO. I, 28TH REG. (1842–08/13/1862).
Robert W. Brown e. in Yadkin Co. at age 19, where he resided, on 8-13-1861. He was wounded in the right shoulder at Frayser's Farm, VA, 6-30-1862, and d. in a Richmond, VA, hospital 8-13-1862 of wounds received (NCT VIII, 208). He is believed to be the Robert W. Brown, b. 6-8-1842, d. ca. 1865, the s. of Jacob and Elizabeth Calloway Brown, and a brother to George Washington Brown. Others in this family were Enoch J. Brown; Hanna Brown; James F. Brown, who m. Sarah Ray; Christina who m. Eli Smith about 1869; Thomas T. m. Caroline Davis; Elizabeth Jane Brown, who m. William Pleas Brendle; and John Conrad Brown, who m. Priscilla Adams, ca. 1880 (per Neish Brown).

BROWN, SQUIRE; CO. F, 28TH REG. (1837–02/15/1863).
Squire Brown was a Yadkin farmer before enlisting at age 25 on 4-27-1862. Reported AWOL Nov.-Dec. 1862. D. near Camp Gregg, VA, 2-15-1863, cause not reported (NCT VIII, 176).

BROWN, THOMAS J.; CO. A, 1ST BAT. SHARPSHOOTERS (05/30/44–10/12/1912; Comanche Co., TX).
Thomas Brown e. in at Kinston, Lenoir Co., on 4-20-1864. Present on company rolls through Dec. 1864 (NCT III, 71). He was one of ten ch. b. to Joseph Joel and Elizabeth Wagoner Brown (dau. of John and Polly Wagoner). The ch. were: Mary, Louisa, Christina, John (killed at Manassas), Thomas, Susan, Nancy, Martha, Elizabeth, and Dinah. Thomas Brown moved to Grayson Co., VA, where he lived for two years before moving to Texas. In 1865 he m. Frances Sparks, b. 10-27-1849, d. 1-1-1934, dau. of Daniel and Kizziah Holloway Sparks. Thomas and Frances Brown had ten ch. (per Neish Brown; *History of Texas*, 626–627.).

BROWN, WILLIAM S.; 75TH REG., 18TH BRIG. MILITIA.

BRUNT, WILLIAM; CO. E, 70TH REG *see* Bryant, William Riley.

BRYANT, CHARLES GREENBERRY; CO. B, 21ST REG. (1840–01/25/1862).
Charles Greenberry Bryant e. in Yadkin Co. on 5-12-1861. Present until he d. in camp near Manassas, VA, on 1-25-1862 of "pneumonia" (NCT VI, 552). Charles Greenberry Bryant was the s. of Hugh and Jane Patterson Bryant (1860 Yadkin; *Heritage*, 301). His middle name comes from his grandfather, Greenberry Patterson. His mother also had a brother with the same name, Greenberry Patterson, Jr.

BRYANT, LEWIS; CO. H, 54TH REG. (1834–?).
Lewis Bryant, a Yadkin resident, e. there on 8-29-1862. Reported absent-sick through Dec. 1862. Hospitalized at Richmond, VA, 2-21-1863 with pneumonia. Transferred to a hospital at Salisbury on 3-24-1863. Reported absent-sick through Dec. 1863. Reported AWOL 1-25-1864. Hospitalized at Charlottesville, VA, 7-26-1864 with chronic bronchitis. Transferred to Lynchburg, VA, hospital on 9-26-1864 (NCT XIII, 320). Lewis Bryant m. Mary Jane Morrison on 7-20-1854 in Yadkin Co. (YCMR). Lewis Bryant, at age 16, was living in the Henry Eldridge household, where he was listed as a farmer, and attending school (1850 Surry). Lewis Briant (age 15), is also listed in the household of Susannah Briant, but he may be the same person, at a different house when the census takers came around.

BRYANT, R. A.; CO. D, 44TH REG. (1826–1864/65 ?).
R. A. Bryant e. at age 36 in Wake Co. on 10-17-1862. Wounded at Bristoe Station, VA, on 10-14-1863. Reported absent-wounded through Feb. 1864. Reported AWOL March–Oct. 1864. Pension records indicate he d. during the war of sickness, date not stated (NCT X, 28). This is probably Reubin A. Bryant, b. 1833, s. of Tolliver and Martha Bryant (1850 Surry).

BRYANT, STEPHEN H[UGH].; CO. I, 28TH REG. (1839–?).
Stephen H. Bryant e. in Co. I, 28th Reg. at age 23 on 3-8-1862. Wounded at the Battle of Second Manassas, VA, 8/27–30/1862. Bryant trans. to Co. A, 44th Reg. NC Troops Mar.–Dec. 1863. He was present through Oct. 1864, and was captured near Petersburg ca. 4-3-1865. He was confined at Ft. Delaware, DE, then Elmira, NY, until released on 7-3-1865, after taking the Oath of Allegiance (NCT X, 401). Stephen H. Bryant was the s. of Hugh and Jane Patterson Bryant. Stephen H. Bryant m. Deborah Farrington on 6-9-1861 in Yadkin Co., the dau. of Nathan and Rachel Caroline Groce Farrington. Stephen and Deborah were the parents of Dr. Charles Greenberry Bryant, Clinton Bryant, and James G. Bryant (d. in 1953 in Washington, DC).

BRYANT, WILLIAM F.; CO. H, 54TH REG.
(06/06/1841–03/19/1938; Fall Creek Bapt.).
William F. Bryant, a Yadkin Co. farmer, e. at age 19 on 3-17-1862. Reported present in June 1862. Deserted on 12-18-1862, but returned to duty on 10-1-1863. Deserted at Goldsboro on 1-26-1864 (NCT XIII, 320). William F. Bryant was the s. of John (Jack) and Caroline Patterson Bryant (*Heritage*, 301). He m. on 12-23-1860 Mary S. Wagoner, b. 3-22-1844, dau. of John and Polly Weatherman Wagoner (YCMR).

BRYANT, WILLIAM RILEY; CO. E, 70TH REG. (1/02/1845–03/14/1927; Mitchell's Chapel Meth.).
William Riley Bryant served in the Confederate Army from 1862 through 1865. He was stationed at Raleigh, NC, and also at Petersburg, VA. He was a guard and never in battle, "for which he was grateful, since he didn't believe in killing" (*Heritage*, 751). William Riley Bryant, b. 1-2-1845, d. 3-14-1927, was the s. of Hugh and Jane Patterson Bryant, and the brother of Stephen H. Bryant (*Heritage*, 301). He was the grandson of Greenberry and Rebecca Bohannon Patterson on his mother's side, and the grandson of Charles and Anne Adams Bryant on his father's side. He e. at age 17 and served as a provisions guard. "Uncle Billy," as he was called, returned to school after the war, and became a Methodist preacher. He m. first on 2-11-1869 in Yadkin Co. Mary Ann Brindle, dau. of William and Nancy Brindle (Brindal). They had two boys. One d. at about age 10, and the other became a Baptist preacher and moved to near Elkin in Wilkes Co. William R. Bryant m. his second wife, Tennessee Williams (b. 5-28-1880, d. 3-14-1931) on 7-4-1904. She met her future husband, who was 45 years her senior, at a revival he was holding. William and Tennessee had twins, at birth one weighed 7 lbs. and the other weighed less than 2 lb. The former is Jennie Bryant Foster, who was still living in 1995 in Winston-Salem, NC. The smaller one also lived. He was drawing a Confederate pension by 1910 in Yadkin Co. (see Appendix F; Hoots, 218).

BUCHANNON (BUCHANNAN), WILLIAM; CO. I, 28TH REG. (1839–?).
William Buchannon, is listed as age 11, residing in the James Vanhoy household in the 1850 Surry Census. He e. at age 22 on 8-13-1861. He was captured at Hanover Court House, VA, 5-27-1862, and confined at Ft. Monroe, VA, and then Ft. Columbus, NY Harbor. Paroled and trans. to Aiken's Landing, James River, VA, for exchange on 8-5-1862. He was reported AWOL about 10-31-1862, but returned to duty Jan.-Feb. 1863. Reported missing at Gettysburg, PA, July 1-3, 1863 (NCT VIII, 208).

BUNDY, HENRY; CO. I, 28TH REG. (1838–?).
Henry Bundy resided in Yadkin Co. where he e. at age 23 on 8-13-1861. He was captured at Hanover Court House, VA, 5-27-1862. Confined at Ft. Monroe, VA, and Ft. Columbus, NY Harbor, paroled and trans. Aiken's Landing and exchanged 8-5-1862. Returned to duty before 11-1-1862 and captured again at Gettysburg, PA, 7-3-1863. Confined at Ft. Delaware, DE. Transferred to Point Lookout, MD, Oct. 15-18, 1863. Released 1-25-1864 after joining the U.S. Army. Unit to which he was assigned was not stated (NCT VIII, 208). Henry Bundy (Bunda) m. Sarah Nichols on 9-29-1856 (YCMR).

BUNDY, NATHAN; CO. I, 28TH REG.
(1841–?).
Nathan Bundy, a Yadkin resident, e. at age 21, 3-8-1862. He was captured at Hanover Court House, VA, 5-27-1862, and confined at Ft. Monroe, VA, then Ft. Columbus, NY Harbor. Paroled and trans. to Aiken's Landing, James River, VA, and exchanged 8-5-1862. Reported AWOL before 11-1-1862, and listed as a deserter 10-1-1863 (NCT VIII, 208).

BURCH, JESSE W.; CO. A, McRAE'S BAT. CAVALRY.
Jesse W. Burch, b. in Yadkin Co., was a farmer when he e. in Burke Co. at age 41, on 10-14-1863. Present until trans. to Co. D, 9th Reg (1st Reg. NC Cavalry), when this battalion was disbanded in June 1864 (NCT II, 698).

BURGESS, E[DWARD]. T.; CO. I, 28TH REG.
(04/08/1816–01/18/1892; Zion Bapt., Iredell Co., NC).
NC pension records indicate that E. T. Burgess served in this company. Edward T. Burgess, age 44, was living in Yadkin Co. when the 1860 census was taken, with wife Nancy P. Burgess (age 30), and ch.: John B. (4), James C. (9/12), and Catharine G. Burgess (age 50, mother/sister?). Edward T. Burgess m. Nancy A. Windsor on 12-30-1850 (Surry Co. Marriages). She was b. 4-8-1816, d. 1-18-1892, dau. of Jesse and Sarah Morgan Windsor. They had five ch. (Cook, *Descendants of Isaac Windsor*, 31).

BURGESS, HENRY H.; CO. I, 18TH REG.
(1832–02/24/1863).
Henry H. Burgess, a Yadkin resident, e. at age 30 in Wake Co. on 9-10-1862. Present until he was wounded in the left thigh at Fredericksburg, VA, 12-13-1862. Died in a Richmond, VA, hospital on 2-24-1863 of "pyremia & hectic fever" (NCT VI, 403). Henry H. Burgess was b. about 1840, and was in the household of William and Elizabeth Burgess (1850 Surry). He was the brother of William A. and Robert C. Burgess, who also served in the same company/regiment.

BURGESS, J[OHN]. M.; CO. A, 9TH BAT. HOME GUARD
A John M. Burgess is bur. at Flat Rock Baptist Church (born 8/18/1842, d. 7/24/1904). There is also a J. M. Burgess (born 1-31-1825, d. 5-26-1895) who is bur. at Zion Baptist Church, in Iredell Co. Because of the close proximity, and the age at enlistment is unknown, it is difficult to determine which is the one who e. in Co. A, 9th Battalion. John M. Burgess m.

Fanny Jane Johnson on 12-19-1865 in Yadkin Co. There is also a marriage between J. M. Burgess, s. of William and Elizabeth Burgess to J. M. Myers, dau. of Shade and Cissey Myers, which took place on 11-5-1868 (YCMR).

BURGESS, ROBERT C.; 75TH REG. 18TH BRIG. MILITIA (1835–?).
Robert C. Burgess, a Yadkin resident, e. in Wake Co. age 27 on 9-10-1862. Present until wounded in the hand and/or left shoulder at Fredericksburg, VA 12-13-182. Returned to duty Jan.–April 1863. Present until he deserted to the enemy on or about 6-11-1864. Took Oath of Allegiance on 6-15-1864 (NCT VI 403). Robert C. Burgess served earlier in the Yadkin Co. Militia, 75th Reg., 18th Brig., enlisting on 2-8-1862. Robert was b. ca 1835, and was in the William and Elizabeth Burgess household when the 1850 Surry Census was taken. His brothers, William A. and Henry H. also served. Robert C. Burgess m. Mattie Thomasson, dau. of C. A. and Margaret Bell, on 4-6-1869 (YCMR).

BURGESS, WILLIAM A.; CO. I, 18TH REG. (1832–?).
William A. Burgess e. at age 30 on 9-10-1862 in Wake Co. Present until wounded in the right shoulder at Fredericksburg, VA, 12-13-1862. Returned to duty 2-25-1863, and present until wounded again at Chancellorsville, VA, 5-3-1863. Reported absent-wounded through August 1863. Deserted and "joined the Quakers" on or about 6-13-1863. Returned to duty 9-13-1864, and was present until he deserted to the enemy about 2-12-1865. Took Oath of Allegiance about 2-17-1865 (NCT VI, 403). William A. Burgess, b. ca. 1832, was living with his brothers, Robert C. and Henry H. in the household of his parents, William and Elizabeth (1850 Surry).

BURNS, JOHN; CO. I, 28TH REG.
John Burns e. in Yadkin Co. 8-13-1861, and was present through Dec. 1861 (NCT VIII, 208).

BYERLY, EPHRAIM; CO. A, 21ST REG.
Ephraim Byerly resided in Yadkin Co. before enlisting at Camp Goodwin, VA, at age 17 on 1-20-1865. Present until wounded in the hand at Hatcher's Run, VA, on 2-5-1865. Hospitalized at Richmond, VA, until furloughed for 60 days on 2-11-1865 (NCT VI, 542).

CALAWAY, CHARLES M.; CO. I, 28TH REG. (1843–?).
Charles M. Calaway (Calloway) e. at Liberty Mills, VA, 12-20-1863, and was captured at Petersburg, VA, 4-2-1865. Confined at Ft. Delaware, DE, until released June 1865, after taking the Oath of Allegiance (NCT VIII, 208). He may be the s. of Daniel and Mary Brown Calloway, as there is a Charles M. C. Calloway (age 7) listed as a child in the household (1850 Surry).

CALLOWAY, B[ARTLEY]. C.; CO. A, 21ST REG. (11/29/1838–05/29/1897; Mitchell's Chapel Meth.).
B. C. Calloway e. in Yadkin Co. on 10-1-1863. He was present until he deserted on 6-21-1864 (NCT VI, 543). He was the s. of James and Sarah Groce Calloway (1850 Surry). Bartley Calloway m. Grace Wagoner, b. 7-6-1846, d. 1-6-1909, and they had several ch. (*Heritage*, 308).

CARLTON, C. WINSHIP; CO. G, 44TH REG. (1835–12/13/1863).
C. Winship (Winshell/Winchel?) Carlton e. at Camp Holmes at age 27, on 10-20-1862. He was present until captured at Bristoe Station, VA, 10-14-1863. Confined at Old Capitol Prison, Washington, DC. He was hospitalized at the prison on 12-7-1863 with "pleurisy and pericarditis," and d. 12-13-1863 (NCT X, 456). One Winshell Carlton (probably the same as C. Winship Carlton) m. Sarah Brooks on 6-9-1855 in Yadkin Co. Winchel Carlton, age 18, was living with his parents, Moses and Mary Carlton (1850 Surry).

CARLTON, SAN[D]FORD B.; CO. I, 28TH REG. (04/08/1841–05/05/1865).
Sandford B. Carlton, a Yadkin resident, e. at age 19 on 8-13-1861. He was captured at Hanover Court House, VA, 5-27-1862, and confined at Ft. Monroe, VA, then Ft. Columbus, NY Harbor. Paroled and trans. to Aiken's Landing, James River, VA, and exchanged 8-5-1862. Wounded at Chancellorsville, VA, 5/1–3/1863. Reported absent-sick Sept.–Oct. 1864, and AWOL 11-15-1864 through Feb. 1865 (NCT VIII, 208-209). Sanford was the s. of Bloom and Elizabeth Carlton, and was b. ca. 1841, according to the 1850 Surry Census. (Rita H. Townsend, *Hutchins/Hutchens*, vol. I, 173).

CARRENDER, JAMES L.; CO. G, 54TH REG. (1836–12/13/1862).
James Carrender e. in Wilkes Co. on 4-5-1862. He was reported present in June of 1862. He was killed at Fredericksburg, VA, on 12-13-1862 (NCT XIII, 308).

CARTER, ABEL DUNCAN; 75TH REG., 18TH BRIG. MILITIA (07/10/37–7/27/1915; Swaim's Bapt.).
Abel D. Carter, the s. of James C. and Rhoda Poenix Carter, m. Nancy E. Fleming on 12-21-1865 in Yadkin Co. (YCMR). She was was b. 5-26-1847, d. 1-2-1919, and was the dau. of David and Eliza Nicholson Fleming (per Craaybeek).

CARTER, EUGENE; CO. F, 28TH REG. (1842/43/44–1891).
Eugene Carter e. in Yadkin Co. at age 17 on 6-18-1861, in Co. F, 28th Reg. Discharged on 9-21-1861 because of disability (NCT VIII, 176). Eugene Carter may have reinlisted at Camp Vance on 4-11-1862 (1863?), in Co. G, 54th Reg., but he is not listed on company records until Sept. 1864. He was

wounded in the neck at Winchester or Fishers Hill in VA about Sept. 19–22, 1864. He was hospitalized at Charlottesville, VA, on 9-26-1864, then trans. to a hospital in Richmond. On 10-13-1864 he was trans. to another hospital (NCT XIII, 308). Eugene Carter, age 7, is listed in the household of his parents, Hugh and Anna (Sprinkle?) Carter (1850 Surry). Eugene m. first Sarah Elizabeth Permelia Hutchens, dau. of Amos and Sarah Rhodes Hutchens, on 11-1-1864. His second wife was Matilda Tate, dau. of John and Matilda Tate, who he m. on 2-23-1873 in Yadkin Co. (YCMR; Wanda Craaybeek). Eugene was the brother of John Wesley Carter, listed below.

CARTER, JOHN A[NDREW].; CO. F, 28TH REG. (1839/1840–MAY 1917; Randolph Co., IN).
John A. Carter m. Susannah North on 5-27-1866 in Yadkin Co. He was a Yadkin Co. farmer before enlisting at age 21 on 6-18-1861. Discharged on 1-12-1862 (NCT VIII, 176). He then e. in Co. A, 54th Reg. in Yadkin Co. on 5-2-1862. Present through Feb. 1863. Wounded in both hips near Fredericksburg, VA, about 5-4-1863. Hospitalized at Richmond, VA. Furloughed for 40 days on 6-11-1863. Returned to duty Nov.-Dec. 1863. Captured at Stephenson's Depot, VA, 7-20-1864. He was confined at Camp Chase, OH, 7-28-1864, and paroled on 3-2-1865, and received at Boulware's Wharf, James River, VA, about 3-11-1865 for exchange. Returned to duty before 3-15-1864 when he was captured at Ft. Stedman, VA, and confined at Point Lookout, MD, 3-28-1865. Released from there on 6-24-1865 after taking the Oath of Allegiance (NCT XIII, 251). John A. Carter, age 10, is listed in the household of his parents, Isaac T. and Louisa (Lynch) Carter (1850 Surry). He was the brother of Logan C. Carter (per Wanda Craaybeek).

CARTER, JOHN W[ESLEY].; CO. A, 60TH REG. (1844–1921; Baltimore Meth.).
John W. Carter's tombstone states that he served in the CSA. He may have been the J. W. Carter who e. on 4-12-1862 in Buncombe Co. (Moore's *Roster*, vol. IV, 675). John Wesley Carter, age 6, was living in the household of his parents, Hugh and Anna (Sprinkle?) Carter in 1850. He is the brother of Eugene Carter (listed above). John W. Carter m. first Emily J. Phillips on 6-14-1866. His second wife was Rebecca Davis, b. 8-12-1873, d. 1-31-1846, bur. at Forbush Baptist Church, Yadkin Co. (YCMR; 1850 Surry; Craaybeek).

CARTER, JOSHUA E.; CO. H, 54TH REG. (1835–03/16/1863).
Joshua E. Carter was a day laborer in Yadkin Co. before enlisting there at age 25 on 3-17-1862. Reported present in June, but was hospitalized on 11-9-1862 in a Richmond, VA, hospital with tonsillitis. Returned to duty before 1-1-1863. Hospitalized again at Richmond on 3-1-1863 and d. in the hospital there about 3-16-1863 of "pneumonia" (NCT XIII, 320).

CARTER, LOGAN C.; CO. A, 54TH REG. (1843–02/26/1864).
Logan C. Carter, b. in Yadkin Co., was a farmer before enlisting there at age 19 on 5-3-1862. Reported present through Feb. 1863. Reported on duty as a wagoner March-April 1863. Reported present May–Oct. 1863. Captured at Rappahannock Station, VA, 11-7-1863 and confined at Point Lookout, MD, 11-11-1863. Died in hospital there of smallpox on Feb. 25-26, 1864 (NCT XIII, 251). Logan C. Carter was the s. of Isaac Thomas Carter, Sr., and Louisa (Lynch) Carter, and the brother of John Andrew Carter (per Craaybeek).

CARTER, MILES; CO. I, 28TH REG.
Miles Carter resided in Yadkin Co. and e. at Liberty Mills, VA, on 2-29-1864. Captured near Petersburg, VA, on 4-2-1865. Confined at Ft. Delaware, DE, until released on 6-19-1865, after taking the Oath of Allegiance (NCT VIII, 209).

CARTER, THOMAS J.; CO. A, 1ST BAT. SHARPSHOOTERS.
Thomas J. Carter e. "at camp in Virginia" on 11-1-1863. Deserted on 12-26-1863, and reported as a deserter until dropped from company rolls 8-31-1864 (NCT III, 71).

CARTER, WILLIAM M.; CO. B, 38TH REG. (1840–08/24/1864).
William M. Carter resided in Yadkin Co. where he e. at age 21 on Oct. 16, 1861. Present until wounded at Mechanicsville, VA, on 6-26-1862. Reported AWOL July–Aug. 1862, and from 10-20-1862 through Dec. 1862. Returned to duty Jan.-Feb. 1863. Transferred to Co. I, 28th Reg., NC Troops, on 3-29-1863. (NCT X, 22). Wounded and captured at Gettysburg, PA, 7-3-1863, and confined at Ft. Delaware, DE. Transferred to Point Lookout, MD, Oct. 15-18, 1863. Died at Point Lookout on 8-24-1864. Cause of death not reported (NCT VIII, 209).

CARTWRIGHT, LOUIS (LEWIS) J.; 75TH REG., 18TH BRIG. MILITIA (06/03/1833–02/18/1889; Old Center Meth. Ch. cem.).
Lewis J. Cartwright m. Martha J. Swaim on 12-7-1856 (YCMR). He is probably the brother or the nephew of Thomas D. Cartwright, and was living in his household in 1850 (1850 Surry).

CARTWRIGHT, THOMAS D.; CO. I, 28TH REG. (02/29/1821–09/09/1879; Cartwright Fam. Cem.).
Thomas D. Cartwright e. at Camp Vance on 11-4-1863. He was reported on detail as a "shoemaker at Richmond, Virginia," from 1-8-1864 through Feb. 1864. Captured in a Richmond, VA, hospital on 4-3-1865. Paroled on 5-3-1865 (NCT VIII, 209).

CASEY, DANIEL C.; CO. I, 28TH REG. SERGEANT (1841–after 1864 in Tennessee?).
Daniel C. Casey, a Yadkin resident, e. at age 20, on 8-13-1861. Mustered in as private and was promoted

to sergeant on 4-12-162. Wounded in the shoulder at the Battle of Second Manassas, VA, Aug. 27-30, 1862. Returned to duty before 3-1-1863. Captured at Chancellorsville, VA, 5-3-1863. Paroled and trans. to City Point, VA, where he was received on 5-13-1863 for exchange. Returned to duty before 7-3-1863, when he was captured at Gettysburg, PA, and confined at Ft. Delaware, DE. He was trans. to Point Lookout, MD, on about 10-15-1863, and confined until released from there on 1-25-1864, after taking the Oath of Allegiance, and joining the U.S. service. Unit to which he was assigned not reported (NCT VIII, 209). Daniel C. Casey was b. ca. 1841, and d. sometime after 1864, probably in Tennessee, the s. of Henry W. and Sarah Ann Windsor Casey (Cook, *Descendants of Isaac Windsor*, 18).

CASEY, THOMAS MELMUTH; CO. C, 18TH REG. (03/25/1829-04/14/1915; St. Paul Meth. Ch.).
Thomas M. Casey e. in Wake Co. on 9-10-1862. Present until wounded in the hand at Fredericksburg, VA, on 12-13-1862. Returned to duty May-June 1863. Captured at Gettysburg, PA, on 7-2-1863 and confined at Ft. Delaware, DE, Oct. 15–18, 1863. Paroled from there and trans. to Boulware's Wharf, VA, where he was received about 2-20-1865 for exchange. Reported present with a detachment of paroled and exchanged prisoners at Camp Lee near Richmond, VA, on 2-25-1865 (NCT VI, 403). Thomas M. Casey, the s. of John Casey, Jr., and Jane Walker Casey (*Heritage*, 310), m. Nancy L. Windsor on 1-2-1854 (YCMR), the dau. of Daniel and Sally Arnold Windsor. They had six ch.: William Andrew, James Henry, John Melmuth, Daniel W., Mary Jane, and Sallie A. Casey. Thomas Casey d. of "LaGrippe, and pneumonia" (per Katherine Williams Hege).

CASS, ALFRED; CO. B, 42ND REG. (1823–?).
Alfred Cass e. at age 39 in Petersburg, VA, on 10-16-1862, and was discharged on 9-25-1863 (NCT X, 208).

CASS, BASWELL G.; CO. B, 42ND REG. (1836–?).
Baswell Cass e. at Petersburg, VA, age 26, on 10-16-1862. Present through 3-7-1865 (NCT X, 208).

CASSTEVENS, JOHN MARTIN; CO. H, 21ST REG. (10/09/1832–10/21/1875).
John M. Casstevens e. in Wake Co. on 11-1-1863, and was present through Feb. 1864. In 1860, John M. Casstevens, age 28, was living with wife, Abslea Nichols Casstevens, age 30, and two ch., Mary C. (age 7), and Miles E. (age 2). (William C. Casstevens and Frances H. Casstevens, *Thomas Casteven: A Genealogical History*, 1976, 33; NCT VI, 603, listed as "Castenens, J.W."; 1860 Yadkin).

CASSTEVENS, NATHAN; (04/08/1841–01/27/1863).
Nathan Casstevens d. as a Confederate soldier, either from wounds or disease. He was the s. of John and Elizabeth Casstevens, he was b. ca. 1841. He m. Annie Melissa Calloway. After his death, his young widow m. L. L. Harris (*Thomas Casteven: A Genealogical History*, 37).

CASSTEVENS, WILLIAM EVAN; CO. A, 28TH REG. (02/06/1831–ca. 1900; Mitchell's Chapel Meth.).
William Evan Casstevens, the s. of Martin Luther and Luran Durham Casstevens, m. Gracy Swaim on 12-18-1856 in Yadkin Co. (YCMR) Children were: Mary Elizabeth, Malinda, Charity Ann, Thomas, Nancy Kissiah, Luzane, John Mecans, and William Evan, Jr. (*Thomas Casteven: A Genealogical History*, 33).

CASSTEVENS, WILLIAM G.(C?); (12/30/1842–04/08/1863; Mitchell's Chapel Meth.).
William G. Casstevens, was the s. of Mecans and Elizabeth Casstevens. He d. at age 20, cause unknown. His tombstone reads: "Was conscripted and forst in the rebellon and d. the deth of a soldier" (*Thomas Casteven: A Genealogical History*, 37; 1850 Surry).

CAUDLE, AARON; CO. B, 21ST REG. (?–05/25/1862).
Aaron Caudle e. in Yadkin Co. on 5-12-1861. Present until trans. to Co. A, 1st Battalion NC Sharpshooters on 4-26-1862 (NCT III, 71; VI, 552). Although technically trans., his unit remained with the 21st NC until after one of the battles at Winchester, and he was killed there on 5-25-1862 (see "Biblical Recorder," Sept. 24, 1862, copy courtesy of Cheryl Martin). He was the s. of Aaron Caudle and brother to Simon, Abraham, and Isaac Caudle, who also served.

CAUDLE, ABRAHAM; CO. B, 38TH REG. (1837–?).
Abraham Caudle, a Yadkin resident, e. at age 26 on 2-15-1863. Deserted on 4-21-1863, but returned to duty on 9-29-1863. Present until he deserted again on 7-17-1864. Returned to duty on 9-29-1864, and captured in a Richmond, VA, hospital on 4-3-1865. Confined at Newport News, VA, on 4-24-1865 until released on 6-30-1865, after taking the Oath of Allegiance (NCT X, 23). Abraham Caudle was the s. of Aaron Caudle. Brothers were Simon, Isaac, and Aaron Caudle (per Cheryl Martin).

CAUDLE, D. F.; C. S. NAVY.
D. F. Caudle e. on 7-19-1863 in the CSA Navy at Wilmington (Moore's *Roster*, vol. IV, p. 445).

CAUDLE, ISAAC; CO. A, 1ST BAT. SHARPSHOOTERS
Isaac Caudle e. in Wake Co. on 9-4-1862. Discharged 4-19-1863 (NCT III, 71). Isaac Caudle, the s. of Aaron and Malinda Caudle, m. Mary Catherine Carter on 11-21-1866 (YCMR). Brothers were Simon, Abraham, and Aaron Caudle, who also served (per Cheryl Martin).

CAUDLE, JESSE; CO. B, 56TH REG. (1844–?).
Jesse Caudle e. in Wake Co. on 10-20-1863. He deserted on 1-15-1864 (NCT XIII, 608). This may be the Jesse W. Caudle, b. 1844, the s. of Aaron and Malinda Caudle (1850 Surry).

CAUDLE, MARTIN A.; CO. A, 1ST BAT. SHARPSHOOTERS (1832–?).
M. A. Caudle e. in Wake Co. on 9-4-1862, and was discharged on 4-19-1863. In 1850 Martin A. Caudle was living with Moses Caudle. M. A. Caudle m. Martha Jane Ray (date of bond) 5-5-1858 (YCMR; Martin). On Tuesday, November 1, 1864, M. A. Caudle, aged 33, was discharged from Home Guard duty because he had epilepsy (Bradley, *North Carolina Confederate Home Guard Examinations 1863–1864*, 81).

CAUDLE, LEWIS; CO. C, 13TH REG. (1838–?).
Lewis Caudle lived in Yadkin Co., where he e. on 3-3-1863, at age 25. He deserted on 4-18-1863, but returned during March-Apr. 1864. He was reported "missing" on 5-5-1864 (NCT V, 311). Lewis Caudle may be the s. of William and Nancy Caudle (1850 Surry).

CAUDLE, SOLOMON JACKSON; CO. A, 1ST BAT. SHARPSHOOTERS (1828–?).
Solomon Jackson Caudle e. "at camp in Virginia" on 10-15-1863 (Brandy Station, VA). Present through Dec. 1864. Captured at Farmville, VA, on 4-6-1865, and confined at Newport News, VA, on 4-15-1865. Date of release not reported (NCT III, 71). According to a pay voucher, dated 1-31-1865, Jackson was 5'10" tall, with dark complexion, black eyes, and black hair. He received $72 for service from 8-31-1864 through 12-31-1864. Jackson had, before the war, been commissioned an ensign in the N.C. Militia on 10-10-1852 (*Heritage*, 138–139). Solomon J. Cordle (Caudle), age 22, and wife Mary, age 24, were living in their own household in 1850, and had just m. that year. He may be the s. of Aaron and Malinda Cordle (Caudle) living nearby.

CHAMBERLAIN, ALEXANDER; CO. A, 9TH BAT. HOME GUARD.
Alex Chamberlain and wife Elizabeth's son, Charlie R. m. Lucinda Macemore, dau. of John and Lucinda Macemore, on 8-18-1885 (YCMR).

CHAMBERLAIN, L(EWIS) L.; CO. G, 13TH REG. (1825–?).
Lewis L. Chamberlain, a Yadkin resident, e. at age 27 on 9-27-1862. He was present until reported AWOL from 3-20-1864 through Aug. 1864. Reported "in arrest" in Sept.-Oct. 1864 (NCT V, 349).

CHAMBERLIN, MARTIN; CO. G, 42ND REG. (1833–?).
Martin Chamlin (Chamberlin), a Yadkin Co. resident, e. at Petersburg, VA, on 11-6-1862 at age 28. He deserted on 12-19-1862. He reportedly d. at Weldon, N.C. on 3-15-1863 from "debility" (NCT X, 260). Martin was the s. of John and Ibba Chamberlin (1850 Surry).

CHAMBERLAIN, WILLIAM; CO. A, 1ST BAT. (SHARPSHOOTERS).
William Chamberlain e. in Wake Co. on 9-4-1862. Present until he deserted from Greensboro, NC, on 10-5-1864. Dropped from rolls on 2-28-1865 (NCT III, 71). He may either be the s. of William C. and Sally Chamberlain, listed as William H. H. Chamberlain, age 8, in the 1850 Surry Census, or William Chamberlain, age 26 in 1850, the s. of John and Ibba Chamberlain. The latter is probably the correct family, as there is a smaller brother, Josiah, age 7 also in the household. He may be the Joseph F. Chamberlain listed below. There were only four Chamberlain households listed in 1850 (1850 Surry). One William Chamberlain m. in Yadkin Co. on 5-5-1859 Lucy Brittain (YCMR)

CHAMBERLIN, JOSEPH F.; CO. H, 4TH REG. (?–06/16/1862).
Joseph F. Chamberlain e. at age 18 on 6-13-1861. Wounded at the battle of Seven Pines, VA, on 5-31-1862. He d. in a Richmond, VA, hospital (NCT IV, 86).

CHAMBERLIN, SAMUEL; CO. H, 4TH REG. (1839–05/12/1864).
Samuel Chamberlain lived in Yadkin Co. but e. in Iredell Co. at age 23 on 10-1-1862. Present until he was killed at Spotsylvania Court House, VA, on 5-12-1864 (NCT IV, 86). Samuel Chamberlain, age 9, is listed in 1850 in the household of his parents, John and Ibba Chamberlain. John was a cooper (1850 Surry).

CHAPPEL, CALVIN J.; CO. I, 28TH REG. (1837–?).
Calvin Chappel e. at Camp Gregg, VA, at age 26 on 2-28-1863. Reported AWOL from Oct. 1864 through Feb. 1865. NC pension records indicate he was wounded near Chancellorsville, VA, on 5-4-1863. He may have served previously in Co. G, 44th Reg. NCT (NCT VIII, 209).

CHAPPEL, LEWIS J.; CO. I, 28TH REG. (1837–?).
Lewis Chappel, a Yadkin Co. farmer, e. at age 24 on 8-13-1861. Transferred to Co. B, 38th Reg. on 1-10-1862. Present until he deserted on 8-6-1862 (NCT VIII, 209; X, 23).

CHAPPEL, REUBEN D.; CO. D, 44TH REG. (1842–?).
Reuben D. Chappel e. at age 20 on 10-17-1862. Deserted on 11-16-1862. He then e. at age 22 at Brandy Station, VA, on 11-14-1863. He deserted to the enemy on 11-14-1863 at Racoon Ford on 12-31-1863. Confined at Old Capitol Prison on 1-4-1864, he was released at Washington, DC, on 5-19-1864, after taking the Oath of Allegiance (NCT X, 428; XIII, 380).

H. YADKIN MEN IN THE MILITARY, 1861–1865

CHAPPEL, WILLIAM; CO. I, 28TH REG.
William Chappel, a Yadkin Co. farmer, e. at Camp Holmes on 11-14-1862. Captured near Pickett's Farm, VA, about 7-21-1864, and confined at Point Lookout, MD, on 7-28-1864. Released on 5-13-1865, after taking the Oath of Allegiance (NCT VIII, 209).

CHAPPEL, WILLIAM; CO. H, 54TH REG.
William Chappel e. in Yadkin Co. on 10-13-1863. Captured at Rappahannock Station, VA, on 11-7-1863. Confined at Point Lookout, MD, on 11-11-1863. Paroled at Point Lookout on 3-16-1864. Received at City Point, VA, 3-20-1864 for exchange. Reported AWOL Sept.–Oct. 1864 (NCT XIII, 320).

CHAPPELL, CALVIN; CO. G, 44TH REG.
(1843–?).
Calvin Chappel resided in Yadkin Co. where he e. at age 29 on 10-20-1862. Deserted on 10-29-1862. He may have served later as a Private in Co. I, 28th Reg. NCT (NCT X, 457). Calvin Chappell m. Fanny Groce on 10-6-1858 in Yadkin Co. (bond date).

CHAPPELL, J. C.; CO. I, 28TH REG. (1845–?).
J. C. Chappel lived in Yadkin Co. where he e. at age 18 on 2-28-1863. Deserted on 6-18-1863 (NCT VIII, 209).

CHAPPELL, JAMES R.; CO. I, 28TH REG.
(1831–?).
James R. Chappell lived in Yadkin Co. where he e. at age 30 on 8-13-1861. Wounded in both thighs and both hips and captured at Wilderness, VA, about 5-6-1864 (NCT VIII, 209).

CHAPPELL, JAMES W.; CO. B, 38TH REG.
(1845–?).
James W. Chappel was a Yadkin Co. farmer before enlisting at age 16 on 10-16-1861. Present until discharged on 10-26-1862 because he was underage (NCT X, 23).

CHAPPELL, JULIUS J.; CO. B, 38TH REG.
(1842–07/18/1862).
Julius J. Chappell lived in Yadkin Co. where he e. at age 19 on 10-16-1861. Present until wounded at Frayser's Farm, VA, on 6-30-1862. Hospitalized at Richmond, VA, where he d. about 7-18-1862 of wounds received (NCT X, 23).

CHAPPELL, SOLOMON C.; CO. F, 52ND REG. (07/05/1843–03/15/1907).
Solomon C. Chappel was b. in Yadkin Co., but resided in Wilkes where he was a farmer before enlisting at age 19 on 4-5-1862. Wounded in the right side and captured at Gettysburg, PA, on 7-2-1863. He was hospitalized at Gettysburg, before being captured and trans. to Davids Island, NY Harbor, where he arrived about 7-20-1863. Paroled there and trans. to City Point, VA, where he was received on 9-8-1863 for exchange. Returned to duty Jan.–Feb. 1864. Reported present through Dec. 1864. Captured at or near Amelia Court House, VA, on 4-4-1865, and confined at Point Lookout, MD, on 4-13-1865. He was released on 6-24-1865 after taking the Oath of Allegiance (NCT XII, 469). Solomon Cephas Chappel was the s. of William J. and Mary Swaim Chappel (YCHGSJ XI [Sept. 1992]: 13).

CHAPPELL, WILLIAM; CO. G, 44TH REG.
(1829–?).
William Chappel, a Yadkin resident, e. at Camp Holmes near Raleigh, at age 33, on 10-20-1862. He was present through Feb. 1863, but deserted before 1-1-1864 (NCT X, 457).

CHEEK, AARON; CO. K, 52ND REG.
(1833–?).
Aaron Cheek e. at Orange Court House, VA, at age 33 on 11-20-1863. Present through Aug. 1864. Wounded in right ankle at Jones' Farm, VA, about 9-30-1864. Reported absent-wounded through Dec. 1864. He survived the war and received a Confederate pension (NCT XII, 513). Aaron Cheek was the s. of John and Mary Cheek(s) (1850 Surry).

CHEEK, JOHN VESTAL; 75TH REG., 18TH BRIG. MILITIA.

CHEEK, JOSEPH C.; CO. B, 38TH REG.
(1838–?).
Joseph C. Cheek lived in Yadkin before enlisting at age 24 on 2-1-1862, as a substitute for Private Isaac Long, Jr., of this company. Deserted on 8-10-1862 (NCT X, 23).

CHEELY, LEWIS JOSEPH ? (01/02/1834–11/30/1905; Greshamville, VA).
He e. at Camp Vance and was captured by forces under Major General W. T. Sherman on 6-28-1864. He was sent to a Federal prison on Lake Michigan. He walked back to Iredell Co., and lived there near Harmony for several years, before returning to Jonesville. A professor at the Jonesville Academy, he was b. in Smoky Ordinary, Brunswick Co., VA, on 1-2-1834. He came to Jonesville and m. Mary Elizabeth Virginia Morrison on 12-22-1858. They had 10 ch. After the death of his first wife, Lewis moved to Greshamville, GA, to teach school, and there he m. Mary Eugenia Pennington. They had five ch. (*Heritage*, 316–317).

CHILDERS, JAMES F.; CO. I. 28TH REG.
(1838–?).
James F. Childers, b. in Surry Co., resided in Yadkin Co., where he was a farmer before enlisting at age 23 on 8-13-1861. Discharged on 12-14-1861 because of a "variocele" (NCT VIII, 209). James Childers m. Elizabeth Ann Martin on 11-24-1858 (bond date, YCMR).

CHILDRESS, WILLIAM H.; CO. I, 28TH REG. (1842–?).
William H. Childress, a Yadkin resident, e. at age 19

on 8-13-1861. Captured at Hanover Court House, VA, on 5-27-1862. Confined at Ft. Monroe, VA, and then Ft. Columbus, NY Harbor. Paroled and trans. to Aiken's Landing James River, VA, where he was received on 7-12-1862 for exchange. Declared exchanged at Aiken's Landing on 8-5-1862. Returned to duty before 11-1-1862. Wounded at Gettysburg, PA, July 1-3, 1863. Returned to duty and was captured near Petersburg, VA, on 4-2-1865. Confined at Ft. Delaware DE until released on 6-19-1865, after taking the Oath of Allegiance (NCT VIII, 209).

CHOPLIN, JESSE; CO. H, 63RD REG. (5TH CAVALRY) (10/28/1844-04/17/1864; Confederate Cem., Point Lookout, MD).
Jesse Choplin was captured on 9-22-1863 at Madison Court House, VA, and confined at Point Lookout, MD, where he d. on 4-17-1864 of dysentery. He was bur. in the Confederate Cemetery there (NCT, II, 431; Curtis D. Choplin, *An American Tragedy: The Robert Choplin Family in the Civil War*, 1995). The Choplins were from Franklin Co., and their parents, Robert and Ann Winston Choplin, moved to Yadkin Co. about 1840.

CHOPLIN, JOHN; CO. E, 70TH REG. (08/14/1846-10/04/1914; Mt. Pleasant Meth.).
John Choplin was conscripted into Co. E, 70th Regiment (see Special Orders No. 22, Conscript Office, Raleigh, NC, dated 9-30-1864, original in possession of Cheryl Lynn Martin), which was a consolidation of Junior Reserve Units. He m. Sarah A. Norman on 4-5-1874 (YCMR), dau. of John and Nancy Norman (*Heritage*, 320; Choplin, *An American Tragedy*).

CHOPLIN, JOHN WESLEY; CO. F, 28TH REG. (05/29/1839-12/19/1917; Prospect Meth.).
John Wesley Choplin was one of six brothers who served in the Confederate Army, the s. of Robert and Ann Winston Choplin. He was first wounded at the Battle of Gaines' Mill on 6-27-1862 during the Seven Days' Battles. He was wounded again in the elbow at Ox Hill, VA, on 9-1-1862. He was reported absent, absent-wounded without leave through Dec. 1862. Wesley was detailed as a hospital guard on 10-17-1863. He continued through the war and was paroled at Greensboro on 5-3-1865. He m. Susannah A. Taylor on 10-27-1857 (YCMR) (Choplin, *An American Tragedy*; NCT VIII, 176).

CHOPLIN, JOSEPH; CO. F, 28TH REG. SERGEANT (02/15/1838-06/27/1862).
Joseph Choplin e. in Yadkin Co. at age 23 on 6-18-1861. He mustered in as corporal and was promoted to sergeant on 4-12-1861. He was reported missing in action at Gaines' Mill, VA, on 6-27-1862 (NCT VIII, 176). He was the s. of Robert and Ann Winston Choplin (NCT VIII, 176; Choplin, *An American Tragedy*).

CHOPLIN, ROBERT; CO. F, 28TH REG. (03/03/1843-08/03/1862).
Robert Choplin e. at age 18 on 6-18-1861. Wounded at Gaines' Mill, VA, 6-27-1862, he d. in Richmond VA, about 8-3-1862 of wounds and or disease (NCT VIII, 176; Choplin, *An American Tragedy*).

CHOPLIN, SIDNEY; CO. F, 28TH REG. (10/02/1836-07/01/1863).
Sidney Choplin, b. in Franklin Co., but lived in Yadkin Co., e. at age 24 on 6-18-1861. He was killed at Gettysburg, PA, July 1-3, 1863 (NCT VIII, 176). He was one of six brothers, the s. of Robert and Ann Winston Choplin. Sidney had been a schoolmaster before enlisting (Choplin, *An American Tragedy*).

CLOER, WASHINGTON FALLS; CO. E, 49TH REG. (09/15/1836-01/02/1925; Fall Creek Bapt.).
Washington Falls and wife, Almeda Cloer had two boys to marry in Yadkin Co. Eddy Cloer m. Fanny Benge on 4-28-1900 (YCMR) and James Cloer m. Junesann Benge on 2-24-1900 (YCMR).

COCHRAN, DANIEL; CO. A, 1ST BAT. SHARPSHOOTERS (?-before 06/30/1864).
Daniel Cochran e. "at camp in Virginia" on 1-20-1864. Company muster rolls state he was "wounded and d. in enemy lines" sometime between Feb. 28 and June 30, 1864 (NCT III, 71). He may be the s. of John and Mary Cochran, b. about 1844 (1860 Yadkin).

COCKERHAM, DAVID; CO. I, 28TH REG. CORPORAL (1831-?).
David Cockerham, a Yadkin resident, e. there at age 30 on 8-13-1861. Mustered in as private, promoted to corporal March 1863-Oct. 1864. Captured at New Bern on 3-14-1862. Confined at Ft. Columbus, NY Harbor. Paroled and trans. to Aiken's Landing, James River, VA, where he was received on 7-12-1862 for exchange. Declared exchanged on 8-5-1862. Returned to duty before 2-28-1863. Captured near Petersburg, VA, on 4-2-1865. Confined at Point Lookout, MD, until released on 6-24-1865, after taking the Oath of Allegiance (NCT VIII, 209). David Cockerham m. Nancy P. Reece on 9-9-1850 (YCMR).

COCKERHAM, DAVID S.; CO. H, 54TH REG. CAPTAIN (01/05/1824-?).
David S. Cockerham, b. in Surry Co. on 1-5-1824, resided in Yadkin Co. where he was a physician before enlisting at age 38. Appointed captain on 3-21-1862. Present or accounted for through Oct. 1863. Captured at Rappahannock Station, VA, 11-7-1863, and confined at Old Capitol Prison, Washington, DC, 11-8-1863. Trans. to Johnson's Island, OH, where he arrived on 11-14-1863. Transferred to Baltimore, MD, 2-9-1864, then to Ft. Delaware, DE, on 6-23-1864. Transferred again to Hilton Head, SC, on 8-20-1864. Confined at Ft. Pulaski, GA, about 10-20-1864. Paroled at Charleston, SC, 12-15-1864. Survived the war (NCT XIII, 318). David S. Cockerham m. first on 3-5-1858 P. M. Jones, dau. of

Jonathan and Hannah Jones. She d. on 6-19-1858, and he m. on 11-17-1867 Amanda J. Long, dau. of Isaac and Sarah Long (YCMR). Cockerham was a physician before entering the Confederate Army.

COLLINS, DAVID D.; CO. B, 38TH REG. (1838–?).
David D. Collins, a Yadkin Co. farmer, e. at age 23 on 10-16-1861. Present until he deserted on 4-11-1864. Returned to duty on 9-18-1864. Surrendered at Appomattox Court House, VA, on 4-9-1865 (NCT X, 23).

COLLINS, LEWIS W.; CO. B, 38TH REG. (1842–?).
Lewis W. Collins lived in Yadkin where he e. at age 19 on 10-16-1861. Present until captured at Warrenton, VA, on 9-29-1862. Paroled about same date. Reported AWOL on 10-1-1862. Returned to duty March-Apr. 1863. Captured at Falling Waters, MD, on 7-14-1863. Sent to Baltimore, MD, and confined at Elmira, NY, on 8-18-1864. Released from there about 6-12-1865, after taking the Oath of Allegiance. N.C. pension records indicate he was wounded at Gettysburg, PA, on 7-1-1863 (NCT X, 23).

COLLINS, OBEDIAH; CO. B, 38TH REG. (1832–?).
Obediah Collins lived in Yadkin Co. where he e. at age 30 on 4-19-1862. Reported AWOL on 8-18-1862. Returned to duty in Sept. 1863. Present until 9-19-1864 when he was reported AWOL (NCT X, 23). Obediah Collins m. Mary Ann Far (Fair/Farris?) 5-2-1852 in Yadkin Co. Obediah was the s. of John and Susannah Collins, and was listed (at age 17) at the house next door to theirs in 1850 (1850 Surry).

COLLINS, WILLIAM H.; CO. A, 1ST BAT. SHARPSHOOTERS.
William H. Collins e. in Wake Co. on 9-4-1862. Present through Feb. 1864, when he was reported as absent-wounded in General Hospital, Goldsboro, NC (NCT III, 71).

COLVARD, BENJAMIN G.; CO. F, 28TH REG. (05/04/1837–05/10/1899; Colvard Fam. Cem.).
Benjamin Colvard, a Yadkin Co. farmer, e. there at age 19 on 4-1-1862. Wounded in the forearm and captured at Hanover Court House, VA, on 5-27-1862, he was confined at Ft. Monroe, VA, then Ft. Columbus, NY Harbor. Transferred to Ft. Delaware, DE, on 8-23-1862, then he was paroled and trans. to Aiken's Landing, James River, VA, on 10-2-1862 for exchange. Exchanged there on 11-10-1862. Reported absent-wounded through Dec. 1862. Company records to not indicate whether he returned to duty, but he was discharged on 1-3-1864 because of wounds received at Hanover Court House (NCT VIII, 176). Benjamin Colvert (Colvard), age 13, was living in the household of his parents, William J. and Martha Colvert in 1850 (1850 Surry). B. G. Colvard m. Marietta Williams on 11-14-1861 (YCMR; 1850 Surry).

COLVARD, ISAAC W.; CO. B, McRAE'S BAT. NC CAVALRY.
Isaac W. Colvard e. in Co. B, McRae Battalion, NC Cavalry. He deserted to the enemy and was confined at Knoxville, TN, on 8-5-1864, where he took the Oath of Allegiance on 8-8-1864. He was sent to Chattanooga, TN, on 8-9-1864 (NCT II, 698). Isaac W. Colvard m. Nancy J. Poindexter on 9-22-1865 (bond date; YCMR).

COLVARD, JOHN S.; CO. F, 28TH REG. (1839–?).
John S. Colvard e. in Yadkin Co. at age 22 on 6-18-1861. Deserted on 6-3-1863. Went over to the enemy about 7-31-1864. Took the Oath of Allegiance at Louisville, KY, on 8-10-1864 (NCT VIII, 176).

COLVARD, THOMAS E.; CO. F, 28TH REG. (1835–?).
Thomas E. Colvard, a Yadkin Co. farmer, e. at age 26 on 6-18-1861. Hospitalized in Richmond, VA, on 12-15-1862 with gunshot wound of the forefinger, place and date of wound not reported. Transferred to hospital at Danville, VA, on 1-8-1863. Deserted from the hospital on 3-24-1863. Went over to the enemy on an unspecified date and was confined at Knoxville, TN, on 7-31-1864. Took Oath of Allegiance at Louisville, KY, on 8-10-1864 (NCT VIII, 176–177).

COLVARD, WILLIAM M.; CO. F, 28TH REG. (1837–?).
William M. Colvard e. in Yadkin Co. at age 24 on 6-18-1861. He was present or accounted for through Dec. 1862. Deserted on 6-5-1863 and went over to the enemy. Confined at Knoxville, TN, on 7-31-1864, and took the Oath of Allegiance there on 8-10-1864 (NCT VIII, 177). He is probably William, age 14, the s. of Thomas and Levina Calvert (Colvard/Calvard/Colvert) (1850 Surry).

COMER, JAMES Q.; CO. I, 28TH REG. CORPORAL (06/29/1829–06/21/1897; Flat Rock Bapt. Ch.).
James Comer, a Yadkin resident, e. there at age 32 on 8-13-1861. Mustered in as private and promoted to corporal on 10-3-1861. Captured at Hanover Court House, VA, on 5-27-1862. Confined at Ft. Monroe, VA, and then Ft. Columbus, NY Harbor. Paroled and trans. to Aiken's Landing, James River, VA, where he was received 7-12-1862 for exchange. Declared exchanged on 8-5-1862. Reduced in rank before 11-1-1862. Reported AWOL Jan.–Feb. 1863. Reported present for duty during Sept.–Dec. 1864. Deserted on 1-11-1865 (NCT VIII, 209). James Q. Comer was a preacher. He and wife, Lucinda (born 2-15-1864, d. 9-23-1918), are both bur. at Flat Rock Baptist.

CONNALLY, JOHN KERR; CO. B, 21ST REG. COLONEL (09/13/1839–01/31/1904; Riverside Cem., Asheville, NC).
John Kerr Connally resided in Little Yadkin Township of Yadkin Co. (Panther Creek), where he e. at age 21. Appointed captain from 5-12-1861. Present until he was defeated for reelection about 4-26-1862. Later served as colonel of the 55th Regiment NC Troops. He was appointed colonel on 5-19-1862. Wounded in left arm and right hip at Gettysburg, PA, on 7-1-1863. Arm amputated. Captured near Cashtown, PA, about 7-5-1863, and hospitalized at Gettysburg. Transferred to hospital at Baltimore, MD, where he arrived 8-5-1863. Transferred to Ft. McHenry, MD, on 10-22-1863, then to Point Lookout, MD, on 1-23-1864. Paroled at Point Lookout on 3-3-1864, and received at City Point, VA, on 3-6-1864 for exchange. Reported in Danville, VA, hospital on June 2–4 through 9-15-1864, still suffering from wounds received at Gettysburg. Reported on duty commanding a brigade of Junior Reserves at Wilmington in Nov. 1864. Resigned on 2-9-1865 as a result of a dispute over his status as a Junior Reserves officer. Resignation accepted on 3-7-1865. Paroled at Richmond, VA, on 4-26-1865 or 5-30-1865. He is mentioned in dispatches for "conspicuous gallantry" at Gettysburg. *Official Records*, series I, XXVII, part II, 637) (NCT VI, 551; VIII, 430). The Rev. A. A. Tyson was quoted in the Asheville *Citizen Times* of Feb. 2(3?), 1904, and he described Connally's actions at Gettysburg: "I was orderly on the first day's fight to Col. Connally and was in charge of his horse when he led the regiment in the charge of Reynolds' brigade posted on the Gettysburg hills. The color-bearers were shot down one after another and Col. Connally himself seized the flag and bore it on. He was shot twice and fell with a shattered arm. I took Col. Connally to the field hospital and when the army returned I volunteered to remain with him." John Kerr Connally was b. in Mt. Pierson, Madison Co., TN, on 9-2-1839, the s. of Thomas D. Connally and Frances Kerr. He was m. to Alice Thomas in 1865. They had three dau.: Mrs. Mary Connally Coxe, Mrs. Thomas P. Cheesborough, and Mrs. Walter Andrews of Washington. After the war, Connally moved to Texas and practiced law. He later returned to VA where he resumed his practice and was elected to the VA State Senate.(Obituary, the Richmond *Times-Dispatch*, Feb. 1, 1904.) (Information from Mr. and Mrs. Lanier Williams, and Confederate Rolls of Prisoners of War, Hospital Registers, other original reports, and obituaries were also consulted.)

CONRAD, AUGUSTINE EUGENE (?01/08/1828–03/27/1917; Lewisville, NC).
Augustine Eugene Conrad, the s. of John Joseph and Keziah Harding Conrad, was privately educated at "Glenwood," the home of Tyre Glenn. He attended Emory and Henry College in VA. Upon graduating, he taught several years in a school on his father's land. He operated a large farm and ran two grist mills and ran Conrad's Ferry. During the Civil War, he served under General P. G. T. Beauregard. His home, "Pilot View" is situated on the Forsyth side of the river, once part of Yadkin Co. He m. first Parmelia A. Shore on 2-27-1851 in Surry Co. They had five ch. He and his second wife, Nannie Moore Roberts, had one child. They were m. in 1889 (O'Daniel and Patton, *Kinfolk of Jacob Conrad*, 96–98; 1850 Surry).

CONRAD, F. S.(SIDNEY FRANCIS); CO. E, 70TH REG. (09/24/1846–08/12/1932 Salem Cem., Forsyth Co., NC).
Sidney Francis Conrad is incorrectly listed as F. S. Conrad. He was the s. of John Joseph and Elizabeth Stauber Conrad. He entered the Confederate Army at age 17 at Camp Vance near Morganton on 5-1-1864. He was captured shortly thereafter in "Kirk's Raid" and with a few others from his company, escaped. He was then sent to guard prisoners at Salisbury. He was elected captain of his company (Ninth Battalion of Junior Reserves), and was sent to Wilmington. They saw action at Ft. Fisher, Kinston, and at Bentonville, the last major battle of the war. Upon returning home after being discharged, he encountered Stoneman's men and "was in their hands twice, but managed to escape, and bushwhacked them into a final farewell shot of twelve buckshots." After the War, Sid entered Wake Forest College and Southern Baptist Seminary at Greenville. S.C. He then began a career as a pastor in Greensboro, N.C., and in other .cities. He helped organize several churches, including Huntsville Baptist in 1883. He m. Isabella Hinton Buchanon in 1876, and they had four ch.: William Broadus, Dallas Kerr, Frederick Sidney, and Elizabeth (O'Daniel and Patton, *Kinfolk of Jacob Conrad*, 339–352; 1850 Surry; Moore's *Roster,* vol. IV, 302; Clark, vol. I, 396).

CONRAD, JAMES DALLAS; CO. F, 28TH REG. (12/20/1844–09/16/1863; Conrad Cem.).
James D. Conrad e. in Yadkin Co. at age 18 on 7-1-1863. Wounded and captured at Gettysburg, PA, between July 1 and July 3, 1863. He d. at Gettysburg on 9-16-1863 of wounds (NCT VIII, 177). He was the s. of John Joseph Conrad and his second wife, Elizabeth Stauber (1810–1900). James Dallas was the brother of Sidney Francis Conrad and the half-brother of Augustine Eugene, John Thomas, and William Alexander Conrad, all of whom served in the Confederate Army (O'Daniel and Patton, *Kinfolk of Jacob Conrad*, 3, 434; 1850 Surry).

CONRAD, JOHN THOMAS; CO. F, 28TH REG. 1ST LIEUTENANT (06/04/1837–05/02/1913; Kimbrough Fam., Forsyth Co., NC).
John Thomas Conrad lived in Yadkin Co. and e. at "Camp Enon" (in Yadkin Co. ?) at age 23 on 8-10-1861. Mustered in as private and promoted to 2nd lieutenant on 9-5-1861. Elected 1st lieutenant on 4-12-1862. Present or accounted for through Dec. 1862. Furloughed home and "remained overtime." He was dropped from the rolls about 4-27-1863 (NCT VIII, 174). John Thomas Conrad was the s. of John Joseph

Conrad and Keziah Harding Conrad (*Heritage*, 325). He m. Sarah Catherine Kimbrough, dau. of Ormon and Sarah Taylor Kimbrough. John Thomas attended Wake Forest College. After enlisting in Co. F., 28th Reg., he received a 7-day leave of absence when his first child was b. in Dec. 1861. His wife attended Salem Female Academy, where she was taught the arts of weaving, sewing and embroidery. During the war she used those skills to make clothing from leather and cow hair. After the war, John Thomas farmed, was a justice of the peace, and was active in the Enon Baptist Church. He and Sallie spent their later years in Florida with their son, Alex E. (O'Daniel and Patton, *Kinfolk of Jacob Conrad*, 166–174; 1850 Surry).

CONRAD, W. AUGUSTUS; CO. B, 21ST REG. CORPORAL (04/01/1842–01/12/1862; Bethania Moravian Cem., Forsyth Co., NC).
William Augustus Conrad, a Yadkin resident, e. there on 5-12-1861. Mustered in as corporal. Present until he d. in a Richmond, VA, hospital 1-12-1862 of "typhoid pneumonia" (NCT VI, 552). William Augustus Conrad was the s. of Isaac Conrad (1807–1805) and wife Antoinette Transou (O'Daniel and Patton, *Kinfolk of Jacob Conrad*, 434, 441).

CONRAD, WILLIAM ALEXANDER; HOME GUARD (12/24/1829–10/16/1864; Lewisville Bapt., Lewisville, NC).
William Alexander Conrad, s. of John Joseph and Keziah Harding Conrad, and brother of Augustine Eugene Conrad, was a member of the Home Guard during the Civil War. William Alexander was killed by some "deserters" who were going west by way of Conrad's Ferry. He tried to head them off, and found them crossing in a small boat. One of them shot him and the wound proved fatal several months later. He was shot in July and d. on 10-16-1864, leaving a young wife and several small ch. The deserters were Union men who had escaped from prison and were on their way to Ohio (O'Daniel and Patton, *Kinfolk of Jacob Conrad*, 131).

COOK, ALVIN; CO. G, 44TH REG. (1841–?).
Alvin Cook e. at Camp Holmes on 10-14-1862. Reported AWOL on 10-20-1862, but returned to duty on 12-1-1863. Present until he trans. to Co. I, 28th Reg. (NCT X, 458). After transferring to Co. I, 28th Reg. on 10-1-1864, Cook was present or accounted for through Feb. 1865 (NCT VIII, 209). Alvin Cook was the s. of Thomas J. and Elizabeth Cook (1850 Surry).

COOK, BURTON; CO. G, 54TH REG. (1842–?).
Burton Cook e. in Wilkes Co. at age 20 on 4-5-1862. He was discharged on 6-4-1862 because of "inability" (NCT XIII, 309). One B. Cook, age 26, was examined on 11-1-1864 at Yadkinville and exempt from service in the Home Guard because of "deformity of right foot" (Bradley, *North Carolina Confederate Home Guard Examinations 1863–1864*, 81). Burton Cook m. Harriet Cook on 2-20-1860 (YCMR).

COOK, COLUMBUS L.; CO. B, 38TH REG. (1825–?).
Columbus L. Cook, b. in Wilkes Co., resided in Yadkin Co., where he was a physician before e. in Yadkin at age 36. Elected captain on 10-16-1861. Resigned on 7-12-1862 because of the "unp[rotected condition" of his family, because he was "over the Conscription age," and because he had been "diseased for some time." Resignation accepted on 7-24-1862 (NCT X, 20).

COOK, HARRISON; CO. D, 44TH REG. (1842–?; ?Swan Creek Bapt.).
Harrison Cook e. at age 20 on 10-17-1862. He deserted on 11-16-1862 (NCT X, 428). Harrison m. Mary Adams on 8-12-1866 (YCMR). She was b. 6-5-1849, d. 7-5-1911, and is bur. at Swan Creek Baptist Church.

COOK, HENRY; CO. D, 44TH REG. (1835–?).
Henry Cook, a Yadkin resident, e. in Wake Co. at age 27 on 10-17-1862. Present through April 1864 (NCT X, 428). Henry Cook m. Susan Shore on 9-12-1858 in Yadkin Co.

COOK, ISOM C.; CO. A, 1ST BAT. SHARPSHOOTERS (12/25/1840–01/07/1910; Town Cem., Yadkinville, NC).
Isam (Isom) C. Cook e. in Wake Co. on 9-4-1862. Wounded near Fredericksburg, VA, on 5-4-1863. Reported absent-wounded through June 1864. Present or accounted for on company rolls through Dec. 1864. Paroled at Appomattox Court House, VA, 4-9-1865 (NCT III, 71). Isom C. Cook m. Sarah E. Suits on 3-3-1867 in Yadkin Co. (bond date). She was b. 6-26-1844, d. 7-24-1933, and was bur. in the Yadkinville Town Cemetery, Yadkinville, NC, also.

COOK, JAMES M.; CO. H, 54TH REG. (1833–?).
James M. Cook, b. in Surry Co., resided in Yadkin Co. where he was a farmer before enlisting at age 29 on 3-17-1862. Reported absent-sick without leave in June 1862. Returned to duty. Wounded near Fredericksburg, VA, about 12-13-1862. Hospitalized at Danville, VA. Returned to duty on 4-10-1863. Reported sick in hospital May–Aug. 1863. Reported AWOL on 9-22-1863. Listed as a deserter on 10-14-1863. Hospitalized at Richmond, VA, on 11-18-1863 with chronic bronchitis. Confined at Castle Thunder Prison, Richmond, VA, on 1-4-1864. Hospitalized at Richmond on 6-16-1864 with an unspecified complaint. Transferred on 6-17-1864. Returned to duty before 10-31-1864. Captured at Ft. Stedman, VA, on 3-25-1865. Confined at Pt. Lookout, MD, on 3-27-1865. Released at Point Lookout on 6-24-1865, after taking the Oath of Allegiance (NCT XIII, 321).

COOK, JOSEPH J.; 75TH REG., 18TH BRIG. MILITIA (01/15/1829–02/21/1909; Buck Shoals Cem.).

Joseph Cook m. Matilda Tulbert (born 12-8-1830, d. 7-27-1895), dau. of James and Elizabeth Howard Tulbert, on 1-32-1853(YCMR). Joseph J. Cook was a blacksmith. He was a captain in the Militia for Buck Shoals Township, and was commissioned 2-8-1862 (Cook, *The Descendants of Claiborne Howard*, 36–40, 50–51).

COOK, ROBERT HENRY; CAPT. WATER'S N.C. VOLUNTEERS (01/14/1833–02/24/1917).
Robert Henry Cook, s. of Lucy Cook, was b. in Franklin Co., NC. He m. Sarah A. Windsor on 10-16-1860 (YCMR). He also served in Co. G, 66th Reg., NC Infantry, and was a member of Company A, Salisbury Prison Guards. He deserted, was captured at Bermuda Hundred, and was taken prisoner. He was then transported to Indiana (Cook, *The Descendants of Isaac Windsor 1753–1821*, 28–29).

COOK, THOMAS J.; CO. G, 54TH REG. MUSICIAN (1822–?).
Thomas J. Cook, b. in Yadkin Co., e. in Wilkes Co. at age 40 as a private on 4-8-1862, as a substitute for Joshua Spicer. He was promoted to musician (drummer) July-Dec. 1862. Present through Feb. 1863, he was hospitalized in Richmond, VA, on 4-25-1863 with chronic rheumatism. He was trans. to a Danville hospital on 5-8-1863, and was discharged from there on 7-1-1863 because of tuberculosis, chronic diarrhea, and old age (NCT XIII, 309). In 1850, Thomas J. Cook was living with wife, Elizabeth and ch.: Martha J. (age 11), Alvin (age 9), Sarah M. (age 2), Mary C. (age 6 months), according to the 1850 Surry Co. census.

COOK, W. P.; CO. H, 54TH REG. (1844–?).
Cook e. in Yadkin Co. on 3-17-1863. Present through Dec. 1863 (NCT XIII, 321). He may be the Pettis Cook, age 23, listed in 1860 (1860 Yadkin). He may be the William P. Cook, b. 1844, who was living in the household of his mother, Rebecca, when the 1850 Surry Co. census was taken.

COOK, WILLIAM; CO. B, 38TH REG. (1844–?).
William Cook, a Yadkin resident, e. at age 18 on 4-12-1862. Wounded at Mechanicsville, VA, on 6-26-1862. Reported absent-sick until 1-18-1864, when he was dropped from the company rolls (NCT X, 23).

COOPER, MARTIN F.; CO. I, 21ST REG. (1836–?).
Martin F. Cooper m. Mary N. Williams on 4-28-1853 in Yadkin Co. He e. in Yadkin Co., age 27, on 12-1-1863. He deserted on 12-5-1863 (NCT VI, 613). In 1850, Martin Cooper was living with parents Martin and Elizabeth Cooper. He was listed in the 1860 Yadkin Co. census, as being 24, and living with wife Mary N., and ch. William E. (age 6), John D. (age 2), Mary S. (age 5/12), and his father Martin Cooper (age 74), his mother Elizabeth (age 68), and his sister Kessiah (age 38). Martin and Mary N. Williams were m. on 4-28-1853 (YCMR; 1850 Surry Division; 1860 Yadkin).

CORAM, JESSE J.; CO. A, 54TH REG. (05/05/1846–09/05/1889; Boonville Cem., Boonville, NC).
Jesse J. Coram was b. in Surry (Yadkin) Co. on 5-5-1846, e. in Yadkin at age 17 on 4-28-1864. Reported present Sept.-Oct. 1864. Hospitalized at Richmond, VA, 3-26-1865, with gunshot wound to left arm. Place and date of wound not reported, but probably at Ft. Stedman, VA, 3-25-1865. Captured in hospital at Richmond on 4-3-1865. Reported still in hospital in Richmond on 5-28-1865. Survived the war and returned to Yadkin Co. (NCT XIII, 251). Jesse Johnson Coram, the s. of Peyton and Mary ("Polly") Johnson Coram, was b. in the Richmond Hill Community near Judge Pearson's Law School (*Heritage*, 326; 1850 Surry). He was never married (*Heritage*, 326).

CORNELIUS, ALVIS E.; CO. F, 28TH REG. (06/12/1841–11/30/1921; Baltimore Meth.).
Alvis E. Cornelius, b. in Forsyth Co., lived in Yadkin Co. where he was a farmer before enlisting there at age 20 on 6-18-1861. Wounded in the ankle and or knee at Cedar Mt., VA, on 8-9-1862. Reported absent-wounded through Dec. 1862. Company records do not indicate whether he returned to duty or not. He was discharged on 8-22-1863 because of disability from wounds (NCT VIII, 177). A. E. Cornelius m. Rachel Steelman on 9-28-1865 (YCMR). Alvis (Alvenius) Cornelius was the s. of William J. and Nancy P. Doub Cornelius. "Alvenius" was a "partial cripple the rest of his life. He was a good farmer and a good citizen" (per William D. Bennet, "Doub Family History," based on research by Olin Doub, who was b. in 1837). His brothers were John Henry and Leonidas.

CORNELIUS, HENRY W. L.; CO. A, 1ST REG.
Henry W. L. Cornelius resided in Yadkin Co. Date of inlistment not given. He appears on a register of rebel deserters and refugees received at Fort Monroe, VA, on 2-17-1864, which states: rebel deserter came into Federal lines, New Bern, North Carolina." He took the Oath of Allegiance at Fort Monroe on 2-24-1864, and was sent to Indianapolis, IN (NCT III, 146).

CORNELIUS, JOHN H[ENRY].; CO. F, 28TH REG. 3RD LIEUTENANT (03/09/1837–?).
John H. Cornelius lived in Yadkin and e. at Camp Enon at age 23 on 8-10-1861. Mustered in as private, promoted to corporal on 10-10-1861. Appointed 3rd lieutenant on 4-12-1862. Wounded in the right thigh and captured at Hanover Court House, VA, on 5-27-1862. Hospitalized at New York City. Transferred to Ft. Delaware, DE, on 8-23-1862. Paroled and trans. to Aiken's Landing, James River, VA, for exchange on 10-2-1862. Exchanged there on 11-10-

1862. Resigned on 3-29-1863 because of wounds received at Hanover Court House (NCT VIII, 174). John Henry Cornelius m. on 2-15-1866 Lucy Cundiff. He was the s. of William J. and Nancy P. Doub Cornelius. John Henry was "one of the first to volunteer for the Civil War. He went through the conflict and came home safe" ("Doub Family History").

CORNELIUS, L. M.; CO. F, 28TH REG. 1ST SERGEANT (1839–11/26/1862).
L. M. Cornelius lived in Yadkin Co. but e. in New Hanover Co. at age 23 on 3-13-1862. Mustered in as private; promoted to 1st sergeant on 4-12-1862. Died in a Staunton, VA, hospital on 11-25-1862 of "febris typhoides" (NCT VIII, 177). Leonidas Cornelius was the s. of William J. and Nancy P. Doub Cornelius, and brother to Alvis and John Henry Cornelius. According to the Olin Doub material, Leonidas Cornelius was "a man of strong mind, and camp life did not suit him" ("Doub Family History").

CORNELIUS, T. R.; CO. E, 70TH REG.
T. R. Cornelius was 4th Sergeant, Co. E, 70th Regiment, Junior Reserves (Moore's Roster, vol. IV, 302).

CORNELIUS, W. D.; CO. B, 21ST REG.
W. D. Cornelius e. in Yadkin Co. on 5-12-1861. Present until he trans. to Co. A, 1st Battalion, NC Sharpshooter on 4-26-1862 (NCT III, 146). Reported as "absent-wounded in General Hospital, Goldsboro, NC," Jan.-Feb. 1864. Present or accounted for on rolls through Dec. 1864 (NCT III, 71; VI, 552). W. D. Cornelius m. Rosannah L. Arey 9-19-1865 (YCMR).

COUCH, ELIJAH M.; CO. B, 21ST REG. (04/14/1841–06/28/1912; Zion Bapt., Iredell Co., NC).
Elijah M. Couch e. in Yadkin Co. on 5-12-1861. Present through Oct. 1861 (NCT VI, 551).

COWLES, ANDREW CARSON; 75TH REG., 18TH BRIG. MILITIA (01/12/1833–01/05/1881; Flat Rock Bapt.).
Andrew Carson Cowles was the s. of Josiah Cowles (from Connecticut) and his second wife, Mrs. Nancy Duvall, a widow, also from Connecticut. Andrew m. Margaret Reynolds of Iredell Co. (Rutledge, 21).

COWLES, HENRY C.; 75TH REG., 18TH BRIG. MILITIA (06/17/1842–?; Statesville, NC).
Henry Clay Cowles, the s. of Josiah and Nancy Caroline Carson Duvall Cowles, of Hamptonville, served in the Militia. After the war he became Clerk of the United States Court for the Western District of North Carolina, a post he held for 43 years. He d. in Statesville, and may be bur. there (Rutledge, 21).

COWLES, MILES MELMOTH; CO. B, 21ST REG. ADJUTANT (04/16/1835–07/09/1862; Flat Rock Bapt.).
Miles M. Cowles lived in Yadkin Co. at Hamptonville, where he e. at age 26. Appointed 1st lieutenant from May 12, 1861. Present until he resigned 9-9-1861. Reason for resignation not reported. He later served as adjutant of the 38th Regiment, NC Troops (NCT VI, 551). Before the war he had been a lawyer. He was wounded and in the Seven Days' Battles around Richmond and d. 10 days after being wounded (Rutledge, 21).

COWLES, WILLIAM H. H.; CO. A, 9TH REG. (1ST CAVALRY) MAJOR (04/22/1840–12/03/1901; Presbyterian Church Cemetery, Wilkesboro, NC).
William H. H. Cowles e. at age 21 on 5-16-1861. He was promoted to captain on 3-1-1862, then major in Oct. 1863, then trans. to Field and Staff of the Regiment (NCT II, 7,10). William Henry Harrison Cowles was the s. of Josiah and Nancy Carson Duvall Cowles. He was b. at Hamptonville, NC. W. H. H. Cowles was "nearly six feel tall, and had brown hair, large blue eyes and fair complexion." He was twice wounded during the war, once through the body and again on the head. He was taken prisoner into Petersburg, paroled and sent home, since it was near the end of the war. After the war, he studied law with Judge Pearson at "Richmond Hill" and was licensed at Wilkesboro. He bought the former Hamilton Brown house, just east of the courthouse, and his office stood in the front yard of the home on Main Street. He was reading clerk of the N.C. Senate 1872-73 and 1873-74. He was solicitor of the 10th Judicial District 1874–1878; United States Congressman (Democrat) from March 4, 1885 to March 3, 1893. He m. first Miss Rosamond Corinna (Cora) Worth of Ashe Co. After her death, he m. a Miss Mary Lura Bost of Catawba Co. There were 11 ch. from the two marriages (*Heritage of Wilkes Co.*, Wilkes Genealogical Society, 1982, 166–167; Rutledge, p. 21).

COX, JAMES; CO. A, 1ST BAT. SHARPSHOOTERS.
James Cox e. "at camp in Virginia" on 11-1-1863. Deserted on 12-26-1863, but returned on 9-25-1864. Reported as "absent, in Pioneer Corps" Aug. 31–Dec. 31, 1864 (NCT III, 71).

COZART, JOHN C.; CO. B, 38TH REG. (1836–06/26/1862).
John C. Cozart (Cozort) lived in Yadkin Co. where he e. at age 26 on 6-1-1862. Killed at Mechanicsville, VA, on 6-26-1862 (NCT X, 23). John Cozart m. Mary E. Peacock on 11-26-1857 (YCMR). He may be the John Cosort, age 13, listed in the 1850 Surry Co. Census as being a s. of William and Mary Cosort.

CRAFT, THOMAS C.; CO. I, 6TH REG. (1834–06/30/1863).

Thomas C. Craft e. in Yadkin Co. at age 28 on 9-15-1862. He d. in Forsyth Co. on 6-30-1863 of "fever" (NCT IV, 371).

CRANFIELD, THOMAS; 75TH REG., 18TH BRIG. MILITIA.
Thomas M. Cranfill m. Lidia Danner on 10-10-1858 (YCMR).

CRATER, RUFUS W.; CO. D, 63RD REG. (5TH CAVALRY) (06/13/1836–05/08/1926; Zion Bapt., Iredell Co., NC).
R. W. Crater e. in Guilford Co. on 7-13-1862, and was present through Oct. 1864 (NCT II, 397). Rufus Weisner Crater, the s. of Jacob and Sarah Weisner Crater, m. Mary Ann Mabry on 12-24-1857, then Martha Louise Myers, b. 11-20-1835, Iredell Co., d. 4-12-1922, Iredell Co., on 3-21-1867 (YCMR). Children were Jacob Lee, who was Yadkin Co. Register of Deeds and Clerk of Court for many years; Parthania, Martha Ellen, and William Andrew Crater (Cook, *Descendants of Isaac Windsor*, 39; *Heritage*, 407). R. W. Crater testified his address was Gwyn Post Office, Yadkin Co., NC., in 1902, and that he had served in Co. D, 63rd Reg., and that he knew John A. Vanhoy who was "a Confederate soldier, having seen him on duty in the service, but that he does not recollect the Co. & Reg. he served in."

CREEDMORE (CREEKMORE), CALEB; CO. B, 38TH REG. (1834–?).
Caleb Creedmore, a Yadkin resident, e. at age 26 on 10-16-1861. Present until he deserted 8-6-1862. Reported present but under arrest Jan.-Feb. 1863. Reported AWOL 8-11-1863, but returned to duty Nov.-Dec. 1863. Wounded near Spotsylvania Court House, VA, 5-21-1864. Reported absent-wounded through Aug. 1864. Reported AWOL 9-18-1864 (NCT X, 23). Creekmore survived the war, and was show on the YCMR as Caleb "Crickmore" who m. Sarah Holliman on 9-10-1865 (YCMR). He was the s. of Nicholas (d. before 1850) and Elizabeth Hinshaw Creekmore.

CREEKMORE, JOSEPHUS; CO. B, 38TH REG. (1843–05/31/1926; Elmwood Cem., Charlotte, NC).
Josephus C. Creekmore e. in Yadkin Co. on 4-19-1862. Present until he trans. to Co. H, 54th Reg., on 11-2-1862. After being trans. he was reported present through Aug. 1863. Reported AWOL about 9-1-1863, but returned to duty Nov.-Dec. 1863, and survived the war (NCT X, 23; XIII, 321). Josephus (Joseph) Creekmore was the s. of Nicholas and Elizabeth Hinshaw. He m. Sarah Jane Brown on 2-24-1865 in Wilkes Co., N.C. (information from Mary Arnold Creedmore, Statesville, NC).

CRESON, SAMUEL D.; CO. F, 28TH REG. CORP. (04/02/1836–04/19/1918; Yamhill Co., Oregon).
Samuel D. Creson e. at Camp Fisher at age 23 on 9-18-1861. Mustered in as private, promoted to corporal Jan.-June 1862. Wounded at Gettysburg, PA, July 1–3, 1863. He deserted to the enemy on 9-10-1863, and took the Oath of Allegiance at Knoxville, TN, on 10-5-1864 (NCT VIII, 177). Samuel D. Creson was the s. of Charles and Elizabeth Rash Creson. He m. Nancy Adaline Hutchens (born 3-20-1850, d. 12-11-1894, dau. of Thompson and Sarah Caroline Phillips Hutchens). They had 7 ch. The oldest, John T., was b. 6-26-1869 in Hardin Co., Iowa, where Samuel moved after the war (Townsend, *Hutchins/Hutchens*, 252, 417; 1850 Surry).

CREWS, EPHRAIM W.; CO. A, 1ST BAT. SHARPSHOOTERS.
E. W. Crews e. "at camp in Virginia" on 1-7-1864. Present through Dec. 1864. Paroled at Appomattox Court House, VA, on 4-9-1865 (NCT III, 71).

CREWS, MATHEW JOHN; CO. B, 21ST REG.
M. J. Crews e. in Yadkin Co. on 5-12-1861. Present until he trans. to Co. A, 1st Battalion, NC Sharpshooters on 4-26-1861. Present in Co. A, 1st Battalion Sharpshooters through Dec. 1864 when he was reported AWOL (NCT III, 71–72; VI, 552).

CREWS, W. A.; CO. B, 21ST REG.
W. A. Crews e. in Yadkin Co. on 5-12-1861. Present until he trans. to Co. A 1st Battalion, NC Sharpshooters, on 4-16-1861. Present through Dec. 1864 (NCT III, 72; VI, 552).

CRUTCHFIELD, ENOCH W.; CO. I, 39TH REG., GEORGIA CSA (1838–11/08/1894).
Enoch W. Crutchfield was the s. of Ira and Mary Reece Crutchfield, b. in Surry (Yadkin) Co. He moved to Gilmer Co., GA, and m. about 1860/1861. Muster rolls for March-April 1864 show him absent-sick and in a hospital since 2-22-1864. Pension records indicate he contracted kidney and lung disease from measles and was disabled for further service.

CRUTCHFIELD, MARTIN A.; CO. I, 39TH REG., GA CSA 1ST SERGEANT (1833/4–06/20/1864).
Martin A. Crutchfield, the s. of Ira and Mary Reece Crutchfield and brother of Enoch W. Crutchfield, was b. 1833/34. The family moved to Giles Co., GA, about 1848. He m. there on 6-20-1864 to Catherine __. He was captured at Vicksburg, MS, on 7-4-1863, and paroled there on 7-8-1863. He was appointed 1st Sergeant in March 1864 and was killed at Powder Springs, GA, on 6-20-1864. Crutchfield is sometimes spelled "Scritchfield" or "Critchfield."

CUMBY, WILEY; CO. D, 21ST REG. (1843–10/19/1864).
Cumby, a Yadkin Co. resident, e. in Forsyth Co. at age 40 on 9-20-1863. He was present until killed at Cedar Creek, VA, on 10-18-1864 (NCT VI, 567). He m. Elizabeth A. Phillips on 4-8-1858 (YCMR).

**CUMMINGS (CUMMINS), WARREN W.;
CO. B, 38TH REG.**
Warren W. Cummings/Cummins/Commins lived in Yadkin Co. where he e. at age 23 on 10-16-1861. Present until he was detached for hospital duty at Richmond, VA, about 12-25-1862. Reported on duty as a nurse or as a guard in the hospital at Richmond through August 1864. Rejoined his company in Sept.-Oct. 1864. NC pension records indicate he was wounded at Gaine's Mill, VA, on 10-16-1862, and was wounded again at an unspecified locality on 6-15-1863 (NCT X, 23).

**CUZZENS, BLOOM S.; CO. F, 28TH REG.
(1836–?).**
Bloom S. Cuzzens lived in Yadkin Co. where he e. at age 25 on 6-22-1861. Deserted about 6-30-1862 (NCT VIII, 177).

**CUZZENS, LEMUEL; CO. F, 28TH REG.
(1839–07/18/1862).**
Lemuel Cuzzens, a Yadkin resident, e. there at age 22 on 6-18-1861. He d. in a Richmond, VA, hospital about 7-18-1862 of "typhoid fever" (NCT VIII, 177).

**DANNER, FRANCIS; 75TH REG., 18TH
BRIG. MILITIA (01/04/1833–11/21/1909;
Courtney Bapt.).**
Francis Danner's wife, Rebecca E. (born 4-2-1842, d. 2-18-1825) is bur. at Courtney Bapt. Church.

**DANNER, G. M.; CO. F, 28TH REG. (?–06/27/
1862).**
G. M. Danner e. in Yadkin Co. on 4-24-1862. He was killed at Gaine's Mill, VA, on 6-27-1862 (NCT VIII, 177).

**DANNER, JOSHUA G.; CO. I, 28TH REG
(1843–07/04/1863).**
Joshua G. Danner lived in Yadkin Co. where he e. at age 19 on 3-18-1862. Wounded at Gettysburg, PA, about 7-3-1863. Died on 7-4-1863 of wounds (NCT VIII, 210).

**DAVIS, ABNER; CO. D, 9TH REG. (1ST CAV-
ALRY) (1823–?).**
Abner Davis e. in Buncombe Co. on 10-14-1863. He was wounded Nov-Dec. 1864. Furloughed from a hospital in Raleigh for 60 days on 1-9-1865 (NCT II, 38). Abner Davis, age 27, is listed in the Jacob and Lucy Davis household in the Boonville area, occupation was a clerk (1850 Surry).

**DAVIS, ALVIS TOBIAS; CO. H, 63RD REG.
(5TH CAVALRY) (06/26/1844–06/30/1890;
Eaton's Bapt., Davie Co., NC).**
He e. in the cavalry at Huntsville at age 17 on 7-15-1862. He was present through Feb. 1865. The only time he was wounded was when he cut his chin on his own sword while crossing a stream and was hospitalized in General Hospital 9, at Richmond, VA, for 18 days (NCT II, 432). Alvis Tobias Davis was the s. of Thomas and Anna Malinda Speas Davis.

He m. Margaret Elizabeth Martin on 11-8-1866, the dau. of Henry P. and Elizabeth Hauser Martin of East Bend (Family Group Sheet, YCHGSJ X [March 1991]: 20). Alvis and wife moved to Davie Co. where they reared 7 ch. (*Heritage*, 335; Casstevens and Bradford, "The Ancestors and Descendants of William Paul Speas, Sr.," 1991, unpublished manuscript).

**DAVIS, DANIEL; CO. F, 28TH REG. (1836–05/
27/1862).**
Daniel Davis e. in Yadkin Co. at age 25 on 6-18-1861. He was killed at Hanover Court House, VA, on 5-27-1862 (NCT VIII, 177).

**DAVIS, DANIEL V.; CO. H, 54TH REG. SER-
GEANT (03/02/1842–11/25/1921; Fork Bapt.,
Davie Co., NC).**
Daniel V. Davis, a Yadkin farmer, e. at age 20 in Yadkin Co. on 3-17-1862. Mustered in as private, and promoted to corporal July-Dec. 1862. Reported present through April 1863. Wounded slightly in right arm near Fredericksburg, VA, 5-4-1863. Returned to duty before 9-1-1863. Promoted to sergeant 10-15-1863. Captured at Rappahannock Station, VA, 11-7-1863. Confined at Point Lookout, MD, 11-11-1863. Paroled at Point Lookout on 3-16-1864, and received at City Point, VA, on 3-20-1864 for exchange. Returned to duty and wounded again in the shoulder at Stephenson's Depot, VA, 7-20-1864. Hospitalized at Winchester, VA. Transferred to a Richmond, VA, hospital on 8-1-1864. Furloughed for 60 days on 8-7-1864. He returned to duty before 10-31-1864. He was captured again at Hatcher's Run, VA, on 2-6-1865, and confined again at Point Lookout on 2-9-1865, until released on 6-11-1865, after taking the Oath of Allegiance (NCT XIII, 321).

**DAVIS, HENRY A.; CO. B, 38TH REG. (1834–
03/28/1865; Rowan Co., NC).**
Henry A. Davis lived in Yadkin Co. where he e. at age 28 on 4-19-1862. Reported AWOL on 8-18-1862. Returned to duty Jan.-Feb 1863 and deserted on 6-15-1863. Returned to duty 9-27-1863. Present until captured at Spotsylvania Court House, VA, on 5-21-1864. Confined at Point Lookout, MD, on 5-30-1864. Paroled about 3-17-1865. Received at Boulware's Wharf, James River, VA, on 3-19-1865 for exchange. Hospitalized at Salisbury, NC, where he d. on 3-28-1865 of "diarrhoea chronic" (NCT X, 23). Henry A. Davis (age 25) m. Mary McBride (age 22) on 1-3-1861 (YCMR).

**DAVIS, HORACE; CO. F, 42ND REG.
(1835–?).**
Horace Davis e. at Petersburg, VA, on 11-17-1862. Present through Oct. 1864. He was 44 years old in 1864 (NCT X, 252). He is probably the Horace Davis, listed as age 15, living with his parents, Samuel L. and Nancy Davis, in the 1850 Census (1850 Surry).

DAVIS, J. A.; CO. B, 21ST REG.
J. A. Davis e. in Yadkin Co. on 5-12-1861. Present through Oct. 1861 (NCT VI, 552).

DAVIS, JAMES; 75TH REG., 18TH BRIG. MILITIA.

DAVIS, JESSE; CO. F, 28TH REG.
Jesse Davis lived in Yadkin where he e. on 11-5-1863. He was captured in a Richmond, VA, hospital on 4-3-1865. Transferred to Newport News, VA, on 4-23-1865, where he was released on 6-30-1865, after taking the Oath of Allegiance (NCT VIII, 177).

DAVIS, LUCKETT C.; CO. B, 38TH REG CORP. (1835–07/06/1912; Dixon Cem.).
Luckett C. Davis, a Yadkin Co. resident, e. at age 26 on 10-16-1861. Mustered in as corporal. Reduced to ranks before 4-1-1862. Present until wounded in left leg at Chancellorsville, VA, about 5-3-1863. Reported absent-wounded or absent-sick until 1-31-1864, when he was discharged because of disability (NCT X, 23–24). He was probably the s. of Thomas C. and Nancy Davis, and was 15 years old when the 1850 Census was taken (1850 Surry). If so, he m. Jane Dixon on 1-13-1855 (YCMR). Jane d. 12-7-1915, age 87 years, and is bur. beside him in the Dixon Cemetery, on Speer Bridge Road.

DAVIS, MARTIN; CO. A, 1ST BAT. SHARPSHOOTERS.
Martin Davis e. in Lenoir Co. on 7-21-1864. He was present through Dec. 1864, and paroled at Appomattox Court House, VA, on 4-9-1865 (NCT III, 72). Martin Davis' widow Lucy applied for a Confederate widow's pension on 3-27-1904 from Boone Co., Arkansas. In support of her claim, M. L. Woodhouse, a member of the pension board, testified in a letter to "Any Pension Board" that Lucy Davis was the widow of Martin Davis, and was living in Arkansas (copy of her pension application and the letter from the pension board courtesy of Frederick DeBow Fulkerson, 9211 E. 38th Street, Tulsa, Oklahoma 74145).

DAVIS, ROBERT J.; CO. ?, 23RD. REG. (1837–?).
Robert J. Davis lived in Yadkin Co. His date and place of enlistment was not reported. He was either captured or deserted, and took the Oath of Allegiance in Louisville, KY, on 6-15-1864. No further information regarding his service record (NCT VII, 244). According to the census, Robert J. Davis was in the household of Daniel (age 71), and Mary Davis (age 59) (1850 Surry).

DAVIS, SAMPSON; CO. G, 38TH REG.
Sampson Davis lived in Yadkin Co. before enlisting at Camp Holmes on 7-30-1864. He deserted to the enemy about 2-5-1865, and was confined in prison at Washington, DC, on 2-13-1865. He was released later after taking the Oath of Allegiance (NCT X, 71).

DAVIS, SAMUEL A.; CO. G, 4TH REG. (1828–?).
Samuel A. Davis e. at age 34 on 6-5-1861. Present through Aug. 1864 (NCT IV, 78).

DAVIS, SAMUEL L.; CO. I, 28TH REG. (11/02/1837–06/02/1897; Center Meth. Ch.).
Samuel L. Davis was b. in Mecklenburg Co., but resided in Yadkin Co., where he was a farmer before enlisting in Yadkin Co. at age 23 on 9-3-1861. Discharged 2-3-1862 because of "chronic rheumatism of the lower extremities" (NCT VIII, 210). Samuel L. Davis, was the s. of Joshua and Jane Davis. He m. Rebecca M. Hobson on 12-25-1892 (YCMR) (per Groce).

DAVIS, THOMAS; CO. D, 21ST REG. (1830–?).
Thomas Davis, a Yadkin Co. farmer, e. at age 43 on 9-20-1863. He was captured at Fisher's Hill, VA, on 9-22-1864, and confined at Point Lookout, MD. He was paroled and trans. to Boulware's Wharf, James River, VA, on 1-21-1865 for exchange. He was hospitalized at Richmond, VA, that day with chronic diarrhoea, and was furloughed on 1-26-1865 (NCT VI, 567). Thomas Davis m. Anna Malinda Speas. They had a number of ch. (1850 Surry). One, Alvis T. Davis, also served in the CSA.

DAVIS, THOMAS J.; 75TH REG., 18TH BRIG. MILITIA.
T. J. Davis m. Lucinda Reece on 12-24-1865 (YCMR).

DAVIS, THOMAS L.; CO. A, 21ST REG.
Thomas L. Davis e. in Yadkin Co. on 10-1-1863. Present until he deserted on 12-8-1864 (NCT VI, 543).

DAVIS, THOMAS W.; CO. F, 28TH REG. (1816–?).
Thomas W. Davis, a Yadkin Co. farmer, e. there at age 45 on 6-18-1861. He was discharged on 11-7-1861 because of an "ulcer upon the sole of the foot which had been in a state of ulceration for the last five months and interferes with the use of his foot" (NCT VIII, 177). Thomas W. Davis m. Minerva Butner on 4-29-1855 (YCMR).

DAVIS, WILLIAM A.; CO. I, 28TH REG.
William A. Davis, according to company records, reported e. at Camp Holmes on 8-20-1862. He was not on the rolls for Sept.–Oct. 1864, but was present through Feb. 1865 (NCT VIII, 210).

DAY, JOHN A.; CO. H, 54TH REG. (09/11/1840–02/08/1914).
John A. Day e. in Yadkin Co. age 21 on 3-17-1862. Reported present in June 1862. Wounded at Fredericksburg, VA, 12-13-1862. Hospitalized at Richmond, VA. Returned to duty on 1-10-1863. Deserted near Staunton, VA, 6-28-1863. Returned to duty on August 28, 1863. Captured at Rappahannock

Station, VA, 11-7-1863. Confined at Point Lookout, MD, 11-11-1863. Released from there on 1-23-1864, after taking the Oath of Allegiance and joining the U.S. Army. Assigned to Co. C, 1st Reg. U.S. Volunteer Infantry (NCT XIII, 321). John A. Day was b. ca. 1841, and is listed in the household of his parents, Samuel and Jane Day in the 1850 Surry census. His father Samuel was a miller.

DEGISNO (DEZERN), JESSE FRANKLIN; 75TH REG., 18TH BRIG. MILITIA (01/06/1828–04/28/1917; Douglas Cem.).
Jesse Franklin Dezern m. Telitha J. (5/1/1836–10/1/1897), both bur. in Douglas Cemetery (Hoots, 377). His name is incorrectly spelled in the records. Jesse is the s. of Ephraim Frank and Phebe Fearrington Dezern ("Poindexter," 139) He is bur. in the Douglas Cemetery where his brother, Joseph Francis (born 1-7-188, d. 4-3-1917) and Joseph's wife are bur. ("Poindexter," 139).

DENNY (DENNIE), C. W.; CO. B, 42ND REG. (1842–?; ?St. Paul's Meth. Ch.).
C. W. Dennie (Denny) resided in Yadkin Co., but e. at Petersburg, VA, on 10-16-1862. Deserted in May 1863. He went over to the enemy on an unspecified date. Confined at Knoxville, TN, on 7-31-1864. Transferred to Chattanooga, TN, on 8-2-1864. Confined at Louisville, KY, on 8-9-1864. He was released at Louisville about 8-16-1864, after taking the Oath of Allegiance (NCT X, 209). C. W. Dennie (Calvin Denny) is probably the s. of James and Elizabeth Denny.

DENNY, EMMITT; CO. B, 21ST REG. SERGEANT (03/25/1836–08/10/1913; St. Paul's Meth. Ch.).
Emmitt Denny e. in Yadkin Co. on 5-12-1861. Present until he trans. to Co. A, 1st Battalion, NC Sharpshooter on 4-26-1861. Promoted from corporal to sergeant in May 1863. Wounded near Fredericksburg, VA, on 5-4-1863. Present on company rolls through Dec. 1864. Denny was wounded slightly in the hand near Fredericksburg, VA, on 5-4-1863 (NCT III, 72, 678; VI, 552).

DENNY, JAMES; CO. A, 1ST BAT. SHARPSHOOTERS (ca. 1827–?).
James Denny e. on 2-15-1864. Present on company rolls through Dec. 1864 (NCT III, 72). He was s. of Stephen and Susannah Denny. James m. Mary Johnson, dau. of Reuben and Catharine Johnson on 10-19-1852 in Iredell Co. James Denny d. in McDowell Co., NC (Cook, *Descendants of Isaac Windsor*, 6).

DENNY, MARTIN; CO. B, 38TH REG. (02/09/1847–12/02/1917; St. Paul's Meth. Ch.).
Pension records indicate he served in this company (NCT X, 24). Martin Denny, s. of Stephen and Susan Denny, m. Catherine Windsor, dau. of S. B. and Sarah Windsor, on 10-15-1871 (YCMR). Catherine Windsor Denney (born 2-28-1842, d. 12-27-1934) is also bur. at St. Paul's Methodist Church, near Windsor's Crossroads.

DENNY, PINKNEY C(ALDWELL).; CO. B, 38TH REG. (ca. 1830–02/06/1862).
Pinkney C. Denny was a Yadkin Co. carpenter before enlisting at age 30 on 10-16-1861. Died at Camp Mangum near Raleigh, NC, about 2-6-1862 of disease (NCT X, 24). Pinkney Caldwell Denny, s. of ___ and Jane Denny, m. Esther Ann Johnson on 8-27-1858 in Yadkin Co. They were the parents of Martha Jane Denny, b. May 1858 in Davie Co., NC (information from Barbara DeHart, 29918 SE Davis Rd., Estacada, OR 97023-9704, submitted on pedigree chart to the Yadkin County Historical & Genealogical Society, published in YCHGSJ XI [June 1992]: 22; 1850 Surry).

DENNY, URIAH; CO. A, 26TH REG. (1826–?).
Uriah Denny, a Yadkin resident, e. in Ashe Co. at age 35 on 5-17-1861. He was present until he was wounded in the right leg at Gettysburg. There he was captured between July 1 and 3, 1863. He was hospitalized at Gettysburg. He was paroled March-June 1864. Reported absent on parole through June of 1864 (NCT VII, 471). Uriah C. Denny was the s. of Edmund and Sarah Denny (1850 Surry).

DICKENSON (DICKERSON), ISAAC D.; CO. I, 28TH REG. (1838–?).
Isaac D. Dickenson (Dickerson) lived in Yadkin Co. where he e. at age 23 on 8-13-1861. He was captured at Hanover Court House, VA, 5-27-1862, and confined at Ft. Monroe, VA. He was then trans. to Ft. Columbus, NY Harbor. Paroled and trans. to Aiken's Landing, James River, VA, where he was received on 7-12-1862 for exchange. Exchanged on 8-5-1862. Returned to duty before 11-1-1862. Wounded at Chancellorsville, VA, May 2–3, 1863. Detailed as a shoemaker at Richmond, VA, in Feb. 1864. Reported "absent on detail" at Richmond through Feb. 1865 (NCT VIII, 210).

DICKERSON, ALPHONSO; CO. A, 9TH REG. (1ST CAVALRY) CORPORAL (1828–?).
Alphonso Dickerson e. at age 22 on 5-24-1861. He deserted before being mustered in and never arrested (NCT II, 13). Later, he was conscripted and assigned to Co. G, 2nd Bat. NC Infantry. He e. in this company in Forsyth Co. at age 30 on 2-15-1863 as a private. Appointed corporal on 3-23-1863, but deserted on 4-26-1863 (NCT III, 322). Alfonso Dickerson, age 22, and wife, Lucinda, age 26 (1850 Surry).

DICKERSON, DAVID A.; CO. I, 28TH REG. (?–01/24/1865).
David A. Dickerson, a Yadkin resident, e. at age 23 on 3-8-1862. Captured on an unspecified date and paroled and trans. to Aiken's Landing, James River, VA, where he was received for exchange on 9-21-1862. Returned to duty before 11-1-1862. Reported present Sept.-Dec. 1864. Hospitalized at Richmond, VA, 1-10-1865 with "diarrhoea" and d. on 1-24-1865 (NCT VIII, 210).

DICKERSON, JAMES; CO. A, 9TH BAT. HOME GUARD.
James Dickerson, age 37 in 1850, was a miller. He was living with wife Catherine, and ch.: Elizabeth A., David A., Isaac D., Lucinda J., and William J. when the census was taken (1850 Surry).

DICKSON, HENRY; CO. I, 28TH REG.
Henry Dickson (Dixon) e. at Petersburg, VA, on 9-22-1864. Reported AWOL on 12-15-1864 (NCT VIII, 210). Henry Dixon (Dickson) m. Elizabeth Jane Williams (born 1-10-1827, d. 7-25-1867). She is bur. in the Lynch Cemetery.

DINGLER, MILUS M.; CO. H, 4TH REG. (1833–12/13/1862).
Milus M. Dingler lived in Yadkin Co. but e. in Iredell Co. at age 28 on 6-13-1861. Killed in battle near Fredericksburg, VA, on 12-13-1862 (NCT IV, 87).

DINKINS, CHAPMAN; CO. B, 38TH REG. (1826–?).
Chapman Dinkins e. at age 35 in Yadkin Co. Present until he deserted on 9-17-1862. Reported present but under arrest Nov.-Dec. 1862. Returned to duty Jan.-Feb. 1863. Deserted again on 6-24-1863. Took Oath of Allegiance at Bermuda Hundred, VA, about 10-13-1864 (NCT X, 24). Chapman Dinkins m. Lydia Jane Bovender on 9-4-1846 in Surry Co. She was the dau. of John and Rachel Brown Bovender. They had at least two ch.: Amanda E., b. 1847, d. before 1860, and Mary A., b. 1849.

DINKINS, JOHN A.; CO. B, 38TH REG. (?–1908).
Dinkins e. at Camp Holmes on 7-4-1864, and deserted 8-8-1864. He went over to the enemy on 10-13-1864. He was released on an unspecified date at Bermuda Hundred after taking the Oath of Allegiance (NCT X, 24). John Dinkins began drawing a Confederate Veterans' pension in 1905, but was dropped from the rolls by 1908, because he was deceased.

DINKINS, LEROY; CO. B, 38TH REG. (01/16/1835–03/09/1911; Dinkins Cem.).
Leroy Dinkins e. at Camp Holmes near Raleigh on 7-6-1864. Present through Oct. 1864 (NCT X, 24). Leroy Dinkins m. Biddy Hutchens on 4-2-1861 (YCMR). Biddy Hutchens Dinkins (born 5-20-1840, d. 4-12-1904) is bur. in the Dinkins Cemetery near Shacktown.

DINKINS, MILLS; CO. B, 38TH REG.
Mills Dinkins e. at Camp Vance on 9-27-1864. Present through Oct. 1864 (NCT X, 24). Mills Dinkins m. Mary Fortner on 3-10-1861 (YCMR).

DINKINS, THOMAS; CO. B, 38TH REG. (1826–?).
Thomas Dinkins, a Yadkin resident, e. there at age 36 on 4-19-1862. Deserted on 8-6-1862. Returned to duty Jan.-Feb. 1863. Nominated for the Badge of Distinction for gallantry at Chancellorsville, VA, on May 1–4, 1863. Captured near Gettysburg, PA, about 7-5-1863. Confined at Ft. Delaware, DE, about 7-7-1863. Transferred to Point Lookout, MD, Oct. 15–18, 1863. Paroled there about 11-1-1864, and trans. to Venus Point, Savannah River, GA, where he was received on 11-15-1864 for exchange (NCT X, 24).

DIXON, GILES; CO. A, 1ST BAT. SHARPSHOOTERS (1832–?).
Giles Dixon e. "at camp in Virginia" on 11-1-1863. Present until he deserted on 3-1-1864. He undoubtedly returned to duty, and deserted again on 10-1-1864. Dropped from company rolls 2-28-1865 (NCT III, 72). Giles, b. ca. 1832, was the s. of John and Mary Dixon (1850 Surry).

DIXON, JOHN; CO. C, 26TH REG. (1839–?).
John Dixon lived in Yadkin Co., but e. at Camp Holmes at age 23 on 10-17-1862. Present until wounded at Gettysburg, PA, on 7-3-1863. Returned to duty Nov.-Dec. 1863. Present until captured near Spotsylvania Court House, VA, on 5-12-1864, and confined at Point Lookout, MD, then trans. to Elmira, NY, on 8-8-1864. Paroled there on 2-9-1865 and trans. to Cox's Wharf, VA, where he was received about 2-20-1865 for exchange (NCT VII, 497).

DIXON, WILLIAM S.; CO. F, 28TH REG. (1844–?).
William S. Dixon, a Yadkin Co. resident, e. in Alamance Co. at age 18 on 10-1-1862. He was wounded at Gettysburg, PA, on 7-1-1863. He returned to duty and was present through Feb. 1865 (NCT VIII, 177).

DOBBIN (DOBBINS), L. S.; CO. B, 21ST REG.
L. S. Dobbins e. in Yadkin Co. on 5-12-1861. Present through Oct. 1861 (NCT VI, 552).

DOBBINS, JAMES; CO. I, 28TH REG. (1842–05/27/1863).
James Dobbins e. at age 20 on 9-20-1862. Died in Richmond, VA, hospital on 5-27-1863 of "fever" (NCT VIII, 210).

DOBBINS, JOHN; CO. H, 10TH REG. (1ST REG. ARTILLERY) (1845–03/05/65).
John Dobbins e. in Wayne Co. on 2-10-1863. He deserted on 6-16-1863, but returned to duty on 11-1-1863. He was courtmartialed and sentenced to be shot, but his sentence was reduced and he was imprisoned instead at Salisbury, NC, where he d. of pneumonia on 3-5-1865 (NCT I, 129). John Dobbins may be the s. of Pleasant and Elizabeth Dobbins (1850 Surry).

DOBBINS, L. B.; CO. B, 21ST REG.
L. B. Dobbins e. in Yadkin Co. on 5-12-1861. Present until he trans. to Co. A, 1st Battalion, NC Sharpshooters, on 4-16-1861. Reported missing in action at the Battle of Second Manassas, VA, on 8-28-1862.

Declared exchanged at Richmond, VA, on 9-19-1862. Present or accounted for on company rolls through Dec. 1864 (NCT III, 72; VI, 552).

DOBBINS, LEVI; CO. I, 28TH REG. (1840/41–?).
Levi Dobbins, a Yadkin Co. farmer, e. at age 20 on 3-8-1862. Captured near Winchester, VA, about 12-3-1862. Paroled at Winchester on 12-4-1862. Discharged on 5-1-1863 because of gunshot wounds of left arm and right hip, date and place of wound not reported (NCT VIII, 210). Levi Dobbins, age 9, was listed in the household of his parents, Joel and Sarah Dobbins (1850 Surry).

DOBBINS, MILAS; CO. I, 28TH REG. (1842–?).
Milas Dobbins lived in Yadkin Co., where he e. at age 19 on 8-13-1861. Captured at Hanover Court House, VA, on 5-27-1862. Confined at Ft. Monroe, VA, then Ft. Columbus, NY Harbor. Paroled and trans. to Aiken's Landing, James River, VA, where he was received on 7-12-1862 for exchange. Exchanged there on 8-5-1862. Deserted in October 1862 (NCT VIII, 210). This may be Miles Dobbins, age 7, listed with his parents, Pleasant and Elizabeth Dobbins (1850 Surry).

DOBBINS, WILLIAM; CO. I, 28TH REG. (1843–?).
William Dobbins e. at age 19 on 3-8-1862. Captured near Pickett's Farm, VA, about 7-21-1864. Confined at Point Lookout, MD. Paroled and trans. to Boulware's Wharf, James River, VA, where he was received on 3-16-1865 for exchange (NCT VIII, 210).

DONATHAN, ELIJAH; CO. B, 38TH REG. (1818–?).
Elijah Donathan e. in Yadkin Co. at age 44 on 4-21-1862 as a substitute. He deserted on 8-6-1862, but returned to duty Jan.-Feb. 1863. Reported under arrest from 4-22-1863 through Oct. 1863. Returned to duty Nov.-Dec., but deserted again on 4-11-1864 (NCT X, 24).

DONATHAN, JACOB; CO. B, 38TH REG. (1846–?).
Jacob Donathan e. in Yadkin Co. at age 16 on 4-21-1862 as a substitute. He deserted on 8-6-1862, but returned to duty Jan.-Feb. 1863. Reported under arrest from 4-22-1863 through Oct. 1863. Returned to duty Nov.-Dec. 1863, then deserted again on 4-11-1864 (NCT X, 24).

DONATHAN, JOHN; CO. F, 28TH REG. (1845–?).
John Donathan e. at age 17 on 4-1-1862. He was wounded in the left hand at Wilderness, VA, on 5-5-1864. Returned to duty on an unspecified date. Hospitalized at Richmond, VA, on 10-2-1864 with a gunshot wound of left side. Place and date of wound not reported. He was captured in a Richmond hospital on 4-3-1865, and confined at Newport News, VA, on 4-24-1865. He was released on 6-16-1865, after taking the Oath of Allegiance (NCT VIII, 177).

DONATHAN, LEWIS; CO. F, 28TH REG. (1843–09/03/1862).
Lewis Donathan resided in Yadkin Co. where he e. at age 18 on 6-18-1861. Wounded at Cedar Mountain, VA, on 8-9-1862, he d. in a Staunton, VA, hospital on 9-3-1862 of wounds (NCT VIII, 177).

DONATHAN, WILLIAM; CO. F, 28TH REG. (1811–09/26/1862).
William Donathan lived in Yadkin Co. where he e. at age 50 on 6-18-1861. Wounded in the knee and feet at Ox Hill, VA, on 9-1-1862. He was hospitalized at Charlottesville, VA, where he d. on 9-26-1862 of "erysipelas" (NCT VIII, 177).

DOSS, FRANCIS M.; CO. A, 21ST REG. (1844–09/13/1861).
Francis M. Doss, a Yadkin resident, e. in Davidson Co. at age 17 on 5-18-1861. Present until he d. near Thoroughfare, VA, on 9-13-1861 of "typhoid fever" (NCT VI, 543).

DOUGLAS, ANDERSON; CO. F, 28TH REG. (07/22/1848–05/04/1919; Yadkinville Town Cem.).
Anderson Douglas e. in Yadkin Co. on 10-27-1863. He was wounded in the right arm at Ream's Station, VA, on 8-25-1864, and his arm was amputated. He was reported absent-wounded on 5-28-1865. Anderson returned to Yadkin Co., and received a Confederate veterans pension for a number of years. Anderson was the s. of John and Elizabeth Douglas. He m. Martha Lucretia Mackie, dau. of R. W. and Sarah Mackie, on 5-30-1880 (YCMR).

DOUGLAS, JOHN HENRY; 75TH REG., 18TH BRIG. MILITIA (08/29/1839–07/29/1903; Douglas Cem.).
John Henry Douglas was the s. of Andrew and Rebecca Kerr Poindexter Douglas. He m. Sallie A. Hall (Hoots; "Poindexter," 139). Another John Douglas was the brother of Anderson and Sanford, and the s. of John and Jane Douglas of near Yadkinville.

DOZIER, NATHAN C.; CO. I, 28TH REG. (1843–?; Ashland, Oregon).
Nathan C. Dozier, a Yadkin resident, s. of Dr. Nathan Bright Dozier and Olive Vestal Dozier, of Booville, e. in New Hanover Co. at age 18 on 10-1-1861. He was captured, paroled and trans. to Aiken's Landing, James River, VA, where he was received on 9-7-1862 for exchange. Exchanged there on 9-21-1862. Returned to duty before 11-1-1862. Wounded at Gettysburg, PA, July 1–3, 1863. Returned to duty. Wounded again in the right foot at Jericho Mills, VA, on 5-23-1864. Reported absent-wounded Nov.-Dec. 1864. Retired to the Invalid Corps on 2-18-1865, because of disability (NCT VIII, 210). His brother, Smith W. Dozier served in the same company (1860 Yadkin; *Heritage*, 357).

DOZIER, SMITH W.; CO. I, 28TH REG. CORPORAL
Smith W. Dozier, s. of Dr. Nathan Bright and Olive Vestal Dozier, and brother of Nathan C. Dozier, e. at age 19 on 8-13-1861. He mustered in as private. Captured at Hanover Court House, VA, on 5-27-1862. Confined at Ft. Monroe, VA, then Ft. Columbus, NY Harbor. Paroled and trans. to Aiken's Landing, James River, VA, for exchange. Exchanged there on 8-5-1862. Promoted to corporal on 8-29-1862. Returned to duty before 11-1-1862. Transferred to the C.S. Navy on 4-3-1864 (NCT VIII, 210).

DRAPER, JESSE; CO. I, 28TH REG. (1838–07/04/1862).
Jesse Draper, a Yadkin resident, e. there at age 23 on 8-13-1861. Died in Richmond, VA, hospital on 7-4-1862 of "typhoid fever" (NCT VIII, 210). Jesse Draper m. Sarah J. Shaw on 6-26-1857 (YCMR).

DUDLEY, JAMES; CO. C, 26TH REG. (08/31/1836–03/17/1919; Wilson-Hauser Cem.).
James Dudley had previously lived in Yadkin Co. with the John F. Felts family where he worked as a laborer. He may be the s. of Charles Dudley, listed as a "shoemaker" and living in the part of Surry Co. that is now Yadkin. By 1860, he was living in Wilkes Co. where he e. at age 28 on 6-12-1861. Present until wounded at Gettysburg, PA, 7-1-1863. Returned to duty prior to 1-1-1864. Present until captured on the South Side Railroad near Petersburg, VA, on 4-2-1865, and confined at Hart's Island, NY Harbor, until released about 6-19-1865, after taking the Oath of Allegiance (NCT VII, 497). After the war, he m. a Yadkin Co. girl and settled in Yadkin Co. James Dudley m. Mary Shore on 10-22-1866 (YCMR; 1850 Surry).

DULL, A. N.; CO. I, 28TH REG. (1838–07/27/1862).
A. N. Dull, a Yadkin Co. resident, e. there at age 24 on 3-8-1862. Killed near Gaines' Mill, VA, about 6-27-1862.

DULL, GEORGE E.; CO. B, 21ST REG. (Forsyth Co., NC).
George E. Dull e. in Yadkin Co. on 5-12-1861. Present until he trans. to Co. A, 1st Battalion, NC Sharpshooter. Deserted on 8-17-1862 (NCT III, 72; VI, 552). George E. Dull m. Emily H. Hauser on 12-24-1865 (YCMR).

DURHAM, T. L.; CO. B, 44TH REG. (?–05/14/1864).
T. L. Durham, a Yadkin Co. resident, e. there at age 28 on 11-18-1862. He deserted on 2-9-1863. He is reported to have d. in a Staunton, VA, hospital on 5-14-1864 of a gunshot wound. Place, date, circumstances of wound not reported (NCT X, 412).

DUVALL, ROBERT C.; C. S. NAVY (11/15/1819–02/04/1863; Flat Rock Bapt.).
Capt. Robert C. Duvall was the stepson of Josiah Cowles of Hamptonville. He was among the first officers commissioned to serve in the North Carolina navy (D. H. Hill, Jr., *From Bethel To Sharpsburg*, Vol. 1, p. 158, Raleigh, NC, 1926). Duvall commanded a ship in the North Carolina Confederate Navy during the War. He had previously been in the U.S. Navy. He d. in Raleigh on 2-4-1863 of an "incurable" disease. Duvall's ship was an 85-ton iron-propeller vessel called the *Beaufort* (Yadkinville, N.C., *Yadkin Ripple*, 11-15-1984, by Charles Mathis, "Noted Commander Lies at Flat Rock"; Salem, N.C., *People's Press*, May 24, 1861, p. 1).

EDDLEMAN, HORACE; CO. B, 38TH REG. SERGEANT (1837–?).
Horace Eddleman e. in Yadkin Co. at age 24 on 10-16-1861. Mustered in as private, and promoted to corporal on 7-29-1862. Present until he deserted on 9-17-1862. Reduced to ranks in Nov.1862–Feb. 1863. Returned to duty Jan.-Feb. 1863, and promoted to Sergeant on 10-4-1863. Present through Oct. 1864 (NCT X, 24). (See Letter, Appendix A.)

EDDLEMAN, THOMAS W.; CO. B, 38TH REG. (1844–?).
Thomas W. Eddleman lived in Yadkin where he e. at age 19 on 9-24-1863. Present through Oct. 1864 (NCT X, 24). He was the s. of Peter and Rebecca Eddleman and m. Sarah A. Eller, dau. of Abraham and Elizabeth Eller, on 6-28-1869 (YCMR).

ELLER, HENRY P.; CO. I, 28TH REG. (1843–?).
Henry P. Eller, a Yadkin Co. farmer, e. there at age 18 on 8-13-1861. Captured at Hanover Court House, VA, about 5-27-1862, and confined at Ft. Monroe, VA, before being trans. to Ft. Columbus, NY Harbor. Paroled and trans. to Aiken's Landing, James River, VA, for exchange, where he was received on 7-12-1862. Exchanged on 8-5-1862, and returned to duty before 11-1-1862. Captured near Gettysburg, PA, 7-3-1863. Confined at Ft. Delaware, DE, then trans. to Point Lookout, MD, in Oct. 1863. Released from there on 1-25-1864, after taking the Oath of Allegiance and joining the U.S. Army. He was assigned to Co. G, 1st Reg. U.S. Volunteer Infantry (NCT VIII, 211).

ESTEP, SOL; CO. A, 9TH BAT. HOME GUARD

EVANS, DENSON; CO. D, 44TH REG. (1839/40–02/25/1863).
Denson Evans e. in Wake Co. at age 24 on 10-17-1862. He was present or accounted for until he d. in a hospital at Weldon, NC, on 2-25-1863 of "lumbar abscess" (NCT X 429). Denson Evans, age 10, was living with his parents, Stephen and Margaret Evens (1850 Surry).

EVANS, FRANKLIN; CO. D, 44TH REG. (03/13/1840–09/06/1920; Shady Grove Bapt.).
Franklin Evans e. at age 21 on 10-17-1862. He deserted

on 11-12-1862 (NCT X, 429). Franklin Evans was b. in Knobs Township, 3-13-1840, and was killed 9-6-1920 by being run over by a freight train in Elkin, NC. He was a licensed government "still" operator for many years. He m. Eliza Roberson, b. 4-3-1841, d. 1-16-1919, on 9-28-1865 (YCMR). They were the parents of 7 ch.: Manuel Wilson, William Reeves, Ada Safronia, Wesley Monroe, Franklin Winfield, Preston, and Emily O'Tilly Evans (*Heritage*, 359-360). Franklin is probably the s. of Stephen and Margaret Evens (Evans) (1850 Surry).

EVANS, IREDELL C.; CO. I, 28TH REG. (1843-?).
Iredell Evans lived in Yadkin Co. where he e. at age 18 on 8-13-1861. Present through Feb. 1865 (NCT VIII, 211). Iredell C. Evans, b. ca. 1842, was the s. of Thomas and Sally Evans. Iredell m. Lucy Coram on 9-9-1866 (YCMR; 1850 Surry).

EVERAGE (EVERIDGE), JOSEPH; CO. I, 28TH REG. (1834-?).
James Everage lived in Yadkin Co. where he e. at age 27 on 8-13-1861. Captured at Hanover Court House, VA, on 5-27-1862, and confined at Ft. Monroe, VA, then Ft. Columbus, NY Harbor. Paroled and trans. to Aiken's Landing, James River, VA, where he was received on 7-12-1862 for exchange. Declared exchanged there on 8-5-1862. Returned to duty and was wounded at Chancellorsville, VA, on 5-2/3-1863. Deserted on 7-15-1863. Hospitalized at Richmond, VA, on 5-18-1865 with a gunshot wound of the right leg. Place and date of wound not reported. Returned to duty before 11-1-1864. Present through Feb. 1865. Hospitalized again at Richmond on 3-10-1865 with gunshot wound of right leg. Place and date not reported. Captured in hospital at Richmond on 4-3-1865. Transferred to Newport News, VA, on 4-23-1865. Released on 6-30-1865 after taking the Oath of Allegiance (NCT VIII, 211).

EVERIDGE, JAMES; CO. A, 9TH BAT. HOME GUARD (05/16/1819-03/16/1897; Cook Fam. Cem.).
James Everidge, the s. of Richard and Elizabeth Benge Everidge, married Sarah M. Denny on 6-14-1875 (YCMR). She was the dau. of Steven and Elizabeth Windsor Denny. James also m. Mary Drusilla Windsor, b. ca. 1832, d. ca. 1886, dau. of James Riley Windsor and Nancy A. Bell Windsor, on 6-7-1885 (YCMR). James was m. three times, name of third wife has not been located as yet (Cook, *The Descendants of Isaac Windsor*, 9, 23).

FAIT (TATE?), R. C.; CO. E, 70TH REG.

FARRINGTON, NATHAN HAYNES; CO. I, 28TH REG. (1840-?; Denton Co., TX).
Nathan Haynes Farrington was a Yadkin Co. farmer before enlisting there at age 22 on 3-8-1862. Discharged on 7-18-1862 because of "scrotal hernia of the left side" (NCT VIII, 211). Nathan Haynes Farrington, the s. of William S. and Keturah Haynes Farrington, m. Rachel Carolyn Gross, b. 7-5-1836, the dau. of Henry and Lucy S. Swaim Groce. Nathan and Caroline Farrington moved to Denton Co., TX in 1890. Their ch. were: Martha Jane, George Washington, William Starbuck, Evan Jones, Lucy Kitura, Ida Cora, Oliver Cromwell, Caleb Scott, Deborah Victoria, Docia Novelle, and John Claiborne (Information from Margaret Farrington Jagmin, Dallas, Texas, published in YCHGSJ IX [Dec. 1990]: p. 10; *Heritage*, p. 361; Wellborn, *Simon Groce*, p. 5).

FARRINGTON, WILLIAM CLAIBORNE; CO. B, 38TH REG. (?-01/03/1923; Columbia, SC?).
William C. Farrington e. at Camp Holmes near Raleigh on 7-10-1864. Deserted on 7-12-1864 (NCT X, 24). He was b. about 1846, the s. of William Starbuck and Keturah Haynes Farrington. William C. Farrington m. on 5-14-1860 (YCMR) Priscilla Swaim (*Heritage*, 361).

FARRINGTON, WILLIAM S.; CO. A, 1ST BAT. SHARPSHOOTERS
William S. Farrington e. in Wake Co. on 9-4-1862. Present through Dec. 1864 (NCT III, 72).

FARRIS, ARCHIBALD; CO. A, 1ST BAT. SHARPSHOOTERS
Archibald Farris was paroled at Appomattox Court House, VA, on 4-9-1865 (NCT III, 72).

FARRIS, COOLY D.; 75TH REG., 18TH BRIG. MILITIA

FARRIS, ENOCH H.; CO. I, 28TH REG. (1843-05/05/1864).
Enoch H. Farris, a Yadkin native, e. there at age 18 on 8-13-1861. Captured at Hanover Court House, VA, about 5-27-1862, and confined at Ft. Wool, VA. Paroled from there and trans. to Aiken's Landing, James River, VA, where he was received on 8-26-1862 for exchange. Exchanged there on 11-10-1862. Returned to duty. Hospitalized at Danville, VA, on 1-1-1863 with gunshot wound, place and date not reported. Returned to duty on 1-17-1863. Killed near Wilderness, VA, on 5-5-1864 (NCT VIII, 211).

FARRIS, JOSEPH; CO. I, 28TH REG. (1842-?).
Joseph Farris, a Yadkin resident, e. there at age 19 on 8-13-1861. Wounded at Sharpsburg, MD, on 9-17-1862. Died of wounds, date and place of death not reported (NCT VIII, 211).

FARRIS, PRESTON T.; CO. I, 28TH REG. (1845-?).
Preston T. Farris resided in Yadkin, but e. at Liberty Mills, VA, at age 18 on 9-8-1863. Captured at Spotsylvania Court House, VA, on 5-12-1864, and confined at Point Lookout, MD. Transferred to Elmira, NY, on 8-10-1864 and held there until released on 7-11-1865, after taking the Oath of Allegiance (NCT VIII, 211).

FARRIS, WILLIAM D.; CO. I, 28TH REG. SERGEANT (1829–06/27/1862).
William D. Farris e. in Yadkin Co. at age 33 on 8-13-1861. Mustered in as corporal. Promoted to sergeant before 12-31-1861. Killed at Gaine's Mill, VA, about 6-27-1862 (NCT VIII, 211). He m. Seleana E. Jenkins on 3-14-1862 (YCMR).

FAULKNER, THOMAS; CO. B, 21ST REG. (1835–?).
Thomas Faulkner e. in Yadkin Co. on 5-12-1861. Present until wounded at Sharpsburg, MD, on 9-17-1862 (NCT VI, 552). He is probably the Thomas Forkner listed as age 15 in the James and Sarah Forkner household (1850 Surry).

FAULKNER/FORKNER, JAMES; CO. B, 44TH REG. (1837–?).
James Faulkner (Forkner) e. at age 26 on 11-28-1863. He was present through 11-28-1863, then was listed as AWOL. He was wounded near Racoon Ford or at Richmond in June 1863 or on 6-10-1864, per pension application (NCT X, 413; Yadkin Co. Pension Records)). He is probably the s. of James Forkner and wife Sarah, b. 1829 (see 1850 Surry). Thomas Forkner, age 15 was also in the household, a brother.

FELTS, JAMES E.; CO. B, 38TH REG. 3RD LIEUTENANT (1837–?).
James E. Felts was a Yadkin farmer before enlisting at age 24 on 10-16-1861. Mustered in as corporal and elected 3rd lieutenant about 8-2-1862. Present until wounded at the Battle of Second Manassas, VA, on Aug. 29-30, 1862. "Dropped" from company rolls on 1-6-1863, reason not reported (NCT X, 21). James E. Felts, b. 1836, was the s. of Willie and Matilda Felts (1850 Surry).

FELTS, WILLIAM H.; CO. B, 38TH REG. (1842–07/04/1862).
William H. Felts e. in Yadkin Co. at age 21 on 10-16-1861. Wounded at Mechanicsvile, VA, on 6-26-1862. D. at Richmond, VA, on 7-4-1862 of wounds received (NCT X, 24).

FLEMING, J. C.; CO. A, 9TH BAT. HOME GUARD (1837–1904; East Bend Bapt., East Bend, NC).
This might be John C. Fleming, s. of David J. and Eliza S. Fleming, b. 1837, of the Hamptonville area, instead, and a brother to Samuel Franklin Fleming. If so, the date of death is wrong.

FLEMING, JOHN W.; CO. F, 28TH REG. CORPORAL (12/25/1844–10/16/1925; East Bend Bapt. Ch.).
John W. Fleming served in this company, according to pension records (NCT VIII, 177). He is probably the John W. Fleming, age 5, listed in the household of parents Sampson and Joanna Tull Fleming (1850 Surry).

FLEMING, M. R.; CO. H, 10TH REG. (1ST ARTILLERY).
M. R. Fleming e. in Yadkin Co. on 2-26-1863. Present or accounted for through Feb. 1865 (NCT I, 129).

FLEMING, SAMUEL FRANKLIN; CO. H, 63RD REG. (5TH CAVALRY) SERGEANT (04/03/1835–09/03/1923; Nicholson Family Cem., Iredell Co., NC).
S. F. Fleming e. in Davie Co. at age 27 on 7-9-1862. Mustered in as sergeant. Wounded and captured at Middleburg, VA, on 6-17-1863, and exchanged on 6-30-1863. Wounded at Ground Squirrel Church, VA, on 5-11-1864, and again on the Weldon Railroad on 8-21-1864. Present or accounted for through Feb. 1865 (NCT II, 432). According to his obituary, Samuel Franklin Fleming, a member of J.E.B.Stuart's Confederate Cavalry, was wounded five times and also sustained a deep sabre cut across the head and forehead (Clark, *Histories of the Several Regiments*, Vol. III, 601) in the fighting around Todd's Tavern in 1864. He carried two bullets to his grave: one lodged just above his eye, which he received at Petersburg, VA, and the other in his foot, which he received in the fighting at Five Forks, VA (at Middleburg, according to Clark, *Histories*, Vol. III, 586). He had two horses shot out from under him at Petersburg. Samuel Franklin Fleming was the s. of David and Eliza S. Nicholson Fleming, dau. of John Nicholson. He was one of nine ch. Samuel Franklin m. on 3-30-1858 Phoebe Ellen Brunt. They had a dau., Lelah Cordelia, who was b. before Samuel left for the war. After the war, he returned home and fathered six more ch.: William Franklin, Mary Bettie, Anna Eliza, Araminta Jane, Thomas Jefferson and Leonidas Calvin. After his wife d., Samuel m. second on 3-11-1896 Mary S. Hauser, dau. of John Nicholson, who d. in 1901. He m. again on 10-5-1904. There were no ch. by the last two marriages. He d. at age 88 near Hamptonville, NC (*Heritage*, 363; NCT II, 432; obituary, 9-4-1823).

FLEMING, WINSTON; 75TH REG., 18TH BRIG. MILITIA (05/20/1822–12/03/1896; Mt. Pleasant Meth. Ch.).
Winston Fleming m. Mary Ann Williams, dau. of Jesse and Ruth Martin Williams on 10-10-1844. They had 12 ch. He served as a captain of the Home Guard during the Civil War, commissioned on 3-10-1862, for the Fall Creek area (*Heritage*, 365; Townsend, *Hutchins/Hutchens*, Vol. II, 276).

FLETCHER, JOHN F.; CO. F, 28TH REG. (1843–?).
John F. Fletcher was a Yadkin Co. shoemaker before enlisting there at age 18 on 6-18-1861. He mustered in as corporal, but was discharged on 3-12-1862 because of an "inguinal hernia of the left side" (NCT VIII, 177). John Fletcher, age 6, was listed in the household of his parents A. E. and Lucinda Fletcher in the 1850 census. A. E. Fletcher's occupation was "shoemaker" (1850 Surry).

FLINN (FLYNN), JESSE F.; CO. F, 28TH REG. (1840–?).
Jesse Flinn lived in Yadkin Co. and e. at Camp Enon at age 21 on 6-18-1861. He deserted on 4-4-1863 (NCT VIII, 178).

FLINN, RILEY; CO. G, 42ND REG. (1832–?).
Riley Flinn lived in Yadkin Co. but e. at Petersburg, VA, on 11-6-1862. He was 30 years old. Riley was present through Oct. 1864. He was hospitalized at Greensboro, NC, in March of 1865, with an unspecified illness or injury (NCT X, 261).

FLINN (FLYNN), WILLIAM C.; CO. F, 28TH REG. (1840–?).
William C. Flinn, a Yadkin Co. farmer, e. there at age 22 on 4-27-1862. He was discharged on 7-21-1862 because of a "chronic cough" and debility (NCT VIII, 178). William C. Flinn, age 18, is listed as living in the household of Catherine Flin, age 38 (1850 Surry).

FORTNER, ALEXANDER; CO. F, 28TH REG. (1840–07/03/1863).
Alexander Fortner lived in Yadkin Co. where he e. at age 21 on 6-18-1861. He was hospitalized at Charlottesville, VA on 9-12-1862, with gunshot wound, place and date of wound not stated. He returned to duty about 11-1-1862. He was killed at Gettysburg, PA, on 7-3-1863 (NCT VIII, 178).

FORTNER, PATRICK H.; CO. A, 21ST REG. (1830–1895; Crab Creek Bapt., Alleghany Co., NC).
Patrick H. Fortner, a Yadkin resident, e. on 10-1-1863. Present until captured near Ft. Stedman, VA, on 3-25-1865. Confined at Point Lookout, MD, until released on 6-26-1865, after taking the Oath of Allegiance (NCT VI, 544).

FRASIER, LEANDER; CO. I, 28TH REG. (1839–12/20/1862).
Leander Frasier e. in Yadkin Co. at age 22 on 8-13-1861. Died in a Richmond, VA, hospital about 12-20-1862 of "pneumonia typhoides" (NCT VIII, 211).

FRAZIER, ALFRED; CO. B, 38TH REG. (1834–01/20/1863).
Alfred Frazier e. at age 27 on 10-16-1861. Present until wounded at Shepherdstown, WV, on 9-20-1862. Died on 1-20-1863, place and cause not reported. He is listed in the household of Susannah Frasier, age 58, in 1850 (1850 Surry).

FREEMAN, JESSE; CO. I, 28TH REG.
Jesse Freeman e. in Yadkin Co. where he resided on 8-13-1861. Deserted on 9-21-1861 (NCT VIII, 211).

FREEMAN, JOHN W.; CO. F, 28TH REG. (1844–09/05/1862).
John W. Freeman, a Yadkin resident, e. there at age 17 on 6-18-1861. He d. in a Richmond, VA, hospital on 9-5-1862 of "febris typhoides" (NCT VIII, 178).

FREEMAN, WILLIAM; CO. C, 4TH REG. (1813–05/13/1864).
William Freeman, a Yadkin resident, e. in Iredell Co. at age 48 on 6-7-1861. He was reported AWOL from 11-28-1862 until 4-11-1863. Reported absent-sick on 4-12-1863 through 10-31-1863. Rejoined his company in Nov.-Dec. 1863. He was killed at Spotsylvania Court House, VA, on 5-13-1864 (NCT IV, 39).

GABARD, RICHMOND MURPHY; 75TH REG., 18TH BRIG. MILITIA (01/26/1826–12/11/1915; Yadkinville Town Cem.).
Richmond Murphy Gabard (whose name is generally misspelled as "Richard") had moved to Yadkin Co. from Davie Co. He was living in Yadkin in 1860, age 34. He m. Malinda C. Hawkins (born 4-30-1829, d. 8-21-1891). Both are bur. in the Yadkinville Town Cemetery. Gabard was one of the members of the Militia present at the shootout at the Bond School in Feb. 1863.

GARNER, FRANCIS ARMSTEAD; CO. B, 38TH REG. (08/12/1834–01/03/1926; Courtney Bapt., Yadkin Co. NC).
Francis A. Garner lived in Yadkin Co. where he e. at age 24 on 2-15-1863. Wounded at Chancellorsville, VA, on 5-3-1863. Returned to duty prior to July 1, 1863, when he was reported missing at Gettysburg, PA. Reported AWOL through Feb. 1864. Returned to duty March-Apr. 1864. Captured at the Wilderness, VA, on May 5-6, 1864, and confined at Point Lookout, MD, 5-17-1864. Transferred to Elmira, NY, on 8-10-1864. Released at Elmira on 6-16-1865, after taking the Oath of Allegiance (NCT X, 24). He was the s. of John and Amy Stanley Garner, and the brother of William Washington Garner (per Edith Garner Sharpless). Francis A. Garner m. Mary J. May, dau. of Henry and Jane May, on 4-6-1871 (YCMR).

GARNER, WILLIAM WASHINGTON; CO.B, 38TH REG. (02/11/1833–10/03/1883; Courtney Bapt. Yadkin Co., NC).
William W. Garner e. at Camp Vance on 3-4-1864, and deserted on 4-11-1864 (NCT X, 24). William Washington Garner, brother of Francis A. Garner, was the s. of John and Amy Stanley Garner. William W. Garner m. Martha Reavis on 12-2-1858. She d. in January 1863, leaving 3 small ch. After Martha d., William W. Garner m. second Phobe (Frances?) Adams on 1-15-1868, dau. of Daniel and Martha Adams (YCMR; and Sharpless).

GENTRY, ALFRED D.; 75TH REG., 18TH BRIG. MILITIA (10/10/1836–01/09/1923; Asbury Meth.).
A. D. Gentry m. Martha E. Stokes on 7-28-1859. An "Alford" D. Gentry m. Martha Poenix on 1-10-1864 (YCMR), probably the same person. Alfred Gentry, age 14, is living with his parents, Gardner and Susannah Gentry in 1850 (1850 Surry).

GENTRY, FRANCIS LEE; CO. G, 44TH REG.
(06/14/1840–04/12/1917; Flat Rock Bapt.).
F. L. Gentry e. at Camp Holmes at age 25 on 11-28-1862. Present until he deserted on 6-9-1863 (NCT X, 459). NC Pension records indicate that he also served in Co. I, 28th Reg. (NCT VIII, 211). Francis Lee Gentry was the s. of William and Lucy Myers Gentry. He m. first Sarah T. ("Tempy") Caisey (Casey) on 6-7-1865 (YCMR), dau. of Jesse M. and Margaret C. Windsor Casey. He was m. 3 times, and all his wives were sisters. His second wife was Robena Elizabeth Casey (m. 4-8-1877); third wife was Margaret Jerusha Casey (m. 10-10-1878), dau. of Jesse M. and Margaret Windsor Casey (Groce; Cook, *Descendants of Isaac Windsor*, 17–18).

GENTRY, JOHN W.; CO B. 38TH REG.
John W. Gentry e. at Camp Vance on 3-4-1864. Deserted on 4-11-1864 (NCT X, 24). J. W. Gentry m. Emeline West on 6-3-1866 (date of bond, YCMR).

GENTRY, ROBERT W.; CO. I, 28TH REG.
Robert W. Gentry e. in Yadkin Co. on 8-13-1861. Present through Feb. 1863 (NCT VIII, 211). He may really be the same as William R. Gentry listed below.

GENTRY, WILLIAM R.; CO. I, 28TH REG.
(06/01/1835–1922; Center Meth.).
William R. Gentry e. in Yadkin Co. at age 26 on 8-13-1861. Mustered in as sergeant but was reduced to ranks Nov. 1861–Oct. 1862. Reported AWOL from 9-27-1864 through Feb. 1865 (NCT VIII, 211). William R.(Robert?) Gentry was the s. of William and Lucy Myers Gentry and the brother of Francis Lee Gentry. He m. Sarah Reinhardt Branon (per Nina Long Groce).

GINNINGS, JAMES A. *see* Jennings, James A.

GODFREY, JOSEPH N.; CO. I, 18TH REG.
(1842–?).
Joseph N. Godfrey e. on 9-10-1862 at age 18. Present until he deserted on 7-20-1863. Returned to duty on 11-1-1863. Present until wounded near the Wilderness, VA, on 5-5-1864. Reported absent-wounded through June 1864 (NCT VI, 405). He was the s. of James and Martha Godfrey (1850 Surry).

GODFREY, STEPHEN A.; CO. I, 18TH REG.
(1836–?).
Stephen A. Godfrey e. in Wake Co. at age 25 on 9-10-1862. Present until wounded in the neck at Fredericksburg, VA, on 12-13-1862. Returned to duty March-Apr. 1863, and was present until he deserted on 7-1-1863. Returned to duty on 11-1-1863, and was present until captured on the Petersburg-Weldon Railroad on 6-22-1864. Confined at Point Lookout, MD, until paroled and trans. to Boulware's Wharf, James River, VA, where he was received 3-16-1865 for exchange (NCT VI, 405). Stephen was the s. of James and Martha Godfrey and the brother of Joseph N. Godfrey, of the same company.

GODFREY, THOMAS N[EWTON].; CO. D, 63RD REG. (5TH CAVALRY) (08/19/1831–12/28/1914; Zion Bapt., Iredell Co., NC).
T. N. Godfrey e. in Guilford Co. on 7-18-1862. Present through Dec. 1863. Admitted to a hospital in Richmond, VA, on 12-20-1863 with "lumbago" and "typhoid fever." Furloughed on 2-10-1864. Detailed as hospital steward at Raleigh on 9-5-1864 (NCT II, 398). Thomas N. Godfrey, s. of James and Martha (Shannon?) Godfrey, m. Sarah Ann Jackson on 12-20-1853 (YCMR). His second wife was Meekly Ann L. Johnson widow of Jacob D. Johnson. Thomas began drawing a Confederate Veterans' Pension in 1905 (*Heritage*, 442; Martin).

GORDEN, M.; CO. A, 21ST REG.
M. Gorden e. in Yadkin Co. on 10-7-1863. Present until he deserted on 8-8-1864 (NCT VI, 544).

GOUGH, JOHN; CO. H, 63RD REG.(5TH CAVALRY) (08/26/1844–09/11/1888; Deep Creek Bapt.).
John Gough (incorrectly listed as "Gaugh" in NCT) e. in Company H, 63rd Regiment, NC Cavalry on 7-30-1862. The company was known as "Capt. William E. Booe's Partisan Rangers, NC Volunteers. The company was organized on 7-8-1862, and the men e. at Farmington and Mocksville, both in Davie Co. John was captured at Hagerstown, MD, on 7-12-1863 and confined at Point Lookout, MD until paroled and exchanged at City Point, VA. on 3-20-1864. He was reported as a deserter on the July-Aug. Muster roll (NCT II, 433). John Gough was the s. of William H. and Christina Shore Gough. He m. Jane "Jennie" Shore on 12-3-1865 (YCMR). She was b. 10-9-1843, d. 11-5-1916. Both are bur. at Deep Creek Baptist Church Cemetery, Yadkin Co. They were the parents of 7 ch. (per Alice Brumfield).

GOUGH, JOHN E.; 75TH REG., 18TH BRIG. MILITIA (10/11/1822–10/13/1888; Sandy Springs Bapt., Iredell Co., NC).
John E. Gough, the s. of Thomas and Rachel Williams Gough, m. on 12-25-1844 in Surry Co., Sarah Mackie, b. 6-5-1823, d. 12-25-1886, dau. of William and Elizabeth Mackie. They had 11 ch. Originally from the South Deep Creek section of the Co., John E. moved to Hamptonville where he worked as a hatter (*Heritage*, 374).

GOUGH, MARTIN FRANKLIN; CO. F, 28TH REG. (05/15/1844–01/12/1930; Boonville Bapt., Boonville, NC).
Martin Franklin Gough e. in Yadkin Co. at age 17 on 6-18-1861. He was wounded at Gettysburg, PA, July 1–3, 1863. Returned to duty and was present through Feb. 1865 (NCT VIII, 178). A chapter of the Daughters of the Confederacy is named for him.

GOUGH, SAMUEL; 75TH REG., 18TH BRIG. MILITIA

H. YADKIN MEN IN THE MILITARY, 1861–1865

GRANT, WILLIAM H.; CO. A, 9TH REG. (1ST CAVALRY) (1845–?).
William H. Grant e. at age 18 on 12-1-1862. He was captured at Gettysburg, PA, on 7-3-1863, and confined at Ft. Delaware, DE, then Point Lookout, MD. Paroled on 5-8-1864, and exchanged at Aiken's Landing, VA. Present or accounted for through Dec. 1864 (NCT II, 14). He is probably the s. of James S. and Jane Grant. His father is listed as a "manufacturer of cotton" (1850 Surry), in the Hamptonville area. The cotton mill is believed to have been at Buck Shoals, and was destroyed during Stoneman's Raid, in 1865.

GRAY, C. L.; CO. E, 70TH REG.

GREEN, RICHARD G.; CO. D, 5TH BAT. CAVALRY (1828–?).
Richard G. Green, a Yadkin Co. teacher, e. in Campbell Co., TN, on 7-25-1863. He trans. from Co. D, 5th Battalion NC Cavalry, on 8-3-1863 to Co. B, 65th Reg. (6th NC Cavalry). He was captured near Jacksboro, TN, on 8-27-1863 and confined at Camp Chase, OH, then trans. to Rock Island, IL, on 1-22-1864. There he joined the U.S. Army and mustered into Co. I, 3rd Reg., U.S. Volunteer Infantry on 10-31-1864 (NCT II, 361, 466). Richard Green, age 22, was living with his parents James and Mary Green (1850 Surry).

GREEN, SOLOMON; CO. H, 10TH REG. (1ST ARTILLERY) (1833–?).
Solomon Green e. in Wayne Co. on 2-10-1863. He was present or accounted for through Feb. 1863. Solomon, the s. of James and Mary Green, was living with them at age 17 in 1850 (NCT I, 130; Surry 1850).

GROSE (GROCE), A.; CO. G, 44TH REG. (1833–?).
A. Groce, a Yadkin resident, e. on 10-14-1862 at age 29. Deserted on 10-23-1863 (NCT, X, 459).

GROSE (GROCE/GROSS), ALFRED; CO. B, 38TH REG. (1842–03/07/1863).
Alfred Groce e. in Yadkin Co. at age 19 on 10-16-1861. Wounded at Mechanicsville, VA, on 6-26-1862. Returned to duty Sept.-Oct. 1862. Died in a Richmond, VA, hospital about 3-7-1863 of "typhoid fever" (NCT X, 24). Alfred Gross, age 7 (b. 1843), was in the household of John and Mary Gross in 1850 (1850 Surry).

GROSE (GROCE), JOHN; CO. B, 38TH REG. SERGEANT (1840–?).
John Gross e. at age 21 in Yadkin Co. on 10-16-1861. Mustered in as private, promoted to corporal in April-June 1862. Promoted to sergeant on 5-10-1863. Captured at the Wilderness, VA, on 5-6-1864. Confined at Point Lookout, MD, on 5-17-1864. Transferred to Elmira, NY, on 8-10-1864. Released at Elmira on 5-23-1865, after taking the Oath of Allegiance (NCT X, 25). John Gross, b. ca. 1835, was the s. of Henry and Lucy S. Swaim Gross (Wellborn, *Simon Groce*, 5).

GROSE (GROCE), W.; CO. G, 44TH REG.
W. Grose e. at Camp Holmes on 10-4-1862. Reported AWOL from 10-20-1862 through 12-1-1863. Dropped from company rolls before 3-1-1864 (NCT X, 459).

GROSS (GROCE), C. L.; CO. G, 44TH REG. (1838–?).
C. L. Gross, a Yadkin resident, e. at Camp Holmes near Raleigh, age 24, on 10-4-1862. Deserted on 1-9-1863, but returned to duty on an unspecified date. Reported AWOL Nov. 1863–Mar. 1864 (NCT X, 459). This may be the Calvin L. Gross, b. about 1832, the s. of Moses C. and Sarah Holcomb Groce, who m. Nancy C. Swaim, on 3-14-1853 (YCMR; Wellborn, *Simon Groce*, 5).

GROSS (GROCE), MELMUTH; CO. F, 42ND REG. (?–03/08/1863).
Melmuth Groce e. at Petersburg, VA, on 11-18-1862. Present until he d. on 3-8-1863. Place and cause not reported (NCT X, 253). Melmuth Elias Gross, the s. of Jacob and Rachel Renegar Gross, m. Levina Armstrong on 4-6-1854 (YCMR; Nina Long Groce).

GROSS (GROCE), NATHAN W.; CO. G, 44TH REG. (1836–?).
Nathan Gross was a Yadkin farmer before enlisting at Camp Holmes, age 26, on 10-14-1862. Present through Oct. 1864. Confederate medical records indicate he was hospitalized in Danville, VA, on 1-17-186? with gunshot wound of finger, and deserted 9-1-186? (NCT X, 459).

GROSS (GROCE), WILLIAM E.; CO. I, 28TH REG. (?–06/29/1864).
W. Gross e. about 2-14-1862. Died in a Richmond, VA, hospital on 6-29-1864 of "rubeola" (NCT VIII, 211). William E. Gross was the s. of Henry and Lucy Swain Gross (information from niece Vallie Hinshaw, per Nina Long Groce).

HAIR(E), RISDON ODELL; CO. B, 38TH REG. 1ST LIEUTENANT (1832–05/02/1863).
Risdon O. Hair, a Yadkin Co. carpenter, e. at age 29 on 10-16-1861. Mustered in as sergeant. Elected 3rd lieutenant on 4-18-1862. Promoted to 1st lieutenant on 7-29-1862. Present until killed at Chancellorsville, VA, on 5-2-1862 (NCT X, 21). Risdon D. Hair m. Sarah Gross on 9-21-1856 (YCMR). He was the s. of Abner and Olivia Haire and the brother of Abner Stokes Haire (*Heritage*, 378; Nina Long Groce).

HALE, WILLIAM D.; CO. F, 28TH REG. (1840–01/25/1865).
William D. Hale e. in Yadkin Co. at age 21 on 6-18-1861. Reported absent-wounded Nov.-Dec. 1862, place and date of wound not reported. Returned to duty and was wounded in the chest at Chancellorsville, VA, May 2-3, 1863. Returned to duty on

an unspecified date before 8-15-1863. Captured near Pickett's Farm, VA, about 7-21-1864, and confined at Point Lookout, MD. He was paroled and trans. to Venus Point, Savannah River, GA, where he was received 11-15-1864, for exchange. Captured at Savannah on 12-21-1864, and d. in a Federal hospital at Savannah on 1-25-1865 of "debility" (NCT VIII, 178).

HALL, DANIEL C.; CO. I, 28TH REG. (09/25/1843–06/25/1911; Boonville Bapt., Boonville, NC).
Daniel C. Hall, a Yadkin resident, e. there at age 18 on 3-8-1862. Wounded and captured at Gettysburg, PA, on July 1-5, 1863. Hospitalized at Davids Island, NY Harbor, about 7-17-1863. Paroled there and trans. to City Point, VA, where he was received 9-8-1863 for exchange (NCT VIII, 211). Daniel C. Hall m. Nancy Jane Caudle on 4-21-1867 (YCMR). A copy of the obituary published in a Boonville, NC, newspaper (name unknown), vol. I, no. 26, dated July 30, 1911, stated that: "Mr. D. C. Hall, Passes: An Ex-Confederate Veteran. At his home near Deep Creek Church, Uncle Daniel Hall, an ex-confederate veteran, who had been suffering with a heart disease for the past three years, and who had been very ill for the last two weeks, died Friday night at two o'clock."

HALL, JAMES SANFORD; CO. F, 28TH REG. (1840–?).
James Sanford Hall e. in Yadkin Co. at age 24 on 4-27-1864. Captured near Deep Bottom, VA, in Aug. 1864, he was confined at Point Lookout, MD, until paroled and trans. to Venus Point, Savannah River, GA, for exchange. He arrived there 11-15-1864 for exchange. Reported absent-sick through Feb. 1865 (NCT VIII, 178).

HALL, LEWIS W.; CO. F, 28TH REG. (11/03/37–02/20/1909; Friendship Bapt. Ch.).
Lewis W. Hall e. at age 21 on 6-18-1861. He deserted about 1-2-1862 (NCT VIII, 178, 211). He e. in Co. G, 18th Reg. (8th NC Volunteers) at Camp Vance on 8-25-1864, and was present until he trans. to Co. I, 28th Reg. about 9-1-1864 (NCT VI, 383). Present in Company I, 28th Reg., through Feb. 1865 (NCT VIII, 211).

HALL, RALEIGH W.; CO. A, 54TH REG. (ca. 1826–?).
Raleigh Hall was the s. of Jacob and Mary Hall, and was a Yadkin Co. farmer before enlisting at age 38 on 5-3-1862. He was sent home on a "wheat furlough" 6-10-1862, and was reported AWOL 6-25-1862. Returned to duty on 10-8-1863. Captured at Rappahannock Station, VA, 11-7-1863, and confined at Point Lookout, MD, 11-11-1863. Paroled about 3-9-1864, and trans. to City Point, VA, 3-15-1864 for exchange. Returned to duty, and was reported AWOL again on 5-3-1864 (NCT XIII, 252; 1850 Surry). R. W. Hall m. 1st Varina Whiteker on 1-21-1855; then Vicey Scott on 12-1-1861 (YCMR).

HALL, RICHMOND; CO. I, 28TH REG.
Richmond Hall e. at Camp Holmes on 11-30-1863. Deserted on an unspecified date, but returned to duty on 9-9-1864. Transferred to Co. G, 44th Reg. about 10-1-1864. Present through Oct. 1864. (NCT VIII, 211; X, 459).

HALL, THOMAS; CO. F, 28TH REG.
Thomas Hall e. in Yadkin Co. on 9-28-1863, and deserted on 5-4-1864 (NCT VIII, 178).

HALL, THOMAS GILLIAM; CO. F, 28TH REG. (9/06/1828–10/06/1899; Friendship Bapt. Ch.).
Thomas G. Hall e. in Yadkin Co. on 4-27-1864 and was captured near Fussell's Mill, VA, about 8-16-1864. He was confined at Point Lookout, MD, until paroled and trans. to Boulware's Wharf, James River, VA. He arrived there 3-18-1865 for exchange (NCT VIII, 178). He was the s. of Thomas Hall III and Rebekah Martin Kerr Hall. At time of his enlistment, Thomas G. Hall was working at Salem College, [Winston-]Salem, NC. After the war, he returned to Yadkin Co. and m. Biddie Nading Hauser on 4-4-1866, and they had one child, Charles Aquilla, b. 6-11-1867 (Irene Hall Jenkins, Winston-Salem, NC; *Heritage*, 379). Mrs. Jenkins has a copy of the "Oath of Allegiance" signed by Thomas Gilliam Hall. They lived near Siloam in a lovely two-story clapboard house, which is still standing.

HAMBERT, STEPHEN; CO. E, 70TH REG.
Stephen Hambert e. in Yadkin Co. on 5-1-1864 in Co. E, 70th Regiment, Junior Reserves (Moore's *Roster*, Vol. IV, 303).

HAMMONDS, J. M.; CO. B, 21ST REG. CORPORAL (1838–?).
J. M. Hammonds e. in Yadkin Co. on 5-12-1861. Present until he trans. to Co. A, 1st Battalion, NC Sharpshooters, on 4-26-1862. Transferred as corporal. Reduced to ranks in May 1863. Present or accounted for until Dec. 1864 (NCT III, 72; VI, 552). James M. Hammons, age 12 and going to school, was listed in the household of his father, Samuel, and mother, Celia (1850 Surry). Samuel was a "forge hammerman."

HAMPTON, ALFRED (ALFORD); CO. A, 9TH BAT. HOME GUARD (02/22/1832–07/21/1892; Flat Rock).
Alfred Hampton, a member of the Home Guard, was the s. of Dr. John Beavers Hampton and Elender Holcomb Long. Alfred m. Jane Patterson (born 6-14-1837, d. 12-26-1906). (Gerald W. Cook, "Five Generations of the Hamptonville, Yadkin Co., NC Hampton Family" in YCHGSJ XIV, no. 4 [September 1995]:9–25; and R.D.W.Connor, *History of North Carolina*, 1919, Vol. V, 93).

HAMPTON, JAMES PRESTON; CO. B, 21ST REG. 2ND LIEUT. (03/19/1842–04/18/1899; Island Ford Bapt.).

James Preston Hampton e. at age 20 in Co. B, 21st Regiment on 5-12-1861. Mustered in as sergeant and was promoted to 1st sergeant in Nov.-Dec. 1861. Present until discharged on 11-18-1861. Reason not given. He was b. in Surry Co., was a farmer before enlisting at age 21. He then e. in Co. H, 54th Regiment and was appointed 2nd lieutenant on 3-31-1862. Present through June 1862. Resigned on 8-29-1862 because of "chronic diarrhoea." Resignation accepted on 10-7-1862 (NCT VI, 552; XIII, 318). James Preston Hampton, of Hamptonville, was the s. of Henry Gray and Charlotte T. Hicks Doby Hampton. His father, Henry G., was first sheriff of Surry Co. and later of Yadkin after its formation. James Preston Hampton m. first Sarah Elizabeth Gaither of Davie Co. on 11-23-1869 at Mocksville, N.C. (from the *Daily Sentinel*). His second marriage was to Emma Ray on 1-12-1887 (YCMR). By his first wife, James Preston Hampton had five ch. (Cook, "Five Generations of the Hamptonville, Yadkin Co., NC Hamptons," 9–25).

HAMPTON, JOHN A.; 75TH REG., 18TH BRIG. MILITIA (03/08/1836–12/04/1917; Flat Rock Bapt. Ch.).
John Adams Hampton, the s. of Dr. John Beavers Hampton and Elender Holcomb Long (therefore the brother of Alfred/Alford Hampton), m. Cynthia Carolina Brown on 12-2-1872 at the home of her father, the Rev. W. G. Brown. Ceremony was performed by the Rev. Samuel May. Their ch. were: Green Brown, Frank Armfield, Jordan Sanford, Leroy John, Parks Gwaltney, Nellie Priscilla, Maggie Cowles, Belle Boyd, Caroline Jane, Winnie Davis, and Docia Hampton (from John A. Hampton Family Bible, published in the YCHGSJ X [March 1991]: 13–15; Cook, "Five Generations," 9–25).

HAMPTON, THOMAS D.; CO. H, 54TH REG. 1ST SERGEANT
Thomas D. Hampton originally served as a 1st lieutenant in the 75th Reg. 18th Brig. Yadkin Co. Militia. enlisting on 2-8-1862 for the Jonesville District. He was a farmer before enlisting in Yadkin Co. at age 27 on 3-17-1862. Mustered in as 1st sergeant, but reduced in ranks Mar.-Apr. 1863. Reported present through Oct. 1864. Wounded in the left shoulder at Hatcher's Run, VA, 2-6-1865. Hospitalized at Petersburg, VA, then trans. to hospital at Salisbury, NC, on 2-18-1865 (Confederate Militia Officers Roster, NCT XIII, 322). He survived the war by at least five years. Thomas D. Hampton was the s. of Henry Gray and Charlotte T. Hicks Doby Hampton. Thomas m. on 10-18-1870 Susan T. Sisk, dau. of Pendleton and Mary Sisk (YCMR; Cook, "Five Generations," 13).

HANCOCK, JOHN A.; CO. D, 52ND REG. (1842–07/01/1863; Oakwood Cem., Raleigh, NC).
John A. Hancock, a private, e. on 10-21-1862 in Co. D, 52nd Reg. He was killed at Gettysburg, PA, on 7-1-1863, and was bur. in Oakwood Cemetery, Raleigh, NC (information from Hunter Edwards and Jeff Stepp) (NCT XII, 450). John A. Hancock was the s. of Andrew and Nancy Hancock (1850 Surry).

HANCOCK, WILLIAM A.; CO. B, 38TH REG. (1831–?).
William A. Hancock e. in Yadkin Co. at age 32 on 2-15-1863. Present until captured at the North Anna River, VA, on 5-24-1864. Confined at Point Lookout, MD, on 5-30-1864. Released on 10-15-1864, after joining the U.S. Army. Unit to which he was assigned not reported (NCT X, 25). William A. Hancock m. Salley E. Head on 7-6-1854 (YCMR).

HARDING, GREENBERRY PATTERSON; CO. I, 28TH REG. SERGEANT (11/24/1842–12/27/1931; Farmington Meth., Davie Co., NC).
Greenberry Patterson Harding (listed incorrectly "Green Berry" in NCT), e. at age 18 on 3-8-1862. Mustered in as private. He was wounded at Gaines' Mill, VA, about 6-27-1862, but returned to duty on an unspecified date. Wounded again at Fredericksburg, VA, about 12-13-1862. Returned to duty before 3-1-1863. Promoted to sergeant in March 1863-Oct. 1864. He reportedly was wounded three times at Gettysburg, PA, July 1–3, 1863. Returned to duty, and wounded again at Gravel Hill, VA, on 7-28-1864. Retired from service on 12-18-1864, because of disability (NCT VIII, 212). A family legend is that he and his brother Samuel each purchased a slave out of the money they received when they enlisted. He was the s. of William and Jane Elizabeth Speer Harding, and grew up in the Huntsville area. After the war, he returned to Yadkin Co. where he was tax collector for Forbush Township. He m. Elizabeth Jane Steelman, dau. of James and Phisa B. Steelman, on 9-17-1876 (YCMR), and they moved to Farmington, Davie Co., NC (*Heritage*, 384; Harding Family Bible).

HARDING, SAMUEL SPEER; CO. I, 28TH REG. SERGEANT (09/16/1838–08/25/1864; Speer-Harding Cem.).
Samuel Speer Harding lived in Yadkin Co. before enlisting at age 23 on 8-31-1861 for one year. Company pay vouchers show that he went home on a 7-day furlough in the fall of 1861. He mustered in as private and was promoted to sergeant on 4-12-1862. He reenlisted on August 13, 1862, for "2 years or the war." In addition to $50 bounty for enlistment, as a private, he received $17 per month. At the time of his death, he was "indebted to the Confederate States for stoppage on account of clothing drawn by him to the amount of forty-six (46) dollars." S. S. Harding was killed at Ream's Station, VA, on 8-25-1864 (NCT VIII, 212; Company Muster Rolls). His body was brought back to Yadkin Co. for burial by his father, William Harding, and younger brother, Thomas R. Harding. He was the s. of William and Jane Elizabeth Speer Harding, and brother of Greenberry Patterson Harding (*Heritage*, 384; Harding Family Bible).

HARDING, THOMAS RENNY; HOME GUARD (07/30/1855–02/04/1929; Yadkinville Town Cem.).
Thomas Renny, although a young boy at the time, probably was among those who attempted to block Stoneman's men when they crossed into Yadkin Co. at Shallowford in April of 1865, because he lived nearby at Huntsville. According to his ch., he was a member of the Home Guard. He m. Effie Morrison Kelly on 12-6-1892, dau. of Leonard D. and Mary Philadelphia White Kelly, and they were the parents of 9 ch., among them the author's father, Attorney F. D. B. Harding (*Heritage*, 383–386, 388; Harding Family Bible; Harding Family Papers).

HARE (HAIRE), ABNER S(TOKES); CO. B, 38TH REG. (1838–06/29/1862).
Abner Hare (Haire) e. at age 27 on 10-16-1861. He was wounded at Mechanicsville on 6-26-1862, and d. in a Richmond, VA, hospital on 6-29-1862 of wounds (NCT X, 25). For letters he wrote home, see *Heritage*, p. 143. From his letters to wife "Ellan P. Haire," it is evident that he was stationed at Camp Mangum, Wake Co., NC, Weldon, NC (Halifax Co.), Camp Mason near Goldsborough, NC, and near the Rappahannock in VA. He mentions one son (Abner Columbus) in his letters. Abner Stokes Haire was the sixth child of Abner and Olivia Haire. A. S. Haire m. Ellen Phoebe (or Phoebe Ellen) Farrington on 11-15-1858 (YCMR). She was b. 6-20-1841, d. 2-14-1920, the dau. of Alexander and Margaret Farrington. Abner's brother was Ridson Odell Hair, who also served (*Heritage*, 378). Phoebe Ellen Farrington m. Jacob Hoots second, and Spencer Williams third whom she m. on 4-7-1879 (YCMR; 1850 Surry).

HARP, ALVIN; CO. H, 10TH REG. (1ST ARTILLERY) (1838–01/16/1923; Salem Cem., Forsyth Co., NC).
Alvin and his brother Henry e. in Wayne Co. on 2-10-1863, in an artillery unit, deserted Feb. 1863 (NCT I, 130). Alvin Harp, s. of Harbert and Elizabeth Harp, m. Louisa M. Danner on 3-9-1857 (YCMR). He was living in Yadkin Co. in 1860 with his wife and small son, James M. Alvin was a "mechanic." A sister, Hannah, m. J. W. Hutson (per Ken Harpe, Mocksville, NC).

HARP, HENRY; CO. H, 10TH REG. (1ST ARTILLERY) (1838/39–1877; Courtney Bapt. Ch.).
Henry Harp e. on 2-10-1863 in Wayne Co.; deserted in Feb. 1863 (NCT I, 130). Henry Harp, the s. of Harbert and Elizabeth Harp, m. Lucy Jane Danner, and they had 6 ch. He was the brother of Alvin Harp. They moved to Davie Co., then to Winston-Salem, NC (information from Ken Harpe, Mocksville, NC). He is believed to be bur. at Courtney Bapt. Church in an unmarked grave.

HARRIS, HIRAM; CO. D, 44TH REG. (1839–?).
Hiram Harris, a Yadkin resident, e. in Pitt Co. at age 23 on 10-17-1862. Present through April 1864. (NCT X, 430).

HARRISON, JOHN M.; CO. B, 44TH REG. (1834–09/20/1863).
John M. Harrison e. at age 28 on 11-28-1862. He was "under arrest" in 1863. Court martialed about 9-10-1863 for "mutinous language," he was sentenced to be executed and was "shot to death" on 9-20-1863 (NCT X, 413). See letters from Harrison to wife in Appendix A.

HARRISON, W. D.; CO. B, 21ST REG.
W. D. Harrison e. in Yadkin Co. on 5-12-1861. Present until discharged on 8-20-1861 because of disability (NCT VI, 553).

HARVILL(E), JOHN; CO. I, 28TH REG. (1829–08/22/1864).
John Harvill(e) lived in Yadkin Co. where he e. at age 35 on 3-8-1862. Deserted on 4-5-1863. Returned to duty. Wounded in the thigh near Petersburg, VA, about 8-22-1864. Died of wounds. Place and cause of death not reported (NCT VIII, 212).

HARVILLE, WILLIAM; CO. I, 33RD REG. (1823–07/21/1865).
William Harville e. in Forsyth Co. at age 39 on 7-8-1862 as a substitute. Present until he deserted on 3-15-1863. Returned to duty on 11-15-1863. Present until captured near Jarratt's Station, VA, on 4-2-1865. Confined at Hart's Island, NY Harbor, on 4-7-1865, then trans. to Davids Island, NY Harbor, on 7-1-1865, where he d. in a hospital on 7-21-1865 of "erysipelas" (NCT IX, 225).

HAUSER, EDWIN T.; CO. B, 21ST REG. SERGEANT (05/24/1840–04/11/1866; Hauser-Wilson Cem.).
Edwin T. Hauser, a Yadkin Co. farmer before enlisting at age 21 on 5-12-1861, mustered in as sergeant. Present until discharged on 2-1-1862 because of disability (NCT VI, 553). He was the brother of John Henry Hauser, and both were the sons of T. C. Hauser, Yadkinville plantation owner, and wife, Mary "Polly" Lydia Doub Hauser. Edwin m. Mary Nicholson, b. 8-26-1844. They had one child, Edwin Theophilus, Jr., b. 7-24-1866 (*Heritage*, 395). Doub family data states that Edwin was often called "Doub" because he looked like members of the Doub family.

HAUSER, JOHN HENRY; CO. B, 21ST REG. (08/23/1847–04/29/1930; Hauser-Long Fam. Cem.).
John Henry Hauser e. first in Yadkin Co. on 5-12-1861, at age 13. Present through Oct. 1861. He later reenlisted. in Co. A, 1st Battalion, NC Sharpshooters on 9-1-1864 in Forsyth Co. and was present on the rolls through Dec. 1864 (NCT III, 72; VI, 553). John Henry Hauser was the brother of Edwin T. Hauser, and the s. of Theophilus Christian Hauser

and wife Mary Lydia Hauser. He m. Flora A. Transou on 2-9-1871, dau. of Ephrim and Adelaide Cooper Transou. They had 8 ch. (*Heritage*, 395, 396-397).

HAWKINS, WESLEY; CO. H, 21ST REG.
Wesley Hawkins, a Yadkin Co. farmer, e. in Wake Co. on 11-1-1863. He was captured at Fisher's Hill, VA, on 9-22-1864, and confined at Point Lookout, VA, until released on 5-12-1865, after taking the Oath of Allegiance. He previously served in Co. H, 57th Reg. (NCT VI, 604).

HAYNES (HANES), ALFRED M.; CO. B, 38TH REG. (01/15/1840-03/27/1909; Flat Rock Bapt. Ch.).
Alfred M. Haynes, a Yadkin Co. farmer, e. on 10-16-1861. Discharged about 2-1-1862, after providing George C. Poplin as a substitute (NCT X, 25).

HAYNES (HANES), ANDERSON H.; CO. I, 28TH REG. (1838-?).
Anderson H. Haynes e. in Yadkin Co. at age 23 on 8-13-1861. Captured at Hanover Court House, VA, on 5-27-1862. Confined at Ft. Monroe, VA, and Ft. Columbus, NY Harbor. Paroled and trans. to Aiken's Landing, James River, VA, where he was received on 7-12-1862 for exchange. Returned to duty before 11-1-1862. Hospitalized at Richmond, VA, on 5-18-1864 with gunshot wound of left arm. Place and date of wound not reported. Company records do not state whether he returned to duty. Reported AWOL from Nov. 1864 through Feb. 1865 (NCT VIII, 212). Anderson Haynes m. Nancy Chamberlain on 1-28-1864 (YCMR).

HAYNES (HANES), ASBURY; 75TH REG., 18TH BRIG. MILITIA.

HAYNES (HANES), GEORGE W.; CO. I, 28TH REG.
George W. Haynes e. at Camp Holmes on 2-7-1864. Company records indicate he was captured on 5-12-1864. However, records of the Federal Provost Marshal do not substantiate that report (NCT VIII, 212).

HAYNES (HANES), J. S.; CO. A, 9TH BAT. HOME GUARD.

HAYNES (HANES), JAMES; CO. B, 1ST BAT. SHARPSHOOTERS.
James Hanes e. in Iredell Co. on 9-11-1862. Present on company muster rolls through Feb. 1864 (NCT III, 79).

HAYNES (HANES), JOHN; CO. A, 9TH BAT. HOME GUARD (08/12/1815-05/29/1870; Flat Rock Bapt.).

HAYNES (HANES), JOHN, JR.; CO. B, 38TH REG. (1843-03/06/1862).
John Haynes, Jr., was a Yadkin Co. farmer before enlisting at age 18 on 10-16-1861. He d. at Petersburg, VA, about March 6-7, 1862 of "pneumonia" (NCT X, 25).

HAYNES (HANES), LEWIS F.; CO. B, 38TH REG. 1ST LIEUTENANT (07/29/1862; Flat Rock Bapt.).
Lewis F. Haynes, a Yadkin Co. farmer, e. at age 19. He was elected 3rd lieutenant on 10-16-1861. Elected 2nd lieutenant on 4-18-1862. Promoted to 1st lieutenant on 7-19-1862. Died "in camp" on 7-19-1862 of disease (NCT X, 21). L. F. Haynes, the s. of John and Rebecca Haynes, m. Nancy Evans on 4-1-1852 (YCMR).

HAYNES (HANES), SAMUEL A.; CO. H, 54TH REG. 1ST SERGEANT (1841-09/19/1864).
Samuel A. Haynes, a Yadkin Co. farmer, e. at age 21 on 3-19-1862. Mustered in as corporal and promoted to sergeant July-Dec. 1862. Reported present through Apr. 1863. Captured near Fredericksburg, VA, 5-4-1863, and confined at Old Capitol Prison, Washington, DC. Transferred to Ft. Delaware, DE, 5-7-1863. Paroled from there and trans. to City Point, VA, for exchange on 5-23-1863. Returned to duty before 9-1-1863. Present until hospitalized at Richmond, VA, 5-16-1864 with gunshot wound of left wrist. Place and date of wound not reported (probably at Drewry's Bluff, VA, the same date). Returned to duty and was promoted to 1st sergeant. Killed at Winchester, VA, 9-19-1864 (NCT XIII, 322). Samuel A. Haynes was the s. of Thomas B. and Nancy Ball Haynes, b. ca. 1839 in Surry (now Yadkin) Co. He was the brother of William L. Haynes of the same company (1850 Surry).

HAYNES (HANES), SANDY; CO. A, 9TH BAT. HOME GUARD.

HAYNES (HANES), THOMAS F.; CO. I, 28TH REG. (1836-?).
Thomas F. Haynes lived in Yadkin where he e. at age 25 on 8-13-1861. Present or accounted for until he surrendered at Appomattox Court House, VA, on 4-90-1865 (NCT VIII, 212).

HAYNES (HANES), THOMAS L.; CO. B, 21ST REG.
Thomas L. Haynes trans. from Co. B, 21st Reg. to Co. A, 1st Battalion Sharpshooters, on 4-26-1862. Present or accounted for through Dec. 1864 (NCT III, 72). Thomas L. Haynes e. in Yadkin Co. on 5-12-1861 and was present until he trans. to Co. A, 1st Battalion, NC Sharpshooters, on 4-26-1862 (NCT VI, 553).

HAYNES (HANES), WILLIAM L.; CO. H, 54TH REG. (1841-?).
William L. Haynes e. in Yadkin Co. on 8-29-1862. Present through Dec. 1863. Captured at Cedar Creek, VA, 10-19-1864 and confined at Point Lookout, MD, 10-28-1864. Paroled at Point Lookout on 3-28-1865 and received at Boulware's Wharf, VA,

on 3-20-1865 for exchange (NCT XIII, 322). William L. Haynes was the s. of Thomas B. and Nancy Ball Haynes (Hanes), and the brother of Samuel L. Haynes of the same company.

HAYNES (HANES), WILLIAM L.; CO. B, 38TH REG. (1837–?).
William L. Haynes e. in Yadkin Co. at age 24 on 10-16-1861. Present until captured at Wilderness, VA, about 5-6-1864. Confined at Point Lookout, MD, on 5-17-1864. Transferred to Elmira, NY, on 8-10-1864. Paroled at Elmira and trans. to James River, VA, on 2-20-1865 for exchange (NCT X, 25).

HAYNES (HANES), WILLIAM M.; CO. F, 28TH REG.
William M. Haynes e. in Stokes Co. on 10-19-1864. Present or accounted for through Feb. 1865 (NCT VIII, 178).

HAYNES (HANES), WILLIAM R.; CO. B, 38TH REG. (?–08/11/1862).
William R. Haynes, a Yadkin farmer, e. there at age 18 on 10-16-1861. Wounded at Mechanicsville, VA, on 6-26-1862. Hospitalized at Richmond, VA, where he d. on 8-11 (or 16), 1862, of wounds (NCT X, 25).

HAYNES (HANES), WILSON C.; CO. G, 44TH REG. (1835–?).
Wilson C. Haynes e. at Camp Holmes, age 27, on 10-14-1862. Present through Oct. 1864. Reported absent-sick during much of the time (NCT X, 459).

HEAD, A. E.; CO. F, 28TH REG. (01/08/1828–03/11/1917; Baltimore Meth. Ch.).
A. E. Head e. in Yadkin Co. where he lived at age 25 on 3-25-1862. He was wounded in the shoulder at Ox Hill, VA, on 9-1-1862. Hospitalized at Danville, VA. He deserted from the Danville hospital on 10-16-1862, but returned to duty Jan.–July 1863. He deserted again on 7-19-1863 (NCT VIII, 178). Augustus E. Head, age 13, was living in the household of his mother, Jinsey Head, in 1850, with other brothers as sisters (see below). Augustine (Augustus) E. Head m. Malinda Lakey on 5-18-1858 (YCMR; 1850 Surry).

HEAD, BENJAMIN C.; CO. F, 28TH REG. (1835–12/07/1862).
Benjamin C. Head, a Yadkin Co. farmer, e. at age 26 on 6-18-1861. He d. "at home" on 12-17-1862 of disease (NCT VIII, 178). Benjamin C. Head, age 15, was living in the household of his mother, Jinsey Head in 1850, along with brother Willie L. Benjamin m. Nancy M. Parker on 7-30-1858 (YCMR).

HEAD, WILEY L.; CO. F, 28TH REG. (1841–05/05/1863).
Wiley L. Head lived in Yadkin Co. where he e. at age 20 on 6-18-1861. He d. at Hanover Junction, VA, 5-5-1863 of "fever" (NCT VIII, 178). Willie L. Head, age 8, was living in the household of his mother, Jensey Head in 1850, with other brothers (Augustus and Benjamin) and sisters (1850 Surry).

HELTON, DAVIS; CO. G, 54TH REG. (?–01/18/1864).
Davis Helton was b. in Surry and lived in Yadkin Co. where he was a tenant farmer. He e. in Wilkes Co. on 4-21-1862. He was reported absent sick in June 1862, and reported AWOL later. He returned to duty on 2-10-1863. He then deserted from a camp near Fredericksburg, VA, on 5-31-1863. He returned to duty and deserted again on 12-16-1863. He was hospitalized at Charlottesville, VA, on 1-7-1864, and d. in a hospital there of pneumonia (NCT XIII, 311).

HELTON, JOSEPH B.; CO. B, 38TH REG. (1826–10/01/1862).
Joseph B. Helton e. at age 35 in Yadkin Co. on 10-16-1861. Present until he d. in a Richmond, VA, hospital on 10-1-1862 of "typhoid fever" (NCT X, 25).

HENDRIX, CLEOPHUS D.; CO. I, 28TH REG. 1ST SERGEANT (03/23/1831–02/15/1899; Boonville Bapt. Ch. cem.).
Cleophus Dioclecian Hendrix, the s. of Henry and Anna Jenkins Ross Hendrix, lived in the Center Community and later in Boonville, NC (*Heritage*, 399) He e. in Yadkin Co. at age 30 on 8-13-1861. Mustered in as musician, but was reduced to ranks Jan.–Oct. 1862. Captured at Hanover Court House, VA, on 5-27-1862. Confined at Ft. Monroe, VA, at Ft. Columbus, NY Harbor. Paroled and trans. to Aiken's Landing, VA, where he was received on 7-12-1862 for exchange. Exchanged there on 8-5-1862. Returned to duty before 11-1-1862. Promoted to sergeant in Nov. 1862-Feb. 1863. Promoted to 1st sergeant March 1863-Oct. 1864. Wounded in left leg and captured at Gettysburg, PA, July 3–5, 1863. Hospitalized at Gettysburg before being trans. to a hospital at Chester, PA, where he arrived 7-15-1863. Transferred then to Point Lookout, MD, on 10-2-1863. Paroled there and trans. to City Point, VA, where he was received on 3-6-1864 for exchange. Retired to Invalid Corps on 9-19-1864 because of disability (NCT VIII, 212). He returned to Boonville, NC, where he was the postmaster from 1872 until 1891, and again from 1894 to 1898 (Rutledge, 52). C. D. Hendrix m. Elizabeth Gentry (the dau. of William and Cynthia Hanes Gentry) on 3-9-1854 (YCMR). He made coffins, and handcrafted furniture (*Heritage*, 399–400). He was the ancestor of Mrs. Carmen Frye Richardson, a noted musician in her own right, and choral director in the Yadkin Co. public schools for a number of years.

HENDRIX, JOSIAH F.; CO. G, 37TH REG. (?–07/30/1864).
Josiah F. Hendrix e. in at Camp Vance on 9-6-1862. He was wounded near Gravel Hill, VA, on 7-28-1864, and d. at Chaffin's Bluff, VA, on 7-30-1864 of wounds. He m. Elizabeth A. Johnson on 10-5-1856 (YCMR). After his death, Elizabeth Ann Johnson Hendrix m. his brother, Jesse Harrison Hendrix on

11-7-1869 (YCMR). He was b. 9-30-1845 in Wilkes Co., d. April 1917, Anderson, Madison Co., Indiana, where he and Elizabeth had moved with her two ch. by her first marriage (Cook, *Descendants of Isaac Windsor*, 34).

HENDRIX, S. E.; CO. B, 21ST REG.
S. E. Hendrix e. in Yadkin Co. on 5-12-1861. Present until he trans. to Co. A, 1st Battalion, NC Sharpshooters, on 4-26-1862 He trans. from Co. B, 21st Reg. to Co. A, 1st Battalion Sharpshooters, on 4-26-1862. He deserted on 6-2-1862 (NCT III, 72; VI, 553).

HICKS, THOMAS R.; CO. F, 28TH REG. (1842–06/27/1862).
Thomas R. Hicks resided in Yadkin Co. where he e. at age 19 on 6-18-1861. He was killed at Gaine's Mill, VA, on 6-27-1862 (NCT VIII, 179).

HILL, B. J.; CO. H, 54TH REG. (ca. 1834–?).
B. J. Hill shown on Moore's Roster of Co. H, 54th (NCT XIII, 545, but not on NCT list for same company/regiment). This may be Benton Hill, b. ca. 1834, the s. of Erasmus and Sarah Hill, and the brother of Nathan Hill, below. B. Hill is also shown as a private in Co. H, 63rd Reg., 5th N.C. Cavalry (NCT II, 433).

HILL, N. A.; CO. B, 21ST REG. (ca. 1838–09/10/1861).
N. A. Hill e. in Yadkin Co. on 5-12-1861. Present until he d. on 9-10-1861, place and cause not reported (NCT VI, 553). This may be Nathan Hill, b. ca. 1838, the s. of Erasmus and Sarah Hill (1850 Surry).

HILL, WILLIAM H.; CO. I, 35TH REG.
William H. Hill lived in Yadkin Co. before enlisting at age 18 at Camp Holmes near Raleigh on 5-6-1863. He was wounded near the Globe Tavern, VA, on 8-21-1864. He was reported absent-wounded or AWOL through Feb. 1865. He was paroled at Salisbury, NC, in 1865 (NCT IX, 445).

HINSHAW, JAMES; CO. I, 28TH REG. (1845–?).
James Hinshaw e. at Liberty Mills, VA, on 3-1-1864. Paroled at Burkeville Junction, VA, April 14-17, 1865 (NCT VIII, 212). He may be the "James P. Hinshaw," age 15, living in the household of John Hinshaw (age 25) and Hannah Hinshaw (age 56) (household #500, 1860 Yadkin, Chestnut Ridge Post Office).

HINSHAW, JESSE; CO. H, 3RD REG. (1840–07/01/1862).
Jesse Hinshaw, a Yadkin farmer, e. at age 21 on 5-10-1861, and was present until killed on 7-1-1862 at Malvern Hills, VA (NCT III, 571).

HINSHAW, L.; CO. B, 38TH REG.
L. Hinshaw e. at Camp Vance on 7-14-1864 for the war. Deserted on 8-26-1864 (NCT X, 25).

HINSHAW, MARTIN; CO. H, 10TH REG. (1ST ARTILLERY) (1837–?).
Martin Hinshaw e. in Wayne Co. on 2-10-1863. He deserted in June 1863. Martin was the s. of John and Hannah Hinshaw. He was living with them, attending school, and in the house with other brothers and sisters, including brother Pleasant J., in 1850 (NCT I, 131; Surry 1850).

HINSHAW, P[LEASANT]. J.; CO. H, 10TH REG. (1ST ARTILLERY) (1844–?).
Pleasant J. Hinshaw e. in Wayne Co. on 2-10-1863 for the war. He deserted in June 1863, along with his brother Martin Hinshaw, who deserted at the same time. Pleasant was the s. of John and Hannah Hinshaw, and was living with them in 1850 (NCT I, 131; Surry 1850).

HOBSON, DAVID F[RANCIS].; CO. I, 28TH REG. CORP. (05/25/1841–02/25/1930; Forbush Bapt.).
David F. Hobson e. in Yadkin Co. at age 21 on 9-3-1861. Mustered in as private and promoted to corporal March 1863-July 1864. Wounded near Chancellorsville, VA, about May 1-4, 1863. Returned to duty. Present through Feb. 1865 (NCT VIII, 212). David F. Hobson, the s. of David Hobson, Jr., and Matilda Lakey Hobson, m. Aggie Pauline Williams, b. 10-17-1837, d. 5-25-1909, dau. of Joshua Lace and Sarah Hutchens Williams on 4-10-1860 (YCMR; *Heritage*, 407; Earl H. Davis and Marie Davis Wiles, *Descendants of George and Elizabeth Hobson*, 1978, 333).

HOBSON, GEORGE DICK; 75TH REG., 18TH BRIG. MILITIA (10/18/1837–07/09/1907; Union Cross Friends).
George Dick Hobson may be George D. Hobson, s. of John and Susanna Fleming Hobson, b. 10-18-1837, d. 7-9-1907, m. Rachel Warden, dau. of Iredell and Mary Warden. She d. 11-19-1934 at East Bend, NC., and they are bur. in the Union Cross Friends Church Cemetery.

HOBSON, J. D.; CO. A, 1ST BAT. SHARPSHOOTERS CORPORAL.
J. D. Hobson e. in Wake Co. on 9-4-1862. Mustered in as private. Present through Dec. 1864. Appointed corporal Jan.-Feb. 1865. Wounded at Petersburg, VA, on 4-2-1865, and admitted to General Hospital, Danville, VA, on 4-5-1865 (NCT III, 73).

HOBSON, JESSE F.; CO. I, 28TH REG. (09/16/1834–11/25/1911; Forbush Bapt. Ch.).
Jesse F. Hobson e. in Yadkin Co. on 10-8-1863. Present through Feb. 1865 (NCT VIII, 212). Jesse F. Hobson was the s. of David Lacey Hobson, Jr., and wife, Matilda Lakey Hobson. His brothers, John Ellet and David Francis, also served in the same company (per Jay Hobson, Columbus, GA).

HOBSON, JOHN E[LLET].; CO. I, 28TH REG. (12/05/1837–02/25/1901; Forbush Bapt.).

John E. Hobson e. in Yadkin Co. at age 24 on 9-3-1861. Retired to the Invalid Corps on 12-7-1864, because of disability (NCT VIII, 212). He was the s. of David Hobson, Jr., and Matilda Lakey Hobson, and the brother of David Francis and Jesse F. Hobson, both of whom also served in Co. I, 28th Reg. (*Heritage*, 407). After the war, John Ellet Hobson m. Mary Jane Brown and they lived out their lives in Yadkin Co., where he was a merchant/farmer.

HOBSON, JOHN P.; CO. A, 54TH REG. (1842–?).
John P. Hobson was a Yadkin Co. farmer before enlisting at age 20 on 5-2-1862. He was hospitalized at Richmond, VA, on 10-28-1862 with typhoid fever. Furloughed on 11-4-1862, and returned to duty Jan.-Feb. 1863. Reported present until captured at Rappahannock Station, VA, 11-7-1863. Confined at Point Lookout, MD, 11-11-1863. Paroled on 3-9-1864 and trans. to City Point, VA, 3-15-1864, for exchange. Reported under arrest in Sept.-Oct. 1864, reason for arrest not stated. Returned to duty and was captured at Farmville, VA, 4-6-1865. Confined at Newport News, VA, 4-14-1865. Released at Newport News on 6-26-1865 after taking the Oath of Allegiance. NC pension records indicate he was wounded at Williamsport, MD, in June 1863 (NCT XIII, 252).

HOBSON, JOHN W.; CO. B, 21ST REG. SERGEANT (11/01/1840–01/13/1919; Union Grove Bapt.).
John W. Hobson e. in Yadkin Co. on 5-12-1862, and was present until he trans. to Co. A, 1st Battalion, NC Sharpshooters on 4-26-1862. He was present through Dec. 1864, and was paroled at Appomattox Court House, VA, on 4-9-1865 (NCT III, 73; VI, 553). John's company served in many battles, including Chancellorsville, Gettysburg, and Petersburg. He served under General Thomas J. (Stonewall) Jackson at one time. He was the s. of George and Zilpha Williams Hobson. He m. Sarah Poindexter. After the war, John m. Melissa Fleming, and they were the parents of 10 ch. (*Heritage*, 408; "Poindexter," 38).

HOBSON, TYRA C.; CO. B, 21ST REG. (04/14/1843–03/01/1925; Union Grove Bapt.).
Tyra C. Hobson trans. to Co. A, 1st Battalion NC Sharpshooters, on 4-26-1862. However, records of Co. B, 21st Reg., do not indicate he served in that company (NCT VI, 553). He was present in Co. A, 1st Battalion, through Dec. 1864, and was paroled at Appomattox Court House, VA, on 4-9-1865 (NCT III, 73). Tyra Caswell Hobson, b. 4-14-1843, d. 3-1-1925, s. of George and Zelpha Hobson, and the brother of John W. Hobson of the same company and regiment. He m. first Malinda Tennessee Bovender, b. 12-1-1849, d. 5-19-1884. He m. second Millie Norman, b. 2-2-1855, and they had 5 ch.: David Caswell, Delia, Laura, Carrie, and Pleas E. Hobson ("Bovender"; *Heritage*, 408, 410–411).

HOLCOMB, BLOOM VIRGIL; CO. I, 28TH REG. SERGEANT (1845–?).
Bloom Virgil Holcomb e. in Yadkin Co. at age 18 on 2-28-1863. Mustered in as private. Wounded near Gaines' Mill, VA, about 7-28-1864. Returned to duty before 11-1-1864. Promoted to sergeant on 11-21-1864. Captured near Petersburg, VA, on 4-2-1865, and confined at Ft. Delaware, DE, until released on 6-19-1865, after taking the Oath of Allegiance (NCT VIII, 212). He was the s. of Col. George and Anna Long Holcomb (*Heritage*, 414). Bloom Virgil Holcomb m. Beckie Kirkman, dau. of Roddy and Nancy Kirkman, on 9-18-1872 (YCMR).

HOLCOMB, C. J.; CO. G, 44TH REG. (?–08/15/1863).
C. J. Holcomb e. at Camp Holmes near Raleigh on 11-28-1862. He d. in a Richmond, VA, hospital on 8-15-1863 of "febris typhoides" (NCT X, 460).

HOLCOMB, CALVIN M[ONROE].; CO. I, 28TH REG. SERGEANT (11/23/1841–08/12/1918; Mitchell's Chapel Meth.).
Calvin Monroe Holcomb e. in Yadkin Co. at age 20. Mustered in as private. Reported absent-wounded May–Oct. 1862. Place and date of wound not reported. Returned to duty before 3-1-1863. Wounded again at Chancellorsville, VA, about May 1–4, 1863. Returned to duty. Reported present for duty Sept.-Dec. 1864. Promoted to sergeant Jan. 1865. Retired to Invalid Corps 1-28-1865. Roll of Honor indicates he was wounded in the foot "near the Rappahannock" River, date not given (NCT VIII, 212-213). Calvin Monroe Holcomb was the s. of Col. George and Anna Long Holcomb. He m. Anna Patience Casstevens, dau. of Mecans and Elizabeth Casstevens on 7-20-1870 (YCMR), and they had six ch. He m. second Ella Long on 10-11-1915. He practiced medicine in Yadkin Co. for many years after the War (YCMR; *Heritage*, 414). Children were: Margaret Alice, Lelah Victoria, Marvin Peeler, and George Mecans Holcomb (*Thomas Casteven: A Genealogical History*, 37–38).

HOLCOMB, D. G. J.; CO. B, 5TH REG. (1834–?).
D. G. J. Holcomb (listed as G. D. J. on 1850 Surry Census) e. on 7-14-1864. He was present until he deserted on 11-6-1864. Holcomb was the s. of George and Ann Holcomb (1850 Surry).

HOLCOMB, DANIEL F.; CO. I, 28TH REG. 1ST LIEUTENANT (1836–12/08/1863).
Daniel F. Holcomb e. in Yadkin Co., age 25. He was appointed 1st lieutenant on 8-13-1861. Defeated for reelection when the regiment was reorganized on 4-12-1862. Continued to serve in this company with rank of private. (NCT, 207, 213). He d. in Richmond, VA, hospital of "smallpox" on 12-18-1863.

HOLCOMB, ELIAS D.; CO. B, 38TH REG. (1837–?).
Elias D. Holcomb e. at age 24 on 10-16-1861 in

Yadkin Co. Wounded in left ankle and both thighs at Mechanicsville, VA, on 6-26-1862. Reported absent-wounded or absent-sick until 10-1-1864, when he was reported AWOL (NCT X, 25).

HOLCOMB, JAMES N.; CO. B, 38TH REG. MUSICIAN (1839–03/03/1862).
James N. Holcomb e. in Yadkin Co. at age 22 on 10-16-1861. Mustered in as musician (camp drummer). Died at Petersburg, VA, about 3-4-1862 of "pneumonia" (NCT X, 25). This may be James Newton Holcomb, b. ca. 1838, the s. of Phillip and Rhoda Lewis Holcomb (L. Margaret Wellborn, *William Holcomb*, 19).

HOLCOMB, JAMES WESLEY; CO. I, 28TH REG. (Robeson Co., NC).
James Wesley Holcomb e. at Camp Holmes on 11-14-1863. Captured near Petersburg, VA, on 4-2-1865. Confined at Ft. Delaware, DE, until released on 6-19-1865, after taking the Oath of Allegiance (NCT 213).

HOLCOMB, JOHN T.; CO. I, 28TH REG. 3RD LIEUTENANT (1838–04/29/1864; Center Meth. Ch.).
John T. Holcomb lived in Yadkin Co. where he e. at age 22. Elected 3rd lieutenant on 8-13-1861. Defeated for reelection when the regiment was reorganized on 4-12-1862. Continued serve with rank of private. Captured at Gettysburg, PA, July 1–5, 1863, and confined at Davids Island, NY Harbor. Paroled and trans. to City Point, VA, where he was received on 9-16-1863 for exchange. Company records do not indicate whether he returned to duty. He d. in a Lynchburg, VA, hospital on 4-29-1864 of "hepatitis acuta" (NCT VIII, 207, 213.) John T. Holcomb, the s. of George D. and Anna Long Holcomb, m. Rhoda E. Vestal 12-29-1862 (bond date, YCMR). Tombstone has date of death as 4-28-1863, but other sources say 4-29-1863 (per Nina Long Groce).

HOLCOMB, JONES; CO. I, 28TH REG. (1842–07/03/1863).
Jones Holcomb e. in Yadkin Co. at age 19 on 8-13-1861. Killed at Gettysburg, PA, on 7-3-1863 (NCT VIII, 213). Jones Holcomb, b. ca. 1842, was the s. of George and Anna Long Holcomb (1850 Surry).

HOLCOMB, LEANDER; CO. I, 28TH REG. (1838–?).
Leander Holcomb e. in Yadkin Co. at age 23 on 8-13-1861. Deserted on 6-18-1863. Returned to duty, then trans. to Co. G, 44th Reg. Jan-Feb. 1864. Retired to Invalid Corps on 10-17-1864, reason not given (NCT VIII, 213; X, 460). A Leander Holcomb, age 15, was listed in 1850 in the household of John S. and Anna Holcomb (perhaps grandparents). He may be Leander Franklin holcomb, b. ca. 1840, the s. of William and Mary A. Lewis Holcomb (1850 Surry; Wellborn, 19).

HOLCOMB, LEWIS B.; CO. H, 3RD. REG.
Lewis Holcomb e. on 10-27-1863. He deserted at Racoon Ford, VA, on 11-15-1863. Enlisted at Camp Vance on 2-24-1864. Captured at the North Anna River, VA, on 5-24-1864. Confined at Point Lookout, MD on 5-30-1864. Paroled from there about 3-14-1865. Received at Boulware's Wharf, James River, VA, on 3-16-1865 for exchange (NCT X, 25, 571). Lewis Holcomb m. Martha L. Flyn on 12-25-1856 (YCMR).

HOLCOMB, M. J.; CO. I, 6TH REG. (1842–10/26/1862).
M. J. Holcomb e. in Yadkin Co. at age 20 on 9-15-1862. He d. at Winchester, VA, on 10-26-1862 of disease (NCT IV, 372).

HOLCOMB, PLEASANT H.; CO. B, 38TH REG. 1ST SERG. (09/06/1832–11/03/1913; Center Meth.).
Pleasant Henderson Holcomb e. at age 25 on 10-16-1861. Mustered in as private, promoted to 1st sergeant before 4-1-1862. Present until discharged on 5-12-1862, after providing a substitute (NCT X, 25). He reenlisted in Co. A, 72nd, N.C. Regiment on 3-17-1864 (Wellborn, 16). He was the s. of John B. and Fannie Brittain/Brittin Holcomb (1850 Surry). On 9-10-1856 he m. Martha Long, dau. of John and Nancy Davis Long. He had three ch. b. before the war: Nancy Obitha (1857); John (1859), and Miles (1861). Five ch. were b. during and after the war: Hilary (1863); Charles D. (1865); Malinda (1869); Anna (1871), and Emma (1873). At age 73 Pleasant ("Pleas") Holcomb applied for a pension and stated that his left arm was missing "between wrist and elbow" and that his eyesight was so bad he could not perform manual labor. His pension application was approved. After Pleasant's death, his widow Martha, age 73, applied for a pension. She d. in 1919 and is bur. at Center Methodist Church beside her husband. (YCMR; Rich Long, 150 South 363 Place, Federal Way, WA 98003).

HOLCOMB, THOMAS FRANKLIN; CO. F, 37TH BAT. VA CAVALRY (04/26/1846–02/26/1924; Mt. View Bapt.).
T. F. Holcomb e. in Yadkin Co. on 11-1-864 in Co. F, 37th Battalion, VA Cavalry. He was absent on "horse detail" on the Dec. 1864 roll (Scott, *36th and 37th VA Cavalry*, 1986). Thomas F. Holcomb, the s. of Raleigh Leroy and Wincy Jowers Holcomb, m. Sarah Long on 3-5-1866 (YCMR). She was b. 8-1-1851, d. 6-13-1883, and was bur. in the Harmony Grove Friends Church Cemetery, Yadkinville, NC. They were the parents of seven ch., including John D. Holcomb, Sr., later a Yadkinville merchant, who was b. 5-20-1877. Thomas Franklin Holcomb participated in many of the battles around Richmond and Petersburg, VA. He was at the battle of Gettysburg, PA, in 1863. After the war, he served as United States Department of Revenue store-keeper and gauger until 1910, and lived near Mountain View

Baptist Church. He was court bailiff in his latter years. He m. second Martha (Alcie) Jane Hutchens, b. 11-27-1864, d. 10-21-1919, bur. in Mountain View Baptist Church Cemetery, Yadkin Co. They had 18 ch. (*Heritage*, 416; Wellborn, 19).

HOLCOMB, W. J.; CO. G, 44TH REG. (1842–09/16/1863).
W. J. Holcomb e. at age 20 on 11-20-1862, and d. on 9-16-1863. Place of death not stated (NCT X, 460).

HOLCOMB, WILLIAM B.; CO. A, 9TH BAT. HOME GUARD (03/18/1827–01/02/1899; Center Meth.).
William B. Holcomb, age 27, was a tanner in 1850, and was probably exempt from military duty other than the Home Guard. He was living in the household of his parents, John and Fanny Brittain Holcomb. Brothers were John B., Samuel, and Pleasant (see above). William B. Holcomb m. Malinda Elizabeth Vestal on 2-15-1852. They had ten ch. (YCMR; Wellborn, 15).

HOLCOMB, WILLIAM M.; CO. I, 28TH REG. (05/08/1842–02/05/1918; Swan Creek Bapt. Ch.).
William M. Holcomb e. at Camp Holmes on 11-14-1863. Captured at Richmond, VA, on 4-3-1865, and confined at Newport News, VA, on 4-24-1865. Released on 6-3-1865, after taking the Oath of Allegiance. NC Pension records indicate he was wounded "in battle of Horse Shoe" in 1863 (NCT VIII, 213). His wife, Julia A. (born 3-25-1856, d. 10-3-1912) is bur. at Swan Creek Bapt. Church, near Jonesville, NC.

HOLCOMB(E), WILLIAM T.; CO. D, 44TH REG. (?–05/22/1938?; Oakwood Cem., Raleigh, NC).
William T. Holcomb(e) resided in Yadkin Co. but e. in Wake Co. at age 26 on 12-17-1862. Present until he "d. at home" on 3-9-1864. Cause of death not given (NCT X, 430). William T. Holcomb d. 5-22-1938, and was bur. in Oakwood Cemetery, Raleigh, NC. Cemetery records and information from Mr. Hunter Edwards state he served in Co. I, 28th Regiment, but this is in error. William M. Holcomb served in Co. I, 28th. (William T. Holcomb m. on 3-15-1860 Mary M. Stokes. On 4-7-1867 William T. Holcomb m. Mary Swaim—same man or different? See Yadkin Co. Marriage Register.) William T. Holcomb, age 12, is listed in the William and Elizabeth Holcomb household in 1850 (1850 Surry), along with brothers, Lewis, James, George D., Daniel L. M., Anderson F., and Lucratus.

HOLDEN, WILLIAM S.; CO. A, 1ST BAT. SHARPSHOOTERS (1850–?).
William S. Holden e. in Wake Co. on 9-4-1862. Present until he deserted in April 1864. Dropped from the company rolls 2-28-1865 (NCT III, 73). He may be the William S. Holden, b. 1817, who was living with wife Susan and son, Isaac N. D. Holden (b. 1850) is listed in the 1850 census (1850 Surry).

HOLDER, JOHN C.; CO. I, 33RD REG. CAPTAIN (1826–?).
John C. Holder was b. in Forsyth (Stokes) Co., but resided in Yadkin Co., where he was a teacher before enlisting in Forsyth on 7-1-1861. He mustered in as a private, but was promoted to corporal on 2-1-1862. He was present until captured at New Bern on 3-14-1862. Federal Provost Marshall records do not substantiate this. He was listed as a deserter and dropped from company rolls on for Nov.-Dec. 1862 (NCT IX, 225).

HOLLEMAN (HOLOMAN), ASA; CO. H, 44TH REG. (05/08/1842–02/05/1818; Swan Creek Bapt. Ch.).
Asa Holleman e. originally at Camp French at age 18 on 10-14-1862. Reported under arrest at Petersburg, VA, Jan.-Feb. 1863. Reported present for duty Nov.-Dec. 1863. Deserted on April 25, 1864. It appears that he then e. in Co. H, 44th Reg., where he is listed as "Alsa" Holoman in NCT XIII, p. 322, Holomon e. on 6-7-1864 in Yadkin Co. and deserted on 6-14-1864 (NCT X, 471; XIII, 322). The only Holoman family in the 1850 Surry Census (Yadkin portion) was that of Bennet Holomon and wife, Harriett, and Asa, one of four ch., is listed as being six years old, and was attending school (1850 Surry). Asa Holleman, s. of Bennett and Harriet Holleman, m. J. A. Swaim, dau. of Lewis and Milly Swaim, on 5-14-1874 (YCMR).

HOLLOMAN, JOHN; CO. I, 3RD REG.
John Holloman e. in Wake Co. on 10-27-1863. He was wounded at the Battle of the Wilderness in VA on 5-5-1864. Reported absent wounded through Dec. 1864 (NCT III, 582).

HOOTS, JOHN ANDERSON; CO. D, 1ST BAT.? (02/17/1845–03/31/1928; Mt. Zion Bapt., Iredell Co., NC).
John Anderson Hoots served in the military two years before his first marriage. He was the s. of Anderson and Nancy Catherine Gough Hoots. John A. Hoots was m. three times: 1) Mary E. Long on 4-12-1866; 2) Nancy Reavis on 3-27-1874; 3) Sarah (Sallie) E. Burgess, dau. of Edward Thomas Burgess and Nancy A. Windsor Burgess on 2-2-1897 (YCMR). He had three ch. by first marriage, only one survived—John Franklin Hoots. There were 9 ch. by his second marriage, and by his third marriage there were two ch. (information from Laura Ann Hoots Winslow; Cook, *Descendants of Isaac Windsor*, 31).

HOOTS, WILLIAM F.; CO. F, 42ND REG.
William F. Hoots e. in Rowan Co. on 12-4-1862. Present until discharged on 5-30-1863 because of disability (NCT X, 253).

HORTON, R. B.; CO. G, 44TH REG. (1842–04/10/1863).
R. B. Horton, a Yadkin resident, e. at Camp Holmes at age 20 on 10-14-1862. Present until he d. at Wilson

on 4-10-1863 of "typhoid fever" (NCT X, 460). This is probably Reuben Horton, b. 1843, s. of James and Margaret Horton (1850 Surry).

HOWARD, A. M.; CO. D, 63RD REG. (5TH CAVALRY) (1841–?).
A. M. Howard e. in Guilford Co. on 7-18-1862, and was present through some time in 1863, when he was reported "absent, at home, sick." This may be Alfred M. Howard, who, at age 9 years, was living with parents Larkin and Sally Howard at home in 1850 (NCT II, 398; 1850 Surry).

HOWELL, J. B.; CO. B, 21ST REG. (?–09/18/1861).
J. B. Howell e. in Yadkin Co. and was present until he d. on 9-18-1861, place and cause of death not reported (NCT VI, 553).

HUDSPETH, DIRIT (DARRETTE) D.; CO. I, 28TH REG. (1819–10/31/1861).
Dirit D. Hudspeth e. in Yadkin Co. at age 42 on 8-13-1861. Died in Wilmington, NC, about 10-31-1861 of "fever" (NCT VIII, 213). D. Hudspeth m. Catharine Collins on 9-14-1861 (YCMR).

HUDSPETH, JAMES; CO. I, 28TH REG. (1837–05/05/1862; Yadkin Co., NC).
James Hudspeth e. in Yadkin Co. at age 24 on 8-13-1861. Captured at Hanover Court House, VA, on 5-27-1862, he was confined at Ft. Monroe, VA, and then Ft. Columbus, NY Harbor. Paroled and trans. to Aiken's Landing, James River, VA, where he was received for exchange on 7-12-1862. Declared exchanged there on 8-5-1862. Died "at home" on 9-6-1862 of disease (NCT VIII, 213).

HUDSPE(A)TH, L. D.; CO. I, 28TH REG. (1840–01/05/1863).
L. D. Hudspe(a)th e. in Yadkin Co. at age 22 on 3-8-1862. Died in a Richmond, VA, hospital on 1-5-1863 of "febris typhoides" (NCT VIII, 213).

HUNT, LEANDER GWYNN; CO. B, 27TH REG. HOSPITAL STEWARD (11/05/1837–12/02/1896; Huntsville Bapt. Ch.).
Leander Gwynn Hunt e. at Fort Macon when he was 25 on 5-1-1861. He was present until captured at New Bern on 3-14-1862. Confined at Ft. Columbus, NY Harbor, until exchanged before 5-18-1862. He was promoted to hospital steward and trans. to Field and Staff of this regiment (NCT VIII, 25). L. G. Hunt returned to Yadkin after the war and became a doctor. He m. Miss Mary (Molly) Martin of Huntsville, and they purchased the Dalton House (commonly referred to as the "Hunt House"). They had one child, Daisy.

HUNT, NATHAN G.; CO. B, 21ST REG. CAPTAIN (1841–?).
Nathan G. Hunt, a Yadkin resident, e. at age 20. Appointed 3rd lieutenant to rank from 5-12-1861, and then promoted to 1st lieutenant on 9-10-1861. Present until he trans. to Co. A, 1st Battalion N.C. Sharpshooters on 4-26-1862 (NCT VI, 551). After transferring, he was appointed captain to rank from 4-26-1862. Resigned 6-27-1862 (NCT III, 70). He was also a major of Co. A, 9th Battalion, Home Guard (Cook, *The Last Tarheel Militia 1816–1865*). Nathan Hunt was the s. of Pleasant and Charity Hunt (1850 Surry).

HUNT, RICHARD; CO. F, 28TH REG. (05/01/1832–03/01/1881; Hunt Cem.).
Richard Hunt e. in Yadkin Co. on 6-18-1861. He deserted on 6-5-1863, but returned to duty. Captured at Wilderness, VA, on 5-6-1864, he was confined at Point Lookout, MD, before being trans. to Elmira, NY, on 8-10-1864. He was released from there on 5-19-1865, after taking the Oath of Allegiance (NCT VIII, 179).

HUNT, WILLIAM J. H.; CO. B, 27TH REG. (1844–06/03/1864).
William J. H. Hunt, a Yadkin resident, e. at Martinsburg, VA, at age 18 on 9-22-1862. He was wounded at the Wilderness, VA, about 5-5-1864. He returned to duty before 6-3-1864, when he was killed by a sharpshooter at Cold Harbor, VA (NCT VIII, 25).

HUNTER, THOMAS M.; CO. D, 21ST REG. (1818–?).
Thomas M. Hunter e. at age 45 on 9-20-1863 (NCT VI, 568).

HURT, ROBERT CALVIN; CO. H, 54TH REG. (1833–02/19/1863).
Robert Calvin Hurt was a tenant farmer in Surry Co. before enlisting in Yadkin Co. at age 29 on 3-17-1862. Reported present through Dec. 1862. He d. 2-19-1863. Place and cause of death not reported (NCT XIII, 322). According to the 1850 Surry Census (Yadkin Co. portion), Robert C. Hurt was 17 years old and living in the household of his parents, Joel and Dicy Hurt. He was also attending school in 1850 (1850 Surry).

HUTCHENS, B. F.; CO. A, 1ST BAT. SHARPSHOOTERS.
B. F. Hutchens e. on 3-15-1864. Present on company rolls through Dec. 1864 (NCT III, 73). Benjamin F. Hutchens, s. of Strangeman and Laney Hutchens, m. Margaret Hutchens, dau. of W. L. and Lethy Hutchens, on 10-30-1869 (YCMR).

HUTCHENS, COLUMBUS V.; CO. I, 28TH REG. (1840–?).
Columbus V. Hutchens e. in Yadkin Co. at age 21 on 8-13-1861. Captured at New Bern on 3-14-1861, he was confined at Ft. Columbus, NY Harbor. Paroled, he was trans. to Aiken's Landing, James River, VA, where he was received on 7-12-1862 for exchange. Exchanged on 8-5-1862, he returned to duty before 11-1-1862. Present through Feb. 1863 (NCT VIII, 213).

HUTCHENS, DANIEL V.; CO. A, 1ST BAT. SHARPSHOOTERS.
Daniel V. Hutchens e. in Yadkin Co. on 6-1-1862. Reported present through Jan.-Feb. 1864, then was reported as "absent wounded in General Hospital at Goldsboro, NC. Reported absent on furlough through June 1864, and was present July-Aug. 1864, according to muster rolls. Deserted at Greensboro, NC, on 10-5-1864, and dropped from the rolls on 2-28-1865. Captured at Five Forks, VA, on 4-1-1865, and confined at Hart's Island, NY Harbor, on 4-7-1865. Released after taking the Oath of Allegiance on 6-17-1865 (NCT III, 73). Daniel V. Hutchens m. Jane Reynolds on 8-15-1863 (date of bond, YCMR).

HUTCHENS, HENRY R.; CO. B, 21ST REG.
Henry R. Hutchens e. in Yadkin Co. on 5-12-1861, and was present until trans. to Co. A, 1st Battalion, NC Sharpshooters, on 4-26-1861. Present in Co. A, 1st Battalion Sharpshooters, after transfer until reported AWOL, "furlough expired" Jan-Feb. 1864. Reported as such until July-Aug. 1864, with remark that he was AWOL. Dropped from rolls on 8-31-1864 (NCT III, 73; VI, 553).

HUTCHENS, HEZ; CO. A, 21ST REG.
Hez (Hezekiah?) Hutchens e. in Yadkin Co. on 10-1-1863. Present until he deserted on 12-8-1864 (NCT VI, 546). Hezekiah Hutchens m. Lucyan E. Davis on 8-11-1859 (YCMR).

HUTCHENS, ISAAC; CO. I, 28TH REG. (1844–?).
Isaac Hutchens e. in Yadkin Co. at age 18 on 3-8-1862 as a substitute. Present until he surrendered at Appomattox Court House, VA, on 4-9-1865 (NCT VIII, 213).

HUTCHENS, JOHN C.; CO. B, 21ST REG.
John C. Hutchens e. in Yadkin Co. on 5-12-1861, and was present until he trans. to Co. A, 1st Battalion, NC Sharpshooters, on 4-26-1862. After transfer to Co. A, 1st Battalion Sharpshooters, he deserted from Greensboro, NC, on 10-5-1864, and was dropped from company rolls on 2-28-1865 (NCT III, 73; VI, 553).

HUTCHENS, JOHN F.; CO. B, 21ST REG. (?–09/23/1862).
John F. Hutchens e. in Yadkin Co. on 5-12-1861 and was present until he trans. to Co. A, 21st Battalion, NC Sharpshooters, on 4-26-1861. After transfer, John F. Hutchens d. at the General Hospital in Danville, VA, on 9-23-1862 of "chronic diarrhoea" (NCT III, 73; VI, 553).

HUTCHENS, JOSEPH ELLIS; CO. B, 38TH REG. (1840–07/14/1862).
Joseph Ellis Hutchens e. in Yadkin Co. at age 22 on 4-21-1862. Wounded at Mechanicsville, VA, on 6-26-1862. Hospitalized at Richmond, VA, where he d. about 7-14-1862 of wounds (NCT X, 26). Joseph E. Hutchens m. Nancy Shermer on 10-2-1858 (YCMR; Townsend, *Hutchins/Hutchens*, Vol. I, 105).

HUTCHENS, RICHARD H.; CO. F, 28TH REG. (1841–?).
Richard H. Hutchens e. in Yadkin Co. at age 20 on 6-18-1861. He was reported absent-wounded Nov.-Dec. 1862, place and date of wound not reported. Returned to duty. He was captured near Gettysburg, PA, between July 1–5, 1863, and confined at Davids Island, NY Harbor. Paroled and trans. to City Point, VA, he was received there on 8-28-1863 for exchange. He returned to duty. Reported absent on detail from Sept.-Oct. 1864 through Feb. 1865. He surrendered at Appomattox Court House, VA, on 4-9-1865 (NCT VIII, 179). R. H. Hutchens m. Nancy Jane Melton on 12-23-1866, and they had 6 ch. (YCMR; Townsend, *Hutchins/Hutchens*, Vol. I, 115, 241).

HUTCHENS, SAMUEL G.; CO. F, 28TH REG. (1843–?).
Samuel G. Hutchens lived in Yadkin where he e. at age 18 on 6-18-1861. He was furloughed for 20 days 12-7-1862, but failed to return (NCT VIII, 179).

HUTCHENS, THEOPHILUS C.; CO. D. 23RD REG. ? (01/19/1849–11/14/1934; Deep Creek Bapt.).
T. C. Hutchens e. in Co. D, 23rd Reg. on or about 6-1-1863 (NCT VII, 179). Theophilus C. Hutchens was b. either January 19 or January 26, 1849, and d. 11-15-1934. He was the s. of Alexander and Catherine Wishon Hutchens. He was m. twice. His first wife was Eliza Caroline (Catherine?) Groce, dau. of Abe and Louisa Gross (born 2-20-1857, d. 6-20-1912), whom he m. on 3-20-1887. They had two ch.: Eliza (Mrs. Lloyd Markland) of Advance, and Charlie B. Hutchens, of Yadkinville (Townsend, *Hutchins/Hutchens*, Vol. I, 223).

HUTCHENS, VESTAL C.; CO. I, 28TH REG.
Vestal C. Hutchens e. in Yadkin Co. on 9-7-1862. Present through Dec. 1861. No further record (NCT VIII, 213).

HUTCHENS, WILLIAM; CO. A, 1ST BAT. SHARPSHOOTERS.
William Hutchens e. in Yadkin Co. on 6-1-1862. Present through Dec. 1864 (NCT III, 73).

HUTCHENS, WILLIAM D. H.; CO. F, 28TH REG. (?–06/23/1864).
William D. Hutchens e. in Yadkin Co. on 11-5-1863. He was wounded in the breast near Petersburg, VA, on 6-22-1864, and d. on 6-23-1864 of wounds (NCT VIII, 179).

HUTCHINGS, C. B.; CO. B, 28TH REG.
C. B. Hutchings (Hutchens) lived in Yadkin Co. Date and place of his enlistment was not reported. He deserted to the enemy and was confined at

Louisville, KY, on 8-9-1864. He took the Oath of Allegiance there on 8-16-1864 (NCT VIII, 132).

HUTCHINS, SAMUEL; CO. F, 44TH REG. (1836–?).
Samuel Hutchens lived in Yadkin Co. where he e. at age 26 on 12-1-1862. Present until furloughed for 40 days about 8-28-1862 (NCT X, 450).

HUTCHINSON, JAMES; CO. B, 38TH REG. (1822–?).
James Hutchinson (Hutchens?) resided in Yadkin Co. where he e. at age 40 on 4-21-1862 for the war as a substitute. He was discharged about 8-10-1862, reason not stated (NCT X, 26).

IDOL, BARNETT VIRGIL; 75TH REG., 18TH BRIG. MILITIA.

IDOL, JESSE C.; CO. H, 21ST REG. 1ST SERGEANT (1838–?).
Jesse Idol e. at age 24 in Wake Co. on 6-5-1861. He was promoted to sergeant Sept.-Oct. 1861, and promoted to 1st sergeant Nov. 1861. Wounded in the shoulder at Cedar Mountain, VA, on 8-9-1862. Returned to duty before 3-1-1863. Present until wounded in the leg at Gettysburg on 7-1-1863. Returned to duty. Wounded again at Winchester, VA, on 9-19-1864. Reported absent-wounded through Oct. 1864. Transferred to a cavalry unit on 2-28-1865 (NCT VI, 605). J. C. Idol m. Frances Jane Reece on 9-27-1866 (YCMR).

INSCORE, JAMES; CO. B, 38TH REG. (1840–?).
James Inscore e. in Yadkin Co. at age 21 on 10-16-1861. Deserted about 11-6-1861 (NCT X, 26). He may be the James R. Inscore who e. in Yadkin Co. on 10-27-1863 in Co. H, 3rd Regiment. He deserted from this company on 11-15-1863 at Racoon Ford, VA (NCT III, 571). James Inscore m. Anna C. Shore 4-2-1863 (bond date, YCMR).

IRELAND, JACKSON; CO. B, 38TH REG. (1834–?).
Jackson Ireland was a Yadkin Co. shoemaker/farmer before enlisting at age 27 on 10-16-1861. Reported AWOL in Aug. 1862. Returned to duty Nov.-Dec. 1862. Deserted again at Chancellorsville, VA on 5-3-1863 (NCT X, 26). Jackson Ireland m. Jane Vanhoy on 3-17-1865 (YCMR).

IRELAND, N.; CO. A, 9TH BAT. HOME GUARD.
This is probably Nehemiah Ireland, s. of William and Sally Whittington Ireland (*Heritage*, 434).

IRELAND, SAMUEL; CO. A, 9TH BAT. HOME GUARD.
Samuel is probably the s. of William and Sally Whittington Ireland and a brother to Nehemiah Ireland. He m. Nancy Wagoner Adams, a widow with six ch. (*Heritage*, 434)

IRWIN, SAMUEL; CO. B, 21ST REG. (?–09/22/1861).
Samuel Irwin e. in Yadkin Co. on 5-12-1861 and was present until he d. on 9-22-1861, place and cause not reported (NCT VI, 553).

JACKS, ALEXANDER; CO. D, 44TH REG. (02/09/1847–06/02/1926; Flat Rock Bapt.).
Alexander Jacks, a Yadkin resident, e. in Wake Co. at age 21 on 12-12-1862. Present until he deserted on 5-26-1863 (NCT X, 430). Alexander Jacks, age 6, was living in the household of Martha Jacks, age 57, and Fanny Jacks, age 25, with a little sister, age 3 (1850 Surry).

JACKS, MARTIN; CO. A, 9TH BAT. HOME GUARD.

JACKSON, WILLIAM B.; CO. G, 42ND REG. (?–02/28/1863).
William B. Jackson, a Yadkin resident, e. at Petersburg, VA, at age 19 on 11-6-1862. He d. in a Weldon, NC, hospital on 2-28-1863 of "bilious fever" (NCT X, 262).

JARRATT, ISAAC AUGUSTUS; CO. C, 26TH REGIMENT CAPTAIN (05/13/1841–02/17/1890; Clingman-Lanier Cem., Forsyth Co., NC).
Isaac Augustus ("Gus") Jarratt entered service as a private in Co. C, 26th Reg. at Bogue Banks, Carteret Co., on 10-8-1861, at age 21. He volunteered for a period of three years or the duration of the war. He mustered in as private and was promoted to corporal before 11-1-1861. He was elected 3rd lieutenant about 4-21-1862, and was appointed captain on 10-18-1862. He was present or accounted for until wounded in the face and hand at Gettysburg, PA, July 1–3, 1863. He returned to duty on an unspecified date. He was hospitalized at Richmond, VA, on 5-11-1864 with a gunshot wound of the left leg. Place and date of wound not reported. He returned to duty before 9-26-1864, and was present until he resigned on 1-8-1865. In his letter of resignation, no reason was given (NCT VII, 494). He asked to be reassigned to Co. D, Cavalry. He may have resigned due to injuries sustained at Gettysburg. On January 22, 1865, Gus Jarratt received $338 for service during the period 11-1-1865 through 1-18-1865—two months and 18 days. His salary was $130 per month. Jarratt was listed in the Roll of Honor. He served in the 26th Regiment, which was part of MacRae's Brigade, Heth's Division, A.P. Hill's Corps, Army of Northern Virginia. Isaac Augustus Jarratt graduated from the University of North Carolina at Chapel Hill in 1861, the class known as the "class that went to war." Unfortunately, he never received his diploma. Isaac Augustus Jarratt, the s. of Isaac C. Jarratt and Harriett Ann Bates Cash. "Gus," as he was called, was wounded twice at the Battle of Gettysburg. After the War, he m. a girl from another prominent Huntsville family, Sarah Ellen Puryear, on 4-20-1869 (YCMR), dau. of Richard C. and

Elizabeth Ann Clingman Puryear of the Shallow Ford Plantation. They had three ch.: Atty. Richard Clausel, Harriett, and Augustus Henry "Hal" Jarratt (*Heritage*, 436; and Frances Grey Jarratt, East Bend, NC).

JARRATT, ISAAC C.; MILITIA (12/18/1794–03/20/1880; Jarratt Fam. Cem.).
Isaac C. Jarratt, a prominent man in the eastern part of the county, was the s. of Killian and Ester Clingman Jarratt (sister to Jacob and Peter Clingman). Isaac was a drummer boy in the War of 1812. He became a slave trader and became a wealthy man before the war. He m. Harriet Ann Bates Cash, of South Carolina. After his marriage, Isaac purchased a large tract of land and a large house built by Davis Durret (which still stands near Enon on Old Highway 421). During the war, Isaac was a captain of the Home Guard, and because of this, he was denied a Federal pension for his War of 1812 service (*Heritage*, 435–436).

JARRATT, JOHN CLINGMAN; 75TH REG., 18TH BRIG. MILITIA (04/30/1835–07/22/1869; Jarratt Fam. Cem.).
John Clingman Jarratt was the s. of Isaac and Harriett Ann Bates Cash Jarratt.

JARVIS, ENOCH; 75TH REG., 18TH BRIG. MILITIA (1827–?).
Enoch Jarvis, the oldest s. of Bryant and Peggy Danner Jarvis, m. Sarah Baity (*Heritage*, 449–450) Enoch Jarvis was a cooper. In 1850, he was living with wife, Sarah A., and dau. Mary, age 2 months (1850 Surry).

JARVIS, LUCKET C.; CO. I, 28TH REG. (1836–?).
Lucket C. Jarvis e. in Yadkin Co. at age 25 on 3-8-1862. Captured at Hanover Court House, VA, on 5-27-1862, and confined at Ft. Monroe, VA, then Ft. Columbus, NY Harbor. Paroled and trans. to Aiken's Landing, James River, VA, where he was received on 7-12-1862. Declared exchanged there on 8-5-1862, and returned to duty before 11-1-1862. Died in a Richmond, VA, hospital on 6-24-1863 of "febris typhoides" (NCT VIII, 213). Lucket C. Jarvis was b. about 1836, the s. of Bryant and Margaret (Peggy) Danner (1850 Surry).

JARVIS, SIMEON A.; CO. H, 54TH REG. 2ND LIEUTENANT (1844–?).
Jarvis, b. in Forsyth Co., resided in Yadkin Co. where he was a farmer before enlisting in Yadkin Co. at age 18 on 3-17-1862. Mustered in as corporal, and promoted to sergeant July–Dec. 1862. Hospitalized at Richmond, VA, 12-8-1862 with pneumonia. Returned to duty on 1-15-1863. Appointed 3rd lieutenant on 3-9-1863. Promoted to 2nd lieutenant on 4-18-1863. Present on muster rolls through Oct. 1863. Captured at Rappahannock Station, VA, 11-7-1863, and confined at Old Capitol Prison, Washington, DC. Transferred to Johnson's Island, OH, 11-11-1863. Released from there on 6-13-1865, after taking the Oath of Allegiance (NCT XIII, 318).

JARVIS, WILLIE L.; CO. I, 28TH REG. (10/14/1833–02/15/1885; Courtney Bapt.).
William L. Jarvis e. in Yadkin Co. at age 25 on 8-13-1861. Mustered in as corporal, but reduced to ranks Nov.–Dec. 1861. Captured at New Bern on 3-14-1862, and confined at Ft. Columbus, NY Harbor. Paroled and trans. to Aiken's Landing, James River, VA, on 7-12-1862. Exchanged there on 8-5-1862. Returned to duty before 11-1-1862. Captured again near Petersburg, VA, on 4-2-1865, and confined at Ft. Delaware, DE, until released on 6-19-1865, after taking the Oath of Allegiance (NCT VIII, 213). He was the s. of Bryant and Margaret Danner Jarvis (1850 Surry). His wife, Mary E. Jarvis (born 6-13-1844, d. 10-15-1880), is bur. with him at Courtney Bapt. Church, Yadkin Co., NC.

JAYNES (JOYNER?), ABRAHAM CO. I, 28TH REG. (1835–?).
Abraham Jaynes (Joyner?) e. at Camp Holmes on 10-14-1863. Reported AWOL in Dec. 1864 (NCT VIII, 213). Abraham Joyner m. Mary Colvard on 3-31-1855 (YCMR). In 1850, there was an Abraham Joyner, age 15, living in the household of John and Mary Dixon and attending school There are no "Jaynes," and this may be a misinterpretation of the name "Joyner."

JEFFERSON, ZACHARIAH M.; CO. H, 54TH REG. (1829–1913; Boonville Town Cem.).
Jefferson, b. ca. 1829, the s. of William and Catherine Jefferson, was living in their household in 1850. He is listed as a farmer and was attending school (1850 Surry). He e. in Yadkin Co. on 8-29-1862 and was wounded near Fredericksburg, VA, about 12-13-1862. Returned to duty before 3-1-1863. Wounded again in the finger near Fredericksburg, VA on 5-24-1863. Hospitalized at Danville, VA. Deserted on 5-25-1863. Transferred to Co. I, 28th Reg., on 10-30-1863. He was paroled at Lynchburg, VA, 4-15-1865 (NCT VIII, 213; XIII, 322–323). Zachariah Jefferson m. Margaret J. Plummer on 8-21-1851 (YCMR; Hoots).

JENKINS, ROBERT M.; CO. I, 28TH REG. (1840–?; Wake Co., NC).
Robert M. Jenkins resided in Yadkin Co. where he e. at age 22 on 3-8-1862. He was wounded at Chancellorsville, VA, May 2–3, 1863. Transferred to Co. H, 9th Reg., NC State Troops (1st Reg. NC Cavalry) on 10-31-1863 (NCT II, 75). He may have previously served in Co. D, 21st Reg. (NCT VIII, 214).

JENKINS, SAMUEL P.; CO. H, 54TH REG.
Samuel P. Jenkins was b. in Surry Co. and was a farmer before enlisting in Yadkin Co. at age 18 on 3-17-1862. He was reported absent-sick in June 1862. Returned to duty. He was wounded in the arm at Fredericksburg, VA, on 12-13-1862, and hospitalized at Richmond, VA. Furloughed for 30 days on 1-10-

1863, he returned to duty March-April 1863, and was present through Oct. 1863. Captured at Rappahannock Station, VA, on 11-7-1863, and confined at Point Lookout, MD, on 11-11-1863. Paroled there on 3-16-1864, and trans. to City Point, VA, for exchange. He returned to duty and was captured again at Fisher's Hill, VA, on 9-22-1864. Again, he was confined at Point Lookout, MD, on 10-3-1864, and held until paroled on 3-17-1865. He was received at Boulware's Wharf, James River, VA, on 3-19-1865, for exchange (NCT XIII, 323). Samuel P. Jenkins m. Milly Cecil on 9-10-1865 (YCMR).

JENNINGS, DAVID H.; CO. I, 28TH REG. (1840-?).
David H. Jennings lived in Yadkin Co. where he e. at age 21 on 9-3-1861. He was wounded at Frayser's Farm, VA, on 7-30-1862. Reported AWOL Jan.-Feb. 1863 (NCT VIII, 214).

JENNINGS, JAMES A.; CO. B, 1ST REG. (1837-?).
James A. Ginnings (Jennings) resided in Yadkin Co. but e. in Wilkes Co. at age 25 on 1-16-1862. He was wounded in action at Ellerson's Mill, VA, on 6-26-1862. Detailed as brigade butcher in Sept. 1862. He was reported absent on detail through Feb. 1864, and as absent sick from Feb. through Dec. 1864. On another page, he is listed as James A. Jennings, and says he was paroled at New Market, VA, on 4-19-1865, as an employee of the Commissary Dept. This is probably the same person (NCT III, 159, 160). James A. Jennings (Jinnings) was 13 years old, attending school, and living with his parents, Anderson and Lydia Jinnings in 1850 (Surry 1850).

JENNINGS, JOHN W.; CO. I, 28TH REG. (1844-11/24/1863).
John W. Jennings, a Yadkin resident, e. there at age 18 on 3-8-1862. Wounded in the leg at Chancellorsville, VA, May 2-3, 1863, and hospitalized at Richmond, VA, he d. on 11-24-1863 of wounds received (NCT VIII, 214).

JENNINGS, S. W.; CO. I, 28TH REG. (1832-06/29/1862).
S. W. Jennings lived in Yadkin Co. where he e. at age 30 on 3-8-1862. He was captured at Hanover Court House, VA, on 5-27-1862, and confined at Ft. Monroe, VA, then Ft. Columbus, NY Harbor. He d. at Davids Island, NY Harbor between June 28-30, 1862, of "fever" (NCT VIII, 214).

JESTER, ALEXANDER Z.; CO. D, 52ND REG. (1841-?).
Alexander Z. Jester e. at age 20 at Petersburg, VA. He was wounded and captured at Gettysburg, PA, 7-3-1863. He was confined at Ft. Delaware, DE, about 7-10-1863, then trans. to a hospital in Chester, PA, on 7-19-1863. He was paroled there and arrived at City Point, VA, on 9-23-1863 for exchange. Reported absent on parole through April of 1864. He was reported AWOL May-Dec. 1864.

JESTER, JAMES; 75TH REG., 18TH BRIG. MILITIA (09/28/1833-12/05/1920; Union Grove Bapt.).
James Jester's wife, Mary Eliza Jester, was b. 4-5-1838, d. 4-29-1904. She is also bur. at Union Grove Bapt. Church.

JESTER, JOSEPH J.; CO. A, 54TH REG. (1835-?).
Joseph J. Jester was a Yadkin farmer before enlisting at age 27 on 5-3-1862. Deserted about 6-10-1862. Returned to duty before 1-1-1863, and captured near Fredericksburg, VA, about 5-4-1863. Confined at Old Capitol Prison, Washington, DC, and trans. to Ft. Delaware, DE, 5-7-1863. Paroled at Ft. Delaware and trans. to City Point, VA, where he arrived 5-23-1863. Hospitalized the same day with intermittent fever. Released from hospital on 7-16-1863, but did not return to duty. Reported AWOL through October 1864 (NCT XIII, 253).

JESTER, JOSIAH; 75TH REG., 18TH BRIG. MILITIA (1836-?; Union Grove Bapt.).
Josiah Jester, age 14, is listed in the William and Mary Jester household in 1850 (1850 Surry). Josiah Jester m. Mary C. Reece on 9-13-1855 (YCMR). They had 11 ch. (*Heritage*, 439).

JESTER, SOLOMON, CO. I, 21ST REG. (ca. 1839-?).
Solomon Jester e. in Yadkin Co. on 12-1-1863. He was present until he deserted on 6-20-1864 (NCT VI, 615). Solomon was living in the household of his mother, Mary Jester, age 43, and younger brother Alexander, age 8, when the 1850 Surry Co. Census was taken.

JESTER, WILLIAM A.; CO. A, 54TH REG. (1837-?).
William A. Jester, a Yadkin farmer, e. at age 25 on 5-3-1862. Deserted on 11-14 or 12-14-1862. Returned to duty Jan.-Feb. 1863. Present through Dec. 1863. Hospitalized at Raleigh on 6-19-1864 with chronic bronchitis. Returned to duty 8-8-1864. Reported present Sept.-Oct. 1864. Captured near Farmville, VA, 4-6-1865. Confined at Newport News, VA, 4-14-1865. Released from there 6-26-1865 after taking the Oath of Allegiance (NCT XIII, 253).

JESTER, WILLIAM AARON; 75TH REG., 18TH BRIG. MILITIA (?-04/28/1865).
William Aaron Jester, b. ca. 1832, m. Mary Ann Kerr His brother, Elkana Jester was b. 1828, d. 1-5-1863. Both were the s. of Jacob and Fannie Brogdon Jester.

JOHNSON, BROOK; CO. B, 38TH REG.
Brook Johnson e. at Camp Holmes near Raleigh on 6-29-1864. Deserted on 7-17-1864 (NCT X, 26).

JOHNSON, E. A.; CO. B, 38TH REG. (06/15/1837-02/18/1892; Zion Bapt., Iredell Co., NC).
NC pension records indicate he served in this company (NCT X, 26). E. A. Johnson's wife, Susanna

M. (born 2-23-1841, d. 12-16-1880). Both are bur. at Zion Bapt. Church, Iredell Co., NC, just south of Windsor's Crossroads.

JOHNSON, JAMES THOMAS; CO. A, 1ST BAT. SHARPSHOOTERS (1840/41–02/16/1863).
J. T. Johnson e. in Wake Co. on 9-4-1862. Died at Guinea Station, VA, on 2-16-1863 (NCT III, 73). James Thomas Johnson was 18 years old in 1860 and living in the household of his parents, John G. and Lena Messick Johnson (1860 Yadkin; Townsend, *Hutchins/Hutchens*, Vol. I, 161).

JOHNSON, JAMES W.; CO. G, 54TH REG. (1842–2/19/1863).
James W. Johnson was b. in Yadkin Co. and was a farmer before he e. in Wilkes Co. on 4-5-1862. He was reported absent-sick in June of 1862, but returned to duty before 1-1-1862. He was hospitalized at Richmond, VA, on 1-26-1863, and d. there on 2-19-1863 of "typhoid fever" (NCT XIII, 312).

JOHNSON, JEREMIAH CARR; CO. B, 21ST REG. (05/19/1839–01/09/1920; Asbury Meth.).
Jeremiah Carr Johnson e. about 9-2-1861 (NCT VI, 553). Jeremiah C. Johnson, the s. of Benjamin Howell and Rebecca Jones Johnson, m. Rebecca Malinda Messick on 5-28-1860 (YCMR; Gerald W. Cook, family data sheets).

JOHNSON, JESSE WILSON; CO. A, 54TH REG. (07/23/1842–?).
Jesse Wilson Johnson lived in Yadkin Co. and was a farmer before enlisting in Yadkin Co. at age 19 on 5-3-1862. Reported present or accounted for on surviving company muster rolls through October 1863. Captured at Rappahannock Station, VA, 11-7-1863, and confined at Point Lookout, MD, 11-11-1863. Paroled at Point Lookout on 3-9-1864. Transferred to City Point, VA, for exchange 3-15-1864. Returned to duty before 7-20-1864 when he was captured again at Stephenson's Depot, VA. Confined at Camp Chase, OH, on 7-28-1864, and paroled the following year on 3-2-1865. Received at Boulware's Wharf, James River, VA, March 10-12, 1865, for exchange. He survived the war (NCT XIII, 253). Jesse W. Johnson, s. of James and Jemima Johnson, m. Rachel M. Evans, dau. of Thomas and Sarah Messick, on 10-3-1867. He was a brother to Thomas Streeter Johnson (YCMR; *Heritage*, 441).

JOHNSON, JOHN; CO. E, 70TH REG.

JOHNSON, JOHN B.; CO. B, 38TH REG.
John B. Johnson e. at Camp Holmes near Raleigh on 6-29-1864. Deserted on 7-12-1864 (NCT X, 26).

JOHNSON, LEWIS W.; CO. I, 28TH REG. CORPORAL (1840–?).
Lewis W. Johnson e. in Yadkin Co. at age 21 on 8-13-1861. Mustered in as corporal, but reduced to ranks Jan.–Oct. 1862. Captured at New Bern on 3-14-1862, and confined at Ft. Columbus, NY Harbor. Paroled and trans. to Aiken's Landing, James River, VA, where he was received on 7-12-1862 for exchange. Exchanged there on 8-5-1862. Returned to duty Jan.–Feb. 1863 after being AWOL for four months. Promoted to corporal March 1863–Oct. 1864. Wounded at Gettysburg, PA, July 1–3, 1863. Company records do not indicate whether he returned to duty. Hospitalized at Richmond, VA, on 5-18-1864 with gunshot wound, place and date of wound not reported. Reported absent-sick Sept. 1864–Feb. 1865. Captured in a Richmond, VA, hospital on 4-3-1865, and paroled on 4-24-1865 (NCT VIII, 214). L. W. Johnson m. T. C. Pardue on 11-6-1860 (YCMR).

JOHNSON, THOMAS STREETER; CO. A, 54TH REG. (08/14/1837–?; Harden Co., Iowa).
Thomas Streeter Johnson, b. 8-14-1837 in Surry (now Yadkin) Co., was a farmer before enlisting in Yadkin Co. at age 24 on 5-3-1862, as a substitute for David Lenard Deafled. Reported present through Feb. 1863. Captured near Fredericksburg, VA, 5-4-1863, and confined at Ft. Delaware, DE, 5-7-1863. Paroled and trans. to City Point, VA, where he was received 5-23-1863 for exchange. Returned to duty prior to 9-1-1863. Hospitalized at Richmond, VA, 10-19-1863 with an unspecified illness. Transferred to another hospital on 10-20-1863. Returned to duty Nov.–Dec. 1863. Captured at Fisher's Hill, VA, 9-22-1864. Confined at Point Lookout, MD, 10-3-1864. Paroled 11-1-1864 and trans. to Venus Point, Savannah River, GA, 11-15-1864 for exchange (NCT XIII 253). Thomas Streeter Johnson, the s. of James and Jemima Reece Johnson, m. 1st Elizabeth Adams. He m. 2nd, Nancy Desern on 3-11-1866. He moved to Union, Iowa, in 1865 with the rest of his family, and is bur. there (YCMR; *Heritage*, 440–441).

JOHNSON, WILEY F.; CO. B, 21ST REG.
Wiley F. Johnson e. in Yadkin Co. on 5-12-1861 and was present until he trans. to Co. A, 1st Battalion, NC Sharpshooters, on 4-26-1862. Present in Co. A, 1st Battalion, through Dec. 1864 (NCT III, 73; VI, 553). Wiley F. Johnson m. Emily C. Lewis on 7-11-1865 (YCMR). Wiley F. Johnson, b. ca. 1839, was the s. of John George and Verlinda Louisa Messick Johnson (Cook, *Descendants of Isaac Windsor*, 13–14).

JOHNSON, WILLIAM; CO. H, 10TH REG. (1ST REG. ARTILLERY) (1841–?).
A number of Yadkin Co. men e. in Wayne Co. on 2-10-1863, as did William Johnson (NCT I, 131). He deserted July-Aug. 1863. William may be the s. of John B. and Elizabeth Johnson.

JONES, BENJAMIN FRANKLIN; 75TH REG., 18TH BRIG. MILITIA.

JONES, CORNELIUS; CO. E, 70TH REG. JUNIOR RESERVES.

Cornelius Jones may be the same as Cornelius J. Jones, listed below.

JONES, CORNELIUS J.; CO. B, 44TH REG. (1836–?).
Cornelius J. Jones e. in Edgecombe Co. at age 27 on 11-28-1863. He was present until he deserted on 4-10-1863. Returned to duty and d. "in camp," cause not reported (NCT X, 414). C. J. Jones m. M. S. Salmons on 2-18-1861 (YCMR). Cornelius Jones, s. of Roland and Rosannah Johnson Jones, age 14, was listed in their household in 1850 (1850 Surry).

JONES, JESSE SANDFORD; 75TH REG., 18TH BRIG. MILITIA.
J. S. Jones m. Sarah L. Glen on 2-7-1861 (YCMR).

JONES, JOHN H.; CO. E, 70TH REG.
John H. Jones also served in Co. B, 44th Reg. N.C. Troops (NCT X, 414).

JONES, PRESTON C.; 75TH REG., 18TH BRIG. MILITIA (03/02/1840–01/11/1919; Greenwood Cem., North Wilkesboro, NC).
Preston Cadwallader Jones was b. in Yadkin Co. He was a farmer by occupation (NC Militia Officers Roster, 208)

JONES, WILSON; CO. B, 38TH REG. (?–04/29/1865).
Wilson Jones's date and place of enlistment not reported. Captured near Petersburg, VA, about 4-3-1865. Confined at Hart's Island, NY Harbor, on 4-11-1865. He d. there on 4-29-2865 of "chronic diarrhoea" (NCT X, 26).

JOYCE, ABNER R.; CO. I, 28TH REG. (1842–?).
Abner R. Joyce resided in Yadkin Co. but e. in New Hanover Co. at age 19 on 10-8-1861. Wounded at Chancellorsville, VA, on 5-3-1863. Returned to duty before 7-2-1862, when he was wounded at Gettysburg, PA. Recovered and returned to duty on an unspecified date. Reported present Sept. 1864–Feb. 1865. Surrendered at Appomattox Court House, VA, on 4-9-1865 (NCT VIII, 214). A. R. Joyce, s. of Absalom and Sarah Joyce, m. E. E. Jenkins, dau. of C. and Emily Jenkins on 12-21-1871 (YCMR).

JOYCE, ROBERT H.; CO. I, 28TH REG. 1ST SERGEANT (?–06/22/1864).
Robert H. Joyce resided in Yadkin Co. where he e. at age 25 on 9-3-1862. Captured at Hanover Court House, VA, about 5-27-1862. Confined at Ft. Columbus, NY Harbor, until exchanged. Transferred to Co. B, 38th Reg. NC Troops on 3-25-1863. After transferring with a rank of private, he was promoted to sergeant on 10-4-1863, and promoted to 1st sergeant on 4-7-1864. Killed near Petersburg, VA, on 6-22-1864 (NCT VIII, 214; X, 26).

JOYCE, WILLIAM A.; 75TH REG., 18TH BRIG. MILITIA (1831–1866).
W. A. Joyce, 1831–1866, m. first Betty York, and second, Mollie J. Wilson (dau. of Dr. George F. Wilson) on 8-15-1861 (YCMR). He lived in Yadkinville in the Joyce-Holton House (*Architectural History of Yadkin Co.*; Brumfield's, *Judge Richmond Pearson*, 78).

JOYNER, ANDREW Z.; CO. B, 38TH REG. (1842–?).
Andrew Z. Joyner, a Yadkin resident, e. there at age 21 on 2-15-1863. Deserted about 7-20-1863 (NCT X, 26). Andy Z. Joyner m. Mary Jane Allen 01-04-1866 (YCMR). He is probably the Andrew Joyner, age 9, listed in the household of his parents, Zachariah and Rebecca Joyner, in 1850 (1850 Surry).

JOYNER, DAVID W.; CO. F, 28TH REG. CORPORAL (1838–?).
David W. Joyner e. at age 23 on 6-18-1861. Mustered in as private. Captured at Hanover Court House, VA, on 5-27-1862. Confined at Ft. Monroe, VA, then Ft. Columbus, NY Harbor. Paroled and trans. to Aiken's Landing, James River, VA, where he was received on 7-12-1862 for exchange. Exchanged on 8-5-1862. Returned to duty before 11-1-1862. Promoted to corporal Jan. 1863–Oct. 1864. Captured near Petersburg, VA, on 4-2-1865, and confined at Point Lookout, MD, until released on 6-28-1865, after taking the Oath of Allegiance (NCT VIII, 179). D. W. Joyner m. Martha W. Myers on 12-13-1866 (YCMR). He may be the s. of Zachariah and Rebecca Speece Joyner (*Heritage*, 449). Also, a David W. Joyner, s. of Timothy and Frances Joyner m. Rody Hutchens, dau. of Isaac and Susannah Hutchens, on 12-23-1875.

JOYNER, E. A. K.; CO. B, 38TH REG. (1842–?).
E. A. K. Joyner e. at Camp Holmes near Raleigh at age 21 on 2-15-1863. Deserted about 7-20-1863 (NCT X, 26). His wife's first name was Joanna, and s. Emory A. m. Lydia M. Spillman on 2-27-1883 (YCMR).

JOYNER, GILES A.; CO. B, 38TH REG. (1839–?).
Giles A. Joyner e. in Yadkin Co. where he resided at age 24 on 2-15-1863. Wounded at Chancellorsville, VA, on 5-2-1863 and "not heard from since" (NCT X, 26).

JOYNER, JOHN S.; CO. F, 28TH REG. (1943–08/06/1862).
John S. Joyner e. at age 18 on 6-18-1861. He d. in a Richmond, VA, hospital on 8-6-1862 of "febris typhoides" (NCT VIII, 179).

JOYNER, JOHN T.; CO. F, 28TH REG. (04/13/1844–08/30/1903; Hunt Cem., Yadkin Co., NC).
John T. Joyner, a Yadkin farmer, e. at age 17 on 4-23-1862, as a substitute. He was discharged on 7-24-1862 because of disease of the left lung (NCT VIII, 179).

JOYNER, TIMOTHY; CO. F, 28TH REG. (1843–06/13/1863).
Timothy Joyner e. in Yadkin Co. at age 18 on 6-18-1861. He was wounded at Ox Hill, VA, on 9-1-1862. He d. "at home" about 6-13-1863 of wounds (NCT VIII, 179).

KELLY, COLUMBUS C.; CO. D, 18TH REG. (05/10/1837–1901; Ashe Co., NC).
Christopher Columbus Kelly (instead of Columbus C.) e. in Wilkes Co. at age 25 on 9-5-1862. Present until he deserted on 7-5-1863 (NCT VI, 349). The s. of Thomas S. Kelly (a wagon maker, b. 6-13-1814, d. 10-11-1875, age 61 years) and wife, Nancy Melraney (?) (See 1850 Surry). Thomas S. Kelly is believed to be the s. of Thomas D. Kelly, of the Huntsville area. He m. about 1860 in Wilkes Co., NC, Elizabeth Merrimon (Meriman), b. 1842, Reddies River, Wilkes Co., d. 7-9-1890, dau. of Owen and Jane Merrimon. Christopher Columbus Kelly's second wife was Lena Caroline Brown, whom he m. on 7-18-1893. She d. in 1938 in Ashe Co., NC. The ch. by his first wife were: Lewis Wade, Virginia Lee, Wiley Thomas Richard, Lucy Ann, Mary Ellen, Owen, Barnett Virgil, Charlie Lawson and Edwin Foster Kelly. By his second wife there were two ch.: John Cottrell and Hattie Mae Kelly (information from a descendant, William Owen Kelley, Rt. 2, Box 84, Branford, FL 32008).

KELLY, JOHN C.; CO. F, 28TH REG. QUARTERMASTER SERGEANT (ca. 1820–?).
Kelly was b. in Yadkin Co. and was a schoolteacher before enlisting in Yadkin Co. at age 44 in May 1861. Mustered in as ordnance sergeant. He was promoted to quartermaster sergeant on 10-9-1861, and trans. to Field and Staff. He was discharged 6-10-1862 by reason of "predisposition to disease of the lungs, accompanied with debility" (NCT VIII, 112, 179). This is probably the John C. Kelly who was 40 (born ca. 1820) in 1860, who m. Sarah A. Baker on 8-11-1859 and lived at East Bend. He was the s. of William D. and Elizabeth Creson Kelly. He was a double first cousin to another John C. Kelly, the s. of Leonard Davis Kelly, Sr., and wife, Rachel Creson Kelly. The second John C. Kelly (born ca. 1824, age 36 in 1860) was the brother of Leonard Davis Kelly, Jr., and Samuel L. Kelly. (See articles on the Kelly family in the *Heritage*, 451; also see "The History of the Kelly Family," compiled by Frances H. Casstevens, unpublished manuscript, 1995.)

KELLY, LEONARD DAVIS II; 75TH REG., 18TH BRIG. MILITIA (05/14/1830–11/23/1876; Yadkinville Town Cem.).
A member of the State Militia, Leonard Davis Kelly was reportedly at the shootout at the Bond School House, although his name does not appear on any of the available documentation. He had moved to Yadkinville from Huntsville and was a tobacconist. He was the s. of Leonard Davis Kelly and Rebecca Creson Kelly. He m. Mary Philadelphia White on 4-10-1853 (YCMR), dau. of William White, the builder of the first Yadkin Co. court house. Kelly owned several lots in the original town of Yadkinville (#25 and #26), and was granted a license to sell "spiritous liquors" in the town, according to the Commissioner Minutes. One of his sons, William Lee Kelly, was later Sheriff of Yadkin Co. Another son, Newton, was the county jailer and after Leonard's death, his widow cooked for the prisoners (*Heritage*, 451; "The History of the Kelly Family," compiled by Frances H. Casstevens, 1995, unpublished manuscript).

KELLY, SAMUEL L.; CO. B, 38TH REG. CORPORAL (1835–ca. 1865; Yadkin Co., NC?).
Samuel L. Kelly was a Yadkin Co. farmer before enlisting at age 28 on 10-16-1861. Mustered in a private. Reported AWOL on 8-20-1862, but returned to duty Jan.-Feb.1863. Promoted to corporal March-April 1863. Hospitalized at Richmond, VA 5-6-1863 with a wound of the left side, date and place wound sustained not reported. Deserted on 6-15-1863. Returned to duty on 9-29-1863. Reduced to ranks on 10-4-1863. Present through Oct. 1864. Reported absent on hospital duty much of that time (NCT X, 26). Samuel L. Kelly, the s. of Leonard Davis and Rebecca Creson Kelly, m. Nancy Caroline Whitaker on 11-8-1855. There is one girl living with Samuel L. and Caroline in 1860: Rebecca, b. 1856 (1860 Yadkin; YCMR; *Heritage*, 451). An aunt related the story shortly before she d. that Samuel L. Kelly had come home from the war on sick leave and was killed by the Home Guard. This is unverified.

KELLY, THOMAS; CO. A, 54TH REG. (6/13/1814–10/11/1875).
Thomas Kelly was b. in Surry (Yadkin) Co., and e. at age 52 on 5-2-1862 as a substitute for James Patterson. Hospitalized at Richmond, VA, 12-12-1862 with pneumonia. Transferred to another hospital on 1-18-1863. Discharged at Huguenot Springs, VA, 3-9-1863 because of "amaurosis (NCT XIII, 253). Thomas Kelly (born 6-13-1814 d. 10-11-1875?, bur. in Kelly Cemetery across the river in Little Yadkin Township in a cemetery next to the Lanier Clingman Cemetery) may be the s. of Thomas D. Kelly (*Heritage*, 450). He is listed in 1860 Yadkin cendud with ch.: Christopher (Columbus), Pleasant C., Mary W., Juliette, Eliza, and Milly. His occupation was "wagonmaker." Thomas Kelly is listed in the 1870 Yadkin Co. Census, age 56, with wife Jane, age 35, and dau. Juliet, age 24, and two grandchildren, John (age 3), and Edward (age 1).

KELLY, WILLIAM D.; CO. F, 28TH REG. (1841–03/10/1864).
William D. Kelly lived in Yadkin Co. where he e. at age 20 on 6-18-1861. Mustered in as corporal, but was reduced to ranks Jan.–June 1862. Wounded and captured at Gettysburg, PA, on 7-3-1863. Confined at Ft. Delaware, DE, then trans. to Point Lookout, MD, about 10-15-1863. Died at Point Lookout on

3-10-1864, cause of death not reported (NCT VIII, 179). William D. Kelly, age 18 (born 1842) was living in the household of John C. Kelly and wife, Sarah A. Baker Kelly, at East Bend when the 1860 Yadkin Co. Census was taken. He may be the s. of John C. Kelly by an earlier marriage. The 1850 Census of Surry Co., Northern Division, shows John Kelly, age 32, with wife, Martha, age 30 (who was b. in Georgia), and ch.: William, age 9 (born in Georgia), and Malinda J., age 7 (born in Alabama). The father, John, is the s. of William D. Kelly and Elizabeth Creson. This family moved from the Huntsville area to Rockford sometime between 1840 and 1850.

KIMBROUGH, JOHN ANDERSON; CO. I, 33RD 2ND LIEUTENANT (1840–?).
John Anderson Kimbrough was living in Yadkin Co. before he e. in Lenoir Co. at age 18 on 3-15-1862. He was promoted to musician before 5-1-1862, and trans. to the regimental band (NCT IX, 227). John A. Kimbrough was appointed 2nd lieutenant to rank from 11-30-1864. He trans. to Co. E, 16th Battalion N.C. Cavalry on 12-06-1864 (NCT IX,122). John A. Kimbrough was the s. of John and Amy Kimbrough (1850 Surry).

KIMBROUGH, LEWIS W.; CO. I, 33RD REG. MUSICIAN (1844–06/02/62).
Lewis W. Kimbrough, a Yadkin resident, e. in Lenoir Co. at age 18 on 3-15-1862. Promoted to musician before 5-1-1862, and trans. to the regimental band (NCT IX, 227). Lewis Kimbrough was present until he d. at Gordonsville, VA, on 6-2-1862 of typhoid fever. He "possessed many high and noble qualities." Lewis Kimbrough was the s. of John and Amy Kimbrough and was 6 years old in 1850 (1850 Surry).

KIMBROUGH, NATHANIEL; 75TH REG., 18TH BRIG. MILITIA.

KINYON, JOHN HENDRICKS; CO. F, 28TH REG. ASSISTANT SURGEON (10/04/1825–07/27/1903; Centerville, Johnson Co., MO).
John Hendricks Kinyon was a physician before enlisting in Yadkin Co. at age 33. Appointed captain on 6-18-1861. Resigned on 3-28-1862 to apply for a medical position. Appointed assistant surgeon of the 66th Regiment, N.C. Troops, on 8-16-1862 (NCT VIII, 174). He served as a surgeon in the hospitals at Richmond, VA. Kinyon, b. in Davie Co., m. Elizabeth Ann Conrad, b. 1-22-1835 in Stokes (Forsyth) Co., the dau. of John Joseph and Keziah Harding Conrad. Dr. Kinyon received his A.B. from Union College, Schenectady, NY, and studied law at Columbia University. After returning to NC, he decided to study medicine at Bellevue Medical School. He practiced at Enon until the war broke out. After the war, he took his wife and ch. and moved to Johnson Co., Missouri, where he was the only physician in a 40-mile radius. They lived in a log cabin on the Post Oak Road near Centerview, MO. He d. at age 78, and both he and his wife are bur. at Centerview Cemetery ("The Harding Family," unpublished manuscript by Frances H. Casstevens; *Kinfolk of Jacob Conrad*, 156–159).

KIRK, FRANKLIN WESLEY; 75TH REG., 18TH BRIG. MILITIA.

KIRK, JAMES M.; CO. F, 28TH REG. (04/02/1842–?; Friendship Bapt. [tombstone]).
James M. Kirk e. in Yadkin Co., where he lived, at age 19 on 6-18-1861. Captured near Petersburg, VA, on 4-2-1865, and confined at Point Lookout, MD, until released on 6-28-1865, after taking the Oath of Allegiance (NCT VIII, 179). James M. Kirk survived the war and d. sometime after 1877. He m. Martha ("Mattie") A. Poindexter on 10-5-1865, the dau. of Thomas H. and Amelia Dull Poindexter. Both are bur. at Friendship Bapt. Church ("Poindexter," 66–67).

KIRK, JOHN P.; CO. F, 28TH REG. (?–05/05/1864).
John P. Kirk e. in Yadkin Co. on 11-5-1863. He was killed at Wilderness, VA, on 5-5-1864 (NCT VIII, 179).

KITTLE (KETTLE), COSTIN; CO. F, 28TH REG. MUSICIAN (1837–?).
Costin Kittle lived in Yadkin Co. and e. there at age 24 on 6-18-1861. Mustered in as musician (fifer) but reduced to ranks July–Oct. 1862. Reported missing at Fryser's Farm, VA, on 6-30-1862 (NCT VIII, 179). Costin Kittle, b. ca. 1836, was the s. of William and Mary Kittle, and a brother to Eugene Kittle and Joseph Kittle listed below (1850 Surry).

KITTLE (KETTLE), EUGENE; CO. F, 28TH REG. MUSICIAN (1835–?).
Eugene Kittle, a Yadkin farmer, e. there at age 26 on 6-18-1861, mustering in as musician (drummer). He was reduced to ranks Jan–June 1862, and discharged 6-10-1862 because of "chronic diarrhoea & debility (NCT VIII, 179–180). Eugene Kittle, b. ca. 1834, was the s. of William and Mary Kittle. Eugene m. Nancy Anne Gibbs on 4-17-1864 (YCMR; 1850 Surry).

KITTLE (KETTLE), JOSEPH; CO. F, 28TH REG. (1841–?).
Joseph Kittle, a Yadkin Co. carpenter, e. at age 21 on 4-5-1862. Discharged on 7-7-1862 because of "chronic disease of lungs or phthsis pulmonalis" (NCT VIII, 180). Joseph Kittle, b. ca. 1838, was the s. of William and Mary Kittle (1850 Surry).

KNOTT (NOTT), JOHN; CO. A, 6TH REG. (03/18/1843–?; Champaign, Illinois).
John Knott e. at age 18 on 9-15-1862 in Yadkin Co. He was captured at Rappahannock Station, VA, in Nov. 1863 and confined at Point Lookout, MD, until paroled and trans. to Aiken's Landing, James River, VA, on 2-24-1865. Exchanged before 3-4-1865, when he was admitted to a Richmond, VA, hospital (NCT IV, 278). John was the oldest child of James and

Louvicia Rice Knott. He was b. in Guilford Co. and moved with his parents when about five years old to what is now Yadkin Co. After the war, he returned to Yadkin Co. and m. Ellen Cowl(e) on 10-15-1865 (YCMR). They had 9 boys, all b. in Yadkin Co. This family moved to Champaign Co., Illinois. After Ellen's death, John m. Kate Lamphier (*Heritage*, 453).

LADD, MILES W.; CO. I, 28TH REG. (11/27/1842–09/25/1861).
Miles W. Ladd e. in Yadkin Co. at age 19 on 8-13-1861. He d. near Hamptonville on 9-25-1861 of "typhoid fever." He was "A young man of excellent qualities, strictly moral and pious in the fullest sense of the word.... In his death the State has lost a brave and efficient soldier—his parents a kind and obedient son" (NCT VIII, 214). Miles Ladd, age 7, was living with his mother, Rebecca, and sister, Jane, in the Thomas and Jane Patterson household near Windsor's Crossroads. He was listed as attending school.

LADD, THOMAS; CO. D, 44TH REG. (1827–?).
Thomas Ladd e. in Wake Co. at age 35 on 12-1-1862. Reported AWOL on 1-18-1863 (NCT X, 430).

LAKEY, ABRAM PHILLIPS; CO. G, 21ST REG. (1826–?).
Abram (Abraham) Phillips Lakey e. in Yadkin Co. on 10-1-1863. Captured at Fisher's Hill, VA, on 9-22-1864, and confined at Winchester, VA. He was released on 4-25-1865 (NCT VI, 595). He was one of four brothers (Abraham P., William D., Francis M., and John L.) who e. in the same company, the s. of Abraham and Nancy Phillips Lakey. Abraham's second wife was Rosy Sears, who he m. on 8-19-1879 (YCMR; *Heritage*, 459).

LAKEY, ELLIS; CO. H, 63RD REG. (5TH CAVALRY) (1835–?).
Ellis Lakey e. in Davie Co. on 7-18-1862. He was wounded and captured at Upperville, VA, on 6-21-1863, and confined at Old Capitol Prison, Washington, DC, until paroled and exchanged at City Point, VA, on 6-30-1863. He was present or accounted for through Feb. 1865. Paroled at Salisbury, NC, in 1865 (NCT II, 434). Ellis Lakey, age 15, was living in the household of his mother, Mary Lakey, and brothers Elkanah and William in 1850 (1850 Surry).

LAKEY, FRANCIS M(ARION).; CO. G, 21ST REG. (09/17/1832–12/08/1917).
Francis M. Lakey e. on 10-1-1863, and was present until he deserted to the enemy on 2-25-1864. Confined at Ft. Monroe, VA, he was released on 3-3-1864, after taking the Oath of Allegiance (NCT VI, 595). F. M. Lakey, the s. of Abraham and Nancy Phillips Lakey, m. Nancy M. Hall on 9-20-1855 (YCMR; *Heritage*, 459; 1850 Surry).

LAKEY, JESSE FRANKLIN; CO. B, 38TH REG. (1846–1872/3; Enon Bapt. (tombstone, no dates).
Jesse Franklin Lakey e. at Camp Vance on 9-27-1864. Present through Oct. 1864 (NCT X, 26). He was the s. of Jesse Francis and Icy (Hester?) Lakey (*Heritage*, 459–460; 1850 Surry).

LAKEY, JOHN L.; CO. G, 21ST REG. (03/23/1844–04/10/1881).
John L. Lakey e. in Yadkin Co. on 10-1-1863. Captured at Sayler's Creek, VA, on 4-6-1865, and confined at Newport News, VA, until released on 6-27-1865, after taking the Oath of Allegiance (NCT VI, 595). John L. Lakey was the s. of Abraham and Nancy Phillips Lakey. He m. Mahala Patterson on 10-29-1869 (*Heritage*, 459; 1850 Surry).

LAKEY, WILLIAM D.; CO. G, 21ST REG. (1831–?).
William D. Lakey e. in Yadkin Co. on 10-1-1863. Present until court-martialed about 12-8-1864. Reason for court-martial not given. Dropped from the rolls of the company prior to 3-1-1865 (NCT VI, 595) William D. Lakey was the s. of Abraham and Nancy Phillips Lakey (*Heritage*, 459).

LANE, THOMAS; CO. I, 33RD REG. (1823–?).
Thomas Lane, b. in Yadkin Co., but resided in Surry, where he was a farmer before enlisting in Forsyth Co. at age 38 on 9-15-1861. Present through Feb. 1862. Reported AWOL from July 1862 through Aug. 1863. Returned to duty Sept.-Oct. 1863. Present until wounded in the right thigh at Spotsylvania Court House, VA, on 5-12-1864. Reported absent-wounded through Feb. 1865 (NCT IX, 227).

LANGLEY, C(HARLES) A.; CO. H, 63RD REG. (5TH CAVALRY) (1838–?).
C. A. Langley e. in Davie Co. at age 24 on 7-18-1862. He was captured at Madison Court House, VA, on 9-22-1863, and confined at Old Capitol Prison, Washington, DC, until transferred to Point Lookout, MD, on 9-26-1863. He was transferred to Elmira, NY, on 8-16-1864, where he remained until paroled and exchanged at Venus Point, Savannah River, GA, on 11-15-1864 (NCT II, 434). Charles A. Langley, age 12, was living with his parents, Charles and Nancy, and brothers James W. and Pleasant D. in 1850 (1850 Surry).

LASH, WILCHER; CO. B, 38TH REG. (1842–?).
Wilcher Lash e. in Yadkin Co. at age 19 on 2-15-1863. Deserted to the enemy at Chancellorsville, VA, May 2-4, 1863. Sent to Washington, D.C. Released on an unspecified date after taking the Oath of Allegiance. Wilcher Lash was the s. of George and Mary Lash, and was listed as 8 years old in 1850 (NCT X, 26; 1850 Surry).

LAUGENHOUR, ANDREW LAFAYETTE; 75TH REG., 18TH BRIG. (07/09/1831–11/19/1933; Sandy Springs).

Andrew Lafayette Laugenhour m. Eliza D. Ledford (b. 4-22-1832, d. 12-20-1904), buried Sandy Springs Bapt. Church, Iredell Co., NC.

LAWRENCE, LEE; CO. B, 21ST REG.
Lee Lawrence e. in Yadkin Co. on 5-12-1861 and was present until he transferred to Co. A, 1st Battalion NC Sharpshooters, on 4-26-1862. He was present in Co., A, 1st Battalion Sharpshooters, through Dec. 1864. Paroled at Appomattox Court House, VA, on 4-9-1865 (NCT III, 73; VI, 553).

LEAGANS, ANANIAS; CO. I, 28TH REG.
(12/25/1820–05/31/1890; Deep Creek Bapt., Yadkin Co., NC).
Ananias Leagans (Legans) lived in Yadkin Co. where he e. at age 41 on 3-8-1862. He was captured at Hanover Court House, VA, on 5-27-1862, and confined at Ft. Monroe, VA, then Ft. Columbus, NY Harbor. He was paroled and transferred to Aiken's Landing on 8-5-1862. Detailed as a shoemaker at Salisbury in Feb. 1863. He was reported absent on detail through Feb. 1865 (NCT VIII, 214).

LEAGANS, JAMES M.; CO. I, 28TH REG.
James M. Leagans e. on 8-13-1861. He was captured at Hanover Court House, VA, on 5-27-1862, and confined at Ft. Monroe, VA, then Ft. Columbus, NY Harbor. Paroled and transferred to Aiken's Landing, James River, VA, where he was received on 7-12-1862 for exchange. Returned to duty. Wounded in the neck and shoulder at Fredericksburg, VA, on 12-13-1862. Returned to duty on 2-10-1863. Reported AWOL from 7-1-1863 to 1-5-1864. Reported present for duty Nov. 1864–Feb. 1865 (NCT VIII, 214).

LEAGANS, MATTHEW; CO. I, 28TH REG.
(1842–?).
Matthew Leagans lived in Yadkin Co. where he e. at age 19 on 8-13-1861. Deserted on 7-15-1863 (NCT VIII, 214).

LEAMON (LEEMON), JAMES D.; CO. D, 52ND REG. (1828–07/01/1863; Oakwood Cem., Raleigh, NC).
James D. Leaman, a Yadkin Co. resident, e. at age 35 on 10-21-1862. He was killed at Gettysburg, PA, on 7-1-1863 (NCT XII, 34). James D. Leaman is buried at Oakwood Cemetery, Raleigh, NC. His body was returned to NC in the 1920s and reburied. James D. Leaman/Leamon m. first on 10-21-1852 Winney Norman; he then m. Sarah Choplin on 4-4-1861 (YCMR) (per Hunter Edwards; Curtis D. Choplin, "An American Tragedy: The Robert Choplin Family").

LEONARD, J. B.; CO. E, 70TH REG. (1845–?).
J. B. Leonard, b. in Orange Co., was a shoemaker before enlisting in Yadkin Co. at age 17 on 3-17-1862. He was discharged on 7-2-1862 because he was underaged (NCT XIII, 323). He probably became a member of Co. E, 70th Regiment, Junior Reserves.

LEWIS, ASA F.; CO. B, 38TH REG. 2ND LIEUTENANT (1843–?).
Asa F. Lewis e. at age 19 on 10-16-1861. Mustered in as sergeant. Elected 3rd lieutenant on 2-28-1863. Promoted to 2nd lieutenant on 5-2-1863. Present until captured at Falling Waters, MD, on 7-14-1863. Confined at Point Lookout, MD, 8-17-1863. Transferred to Johnson's Island, OH, where he arrived 10-23-1863. Released from there on 6-11-1865, after taking the Oath of Allegiance (NCT X, 21). Asa F. Lewis was b. ca. 1843, the s. of Asa and Elizabeth Shinn Lewis (per Douglas Reed Niemeyer).

LEWIS, ELIAS D.; CO. B., FREEMAN'S BAT. INFANTRY (1824–07/14/1864; Confederate Cem., Salisbury, NC).
Elias D. Lewis, b. about 1824, served in Co. B, Freeman's Battalion, Infantry, Capt. Allen's Company. He d. of contagious fever, and was buried at Salisbury, NC, at the Confederate Prison. Elias was the s. of Asa and Elizabeth Shinn Lewis. Elias D. Lewis m. Elizabeth J. Windsor on 1-8-1853 (YCMR), and was the brother of Levi Branson, William T., and Asa F. Lewis (per Niemeyer). Elias and wife Elizabeth had a number of children.

LEWIS, LEVI BRANSON; CO. A, 9TH BAT. CORPORAL (12/01/1829–01/14/1903; Brushcreek Cem., Franklin Co., Missouri).
Levi Branson Lewis is the same as L. B. Lewis. He served both in Co. A, 9th Battalion (Home Guard) and the 75th Reg., 18th Brigade (Militia). Levi was a corporal in the Militia, and a 2nd lieutenant in the Home Guard. The s. of Asa and Elizabeth Shinn Lewis, Levi m. Temperance Mary Ann Windsor (b. 5-20-1839, d. 2-10-1900), dau. of Bennet and Sarah A. Holeman Windsor, on 10-2-1856 (YCMR). After the war, this family moved by covered wagon in 1869 to Missouri (per Niemeyer).

LEWIS, WILLIAM T.; CO. B, 38TH REG. SERGEANT (1837–01/20/1863).
William T. Lewis was a carpenter before enlisting in Yadkin Co. at age 24 on 10-16-1861. Mustered in as private, promoted to sergeant on 7-9-1862. Died 1-20-1863 of disease, place and cause not reported (NCT X, 26). William T. Lewis was the s. of Asa and Elizabeth Shinn Lewis, and the brother of all the preceding Lewis boys (per Niemeyer).

LILLINGTON, NICHOLAS WILLIAMS; CO. H, 55TH REG. CAPTAIN (01/03/1845–12/19/1921).
Nicholas W. Lillington, a Yadkin Co. resident (Little Yadkin Township), was appointed 2nd lieutenant on 10-1-1862. Promoted to 1st lieutenant on 3-10-1863. Slightly wounded in the scalp near Suffolk, VA, on 5-1-1863. Returned to duty prior to July 1, 1863. Wounded in the thigh at Gettysburg, PA, on 7-1-1863. Promoted to captain on 7-3-1863. Returned to duty on an unspecified date. Hospitalized at Richmond, VA, on 5-23-1864 with chronic diarrhoea. Transferred to another hospital on 5-24-1864.

Hospitalized at Richmond, VA, on 8-28-1864 with debilities. Transferred to another hospital on 9-5-1864. Was probably absent-sick most of the remainder of the war. He was transferred again to a hospital at Richmond on 1-29-1865 with remittent fever, and to another hospital on 1-31-1865, but he survived the war (NCT XIII, 506; Moore's *Roster* III, 569). Nicholas Williams Lillington, the s. of John A. and Elizabeth Kerr Williams Lillington, m. Sallie Alexander (Smith) Williams, widow of Lewis James Williams and the dau. of W. G. and Eliza Smith, on 12-25-1893 (YCMR). She is buried in the Williams Cemetery, Panther Creek, Forsyth Co., NC. Nicholas's father, John A., was from Wilmington (per Brumfield, "Williams and Henderson Families," 98–100, 108, 126, 167, 171).

LINDLEY, JOHN F.; CO. I, 18TH REG. (1837–?).
John F. Lindley e. in Wake Co. at age 25 on 9-10-1862. Present until wounded in the right hand at Chancellorsville, VA, on 5-3-1863. Reported absent-wounded or absent on light duty through Feb. 1865 (NC Troops VI, 407). John F. Lindley, the s. of Thomas and Rosannah Lindley, m. Cetha Beggarly on 2-15-1855 (YCMR). In 1850, John F. Lindley, age 17, was a farmer, living in his parents household. His father, Thomas, was a wagon maker (1850 Surry).

LINDLEY, JOSHUA A.; CO. B, 38TH REG. (1839–?).
Joshua A. Lindley was a Yadkin Co. farmer before enlisting at age 22 on 10-16-1861. Present until he deserted about 9-26-1862 (NCT X, 26). His brother, John F. Lindley, served in Co. I, 18th Reg. Joshua A. Lindley, age 11, was living in the household of his parents, along with his brother, in 1850 (1850 Surry).

LINDSAY (LINDSEY), A. A.; CO. A, 9TH BAT. HOME GUARD (1834–?).
This is Alfred A. Lindsey, s. of Laban and Margaret. At age 6, he was living in their household in 1850 (1850 Surry).

LINDSAY (LINDSEY), L. L.; CO. A, 9TH BAT. HOME GUARD (1819–?).
This may be Laban Lindsey, father of Alfred A. He was 31 in 1850 (1850 Surry).

LINDSEY, WADE; CO. I, 18TH REG. (01/05/1834–02/01/1891).
Wade Lindsey e. in Wake Co., age 26, on 9-10-1862. Present till wounded in the leg at Chancellorsville. His right leg had to be amputated. Reported absent-wounded until retired from service on 9-10-1864. He later received a pension (NCT VI, 407). His wife, Eliza, began drawing a Confederate widow's pension in 1900. Wade Lindsey was living in the household of Winney, Elizabeth A., Susannah, Mary, and Miriam Lindsey in 1850, and was probably the s. of one of them (1850 Surry).

LINDSY, THOMAS W.; HOME GUARD (ca. 1800–?).
This is probably Thomas Lindley, husband of Rosannah, and father of John F., William C., Joshua A., and three daughters, who was 50 years old in 1850 (1850 Surry).

LINEBERRY, ASBERRY O.; 75TH REG., 18TH BRIG. MILITIA (07/28/1822–?).
The name should correctly be Oren A. Lineberry, b. in Randolph Co., the s. of Francis and Mary Scotten Lineberry. Oren m. Alvira Reece on 12-13-1844, in Randolph. After her death, he moved to Yadkin Co. (after 1850) and m. Mary (Foot) Hurt, widow of James Hurt. Oren had two sons who served in the war. Lewis Lineberry was killed at Chancellorsville and Edwin Culver Lineberry was killed at Kinston, NC (Frances H. Casstevens, *The Descendants of Solomon Lineberry*).

LINEBERRY, EDWIN CULVER; CO. E, 70TH REG. (1848–?).
Edwin Culver Lineberry, the s. of Oren A. and Alvira Reece Lineberry, was b. in Randolph Co. He was killed at the battle of Kinston, NC.

LINEBERRY, LEWIS (LOUIS) S.; CO. B, 27TH REG. (ca. 1845–05-?–1863).
Louis S. Lineberry e. at age 17 in Guilford Co. on 8-17-1862 as a substitute for Private Henry S. Puryear. He was wounded at Bristoe Station, VA, on 10-14-1862. He returned to duty on an unspecified date and was killed at the Wilderness, VA, on 5-5-1864. "A most exellent soldier" (NCT VIII, 26). Lewis Lineberry, s. of Oren A. and Alvira Reece Lineberry, was b. about 1846 in Randolph Co.

LOGAN, FREBORN G.; CO. A, 54TH REG. (1807–?).
Freborn G. Logan was a Yadkin farmer (or shoemaker) before enlisting at age 55 on 5-3-1862 as a substitute for Martin Wilheim Deafled. Reported present through Feb. 1863. Discharged at Staunton, VA, 4-11-1863 because of "chronic rheumatism, general debility [and] effects of age, being fifty-six years old (NCT XIII, 253).

LOGAN, GEORGE T.; CO. A, 54TH REG. (1833–?).
George T. Logan, a farm laborer before enlisting in Yadkin Co. at age 29 on 5-2-1862, he was reported present through Oct. 1863. Reported absent-sick 11-7-1863 through 12-31-1863. Reported AWOL 1-21-1864 through 10-31-1864. Survived the war. NC pension records indicate he was wounded at Chancellorsville, VA, "May 5, 1863 or 1864" (NCT XIII, 253). George T. Logan, s. of John and Rebecca Logan, m. Nancy Wilhelm on 6-7-1855 (YCMR; 1850 Surry).

LOGAN, H. A.; CO. F, 28TH REG. (1842–04/18/1863).
H[ugh]. A. Logan lived in Yadkin Co. where he e. at age 21 on 4-27-1864. He d. "at home" on 4-18-1863,

cause of death not reported (NCT VIII, 180). He may be Hiram A. Logan, b. 1841, s. of George and Mary Logan (1850 Surry).

LOGAN, LARKIN C.; CO. H, 21ST REG. (1841–?).
Larkin C. Logan (a former Yadkin resident who was residing in Surry Co. at the time he e.) was a farmer before enlisting in Wake Co. at age 20 on 6-5-1861. Mustered in as private, promoted to corporal Nov. 1861–Feb. 1863. Present until wounded in the right arm at Gettysburg, PA, on 7-1-1863. Reported absent-wounded until he retired from service on 1-17-1865 because of disability (NCT VI, 606).

LOGAN, RICHARD M.; CO. F, 28TH REG. CORPORAL (04/24/1829–02/21/1878; Logan Family Cem.).
Richard M. Logan e. in Yadkin Co. at age 26 on 6-18-1861. Mustered in as sergeant but reduced to ranks Jan.–June 1862. Promoted to corporal Nov.–Dec. 1862. Reported AWOL from 9-1-1863 through Feb. 1865. Reduced to ranks before 11-1-1864 (NCT VIII, 180). In 1850, Richard M. Logan, age 21, was working as a blacksmith, and living in the household of merchant Richard S. Phillips. Richard M. Logan m. Martha Dorca Hall on 12-9-1852 (YCMR; 1850 Surry).

LONG, DANIEL; 75TH REG., 18TH BRIG. MILITIA.
Daniel Long m. Rachel Rhinehardt on 4-25-1861 (YCMR). She was b. 7-11-1819, d. 8-7-1893, buried at Center Methodist Church, Yadkinville, NC.

LONG, ELLIS; CO. I, 28TH REG. (1841–?).
Ellis Long lived in Yadkin where he e. at age 20 on 8-13-1861. Captured at Fredericksburg, VA, on 12-13-1862. Exchanged about 12-17-1862. Deserted on 7-23-1863. Returned to duty. Reported present Sept. 1864–Feb. 1865. Captured near Petersburg, VA, on 4-2-1865. Confined at Ft. Delaware, DE. Released from there on 6-19-1865, after taking the Oath of Allegiance (NCT VIII, 214). Ellis Long m. Frances Shugart on 3-14-1864 (YCMR).

LONG, FRANCIS; CO. I, 28TH REG. (1843–07/20/1862).
Francis Long e. in Yadkin Co. at age 18 on 8-13-1861. Died about 7-20-1862 of "diphtheria." Place of death not reported (NCT VIII, 214). Francis Long, age 7, is listed in the household of his parents, Danny and Winney Long, in 1850 (1850 Surry).

LONG, FREDERICK; CO. I, 28TH REG. 2ND LIEUT. (1840–10/23/1862; Stonewall Cem., Winchester, VA).
Frederick Long e. in Yadkin Co., age 21, and was appointed 2nd lieutenant on 8-13-1861. Wounded in the back at Shepherdstown, VA, on 9-20-1862. Died at Winchester, VA, on 10-23-1862 of wounds. "He was a brave and gallant officer" (NCT VIII, 207). Frederick Long, b. ca. 1840, was the s. of John and Nancy Davis Long (*Heritage*, 466; Long family records, and "Descendants of Henry Long" by Jasper Long).

LONG, ISAAC, JR.; CO. A, 9TH BAT. HOME GUARD.
Isaac Long, Jr., e. in Co. B, 38th Reg., on 10-16-1861. He was discharged on 2-7-1863 or 3-20-1862 after providing Private Joseph C. Cheek as a substitute (NCT X, 26).

LONG, NATHAN; CO. I, 28TH REG. (1825–?).
Nathan Long e. at Camp Vance on 4-17-1864. He was hospitalized at Richmond, VA, on 4-2-1865 with a gunshot wound. Place or date or wound not reported. Captured in a Richmond, VA, hospital on 4-3-1865, and transferred to Newport News, VA, on 4-23-1865. He was released on 6-30-1865, after taking the Oath of Allegiance (NCT VIII, 214). In 1850, Nathan Long was the head of the household which included wife Nancy A., and sons James F. and George W. (1850 Surry; 1860 Yadkin).

LONG, WILLIAM DOBSON; 75TH REG., 18TH BRIG. MILITIA (11/30/1836–01/01/1865; Swaim's Bapt.).

LYNCH (LINCH), GEORGE; CO. B, 38TH REG.
George Linch (Lynch) e. at Camp Vance on 9-27-1864. Present through Oct. 1864 (NCT X, 26).

LYNCH, PLEASANT H.; CO. F, 28TH REG. (1839–?).
Pleasant H. Lynch e. in Yadkin Co. at age 25 on 2-18-1863. Deserted to the enemy about 4-1-1863, and confined at Ft. Monroe, VA. Released on an unspecified date after taking the Oath of Allegiance (NCT VIII, 180). Pleasant H. Lynch, s. of John C. and Mary Lynch, m. Keziah Binkley on 2-16-1860 (YCMR; 1850 Surry).

LYNCH, THOMAS A.; CO. A, 54TH REG. (1832–12/13/1862).
Thomas A. Lynch, a Yadkin Co. farmer before enlisting on 5-2-1862 at age 29 was killed at Fredericksburg, VA, on 12-13-1862 (NCT XIII, 254).

MCBRIDE, DANIEL B.; CO. I, 28TH REG. (1841–07/03/1862).
Daniel B. McBride lived in Yadkin Co. where he e. at age 20 on 8-13-1861. He was wounded in the abdomen at Frayser's Farm, VA, or Malvern Hill, VA, about 6-30-1862. Hospitalized at Richmond, Va, where he d. on 7-3-1862 of wound (NCT VIII, 214-215).

MCBRIDE, J. L.; CO. B, 21ST REG. CORPORAL (?–10/14/1862).
J. L McBride e. on 5-12-1861. He mustered in as corporal and was present until he transferred to Co. A, 1st Battalion NC Sharpshooters. He d. at Staunton VA, on 10-14-1862 of "febris typhoides" (NCT III, 73; VI, 553).

MCBRIDE, JOHN G.; CO. I, 28TH REG. SERGEANT (1836–?).
John G. McBride lived in Yadkin where he e. at age 25 on 8-13-1861. Mustered in as private. Captured at Hanover Court House, VA, on 5-27-1862. Confined at Ft. Monroe, VA, then Ft. Columbus, NY Harbor. Paroled and transferred to Aiken's Landing on 8-5-1862. Returned to duty before 3-1-1865. Promoted to sergeant March 1863–June 1864. Reported AWOL Nov.-Dec. 1864. Returned to duty Jan.-Feb. 1865. Captured near Petersburg, VA, on 4-2-1865, and confined at Ft. Delaware, DE, until released on 6-19-1865, after taking the Oath of Allegiance (NCT VIII, 215).

MCBRIDE, WILLIAM; CO. E, 70TH REG.

MCBRIDE, WILLIAM D.; CO. B, 44TH REG. (1837–?).
William D. McBride e. at age 25 on 10-1-1862. Deserted on 11-23-1863 (NCT X, 414).

MCCOLLUM, JOHN; CO. F, 28TH REG. (1836–?).
John McCollum e. in Yadkin Co. on 10-27-1863. Reported AWOL on 8-1-1864 (NCT VIII, 180). John McCollum, age 14, was listed in the household of his parents, Michael, and grandmother Catherine McCollum, in the 1850 census (1850 Surry).

MCKAUGHN, B. TEMPLE; CO. I, 28TH REG. (1844–?).
B. Temple McKaughn lived in Yadkin Co. where he e. at age 18 on 3-8-1862. Captured by the enemy on an unspecified date and confined at Ft. Monroe, VA, on 8-26-1862. Paroled on 9-1-1862. Exchanged about 9-21-1862. Returned to duty before 3-1-1863. Wounded at Gettysburg, PA, July 1–3, 1863 (NCT VIII, 215).

MACKIE, NATHAN; CO. B, 24TH REG. (01/03/1829–06/27/1865; Camp Chase, OH).
NC pension records indicate Nathan Mackie e. on 7-1-1863. No further record (NCT VII, 271). Family tradition holds that Nathan Mackie was "conscripted" and d. as a result of wading across the Ohio River, after which he either had pneumonia or measles and d. at Camp Chase, Ohio on 6-2-1865. The family Bible gives dates of birth and death, and the notation that at the time of death, Nathan Mackie was 36 years, 5 months, and 25 days old (items from the files of Andrew Mackie, Yadkinville, NC). Nathan Mackie m. Elizabeth T. Vestal on 12-12-1854 (YCMR).

MACY, H. C.; CO. A, 9TH BAT. HOME GUARD.

MACY, THOMAS E.; CO. B, 38TH REG. (1842–?).
Thomas E. Macy e. in Yadkin Co. on 10-16-1861 at age 19. Enlisted in Co. I, 28th Reg. on 11-12-1861, apparently while still a member of this company. Discharged from this company on 1-10-1862 after providing a substitute. Macy was reported AWOL May–Oct. 1862. Returned to duty before 2-28-1863. Hospitalized at Richmond, VA, on 5-18-1864 with gunshot wound, place and date not reported. Reported on duty as a prison guard at Salisbury during Sept. 1864–Feb. 1865 (NCT VIII, 215; X, 27). T. E. Macy m. Martha M. Fleming on 9-19-1865 (YCMR).

MACY, WILLIAM L.; CO. B, 38TH REG. (09/08/1837–08/13/1908; Perry Shermer Cem.).
William L. Macy e. in Yadkin Co. on 10-16-1861 at age 24. He also e. in Co. I, 28th Reg., on 11-12-1861 while still a member of this company. Discharged from this company on 1-10-1862 after providing a substitute. He was captured at Hanover Court House, VA, on 5-27-1862, and confined at Ft. Monroe, VA, then Ft. Columbus, NY Harbor. Paroled and transferred to Aiken's Landing, James River, VA, where he was received on 7-12-1862 for exchange. Exchanged on 8-5-1862. Returned to duty before 3-1-1863. Hospitalized at Richmond, VA, on 4-21-1864 with gunshot wound of left thigh, place and date of wound not reported. Reported absent-sick Sept.–Oct. 1864 through Feb. 1865. Captured near Petersburg, VA, on 4-2-1865, and confined at Ft. Delaware, DE, until released on 6-19-1865, after taking the Oath of Allegiance (NCT VIII, 215; X, 27). William L. Macy m. Elizabeth Shermer on 11-26-1862 (bond date, YCMR).

MAHATHY, FINLY; CO. A, 9TH BAT. HOME GUARD (1847–?).
This may be William F. Mahaffy, s. of Sally Mahaffy, who, at age 3, was living with her in 1850 (1850 Surry). There were only two families with this name in 1850: Moses Mahaffa and Sarah Mahaffy.

MARLER, H. FRANKLIN; CO. D, 52ND REG. (1838–?).
H. Franklin Marler, a Yadkin resident, e. at Camp French near Petersburg, VA, at age 23 on 10-21-1862. Reported AWOL through Aug. 1863. Dropped from company rolls in Sept.-Oct. 1863 (NCT XII, 451). This may be Henry Francis Marler, the s. of John and Mary Wentworth Poindexter Marler, b. 1838, d. after 1880, m. on 3-20-1859 Elizabeth J. Martin ("Poindexter," 89; YCMR).

MARLER, JAMES NICHOLSON; CO. F, 28TH REG. CORPORAL (05/23/1845–05/28/1878; Yadkinville Town Cem., Yadkinville, NC).
James N. Marler e. at age 16 on 8-5-1861. Mustered in as private and promoted to corporal on 5-11-1863. Captured near Petersburg, VA, on 4-2-1865, and confined at Point Lookout, MD, until released on 6-15-1865, after taking the Oath of Allegiance (NCT VIII, 180). James Nicholson Marler was the s. of John and Mary Wentworth Poindexter Marler. He m. Laura A. Tulbert on 1-26-1873 (YCMR), the dau. Thomas L. and Levicy Jane Bryant Tulbert. The house in which Laura was born, "The Tulbert

House," is still standing and is part of the Charles Bruce Davis Museum of Art, History, and Science, Inc. ("Poindexter," 88–90).

MARLER, JOSEPH F.; CO. F, 28TH REG. (1827–02/25/1865).
Joseph F. Marler e. at age 34 on 6-18-1861, and was captured at Wilderness, VA, or at Spotsylvania Court House, VA, May 6–12, 1864. He was confined at Point Lookout, MD, before being transferred to Elmira, NY, on 7-25-1864. He d. at Elmira on 2-25-1865 of "pneumonia" (NCT VIII, 180).

MARLER, WILLIAM A.; CO. F, 28TH REG. 2ND LIEUTENANT (1839–12/01/1909; Harmony Grove Friends, Yadkinville, NC).
William A. Marler transferred from Co. F, 28th Reg. to Co. H, 63rd (5th NC Cavalry). He mustered in as private and was appointed sergeant Nov.-Dec. 1862. Promoted to 1st sergeant May 1863. Transferred to Co. F, 28th Reg. in June 1863 upon appointment as 2nd lieutenant to rank from 4-9-1863 (NCT II, 434). He was captured at Gettysburg, PA, 7-3-1863, and confined at Ft. Delaware, DE, until transferred to Johnson's Island, Ohio. He was paroled and transferred to Cox's Wharf, James River, VA, where he was exchanged on 3-22-1864 (NCT III, 174). William A., the s. of John and Mary Marler, returned to Yadkin Co. where he m. Sarah M. Phillips, dau. of Thomas J. and Kezziah Phillips, on 12-19-1876 (YCMR; "Poindexter," 90).

MARSHALL, HENRY; 75TH REG., 18TH BRIG. MILITIA.

MARTIN, ALFRED W.; CO. I, 28TH REG. (1840–?).
Alfred W. Martin lived in Yadkin Co. where he e. at age 21 on 8-13-1861. Deserted on 8-5-1862 (NCT VIII, 215). Alfred W. Martin, age 10, was listed in the household of his parents, Meredith and Rose Martin, in the 1850 census (1850 Surry).

MARTIN, DOCTOR ALEXANDER; HOME GUARD (03/09/1836–02/08/1919; East Bend Bapt., East Bend, NC).
Doctor ("Dock") Alexander Martin was a deputy sheriff during the war and a member of the Home Guard. He was the s. of John and Jane Kerr Martin of East Bend. He m. Virginia Poindexter on 9-20-1865 (YCMR; *Heritage*, 490; "Poindexter," 97).

MARTIN, GILBERT; CO. F, 28TH REG. (1828–?).
Gilbert Martin was a Yadkin Co. farmer before enlisting at age 33 on 6-18-1861. He was discharged on 11-7-1861 because of "an affliction of the spine of some eight years standing & which interferes with the use of his lower limbs" (NCT VIII, 180). Gilbert was the s. of John and Jane Kerr Martin. He m. Betsy Baker in Surry Co. on 5-11-1850, and they had one s. and four daughters. After he returned from the war, he d. of typhoid fever (*Heritage*, 490). Gilbert was 6 feet 2 inches tall. He had a reddish complexion, blue eyes and sandy hair (NC State Archives, Confederate Records, submitted by Jane Smith Hill, Winston-Salem, NC).

MARTIN, I. H.; CO. E, 70TH REG.

MARTIN, J. W.; CO. H, 63RD REG. (5TH CAVALRY).
J. W. Martin e. on 7-18-1862. He was hospitalized at Danville, VA, on 5-18-1864 with a gunshot wound to hand. He was reported as a deserter July-Aug. 1864 (NCT II, 434).

MARTIN, JOHN A.; CO. A, 9TH REG. (1ST CAVALRY).
John A. Martin e. at age 22 on 5-25-1861. Present through Dec. 1864 (NCT II, 15).

MARTIN, JOHN B.; CO. B, 38TH REG. SERGEANT (08/24/1830–02/16/1910).
John B. Martin e. at age 31 on 10-16-1861, mustering in as corporal. Promoted to sergeant April-June 1862. Present until wounded at Gettysburg, PA, July 1–3, 1863. Returned to duty before 9-1-1863. Captured at the Wilderness, VA, on 5-6-1864, and confined at Point Lookout, MD, on 5-17-1864 before being transferred to Elmira, NY, on 8-10-1864. He was released 5-29-1865, after taking the Oath of Allegiance (NCT X, 27). John Brittain Martin was b. 8-14-1830, the s. of Morgan and Mary Brittain Martin (*Heritage*, 488).

MARTIN, JOHN H.; CO. F, 28TH REG. (06/27/1842–04/28/1919; Flat Rock Bapt., Yadkin Co., NC).
John H. Martin e. in Yadkin Co. on 4-27-1864. Reported AWOL on 10-16-1864 (NCT VIII, 180).

MARTIN, JOHN H., JR.; CO. I, 28TH REG. (1843–?).
John H. Martin e. in Yadkin Co. at age 18 on 8-13-1861. Captured at Hanover Court House, VA, on 5-27-1862, and confined at Ft. Monroe, VA, then Ft. Columbus, NY Harbor. Transferred to Aiken's Landing, James River, VA, where he was received on 7-12-1862 for exchange. Exchanged there on 8-5-1862, he returned to duty before 11-1-1862. He was captured again at Wilderness, VA, on 5-6-1864, and confined at Point Lookout, MD. Paroled and transferred to Boulware's Wharf, James River, VA, where he was received about 2-20-1865 for exchange (NCT VIII, 215).

MARTIN, MORGAN C. M.; CO. B, 38TH REG. (08/31/1845–12/21/1932; Harmony Grove Friends).
Morgan Calvin Miles ("Mack") Martin e. in Yadkin Co. at age 18 on 9-15-1863. Present through Oct. 1864. Surrendered at Appomattox Court House, VA, on 4-9-1865 (NCT X, 27). M. C. Martin m. S. C. Long on 7-10-1866 (date of bond, YCMR). Morgan Calvin "Mack" Miles Martin was the s. of Morgan

and Mary Brittain Martin. He was a brother to John Brittain, William Leander, Wiley Clingman, and Thomas Alfred Martin. "Mack" Martin followed his brother to Missouri and lived there for a while. Then he went to western Nebraska to homestead, became discouraged, and returned to Missouri, before returning to Yadkinville where he m. on 7-10-1866 Sarah (Sally) C. Long. She was the dau. of Daniel Long who lived near Cox's Mill (*Heritage*, 488–489; 1850 Surry).

MARTIN, P. R.; CO. I, 44TH REG. (1838–?).
P. R. Martin lived in Yadkin Co. where he e. at age 24 on 12-10-1862. Listed as a deserter in Jan. 1863 (NCT X, 480).

MARTIN, REPS; CO. F, 28TH REG. (01/13/1826–05/29/1911; East Bend Bapt., East Bend, NC).
Reps Martin was a Yadkin Co. farmer before enlisting at age 35 on 6-18-1861. Mustered in as sergeant but reduced to ranks Jan.–June 1862. Discharged on 6-10-1862 because of "predisposition to disease of the lungs, accompanied with a severe cough of long standing" (NCT VIII, 180). Reps Martin was the s. of John and Jane Kerr Martin of East Bend. He m. Nancy Elizabeth Poindexter on 9-20-1848 (Surry Marriage Register). They had 7 sons and 2 daughters. Reps was treasurer of Yadkin Co. from 1870 to 1872 (*Heritage*, 491).

MARTIN, REUBEN BENNETT; CO. F, 28TH REG. (1834–05/23/1864; Spotsylvania Court House, VA).
(Reuben) Bennett Martin e. in Yadkin Co. at age 29 on 2-1-1863. He was killed at Jericho Mills, VA, on 5-23-1864 (NCT VIII, 180). Reuben Bennet Martin m. Martha Truelove, b. ca. 1834, on 1-10-1856 (YCMR). They had two sons (*Heritage*, 490; Casstevens, "The Poindexter Family," 84).

MARTIN, THOMAS ALFRED; CO. B, 38TH REG. CORPORAL (09/21/1842–03/11/1907; Guilford, MO).
Thomas Alfred Martin e. in Yadkin at age 21 on 9-1-1862. Mustered in as private; promoted to corporal March–April 1863. Present until wounded at Gettysburg, PA, 7-1-1863. Returned to duty Nov.–Dec. 1863. Captured at Wilderness, VA, 5-6-1864, and confined at Point Lookout, MD, on 5-17-1864. Transferred to Elmira, NY, on 8-10-1864, and released from there on 5-19-1865 after taking the Oath of Allegiance (NCT X, 27). Thomas Alfred Martin was the s. of Morgan and Mary Brittain Martin, and a brother to John B., William Leander, Wiley Clingman, and Morgan C. M. Martin (*Heritage*, 488). After the death of his mother in 1866, Thomas Alfred Martin moved to Missouri near his Brittain cousins. There he taught school and farmed. There he m. on 9-24-1874 in Clyde, Missouri, Jemima Ann Weathermon (b. 7-21-1855, d. 3-20-1926), dau. of Isaac Newton and Saran Ann Hobson Weathermon (*Heritage*, 488–489).

MARTIN, W. C.; CO. A, 9TH BAT. HOME GUARD.

MARTIN, WILEY C[LINGMAN].; CO. B, 38TH REG. (02/24/1837–01/03/1872; Martin Fam. Cem.).
Wiley C. Martin, a Yadkin Co. farmer, e. there at age 24 on 10-16-1861. Present until discharged on 5-6-1862 because of "disability & disease" (NCT X, 27). Wiley Clingman Martin was the s. of Morgan and Mary Brittain Martin, and a brother to John B., William Leander, Thomas Alfred, and Morgan Calvin Miles Martin. Wiley C. Martin m. Louisa J. Denny on 1-18-1865 (bond date, YCMR). After Wiley Clingman's death, his widow went to Missouri where she m. Allen Gentry on 9-24-1874 (*Heritage*, 488).

MARTIN, WILLIAM; CO. A, 9TH BAT. HOME GUARD.

MARTIN, WILLIAM L[EANDER].; CO. B, 38TH REG. (11/17/1834–05/10/1863; Martin Fam Cem.).
William L. Martin e. in Yadkin Co. at age 26, on 4-19-1862. Present until wounded at Chancellorsville, VA, 5-3-183. He d. at Hamilton's Crossing, VA, 5-10-1863 of wounds (NCT X, 27). William Leander Martin was the s. of Morgan and Mary Brittain Martin, and a brother to John B., Wiley Clingman, Thomas Alfred and Morgan C. M. Martin who all served in Co. B, 38th Reg. (*Heritage*, 488).

MARTIN, WILLIAM LEE; CO. A, 9TH REG.(1ST CAVALRY) SERGEANT (12/24/1829–03/18/1909; Flat Rock Bapt. Ch.).
William Lee Martin e. at age 31 on 5-25-1861. Mustered in as private, appointed sergeant Sept.–Oct. 1862. Captured at Gettysburg July 3–4, 1863, and confined at Point Lookout, MD. Exchanged at Cox's Landing, VA, on 2-14-1865. Admitted to a Richmond, VA, hospital on 2-19-1865, then furloughed for 40 days on 2-10-1865 (NCT II, 15).

MASON, A[NDREW]. J.;CO. F, 13TH REG. (1830–?).
A. J. Mason e. at Camp Vance near Morganton on 1-25-1864. He was present through Feb. 1864, but deserted before 5-1-1864 (NCT V, 343). Mason was living next door to his mother, Elen Mason in 1850 (1850 Surry Census).

MATTHEWS, BRADLEY; 75TH REG., 18TH BRIG. MILITIA (1834–?).
Bradley Mathis (Matthews), s. of Alfred Mathis, m. Emma Messick, dau. of Bethel Messick on 8-7-1879 (YCMR). In 1850, Bradley Mathis (Matthews), age 16, was living in the household of his parents, Bradley and Martha Mathis (Matthews) (1850 Surry).

MATTHEWS, HENRY DENSON; CO. F, 28TH REG. (08/24/1843–05/05/1864).

Henry D. Matthews e. in Yadkin Co. on 9-28-1863. He was killed at Wilderness, VA, on 5-5-1864 (NCT VIII, 180). Henry Denson Matthews was the s. of Absalom and Mitty Poindexter Matthew, and brother to Thomas A. F., John V. and Joseph M. Matthews (*Heritage*, 498; "Poindexter," 74; 1850 Surry).

MATTHEWS, J. T. S.; CO. I, 21ST REG. (1845–?).
J. T. S. Mattthews e. in Yadkin Co. on 11-1-1863. Present till hospitalized at Danville, VA, on 7-1-1864 for gunshot wound to right foot. Deserted from the hospital on 8-19-1864 (NCT VI, 616). NC pension records indicate he served in Co. F, 28th Reg. (NCT VIII, 180). James T. Stokely Matthews, the s. of James Matthews, m. Curlista Jane Martin, b. 6-30-1849, d. 2-6-1927, dau. of Reps and Nancy Elizabeth Poindexter Martin, on 12-13-1866 (YCMR; "Poindexter," 42–43; 1850 Surry).

MATTHEWS, JAMES; CO. D, 21ST REG. (1836–1/1/1865).
James Matthews e. at age 18 while a resident of Yadkin Co. on 9-20-1863. He d. before 1-1-1865, but place, date, and cause of death were not reported (NCT VI, 569). James was probably the s. of Hezekia and Rebecca Matthews (1850 Surry).

MATTHEWS, JOHN VINCENT; CO. F, 28TH REG. (04/17/1841–07/31/1895; Prospect Meth. Ch.).
John Vincent Matthews e. in Yadkin Co. on 9-28-1863. He was captured near Petersburg, VA, on 4-2-1865, and confined at Point Lookout, MD, until released on 6-29-1865, after taking the Oath of Allegiance (NCT VIII, 180). John Vincent, the s. of Absalom and Amitty Poindexter Matthews, m. Martha Warden, b. 1842, on 2-14-1867 (YCMR). She was the dau. of Iredell and Mary Ann Bovender Warden. They had six ch.: Henry, Abram, Richard, Lillie, Julius, and Preston Matthews. During his life, John Vincent Matthews was a soldier, farmer, teacher, clerk, surveyor, and church leader (*Heritage*, 502; 1850 Surry).

MATTHEWS, T. C.; CO. I, 21ST REG.
T. C. Matthews e. in Yadkin Co. on 11-1-1863. Reported absent-wounded Sept.-Oct. 1864 through Feb. 1865. Place and date of wound not reported (NCT VI, 616). Pension records indicate he served in Co. F, 28th Reg. (NCT VIII, 180).

MATTHEWS, THOMAS A. P. F[RANKLIN].; HOME GUARD (01/05/1834–03/09/1916; Prospect Meth. Ch.).
Thomas A. P. F. Matthews, the oldest child of Absalom and Mitty Poindexter Matthews, was a farmer, teacher, a magistrate, as well as a member of the Home Guard during the Civil War. He m. three times, first to Sarah Jester, second to Permelia Carter, and third to Lucinda Hunt. Thomas and Sarah Jester Matthews had seven ch.: William Anderson, Francis Marion, Martha, James, Robert, Thomas, and Wesley (*Heritage*, 499; "Poindexter," 69; 1850 Surry).

MAY, F[REDERICK]. L.; CO. H, 63RD REG. (5TH CAVALRY) (1842–?).
F. L. May e. in Davie Co. at age 20 on 7-18-1862. He was captured at Catletts Station, VA, on 10-14-1863, and confined at Old Capitol Prison, Washington, DC, until transferred to Point Lookout, MD, on 10-27-1863. He remained there until paroled and exchanged at Venus Point, Savannah River, GA, on 11-15-1864 (NCT II, 434).

MAY, HENRY D.; CO. A, 1ST BAT. SHARPSHOOTERS.
H. D. May e. "at camp in Virginia" on 3-17-1864. Present through Dec. 1864 (NCT III, 73). Henry D. May m. Sarah Wilkins on 1-25-1866 (YCMR).

MAY, J. M.; CO. A, 1ST BAT. SHARPSHOOTERS (1842–?).
J. M. May e. in Wake Co. on 9-4-1862. Present through Dec. 1864 (NCT III, 73). J. M. is probably James Madison May, b. 1842. James M. May m. Sarah J. Casey on 1-2-1862 (YCMR). He was probably the s. of Samuel and Lydia May (1850 Surry).

MAY, JAMES F.; CO. A, 1ST BAT. SHARPSHOOTERS (1847–?).
James May e. at "camp in Virginia" on 3-15-1864. Present through Dec. 1864 (NCT III, 73). He was living in Yadkin Co. in 1860, where he was listed as being 13 years old, b. 1847.

MAY, MONROE; CO. B, 21ST REG. SERGEANT (1840–?).
Monroe May e. in Yadkin Co. on 5-12-1861 as a private and was promoted to sergeant on 10-31-1861. Present until he transferred to Co. A, 1st Battalion NC Sharpshooters. As a member of Co. A, 1st Battalion Sharpshooters, he was present through Dec. 1864. May was wounded and captured at Hatcher's Run on 2-6-1865, and confined at U. S. Army General Hospital, West's Buildings, Baltimore, MD, until transferred to Ft. McHenry, MD, on 5-9-1865. Released after taking the Oath of Allegiance on 6-10-1865. He is the s. of Samuel and Lydia May (NCT III, 73; VI 553; 1850 Surry).

MAY, STANLEY S.; 6TH MISSOURI (08/23/1835–10/01/1936; Courtney Bapt. Ch.).
Stanley Samuel May was living in Oseola, Missouri, in 1861 where he e. in the CSA, the 6th Missouri Regiment. May fought in battles in five or six Southern states, and was at the Siege of Vicksburg, which lasted 48 days. He was captured at Vicksburg and then exchanged. The worst battle he was in was that of Franklin, TN, where all but 4 men and 2 officers in his company were killed or wounded. He continued to serve in the CSA until the surrender in April 1865. Then, he returned to NC and m. Nancy Gabard in 1867. He worked with his father building

wagons and caskets. Samuel May attended the first free schools. He also taught school in Davie Co. and in the Boonville area of Yadkin Co. He was ordained a Baptist minister in 1875, and for 60 years pastored many churches in Yadkin Co. He preached his last sermon at Huntsville Baptist Church. May attended a Confederate reunion at the Robert E. Lee Hotel in Winston-Salem in 1930. He was the oldest active Confederate veteran in NC then at age 95 (from granddaughter Mattie May Reavis, 1016 Lone Hickory Road, Yadkinville, NC 27055). May lived to be 101 years old (Rutledge, 169-170). Stanley Samuel May, the s. of William and Mary Magdalene May, m. Elizabeth Cranfield on 2-8-1852 (YCMR; 1850 Surry).

MAYNARD, WILLIAM; CO. A, 1ST BAT. SHARPSHOOTERS (?-01/13/1864).
William Maynard e. "at camp in Virginia" on 11-1-1863. Died 1-13-1864 "at winter quarters in Virginia" (NCT III, 74). He was the s. of Horace L. and Tennessee Maynard.

MELTON, RICHARD GREENE; CO. I, 28TH REG. (1827-07/27/1862?; Government Cem.?, Danville, VA).
Richard Greene Melton, a Yadkin resident, e. at age 35 on 3-8-1862. He d. in a Richmond, VA, hospital on 7-27-1862 or 8-9-1862 of "diarrhoea" or "erysipelas" (NCT VIII, 215). Richard Melton, the s. of Ishom and Susannah Melton, m. Elizabeth Spillman on 4-22-1852 (YCMR). She was the dau. of Samuel and Alley Hutchens Spillman (*Heritage*, 383; 1850 Surry). He was a brother of Zachariah Melton, who served in the same company.

MELTON, ZACHARIAH; CO. I, 28TH REG. (1839-?).
Zachariah Melton lived in Yadkin Co. where he e. at age 23 on 3-8-1862. He was captured at Hanover Court House, VA, on 5-27-1862 and confined at Ft. Monroe, VA, then Ft. Columbus, NY Harbor. He was paroled and transferred to Aiken's Landing, James River, VA, where he was received on 7-12-1862 for exchange. Exchanged on 8-5-1862. Reported AWOL Jan.-Feb. 1863. Returned from desertion on 9-22-1864. Transferred to Company G, 52nd Reg., on the same date. He was reported present in Co.G, 52nd Reg. Nov.-Dec. 1864 (NCT VIII, 215; XII, 486). He was the s. of Ishom and Alley Hutchens Spillman and the brother of Richard Greene Melton. Her m. Nancy __ (Jackson, *Heritage of Surry County*, 383; 1850 Surry). The 1850 Surry Co. census gives his age as 17 (b. 1833).

MESSICK, BETHEL HAMILTON; CAPT. H.P. ALLEN'S CO. (09/15/1832-04/04/1911; Hollywood Cem., Elkin, Surry Co., NC).
Bethel Hamilton Messick was a private in Captain Allen's company, part of the local defense. He served part of his time as a prison guard at Salisbury, NC. He was a carpenter by trade, and made furniture in addition to operating a farm. Bethel m. Susan Ann Ray (b. 6-30-1830, d. 12-7-1877) on 8-10-1856 (YCMR). He then m. her sister as his second wife was Laura Cinderella Ray Holcomb, on 12-18-1881 in Yadkin Co. He had three ch.: Mary E.; Richard R. (b. 6-14-1861, d. 1-19-1904), and Lamyra Jane (b. 7-5-1863, d. 3-1-1840). He and most of the family are buried at Hollywood Cem., Elkin, NC (information submitted by Larry Messick; YCHGSJ V [March 1986]: 9; Jennings, *Messick Ancestral File 1664-1988*.

MESSICK, GEORGE T.; CO. H, 21ST REG. (1836-?).
George T. Messick e. in Wake Co. on 11-1-1863. Present until wounded at Plymouth, NC, on 4-18-1864. Paroled at Appomattox Court House, VA, on 4-9-1865 (NCT VI, 606). George T. Messick m. Amedia Ray on 11-17-1861 (YCMR). George T. Messick, age 14, was living in the household of his parents, William J. and Mary E. Messick in 1850 (1850 Surry).

MESSICK, JAMES J.; CO. B, 52ND REG. (1837-?).
James J. Messick e. in Wake Co. at age 25 on 10-8-1862. Present through Feb. 1863. Wounded and captured at Gettysburg, PA, about 7-3-1863. Confined at Ft. Delaware, DE, about 7-10-1863. Released from there on 5-5-1865, after taking the Oath of Allegiance (NCT XII, 434). In 1850, James J. Messick, age 13, was attending school and living in the household of his parents, Nelson and Sarah Messick (1850 Surry).

MICHAELS (MIKLES), JOHN; CO. A, 54TH REG. (1839-05/28/1863).
John Michaels, a Yadkin farmer, e. at age 23, on 5-3-1862. He deserted on 6-1-1862. Returned to duty prior to 1-1-1863. Hospitalized at Richmond, VA, 4-28-1863, with typhoid fever, and d. in the hospital 5-28-1863 of "erysipelas"(NCT XIII, 254). John Mikels m. Jane Cordle (Caudle) on 1-23-1853 (YCMR).

MICHAELS (MIKLES), NICHOLAS; CO. F, 28TH REG. (1838-?).
Nicholas Michaels (Mikles) lived in Yadkin Co. where he e. at age 24 on 6-18-1861. Wounded in the left hand, he was captured near Hanover Court House, VA, about 5-27-1862, and confined at Ft. Monroe, VA, then Ft. Columbus, NY Harbor. He was transferred to Aiken's Landing, James River, Va, arriving 7-12-1862, and exchanged there on 8-5-1862. He returned to duty Nov.-Dec. 1862, and deserted 5-27-1864 (NCT VIII, 180). Nicholas Mikels (Michaels), s. of Jesse and Nancy Michael, m. Sarah Taylor on 12-15-1865 (YCMR; 1850 Surry).

MILLER, DANIEL W.; CO. A, 21ST REG. (05/05/1821-08/10/1897; Huntsville Bapt., Yadkin Co., NC).
Daniel Miller e. in Yadkin Co. on 10-1-1863. Present

until captured at Cedar Creek, VA, on 10-19-1864. Confined at Point Lookout, MD, until paroled and transferred to Boulware's Wharf, James River, VA, where he was received on 3-30-1865 for exchange (NCT VI, 547–548). Daniel W. Miller m. Catharine Grose on 12-13-1853 (YCMR).

MILLER, GAITHER WILLIAM; CO. A, 9TH BAT. HOME GUARD (03/10/1828–03/12/1906; Flat Rock Bapt.).
Gaither W. Miller m. Mary A. Haynes on 9-25-1855 (YCMR).

MILLER, WILLIAM HENRY; CO. F, 28TH REG. (1820–1905; Randolph Co., NC).
William Henry Miller e. in Yadkin Co. at age 43 on 11-5-1863. He was captured in a Richmond, VA, hospital on 4-3-1865, and confined at Point Lookout, MD, until being released about 6-26-1865, after taking the Oath of Allegiance (NCT VIII, 180). William Henry Miller, m. Catharine Martin (b. 7-27-1827, d. 12-21-1895) on 12-14-1845 in Surry Co., NC. His second wife was Martha Prim Sprinkle. His ch. were: Mary Elizabeth (b. 1848), William Farley (1850–1906), John (b. 1852), Lee Roy (b. 1854), Robert Henry (1855–1917), Matthew Moses (1856–1896), Isaac Shubel (1858–1932); Phillip Snide (3-26-1860/4-30-1926), Joel A., Emma (1871–1958), and Lucy. After his second marriage, he moved to Randolph Co. and d. there about 1905 (per Dorma Hilliard, Olivia, NC) He may be listed as "H. Miller" in the 1880 Yadkin Co. Census, Fall Creek Township, and was living with wife Catherine and 6 children (1880 Yadkin Co. Census, transcribed by McCracken, 1991). William Miller, age 29 in 1850, born 1821, living with wife Catherine, age 28, and dau. Mary E. in the East Bend area next to John G. Poindexter, Henry Martin, and Charlotte Poindexter (1850 Surry).

MINESH, GEORGE W. see MINISH, GEORGE

MINISH, GEORGE W.; CO. B, 38TH REG. (1846–?).
George Minnish (Minish/Minesh), was b. ca. 1846, the s. of Joshua and Martha Messick Minnish (1850 Surry). He e. in Yadkin Co. age 17 (he was probably only 15), on 10-16-1861 in Co. B, 38th Reg. He deserted about 11-6-1861. He is probably the same George W. Minesh who e. at age 16 on 3-17-1862 in Co. H, 54th Reg. He was discharged before 7-2-1862 "by reason of being underage" (NCT X, 27, XIII, 324).

MINISH, THOMAS R.; CO. H, 54TH REG. CORPORAL (12/26/1838–06/02/1907; Fall Creek Bapt.).
Thomas R. Minish was b. in Surry Co. on 12-26-1838, the s. of Joshua and Martha Messick Minish. George Minnish/Minish was his brother. T. R. was a Yadkin Co. farmer before enlisting at age 23 on 4-28-1862. Mustered in as private. Present through Oct. 1863. Promoted to corporal on 10-20-1863. Captured at Rappahannock Station, VA, 11-7-1863. Confined at Point Lookout, MD, until paroled about 3-16-1864 and transferred to City Point, VA, on 3-20-1864 for exchange. Returned to duty prior to 7-20-1864. He was wounded in the right hand and both thighs at Stephen's Depot, VA, and hospitalized in Winchester, VA. Reported absent-wounded through Oct. 1864. Survived the war (NCT XIII, 324). Minish returned to Yadkin Co. to live out his life and raise a family. He ran a store, an inn, and a livery stable. He m. Louise Jane Jenkins on 2-7-1860 (YCMR). She was b. 11-22-1863 and d. 12-26-1917 (*Heritage*, 508; Cook, *Descendants of Isaac Windsor*, 13).

MITCHELL, HIRAM; CO. F, 28TH REG. (1838–02/25/1862; Yadkin Co., NC).
Hiram Mitchell e. at age 22 on 6-18-1861. He d. in Yadkin Co. about 2-25-1862, cause of death not reported (NCT VIII, 180). Hiram Mitchell, at age 12, was in the house of his parents, William and Elizabeth Mitchell.

MITCHELL, SAMUEL; CO. B, 38TH REG. (1838–?).
Samuel Mitchell e. in Yadkin Co. at age 23 on 10-16-1861. Reported AWOL on 8-18-1862. Captured by the enemy on an unspecified date. Paroled and transferred to Aiken's Landing, where he was received on 9-7-1862 for exchange. Reported AWOL through Dec. 1862. Returned to duty Jan.-Feb. 1863. Wounded at Chancellorsville, VA, 5-3-1863. Returned to duty Sept.-Oct. 1863. Captured again at Spotsylvania Court House, VA, on 5-21-1864. Confined at Point Lookout, MD, on 5-30-1864. Paroled from there on 3-14-1865 and received at Boulware's Wharf, James River, VA, on 3-16-1865 for exchange (NCT X, 27). Samuel Mitchell may be the brother of Hiram Mitchell (above), and the s. of William and Elizabeth Mitchell, and therefore b. ca. 1836 (1850 Surry).

MOCK, JOHN; CO. I, 28TH REG. (1824–08/11/1862).
John Mock, b. in England, lived in Yadkin Co. where he e. at age 38 on 3-8-1862. Captured at Hanover Court House, VA, on 5-27-1862, he was confined at Ft. Monroe, VA, then Ft. Columbus, NY Harbor. Paroled and transferred to Aiken's Landing, James River, VA, where he was received on 8-5-1862 for exchange. Hospitalized in Richmond, VA, on 8-7-1862 with "phthisis," he d. 8-11-1862 (NCT VIII, 215).

MONDAY, FRANK; CO. A, 1ST BAT. SHARPSHOOTERS (1823–?).
Frank Monday (Mundy) e. "at camp in Virginia" on 11-1-1863. Deserted in Orange Co., VA, on 12-26-1863. Returned and deserted a second time on 10-11-1863. Dropped from the company rolls as a deserter on 2-28-1865 (NCT III, 74). Frank Monday,

age 27, was living with wife, Mary, and daughters, Amanda (age 2), and Saran E. (age 4 months), in 1850 (1850 Surry).

MONEY, BENJAMIN J.; CO. B, 38TH REG. (04/11/1834–04/11/1881; Mt. Pleasant Meth.).
Benjamin Money, a Yadkin resident, e. there at age 26 on 4-19-1861. Reported sick from 7-26-1862 to 9-24-1864, when he was reported AWOL. Returned to duty about 10-29-1864 (NCT X, 27). Benjamin J. Money m. Mary G. Nicols on 3-2-1856 (YCMR).

MONEY, DANIEL W.; CO. B, 38TH REG. (1813–?).
Daniel W. Money e. in Yadkin Co. at age 48 on 1-16-1861. Present until 8-20-1862 when he was reported AWOL. Discharged 12-6-1862 because he was "overage" (NCT X, 27).

MONEY, HOWELL; CO. H, 54TH REG. (1832–?).
Howell Money e. in Yadkin Co. 8-29-1862. Deserted on 12-18-1862. Returned to duty 2-11-1863. Deserted near Fredericksburg, VA, 5-18-1863. Returned to duty 9-23-1863. Captured at Rappahannock Station, VA, 11-7-1863, and confined at Point Lookout, MD, on 11-11-1863. Paroled there about 3-16-1864. Received at City Point on 3-20-1864 for exchange. Returned to duty. Reported absent-wounded Sept.-Oct. 1864. Place/date of wound not reported. Returned to duty. Surrendered at Appomattox Court House, VA, 4-9-1865 (NCT XIII, 324). Howell Money m. Anne Cheek on 7-3-1855 (YCMR). According to the 1850 Surry Co. Census, Howell was b. ca. 1832, the s. of William and Catherine Money. Howell Money m. Elizabeth Money, dau. of Stephen and Nancy Evans on 1-14-1877 (YCMR).

MONEY, HUGH; CO. H, 54TH REG.
Hugh Money e. in Yadkin Co. on 9-25-1862. Reported present through Oct. 1683. Captured at Rappahannock Station, VA, on 11-7-1863. Confined at Point Lookout, MD, 11-11-1863. Paroled from there about 3-16-1864. Received at City Point, VA, 3-20-1864 for exchange. Returned to duty. Wounded severely in arm at Winchester or Fisher's Hill, VA, 9/19–22/1864 (NCT XIII, 324). Hugh Money, s. of Frederick and Susan Money, m. Eliza A. Gross, dau. of Henry and Lucy Gross, on 10-9-1868 (YCMR).

MONEY, JAMES P.; CO. H, 54TH REG. (1836–?).
James P. Money was a farmer before enlisting in Yadkin Co. at age 26 on 4-28-1862. Reported absent-sick in June 1862. Deserted on 12-18-1862. Returned to duty 2-11-1863. Deserted near Fredericksburg, VA, 5-18-1863. Returned to duty on 9-23-1863. Captured at Rappahannock Station, VA, 11-7-1863, and confined at Point Lookout, MD, 11-11-1863. Paroled at Point Lookout about 3-16-164. Received at City Point, VA, 3-20-1864 for exchange. Returned to duty before 9-19-1864. Captured again at Winchester, VA, and confined at Point Lookout on 9-26-1864. Paroled from there on 2-18-1865, and received at Boulware's Wharf, James River, VA, about 2-21-1865, for exchange (NCT XIII, 324). James P. Money, b. ca. 1834, was the s. of William and Catherine Money and the brother of Howell Money (1850 Surry).

MONEY, LEWIS; CO. B, 38TH REG. (1827–?).
Lewis Money lived in Yadkin Co. where he e. at age 34 on 10-16-1861. Discharged on 6-22-1862 because of disability. He later have served as a private in Co. H, 3rd Reg. NC State Troops. He e. in Yadkin Co. on 10-17-1863 in Co. H, 3rd Reg. Deserted on 11-25-1863 near Morton's Ford, VA (NCT III, 573; X, 27).

MONEY, MOSES; CO. E, 54TH REG. (1826–?).
Moses Money, born in Surry, resided in Yadkin Co., where he was a farm laborer. He e. in Wilkes Co. at age 36 on 4-2-1862. He was discharged on 5-28-1862 because he was overage (NCT XIII, 292).

MONEY, WILLIAM L.; CO. H, 54TH REG. (1839–?).
William L. Money e. in Yadkin Co. at age 24 on 4-28-1863. Reported absent-sick in June 1862. Deserted on 12-18-1862. Returned to duty on 2-11-1863. Wounded in the arm near Fredericksburg, VA, 5-4-1863. Deserted on 5-18-1863. Returned to duty on 9-23-1863. Captured at Rappahannock Station, VA, 11-7-1863. Confined at Point Lookout, MD, 11-11-1863 until paroled on 2-18-1865. Received at Boulware's Wharf, James River, VA, about 2-21-1865 for exchange (NCT XIII, 324). William L. Money m. Mary Jane Whitehead on 10-28-1860 (YCMR).

MONEY, ZEB; CO. A, 9TH BAT. HOME GUARD.

MOORE, ISAAC; CO. I, 28TH REG. (1825–?).
Isaac Moore lived in Yadkin Co. where he e. at age 37 on 3-8-1862. He was captured near Petersburg, VA, on 4-2-1865, and confined at Ft. Delaware, DE, until released on 6-19-1865, after taking the Oath of Allegiance (NCT VIII, 215). Isaac Moore, s. of Isaac and Sarah Moore, m. Rebecca Pendry, dau. of Andrew and Jane Pendry on 5-31-1868 (YCMR).

MOXLEY, DANIEL; CO. A, 1ST BAT. SHARPSHOOTERS (12/22/1821–11/11/1913; Moxley Fam. Cem.).
Daniel Moxley e. "at camp in Virginia" on 11-1-1863. Captured at New Bern, NC, on 2-3-1864, and confined at Point Lookout, MD, on 2-27-1864. Released after taking the Oath of Allegiance at Point Lookout, MD, on 6-12-1865 (NCT III, 74). Daniel Moxley and his sister, Sallie, came to Yadkin Co. from Alleghany. He m. four times, first to Mary Shore (1823–1874), and they had three ch. By his last wife, Rachel Wooten he had one s., John H. Moxley (1850 Surry; 1860 Yadkin).

MURPHY, ABRAHAM; CO. F, 28TH REG. (1833–03/06/1863).

Abraham Murphy lived in Yadkin Co. where he e. at age 28 on 6-18-1861. He d. at Camp Green, VA, on 3-6-1863 of "pneumonia" (NCT VIII, 180). Abraham Murphy m. Anna Irene Bovender, dau. of John and Rachel Brown Bovender, on 11-24-1853 (YCMR). She m. second on 1-11-1865 Henry Hutchens, s. of Samuel and Lettie Allgood Hutchens ("Bovender Genealogy," unpublished manuscript by Frances H. Casstevens, and YCMR).

MURPHY, BENJAMIN; CO. F, 28TH REG.
(08/26/1832–02/10/1913; Enon Bapt. Ch.).
Benjamin Murphy lived in Yadkin Co. where he e. at age 30 on 11-5-1863. Reported AWOL from 3-2-1864 through 9-10-1864. Present or accounted for through Feb. 1865. He was captured near Petersburg, VA, on 4-2-1865, and confined at Point Lookout, MD, until released on 6-29-1865, after taking the Oath of Allegiance (NCT VIII, 181).

MURRAH, MILTON; CO. F, 28TH REG.
(1839–05/03/1863).
Milton Murrah (Murry?) lived in Yadkin Co. where he e. at age 22 on 6-18-1861. He was killed at Chancellorsville, VA, on 5-3-1863 (NCT VIII, 181).

MYERS, ALEXANDER H.; CO. F, 44TH REG.
(1841–?).
Alexander H. Myers e. on 12-1-1862 at age 21. He deserted but returned to duty prior to 3-1-1862 (NCT X, 451).

MYERS, ALVIS GRAY; CO. D, 42ND REG. (10/18/1842–12/02/1907; Zion Bapt., Iredell Co., NC).
Alvis Gray Myers, a Yadkin Co. resident, e. in Rowan Co. at age 20, on 3-4-1862. Present through Oct. 1864 (NCT X, 236). A. G. Myers may have m. M. J. McCary on 11-1-1866 (YCMR). He was the s. of Shadrack and Mary Hesa Windsor Myers. Alvis is known to have m. Louise A. Redmond, b. 6-12-1851, d. 7-4-1921, and their ch. were Minnie Myrtle and Sallie (Cook, *Descendants of Isaac Windsor*, 15, 40; 1850 Surry).

MYERS, FREDERICK A.; CO. F, 28TH REG.
SERGEANT (1840–?).
Frederick A. Myers lived in Yadkin Co. where he e. at age 21 on 6-18-1861. Mustered in as private and promoted to corporal Jan.–June 1862. Promoted to sergeant on 5-11-1863. Captured near Petersburg, VA, on 4-2-1865, he was confined at Point Lookout, MD, until released on 6-29-1865, after taking the Oath of Allegiance (NCT VIII, 181). F. A. Myers m. L. A. Kinyoun on 8-4-1864 (YCMR).

MYERS, GEORGE D.; CO. F, 28TH REG.
(1842–?).
George D. Myers lived in Yadkin Co. where he e. at age 19 on 6-18-1861. He was wounded in the left shoulder at Ox Hill, VA, on 9-1-1862. He "went home on furlough on October 1, 1862, & never returned" (NCT VIII, 181). George D. Myers m. Mary F. Williams in 1865 (YCMR).

MYERS, JOHN; CO. I, 28TH REG. (?–12/18/1862).
John Myers e. at age 23 on 3-8-1862. He d. in a Lynchburg, VA, hospital about 12-18-1862 of "pneumonia" (NCT VIII, 215).

MYERS, THOMAS P.; CO. B, 38TH REG.
(1838–?).
Thomas P. Myers e. in Yadkin Co. at age 23 on 10-16-1861. Deserted about 12-15-1861. He e. in Wilkes Co. at age 21 on 3-8-1862 in Co. B, 1st Reg. NC Troops. Wounded in action at Ellerson's Mill, VA, on 6-16-1862. Reported missing in action at Sharpsburg, MD, on 9-17-1862, and dropped from rolls as a deserter on 11-1-1862 (NCT III, 162; X, 27).

MYERS, WILLIAM H.; CO. F, 28TH REG.
(09/17/1845–09/15/1933; Enon Bapt. Ch.).
William H. Myers, a Yadkin resident, e. there at age 17 on 11-5-1863. Captured near Petersburg, VA, on 4-2-1865, and confined at Point Lookout, MD, until released on 6-29-1865, after taking the Oath of Allegiance (NCT VIII, 181).

NANCE, JOSEPH W.; CO. F, 28TH REG.
CORPORAL (1830–10/25/1864).
Joseph W. Nance lived in Yadkin Co. where he e. at age 31 on 6-18-1861. Mustered in as private, he was promoted to Corporal Jan. 1863–Oct. 1864. Captured near Petersburg, VA, on 7-29-1864, he was confined at Point Lookout, MD, until released on 6-29-1865, after taking the Oath of Allegiance (NCT VIII, 181).

NANCE, RICHARD S.; CO. A, 28TH REG.
Richard Nance, b. in Yadkin Co., but resided in Surry, where he farmed, before enlisting at age 22 on 5-4-1861. Present until wounded in the left arm at Malvern Hills, VA, 7-1-1862. Left arm amputated. Discharged 1-26-1863 because of disability (NCT VIII, 120).

NAYLOR, ERVIN E.; CO. H, 54TH REG.
(1823–?).
Ervine E. Naylor, b. in Surry, resided in Yadkin Co., where he was a day laborer or farmer before enlisting in Yadkin Co. at age 37 on 3-17-1862. Discharged before 5-23-1862, because he was overage (NCT XIII, 325). In 1850, Irvin E. Naylor, age 27, was a miller, and lived with wife Catharine, and ch., Cyntha, Harriet J., and Melvina C. (1850 Surry).

NAYLOR, JOSEPH R.; 75TH REG., 18TH
BRIG. MILITIA (1817–?).
Joseph Naylor, age 33, was a farmer in 1850, and living with wife, Mary, age 25, and ch.: Sarah A., Mary J., Charles W., and Susan C. (1850 Surry).

NEWMAN, WILLIAM; CO. H, 54TH REG.
(1840–?).
William Newman e. in Yadkin Co., age 22, on 8-29-1862. Reported present through April 1863. Captured near Fredericksburg, VA, 5-4-1863, and confined at the Old Capitol Prison, Washington, DC.

Transferred to Ft. Delaware, DE, 5-7-1863. Paroled at Ft. Delaware, and transferred to City Point, VA, where he was received 5-23-1863 for exchange. Deserted on 5-25-1863. Returned to duty 9-23-1863. Captured at Rappahannock Station, VA, 11-7-1863, and confined at Point Lookout, MD, 11-11-1864. Paroled there about 3-16-1864. Received at City Point on 3-20-1864 for exchange. Returned to duty and was present Sept.-Oct. 1864. Surrendered at Appomattox Court House, VA, on 4-9-1865. NC Pension records indicate he was wounded in the left arm by a shell at Winchester, VA, in June 1863 (NCT XIII, 325). William Newman is probably the s. of Avery and Elizabeth Newman, and was listed in their household in the 1850 Surry Census, which gives his age as 10.

NICHOLS, JESSE; CO. I, 28TH REG. (1838–?).
Jesse Nichols, a Yadkin resident, e. there at age 23 on 8-13-1861. Present through Dec. 1861. Discharged on an unspecified date after providing a substitute (NCT VIII, 216). Jesse W. Nichols m. Betsy Ann Dickerson on 11-28-1855 (YCMR).

NICHOLS, MARTIN S.; CO. G, 18TH REG. (1835–?).
Martin Nichols lived in Yadkin Co., but e. in Wake Co. on 9-27-1862. He was present until reported AWOL on 4-15-1863 through Oct. 1863. He returned to his company Nov.-Dec. 1863, and continued to be present until wounded in the left arm and side at the Wilderness, VA, on 5-6-1864. He was reported absent-wounded through Oct. 1864 (NCT V, 352). He may be the s. of Nancy Nichols, b. in 1838, according to the 1850 Census (1850 Surry).

NICHOLS, WILLIAM; CO. I, 28TH REG. (?–06/30/1862).
William Nichols e. in Yadkin Co. on 8-31-1861. He was killed at Frayser's Farm, VA, on 6-30-1862 (NCT VIII, 216).

NICHOLSON, JAMES G.; CO. F, 28TH REG. (1834–?).
James G. Nicholson lived in Yadkin Co. where he e. at age 27 on 6-18-1861. He was captured at Hanover Court House, VA, on 5-27-1862, and confined at Ft. Columbus, NY Harbor. He was exchanged and returned to duty before 11-1-1862. He was captured near Petersburg, VA, on 4-2-1865, and confined at Point Lookout, MD, until released on 6-29-1865, after taking the Oath of Allegiance (NCT VIII, 181). Before the war, James G. Nicholson lived at East Bend, NC, where, at age 27, his occupation was "tobacconist." J. G. Nicholson, s. of Isaac and Elizabeth Nicholson, m. E. C. Fleming, dau. of Jeff and Lucy Fleming, on 2-19-1885. He m. C. J. Matthews, dau. of Reps and Nancy Martin, on 9-23-1888 (YCMR).

NICHOLSON, JOHN P.; CO. I, 33RD REG.
Acting Assistant Surgeon (02/13/1836–11/10/1930; Nicholson Cem., Iredell Co., NC?).
John P. Nicholson, b. in Iredell Co., was a doctor before enlisting in Forsyth Co. at age 24 on 9-15-1861. Mustered in as corporal. Detailed as hospital steward and transferred to Field and Staff of the Regiment on 1-1-1862. Reduced to ranks and transferred back to this company May–Oct. 1862. Reported on duty as acting Assistant Surgeon of the regiment Sept-Oct. 1863. Present until promoted to Commissary Sergeant on 11-1-1864, and transferred to Field and Staff of regiment (NCT IX, 229). Nicholson also practiced medicine in East Bend for a number of years. John P. Nicholson m. P. A. V. Martin on 12-7-1859 (YCMR). John Pinkney Nicholson attended school at East Bend at the Academy, after which he studied medicine under Dr. Evan Benbow. Later, Nicholson graduated from Jefferson College in Philadelphia in 1858. He returned to East Bend to practice. He practiced medicine for 62 years, and was a licensed a preacher in 1867 (Rutledge, pp. 98–99).

NORMAN, ELLIS; CO. D, 21ST REG. (04/26/1844–01/05/1917; New Home Meth., Yadkin Co., NC).
Ellis Norman, a Yadkin resident, e. in Co. D, 21st Regiment, but place and date not given. He deserted to the enemy on 6-11-1864, and took the Oath of Allegiance in Knoxville, TN (NCT VI, 570). Ellis Norman, the s. of David C. and Milly Norman, m. Octavia S. Poindexter, b. 8-19-1848, d. 7-29-1867, dau. of Denson A. and Sarah Jones Poindexter, on 12-21-1865. Ellis m. second 7-30-1870 Susannah (Susan) Alsey Poindexter, b. 12-18-1853, d. 4-11-1939, dau. of Thomas C. M. and Sarah Poindexter. (YCMR; 1850 Surry). They are buried at New Home Methodist Church, Smithtown, NC (Hoots, 257).

NORMAN (NORMON), FREDERICK; CO. B, 38TH REG. (1840–?).
Frederick Norman/Normon e. at Camp Holmes, near Raleigh, on 7-30-1864. He deserted about 8-3-1864 (NCT X, 28). Frederick Norman m. Nancy Dinkins on 11-15-1861 (bond date, YCMR). He may be the Frederick Norman, age 10, listed in the household of James and Patience Norman in 1850 (1850 Surry).

NORMAN, GEORGE; CO. B, 38TH REG. (1838–?).
George Norman, a Yadkin Co. farmer, e. at age 23 on 10-16-1861. He was discharged on 6-21-1862 because of disability (NCT X, 27).

NORMAN, HENRY I.; CO. F, 28TH REG. (1844–?).
Henry I. Norman e. in Yadkin Co. at age 19 on 2-18-1863. He deserted on 9-12-1863, but returned to duty about 9-15-1864. He was captured near Petersburg, VA, on 4-2-1865, and confined at Point Lookout, MD, until released on 6-29-1865, after taking the Oath of Allegiance (NCT VIII, 181).

NORMAN, THOMAS A.; CO. A, 44TH REG. (10/09/1836–03/15/1917; Baltimore Meth., Yadkin Co., NC).

Thomas A. Norman e. at Camp French on 3-25-1862. Captured at the South Anna Bridge, VA, on 6-26-1863. Paroled on 6-29-1863 and transferred to Co. I, 28th Reg., in July of 1863 through May 1864. Captured at Wilderness, VA, on 5-12-1864. Confined at Point Lookout, MD, before being transferred to Elmira, NY, on 8-10-1864. Released on 6-12-1865, after taking the Oath of Allegiance (NCT VIII, 216; X, 406).

NORMAN, W. A.; CO. F, 51ST REG.
W. A. Norman, a Yadkin resident, e. at Camp Holmes on 2-10-1864. He deserted on 4-18-1864, and went over to the enemy. He was confined at Knoxville, TN, on 6-11-1864, then transferred to Louisville, KY, where he took the Oath of Allegiance on 6-16-1864, and was released (NCT XII, 336).

NORMAN, WILLIAM; CO. F, 28TH REG.
(1825–03/25/1863).
William Norman, a Yadkin Co. farmer, e. there at age 36 on 6-18-1861. He d. at Camp Gregg, VA, about 3-25-1863 of "pneumonia" (NCT VIII, 181).

NORMAN, WILLIAM; CO. B, 21ST REG.
(?–09/27/1861).
William Norman e. in Yadkin Co. on 5-12-1861 and was present until he d. on 9-27-1861, place and cause of death not reported (NCT VI, 553). He may be the William Norman, b. 1836, the s. of James and Patience Norman (1850 Surry).

NORMAN, WILLIAM H.; CO. B, 38TH REG.
(1842–07/01/1863).
William H. Norman e. in Yadkin Co. at age 22 on 1-1-1863. He was killed at Gettysburg, PA, on 7-1-1863 (NCT X, 27–28). William H. Norman m. Mitty Kerr on 12-15-1859 (bond, YCMR).

NORMAN, WILLIAM P.; CO. G, 42ND REG.
(1842–?).
William P. Norman lived in Yadkin Co.. He e. at Petersburg, VA, at age 32 on 11-6-1862. He deserted shortly after on 11-27-1862 (NCT X, 263). William is probably the s. of George and Louisa Norman (1850 Surry).

NORTH, JOHN; 75TH REG., 18TH BRIG. MILITIA.
John North m. Joanna Lynch on 12-18-1851 (YCMR).

NORTH, T. E.; CO. K, 38TH REG.
T. E. North lived in Yadkin where he e. on 4-1-1864 (NCT X, 102).

NORTH, WILLIAM S.; CO. A, 1ST BAT. SHARPSHOOTERS (02/11/1840–11/02/1910; Baltimore Meth. Ch.).
William S. North e. "at camp in Virginia" on 11-1-1863. Deserted on 2-1-1864 at Bachelor's Creek, NC, and voluntarily gave himself up to the Federal forces. Provided transportation to Indianapolis, IN, on 2-24-1864 (NCT III, 74). William S. North, the s. of Jonathan and Ann Hobson North (1860 Yadkin), m. Sarah Ann Almeda Carter, dau. of Isaac and Louisa Carter, on 6-11-1871 (YCMR).

OAKLEY, JAMES; CO. D, 42ND REG.
(1825–?).
James Oakley, a Yadkin resident, e. in Rowan Co. at age 37 on 3-4-1862. Present until July-Aug. 1862, when he was listed as a deserter. Returned to duty on 2-24-1863. Deserted again on 6-1-1863 (NCT X, 236).

OSBORN, EZEKIEL N.; CO. H, 54TH REG. 3RD LIEUTENANT (1845–?).
Ezekiel N. Osborn, b. in Stokes Co., resided in Yadkin where he was a harness maker before enlisting in Yadkin Co. at age 17 on 4-18-1862. Mustered in as private, and promoted to corporal Mar.-April 1863. Appointed 3rd lieutenant on 5-19-1863. Present through Oct. 1863. Captured at Rappahannock Station, VA, 11-7-1863 and confined at Old Capitol Prison, Washington, DC, 11-8-1863. Transferred to Johnson's Island, OH, 11-11-1863, and released 6-13-1865, after taking the Oath of Allegiance (NCT XIII, 318).

OSBORNE, DAVID D.; CO. B, 21ST REG. 2ND LIEUTENANT.
David D. Osborn resided in Yadkin Co. where he e. on 5-12-1861. He mustered in as sergeant and was present until appointed 3rd lieutenant and transferred to Co. A, 1st Battalion NC Sharpshooters on 4-26-1862 (NCT VI, 553). Appointed 2nd Lieutenant on 6-27-1862, he was present through Dec. 1864. Paroled at Appomattox Court House, VA, on 4-9-1865 (NCT III, 70).

OVERBEY (OVERBY), ALBERT M. CO. B, 21ST REG. (02/17/1834–07/27/1923; East Bend Bapt.).
Albert M. Overby e. on 5-12-1861 in Yadkin Co. and was present until discharged in Sept. 1861, reason not given (NCT VI, 553). Albert's wife, Malinda J., was b. 5-31-1828, d. 1-31-1898.

OVERBEY (OVERBY), E. I.; CO. B, 21ST REG. (?–09/20/1861).
E. I. Overby e. in Yadkin Co. on 5-12-1861 and was present until he d. on 9-20-1861, place and cause of death not reported (NCT VI, 553).

PARDUE, ALISON; 75TH REG., 18TH BRIG. MILITIA.

PARDUE, THOMAS; CO. G, 54TH REG.
(02/20/1827–10/10/1910; Oak Grove Bapt. Ch.).

PARDUE, THOMAS C.; CO. A, 21ST REG.
(Union Cross Friends, Yadkin Co., NC).
Thomas C. Pardue, a Yadkin resident, e. there on 10-1-1863. Present until he deserted on 5-6-1864. Took the Oath of Allegiance in Knoxville, TN, on 12-10-1864 (NCT VI, 548). Thomas C. "Pardew" m. Mary

Green on 7-4-1861 (YCMR). She and his s., Andrew, are buried at Union Cross Friends Church, Yadkin Co., NC.

PARKS, WILBORN; CO. E, 70TH REG.

PATTERSON, A[MOS]. C.; CO. A, 1ST BAT. SHARPSHOOTERS.
A. C. Patterson e. "at camp in Virginia" on 11-1-1863. Present until he deserted on 3-1-1864. Dropped from the rolls for desertion on 8-31-1864 (NCT III, 74). This is probably Amos C. Patterson, b. 1825, s. of Jesse and Nancy Patterson (1850 Surry).

PATTERSON, J. C.; CO. F, 28TH REG.
J. C. Patterson lived in Yadkin Co., but place and date of enlistment not reported. He deserted to the enemy on an unspecified date, and took the Oath of Allegiance at Louisville, KY, on 8-16-1864 (NCT VIII, 181).

PATTERSON, J. L. CO. A, 54TH REG.
J. L. Patterson e. in Yadkin Co. 5-3-1863. Reported absent-sick without leave. Failed to report for duty and was dropped from company rolls prior to 9-1-1863 (NCT XIII, 255).

PATTERSON, JESSE D.; CO. A, 54TH REG. (12/10/1841–3/10/1928; Forbush Friends Ch.).
Jesse Patterson farmed in Yadkin Co. before enlisting at age 22 on 5-3-1862. Reported absent on sick furlough 6-10-1862. Reported AWOL 7-10-1862 through 10-31-1863. Dropped from company rolls Nov.-Dec. 1863 (XIII, 255). Jesse D. Patterson was the s. of Joshua and Mary Williams Patterson. Jesse m. Mary Ann Allgood and they had one dau. (per Mrs. F. A. Phillips, Mt. Airy, Doris George Bohannon, Jim and Barbara Frost).

PATTERSON, WILLIAM W.; 75TH REG., 18TH BRIG. MILITIA (05/31/1824–12/21/1902; Forbush Friends Ch.).
William Williams Patterson, a resident of the Baltimore community and a member of the Militia, m. Rebecca Davis (1829–1911). After the war, he was instrumental in organizing the Republican Party in Yadkin Co.. William Williams Patterson was the s. of Joshua and Mary ("Polly") Williams Patterson. He m. on 4-6-1844 Rebecca Davis. In 1850, William Williams Patterson, a farmer, was living with wife, Rebecca, daughters Sarah L., age 5; and Elizabeth T., age 1 (Patterson family data based on family research by Frances H. Casstevens and others; 1850 Surry).

PEAL (PEELE), D.; CO. F, 28TH REG.
D. Peal (Peele), place and date of enlistment not reported, but he was hospitalized at Richmond, VA, on 3-28-1865 with a gunshot wound of the right leg. Place and date of wound not reported. He was captured in a Richmond, VA, hospital on 4-3-1865 (NCT VIII, 181).

PEARSON, JOHN W.; CO. I, 28TH REG. 1ST SERGEANT (1845–?).
John W. Pearson e. in Yadkin Co. where he resided at age 18 on 8-13-1861. Mustered in as 1st sergeant but reduced to ranks on 10-8-1861. He was appointed drillmaster and transferred to 31st Reg. in Dec. 1861. However, records of the 31st do not indicate he served with them (NCT VIII, 216). He may very well be the s. of Supreme Court Judge Richmond M. Pearson, and is listed in his household (along with several young men who were "students at law") in 1850 and was five years old (1850 Surry).

PENDRY, ALFRED L.; CO. A, 1ST BAT. SHARPSHOOTERS (1848–?).
Alfred L. Pendry e. at age 15 "at camp in Virginia" on 11-1-1863. Present until he deserted at Lynchburg, VA, on 10-15-1864. Dropped from the rolls for desertion on 2-28-1865 (NCT III, 74). Alfred L. Pendry was living in his parents' home in 1860, that of Andrew and Penna Pendry (1860 Yadkin).

PENDRY, DANIEL C. F.; CO. B, 38TH REG. (1843–?).
Daniel C. F. Pendry e. at age 18 on 10-16-1861 in Yadkin Co.. Present until 8-18-1862 when he was reported AWOL. Returned to duty Jan.-Feb. 1863. Present until he deserted again on 4-16-1864. Returned to duty 8-2-1864 and was placed under arrest (NCT X, 28).

PENDRY, J. C.; CO. B, 21ST REG.
J. C. Pendry e. in Yadkin Co. on 5-12-1861 and was present until he transferred to Co. A, 1st Battalion NC Sharpshooters, on 4-26-1862. He was wounded near Fredericksburg, VA, on 50401863. Present on company rolls through Dec. 1864 (NCT III, 74; VI, 553).

PENDRY, JOHN; CO. B, 38TH REG. (1825–?).
John Pendry lived in Yadkin Co. where he e. at age 36 on 10-16-1861. Present until 8-18-1862 when he was reported AWOL. Captured by the enemy on an unspecified date. Received at Aiken's Landing, James River, VA, on 9-7-1862 for exchange. Reported AWOL through Dec. 1862. Returned to duty Jan.-Feb. 1863. Discharged on 3-13-1863 because he was overage (NCT X, 28). John Pendry, age 26, was living with wife, Lucy, age 30, and ch., Franklin and Rebecca, in 1850 (1850 Surry).

PENDRY, ROBY; CO. I, 28TH REG. (1840–02/04/1862).
Roby Pendry lived in Yadkin Co. where he e. at age 21 on 8-13-1861. He d. at Wilmington, NC, on 2-4-1862 of measles (NCT VIII, 216).

PENDRY, W. A.; CO. B, 21ST REG. (1842–?).
W. A. Pendry e. in Yadkin Co. on 5-12-1861 and was present until he transferred to Co. A, 1st Battalion NC Sharpshooters, on 4-26-1862. Present or accounted for through Dec. 1864 (NCT III, 74; VI, 553). William A. Pendry is listed in the household

of his parents, Andrew and Penny Pendry in 1850 (1850 Surry).

PENDRY, W. F.; CO. D, 44TH REG. (1842–09/11/1863).
W. F. Pendry e. in Wake Co., age 20, on 10-17-1862. Listed as a deserter in Feb. 1863. Returned to duty on 2-25-1863, and d. in a hospital at Gordonsville, VA, 9-11-1863 of pneumonia (NCT X, 431).

PENDRY, WILSON S.; CO. I, 28TH REG. (1838–11/06/1861).
Wilson S. Pendry, a Yadkin resident, e. there at age 23 on 8-13-1861. He d. at Wilmington, NC, on 11-6-1861 of measles (NCT VIII, 216).

PENIX (PENNIX/PINNIX), WILLIAM T.; CO. B, 38TH REG. (?–12/20/1862).
William T. Penix e. in Yadkin Co. on 4-19-1862. Present until 8-18-1862 when he was reported AWOL. Captured by the enemy on an unspecified date. Received at Aiken's Landing for exchange on 9-7-1862. He d. on 12-20-1862, place and cause of death not reported (NCT X, 28).

PERDUE, JAMES N.; CO. B, 38TH REG. (1848–?).
James N. Perdue e. at Camp Holmes, Raleigh, NC, at age 17, on 7-26-1864. Deserted on 8-8-1864 (NCT X, 28).

PETTITT, WILLIAM; CO. F, 28TH REG. (1826–09/01/1862).
William Pettitt, b. in Yadkin (Surry) Co., and e. in Yadkin at age 36 on 8-15-1861. He was killed at Ox Hill, VA, on 9-1-1862 (NCT VIII, 181).

PETTY, ELIJAH; CO. I, 28TH REG. (1844–?).
Elijah Petty, a Yadkin resident, e. there at age 19 on 8-13-1816. Reported AWOL May–Oct. 1862, but returned to duty before 2-28-1863. Deserted on 8-5-1863. Returned to duty on 9-22-1864. Deserted to the enemy on 11-19-1864. Confined at Washington, DC, until released about 11-23-1864, after taking the Oath of Allegiance (NCT VIII, 216). Elijah J. Petty, age 6, was living in the household of his parents, Elisha and Mary Petty in 1850 (1850 Surry).

PETTY, MILES; CO. I, 28TH REG. (1836–?).
Miles Petty e. in Yadkin Co. at age 25 on 8-13-1861. Present through Feb. 1863. Deserted on an unspecified date, but returned to duty on 9-22-1864. Deserted to the enemy on 11-19-1864, and confined at Washington, DC, until released about 11-25-1864, after taking the Oath of Allegiance (NCT VIII, 216). Milas Petty m. Martha Martin 4-7-1867 (YCMR). Milas C. Petty, age 11, was living in the household of his parents, Elisha and Mary Petty, and younger brother, Elijah, in 1850 (1850 Surry).

PETTYJOHN, ANDREW J.; CO. D, 44TH REG. (1823–?).
Andrew Pettyjohn e. in Wake Co. at age 39 on 10-17-1862. Present until he deserted 5-26-1863. Returned to duty and deserted again on 11-17-1863. Returned to duty 12-17-1863. Present until he deserted to the enemy about 3-3-1865. Confined at Washington, DC, 3-7-1865, and released on an unspecified date after taking the Oath of Allegiance (NCT X, 431). Andrew J. Pettyjohn m. Jeny Celia Harris on 12-14-1854 (YCMR).

PETTYJOHN, JAMES; CO. I, 28TH REG. (1840–12/07/1862).
James Pettyjohn, a Yadkin resident, e. there at age 22 on 8-13-1861. Captured at Hanover Court House, VA, on 5-27-1862, and confined at Ft. Monroe, VA, then Ft. Columbus, NY Harbor. Exchanged on an unspecified date. Died in a Richmond, VA, hospital on 12-7-1862 of pneumonia (NCT VIII, 216).

PETTYJOHN, WILLIAM; CO. I, 28TH REG. (1839–12/13/1862).
William Pettyjohn e. in Yadkin Co. at age 22 on 8-13-1861. Captured at Hanover Court House, VA, on 5-27-1862, and confined at Ft. Monroe, VA, then Ft. Columbus, NY Harbor. Paroled and transferred to Aiken's Landing, James River, VA, where he was received on 7-12-1862 for exchange. Exchanged there on 8-5-1862. Returned to duty before 11-1-1862, he was killed at Fredericksburg, VA, on 12-13-1862 (NCT VIII, 216). William Pettyjohn may be the s. of Thomas and Elizabeth Pettyjohn (1850 Surry).

PHILLIPS, ABRAHAM (ABRAM); CO. F, 28TH REG. (09/08/1825–05/05/1864; Kelly Fam. Cem.).
Abraham Phillips e. in Wake Co. on 11-15-1863. He was killed at Wilderness, VA, on 5-5-1864 (NCT VIII, 181). Abraham (Abram) was the s. of William and Sally Glenn Phillips, he was killed in the Battle of the Wilderness, and his body was not recovered, although there is a monument for him and his wife in the Kelly-Phillips Cemetery, near Baltimore Meth. Church, Yadkin Co., NC. Abram's wife, Rachel, was b. 7-14-1828, d. 10-5-1885, is buried in the Kelly-Phillips Cemetery near Baltimore Church (per Edith Garner Sharpless, a Phillips descendant). The 1850 Surry Co. census shows that Abraham, age 24, and wife, Rachel 21, were living in a household with no children (1850 Surry).

PHILLIPS, BENJAMIN A.; CO. F, 28TH REG. (05/08/1833–07/24/03; Baltimore Meth. Ch.).
Benjamin A. Phillips was a Yadkin Co. farmer before enlisting on 4-27-1862. He was wounded in the right arm near the Wilderness, VA, on 5-5-1864, and admitted to the General Hospital, Petersburg, VA, on 8-25-1864, where his right arm was amputated. He was also wounded in his left arm, but retained some use of it. He was furloughed on 9-14-1864, and discharged 1-11-1865, because of disability from wounds. Benjamin A. Phillips, s. of John and Elizabeth Davis Phillips, was b. 5-8-1833 in Yadkin Co., NC, and d. 7-24-1903, Yadkin Co., NC. He is buried in the Baltimore United Methodist Church Cemetery,

Yadkin Co., NC. He returned to Yadkin Co. and resumed his position as constable of the Baltimore District (from which he had resigned in 1858 to take a job as overseerer on the Larkin Lynch plantation). He m. Dicy Ann Hurt on 2-24-1871, and they were the parents of five ch. (NCT VIII, 181; *Heritage*, 540–541).

PHILLIPS, JEREMIAH; CO. C, 72ND REG., 3RD BAT. JUNIOR RESERVES ? (05/24/1827–03/04/1880; Church, Surry Co., NC).
Jeremiah Phillips was the s. of William and Sally Glenn Phillips, and a brother of Abraham (Abram) Phillips listed above. He is bur. at a church on Hwy. 268 between Elkin and Dobson in Surry Co., NC (per Sharpless).

PHILLIPS, JOHN; 75TH REG., 18TH BRIG.

PHILLIPS, ROBERT S.; CO. H, 54TH REG.
Robert S. Phillips (s. of either Abner or John Phillips, per Edith Garner Sharpless), resided in Surry Co. and e. in Yadkin Co. on 9-12-1863 in Co. H, 54th Reg. NC Troops. He was captured at Rappahannock Station, VA, on 11-7-1863, and confined at Point Lookout, MD 11-11-863. Paroled from there about 3-16-1864. Received at City Point, VA, on 3-20-1864, and returned to duty. Reported present Sept.-Oct. 1864. Captured again at Ft. Stedman, VA, on 3-15-1865. Confined at Point Lookout on 3-27-1865 until released from there 6-16-1865, after taking the Oath of Allegiance (NCT XIII, 325).

PHILLIPS, SOLOMON L.; CO. A, 54TH REG. (1826–?).
Solomon L. Phillips was a Yadkin farmer before enlisting at age 36 on 5-2-1862. Hospitalized at Richmond, VA, 9-25-1862. Returned to duty 10-1-1862. Reported present through April 1863. Hospitalized again at Richmond 5-2-1863 with pneumonia. Transferred to Lynchburg, VA, hospital 5-9-1863. Deserted from the hospital 6-30-1863. Returned to duty before 12-31-1863. Wounded in the left arm (compound fracture) and captured at Fisher's Hill, VA, 9-22-1864. Hospitalized at Baltimore, MD. Transferred to Point Lookout, MD, 10-25-1864. Paroled 10-30-1864 and transferred to Venus Point, Savannah River, GA, 11-15-1864 for exchange (NCT XIII, 255). He was the s. of Richard and Nancy Phillips (1850 Surry). Solomon Phillips survived the war (according to Edith Garner Sharpless).

PHILLIPS, W. A.; CO. F, 28TH REG. (1839–?).
W. A. Phillips was a Yadkin Co. farmer before enlisting at age 23 on 4-24-1862 as a substitute. He was discharged on 6-23-1862 because of "general debility" (NCT VIII, 181).

PHILLIPS, WILLIAM D.; CO. H, 3RD REG.
William D. Phillips resided in Yadkin Co. where he e. on 10-27-1863. Present or accounted for until captured at Morton's Ford, VA, on 1-18-1864, he was confined at Old Capitol Prison, Washington, DC. He was released after taking the Oath of Allegiance on 3-15-1864, and was sent to Philadelphia, PA, (NCT III, 574).

PHILLIPS, WILLIAM HENRY; CO. I, 33RD REG. (1843–08/05/1862; Phillips Cem., Stokes Co., NC).
William Henry Phillips was b. in Yadkin Co., but resided in Stokes Co. where he farmed, before enlisting at age 18 on 9-9-1862. He was present until he d. at Gordonsville, VA, about 8-5-1862 of disease (NCT IX, 230). He was the s. of Matthew and Anne Radford Scott Phillips. His body was brought home and was the first one to be buried in the Phillips family cemetery near Pinnacle, Stokes Co., on 12-14-1862 (per Edith Garner Sharpless).

PHILLIPS, WILLIAM MONROE; HOME GUARD (09/12/1849–12/09/36; Harmony Grove Friends).
William Monroe Phillips was the s. of Thomas Jefferson and Keziah William Phillips, of Yadkinville, NC. As a boy of 14, he accompanied the Home Guard to Shallow Ford to construct breastworks in an attempt to stop the advance of U. S. General Stoneman's men in April of 1865. After the war, Phillips graduated from New York Medical College, and practiced medicine in Yadkin Co. Later he moved to Goodson (now Wallace), VA, where he m. Jennie Garrett. He practiced medicine there the rest of his life (*Heritage*, 541–542).

PILCHER, DANIEL; CO. B, 38TH REG. (1834–08/05/1862).
Daniel Pilcher, a Yadkin resident, e. there at age 28 on 4-19-1862. Died in a Richmond, VA, hospital about Aug. 6–7, 1862 of "dysentery" (NCT X, 28). Daniel Pilcher m. Rebecca Adams on 3-4-1858 (bond date, YCMR). Daniel Pilcher was the s. of John and Edith Carringer Pilcher. He d. in Chimbrazo Hospital No. 1, in Richmond, VA, having served only four months, his widow Rebecca received his pay—$39.23 (*Heritage*, 544).

PILCHER, WILEY; CO. I, 28TH REG. (1839–03/20/1862).
Wiley Pilcher, a Yadkin resident, e. there at age 22 on 9-1-1861. He d. at Wilmington, NC, on 3-30- or 4-1-1862 of "fever" (NCT VIII, 216). This may be the "Willie" Pilchard (age 8) in 1850 (1850 Surry), living in the household of Lydia Pilchard, age 50 (widow of James), Alvis (age 23), and Luddy (age 25), which would make him a brother to Daniel Pilcher of Com B, 38th Reg. (*Heritage*, 548; 1850 Surry).

PLOWMAN, HENRY; CO. I, 28TH REG.
Henry Plowman e. at Camp Holmes on 11-30-1863. Transferred to Co. G, 18th Reg. NC Troops (8th Reg., NC Volunteers) on 9-1-1864. Deserted on 9-2-1864 (NCT VI, 386; VIII, 216).

PLOWMAN, JAMES H.; CO. I, 28TH REG.
(03/05/1839–08/15/1901; Plowman Cem.).
NC pension records indicate he served in this company (NCT VIII, 216). However, he may be "Henry" Plowman who e. on 11-30-1863 and transferred to Co. G, 18th Reg. (8th NC Volunteers). James H. Plowman m. Milly P. Norman on 11-14-1861 (YCMR). In the 1850 Surry County Census, there is but one Plowman family, that of John and wife Phoebe. James H., age 9, is one of their children.

PLOWMAN, JOHN W.; CO. I, 28TH REG.
(1841–?).
John W. Plowman, b. in Surry, resided in Yadkin Co., where he was a farmer before enlisting at age 20 on 8-13-1861. Discharged on 12-24-1861 because of "the loss of motion of the left arm ... from an old fracture of the collar bone & rheumatism" (NCT VIII, 216). John W. Plowman, s. of John and Phebe, is listed with his parents in 1850 (1850 Surry), and his age is listed as 6 years old (b. ca. 1844). John Plowman, Jr., m. Polly Jenkins on 12-19-1865 (bond date, YCMR).

PLOWMAN, WILLIAM; CO. I, 28TH REG.
(1835–?).
William Plowman e. at Camp Holmes on 11-30-1863. Captured near Gravel Hill, VA, about 7-28-1864, and confined at Point Lookout, MD. Transferred to Elmira, NY, on 8-8-1864. Released there on 5-9-1865, after taking the Oath of Allegiance (NCT VIII, 216). William W. Plowman, s. of John and Phebe, is listed as 15 years old in 1850 (1850 Surry). William m. Catherine Shore on 10-7-1877 (YCMR).

POINDEXTER, ALBERT; CO. A, 7TH BAT. BLACKSMITH (12/15/1823–08/30/1864).
Albert Poindexter e. in Macon Co. at age 33 on 7-7-1862. He mustered in as blacksmith, and was present until he transferred to Co. E, 65th Reg, NCT (6th Reg. NC Cavalry) on 8-3-1863 (NCT II, 522). After transferring, he was captured in Monroe Co., TN, on 10-20-1863 and confined at Camp Chase, OH, until transferred to Ft. Delaware, DE, on 2-29-1864. He d. there on 8-30-1864 of "erysipelas" (NCT IV, 485). Albert, b. 12-15-1823, was the s. of Thomas and Sarah Nance Poindexter. He m. Lucinda Bovender, dau. of John Bovender, Jr., and wife Rachel Brown Bovender, b. 1-1-1826 in Surry (Yadkin) Co., and probably d. in Macon Co., where Albert and Lucinda had moved to after 1850. They had five ch.: Sarah Elizabeth, John R., James L., Mary, and Albert Lee (Bud) Poindexter. His younger brother, Jasper, served in the same companies. (See letters to Albert and wife in Appendix A.)

POINDEXTER, ALEXANDER ROBY; CO. F, 28TH REG. (07/29/1844–03/19/1926; Boonville Bapt. Ch.).
Alexander Roby's pension records indicate he served in this company (NCT VIII, 181). Alexander Roby Poindexter, the s. of Denson Asburn and Sarah Jones Poindexter, m. on 5-27-1868 Emma Catherine Ireland (b. 8-20-1852, d. 12-10-1936), dau. of Albert M. Ireland. Both are buried at Boonville Bapt. Church cemetery, Boonville, NC ("Poindexter," 58; 1850 Surry).

POINDEXTER, CHARLES A.; CO. F, 28TH REG.
Charles A. Poindexter, a Yadkin resident, e. there on 3-12-1864. He was captured in a Richmond, VA, hospital on 4-3-1865, and transferred to Newport News, VA, on 4-23-1865. He was released on 6-30-1865, after taking the Oath of Allegiance (NCT VIII, 181).

POINDEXTER, ISAAC C.; CO. F, 28TH REG. SERGEANT (10/13/1837–07/29/1916; Friendship Bapt.).
Isaac Columbus Poindexter e. in Yadkin Co. at age 23 on 6-18-1861. He mustered in as private, promoted to sergeant Jan.-April 1862. He was captured at Wilderness, VA, or Spotsylvania Court House, VA, in May of 1864, and confined at Point Lookout, MD, until transferred to Elmira, NY, on 8-15-1864. Paroled at Elmira on 3-14-1865, and transferred to Boulware's Wharf, James River, VA, for exchange on March 18–21, 1865. Captured in a Richmond, VA, hospital on 4-3-1865, and confined at Point Lookout, MD, until released on 7-25-1865 after taking the Oath of Allegiance (NCT VIII, 182). Additional information received from a descendant about Poindexter's military service is as follows. After the Confederates took Harpers Ferry, Isaac Columbus Poindexter participated in A. P. Hill's famous 17-mile march to Sharpsburg to rescue General Lee's army. Returned to duty after being sick and in the hospital. He was promoted to corporal, and took part in Jack's flank attack on U. S. General Hooker at Chancellorsville. At Gettysburg, the 28th Regiment in which he served was one of the last to withdraw from Pickett's Charge. He was promoted to Sergeant in 1864, and was captured at the Wilderness. He was the s. of the Rev. Denson A. and Sarah Jones Poindexter. He m. Mary (Polly) A. Milner Hauser (b. 9-20-1840, d. 3-18-1925), on 11-15-1866 in Surry Co., NC (per Randall G. Poindexter, Boonville, NC; *Heritage*, 557–558; "Poindexter," 51; 1850 Surry).

POINDEXTER, JASPER; CO. A, 7TH BAT.
(1832–?).
Jasper Poindexter e. in Macon Co. at age 30 on 7-7-1862 along with his brother, Albert. He was present until he transferred to Co. E, 65th Reg. (6th Reg. N.C. Cavalry), on 8-3-1863 (NCT II, 522). After transferring he was reported AWOL Sept.–Dec. 1863. Jasper e. in Macon Co. at age 30 on 7-7-1862. He was present until he transferred to Co. E, 65th Reg. (6th Reg. NC Cavalry), on 8-3-1863. Jasper was reported AWOL Sept.–Dec. 1863 (NCT IV, 485, 522). Jasper Poindexter, s. of Thomas and Sarah Nance Poindexter, was b. ca. 1832. In the 1850 Surry (Yadkin) Co. Census, he is living in the household of his parents (1850 Surry). He undoubtedly moved to Macon Co. when his brother Albert and wife

moved there, sometime after 1860 (see letter in Appendix A).

POINDEXTER, JOHN A.; CO. A, 54TH REG. (1838–?).
John A. Poindexter was a Yadkin farmer before enlisting at age 24 on 5-3-1862. Discharged 5-27-1862, reason not given (NCT VIII, 255). There are several John A. Poindexters, and I have not conclusively placed this one as yet. He is probably the John A. Poindexter, b. 1-12-1839, d. 10-14-1886, s. of Thomas H. and Amelia (Milly) Dull Poindexter, who m. Nancy Paulina Allen, dau. of James and Rebecca Allen, on 10-28-1868 (YCMR, "Poindexter," 65; 1850 Surry).

POINDEXTER, JOHN A. H.; CO. F, 28TH REG. 2ND LIEU. (05/17/1829–07/09/1915; Macedonia Meth. Ch.).
John Poindexter e. at age 32, and was appointed 2nd lieutenant 6-18-1861. Resigned 9-5-1861. However, he continued to serve. Promoted to corporal Jan.-June 1862. Hospitalized at Richmond VA, 7-3-1862 with a flesh wound of the hand. Returned to duty 7-4-1862. Promoted to sergeant 7-16-1862. Captured at Burkeville, VA, 4-6-1865. Confined at Point Lookout, MD, until released 6-17-1865 after taking the Oath of Allegiance (NCT VIII, 174, 182). Robert Alexander and Charlotte Martin Poindexter. He m. Julia Ann Caroline Speas (4-17-1831/7-30-1912), dau. of John Henry and Anna Shore Speas. They had no children (YCHGSJ XII [Dec. 1993]: 13; *Heritage*, 551; Eugenia Poindexter, East Bend, NC; "Poindexter," 121).

POINDEXTER, PLEASANT HENDERSON; CO. I, 6TH REG. (03/07/1837–05/11/1913; Macedonia Meth. Ch.).
Pleasant Henderson Poindexter e. in Yadkin Co. at age 26 on 9-15-1862 in Co. I, 6th Reg. Present or accounted for until he transferred to Co. G, 28th Reg. March-April 1863. He was wounded at Gettysburg July 1–3, 1863. Returned to duty in 1863, and surrendered at Appomattox Court House on 4-9-1865 (NCT IV, 376). He was the youngest s. of Robert Alexander and Charlotte Martin Poindexter (YCHGSJ XII [Dec. 1993]: 13; 1850 Surry). Before the War, P. H. Poindexter attended York Institute at Taylorsville, NC. Three of his brothers served in the war (John A. H., Thomas C. M., and William George Washington). P. H. and two other men walked home from Appomattox (per Eugenia Poindexter) to return to his wife Temperance Ann Bagwell, b. 8-11-1841, d. 1913, whom he had m. on 3-7-1861 (*Heritage*, 551–552). According to the Poindexter Family Association Newsletter, No. 1, page 3, July 1987, "Uncle Ples was responsible for passing along the Indian ancestry story as well as other Poindexter history firmly believed by the earlier generations."

POINDEXTER, ROBY H.; CO. G. 28TH REG.
Roby H. Poindexter transferred from Co. G, 28th Reg., to Co. F, 28th Reg., about 9-28-1863. He deserted on 9-13-1864 (NCT VIII, 182). He may be the same as Alexander Roby Poindexter of Co. F, 28th Regiment, NC Troops (see above).

POINDEXTER, THOMAS C. M.; CO. F, 28TH REG. SGT. (05/15/1831–07/10/1862; Macedonia Meth.).
Thomas C. M. Poindexter e. in Yadkin Co. at age 30 on 6-18-1861. Mustered in as sergeant but reduced to ranks Jan.-June 1862. Died in a Richmond, VA, hospital on 7-10-1862 of typhoid fever (NCT VIII, 182). He is believed to have been brought back to Yadkin Co. for burial. According to Eugenia Poindexter, a descendant, Thomas C. M. and his brother William George were brought home by family members in a wagon. It took two days to make the trip, and the two were buried by candlelight because their bodies were so decomposed. Thomas C. M. Poindexter m. Margaret A. Wooten on 1-13-1853 (YCMR). She was b. 6-29-1834, d. 10-14-1861. He was the s. of Robert Alexander and Charlotte Martin Poindexter (YCHGSJ XII [Dec. 1993]: 13; *Heritage*, 551; "Poindexter," 121).

POINDEXTER, WILLIAM G. WASHINGTON; CO. I, 6TH REG. (08/02/1835–07/03/1863; Macedonia Meth.).
William George Washington Poindexter e. in Yadkin Co. at age 28 on 9-15-1862. Present until he transferred to Co. G, 28th Reg., NC Troops, on 3-18-1863 (NCT IV, 377). He was wounded and captured at Gettysburg, PA, on 7-3-1863. Hospitalized at Gettysburg, he d. on 7-5-1863 of wounds. He was the s. of Robert Alexander and Charlotte Martin Poindexter (YCHGSJ XII [Dec. 1993]: 13; 1850 Surry). According to family tradition, he, along with his brother, Thomas C. M. Poindexter, was brought home by wagon and buried in Macedonia Methodist Church cemetery. They were buried at night by candlelight, because the bodies were so decomposed (per Eugenia Poindexter, East Bend, NC). William G. W. Poindexter m. Judetta Varner (or Lizette R. In 1860 census of Yadkin; "Poindexter," 126).

POPLIN, GEORGE C.; CO. B, 38TH REG. (1840–?).
George C. Poplin, a Yadkin resident, e. there at age 22 on 2-1-1862 as a substitute for Private Alfred M. Haynes of the same company. Wounded at Mechanicsville, VA, on 6-26-1862. Returned to duty Sept-Oct. 1862. Present through Oct. 1864. Surrendered at Appomattox Court House, VA, on 4-9-1865 (NCT X, 28). George C. Poplin m. R. C. Poenix on 2-28-1866 (YCMR). George and his brother Stephen H., were the s. of Alston and Mary Poplin (1850 Surry). George is listed as 10 years old in 1850).

POPLIN, STEPHEN H.; CO. B, 38TH REG. 3RD LIEUTENANT (1837–?).
Stephen H. Poplin was a cooper in Yadkin Co. before enlisting at age 24 on 10-16-1861. Mustered in as

sergeant. Present until wounded at Frayser's Farm, VA, about 6-20-1862. Returned to duty Sept.-Oct. 1862. Elected 3rd lieutenant about 5-10-1863. Reported on duty as acting commander of this company July-Dec. 1863. Present until wounded and captured near the Wilderness, VA, about 5-6-1864. "Died in prison," place and date, and cause of death not reported (NCT X, 21). Stephen H. and his brother George Poplin were the sons of Alston and Mary Poplin. The family was living in Surry Co. when the 1850 Census was taken.

POTTER, SHADRACK; CO. C, 44TH REG. (1829-?).
Shardrack Potter, a Yadkin Co. resident, e. at age 33 in Co. C, 44th Reg, on 11-25-1862. He deserted on 1-7-1863 (NCT X, 424). He is also listed as serving in Co. E, 70th Reg.

POTTS, JOHN H.; CO. I, 28TH REG. MUSICIAN (1836-?).
John H. Potts, a Yadkin resident, e. there at age 26 on 3-8-1862. Mustered in as private and promoted to musician before 11-1-1862. Reduced to ranks before 3-1-1863. Deserted on 7-23-1863 (NCT VIII, 216).

POTTS, NICHOLAS H.; CO. F, 28TH REG. (1844-?).
Nicholas H. Potts lived in Yadkin Co. where he e. at age 19 on 6-20-1863. Hospitalized in Richmond, VA, on 6-3-1864 with a gunshot wound, but place and date of wound not reported. He was furloughed on 6-30-1864, and reported AWOL on 8-28-1864 (NCT VIII, 182). Nicholas H. Potts m. Elizabeth M. Spear on 3-25-1866 (YCMR).

PREVETTE (PREWETT), ABRAM; CO. K, 42ND REG. (1831-04/14/1864).
Abram Prevette e. on 10-15-1862 in Wake Co. and deserted on 5-26-1863. Returned to duty on 12-1-1863. Died in a Wilmington hospital on 4-14-1864 of "febris continuaminus" (NCT X, 286). Abraham Prewett (Prevette?), age 19, was living in the house of Nancy and Mary Mitchell and was working as a laborer (1850 Surry).

PREWET, N[ATHAN].; CO. H, 63RD REG. (5TH CAVALRY) (1838-?).
N. Prewet e. in Davie Co. on 7-18-1862. He was present or accounted for through October 1862 (NCT II, 435). Nathan Prewet was the s. of Abraham and Malinda Prewit, and was living in their household in 1850, along with brothers Anderson, and Wilson T. (1850 Surry).

PRIMM, ALFRED R.; CO. G, 38TH REG. (1829-?).
Alfred R. Primm e. at Camp Holmes on 7-20-1864. He was present through 12-5-1865 (NCT X, 74). Primm (Prim) was living in in the Edred Thornton household and working as a laborer in 1850 (1850 Surry). He m. Mary Fletcher on 9-27-1865 (YCMR).

PRUETT (PREWET), ANDERSON; CO. H, 63RD REG. (5TH CAVALRY) (1844-?).
Anderson Pruett (Prewet/Prewit) e. in Davie Co. on 7-18-1862. He deserted in April 1863 and was AWOL through Dec. 1863. In 1864, muster rolls March-August list him as "absent under guard—charge of desertion." He was paroled at Salisbury, NC, in 1865 (NCT II, 435). Anderson Prewet (Pruett/Prewit), age 6, was living in the household of his parents, Abraham and Malinda, with other brothers and sisters, including Nathan (above) (1850 Surry).

PURYEAR, HENRY (HAL); SHEPHERD CLINGMAN'S BRIGADE (1841-?).
Henry S. Puryear e. at Fort Macon at age 20 on 5-1-1862. He was present in this company until discharged about 8-17-1862, after providing Louis S. Lineberry as his substitute (NCT VIII, 28). He then served as an aide to his uncle, Brigadier General Thomas L. Clingman. Henry Shepherd Puryear was the s. of Richard and Elizabeth Ann Clingman Puryear, and grew up at the Shallow Ford Plantation across the river from Huntsville in Little Yadkin Township. Hal never married. In 1850, he was living at home and attending school. After the war, he practiced law in Cabarrus Co. (*Heritage*, 561; 1850 Surry).

RANDLEMAN (RENDLEMAN), GEORGE W.; CO. A, 6TH REG. (1831-?).
George W. Randleman, a Yadkin Co. farmer, e. in Yadkin Co. on 9-15-1862. Captured at Winchester, VA, on 7-20-1864, he was confined at Camp Chase, Ohio, until released after taking the Oath of Allegiance on June 10, 1865. Age given on the oath was 34 (NCT IV, 279).

RASH, RICHARD M.; CO. F, 28TH REG. (1843-?).
Richard M. Rash was b. and lived in Yadkin Co. where he was a farmer before enlisting at age 21 on 6-18-1861. He was captured near Fussell's Mill, VA, about 8-16-1864, and confined at Point Lookout, MD, until released Oct. 14-17, 1864, after taking the Oath of Allegiance, and joining the U. S. Army. He was assigned to Company B, 4th Regiment, U. S. Volunteer Infantry (NCT VIII, 182). R. M. Rash m. Amanda Howell on 11-1-1866 (YCMR). Richard M., age 7 (and his brother Robert B.), were the sons of William B. and Elizabeth A. Rash and are listed in their household in 1850 (1850 Surry).

RASH, ROBERT (B.); CO. F, 28TH REG. (1844-03/06/1862).
Robert Rash was b. in Yadkin Co. where he e. at age 19 on 6-18-1861. He d. in a Wilmington, NC, hospital on 3-6-1862 of typhoid fever and or "dysenteria chron[ic]" (NCT VIII, 182). Robert B. Rash, the s. of William B. and Elizabeth A. Rash was listed as age 6 and living in their household in 1850 (1850 Surry).

REAVES (REAVIS?), JAMES WASHINGTON; CO. I, 28TH REG. (1843–?).
James Washington Reaves (Reavis?) lived in Yadkin Co., where he e. at age 19 on 8-8-1862. Reported AWOL on 2-8-1865 (NCT VIII, 216).

REAVICE (REVIS), CALVIN; CO. E, 70TH REG. (1846–?).
Calvin Reavis, s. of John and Millie Reavis, m. Amanda Whitehead, dau. of Jesse and Lucy Whitehead, on 1-20-1868 (YCMR).

REAVIS, ABRAHAM H.; CO. A, 1ST BAT. SHARPSHOOTERS (Iredell Co., NC).
Abraham H. Reavis e. in Wake Co. on 9-4-1862. Present until reported in Military Prison, Salisbury, NC, under sentence of court-martial on 2-28-1864 through 6-30-1864 muster roll. The same remark was noted through the December 1864 rolls. Captured at Farmville, VA, on 4-6-1865, and confined at Newport News, VA, on 4-13-1865. Released after taking Oath of Allegiance on 6-16-1865 (NCT III, 74).

REAVIS, ASA; CO. H, 3RD REG. (1827–?).
Asa Reavis e. in Yadkin Co. on 10-27-1863. He deserted on 11-15-1863 at Racoon Ford, VA (NCT III, 574). Asa was the s. of William and Jane Reavis (1850 Surry). His brother, David, e. in the same regiment and company.

REAVIS (REVIS), DANIEL; CO. I, 6TH REG.
Daniel Revis (Reavis), a Yadkin resident, e. in Wake Co. on 10-10-1864. Captured near Petersburg VA, on 2-6-1865, and confined at Point Lookout, MD, until released on 6-17-1865, after taking the Oath of Allegiance (NCT IV, 377).

REAVIS, DAVID; CO. H, 3RD REG.
David Reavis e. in Yadkin Co. on 10-27-1863. He deserted on 11-15-1863 at Racoon Ford, VA (NCT III, 574). David was the s. of William and Jane Reavis (1850 Surry). His brother, Asa, e. in the same company.

REAVIS, GILES; CO. A, 1ST BAT. SHARPSHOOTERS (1843–?).
Giles Reavis e. in Wake Co. on 9-4-1862. Present until he deserted on 3-1-1865. Dropped from the rolls for desertion on 8-31-1864. Reported present "in arrest" Aug. 31–Dec. 31, 1864. Sentenced by court-martial on 1-17-1865, and reported as being confined to Castle Thunder, Richmond, VA, as late as 3-15-1865. Paroled at Appomattox Court House, VA, on 4-9-1865. Giles is the s. of John and Milly Reavis, and was listed as 7 years old in 1850. Brother Calvin and sister Nancy were also in the household at that time (NCT III, 74; 1850 Surry).

REAVIS, J. F.; CO. B, 21ST REG.
J. F. Reavis e. in Yadkin Co. on 5-12-1861 and was present until he transferred to Co. A, 1st Battalion NC Sharpshooters, on 4-26-1862. Present through Dec. 1864 (NCT III, 74; VI, 553). J. F. Reavis m. Emeline Hutchens on 6-2-1866 (YCMR).

REAVIS, J. GRANVILLE; CO. B, 21ST REG. 1ST SERG. (08/12/1840–08/14/1892; Courtney Bapt. Ch.).
J. Granville Reavis e. in Yadkin Co. on 5-12-1861, and mustered in as a private; promoted to corporal on 10-31-1861. Present until he transferred to Co. A, 1st Battalion NC Sharpshooters, on 4-26-1862. Transferred as 1st sergeant, and present through Dec. 1864. Paroled at Appomattox Court House, VA, on 4-9-1865 (NCT III, 74; VI, 553). Granville Reavis was the s. of Joel Reavis (1850 Surry).

REAVIS, J. P. H.; CO. A, 1ST BAT. SHARPSHOOTERS.
J. P. H. Reavis e. in Wake Co. on 9-4-1862. Present through Dec. 1864 (NCT III, 74). J. P. H. Reavis m. Mary A. Hutchens on 3-5-1865 (YCMR).

REAVIS, JAMES M.; CO. B, 21ST REG.
James M. Reavis e. in Yadkin Co. on 5-12-1861, and was present until he transferred to Co. A, 1st. Battalion NC Sharpshooters, on 4-26-1862. Present through Dec. 1864 (NCT III, 74; VI, 554). James M. Reavis m. Elizabeth Jane Hair on 11-7-1862 (YCMR).

REAVIS, NATHAN; CO. I, 28TH REG. (1838–11/17/1864).
Nathan Reavis lived in Yadkin Co. where he e. at age 24 on 3-8-1862. Died "at home" on 11-17-1864, cause of death not reported (NCT VIII, 216). He was the s. of Joseph and Caroline Weatherman Reavis.

REAVIS (REVIS), WILLIAM S.; CO. B, 6TH REG.
William S. Revis (Reavis), a Yadkin Co. resident, e. in the Shenandoah Valley, VA, at age 19 on 10-16-1864. Captured near Petersburg, VA, on 2-6-1865, and confined at Point Lookout, MD, until released on 6-17-1865, after taking the Oath of Allegiance (NCT IV, 290).

REECE, A. H.; CO. H., 21ST REG.
A. H. Reece, a Yadkin farmer, e. in Wake Co. on 11-1-1863. Present until captured at Fisher's Hill, VA, on 9-22-1864. Confined at Point Lookout, MD, until released on 5-14-1865, after taking the Oath of Allegiance (NCT VI, 608).

REECE, A. R.; CO. A, 9TH BAT. HOME GUARD.
(He may be the same as Augustus R. Reese of Co. B, 38th Reg.)

REECE, ASBERRY H.; CO. I, 28TH REG. (1841–03/09/1863).
Asberry H. Reece e. at age 21 on 9-10-1862. Died in a hospital at Montgomery White Sulphur Springs, VA, about 3-9-1863 of "smallpox" (NCT VIII, 217). Asberry Reece m. Priscilla Roberson on 12-22-1859 (YCMR).

REECE, ATNEY (ANTHONY); CO. A, 21ST REG. (11/03/1829–03/28/1892; Boonville Bapt. Ch.).
Anthony Reece e. in Yadkin Co. on 10-1-1863. Present until wounded in the chest and right arm and captured at Cedar Creek, VA, on 10-19-1864. Hospitalized at Baltimore, MD, until paroled and transferred to James River, VA, in Feb. 1865 for exchange. Federal hospital records dated 1865 give his age as 36 (NCT VI, 549). Anthony (misspelled Atney in NCT VI, 549), was b. in Surry Co., the s. of Simon (ca. 1809–May 1860) and Mary Elizabeth Woodhouse Reece (12-3-1803/2-7-1889). He was the grandson of Jesse (1784–1864) and Margaret Hadley Reece (1790–ca. 1838), and the great-grandson of Abraham (ca. 1750–1822), and Mary Huff Reece (ca. 1754–ca. 1835). He was the great-great-grandson of Solomon Reece (b. 1725) and Sarah Boone Reece, and the great-great-great-grandson of David Reece (ca. 1700) and Mary Polk, of Wales, England. Anthony's brother, Nathan S. Reece also served (see below). Anthony m. Elizabeth Spence on 12-18-1856 (YCMR). She was b. 11-24-1840, and d. in Hardin Co., Iowa, on 11-27-1911. She is buried in Chester Friends Cem., Providence Township, Hardin Co., IA. They were the parents of 9 children, all b. in Yadkin Co.: Cornelia, Glancy Eugene, Elizabeth, Wiley Ray, Sarah H. J., Cora, Simon Arthur, Carrie Ann, and Charlie Clifton (per Helen M. Reynolds).

REECE, EVAN H.; CO. I, 28TH REG. (12/09/1842–07/30/1927; Boonville Bapt., Boonville, NC).
Evan H. Reece lived in Yadkin Co. where he e. at age 19 on 3-8-1862. He was captured at Hanover Court House, VA, on 5-27-1862, and confined at Ft. Monroe, VA, then Ft. Columbus, NY Harbor. He was paroled and transferred to Aiken's Landing on 7-12-1862, and exchanged on 8-5-1862. He returned to duty before 11-1-1862. Wounded at Gettysburg, PA, July 1-3, 1863, he returned to duty on an unspecified date and surrendered at Appomattox Court House, VA, on 4-9-1865 (NCT VIII, 217). Evan H. Reece, s. of James and Nancy Reece, m. Mary F. Woodhouse, dau. of Anthony and Miranda Woodhouse, on 12-29-1867. He m. Amanda C. Williams, dau. of Lace Williams, on 12-4-1892 (YCMR; 1850 Surry).

REECE, JAMES D.; CO. D, 63RD REG. (5TH CAVALRY) (1831–ca. 1864).
James D. Reece e. in Guilford Co. on 7-18-1862. He was present through December 1862. Claim for balance of pay due him was filed on 1-16-1864, with the notation that he had d. at Kinston, place, date, or cause of death not given (NCT II, 402). He was the s. of James D. and Sally Reece (1850 Surry). His brother, Joel M., served in same company/regiment (see below).

REECE, JOEL ("DECK") DARET; 75TH REG., 18TH BRIG. MILITIA (02/04/1832–02/21/1914; Boonville Bapt. Ch.).
Joel Reece (1850 Surry), was the s. of Joel Reece, the grandson of Daniel Reece, and the great-grandson of Abraham Reece. He was appointed by "Governor Vance as a captain of the Home Guard of North Boonville District during the Civil War" (*Heritage*, 570). Joel D. Reece m. Sarah D. Caudle on 12-30-1852 (YCMR).

REECE, JOEL M.; CO. D, 63RD REG. (5TH CAVALRY) (1833–?).
Joel M. Reece e. in Guilford Co. on 7-18-1862. He was captured near Hagerstown, MD, on 7-12-1863 and confined at Point Lookout, MD. He was paroled and exchanged there on 3-20-1864. He continued to be present until 1865 (NCT II, 402). Joel M. Reece was the s. of John and Sally H. Reece. He m. Mary M. Madison on 11-10-1852 (date of bond, YCMR).

REECE, NATHAN S.; CO. A, 21ST REG. (1831–ca. 02/20/1865).
Nathan S. Reece is first shown on company rolls of 2-16-1864. Died before 2-20-1864. Place and cause of death not reported (NCT VI, 549). Nathan S. Reece, the s. of Simon and Elizabeth Woodhouse Reece, m. Elizabeth Shugart on 3-8-1854 (YCMR). They had no ch. He had a brother, Anthony Reece, who served in the same company (see above), and two sisters, Mary Ann Reece (m. Jeremiah Vestal) and Martha Frances Reece (who m. James Alexander Shugart) (per Helen T. Reynolds).

REECE, T. A.; CO. B, 21ST REG. (1841–01/11/1862).
T. A. Reece e. in Yadkin Co. on 5-12-1861, and was present until he d. in a hospital at Culpeper Court House, VA, on 1-11-1862 of "typhoid pneumonia" (NCT VI, 554). This may be Thomas A. Reece, s. of John and Sally H. Reece, who was 9 years old in 1850 (1850 Surry).

REECE, THOMAS H.; 75TH REG., 18TH BRIG. MILITIA (12/03/1796–10/09/1863; Boonville Bapt. Ch.).

REECE, WINSTON; CO. H, 21ST REG. (1835–?).
Winston Reece e. in Wake Co. on 11-1863. Present until he deserted in June 1864 (NCT VI, 608). Winston Reece m. Mary Jane Dobbins on 1-16-1858 (YCMR). Winston, at age 15, was living in the household of his parents, John and Elizabeth Reece (1850 Surry).

REESE, AUGUSTUS R.; CO. B, 38TH REG. (1843–?).
Augustus R. Reece/Reese was a Yadkin Co. farmer before enlisting at age 18 on 10-16-1861. Present until wounded at Mechanicsville, VA, on 6-26-1862. Reported absent-wounded or absent-sick until discharged about 6-20-1863 because of "anchylosis" from gunshot wound (NCT X, 28). Augustus Reese m. Caroline Blaylock on 1-30-1865 (YCMR). Augustus R. Reese, b. in 1854, was the s. of John and

Sally H. Reese, and was living with them and several siblings in 1850 (1850 Surry).

REID, WILLIAM F.; CO. B, 21ST REG.
(1836–?).
William F. Reed (Reid) e. in Yadkin Co. on 5-12-1861, and was present until he transferred to Co. A, 1st Battalion NC Sharpshooters, on 4-26-1862. Wounded at Winchester, VA, on 9-15-1862. Retired to Invalid Corps on 7-12-1864 (NCT III, 74; VI, 554). A William Reed, age 14, was living in the James and Jane Davis household in 1850, and was attending school. Next door was the household of Nathan and Mary Reed and several younger children. They were probably his parents (1850 Surry).

REYNOLDS, GEORGE T.; CO. I, 28TH REG.
(1842–?).
George T. Reynolds e. in Yadkin Co., where he lived, at age 18 on 3-8-1862. Captured at Hanover Court House, VA, on 5-27-1862, he was confined at Ft. Monroe, VA, then Ft. Columbus, NY Harbor. Paroled and transferred to Aiken's Landing, James River, VA, where he was received on 7-12-1862. He was exchanged there on 8-5-1862. He returned to duty before 11-1-1862, but was reported missing at Gettysburg, PA, in the fighting July 1–3, 1863 (NCT VIII, 217). George T. Reynolds, b. ca. 1842, was the s. of William and Rachel Reynolds (1850 Surry).

REYNOLDS, WILLIAM; MILITIA (11/26/1820–05/14/1890; Town Cem., Yadkinville, NC).
In 1850, William Reynolds, age 29, was living with his wife, Rachel, and children, George T. (age 8), Sarah J. (age 6), Daniel M (age 3), and William S. (age 1). He was a hatter by trade (1850 Surry).

RIGGSBEE (RIGSBY), JOBE; CO. H, 54TH REG. SERGEANT (1839–?).
Jobe Rigsby, a farmer before enlisting in Yadkin Co. at age 23 on 4-13-1862. He mustered in as a private. Reported present on muster rolls through Oct. 1864. Promoted to sergeant before 10-31-1864. Surrendered at Appomattox Court House, VA, on 4-9-1865 (NCT XIII, 326). Jobe Rigsby, age 21, was living in the household of his father, Henry H. Rigsby and mother Nancy S. Rigsby, together with sisters Morning A., and Frances and younger brother William A. in 1860 (1860 Yadkin).

RIGGSBY, CHRISTOPHER COLUMBUS; CO. H, 54TH REG. (1835–10/06/1864).
Christopher C. Riggsby was a farmer before enlisting in Yadkin Co. at age 28 on 4-13-1862. Present through June 1862. Wounded in left leg and left breast at Fredericksburg, VA, 12-13-1862. Hospitalized at Richmond, VA. Furloughed for 60 days 2-13-1863. Returned to duty Sept.-Oct. 1863. Reported present through Dec. 1863. Wounded in foot and left knee at Winchester, VA, 9-19-1864. Hospitalized at Mt. Jackson, VA, where he d. on 10-16-1864 of wounds (NCT XIII, 326). Christopher m. Mary Wagoner on 11-6-1858 (YCMR). C. C. Rigsby, age 25, wife Mary (18), and dau. Nancy M. (7/12 mos), were living in 1860 in Yadkin Co. in the Boonville district (1860 Yadkin).

RILEY, ELDRIDGE; CO. H, 54TH REG.
(1825–?).
Eldridge Riley, b. in Davidson Co., but resided in Yadkin Co. where he was a farmer before enlisting there at age 32 on 4-19-1862. Reported present on company rolls through Oct. 1863. Captured at Rappahannock Station, VA, 11-7-1863. Confined at Point Lookout, MD, 11-11-1863, until released on 6-17-1865, after taking the Oath of Allegiance (NCT XIII, 326). In the 1860 Yadkin Co. Census, Eldridge Riley, age 35, and wife Nancy, age 25, were living in Yadkin Co., together with two small children, Franklin (age 4), and Tessia (age 6 months).

ROBERTS, A. W.; CO. F, 28TH REG. (1837–?).
A. W. Roberts lived in Yadkin Co. and e. in Alamance Co. at age 25 on 10-1-1862. He deserted in March 1863 (NCT VIII, 182).

RODWELL, WILLIAM H.; 75TH REG., 18TH BRIG. MILITIA (1832–?).
William H. Rodwell m. Martha Jane Williams on 5-5-1857 (YCMR). In 1850, William H. Rodwell, age 17, was living in the household of Richard S. Phillips, a merchant. In 1860 William H. Rodwell, age 28, was living in Yadkinville with wife Martha J. and children, Edwin C. (age 3), and Ann (age 6 months). His occupation was "salesman" (1850 Surry, 1860 Yadkin).

ROSE, BENJAMIN L.; CO. H, 54TH REG.
(1826–?).
Benjamin L. Rose, b. in Surry (now Yadkin) Co., was a farmer before enlisting in Yadkin Co. at age 36 on 3-17-1862. Discharged before 7-2-1862, because he was overage (NCT XIII, 326). In the 1860 Yadkin Co. census, Benjamin Rose is listed in Jonesville as 58 years old, living with wife, Martha, age 58; children Isaac, 19; Nancy, 16; Martha, 14; and Wesley, 8.

ROSE, ISAAC W.; CO. I, 28TH REG. MUSICIAN (08/25/1841–05/25/1909; Fall Creek Cem., Yadkin Co., NC).
Isaac Rose, (listed as J. W. Rose in Moore's *Roster*), was s. of Benjamin L. and Martha Rose of Jonesville, e. at age 22 on 8-13-1861. Mustered in as musician, but was reduced to ranks Jan.–Oct. 1862. Captured at Hanover Court House, VA, on 5-27-1862. Confined at Ft. Monroe, VA, and at Ft. Columbus, NY Harbor. Paroled and transferred to Aiken's Landing, James River, VA, and was received 6-10-1863. Returned to duty, but was reported AWOL 9-22-1864 (NCT VIII, 217). Isaac W. Rose, s. of Benjamin and Elizabeth Rose, m. Sarah Wagoner, dau. of Jonathan and Nancy Adams, on 9-15-1867 (YCMR; 1850 Surry).

ROSE, THOMAS A.; CO. I, 28TH REG.
(1839–?).
Thomas A. Rose e. at Camp Holmes on 10-14-1862. Reported AWOL 10-17-1864 (NCT VIII, 217). Thomas Rose m. Elizabeth Adams on 1-1-1858 (YCMR). He was the s. of Benjamin and Patsy Rose, who m. Isey McBride, dau. of Thomas and Sally McBride, on 5-29-1873 (YCMR; 1850 Surry).

ROSS, ALEXANDER; 75TH REG., 18TH BRIG. MILITIA (1831–?).
Alexander Ross m. Elizabeth Harris (who was probably the dau. of David and Martha Harris who were living with her in 1860) on 12-20-1860 (YCMR). He had previously m. Susan Caroline West (m. 1-2-1853, YCMR), who d. in 1857. After the war, Ross and wife are believed to have moved to Surry Co. in the Judeville area or below Roaring Gap (per Clay R. Perkins, 617 Drain Drive, Pasadena, MD 21122, letter dated 3-9-1986). Other sources state that Harriet M. Swaim, b. ca. 1842, the dau. of the Rev. Solomon and Sarah Ann Wagoner Swaim, was m. to Alexander Ross about 1861. She (Harriett Swaim) later m. Martin Pinnix on 9-11-1867 (1860 Yadkin).

ROSS, GABRIEL; CO. D, 44TH REG.
(1839–?).
Gabriel Ross lived in Yadkin Co. and e. in Wake Co. at age 23 on 10-17-1862. Present until he deserted on 5-27-1863. Returned to duty and deserted again about 11-27-1863. Returned to duty on 12-7-1863, and was present until he deserted to the enemy about 3-3-1865. Confined at Washington, DC, on 3-7-1865, and released after taking the Oath of Allegiance (NCT X 432). In 1860, Gabriel was living in the household of Alexander Ross, probably a brother.

ROUGHTON, ELISHA CLARK; 75TH REG., 18TH BRIG. MILITIA (1831–?).
Elisha Roughton m. Abigail Bagby on 10-19-1854 (YCMR). He was the s. of Elisha Roughton, b. in DE, and wife Nancy, and was living with them, at age 19, in 1850. Also in the household was his brother, James L. Roughton (1850 Surry).

ROUGHTON, JAMES L.; CO. I, 28TH REG.
(1836/7–?).
James L. Roughton, a Yadkin resident, e. there at age 23 on 8-13-1861. He was wounded in the right shoulder near Richmond, VA, sometime between 7-25-1862 and 7-1-1862. He returned to duty and was captured by the enemy on an unspecified date. Paroled and transferred to Aiken's Landing, James River, VA, where he was received on 9-7-1862 for exchange. Exchanged on 9-21-1862. Reported AWOL but returned to duty before 3-1-1863. Deserted on 6-20-1863 (NCT VIII, 217). James L. Roughton m. Temperance Shore on 4-5-1866 (YCMR). James L., age 13, was living with his parents, Elisha and Nancy Roughton in 1850 (1850 Surry).

ROYAL, ISAAC R.; CO. A, 1ST BAT. SHARPSHOOTERS (1846–?).
Isaac Royal enlisted in Lenoir Co. on 9-20-1864. Deserted at Greensboro, NC, on 10-11-1864, and was dropped from company rolls for desertion on 2-28-1865 (NCT III, 74). Isaac R. Royal m. Eliza M. Vanhoy on 12-28-1865 (YCMR). He was the s. of Lodewick and Jane Royal, and was probably b. in 1846 (1850 Surry).

ROYAL, JOHN C.; CO. B, 21ST REG. SERGEANT.
John C. Royal e. in Yadkin Co. on 5-12-1861. He mustered in as corporal, and was present until he transferred to Co. A, 1st Battalion NC Sharpshooters, on 4-26-1862. Wounded in the battle at Sharpsburg, MD, on 9-17-1862 and captured. Paroled on 9-27-1862, and discharged about 12-27-1862 because of "gunshot wound of face, probability of loss of sight" (NCT III, 74; VI, 554).

ROYAL, WILLIAM H.; CO. B, 38TH REG.
(?–06/03/1865).
William H. Royal (place and date of enlistment not reported) was captured at Jarratt's Station, VA, on 4-2-1865. Confined at Hart's Island, NY Harbor, 4-7-1865. Died there on 6-3-1865 of "chronic diarrhoea" (NCT X, 28).

ROYAL, WILLIE D.; CO. I, 28TH REG. MUSICIAN (1842–?).
Willie D. Royal e. in Yadkin Co. on 8-13-1861. Mustered in as private, was promoted to musician (drummer) Jan.–Oct. 1862. Captured at Hanover Court House, VA, on 5-27-1862. Confined at Ft. Monroe, VA and Ft. Columbus, NY Harbor. Paroled and transferred to Aiken's Landing, VA, on 7-12-1862 where he was exchanged on 8-5-1863. Returned to duty before 3-1-1863. Captured again at Amelia Court House, VA, on 4-6-1865. Confined at Point Lookout, MD, until released on 6-19-1865, after taking the Oath of Allegiance (NCT VIII, 217). He may be the W. D. Royal m. E. J. Gross on 12-7-1866 (YCMR). In 1850, Willie D. Royal, age 8, is listed in the house of his parents, Lodwick and Jane Royal (1850 Surry).

RUSSELL, GIDEON F.; CO. H, 63RD REG. (5TH CAVALRY) (1836–?).
Gideon Russell e. in Davie Co. on 7-18-1862. He was present until he transferred to Capt. W. M. McGregor's Company of Virginia Horse Artillery on 9-24-1864 (NCT III, 435). Gideon was the s. of Abner and Sarah Russell (1850 Surry).

RUSSELL, RICHARD D.; CO. B, 38TH REG.
Richard D. Russell was b. in Stanly Co. and resided in Yadkin Co. where he e. at age 24 on 10-16-1861. Present until wounded at Mechanicsville, VA, on 6-26-1862. Returned to duty Sept.–Oct. 1862. Deserted on 4-21-1863, but returned to duty 11-7-1863. He deserted again on 4-11-1864 (NCT X, 28).

RUSSELL, WILLIAM T.; CO. E, 33RD REG.
(1842–?).

William T. Russell served in this company and regiment, but date of enlistment not given. However, he was captured near Petersburg, VA, on 4-2-1865, and confined at Point Lookout, MD, on 4-4-1865 and held until paroled on 6-9-1865, after taking the Oath of Allegiance (NCT IX, 181). William T. Russell was the s. of John and Jemima Russell (1850 Surry).

RUTLEDGE, WILLIAM W.; CO. B, 38TH REG.
William W. Rutledge, a Yadkin Co. farmer, e. on 10-16-1861. Discharged about 2-1-1862 after providing William Shores as a substitute (NCT X, 28). W. W. Rutledge was m. three times: one of his wives was Margaret Allgood, whom he m. on 2-28-1860 (YCMR; *Heritage*, 579). A William W. Rutledge, age 44, is listed in the 1850 Surry Co. Census, with no wife, but with sons Thomas, age 18, Wilson, age 16, William C., age 14; and Isaac, age 11 (1850 Surry).

RYNEHART (RINEHARDT), D. D.; CO. A, 21ST REG.
D. D. Rynehart e. in Yadkin Co. on 10-1-1863. Present until he deserted on 5-6-1864 (NCT VI, 549). Daniel Rinehart m. Mary E. Ray on 5-5-1867 (YCMR).

SALMONS, JESSE FRANKLIN; 75TH REG., 18TH BRIG.
According to *The Last Tarheel Militia* by Gerald Cook, Salmons was in charge of the "Holly Springs" district.

SAWYERS, A. F.; CO. B, 21ST REG. (1843–?).
A. F. Sawyers e. in Yadkin Co. on 5-12-1861, and was present until he transferred to Co. A, 1st Battalion NC Sharpshooters, on 4-26-1862. Present through Dec. 1864 (NCT III, 74; VI, 554). An Arch. P. Sawyers, age 17, is listed in 1860 in the Thomas Brown household (1860 Yadkin).

SCOTT, THOMAS G.; CO. I, 28TH REG. (1843–?).
Thomas G. Scott lived in Yadkin Co. before enlisting at age 19 on 3-8-1862. Present or accounted for until he surrendered at Appomattox Court House, VA, on 4-9-1865 (NCT VIII, 217). Thomas G. Scott, the s. of Robert and Martha Scott, m. Alice Harding, dau. of William and Jane Speer Harding, on 3-30-1869 (YCMR). They had one dau., Cora. Scott was at the Battle of Ream's Station and wrote to his future bride's father about the death of his s. and her brother, Samuel Speer Harding who was killed at Ream's Station on 8-25-1864 (see Appendix A for letter).

SEAGRAVES, CURTIS F.; CO. F, 32ND REG.
Curtis F. Seagraves lived in Yadkin Co. at the time of his enlistment on 8-8-1862 near Raleigh. He was present through December 1864, but was reported sick most of that time. He was reported AWOL during Jan.-Feb. 1865 (NCT IX, 63).

SEAGRAVES, FRANK; CO. F, 18TH REG.
Frank Seagraves, a Yadkin Co. resident at the time of his enlistment at Camp Vance on 3-16-1864, was present until reported "missing" on 5-6-1864. However, he took the Oath of Allegiance at Salisbury on 6-15-1865 (NCT V, 344).

SEGRAVES, JOHN G.; CO. A, 9TH BAT. HOME GUARD (1839–?).
John G. Seagraves, age 21, was living in the Alphonso Dickerson household in 1860. His occupation was "carpenter." A George Seagraves was also in the household, and was probably the brother of John.

SEAT(S), NATHANIEL (NED) T.; CO. B, 21ST REG. (11/04/1845–03/19/1922; Huntsville Bapt. Ch.).
Nathaniel (Ned) T. Seat(s) e. at age 25 on 5-12-1861. He was present until transferred to Co. A, 1st Battalion NC Sharpshooters. Present on muster rolls through Dec. 1864 (NCT III, 75–76; VI, 554). Nathaniel T. Seat m. Nancy M. Brann on 10-5-1865 (YCMR).

SHAVER, ALEXANDER; CO. B, 5TH REG. (1825–?).
Alexander Shaver e. in Wake Co. on 7-14-1864. He was present until he deserted on 11-6-1864 (NCT IV, 154). He is listed in the 1850 Surry Census (Yadkin) as living in the household with Lydia Shaver (wife or sister), and three female children: Amanda, Mary, and Nancy Shaver (1850 Surry).

SHAVER, EMBERRY; CO. B, 38TH REG. (1829–?).
Emberry Shaver, a Yadkin resident, e. at age 32 on 10-16-1861. Present until wounded in right knee at Shepherdstown, WV, on 9-20-1862. Reported absent-wounded or absent-sick through Aug. 1863. Reported absent on hospital duty during Sept. 1863–Oct. 1864 (NCT X, 28). Emberry Shaver m. Nancy Dudly on 1-3-1860 (YCMR). In 1850, Emberry Shaver, age 23, was living in the household of Elizabeth Shaver, age 63, probably his mother. In 1860, Emberry, age 31 years old, b. In NC, was living with his wife, Nancy, and two children, James F. (age 2) and Franklin (age 6 months). (1850 Surry; 1860 Yadkin).

SHEEK, ASBERRY; CO. A, 1ST BAT. SHARPSHOOTERS (1846–?).
Asberry Sheek e. "at camp in Virginia" on 1-20-1864. Present on muster rolls through Dec. 1864 (NCT III, 75). Sheek, b. 1846, was the s. of James and Milly Sheek. His brother, Miles, also served in Co. A, 1st Battalion Sharpshooters (1850 Surry; 1860 Yadkin).

SHEEK, MILES C.; CO. A, 1ST BAT. SHARPSHOOTERS CORPORAL (1843–?).
Miles C. Sheek e. in Wake Co. on 9-4-1862. Mustered in as private, appointed corporal on 4-1-1864. Present on company rolls through Dec. 1864. Paroled

at Appomattox Court House, VA, on 4-9-1865 (NCT III, 75). Miles was the s. of James and Milly Sheek. His brother, Miles, also served in Co. A, 1st Battalion Sharpshooters (1850 Surry; 1860 Yadkin).

SHEPHERD, GEORGE W.; CO. F, 28TH REG. (d. 09/07/1864 or 10/01/1864; Yadkin Co., NC).
George W. Shepherd, b. in Franklin Co., but resided in Yadkin, e. in Yadkin at age 22 on 6-18-1861. Captured at Fredericksburg, VA, on 12-13-1862, and exchanged on 12-17-1862. He was reported AWOL before 1-1-1863. Returned to duty but deserted again on 6-23-1863. He was hospitalized at Richmond, VA, on 6-30-1864. Company records do not indicate if he returned to duty, but he d. at home on 9-7- or 10-1-1864 of disease (NCT VIII, 1820).

SHERMER, ISAAC; CO. G, 38TH REG. (1845-?).
Isaac Shermer e. at Camp Holmes on 7-30-1864. He deserted on 8-15-1864 (NCT X, 74). He was the s. of John and Cloe Shermer (1850 Surry).

SHERMER, JAMES; CO. F, 44TH REG. (1841-?).
James Shermer e. at age 21 on 12-1-1862. Deserted but returned before 3-1-1863 (NCT X, 452). James was the s. of John and Cloe Shermer and was living with them and his brothers (John H. and others) in 1860 (1860 Yadkin) when the census was taken. James Shermer m. Nancy Chamberlain on 1-19-1862 (YCMR).

SHERMER, JESSE; CO. B, 38TH REG. (1840-05/02/1863).
Jesse Shermer e. in Yadkin Co. at age 22 on 2-15-1863. He was killed at Chancellorsville, VA, during the fighting of May 2-3, 1863 (NCT X, 28). Jesse Shermer was the s. of Peter and Elizabeth Shermer. He is listed at age 10, in the household of Peter and Elizabeth Shermer (1850 Surry). His brother, Perry, also served in Co. A, 1st Battalion (1860 Yadkin). Date of Jesse's death recorded in Shermer family bible.

SHERMER, JOHN H.; CO. F, 44TH REG. (1837/38/39/40/41/42/43-?).
John H. Shermer e. at age 25 on 12-1-1862, deserted, and returned to duty before 3-1-1863 (NCT X, 452). He is also shown as enlisting in Co. H, 54th Reg. at Raccoon Ford, VA, on 12-5-1863, and deserted from camp near Racoon Ford on 12-26-1863 (NCT XIII, 327). In 1850, John H. Shermer, age 7, is listed in the household of John and Cloe Sprinkle, along with brothers James, Frederick, Isaac, Peter, and sisters Thursey and Sally in Yadkin Co. (1850 Surry, 1860 Yadkin).

SHERMER, PERRY A.; CO. A, 1ST BAT. SHARPSHOOTERS (03/16/1845-03/17/1929; Shermer Fam. Cem.).
Perry Shermer e. "at camp in Virginia" on 11-1-1863. Present until he deserted on 2-23-1864 at Kinston, NC. Muster roll for Aug.31-Dec. 31, 1864 lists him with the remark: "In Military Prison, Salisbury, NC, under sentence of Court Martial." Paroled at Appomattox Court House, VA, 4-9-1865 (NCT III, 75). Perry A. Shermer, the s. of Peter and Elizabeth Shermer (1850 Surry), Louise J. Hoots, dau. of Daniel and Sarah Hoots, on 6-20- 1865 (YCMR). She was b. 11-9-1846, d. 6-7-1904 (Hoots, 394; 1860 Yadkin; Shermer family bible). His brother, Jesse, was killed at Chancellorsville, while serving in Co. B, 38th Reg. NC Troops.

SHIPWASH, GEORGE W.; CO. F, 28TH REG. (1837-?).
George W. Shipwash lived in Yadkin Co. where he e. at age 24 on 6-18-1861. He deserted on 6-30-1862, but returned to duty before 12-31-1862. He deserted again on 7-19-1863. He was captured by the enemy at Culpeper, VA, on 12-4-1863, and confined at Old Capitol Prison, Washington, DC, until released on 3-19-1864, after taking the Oath of Allegiance. Roll of Honor indicates he deserted three times (NCT VIII, 182). George Shipwash m. Elizabeth Martin on 12-6-1859 (bond date, YCMR).

SHORE(S), ALEXANDER F.; CO. I, 28TH REG. (1840-09/11/1862).
Alexander F. Shores lived in Yadkin Co. where he e. at age 21 on 8-13-1861. Mustered in as private, promoted to corporal Jan.-Oct. 1862. Captured at Hanover Court House, VA, on 5-27-1862, and confined at Ft. Monroe, VA, then Ft. Columbus, NY Harbor. Paroled and transferred to Aiken's Landing, James River, VA, where he arrived 7-12-1862 for exchange. Exchanged on 8-5-1862. Returned to duty before 8-28-1862, when he was wounded in the Battle of Second Manassas, VA. He d. on 9-11-1862 of wounds, place and date of death not given (NCT VIII, 217).

SHORE(S), ANDERSON D.; CO. B, 21ST REG. (1832-?; Yadkin Co., NC).
Anderson D. Shore(s), e. in Yadkin Co. on 5-12-1861, and was present through 1-4-1862. After transfer to Co. A, 1st Battalion, he was listed at Second Manassas, VA, on 8-28-1862 (NCT III, 75; VI, 554). Shore served under Capt. J. K. Connally. While in this company, he was reported absent-sick at camp, then that he was in Moore Hospital, Danville, VA, with influenza. He was transferred from there to Culpeper General Hospital in January 1862. Anderson Shore is also listed in Co. I, 28th Reg., as enlisting at age 22 on 8-13-1861, and was killed at the Battle of Second Manassas on Aug. 28-30, 1862 (NCT VIII, 217). This may be the one and the same person, since Shore research Alice Brumfield believes there was only one Anderson Shore, the Anderson Shore, who was b. in 1832, the s. of David L. and Rachel Clanton Shore, who m. Mary Jane Russell about 1850. Anderson and Mary were the parents of four children: David Anderson (b. 8-19-1850), Thomas (b. 1852), Rachel (b. 6-5-1859), Isaac, and Mary Jane (b. 1865). A family tradition is that

Anderson Shore was killed by the Home Guard in 1865 at a place known as "Green Pond" on the Huntsville-Courtney Road (per Alice Brumfield; 1850 Surry).

SHORE(S), CHRISTIAN; CO. H, 54TH REG. (1837–?).
Christian Shores e. in Yadkin Co., age 25, on 3-17-1862. Present through June 1862. Deserted at Fredericksburg, VA, 12-18-1862 (NCT XIII, 327).

SHORE(S), D. A.; CO. E, 70TH REG.

SHORE(S), D. A.; CO. C, 44TH REG. (1839–?).
D. A. Shore e. in Yadkin Co. at age 23 on 10-2-1862. Present until 6-4-1863 when he was reported AWOL (NCT X, 425). He may be the same as D. A. Shore(s) who served in the Reserve unit, Co. E, 70th Reg. (above).

SHORE(S), DAVID; CO. I, 28TH REG. (1842–?).
David Shore e. in Co. I, 28th Reg. at age 19 on 8-13-1861 (NCT VIII, 217). He may be the same as David Shore who e. in Yadkin Co. on 10-1-1863 in Co. A, 21st Reg (VI, 549). While in Co. A, 21st, Regiment, he was present until captured at Bermuda Hundred, VA, about 5-16-1864. Confined at Point Lookout, MD, until released on 6-17-1864, after joining the U. S. Army. Records of Federal Provost Marshal dated 1864 give his age as 22 (NCT VI, 217, 549).

SHORE(S), DAVID K.; CO. H, 54TH REG. (1840–?).
David K. Shore e. in Yadkin Co. on 4-17-1862 for the war, but failed to report for duty. Reported AWOL in June 1862 and dropped from company rolls (NCT XIII, 327). He may be the same as David Shore listed in same company and regiment as enlisting at age 22 on the same day (4-17-1862), and deserted on 7-1-1862 (NCT XIII, 327).

SHORE(S), DANIEL; CO. H, 3RD REG. (?–02/11/1864).
Daniel Shore e. in Yadkin Co. on 10-17-1863, deserted 11-15-1863 at Morton's Ford. He d. 2-11-1865 (NCT III, 575). His widow, Elizabeth Shore, received a pension in Yadkin County.

SHORE(S), ENOCH; CO. H, 63RD REG. (5TH CAVALRY) (1846–?).
Enoch Shore(s) e. in Davie Co. at age 16 on 7-18-1862 as a substitute for Newton Spellman. His name appears on the muster roll dated 9-17-1862, but there is no further record of his service (NCT II, 436). Enoch Shore was the s. (or grandson) of Susannah Shore and was in her house with other brothers and sisters in 1850 (1850 Surry).

SHORE(S), FREDERICK; CO. F, 44TH REG. (1835–05/05/1865).
Frederick Shore e. at age 27 in Yadkin Co. on 12-1-1862. Deserted on an unspecified date. Returned to duty before 3-1-1863. Deserted again. Returned to duty on 3-1-1864. Died at Hanover, VA, before 10-12-1864. Cause of death not reported (NCT X, 452). John E. Tate, Sr., had a letter about Frederick Shore's death: "Frederick Shores, Company F, 44th N. C. Troops McRae's Brigade was killed on the 5th of May 1864, at the second battle of the Wilderness, VA, on the old plank road leading from Orange Courthouse to Fredericksburg, VA. Was shot though the left bre[a]st about six o'clock in the evening. He was good and faithful soldier, was barried [buried] in the grave with Alexander Cline, Burke Valler who belonged to the company. [Signed] G. W. Montgomery, Captain Co. F, 44th N. C. Troops, McRae's, Heath's Division, A. P. Hill's Corps." Frederick Shore(s) was the s. of David L. and Rachel Clanton Shore. He m. Sallie Brilla Dinkins on 12-12-1857 (YCMR), and they had 4 daughters: Louisa (b. 1858), Lucy J. (b. 1860), Amanda (b. 4-2-1861), and Rachel (b. 5-14-1864 who m. a Tate) (per Alice Brumfield; 1850 Surry).

SHORE(S), HENRY; CO. I, 28TH REG. (1840–?).
Henry Shore(s), b. in Surry Co., resided in Yadkin Co., where he was a farmer before enlisting there at age 21 on 8-13-1861. Discharged on 4-14-1862 because of a "scrotal hernia" (NCT VIII, 217).

SHORE(S), ISAAC; CO. C, 44TH REG. (1838–?).
Isaac Shore was "conscripted" in Yadkin Co. at age 27 on 10-20-1862. Present until hospitalized at Charlottesville, VA, on 10-18-1863 with a gunshot wound. Place and date of wound not reported. Returned to duty Jan.-Feb. 1864. Present through April 1864 (NCT X, 425). This Isaac Shore was born about 1838 in Surry (now Yadkin) Co., NC, the s. of David L Shore(s) and Rachel Clanton Shore(s). He m. Catherine Haire, dau. of Abner Haire, on 1-29-1860, and they had James (born 1860), Isaac, and Miles William Shore (born 1863). Catherine Haire Shore, widow of Isaac Shore, m. second William Henry Plowman Miles William m. Julia Steelman on 1-8-1899, and they removed to Texas (per Alice Brumfield).

SHORE(S), ISAAC, JR.; CO. B, 38TH REG. (1838–05/03/1863; Deep Creek Bapt.).
Isaac Shore(s), Jr., lived in Yadkin Co. where he resided at age 24 on 4-19-1862. Reported AWOL on 9-15-1862. Company records indicate he was captured and paroled Nov.-Dec. 1862. However, records of the Federal Provost Marshal do not substantiate that report. Returned to duty in Jan.-Feb. 1863. Killed at Chancellorsville, VA, on 5-3-1863 (NCT X, 28–29).

SHORE(S), J. W.; CO. H, 63RD REG.(5TH CAVALRY) CORPORAL (1832–?).
J. W. Shore(s) e. in Yadkin Co. on 7-18-1862 as a private, appointed corporal on 8-1-1863. Captured at

Hanover Court House on 5-31-1864, and confined at Point Lookout, MD. He was paroled and exchanged at Boulware's Wharf, James River, VA, on 3-16-1865 (NCT II, 436). J. W. Shore is listed as being 28 years old in 1860, and living with wife, Nancy, and children, Louisa A. (age 3), Julius F. (age 2), and Augustine E. (age 2/12) (1860 Yadkin).

SHORE(S), JACKSON; MILITIA.

SHORE, JAMES HENRY?; (02/20/1847–03/01/1889; Boonville Bapt., Boonville, NC).
James Henry Shore, the s. of John Benjamin (Jack) and Eunice Reece Shore (1850 Surry), was conscripted at age 16 in 1863. "He walked to Camp Fisher near Salisbury, NC, where he was inducted and began his training." He was sent to East Tennessee to help General Longstreet, and had to walk over 200 miles. There was a skirmish and James Henry and other were captured. He was marched on foot to Strawberry Plains, TN, to the railroad, where he was put in a cattle car and sent to Camp Douglas Prison on the south side of Chicago, where he was held until the war was over. When he was released, he was sent by train to Greensboro. From there, he walked to Salem, NC, and spent the night at the home of a family friend. Then he walked another 30 miles home to Yadkin Co. He decided to "go West," and spent the next couple of years in San Francisco, worked, and saved his money. After four years in the West, James Henry sold his farm and returned home to marry his sweetheart, Julia Ann Williams, the dau. of Crawford Wade and Nancy Ann Johnson Williams. They were m. on 1-23-1872 (YCMR). They had four children: Martha (b. 12-31-1873, m. George W. Garland, and moved to Monroe, Colorado), Dr. Thaddeus Warshaw (b. 9-9-1876, m. Zetta Woodruff), John Wade (b. 3-20-1879, m. Myrtle Elizabeth Fleming), and Annie Pearl (b. 8-3-1884, who m. Egbert Lawrence Davis) ("The James Henry Shore Family" by Egbert L. Davis, in *Heritage of Yadkin* Co., 588–590).

SHORE(S), JOHN; CO. F, 28TH REG. (1820–?).
John Shore(s) was a Yadkin Co. farmer before enlisting on 11-11-1863 at age 43 in Union Co. He was discharged on 12-21-1863 because of a "double inguinal hernia" (NCT VIII, 182).

SHORE(S), LEWIS; CO. A, 9TH BAT. HOME GUARD (1820–?).
This may be Lewis Shores, age 40, who was living with wife Mary, and children Enoch (age 16), David (age 18), Elizabeth (age 17), Martin (age 14), Louis (age 9), Robert (age 7), Mary (age 6), and Nathan (age 6/12) (1860 Yadkin).

SHORE(S), LEWIS W.; CO. I, 28TH REG. CORPORAL (1844–?).
Lewis W. Shores, e. originally as a private in Co. I, 28th Reg., at age 18 on 8-13-1862 (NCT VIII, 217). He transferred to Co. H, 54th Reg. May–Oct. 1863.

Mustered in as corporal. Captured at Rappahannock Station, VA, 11-7-1863, and confined at Point Lookout, MD, 11-11-1863. Paroled from there 2-24-1865. Received at Aiken's Landing, James River, VA, Feb. 25–March 3, 1865 for exchange. Paroled at Salisbury on 5-24-1865 (NCT XIII, 327).

SHORE(S), MARTIN G.; CO. B, 21ST REG. 1ST LT. (1834–?; Eastside Cem., Rockingham, NC).
Martin G. Shore, a Yadkin Co. farmer, b. in Wilkes Co., e. on 5-12-1861 in Yadkin Co. and was present until he transferred to Co. A, 1st Battalion NC Sharpshooters (NCT VI, 554). He then e. at age 18 on 3-17-1862 in Co. H, 54th Regiment, as a sergeant. Promoted to 2nd lieutenant on 10-8-1862, then to 1st lieutenant on 4-18-1863. Captured at Fredericksburg, VA, on 5-4-1863, and confined in Old Capitol Prison, Washington, DC. Paroled there on 5-18-1863. Returned to duty on 9-1-1863, and present through December 1863. Wounded in left thigh at Cold Harbor on 6-7-1864. Hospitalized in Richmond, VA, and reported absent-wounded 9-10-1864. He resigned on 2-13-1865 because of disability from wounds. Shore previously served in Co. A, 11th Reg. (1st Battalion NC Volunteers) (NCT XIII, 319). In 1860, Martin Shores, age 30, was living with wife, Lucinda (age 25), and children, Matilda and William (1860 Yadkin).

SHORE(S), NATHAN A.; CO. B, 38TH REG. (04/10/1829–09/18/1901; Jack Shore Cem., Yadkin Co., NC).
Nathan A. Shore e. in Yadkin Co. at age 32 on 10-16-1861. Present through Oct. 1864. He was reported absent-sick most of that period (NCT X, 29). Nathan A. Shore was the s. of Sarah Shore(s). He m. Rhoda (Rody) Shugart on 4-2-1857 (YCMR). They were the parents of 3 children: Sylvia (b. 1859), Sarah M. (b. 1863), and Eli (b. 1865) (per Alice Brumfield).

SHORE(S), PHILLIP; CO. H, 54TH REG. (1830–?).
Phillip Shore was a Yadkin Co. farmer before enlisting in Yadkin Co. on 8-29-1862. Hospitalized at Richmond, VA, on 11-17-1862 with typhoid fever. He was discharged 11-17-1862 at Richmond because of a "double inguinal hernia." Discharge certificate gives age at 32 (NCT XIII, 327).

SHORE(S), THOMAS; CO. C, 44TH REG. (1833–?; Old Shore Graveyard, Yadkin Co., NC).
Thomas Shore e. in Yadkin Co. at age 29 on 10-20-1862. Deserted on 11-24-1862 (NCT X, 425). Thomas Shore(s) was b. ca. 1830, the s. of David L. Shore(s) and wife, Rachel Clanton Shore(s). He m. Elizabeth Warden on 3-4-1855 in Yadkin Co.. They had three children: Ire (Ira) (b. 1855), Hugh (b. 1859), and James H. (b. 1860). Thomas is buried in the old Shore graveyard on the north side of Deep Creek (per Alice Brumfield; see also Bertie Shore Allgood, *Shore Family Records*, 47).

SHORE(S), WESLEY M.; CO. B, 38TH REG. (1844–?).
Wesley M. Shore e. in Yadkin Co. at age 17 on 10-16-1861. Present until 9-1-1862 when he was reported AWOL. Returned to duty in Jan.-Feb. 1863. Deserted again on 4-21-1863. Returned to duty 11-7-1863, and deserted on 7-17-1864 (NCT X, 29). Wesley Shore (age 17), who was living in the household of Kitty Shores (age 60), in 1860 (1860 Yadkin).

SHORE(S), WILLIAM; CO. B, 38TH REG. (1844–?).
William Shores, a Yadkin Co. farmer, e. at age 18 on 2-1-1862 as a substitute for Private William W. Rutledge of this company. Discharged on 6-15-1862 because of "disease and disability to perform military duty" (NCT X, 29).

SHORE(S), WILLIAM C.; CO. H, 54TH REG. SERGEANT.
William C. Shores, a Yadkin Co. resident, e. there on 8-29-1862. Mustered in as private. Present through April 1863. Captured near Fredericksburg, VA, 5-4-1863. Confined at Old Capitol Prison, Washington, DC. Transferred to Ft. Delaware, DE, 5-7-1863. Paroled from there and transferred to City Point, VA, where he was received 5-23-1863 for exchange. Returned to duty. Captured at Rappahannock Station, VA, on 11-7-1863. Confined at Point Lookout, VA, on 11-11-1863. Paroled from there about 3-16-1864. Received at City Point on 3-20-1864 for exchange. Returned to duty. Present through Sept.-Oct. 1864. Promoted to sergeant before 10-31-1864. Captured at Ft. Steadman, VA, 3-25-1865. Confined at Point Lookout on 3-27-1865. Released from there 6-19-1865, after taking the Oath of Allegiance (NCT XIII, 327).

SHORE(S), WILLIAM D.; CO. B, 21ST REG.
William D. Shore(s) e. on 5-12-1861, and was present until discharged on 12-16-1862, reason not given (NCT VI, 554).

SHUGART, ELI; CO. B, 38TH REG. (1839–?).
Eli Shugart (Sugart), a Yadkin Co. farmer, e. at age 22 on 10-16-1861. Present through April 1863. Reported absent-sick much of that time. Hospitalized at Richmond, VA, on 5-6-1863 with gunshot wound of left hand. Place and date of wound not reported. Reported absent-wounded or absent-sick through Oct. 1863. Reported AWOL 11-1-1863 until 10-16-1864 (NCT X, 29). Eli Shugart m. Milly Adams on 10-9-1865 (YCMR). Their s., John E., m. Missouri Carter, dau. of George and Julie Carter, on 8-16-1891 (YCMR). He may be the s. of Silva (Williams) Shugart and listed as age 14 in her household in 1850 (1850 Surry).

SHUGART, ENOCH JONES; CO. A, 1ST BAT. SHARPSHOOTERS (1845–?).
Enoch Jones Shugart e. "at camp in Virginia" on 6-15-1863. Present or accounted for on muster rolls through Dec. 1864. Wounded at Hatcher's Run, VA, on 2-6-1865 (NCT III, 75). He was the s. of Enoch and Carolina Davis Shugart, and was b. ca. 1845 (*Heritage*, 593; 1850 Surry).

SHUGART, ISAAC L.; CO. B, 21ST REG. CORPORAL (03/17/1843–01/17/15; Boonville Bapt., Boonville, NC).
Isaac L. Shugart e. in Yadkin Co. on 5-12-1861, and was present until transferred to Co. A, 1st Battalion NC Sharpshooters, on 4-26-1862. Wounded at Hazel River, VA, on 8-22-1862. Present until transferred to C. S. Navy on 4-19-1864 (NCT III, 75; VI, 554). He was the s. of Enoch and Carolina Davis Shugart, and the brother or Enoch Jones, and Lafayette D. Shugart (*Heritage*, 593; 1850 Surry). Isaac L. Shugart m. Nancy R. Turner, dau. of Lewis and Jane Turner, on 1-4-1871 (YCMR).

SHUGART, J[AMES]. ALEXANDER; CO. A, 1ST BAT. SHARPSHOOTERS (01/08/1840–02/03/14; Boonville Bapt. Ch.).
J. A. Shugart e. in Wake Co. on 9-4-1862. Present through Dec. 1864. Admitted to Jackson Hospital, Richmond, VA, on 2-10-1865 with gunshot wound of left arm. Arm amputated and he was furloughed for 60 days on 3-12-1865. Paroled at Appomattox Court House, VA, on 4-9-1865 (NCT III, 75). James A. Shugart, the s. of Enoch and Carolina Davis Shugart, m. Martha J. (Frances) Reece on 12-18-1860 (bond date, YCMR; *Heritage*, 593; 1850 Surry). After the war, when there were no slaves to tend the land, James Alexander went to work on the plantation of Tyre Glenn as a tenant farmer. By saving their money, he and his brother Isaac bought a 320-acre farm together, and then he tried running a tobacco factory for a time. He and his wife were the parents of 10 children (*Heritage*, 596).

SHUGART, LAFAYETTE D.; MILITIA (03/17/1839–05/01/1901; Boonville Bapt., Boonville, NC).
Lafayette D. Shugart is believed to have been at the Bond School House in February when the "shootout" occurred. His name is given as "DeLafayette" on the 1850 Surry Co. Census, which is probably correct. He was probably named after the Frenchman, Marquis de Lafayette (1757–1834), who assisted the colonists during the American Revolution. On later records, Shugart is called "Lafayette D." (1850 Surry). L. D. Shugart, the s. of Enoch and Carolina Davis Shugart, m. Elizabeth Woodhouse on 10-4-1860, and they were the parents of 10 children. During the war, as a member of the Militia/Home Guard he was described by those who knew him "as being kind and understanding but at the same time very persistent and very firm in the executions of his duties in the Home Guard." (YCMR; *Heritage*, 593).

SIZEMORE, ABRAM; CO. H, 3RD REG. (07/25/1832–01/01/1892; Deep Creek Friends, Yadkin Co., NC).

Abram Sizemore e. at age 20 on 7-15-1862. He was captured on 11-18-1863 at Mine Run, VA, and confined in the Old Capitol Prison, Washington, DC. Released on 3-2-1864 after taking the Oath of Allegiance, he was sent to New York (NCT III, 576). Abram (or Abraham) Sizemore m. a Smith. She d. young and he m. her sister, Alcie (Alsey) Smith, on 8-19-1859 (YCMR). She was b. 2-22-1842, d. 4-9-1910. Both are buried at Deep Creek Friends Church, Yadkin Co. He had 7 children in all (*Heritage*, 600; Hoots, 96). He is probably the s. of Isam and Patience Sizemore (1850 Surry).

SMITH, E. D. (D. E.?); CO. H, 44TH REG. (1834–?).
E. D. Smith resided in Yadkin Co. but e. at Camp French at age 28 on 10-14-1862. Present through 11-15-1864. NC pension records indicate he was wounded in the shoulder, hip, and neck at Orange Court House, VA, and at Chicamauga, GA, on unspecified dates (NCT X, 474).

SMITH, EPHRAIM DAVIS; 75TH REG., 18TH BRIG. MILITIA.
Ephraim Davis Smith may be the same as E. D. Smith who served in Co. H, 44th Reg. Ephraim Smith m. Susana Holcomb on 4-24-1856 (YCMR).

SMITH, JACOB; CO. H, 54TH REG. (1844–?).
Jacob Smith, a Yadkin Co. farmer, e. at age 18 on 3-17-1862. Reported AWOL June 1862. Returned to duty before 1-1-1863. Present through Oct. 1863. Hospitalized at Richmond, VA, 11-8-1863 with fever, debility, and an abscess. Furloughed for 30 days on 11-18-1863. Returned to duty. Reported present Sept.-Oct. 1864. He surrendered at Appomattox Court House, VA, 4-9-1965 (NCT XIII, 327).

SMITH, JAMES E.; CO. H, 54TH REG.
James E. Smith e. in Yadkin Co. on 9-23-1863. Died in Prince William Co., VA, on 10-17-1863 of "typhoid pneumonia" (NCT XIII, 327).

SMITH, JAMES T.; CO. B, 21ST REG.
James T. Smith transferred from Co. B, 21st Reg. (11th Reg. NC Volunteers) on 4-26-1862 as private. Promoted to corporal May-Aug. 1863. Present on muster rolls through Dec. 1864 (NCT III, 75). James T. Smith e. in Yadkin Co. on 5-12-1861, and was present until transferred to Co. A, 1st Battalion NC Sharpshooters, on 4-26-1862 (NCT VI, 554).

SMITH, JOHN; CO. F, 28TH REG. (?–08/09/1862).
John Smith e. in Yadkin Co. on 5-8-1862. He d. in a Richmond, VA, hospital on 8-9-1862 of "typhoid fever" (NCT VIII, 182).

SMITH, JOHN; CO. I, 28TH REG. (1844–02/05/1864).
This John Smith, a Yadkin resident, e. at age 18 on 1-6-1862. He d. in a Lynchburg, VA, hospital on 2-5-1864 of a "self-administered overdose of morphine" (NCT VIII, 271).

SMITH, JOHN M.; CO. G, 44TH REG. (1843–?).
John M. Smith and M. Smith appear to be the same person, but both are listed in NCT X, 463. He resided in Yadkin Co. and e. at Camp Holmes at age 19 on 10-14-1862. Listed as a deserted on 10-20-1862. Hospitalized at Richmond, VA, on 6-28-1863 with pneumonia and furloughed on 7-24-1863. Hospitalized again at Charlottesville, VA, on 12-25-1863 with acute diarrhea and furloughed for 60 days beginning on 2-18-1864 (NCT X, 463). He lived long enough to draw a NC pension (NCT X, 463).

SMITH, M.; CO. G, 44TH REG. (1843–?).
M. Smith, listed as a Yadkin Co. resident, e. at Camp Holmes at age 19 on 10-14-1862. He was listed as a deserter on 10-20-1862. He was hospitalized in Richmond, VA, on 6-28-1863 with pneumonia and received a furlough on 7-24-1863. He was hospitalized again at Charlottesville, VA, on 12-25-1863 with diarrhea and furloughed for 60 days on 2-18-1864. There is no further record (NCT X, 462). He may be Matthews Smith, b. ca. 1846, s. of Thomas Smith, both of whom were living in the Elizabeth Shaver (age 63) household in 1850 (1850 Surry).

SMITH, TAPLEY A.; CO. I, 28TH REG. (1840–?; Flat Rock Bapt., Yadkin Co., NC).
Tapley A. Smith, a Yadkin resident, e. at age 21 on 8-13-1861. Reported absent-wounded May–Oct, 1862. Returned to duty before 3-1-1863. Present through Feb. 1865. NC pension records indicated he was wounded in the forehead at "Cedar Mountain, Virginia, May 1, 1864." Roll of Honor indicates he was wounded several times (NCT VIII, 218).

SMITH, WILLIAM M. CO. H, 44TH REG. (1839–?).
William M. Smith resided in Yadkin Co., e. at Camp French at age 23 on 10-14-1862. Deserted on 11-2-1862. Listed as a deserter through Feb. 1863. Reported absent-sick during Nov. 1863–April 1864, and on sick furlough Sept.–Oct. 1864 (NCT X, 474).

SMITH, WILLIAM T.; CO. H, 54TH REG. (1843–?).
William T. Smith e. at Port Royal, VA, at age 20 on 3-1-1863 for the war. Deserted near Fredericksburg, VA 5-11-1863 (NCT XIII, 327). William T. Smith is listed as 10 years old in 1850 (1850 Surry), living in the household of Martha Smith, age 49.

SNOW, ALFRED; COL I, 4TH REG. (1842–12/24/1863).
Alfred Snow lived in Yadkin Co., but he e. in Wake Co. on 9-17-1863. He d. in a Richmond, VA, hospital on 23-24-1863 of "febris typhus" (NCT IV, 102). Alfred was living in Little Yadkin Township with wife Mary and three children in 1850 (1850 Surry).

SNOW, HENRY; CO. A, 1ST BAT. SHARPSHOOTERS (1820 VA–?).
Henry Snow e. at New Market, VA, on 11-1-1864.

Present through Dec. 1864 (NCT III, 75). Henry reportedly e. as a substitute for James Monroe Jones (*Heritage*, 444). In 1860, Henry was living with wife Mary M., and children: Charles P., Margaret E., Sarah, in the East Bend area next to the law school and home of Judge Richmond Pearson (1860 Yadkin).

SNOW, J. C.; CO. B, 21ST REG.
J. C. Snow e. in Yadkin Co. on 5-12-1861, and was present until transferred to Co. A, 1st Battalion NC Sharpshooters, on 4-26-1862. Present in Co. A, 1st Battalion, through Dec. Wounded at Hatcher's Run, VA, 2-6-1865, and confined in General Hospital, Richmond, VA, until furloughed 2-23-1865 (NCT III, 75; VI, 554).

SNOW, JORDAN H., JR.; CO. I, 28TH REG. 1ST LIEUTENANT (1832–?).
Jordan H. Snow, Jr., resided in Yadkin Co. where he e. at age 29 on 8-13-1861. Mustered in as private and was elected 3rd lieutenant on 1-3-1863. Promoted to 1st lieutenant on 6-20-1862. Wounded in the right thigh at Gettysburg, PA, on 7-3-1863. Returned to duty. Captured near Pickett's Farm, VA, about 7-21-1864. Confined at Point Lookout, MD, 7-28-1864. Transferred to Old Capitol Prison, Washington, DC, on 8-4-1864. Transferred to Ft. Delaware, DE, on 8-11-1864. Released on 6-17-1865, after taking the Oath of Allegiance (NC Troops VIII, 207).

SPARKS, ALLEN; CO. A, 1ST BAT. SHARP-SHOOTERS (1846–?).
Allen Sparks e. in Lenoir Co. on 4-20-1864. Deserted at Greensboro, NC, on 10-11-1864, and dropped from rolls for desertion on 2-28-1865 (NCT III, 75). Allen Sparks is believed to be the s. of John and Martha Sparks, and may be the John A. Sparks, age 4, living in their household in the 1850 Surry. In the same household is also William Sparks, probably a brother. William also served in this company.

SPARKS, JAMES T.; CO. E, 26TH REG.?
James T. Sparks was wounded and admitted to a hospital on 11-8-1862. He returned to duty. Captured at Petersburg, VA, on 3-25-1865, he was confined at Point Lookout, MD, until released on 6-20-1865, upon taking the Oath of Allegiance.

SPARKS, JOSEPH; CO. A, 9TH BAT. HOME GUARD (1817–?).
This may be Joseph Sparks, age 33 in 1850, who was living with wife, Martha, and children: Benjamin T., William R., John A., Sarah A., and James L. (1850 Surry).

SPARKS, WILLIAM; CO. A, 9TH BAT. HOME GUARD.

SPARKS, WILLIAM; CO. A, 1ST BAT. SHARPSHOOTERS.
William Sparks e. in Lenoir Co., NC, on 9-10-1864. Deserted at Greensboro, NC, on 10-11-1864, and was dropped from the rolls for desertion on 2-28-1865 (NCT III, 75). William Sparks is probably the s. of John and Martha Sparks (1850 Surry).

SPEAS, WILLIAM HENRY; CO. F, 28TH REG. (04/23/1839–01/07/1863).
William H. Speas lived in Yadkin Co. where he e. at age 22 on 6-18-1861. Mustered in as private, promoted to corporal on 7-10-1862. Died in a hospital in or near Richmond, VA, about 1-7-1863. Cause of death not reported (NCT VIII, 183). William was the s. of John Levi and Mary Phillips Speas. According to the records kept by Dr. John H. Kenyon, he was 5 ft. 11 inches tall (Alice K. Houts, "Yadkin Boys," in YCHGSJ [IV] summer 1963; 1850 Surry).

SPEASE, ISAAC N.; CO. D, 21ST REG. (08/09/1821–12/05/1864; Shore Cem., Yadkin Co., NC).
Isaac N. Spease, a Yadkin resident, e. in Forsyth Co. at age 42 on 9-20-1863. Present through Sept. 1864 (NCT VI, 572). Isaac N. Speas(e) was the s. of John Henry and Anna Shore Speas. Isaac's wife, Elizabeth Jane, was b. 4-14-1822, d. 8-1-1866. In 1850, Isaac Spease, age 28, was living with wife, Elizabeth, and two children, Solomon H., age 4, and Robert M., age 1. Both Isaac and Elizabeth are buried in the Shore Family Cemetery, near Flint Hill, Yadkin Co., NC (Casstevens and Bradford, "The Ancestors and Descendants of William Paul Spease Sr.," unpublished manuscript, 1991; 1850 Surry).

SPEER, ALEX; CO. F, 28TH REG. (1843–05/08/1865).
Alex Speer lived in Yadkin Co. where he e. at age 19 on 4-5-1862. He was captured near Petersburg, VA, on 4-2-1865, and confined at Point Lookout, MD, where he d. on 5-8-1865 of "diphtheria" (NCT VIII, 183). This may be "Sandy Spear," listed as 6 years old in the 1850 Surry Census, living in the household of his parents, John and Jane Spear. John was b. in Ohio.

SPEER, JAMES D.; CO. F, 28TH REG. (05/20/1845–04/10/1931; Lynch Cem., Yadkin Co., NC).
James D. Speer e. in Yadkin Co. on 11-5-1863 for the war. He was captured near Petersburg, VA, on 4-2-1865, and confined at Point Lookout, MD, until released on 6-20-1865, after taking the Oath of Allegiance (NCT VIII, 183). James' wife Mahaley, b. 9-24-1846, d. 11-4-1918, is buried in the Lynch Cemetery, Yadkin Co., NC, also. James may be the s. of John and Jane Spear, listed at 5 years old in 1850 (1850 Surry).

SPEER, JAMES MONROE; 75TH REG., 18TH BRIG. MILITIA (01/09/1843–03/23/1928; Speer Fam. Cem.).
James M. Speer m. Salina F. Dozier (b. 2-28-1848, d. 1-1-1941) on 3-20-1867, the dau. of Dr. Nathan B. and Olive Vestal Dozier (YCMR). He was the youngest child of Aquilla and Elizabeth Ashby Speer. His older brother was Col. William Henry

Asbury Speer. After the war, James farmed and operated a tobacco factory, making plug tobacco called "Speer's Best," which he distributed in North and South Carolina. James and Salina Speer had 11 children (*Heritage*, 612-713, 903-904; 1850 Surry; 1860 Yadkin).

SPEER, LEWIS H.; CO. F, 28TH REG. (1843-?).
Lewis H. Speer was a Yadkin Co. farmer before enlisting there on 6-18-1861. He was hospitalized at Richmond, VA, on 7-2-1863 with gunshot wound of right shoulder, Place and date of wound not reported. He returned to duty on 7-3-1862. He was captured near Fussell's Mill, VA, about 8-16-1864, and confined at Point Lookout, MD, until released on 10-16-1864, after joining the U. S. Army. He was assigned to Company C, 4th Regiment, U. S. Volunteer Infantry (NCT VIII, 183). Lewis Speer, b. 1863, was the s. of John and Jane Speer (Spear), and the brother of Sandy Speer (1850 Surry).

SPEER, SAMUEL HENRY; CO. A, 1ST BATTALION SHARPSHOOTERS (05/10/1823-11/18/1900; Macedonia Meth. Ch.).
Samuel H. Speer e. "at camp in Virginia" on 11-1-1863. Present through Dec. 1864 (NCT III, 75). Samuel H. Speer was the s. of Samuel and Rachael Cain Eddleman Speer. He m. Rachael S. Davis (dau. of Samuel L. Davis. She was b. 3-2-1838 and d. 4-8-1900. He and his family are listed in the 1860 Yadkin Co. census. Children were: Leroy, Ruth E., Nancy E., Comile Margaret, Mary E., Samuel H., Rachael, Rebecca, Willmuth, Permelia and Thomas (*Heritage*, 617; 1850 Surry; 1860 Yadkin).

SPEER, WILLIAM A.; CO. F, 28TH REG. (1845-?).
William A. Speer was a Yadkin Co. farmer and was born there. He e. at age 17 on 4-10-1862, but deserted on 8-7-1862. He returned to duty before 12-31-1862, and was captured at Fussell's Mill, VA, about 8-16-1864. He was confined at Point Lookout, MD, until released on 10-16-1864, after joining the U. S. Army. He was assigned to Company E, 4th Regiment, U.S. Volunteer Infantry (NCT VIII, 183). This may be William Spear, s. of Abraham and Nancy Spear, who was listed as 5 years old, living in their household in 1850 (1850 Surry).

SPEER, WILLIAM H. ASBURY; CO. I, 28TH REG. MAJOR (07/06/1826-08/29/1864; Speer Fam. Cem.).
William H. Asbury e. at age 30. He was appointed captain 8-13-1861. Captured at Hanover Court House, VA, 5-27-1862, and confined at Ft. Monroe, VA, then at Fort Columbus, NY Harbor. He was then transferred to Johnson's Island, OH, where he spent several months. He was paroled and transferred to Vicksburg, MS, and exchanged on 9-20-1862. He returned to duty. He was appointed major on 11-1-1862, and transferred to Field and Staff of the regiment (NCT VIII, 110, 206-207). He was promoted to lieutenant colonel on 3-12-1863. Wounded at Chancellorsville, VA, 5-2/3-1863, but returned to duty before July 1863, when he was wounded again at Gettysburg, PA. Returned to duty, and promoted to colonel 7-9-1864. He was fatally wounded in the head at Ream's Station, VA, near Petersburg, and hospitalized at Petersburg, where he d. 8-29-1864 of wounds received. Speer left a diary and several letters that have been edited and published by a descendant, Professor Allen Speer (see Speer, *Voices from Cemetery Hill*, 1997). William H. Asbury Speer was the s. of Aquilla and Elizabeth Ashby Speer (*Heritage*, 607-609, 611). Before the war, in 1850, William H. A. Speer was living at Jonesville in the house of Joseph R. Parks, a harness maker. Speer's occupation was tanner, and another person in the house, Hardin Laffoon, was a shoemaker. This house was next to or across the street from the residence of Professor William L. Van Eaton, who ran the Jonesville Academy (1850 Surry).

SPENCER, JAMES; CO. H, 54TH REG. (1835-?).
James Spencer e. in Yadkin Co. on 3-17-1862 (NCT XIII, 327). He may be the James Spencer listed as being 15 years old in the 1850 Census (1850 Surry), living in the household of Martha Spencer, age 40.

SPENCER, WILLIAM; CO. E, 70TH REG. (1805 VA-?).
A William H. Spencer, age 55, b. in VA, was living with wife Sarah, 49, and children, Lucy Ann (11), and David S. (7), in the Boonville District, in 1860 (1860 Yadkin). A younger William D. Spencer, was 22 in 1850 (b. 1828) and was living with his new bride, Mahala, whom he had m. within the year (1850 Surry).

SPILLMAN, MATTHEW D.; CO. F, 28TH REG. (02/05/1844-09/19/1923; Spillman Cem., Yadkin Co., NC).
Matthew D. Spillman lived in Yadkin Co. where he e. at age 18 on 2-11-1863. He was wounded and captured at Spotsylvania Court House, VA, on 5-12-1864, and confined at Old Capitol Prison, Washington, DC, on 5-19-1864. He was transferred to Ft. Delaware, DE, on 6-15-1864, and held until he was released on 6-19-1865, after taking the Oath of Allegiance (NCT VIII, 183). In 1860, Matthew D. Spillman, age 15, was living in the household of William Phillips (1860 Yadkin).

SPILLMAN (SPELMAN), THOMAS A.; CO. A, 44TH REG.
Thomas Spelman (Spillman?) e. on 11-25-1862 and was present through Feb. 1863. Listed as AWOL Mar.-April 1864 and Aug.-Oct. 1864. He was listed as a deserter (NCT X, 408).

SPILLMAN, THOMAS ELI; CO. A, 1ST BATT. HARPSHOOTERS (1841-01/01/1864; Orange Co., VA).
Thomas E. Spillman e. "at camp in Virginia" on

11-1-1863. Died in Orange Co., VA, on 1-14-1864 (NCT III, 75; Barry A. Price, Fancy Gap, VA). Thomas E. Spillman, age 9, was listed in the household of parents, Samuel and Ailey Spillman in 1850 (1850 Surry).

SPILLMAN, WILLIAM; CO. F, 28TH REG. CORPORAL (1841–?).
William Spillman, a Yadkin resident, e. there at age 20 on 6-18-1861. He mustered in as private. Reported absent-wounded July–Oct. 1862. Place and date wounded not reported. Returned to duty before 12-31-1862. Promoted to corporal on 5-11-1863. Reported present Sept.-Oct. 1864. Retired to Invalid Corps on 11-9-1864 because of an unspecified disability (NCT VIII, 183).

SPILLMAN, WILLIAM H.; CO. F, 28TH REG. (12/14/1840–08/05/1919; Spillman Cem., Yadkin Co., NC).
William H. Spillman e. in Yadkin Co. at age 21 on 4-18-1862. He was captured at Wilderness, VA, on 5-12-1864, and confined at Point Lookout, MD, until transferred to Elmira, NY, on 8-10-1864. He was released from Elmira on 6-21-1865, after taking the Oath of Allegiance. William H. Spillman was the s. of James and Elizabeth Spillman (NCT VIII, 183; 1850 Surry).

SPRINKLE, ALEXANDER; CO. B, 38TH REG. (1843–?).
Alexander Sprinkle, a Yadkin resident, e. at age 19 on 4-19-1862 for the war as a substitute. Mustered in as private. Present through 9-24-1863. Reported absent-sick during much of that period. Erroneously reported AWOL from 9-25-1863 through Feb. 1864. Rejoined company March-April 1864. Promoted to musician (drummer) on 4-10-1864. Reduced to ranks Sept.-Oct. 1864. Captured at Gill's Mill, VA, on 4-6-1865. Confined at Point Lookout, MD, on 4-14-1865 until released on 6-20-1865, after taking the Oath of Allegiance (NCT X, 29). Alex Sprinkle m. Martha Everidge on 1-3-1867. Alexander Sprinkle, age 5, is listed in the household of Nancy (age 68), Eda (age 42), Charity (age 48), and a number of younger males and females (YCMR; 1850 Surry).

SPRINKLE, C.; CO. E, 70TH REG.

SPRINKLE, CLEM C.; CO. F, 28TH REG. (1840–?).
Clem C. Sprinkle lived in Yadkin Co. where he e. at age 22 on 4-30-1862. He was captured in a Richmond, VA, hospital on 4-3-1865, and confined at Point Lookout, MD, until released on 6-28-1865, after taking the Oath of Allegiance (NCT VIII, 183).

SPRINKLE, GEORGE F.; CO. H, 10TH REG. (1ST ARTILLERY) (1837–?).
George F. Sprinkle e. in Wayne Co. on 2-10-1863. He deserted on 2-15-1863 and returned 11-16-1863. He was present or accounted for through Feb. 1865. He took the Oath of Allegiance at Mocksville on 6-7-1865. George F. Soprinkle was the s. of Michael and Margaret Sprinkle and was living with them, attending school, in 1850. Michael, his father, was a miller (NCT I, 136; Surry 1850).

SPRINKLE, HUGH; CO. C, 30TH REG. (1833–1914).
Hugh Sprinkle e. at Camp Holmes at age 31 on 11-22-1863. He was present until captured at Winchester, VA, on 9-19-1864. He was confined at Point Lookout, MD, on 9-26-1864, until released on 6-20-1865, after taking the Oath of Allegiance (NCT VII, 350). Hugh Sprinkle m. Martha K. Gross/Groce (1837–1909) on 12-27-1855 (YCMR). Hugh built a two-story log house in the 1850s, which has since been torn down. He was one of the "bushwhackers" present at the Bond School House when James West was killed. One of his daughters, Syniscal, m. Sam Joyner (per Lupton Wood).

SPRINKLE, JAMES H.; CO. I, 18TH REG. (1838–09/03/1863).
James H. Sprinkle e. at age 24 on 9-10-1862. Present until wounded at Chancellorsville on 5-3-1863. Leg amputated, and he d. in a Richmond hospital on 9-3-1863 of his wounds (NCT VI, 410). James H. Sprinkle m. Nancy Hutchens on 12-27-1854 (YCMR) She received a Confederate widow's pension.

SPRINKLE, JOHN S.; CO. I, 28TH REG. (1846–05/05/1864).
John S. Sprinkle's date and place of enlistment not reported. He was first listed in the company records in March of 1864. Killed at the Wilderness, VA, on 5-5-1864 (NCT VIII, 218). John S. Sprinkle, age 4, is listed in the household of Michael and Margaret Sprinkle in 1850 (1850 Surry).

SPRINKLE, JOHN T.; CO. F, 28TH REG. (?–07/11/1862).
John T. Sprinkle e. in Yadkin Co. on 4-28-1862. He d. in Richmond, VA, about 7-11-1862 of wounds and/or disease. Please and date wounded not stated (NCT VIII, 183).

SPRINKLE, MODE; CO. I, 18TH REG. (1832–10/05/1864).
Mode (Moses?) Sprinkle e. at age 30 on 9-10-1862. Present until captured at Spotsylvania Court House, VA, on 5-12-1864. Confined at Point Lookout, MD, until transferred to Elmira, NY, on 8-3-1864. Died at Elmira about 10-5-1864 of "chronic diarrhoea" (NCT VI, 410). Sprinkle m. Elizabeth L. Hutchens on 11-22-1853 (YCMR). He m. Elizabeth L. Hutchens on 11-22-1853 (YCMR). She is buried in the Joshua Williams Cemetery in Fall Creek Township, Yadkin Co., NC.

SPRINKLE, WILLIAM R.; CO. B, 38TH REG. (1827–?).
William R. Sprinkle e. at Camp Vance on 9-27-1864 for the war. Surrendered at Appomattox Court

House, VA, on 4-9-1865 (NCT X, 29). William R. Sprinkle m. Lucinda V. Johnson on 12-19-1853 (YCMR). This may be William Sprinkle, age 23, who was living in the house of Joshua and Sarah, in 1850 (1850 Surry).

STARLING, JAMES M. K.; CO. F, 28TH REG. 2ND LIEUTENANT (1839–07/06/1877; Fam. Cem, Surry Co.,NC).
James was reported absent-wounded Nov.-Dec. 1862 (NCT VIII, 174). James M. Starling was the s. of Alfred A. and Rebecca R. Starling. He m. Virginia E. Poindexter (b. 9-28-1851), dau. of William and Mary Poindexter, on 1-16-1869 (YCMR). James was living in his parents' household in 1860 and was listed as a 21-year-old laborer. His sisters were July A., Nancy E., Permelia F., and Luzetta J. and younger brother John W., age 15 (from Terri Stout Stevens, Pfafftown, NC 27040; Clark, *Histories of the Several Regiments,* II, 483; "Poindexter," 69; 1850 Surry; 1860 Yadkin).

STARLING, JOHN W. A.; CO. E, 6TH REG. (1847–?).
J. W. A. Starling e. at Camp Stokes on 11-3-1864. He deserted to the enemy about 3-26-1865. He was released and furnished transportation to Hamilton Co., IN, about 3-30-1865, after taking the Oath of Allegiance (NCT IV, 329). John W. A. Starling was the s. of Alfred and Rebecca Starling. His brother James M. served in Co. F, 28th Reg. (see above) (1850 Surry).

STEELE, JAMES GIDEON, SR.; CO. I, 6TH REG. (1846–?).
James Gideon Steel, Sr., was a Yadkin Co. farmer before enlisting there at age 18 on 1-15-1864. He was captured at Winchester, VA, on 7-20-1864, and confined at Camp Chase, OH, until paroled. He was transferred to Boulware's and Cox's Wharf, James River, VA, where he was received about 3-10-1865 for exchange. NC pension records indicate he was wounded in the ankle in Feb. 1865 while a prisoner of war (NCT IV, 378).

STEELE, WILLIAM D.; CO. I, 6TH REG.
William D. Steele, a Yadkin Co. wagon maker before enlisting in Yadkin Co. at age 28, on 9-15-1862, was captured at Fredericksburg, VA, on 5-3-1863. He was confined at Ft. Delaware, DE, until paroled and transferred to City Point, VA, where he was received 5-23-1863 for exchange. Present until captured at Winchester, VA, on 7-20-1864. He was confined at Camp Chase, OH, until paroled and transferred to Boulware's and Cox's Wharf, James River, VA, were he arrived about 3-10-1865 for exchange (NCT IV, 378).

STEELMAN, A[LEXANDER].; CO. H, 21ST REG. (11/28/1833–01/31/1933; Boonville Bapt., Boonville, NC).
A.(Alexander?) Steelman, a Yadkin resident, e. in Wake Co. on 11-1-1863. Present until he deserted on 6-20-1864. He e. then in Co. F, 37th Battalion, Virginia cavalry (NCT VI, 609). Alexander Steelman was the s. of Bennett and Julia Todd Dobbins (1850 Surry). Alexander m. Almeda Dobbins on 10-10-1861. He m. Elvira Angel, dau. of John and Keziah Angel, second on 11-17-1881 (YCMR; *Heritage*, 630).

STEELMAN, GEORGE; CO. H, 63RD REG. (5TH CAVALRY) (1840–12/26/1864).
George Steelman e. in Davie Co. on 7-15-1862. He was present through Oct. 1864. He was admitted to a hospital in Raleigh, NC, with cirrhosis of the liver, and d. 12-26-1864 (NCT III, 436). George was the s. of Joseph Steelman (1850 Surry).

STEELMAN, J. W.; CO. H, 63RD REG. (5TH CAVALARY) (1844–?).
J. W. Steelman e. in Davie Co. at age 18 on 7-15-1862. He was wounded in action at Upperville, VA, on 6-21-1863, but continued to serve through Dec. 1864 (NCT III, 436). J. W. Steelman was the s. of George and Mary Steelman (1850 Surry).

STEELMAN, JACKSON; CO. H, 63RD REG. (5TH CAV.) (06/21/1838–01/21/96; Sandy Springs Bapt., Iredell Co., NC).
Jackson Steelman, a Yadkin resident, e. at age 26 on 7-18-1862. He was captured at Madison Court House, VA, on 9-22-1863, and confined in the Old Capitol Prison, Washington, DC, then at Point Lookout, MD, on 9-16-1863. Paroled and exchanged at Aiken's Landing, VA, on 5-8-1864. Admitted to a Richmond hospital on 5-8-1864 with pleuritis and furloughed for 30 days on 5-12-1864. Present through Aug. 1864. Admitted to a Raleigh, NC, hospital on 12-12-1864 with an abscess of the left eye. He returned to duty on 12-16-1864, and was present at "the election of officers" Feb. 1865 (NCT II, 436). Jackson Steelman m. Martha Steelman on 1-3-1861 (YCMR), the dau. of George and Nancy Caroline Williams. Martha was b. 7-6-1842, d. 3-15-1924. Jackson Steelman was the s. of Joseph and either his second wife, Elizabeth Steelman or the third wife, Ruth Steelman (Steelman, *Descendants of Mathias and Ruth Steelman,* 49–51).

STEELMAN, SANFORD; 75TH REG., 18TH BRIG. (05/14/1838–08/07/95; Sandy Springs Bapt., Iredell Co.).
Sanford L. Steelman m. Ruth Malinda Jane Williams on 8-19-1860 (YCMR). He was the s. of George and Nancy Caroline Williams (1850 Surry). She was b. 4-10-1843, d. 12-8-1892. Both ar buried at Sandy Springs Baptist Church, Iredell Co., NC. Her sister m. Jackson Steelman (Steelman, *Descendants of Mathias and Ruth Steelman,* 29, 36; 1850 Surry).

STINSON, ABRAHAM; CO. I, 28TH REG. (1836–?).
Abraham Stinson e. in Yadkin Co. on 11-1-1862.

Wounded in the head and leg at the Petersburg & Weldon Railroad near Petersburg, VA, on 6-22-1864, he returned to duty before 11-1-1864. Wounded again in the right leg, he was captured near Petersburg on 4-2-1865. His right leg was amputated, and he was reported in a hospital at Ft. Monroe, VA, through 6-21-1865 (NCT VIII, 218). Abraham Stinson, age 14, was listed in the household of his parents, Moses and Elizabeth Stinson (1860 Yadkin).

STINSON, ELIAS; CO. I, 28TH REG. (1842–12/17/1864 [before]).
Elias Stinson e. in Yadkin Co. at age 19 on 8-13-1861. He was present through Feb. 1863, but d. before 12-17-1864. Place and cause of death not reported (NCT VIII, 218). Elias Stinson m. Ann R. Rodwell on 7-25-1861 (YCMR).

STINSON (STIMPSON?), R. A.; CO. E, 70TH REG.
R. A. Stimpson, s. of Thomas B. and Margaret Stimpson, m. N. R. Carr (Kerr), dau. of Gilliam and Susan R. Carr (Kerr) m. on 12-16-1868 (YCMR). Stinson and Stimpson are often misspelled ("Poindexter," 119).

STOKES, JAMES; CO. I, 28TH REG. (1843–?).
James Stokes, a Yadkin Co. resident, e. in New Hanover Co. at age 19 on 1-1-1862. Reported AWOL May–Oct. 1862, and was listed as a deserter on 5-27-1863 (NCT VIII, 218).

STOKES, JAMES; CO. D, 44TH REG. (1843–?).
James Stokes e. at age 19 on 10-17-1862. Deserted 11-12-1862 (NCT X, 432). He may be the same as James Stokes who e. in Co. I, 28th Reg., above.

STOKES, JAMES D., SR.; CO. B, 38TH REG. (1827–06/26/1862).
James D. Stokes, Sr., a Yadkin resident, e. there at age 35 on 10-16-1861. Present until killed at Mechanicsville, VA, on 6-26-1862 (NCT X, 29). He is probably the James Stokes, age 24, who was living with wife, Caroline, age 26, in 1850 (1850 Surry).

STOKES, JAMES, JR.; CO. B, 38TH REG. (1826–?).
James Stokes, Jr., e. in Yadkin Co. at age 36 on 4-8-1862. Present until he deserted on 6-15-1863. Returned to duty 11-7-1863. Present until 8-28-1864 when he was reported AWOL (NCT X, 29). James Stokes, Jr., m. Sarah Simms on 7-15-1853 (or 8-9-1853, YCMR).

STONE, FRANCIS R.; CO. K, 51ST REG. VIRGINIA INF. (03/06/1828–03/30/1918; Union Church, Ararat, NC).
Francis (Frank) Rutherford Stone, the s. of Enoch Stone, Jr., and Elizabeth Gordon Stone, m. Sarah Caroline Poindexter on 3-4-1852 (YCMR). She was the dau. of Denson Ashburn and Sarah Jones Poindexter. Stone and his wife lived in the East Bend area until sometime after the 1860 census was taken, then they moved north of Pilot Mountain. Francis e. in Co. K, 51st Reg., Virginia Infantry, on 3-3-1862. He was present through 12-24-1864, at which time he was on the receipt rolls for clothing. Both he and his wife are buried at Union Church Cemetery, Ararat, NC. They had several children (Charles H. Stone, *The Stones of Surry*, rev. ed., 1955, 129, 383–385; "Poindexter," 45).

STOWE, GEORGE C.; CO. I, 33RD CAPTAIN (1832–?).
George C. Stowe lived in Yadkin Co. before he e. in Forsyth Co. He was appointed captain on 7-1-1861. Present until wounded and his thumb was shot off near Culpeper, VA, in 1862. He returned to duty before 12-13-1862. Reported absent on detached service January through February 1863. He resigned on 7-2-1863 because of disability from wounds. He later served as an enroling officer in the 9th Congressional District and as captain of Co. A, McRae's Battalion of NC Cavalry (NCT XI, 220). George Stowe was the s. of John and Rachel Stowe (1850 Surry).

STRICKLAND, STEPHEN B.; CO. F, 28TH REG. (1842–07/03/1863).
Stephen B. Strickland was b. in Yadkin Co. where he lived prior to enlisting in Alamance Co. at age 20 on 10-1-1862. He was killed at Gettysburg, PA, 7-3-1863 (NCT VIII, 183). He is probably the s. of Perry and Nancy Strickland (1860 Yadkin).

STRICKLAND, WILLIAM S.; CO. I, 28TH REG. (1845–06/22/1864).
William S. Strickland, a Yadkin resident, e. at Liberty Mills, VA, on 12-17-1863. He was killed in the fighting on the Petersburg & Weldon Railroad near Petersburg, VA, on 6-22-1864 (NCT VIII, 218). William S. Strickland was the s. of Perry and Nancy Strickland, and was living near Boonville when the 1860 Yadkin Co. Census was taken (1850 Surry; 1860 Yadkin).

STUDIVANT, THOMAS F.; CO. A, 21ST REG. (1842–04/17/1865).
Thomas F. Studivan(t) resided in Yadkin Co. where he was a farmer before enlisting there on 10-1-1863. Present until wounded in left thigh and captured at Stephenson's Depot, VA, on 7-20-1864. Confined at Cumberland, MD, and at Wheeling, WV, until transferred to Camp Chase, OH, where he arrived 11-4-1864. Died at Camp Chase on 4-17-1865 of "diarrhoea." Medical records dated 1864 give his age as 22 (NCT VI, 550).

SWAIM, DABNER(DABNEY) CALDWELL; 75TH REG., 18TH BRIG. MILITIA (1839–?).
Dabney C. Swaim, b. ca. 1839, the s. of Michael and Elizabeth Swaim, m. Martha Jane Casstevens, b. ca. 1842, dau. of William and Lucinda Holcomb Casstevens (*Thomas Casteven: A Genealogical History*, 35–36; 1850 Surry). He is probably the brother of Ephraim David Swaim, listed below.

SWAIM, DAVID; 75TH REG., 18TH BRIG. MILITIA (1836–?).
This may be the David Swaim, age 14, listed in the household of Michael Swaim and others (1850 Surry).

SWAIM, EPHRAIM DAVID; 75TH REG., 18TH BRIG. MILITIA (1831–?).
Ephraim David Swaim may be the s. of Michael and Elizabeth Swaim, and listed as 19 years old (b. ca. 1831) in the 1850 Surry Census.

SWAIM, J. F.; CO. H, 54TH REG. (1831–?).
J. F. Swaim, a farmer, e. at age 31 on 3-17-1862. Discharged before 7-2-1862, reason not given (NCT XIII, 328).

SWAIM, JOSEPH/JOSEPHUS CEPHUS; CO. G, 54TH REG. (1836–?).
Joseph C. Swaim e. in Wake Co. on 10-22-1863. He was captured at Rappahannock Station, VA, 11-7-1863, and confined at Point Lookout, MD, on 11-11-1863. He was proled at Point Lookout about 3-16-1864. He was received at City Point, VA, on 3-20-1864 for exchange. He was reported AWOL Sept.-Oct. 1864 (NCT XIII, 316). According to descendants, Joseph (or Josephus or Cephus) Swaim served 4 years in the Confederate Army, and spent 5 months in a Yankee prison. He took the Oath of Allegiance on 9-8-1865 (per the late Mrs. Lexa Cummings Groce and Esther N. Clifton). This may be Joseph (Josephus) Swaim, born ca. 1836, s. of Solomon (the minister), and Sarah Ann Waggoner Swaim.

SWAIM, LEWIS; CO. B, 4TH REG. (1832–?).
L. Swain (Swaim) e. in Yadkin Co. on 9-24-1863. He deserted at Kelly's Ford, VA, on 11-7-1863 (NCT IV, 34). Lewis Swaim was living in Yadkin Co. in 1850 with wife Milly, and 5 children (1850 Surry).

SWAIM, LITTLE M.; CO. I, 28TH REG. CORPORAL (1843–?).
Little M. Swaim e. at age 18 in Yadkin Co. on 8-13-1861. He mustered in as private. He was hospitalized at Richmond, VA, on 9-27-1862 with a gunshot wounds of the shoulder and hip, place and date of wounds not reported. He returned to duty on 11-25-1862. Promoted to Corporal on 12-1-1864, he was captured the next year near Petersburg, VA, on 4-2-1865, and confined at Ft. Delaware, DE, until released on 6-19-1865, after taking the Oath of Allegiance (NCT VIII, 218). He was the s. of Michael and Elizabeth Swaim as enumerated in 1850 (1850 Surry), which gave his age as 7 years at that time (b. 1843).

SWAIM, MICHAEL F.; CO. H, 54TH REG. (1845–?).
A Yadkin farmer, Michael F. Swaim e. at age 17 on 4-17-1862. Reported present through April 1863. Captured near Fredericksburg, VA, 5-4-1863, and confined at Old Capitol Prison, Washington, DC. Transferred to Ft. Delaware, DE, on 5-7-1863. Paroled and transferred to City Point, VA, where he was received on 5-23-1863 for exchange. Returned to duty before 9-1-1863. Captured again at Rappahannock Station, VA, on 11-7-1863, and confined at Point Lookout, MD, on 11-11-1863. Paroled about 3-16-1864 and received at City Point on 3-20-1864 for exchange. Returned to duty on an unspecified date, and reported present Sept.-Oct. 1864. He surrendered at Appomattox Court House, VA, 4-9-1865 (NCT XIII, 328). Michael F. Swaim m. Amanda J. Shaver on 4-8-1865 (YCMR).

SWAIM, MILAS G.; CO. I, 28TH REG. (1844–?).
Milas G. Swaim was a Yadkin Co. farmer before enlisting at age 18 on 3-8-1862. Transferred to Co. G, 44th Reg. March–Dec. 1863. Transferred back to this company on 10-1-1864. Present through Feb. 1865 (NCT VIII, 218; X, 463).

SWAIM, SOLOMON D.; CO. H, 54TH REG. (1830–02/21/1865).
Solomon D. Swaim, a Yadkin farmer, e. at age 32 on 4-17-1862. Reported AWOL in June 1862, but returned to duty. Deserted on 12-18-1862. Transferred to Co. I, 28th Reg. on 10-19-1863. Records of Co. I, 28th, state he e. 7-19-1862, and trans. to Co. G, 44th Reg. March–Dec. 1863. Records of Co. G, 44th Reg. indicate he "Gave himself up voluntarily to the Union pickets near Spotsylvania Court House" VA, May 18–21, 1864. Confined at Point Lookout, MD, on 5-30-1864. Transferred to Elmira, NY, 7-25-1864, where he d. on 2-21-1865 of "pneumonia" (NCT VIII, 218; X, 463; XIII, 328). Solomon D. Swaim (this may be another Solomon) m. Lucinda Calloway on 7-21-1852 (YCMR). One Solomon D. Swaim, Jr., age 26, was living with wife, Sarah L., age 26, s. John and dau. Lucinda in 1850 (1850 Surry).

SWAIM, VIRGIL D.; CO. H, 66TH REG. (08/16/1844–06/29/1922; Swan Creek Bapt., Yadkin Co., NC).
Virgil D. Swaim reportedly served, and he may have e. in Lenoir Co. in Co. H, 66th Reg. (Moore, *Roster*, Vol. IV, 123). He may be the Virgil D. Swaim, b. 8-18-1844, d. 7-29-1922, the s. of Rev. Solomon and Sarah Ann Waggoner Swaim. Virgil D. Swaim m. Dinah McBride ca. 1866 (per Dale E. Wagoner; 1850 Surry).

SWAIM, WILLIAM; CO. I, 28TH REG. (1825–?).
William Swaim, b. in Surry Co., resided in Yadkin Co., where he was a farmer before enlisting there at age 37 on 9-1-1861. Discharged on 6-23-1862 because of a heart condition following an attack of pneumonia (NCT VIII, 218).

SWEENEY (SWINEY), JOHN W.; CO. B, 4TH REG. (1845–?).
John Sweeney lived in Yadkin Co. and e. at Camp

Vance on 10-6-1863. He deserted on 11-25-1865, and was reported captured by the enemy at Culpeper, VA, on 12-4-1863. He was imprisoned at Old Capitol Prison, Washington, DC, until released on 5-15-1864, after taking the Oath. Company muster rolls from April 30 to Aug. 31, 1864, stated that he had "join from desertion" and had been under arrest since 5-4-1864. No further information regarding outcome (NCT IV, 34). Sweeney was the s. of Anderson E. (see below) and Ailsey Sweeney (1850 Surry).

SWINEY (SWEENEY), ANDERSON E.; CO. H, 54TH REG. (1810–?).
Anderson E. Swiney, b. in Surry Co., resided in Yadkin Co. where he was a carpenter before enlisting on 5-23-1862 at age 52 as a substitute for Richard N. Tiddy. Hospitalized at Richmond, VA, 11-9-1862 with rheumatism, he was furloughed for 30 days on 11-26-1862. Reported AWOL on or about 2-28-1863. He returned to duty before 5-1-1863, but deserted on 5-18-1863 near Fredericksburg, VA (NCT XIII, 328). In 1850, Anderson E. Swiney was living with wife, Alsey, and children, Sarah L.(age 9) and John W. (age 5) (1850 Surry). A. E. Swiney m. second Nancy Jacks on 2-20-1863 (YCMR).

TACKET, GEORGE; CO. E, 70TH REG.

TACKETT, B. FRANK; CO. F, 28TH REG. (1845–04/19/1863).
B. Frank Tackett was b. in Yadkin Co. where he lived before enlisting there at age 17 on 4-5-1862. He was reported AWOL Nov.–Dec. 1862, but returned to duty. He d. at Camp Gregg, VA, on 4-19-1863 of "pneumonia" (NCT VIII, 183).

TACKETT, JAMES W.; CO. F, 28TH REG. (1841–?).
James W. Tackett lived in Yadkin Co. where he e. at age 21 on 4-26-1862. He was wounded and captured at Gettysburg, PA, July 1–5, 1863. Hospitalized at Davids Island, NY Harbor, he was paroled and transferred to City Point, VA, where he was received on 8-28-1863 for exchange. Returned to duty on an unspecified date. Reported AWOL 7-1-1864. Returned to duty about 8-13-1864. He was captured near Petersburg, VA, on 4-2-1865, and confined at Point Lookout, MD, until released on 6-21-1865, after taking the Oath of Allegiance (NCT VIII, 183).

TACKETT, JOHN W.; CO. F, 28TH REG. (1841–?).
John W. Tackett lived in Yadkin Co. where he e. at age 20 on 6-18-1861. He was captured at Gettysburg, PA, about 7-4-1863, and confined at Ft. Delaware, DE, before being transferred to Point Lookout, MD, about 10-15-1863. He was paroled and transferred to City Point, VA, where he was received on 3-20-1864 for exchange. Reported AWOL on 4-20-1864. Returned to duty 8-28-1864. Captured near Petersburg, VA, on 4-2-1865, and confined at Point Lookout, MD, until released on 6-20-1865, after taking the Oath of Allegiance (NCT VIII, 183).

TACKETT, THOMAS E.; CO. F, 28TH REG. (1844–?).
Thomas E. Tackett lived in Yadkin Co. where he e. at age 18 on 4-29-1862. He was wounded in the left thigh at Bethesda Church, VA, on 5-31-1864. Returned to duty Aug.-Oct. 1864. Captured near Petersburg, VA, on 4-2-1865, and confined at Point Lookout, MD, until released on 6-21-1865, after taking the Oath of Allegiance (NCT VIII, 184). Thomas Tackett m. Mary Ann Inscore on 10-20-1865 (YCMR).

TALLY (TALLEY), DANIEL D.; CO. B, 38TH REG. (01/10/1841–08/31/1894; Sandy Springs Bapt., Iredell Co., NC).
Daniel D. Tally lived in Yadkin Co. where he e. at age 24 on 10-16-1861. Present until wounded at Mechanicsville, VA, on 6-26-1862. Reported absent-wounded or absent-sick through Aug. 1862. Reported AWOL Sept–Dec. 1862. Returned to duty Jan.-Feb. 1863. Deserted on 4-21-1863. Returned to duty on 11-7-1863. Present through Oct. 1864 (NCT X, 29). D. D. Talley, s. of Isaac and Sarah Talley, m. N. A. Dickerson, dau. of James Dickerson, on 2-6-1870 (YCMR).

TANNER, THOMAS E.; CO. A, 1ST BAT. SHARPSHOOTERS (1838–?).
Thomas E. Tanner e. in Lenoir Co. on 7-21-1864. Present through Dec. 1864, and paroled at Appomattox Court House, VA, on 4-9-1865 (NCT III, 75). He was the s. of Eunice Tanner (1850 Surry; 1860 Yadkin).

TATE, ALFRED O.; CO. B, 38TH REG. (1844–01/04/1864).
Alfred O. Tate, a Yadkin resident, e. there at age 19 on 2-15-1863. Present until he d. on 1-4-1864. Place and cause of death not reported (NCT X, 29). Alfred O. Tate was the s. of John and Matilda Tate, and brother to Lewis F. Tate (see below) (1850 Surry).

TATE, LEWIS (LOUIS) F.; CO. I, 28TH REG. (03/18/1836–08/20/1898; Spillman Cem., Yadkin Co., NC).
Lewis Tate e. at Camp Holmes on 10-8-1863. Deserted on an unspecified date. Returned to duty on 9-22-1864. Reported absent-wounded during Sept. 1864–Feb. 1865, place and date of wound not reported (NCT VIII, 218). Lewis F. Tate, the s. of John and Matilda Tate, m. Rachel C. Hobson on 7-31-1856 (YCMR). Both are buried in the Spillman Family Cemetery, Yadkin Co., NC (1850 Surry).

TAYLOR, FRANCIS W.; CO. F, 28TH REG. (1840–07/25/1864).
Francis W. Taylor was b. in Yadkin Co. where he lived before enlisting there at age 21 on 6-18-1861. He d. in a Richmond, VA, hospital about 7-25-1864 of disease (NCT VIII, 184).

TAYLOR, WILLIAM COLUMBUS; CO. F, 28TH REG. (1846–?).

William Columbus Taylor lived in Yadkin Co. where he e. at age 16 on 4-21-1862 as a substitute. Hospitalized at Danville, VA, about 8-13-1862 with pneumonia. He deserted from the hospital on 10-6-1862. NC pension records indicate he was wounded at Richmond, VA, in June 1862 (NCT VIII, 184). W. C. Taylor m. Martha Norman on 12-05-1865 (YCMR).

TESH, MOSES; 75TH REG., 18TH BRIG. MILITIA (11/07/1818–06/04/1872).
Moses Tesh was b. in Rowan Co. and d. in Yadkin Co. in 1872. He m. Mary "Mollie" Mock (9-12-1819/6-4-1877), dau. of George Mock and granddaughter of Philip Mock. Moses was a blacksmith and lived in 1850 in the Waughtown area of Forsyth Co. By 1860 he was living in the Panther Creek area of Yadkin Co., and in the Forbush Community of Yadkin Co. by 1870. Children were: William Addison (10-12-1843/5-4-1864); Chrissie Jane (11-4-1846/4-27-1823); John Henry (10-21-1849/5-30-1922); Samuel Milton (1-10-1853/11-13-1919); and Mary Frances Tesh (5-17-1857/11-13-1919) (per Peggy J. Tesh, 2500 Bitting Rd., Winston-Salem, NC 27104; YCHGSJ XIII [Sept. 1994]: 10).

TESH (TEASH), WILLIAM A.; CO. I, 28TH REG. CORPORAL (10/12/1843–05/04/1864).
William A. Tesh, resided in Yadkin Co. where he e. at age 18 on 3-18-1862. Mustered in as private and was promoted to corporal Nov. 1862–Feb. 1863. Died "at home" or at Lynchburg, VA, on 5-4-1864, cause of death not reported (NCT VIII, 218). William Addison Tesh was the s. of Moses and Mary Mock Tesh (per Peggy J. Tesh).

THORNTON, JOHN; CO. B, 38TH REG. (1824–?).
John Thornton e. in Yadkin Co. at age 39 on 9-22-1863. Deserted on 4-11-1864. Returned to duty on 6-1-1864. Wounded at Riddell's Shop, VA, on 6-13-1864. Reported absent-wounded through Oct. 1864 (NCT X, 29). In 1850, John Thornton, age 25, was living in the household of his brother, Abraham Thornton, a wagoner. A John "Thorington," age 26, was listed in the household of Jesse and Elizabeth Thorington (1850 Surry). This may be the same person.

TODD, LEANDER A.; CO. I, 28TH REG. 3RD LIEUTENANT (1838–?).
Leander A. Todd e. in Yadkin Co. at age 24 on 3-8-1862. Mustered in as private and was elected 3rd lieutenant on 10-20-1863. Surrendered at Appomattox Court House, VA, on 4-9-1865. According to a descendant, Thelma D. Hutchens, Yadkinville, NC, Leander walked home after the war ended.

TOMLIN, WILLIAM A.; CO. B, 38TH REG. (1830–03/23/1863).
William A. Tomlin e. in Yadkin Co. on 4-19-1862. Deserted on 7-4-1862. Apprehended on an unspecified date. Court-martialed and "found guilty of desertion and inducing others to do so...." Sentenced to be shot. Executed on 2-23-1863. He "fell a lifeless corpse, pierced by ten minnie balls, two of which went through his head." He was 33 years old at time of death (NCT X, 29). W. A. Tomlin m. Delany York on 12-28-1861 (bond date, YCMR).

TRANSOU, EDWIN L.; CO. B, 21ST REG. MUSICIAN (05/16/1835–11/04/1919; Boonville Bapt. Ch.).
Edwin L. Transou (incorrectly spelled "Transon" in Manarin and Jordan, *North Carolina Troops*), e. in Yadkin Co. on 5-12-1861. He mustered in as a musician (drummer), and was present until transferred to Co. A, 1st Battalion NC Sharpshooters, on 4-26-1862. After transferring, Transou was listed on rolls through Dec. 1864 (NCT III, 75; VI, 554). Edwin Lafayette Transou was b. in Wilkes Co. in 1835 and d. in Yadkin Co. He was the s. of James W. Transou, who was b. in Bethania, Forsyth Co., NC. After the war, Edwin m. in 1867 Nancy Gertrude Flynt of Stokes Co. The couple lived in Boonville where he was a tanner. Later they moved to Iowa for a couple of years before moving back to Boonville. Transou also had a brickyard. They were the parents of Mary Elizabeth (who m. John M. Mock), John Byron, Clarence Rufus (who m. Mollie Garwood), and Fannie Leola (who m. Thomas L. Hayes, the Boonville merchant) (*Heritage*, 640).

TRUELOVE, JOHN GEORGE; CO. F, 28TH REG. (?–10/11/1864).
John George Truelove was wounded in the neck at Gettysburg July 1–3, 1863, and wounded in the abdomen at Petersburg, VA, on 6-22-1864. He was hospitalized at Richmond. Furloughed on 8-11-1864, then returned to duty. Wounded again at Jones' Farm, VA, on 9-30-1864. He d. of those wounds, place and date of death not reported. John George was the s. of Austin and Martha Poindexter Truelove. He m. Florina A. Butner, b. ca. 1841. She is buried at East Bend Bapt. Church, East Bend, NC ("Poindexter," 84).

TUCKER, BENJAMIN F.; CO. B, 42ND REG. (1842–?).
Benjamin F. Tucker, a Yadkin Co. resident, e. in Rowan Co. at age 20 on 3-12-1862. Deserted July-Aug. 1862 (NCT X, 239). Benjamin F. Tucker m. Mildred S. Messick on 9-18-1860 (YCMR). In 1850, Benjamin Tucker, age 9, was living in the house of his parents, Thomas and Nelley Tucker (1850 Surry).

TUCKER, ROBERT B.; CO. G, 13TH REG. (1838–?).
Robert B. Tucker, a Yadkin Co. farmer before enlisting in Wake Co. at age 24, on 9-27-1862, was present until discharged at Danville, VA, on 7-23-1863, because of "ascites"(NCT V, 354). Robert was the s. of John and Clary Tucker (1850 Surry).

TULBERT, JOSHUA; CO. A, 9TH BAT. HOME GUARD.

UNDERWOOD, HENRY; CO. B, 38TH REG. MUSICIAN (1817–?).
Henry Underwood e. in Yadkin Co. at age 44 on 10-16-1861. Mustered in as musician (fifer). Reported AWOL about 12-2-1861. Reduced to ranks before 4-1-1862. Returned to duty April–June 1862. Discharged on 10-3-1862 because of disability. He may have later served as a private in Co. H, 5th Reg., Senior Reserves, Co. A, 9th Battalion (Home Guard) (NCT X, 29). The Underwood family cemetery is near Brannon Church, Yadkin Co., NC, where there are tombstones for many of his children.

VANHOY, CALVIN; CO. F, 29TH REG.
Calvin Vanhoy e. at age 25 on 7-2-1862. He was hospitalized at Meridian, MS, on 1-29-1865, with an unspecified wound. He was paroled at Charlotte, NC, on 5-11-1865 (NCT VIII, 285). Calvin Vanhoy applied for a pension on 7-1-1906 in Yadkin Co. He had lived in Yadkin in 1850 but was living in Stanly Co. in 1860 when he e. He returned to Yadkin Co. in 1910. He was the s. of James and Juda Vanhoy (per Martin).

VANHOY, JOHN A.; CO. ?, 3RD REG.?
John A. Vanhoy, a Yadkin resident, reportedly served in the 3rd Regiment, but name of company was not given. He took the Oath of Allegiance in Knoxville, TN, on 6-11-1864 and was sent to Jefferson, IN (NCT III, 600). John A. Vanhoy was the s. of Clayton and Elizabeth Kirk Vanhoy. He m. on 8-8-1858 Theresa D. Nicks. NC pension records of his widow, dated 7-26-1907 state the he e. about 6-13-1863 and served in Co. D, 28th N.C. Reg. until the surrender (per Cheryl Martin, a great-great-great-niece).

VANHOY, JOSEPH L.; CO. B, 1ST BAT. SHARPSHOOTERS (?–d. after 1926).
In Joseph L. Vanhoy's pension application, dated 7-19-1916, he stated he e. about 10-17-1863 in Co. B, 1st Battalion, NC State Troops. He gave his address as Rt. 1, Cycle, NC. Joseph L. Vanhoy m. Sarah C. Durham, dau. of William and Nancy Durham on 11-21-1867 (per Martin).

VEACH, JAMES L.; CO. B, 38TH REG. MUSICIAN (1843–?).
James L. Veach, a Yadkin resident, e. there at age 18 on 10-16-1861. Mustered in as private. Promoted to musician (drummer) on 4-10-1864. Present through Oct. 1864. Surrendered at Appomattox Court House, VA, on 4-9-1865 (NCT X, 29). J. L. Veach, s. of H. H. and Jennette Veach, m. Amanda Caudle, dau. of Moses and Susanna Caudle, on 10-3-1869 (YCMR).

VESTAL, DOBBS (Daniel?) A.; CO. B, 21ST REG. CORPORAL (?–1913; Oaklawn Cem., Plant City, FL).
Dobbs A. Vestal e. in Yadkin Co. on 5-12-1861 and was present until transferred to Co. A, 1st Battalion NC Sharpshooters, on 4-26-1862. Promoted to corporal May–Aug. 1863. Present on rolls through Dec. 1864 (NCT III, 75; VI, 554). Although listed as "Dobbs A. Vestal," in NCT, Vol. VI, 554, this is probably Daniel A. Vestal, who was living in Bowling Green, FL, when he first applied for a pension in 1907 in DeSoto Co., FL, stating that he had been a resident there since Feb. 13, 1897, which he later changed to Jan. 13, 1895. A new Florida law stated that no one who came to Florida after 1895 could receive a pension. However, a letter from the comptroller dated 7-23-1912 notified Mr. Dan Vestal that his pension had been increased to $150 per annum from that date, so he must have received a pension eventually. Dan Vestal m. Permelia (Pamelia) Sprinkle on 3-27-1865, according to her pension claim dated 5-13-1913. She was b. 9-26-1848, d. 4-6-1928, and was buried in Oaklawn Cemetery, Plant City, Hillsborough Co., FL, beside her husband. In his pension application he stated that he had served continuously since enlisting at Yadkinville in May or June 1861 in Co. A, 21st Regiment, and that companies A and B were detached and formed in to the First Battalion of NC Sharpshooters; that he "went through the Virginia Campaigns, rendering faithful service; was shot through the right thigh at Cedar Run, VA," through the stomach at Culpeper Court House, VA, the left hip at Newbern, NC, and "from which I yet suffer always and am crippled...." He added that he was captured just a few days before the surrender on the "banks of the James River near Petersburg, Virginia," and sent to Hart's Island, NY. He was held there until released on the 17th or 18th of June, 1865, and was discharged from said prison and went to New York City where he booked passage on the *Starlight* and sailed for NC, and reached his "ante-bellum home" on July 4th, 1865 (pension papers from the state of Florida, from Eunice Vestal).

VESTAL, GEORGE S.; CO. H, 54TH REG. (1843–?).
George S. Vestal, a Yadkin Co. farmer, e. in Yadkin Co. at age 19 on 4-17-1862. Reported AWOL in June 1862. Returned to duty before 12-13-1862, when he was wounded in the right leg (fracture) at Fredericksburg, VA. Hospitalized at Richmond, VA. Furloughed for 60 days on 6-2-1863. Reported absent-wounded through Dec. 1863. Discharged before 11-1-1864 because of disability from wounds (NCT XIII, 328). George Vestal, b. ca. 1845, was the s. of James and Rebecca Vestal (1850 Surry).

VESTAL, ISAAC; CO. A, 9TH BAT. HOME GUARD.

VESTAL, J. M.; CO. I, 28TH REG. (1837–?).
J. M. Vestal, a Yadkin resident, e. there at age 24 on 8-13-1861. Discharged because of disability, date not given (NCT VIII, 218).

VESTAL, JAMES H.; CO. D, 44TH REG. (1826–?).
James H. Vestal e. in Wake Co., age 36, on 10-17-1862. Present through Feb. 1863. Was apparently killed in action prior to 1-1-1864. Place and date of death not reported (NCT X, 432).

VESTAL, JEREMIAH W.; CO. A, 1ST BAT. SHARPSHOOTERS (01/10/1831–05/19/1881; Deep Creek Friends).
J. W. Vestal e. "at camp in Virginia" on 11-1-1863. Present through Dec. 1864. Took Oath of Allegiance at Hart's Island, NY Harbor, on 6-17-1865. Date and place of capture not reported (NCT III, 75).

VESTAL, JOHN B.; CO. I, 28TH REG. CORPORAL (1834–?).
John B. Vestal e. in Co. I, 28th Reg. in New Hanover Co. at age 27 on 10-8-1861. Transferred to Company B, 38th Reg. before 4-1-1862. He was promoted to Corporal Jan.-Feb. 1863. Wounded in the foot at Chancellorsville, VA, on 5-3-1863. Reported absent-wounded or absent-sick through Aug. 1863. Returned to duty Sept.-Oct. 1863. Reduced to ranks on 10-4-1863. Present through Oct. 1864 (NCT VIII, 218; X, 30).

VESTAL, M. I.; CO. A, 9TH BAT. HOME GUARD.

VESTAL, MARTIN V. B.; CO. I, 28TH REG. (1838–?).
Martin V(an) B(uren) Vestal lived in Yadkin where he e. at age 24 on 3-8-1862. Captured at Fredericksburg, VA, on 12-13-1862, he was exchanged about 12-17-1862. Returned to duty before 3-1-1863. He was captured at Spotsylvania Court House on 5-12-1864; however, Federal Provost Marshall records do not substantiate this (NCT VIII, 218).

VESTAL, MILES J.; CO. I, 28TH REG. SERGEANT (1838–?).
Miles J. Vestal, a farmer before enlisting in New Hanover Co. on 10-8-1862. Mustered in as sergeant, but discharged on 2-15-1862 because of a "scrotal hernia of both sides" at age 24 (NCT VIII, 218).

VESTAL, R. S.; CO. A, 38TH REG. (1844–?).
R. S. Vestal e. at Camp Vance on 7-6-1864. He deserted to the enemy about 9-22-1864, and was confined at Washingrton, DC, on 9-28-1864. He was released after taking the Oath of Allegiance (NCT X, 19). Romulus S. Vestal was the s. of Daniel and Ann Vestal (1850 Surry).

VESTAL, WILLIAM; CO. A, 1ST BAT. SHARPSHOOTERS.
William Vestal e. on 1-20-1864. Present through Dec. 1864 (NCT III, 75–76).

VESTAL, WILLIAM P. D.; CO. B, 21ST REG. (1840–?).
William P. D. Vestal e. in Yadkin Co. on 5-12-1861, and was present until transferred to Co. A, 1st Battalion NC Sharpshooters, on 4-26-1862. Present until he deserted at Lynchburg, VA, on 10-15-1864. Dropped from rolls on 10-15-1864 for desertion (NCT III, 76; VI, 554). William P. D. Vestal, at age 10, was living in the household of his parents, Thomas and Grace Vestal, along with other brothers and sisters (1850 Surry).

WAGONER, CALVIN; CO. I, 28TH REG. (1840–?).
Calvin Wagoner was a Yadkin Co. farmer before enlisting at age 21 on 8-13-1861. Deserted on 7-1-1863. Returned to duty on an unspecified date. Wounded in the right elbow near Ream's Station, VA, about 8-25-1864. Reported absent-wounded until 12-1-1864, when he was reported AWOL (NCT VIII, 218). Calvin Wagoner, the s. of Daniel and Nancy Hoppers Wagoner, m. Jane Moxley on 8-4-1859 (YCMR).

WAGONER, HENRY; CO. A, 1ST BAT. SHARPSHOOTERS.
Henry Wagoner e. "at camp in Virginia" on 1-20-1864. Present on company muster rolls through Dec. 1864 (NCT III, 76).

WAGONER, HENRY S.; CO. H, 44TH REG. (1840–12/22/1864).
H. S. Wagoner e. at Camp French, age 21, in Oct. 1862. Deserted 11-2-1862, returned to duty before 2-28-1863. Present Nov.–Dec. 1863, and deserted 4-25-1864 (NCT X, 474). He is probably the same as Henry Wagoner, a Yadkin Co. farmer, who e. in Co. H, 54th Regiment, on 6-7-1864, and was captured near Winchester, VA, about 7-21-1864. Confined at Atheneum Prison, Wheeling, WV, before being transferred to Camp Chase, OH, 10-6-1864. Died at Camp Chase on 12-22-1864 of "variola." Records of Federal Provost Marshall dated July 1864 give his age as 24 (NCT XIII, 328). Henry S. Wagoner may be the s. of David and Catherine Sperlin Wagoner, b. ca. 1841, d. after 1860 (1850 Surry; 1860 Yadkin).

WAGONER, JACOB M.; CO. I, 28TH REG. (1842–?).
Jacob M. Wagoner, a Yadkin Co. resident, e. there at age 19 on 8-13-1861. Captured by the enemy on an unspecified date and confined at Ft. Monroe, VA. Paroled and transferred to Aiken's Landing, James River, VA, where he was received on 9-7-1862 for exchange. Exchanged there on 9-21-1862. Reported AWOL through Feb. 1863, but returned to duty on an unspecified date. Company records indicate he was captured by the enemy on 7-21-1864; however Federal Provost Marshal records do not substantiate that. NC pension records indicate he was wounded in the hip at Wilderness, VA, on 10-16-1863. He survived the war (NCT VIII, 219). He may be Jacob Wagoner, b. ca. 1841, who m. Sarah Bullard, and was living in the household of parents, Jacob and Mary Brinegar Wagoner in 1850 (1850 Surry).

WAGONER, JAMES; CO. G, 44TH REG. (1839–?).
James Wagoner, Yadkin resident, e. at age 23 in October 1862. He deserted prior to 3-1-1863 (NCT X, 465).

WAGONER, JAMES H.; CO. G, 44TH REG.
(1841–?).
James H. Wagoner, Yadkin resident, e. at Camp Holmes at age 21 on 10-14-1862. He was present until Feb. 1863 when he deserted. Court-martialed on 7-20-1863 (NCT X, 465). He may be James H. Wagoner, b. 6-27-1840, s. of John and Mary Weatherman Wagoner, and may also be the same as "James Wagoner" above.

WAGONER, JOHN W.; CO. I, 28TH REG.
(1842–?).
John W. Wagoner, a Yadkin resident, e. in Orange Co. at age 21 on 9-20-1863. He surrendered at Appomattox, VA, on 4-9-1865 (NCT VIII, 219).

WAGONER, MOSES; CO. H, 44TH REG.
(1834/35/36–09/28/1863).
Moses Wagoner resided in Yadkin Co., e. at Camp French on 10-14-1862. He died in Richmond, VA, hospital on 9-28-1863 of "febris typhoides" (NCT X, 474). He may be the s. of Jacob and Mary Brinegar Wagoner, b. 1834. There is also another Moses Wagoner, b. 1836, the s. of John and Mary Wagoner, so it is impossible to tell which one this is (1850 Surry).

WAGONER, WILLIAM; CO. B, 21ST REG.
(12/14/1842–09/13/1884; Hoppers Fam. Cem., Alleghany Co., NC.).
William Wagoner e. in Yadkin Co. on 5-12-1861 and was present until transferred to Co. A, 1st Battalion NC Sharpshooters, on 4-26-1862. Present on muster rolls through Dec. 1864 (NCT III, 76; VI, 554).

WAGONER, WILLIAM MOSES; CO. H, 44TH REG.
William Moses Wagoner, a Yadkin resident, e. at Camp French on 10-14-1862. Deserted about 11-2-1862 (NCT X, 474).

WALL, JOHN WILLIAM; CO. D, 21ST REG.
(1824–09/20/1863).
John William Wall, e. at age 39 on 9-20-1863. He d. at Orange Court House, VA. Cause of death not reported (NCT VI, 573; see also letters from John W. Wall in Appendix A). John William Wall m. Nancy Agnus ("Aggie")___. They lived behind what is now the home of Thomas Y. Wooten in East Bend. William and Aggie were the parents of three boys: John Belvey, J. Hilery, and William Yancey (*Heritage*, 647). One of the boys, William, m. Sarah P. Davis, dau. of M. D. and Nancy Davis, on 12-23-1883. Another, John B., m. Ellen Smitherman, dau. of A. P. and Sarah Smitherman, on 12-23-1879. William Wall, age 28, b. in VA, was living with Jane Wall, probably his mother, in 1850 in the Little Yadkin Township of what is now Yadkin Co. This may be the same person as John William Wall (YCMR; 1850 Surry).

WARDEN, CARY, SR.; CO. B, 38TH REG.
(1808–?).
Cary Warden, Sr., lived in Yadkin Co. where he e. at age 55 on 10-16-1861. Present through Feb. 1863. Reported absent-sick much of that period. He was discharged on 3-10-1863 because of disability (NCT X, 30). In 1850, Cary Warden was a "collier," and was head of a household consisting of wife, Jane, and a number of children, including son Cary (below) (1850 Surry).

WARDEN, CARY W., JR.; CO. I, 28TH REG.
(1841–11/07/1864).
Cary W. Warden, Jr. e. in Yadkin Co. at age 21 on 8-13-1861. Present until he transferred to Co. B, 38th Reg., before 1-31-1862. Present until he deserted on 7-21-1863. Returned to duty about 11-7-1863. Died near Orange Court House, VA, on 2-27-1864, cause of death not reported (NCT VIII, 219; X, 30). In 1850, Cary, age 9, was living with his parents, Cary and Jane Warden (1850 Surry).

WARDEN, NATHAN C.; CO. A, 38TH REG.
(1847–?).
Nathan C. Warden enlisted at Camp Vance near Morganton, NC, on 7-25-1864. He deserted to the enemy about 10-11-1864. He was confined at Washington, DC, but released after taking the Oath of Allegiance (NCT X, 19).

WEATHERMAN, BARTHOLOMEW W.; CO. I, 28TH REG. (1841–12/12/1864; Woodlawn National Cem., Elmira, NY).
Bartholomew W. Weatherman, a Yadkin resident, was e. there at age 20 on 8-13-1861 by W. H. A. Speer (later Lieutenant Colonel of the 28th Regiment). On 9-8-1862, he entered the Chimborazo Hospital, Richmond, VA, with typhoid fever. He recovered and returned to duty on 11-18-1862.He was hospitalized again on 11-29-1863 at Winder Hospital, Richmond, VA. He returned to duty and was captured near Gravel Hill, VA, near Petersburg, on 7-29-1864, and confined at Pt. Lookout, MD, before being transferred to Elmira, NY, on 8-8-1864. He d. at Elmira, NY, on 12-12-1864 of pneumonia (NCT VIII, 219). Bartholomew W. Weatherman, b. ca. 1841, was the s. of James and Elizabeth Arnold Weatherman. He was e. at Yadkinville on 8-13-1861 by W. H. Asbury Speer (per McCracken; 1850 Surry).

WEATHERMAN, GEORGE P.; 75TH REG., 18TH BRIG. MILITIA (1835–12/30/1863).
This may also be the same George Weatherman who e. in Iredell Co. on 9-17-1862 in Co. B, 1st Battalion Sharpshooters, and d. 12-3-1863 of "variola" (NCT III, 83). George P. Weatherman, age 15, is listed in the Lydia Weatherman household, along with brothers Thomas A., Samuel, John N., and sisters Nancy J., and Rebecca. George P. Weatherman m. Sarah Holcomb on 6-23-1861 (YCMR).

WEATHERMAN, ISAAC; CO. F, 37TH REG. VA CAVALRY (1843–?).
Isaac Weatherman was first in the Home Guard. Then he e. on 8-1-1864 in Yadkin Co. by Lt.

Eldridge, in Co. F, 37th Regiment, Virginia Cavalry. He was the s. of James and Elizabeth Arnold Weatherman, and the brother of Bartholomew, James Wesley, and William R. Weatherman. (per McCracken; 1850 Surry).

WEATHERMAN, JAMES W.; CO. F, 37TH REG. VA CAVALRY (1845–?).
James W. Weatherman e. in Co. F, and was listed as absent on horse detail in December 1864. James Wesley Weatherman, the s. of James and Elizabeth Arnold Weatherman, was b. Dec. 1842, and d. 7-18-1915. His brothers were Samuel, Jacob H., Bartholomew, Isaac and William R. Weatherman. Sisters were Milly and Catherine. James Wesley m. Nancy Loretta Nichols (b. about 1843, d. about 1919), and they were the parents of Ira, Messer D., Marcus Woodriff, Lizzie, Ottis Hopper, and Thomas Bascum Weatherman. He probably left Yadkin Co. after 10-25-1873, at which time he sold land to John W. Casstevens, and moved to Jonesville, VA (per Weatherman; McCracken; 1850 Surry).

WEATHERMAN, ROBERT W.; CO. I, 28TH REG. 1ST SERGEANT (1841–07/19/1863).
Robert W. Weatherman was e. at Yadkinville by W. H. A. Speer, on 8-13-1861. He was 21 years old. Mustered in as private, promoted to sergeant Nov.-Dec. 1861. Promoted to 1st sergeant Jan.–Oct. 1862. Captured at Hanover Court House, VA, on 5-27-1862. Confined at Ft. Monroe, VA, then Ft. Columbus, NY Harbor. Paroled and transferred to Aiken's Landing, James River, VA, where he was received on 7-12-1862 for exchange. Declared exchanged at Aiken's Landing on 8-5-1862. Returned to duty before 11-1-1862. Died in the hospital at Camp Winder, Richmond, VA, 7-19-1863 of chronic diarrhea (NCT VIII, 219). R. W. Weatherman, the s. of Milly Weatherman, m. Sarah J. Brindle on 7-25-1861 (YCMR; 1850 Surry). In 1850, Robert W. Weatherman, age 9, was attending school.

WEATHERMAN, WILLIAM R.; CO. B, 1ST BAT. SHARPSHOOTERS (11/20/1832–7/7/1914; Center Meth. Ch.).
William R. Weatherman e. in Iredell Co. on 9-11-1862. He was wounded in the left hip near Fredericksburg, VA, on 5-4-1863. Present through December 1864 (NCT III, 83). William R. Weatherman was the s. of James and Elizabeth Arnold Weatherman, and brother to Samuel, Jacob H., Bartholomew, Isaac and James Wesley. William R. Weatherman m. Margaret M. Pendry on 12-01-1857 (YCMR).

WEAVER, JAMES M.; CO. I, 28TH REG. (1838–?).
James M. Weaver, a Yadkin resident, e. there at age 23 on 8-13-1861. Captured at Hanover Court House, VA, about 5-27-1862, and confined at Ft. Monroe, VA. He was paroled and transferred to Aiken's Landing, James River, VA, where he was received on 7-12-1862 for exchange. Exchanged there on 8-5-1862. Returned to duty before 11-1-1862. Present or accounted for through Feb. 1863. NC pension records indicate he was wounded at Fredericksburg, VA, and at Wilmington, NC, and that he survived the war (NCT VIII, 219). James M. Weaver m. Martha Burton on 8-5-1863 (bond date, YCMR).

WEBB, THOMAS POINDEXTER; CO. F, 28TH REG. (05/10/1842–09/14/1914; Union Hill Meth. Ch.).
Thomas P. Webb lived in Yadkin Co. where he e. at age 19 on 6-18-1861. Present or accounted for until 2-10-1865, when he was reported AWOL (NCT VIII, 184). Thomas P. Webb, the s. of Andrew and Hannah B. Poindexter Webb, m. Sarah Ann Kirk on 4-17-1864 (YCMR). She was b. 8-18-1838, d. 10-20-1917, the dau. of John and Nancy Kirk. Both are buried at Union Hill Methodist Church, near East Bend, NC ("Poindexter," 90–91; 1850 Surry).

WEBSTER, JOHN; CO. D, 14TH REG. (1836 ENGLAND–?).
John Webster lived in Yadkin Co. He e. at age 28 at Camp Holmes on 8-9-1863. He was present until hospitalized at Richmond, VA, on 6-10-1864, with a gunshot wound. Date, place, and circumstances of wound not reported. He rejoined his company before 9-1-1864, and was paroled at Appomattox Court House, VA, on 4-9-1865 (NCT V, 434). John was the s. of Mary Webster (b. in Ireland). His brother, Ralph G. Webster, served in Co. A, 21st Regiment (see below) (1850 Surry).

WEBSTER, RALPH; CO. A, 21ST REG. (1834 ENGLAND–?).
Ralph Webster e. in Yadkin Co. on 10-1-1863. He was present until he deserted on 5-6-1864 (NCT VI, 551). Ralph G. Webster is listed in the 1850 Surry Census living with his mother, Mary, who was b. in Ireland, and his brother John (above) (1850 Surry).

WELLS, A. M.; CO. E, 70TH REG.

WELLS, E[LISHA]. A.; CO. D, 63RD REG (5TH CAVALRY) (1835–?).
E. A. Wells e. in Guilford Co. on 7-18-1862. He was present through December 1864. E. A. Wells, age 15, was living in the household of his mother, Elizabeth along with other brothers and sisters in 1850, including Matilda, Mahala, Merril, Elbert, Lawson J., Leander M., and Miles M. (see below) (NCT II, 404; 1850 Surry).

WELLS, ELBERT; CO. D, 44TH REG. (1831–?).
Elbert Wells e. in Wake Co. at age 35 on 12-1-1862. Present until discharged on 6-11-1863, reason not stated (NCT X, 433). Elbert Wells m. Avis Messick on 6-12-1860 (YCMR). Elbert Wells, at age 19, was living in his mother's household (Elizabeth Wells), along with a number of sisters and brothers (1850 Surry).

WELLS, L[EANDER]. M.; CO. C, 44TH REG. (1840–?).

L. M. Wells e. at age 38 on 10-20-1862, and deserted on 11-14-1862 (NCT X, 426). Leander M. Wells, age 10, was living in the household of his mother, Elizabeth, along with brother, Elbert, Elisha A., Lawson J., Merrill, and Miles M. Wells, and two sisters (1850 Surry).

WELLS, LAWSON J.; CO. B, 38TH REG. (1838–05/12/1863).
Lawson J. Wells was present until wounded at Mechanicsville, VA, on 6-26-1862. He returned to duty Sept.-Oct. 1862. Present or accounted for until wounded again at Chancellorsville, VA, on May 1–4, 1863. He d. of wounds on 5-12-1863, place of death not reported (NCT X, 30). In 1850, Lawson J. Wells, age 12, was living in his mother's household (Elizabeth Wells), along with brothers Leander M., and Elbert (1850 Surry).

WELLS, MERRILL; CO. H, 21ST REG. (1829–?).
Wells e. in Wake Co. on 11-1-1863. Present until he deserted to the enemy on 5-5-1864. He took the Oath of Allegiance in Knoxville, TN, on 7-25-1864 (NCT VI, 610). In 1850, Merrill Wells was still living in his mother's household, along with younger brothers, Lawson, Leander M., and Elbert (1850 Surry). Merrill Wells m. Marinda Salmons on 2-26-1852 (YCMR).

WELLS, MILAS M.; CO. B, 38TH REG. (1843–09/03/1862).
Milas M. Wells e. in Yadkin Co. at age 19 on 10-16-1861. Present until he d. in a Richmond, VA, hospital on 9-3-1862 of "chronic diarrhoea" (NCT X, 30). In 1850, Miles M. Wells was living in his mother's household (Elizabeth Wells), along with brothers, Merrill, Elbert, Elisha A., Lawson J., and Leander M. (1850 Surry).

WELLS, WILLIAM M.; CO. D, 63RD REG (5TH CAVALRY) (1844–?).
William M. Wells e. in Guilford Co. on 7-18-1862. He was present through August 1864. William M. Wells, age 6, was living with his parents, James and Sarah Wells, brother Miles L., and sister Elizabeth L. in 1850 (NCT II, 405; 1850 Surry).

WEST, ALEXANDER; CO. A, 9TH BAT. HOME GUARD (1827–?).
Alexander West, age 23, a farmer, was living in the household with James West, age 35, Isaiah West, age 87 (who was b. in MD), and Mary West, age 53. Isaiah may be the grandfather, and James a brother. Mary is probably his mother (1850 Surry).

WEST, JAMES PEARSON; MILITIA (10/01/1821–02/12/1863; Flat Rock Bapt. Ch.).
James West was killed at the shootout at the Bond School House on Feb. 12, 1863. He was a justice of the peace and undoubtedly the person in charge of the expedition to arrest some men hiding out to avoid conscription. West is referred to as "Capt." West in some accounts. Although no official record of his being a member of the militia has been found, his widow, Anna, applied for and received a pension for his service as a member of the Home Guard. West m. Anna Penix on 4-18-1852 (YCMR). They had five children: Lee Franklin, James Andrew, William C., Amanda Rachel, and Sophronia West (per Laura Ann Hoots Winslow, 4115 Lee's Corner Rd., Chantilly, VA 22021). In 1850, James West was head of a household that contained Isaiah West, age 87 (b. in MD); Mary West, age 53 (probably his mother); Alexander West, age 23, probably a brother; and several younger sisters and a younger brother (1850 Surry).

WHEELING, GEORGE W.; CO. B, 38TH REG. CORPORAL (1837–06/26/1862).
George W. Wheeling resided in Yadkin Co. where he e. at age 24 on 10-16-1861. Mustered in as private and promoted to Corporal Feb.-Mar. 1862. Present until killed at Mechanicsville, VA, on 6-26-1862 (NCT X, 30).

WHITAKER, HENRY M.; CO. B, 21ST REG. (?–11/23/1862).
Henry M. Whitaker e. on 5-12-1861 in Yadkin Co. and was present until transferred to Co. A, 1st Battalion NC Sharpshooters, on 4-26-1862. Wounded at Hazel River on 8-22-1862 and d. in a hospital at Staunton, VA, on 9-23-1862 of wounds (NCT III, 76; VI, 554).

WHITAKER, JOHN; CO. H, 21ST REG.
John Whitaker resided in Yadkin but e. in Wake Co. on 11-1-1863. Present until captured at Sayler's Creek, VA, 4-6-1865. Confined at Newport News, VA, until released on 6-27-1865, after taking the Oath of Allegiance (NCT VI, 610).

WHITAKER, LORENZO DOW; CO. B, 21ST REG. 4th SERG. (08/07/1842–02/19/1933; Whitaker Cem.).
Lorenzo Dow Whitaker e. in Yadkin Co. on 5-12-1861, at age 19. (He e. along with his cousins, William Asbury Whitaker and Henry Whitaker, all grandsons of Riley Whitaker). At the time of his enlistment, Lorenzo was sick, and the enlistment officer, J. K. Connally noted that Lorenzo was "present sick." Present until he transferred to Co. A, 1st Battalion Sharpshooters, on 4-26-1862. He was wounded at Second Manassas, VA, on 8-28-1862, but was present on company rolls through Dec. 1864 (NCT III, 76; VI, 554). Lorenzo lost an eye, per pension lists. After being wounded, Whitaker was sent to General Hospital #9 in Richmond. Confederate documents state that he was wounded on 8-28-1862. On 10-13-1862, he was released from the hospital and given a 60-day furlough to High Point, NC. He was able to visit the home of his parents and other relatives in Yadkin Co. but had to return to duty shortly before Christmas 1862. He returned to his regiment and continued through 1863, with a brief furlough in the spring of 1864 (YCHGSJ XII, Sept.

1993, 12–14). He was the s. of Robert C. and Catharine Weatherman Whitaker (1850 Surry). Lorenzo m. on 1-14-1866 in Yadkin Co. Lydia Gough, b. 2-10-1843, d. 10-21-1905, on 1-14-1866 (YCMR), the dau. of James Gough, Jr., and Elizabeth Hoots Gough. His second wife was Margaret Adams. The 1880 Yadkin Co. Census, Deep Creek Township, shows "Loranza" D. Whitaker, a farmer (age 38), together with wife Lydia, and children. James L. R. (age 12), Charlie W. D. (age 7), Calvin W. M. (age 5), Frank T. (age 3) and Joshua A. (age 1) (1880 Yadkin, transcripbed by McCracken, 1991).

WHITAKER, ROBERT S.; CO. A, 1ST BAT. SHARPSHOOTERS.
Robert S. Whitaker e. "at camp in Virginia" on 6-15-1863. Present until he deserted on 9-20-1864. He deserted again on 10-11-1864. Dropped from rolls for desertion on 2-28-1865 (NCT III, 76). Robert S. Whitaker m. Nancy Jane Hair on 9-22-1861 (YCMR).

WHITAKER, WILLIAM ASBURY; CO. B, 21ST REG. (?–12/12/1912; St. Paul's Episcopal, Winston-Salem, Forsyth Co., NC).
W. A. Whitaker e. in Yadkin Co. on 5-12-1861. Mustered in as corporal. Present until discharged on 9-23-1861, reason not given. Later served in Co. A, 1st Battalion Sharpshooters, where he was mustered in as musician and continued through June 1864. Listed as private after June 1864. Present through Dec. 1864 (NCT III, 76; VI, 554). (He may be the same as another W. A. Whitaker reported on an "undated" muster roll which states that he e. on 5-12-1861 at Yadkinville for twelve months, with the rank of sergeant.)

WHITE, JOHN R.; CO. G, 38TH REG.
John R. White e. at Camp Holmes near Raleigh 7-30-1864. He deserted to the enemy about 1-18-1865, and was confined in Washington, DC, on 1-24-1865. He was released after taking the Oath of Allegiance (NCT X, 75–76).

WHITE, WILLIAM; MILITIA (04/05/1803–07/17/1867; Haynes-White Fam. Cem, Yadkin Co., NC).
William White, a carpenter/contractor, built the first Yadkin Co. Court House. He m. Mary Philadelphia White, dau. of the Rev. Thomas Haynes, of Hamptonville. In 1850, White, a widower, was head of a household which included Mahala Hanes (probably a relative of his wife's), dau. Mary P., sons Thomas L., age 17, and William age 13, and Gaither Miller. His second wife was Sarah Nicholson. After William d. in 1867, the property was sold. The widow, Sarah, took her children and moved to Wilkesboro so that they could receive an education. Those children became professionals, one of whom was Dr. John Wesley White (Connor, *History of North Carolina*, Vol. IV, 320; 1850 Surry).

WHITE, WILLIAM LEE; CO. I, 33RD REG. 3RD LIEUTENANT.
William Lee White, b. in Yadkin Co., e. in Forsyth. He had been a mechanic before enlisting at age 25 on 7-1-1861. Mustered in as 1st sergeant. Present until captured at New Bern on 3-14-1862. Paroled and transferred to Aiken's Landing, James River, VA, where he was received on 7-12-1862 for exchange on 8-5-1862. He returned to duty before 11-1-1862, and appointed 3rd lieutenant on 4-1-1863. Present until wounded near Chancellorsville, VA, about May 1–4, 1863. Returned to duty before 9-1-1863. Present until wounded in the breast near Wilderness, VA, about 5-6-1864. Returned to duty before 7-28-1864, when he was captured at Gravel Hill, VA, and confined at the Old Capitol Prison, Washington, DC. Transferred to Ft. Delaware, DE, on 8-11-1864, he was released on 6-17-1865, after taking the Oath of Allegiance (NCT IX, 221). William Lee White m. Mary Lou Gray on 6-29-1865 (bond date, YCMR).

WHITEHEAD, CALVIN; CO. I, 28TH REG. (1846–?).
Calvin Whitehead e. at Camp Holmes on 5-4-1864. Deserted on 1-11-1865 (NCT VIII, 219). Calvin Whitehead, the s. of John and Martha Royal Whitehead, m. Julina Dun(n) on 5-27-1863. He m. second Lucinda Willard, dau. of William and Matilda Willard, on 12-17-1871 (bond date, YCMR; *Heritage*, 653; 1850 Surry).

WHITEHEAD, HENRY W.; CO. I, 28TH REG. (01/10/1837–12/24/1935; Center Meth., Yadkin Co., NC).
Henry W. Whitehead e. at age 23 in Yadkin Co. on 3-8-1862. Wounded near Gravel Hill, VA, on 7-28-1864. Returned to duty before 11-1-1862. He was captured near Petersburg, VA, on 4-2-1865, and confined at Ft. Delaware, DE, until released on 6-19-1865, after taking the Oath of Allegiance (NCT VIII, 219). Henry Whitehead, the s. of John and Martha Royal Whitehead, m. Martha Jane Sprinkle on 1-10-1861. He was the brother of Calvin Whitehead (see above) (YCMR; Nina Long Groce).

WHITEHEAD, JAMES S.; CO. I, 28TH REG. (1841–06/27/1863).
James S. Whitehead e. in Yadkin Co. at age 20 on 8-13-1861. Captured at Hanover Court House, VA, on 5-27-1862, he was confined at Ft. Monroe, VA, then Ft. Columbus, NY Harbor. Paroled and transferred to Aiken's Landing, James River, VA, where he arrived on 7-12-1862, and was exchanged on 8-5-1862. Returned to duty before 11-1-1862. Died in a Richmond, VA, hospital about 6-27-1863 of gunshot wound and or fever. Place and date of wound not reported (NCT VIII, 219). James may be the s. of Joel and Margaret Weatherman Whitehead (*Heritage*, 653; 1850 Surry).

WHITEHEAD, JOHN; CO. I, 28TH REG. (05-?-1841?–11/04/1921; Center Meth., Yadkin Co., NC).
John Whitehead's pension records indicate he served in the company (NCT VIII, 219). John Whitehead

was the s. of Joel and Margaret Weatherman Whitehead (*Heritage*, 653). He m. on 12-12-1871 (YCMR) Martha Catherine Weatherman Whitaker (b. ca. 1822). They had two daughters: Maggie Novalla (b. 11-7-1873, d. 8-29-1844) and Allace A. Whitehead (b. Oct. 1879). He applied for a veterans pension on 7-31-1902 and stated he had "a lame leg caused by a chronic sore," also breast trouble and kidney disease," which was verified by Dr. M. A. Royall. On his application, he stated he had served in Co. A, 10th Reg. NC Troops. After his death, his widow Martha, applied for a widow's pension and she stated he had served in Co. I, 28th Reg. His tombstone has the inscription: "Rest soldier rest, Thy warfare is o'er" (per Jody Watts Chadduck; Nina Long Groce).

WHITEHEAD, WILLIAM; CO. B, 21ST REG. (1836–?).
William Whitehead e. in Yadkin Co. on 5-12-1861, and was present until transferred to Co. A, 1st Battalion Sharpshooters. Present through Dec. 1864, and paroled at Appomattox Court House, VA, on 4-9-1865 (NCT III, 76; VI, 554). William (b. 1836?) may be the s. of Joel and Margaret Weatherman Whitehead. He m. on 10-17-1669 Nancy Jane Sprinkle, dau. of Henderson and Elizabeth Sprinkle (YCMR; *Heritage*, 693).

WHITLOCK, A[LEXANDER]. H.; CO. B, 21ST REG. (1839–?).
A. H. Whitlock e. in Yadkin Co. on 5-21-1861 and was present until transferred to Co. A, 1st Battalion Sharpshooters. After transferring, he was wounded at Second Manassas on 8-28-1862. He was wounded a second time at Mine Run, VA, on 11-29-1863. Reported as absent-sick after being wounded at Mine Run. Detained for light duty 2-6-1865 (NCT III, 76; VI, 554). In 1850, Alexander H. Whitlock was living in the household of John (age 53) and Sylva Whitlock (age 45), probably his parents (1850 Surry).

WHITLOCK, ROLAND HIAL; CO. I, 18TH REG. (01/11/1831–02/16/1863).
R. H. Whitlock e. in Wake Co. at age 28 on 9-10-1862. Present until he d. in Lynchburg, VA, hospital on 2-16-1863 of "febris typhoides" (NCT VI, 411). He was the s. of William and Lavisa Johnson Whitlock. In 1850, Roland Whitlock, age 19, was living in his mother's household (1850 Surry). Roland m. Minerva Ann Buchanan in 1857 ("Whitlock Family of Yadkin County, North Carolina, and Descendants," compl. by Mrs. Sherman Whitlock, 332 Louise Ave., High Point, NC 27262; Cheryl Martin).

WILBORN, JAMES; CO. A, 9TH BAT.

WILBORN, THOMAS; CO. A, 9TH BAT.

WILBOURN, JOHN; CO. I, 28TH REG. (?–09/08/1864).
John Wilbourn reportedly served first in Co. I, 28th Reg., then transferred to Co. H, 54th Reg., on 10-17-1863. He was captured at Rappahannock Station, VA, on 11-7-1863 and confined at Point Lookout, MD, on 11-11-1863. He d. there on 9-8-1864, cause of death not reported (NCT XIII, 328).

WILDER (WILES), SAMUEL C.; CO. B, 38TH REG. 1st Lieutenant (1830–?).
Samuel C. Wilder (Wiles?), a Yadkin Co. cabinetmaker, e. at age 31 on 10-16-1861. Mustered in as sergeant. Elected 2nd lieutenant 8-2-1862. Promoted to 1st lieutenant on 5-3-1863. Present until reported missing and presumed dead at Gettysburg, PA, on 7-3-1863 (NCT X, 21).

WILES, ENOCH; CO. D, 21ST REG. (1824–?).
Enoch Wiles e. in Forsyth Co. at age 39 on 9-20-1863. He was reported AWOL Jan-Feb. 1865. In 1850 Enoch Wilds, age 26, was living with wife, Anna, age 22, who was b. in Tennessee, and children Eliza J. and William T. (1850 Surry). Enoch and Nathan Wiles were probably brothers (NCT VI, 574).

WILES, NATHAN; CO. D, 21ST REG. (1823–?).
Nathan Wiles e. in Forsyth Co. at age 40 on 9-20-1863. He was reported AWOL Jan.-Feb 1865 (NCT VI, 574). Nathan Wilds (Wiles), age 24, was living in the household of Thomas J. Patterson in 1850, with Mary J. Wilds (wife?), age 17 and b. in Tennessee, and James Wilds, age 1, probably his s. (1850 Surry)

WILKES, WILLIAM; CO. E, 70TH REG.

WILKINS, MARTIN; CO. A, 1ST BAT. SHARPSHOOTERS (1846–01/19/1865).
Martin Wilkins, b. in Yadkin Co., e. in Wake Co. on 9-4-1862. Reported as "wounded in General Hospital" at Goldsboro Jan.-Feb. 1864. He was wounded slightly in the head near Fredericksburg, VA, on 5-4-1863. Reported as present but under arrest on 2-28 through 6-30-1864. Listed as present on muster rolls of Aug. 31–Dec. 31, 1864. Died in General Hospital, Petersburg VA, 1-19-1865 of "pneumonia." His age was listed as 27 years (NCT III, 76). Martin Wilkins was the s. of Samuel and Mary Wilkins (1850 Surry).

WILLARD, FRANCIS H.; CO. H, 3RD REG.
Francis H. Willard e. in Yadkin Co. on 10-27-1863. Deserted at Racoon Ford, VA, on 9-15-1863 (NCT III, 577). He e. again at Camp Holmes on 7-20-1864, but deserted about 8-2-1864 (NCT X, 76).

WILLARD, J. H.; CO. G, 385H REG.
J. H. Willard e. along with Francis H. and Milton F. Willard on 7-30-1864. He deserted along with Francis Willard on 7-2-1864 (NCT X, 76).

WILLARD, M. F.; CO. H, 10TH REG (1ST ARTILLERY) (?–09/30/1864).
M. F. Willard e. in Wayne Co. on 2-10-1863. Present

or accounted for through February 1865 (NCT I, 137). This may be Miles F. Willard, b. 1840, the s. of William and Matilda Willard (Surry 1850).

WILLARD, M[ILTON]. F.; CO. G, 38TH REG. (1828–10/12/1864).
M. F. Willard e. at Camp Holmes on 7-30-1864. He deserted on 8-17-1864, but returned to duty on 8-30-1864. He was "shot for desertion" on 10-12-1864 (see letter he wrote to his wife in the text, pages 52–53) (NCT X, 76). Milton F. Willard was the s. of Jonathan and Kesiah Willard (1850 Surry). At the time of his death he left a widow and three children orphaned.

WILLIAMS, G. W.; CO. B, 38TH REG. (1846–?).
G. W. Williams e. at Camp Vance at age 18 on 8-14-1864 for the war. Hospitalized at Richmond, VA, on 3-28-1865 with gunshot wound of left foot. Place and date of wound not reported. Captured in hospital at Richmond, VA, on 4-3-1865. Escaped on 5-6-1865 (NCT X, 30).

WILLIAMS, GEORGE D.; CO. F, 28TH REG. (1827–?).
George D. Williams lived in Yadkin Co. where he e. at age 34 on 6-18-1861. Mustered in as sergeant but reduced to ranks on 4-15-1862. Captured at Hanover Court House, VA, on 5-27-1862. Confined at Ft. Monroe, VA, then Ft. Columbus, NY Harbor, before being paroled and transferred to Aiken's Landing, James River, VA. He arrived there on 7-2-1862 for exchange and was released on 8-5-1862. He was discharged 9-18-1862, reason not given (NCT VIII, 184). George D. Williams, s. of Thomas and Rachel Williams, m. R. P. Hunter on 6-23-1867 (YCMR; 1850 Surry).

WILLIAMS, ISAAC D.; CO. A, 54TH REG. (05/04/1843–08/30/1904; Mt. Pleasant Meth., Yadkin Co., NC).
Isaac Williams, b. in Surry (Yadkin) Co., was a farmer before enlisting in Yadkin Co. at age 20 on 5-3-1862. He was reported present on surviving muster rolls through Dec. 1863. Reported present Sept.–Oct. 1864 (NCT XIII, 258).

WILLIAMS, JESSE FRANKLIN; ARMY OF TENNESSEE (03/19/1835–12/16/1917).
Jesse Franklin Williams was serving with the Army of Tennessee and was wounded in the fighting at Chickamauga. He was also in the battle for Chattanooga and was on Missionary Ridge (according to a descendant, Mrs. A. P. Phillips of Mt. Airy). Jesse Franklin Williams was still in the Army when his wife wrote him on 1-1-1865 (numerous letters exist to and from this couple). Jesse Franklin Williams was the s. of Jesse and Ruth Martin Williams. He m. first his third cousin, Martha P. Hutchens (12-17-1837/6-9-1859), dau. of David F. and Martha P. Bales Hutchens. His m. his second wife, Sarah Luzania Patterson, on 12-15-1860 (YCMR). She was the dau. of William Williams and Rebecca Davis Patterson. Their children were: William Pearson (8-30-1863–1945); Lindsey Belton (1-26-1866); John Drewery Gray (9-9-1867); Hiette Sinclair Williams (3-3-1862/10-6-1940); Lela Bannah (12-29-1876/5-12-1956); and Minnie Nevada Williams (5-12-1882/5-28-1949) (Casstevens, "The Harding Family").

WILLIAMS, JOHN L.; CO. F, 28TH REG. (05/15/1843–04/30/1901; Matthews-Williams Cem.).
John L. Williams e. in Yadkin Co. on 10-27-1863. He was furloughed on 2-21-1864, but failed to return to duty, and was listed as a deserter. He went over to the enemy on an unspecified date and took the Oath of Allegiance in Louisville, KY, on 8-16-1864 (NCT VIII, 184). According to Lewis Brumfield, John L. Williams was the s. of Cadmile and Sarah Williams, and he m. Texas Russell in 1884. He is buried in the Matthews Williams graveyard, and she in the Russell Graveyard (Hoots, 391; 1850 Yadkin 1860).

WILLIAMS, JOHN MACINTOSH; MILITIA (11/20/1824–02/12/1863; Isaac Williams Cem.).
John Macintosh Williams was a member of the Militia who were sent to bring in "conscripts" hiding out at the Bond School He was one of two members of the Militia killed by some of the conscripts. He m. Sabrilla Brown (Brumfield, "Timothy Williams Folks," 27–31).

WILLIAMS, JOHN O.; CO. A, 9TH BAT. HOME GUARD (01/10/1844–12/25/1928; Flat Rock Bapt. Ch.).
John O. Williams is buried at Flat Rock Baptist Church. His wife's first name was Caroline. John O. Williams, age 5, was living in his parents household in 1850, that of Hardin and Susannah Williams, with brothers Thomas, Ellis F., and William L. (1850 Surry).

WILLIAMS, LEWIS A.; CO. I, 28TH REG. CORPORAL (04/28/1844–12/07/1861; Deep Creek Friends).
Lewis A. Williams e. at age 19 on 8-13-1861. He mustered in as corporal, but d. at a hospital in Wilmington, NC, about 12-7-1861 of "measles" (NCT VIII, 219). Lewis was the s. of Crawford and Nancy Johnson Williams (Brumfield, "Timothy Williams Folks," 60).

WILLIAMS, THOMAS, JR.; CO. B, 38TH REG. (1843–08/??/1862).
Thomas Williams, Jr., e. in Yadkin Co. at age 18 on 10-16-1861. Present or accounted for until he d. in Richmond, VA, hospital in August of 1862 of disease (NCT X, 30).

WILLIAMS, WILLIAM SANDFORD; 75TH REG., 18TH BRIG. MILITIA (7/20/1831–6/5/1920).

William Sandford Williams became a member of the 75th Regiment, 18th Brigade, Militia, on 3-10-1862, for the Huntsville district. He reportedly was paroled at Appomattox. William Sanford Williams was the s. of Jesse and Ruth Martin Williams, and the brother of Jesse Franklin Williams. He m. Mary Tallulah Hickman, b. 2-22-1857, d. 10-12-1836, and they lived in Graysville, GA, after the war. Children were: Willie Lee; Maymie Frances (b. 11-24-1884, d. 2-23-1860); and Charles H. Williams (all of whom lived in Chattanooga or Catossa Co., GA) (Brumfield, "Timothy Williams Folks," 40).

WILLIAMSON, WILLIAM; CO. B, 21ST REG. (ca. 1841–04/26/1862).
William Williamson e. in Yadkin Co. on 5-21-1861 and was present through Oct. 1861. He d. at Manassas, VA, before 4-26-1862, cause of death not reported (NCT VI, 554). William Williamson, at age 9, was living in the household of Chris Ready, a blacksmith (1850 Surry).

WILLIARD, JOSEPH; CO. A, 21ST REG.
Joseph Williard e. in Yadkin Co. on 10-1-1863. Present until he deserted about 12-28-1863 (NCT VI, 551).

WILSON, HENRY C., M.D.; HOME GUARD (02/16/1830–01/14/78; Wilson-Hauser Cem., Yadkinville, NC).
H. C. Wilson m. Julia Amelia Hauser on 2-16-1858, the dau. of T. C. and Mary Lydia Doub Hauser (bond date, YCMR). He was the s. of Dr. George Follett and Henrietta Sophia Hauser Wilson, and was b. in Bethania, Forsyth Co., NC. Dr. Henry C. Wilson and Julia were the parents of 8 children. The Hauser and Wilson houses were next to each other, and both are still standing on Old Highway 421, just west of Yadkinville, at what was once called "Dowelltown." Dr. Wilson was educated in the Moravian school in Nazareth, PA, and at a school in Vermont. He was practicing medicine in Bethania in 1850, when his parents moved to Yadkin Co. Dr. Henry Wilson was also active incounty government. He was Clerk of Court from 1874 to 1873 (*Heritage*, 663).

WILSON, REUBEN EVERETT; CO. B, 21ST REG. CAPTAIN (12/31/1840–03/08/07; Salem Cem., Winston-Salem, NC).
Reuben Everett Wilson, b. in Stokes Co., but resided in Yadkinville, where he e. at age 20. Appointed 2nd lieutenant to rank from 5-12-1861. Present until he transferred to Co. A, 1st Battalion NC Sharpshooters, on 4-26-1862 (NCT VI, 551). Promoted to captain, Co. A, 1st Battalion Sharpshooters, on 6-27-1862. Wilson was wounded in the right forearm (fracture) and the left leg (fracture) at Cedar Mountain, VA, on 8-9-1862. Reported absent-wounded through Dec. 1863. Returned to duty Jan.-Feb. 1864. Left leg "cut off by a shell" at Petersburg, VA, on 4-2-1865. Hospitalized at Manchester, VA, where he was paroled on 4-29-1865. "Rearrested" ten days later and taken to Libby Prison in Richmond, VA, where he was held there and in other prisons until Dec. 20, 1865 (NCT III, 70, 720; *Confederate Veteran*, VI, No. 5, May 1898, 223). Reuben Everett Wilson was a brother to Dr. Henry C. Wilson, and the s. of Dr. George Follett Wilson and Henrietta Sophia Hauser Wilson, of Bethania. After the War, Reuben went to Augusta GA, and operated a business for 12 to 15 years, but his health failed and he returned to live in Winston-Salem with his sister, Mrs. L. P. Bitting. He never became reconciled to the defeat of the South, and he never wore anything except his Confederate uniform, and he was buried in it in the Salem Cemetery (*Heritage*, 663–664; Winston-Salem *Journal*, March 10, 1907, page 5).

WILSON, WILLIAM HENRY; CO. B, 42ND REG. (1841–?).
William Henry Wilson, a Yadkin Co. resident, e. in Rowan Co. at age 21 on 3-18-1862. Present until July-Aug. 1862, when he was listed as a deserter. Returned to duty before 1-1-1863, and was present until he deserted again on 8-12-1864 (NCT X, 240).

WINDSOR, AMOS A.; CO. D, 42ND REG. (1834–11/25/1863).
Amos A. Windsor e. at Petersburg, VA, on 10-1-1863. Died in a Wilmington, NC, hospital about 11-25-1863 of "pneumonia" (NCT X, 240). Amos A. Windsor was b. ca. 1834 in Surry (now Yadkin) Co., the s. of James Riley Windsor and Nancy A. Bell (Cook, *Descendants of Isaac Windsor*, 9). The 1850 Surry Co. Census shows Amos A. Windsor, age 16, living with parents, James and Susannah Windsor.

WINDSOR, ENOS LAWSON; 75TH REG., 18TH BRIG. MILITIA (01/11/1832–11/18/1906; Zion Bapt., Iredell Co., NC).
Enos Lawson Windsor is listed as a 1st lieutenant in the Militia for the Buck Shoals District. Enos was the s. of Bennet and Sarah A. Holeman Windsor (1850 Surry). He m. first on 5-25-1854 Lettye D. Lewis. He m. second Julia E. Windsor on 5-6-1860 (YCMR; Douglas Reed Niemeyer; Cook, *The Descendants of Isaac Windsor*, 26–27).

WINDSOR, JOHN; CO. A, 9TH BAT. HOME GUARD (10/13/1845–02/07/1904).

WINDSOR, SAMUEL BOONE; CO. B, 38TH REG. (01/16/1827–05/16/1909).
Samuel Boone Windsor, the s. of Bennet and Sarah A. Holeman, m. Sarah Morgan on 3-16-1848 (per Douglas Reed Niemeyer; Cook, *Descendants of Isaac Windsor*, 26). Samuel Boone Windsor's pension records indicate he served in this company (NCT X, 30).

WINDSOR, THOMAS W.; CO. G, 66TH REG. (03/14/1837–06/04/1864).
Thomas W. Windsor e. at Salisbury in Co. G, 66th Reg. He was killed near Kinston, NC. He m. Emeline Elizabeth Buchannan and they had two children. (Cook, *Descendants of Isaac Windsor*, 27).

WINFREY, W. H.; CO. I, 6TH REG. (02/06/1843–09/23/1930; Macedonia Meth., Yadkin Co., NC).
W. H. Winfrey, a Yadkin Co. resident, e. there at age 20 on 9-15-1862. He was captured in a hospital at Gettysburg, PA, on 7-50-1863, and hospitalized at Davids Island, NY Harbor, until paroled and transferred to City Point, VA, where he was received 9-8-1863 for exchange. Captured at Strasburg, VA, on 9-23-1864, and confined at Point Lookout, MD, until released on 6-22-1865, after taking the Oath of Allegiance (NCT IV, 380). He and wife, Ersella J. (b. 4-28-1851, d. 9-11-1883) are buried at Macedonia Methodist Church, near East Bend, NC.

WINTERS, JAMES A.; CO. D, 44TH REG. (1837–05/07/97; Mitchell's Chapel Meth., Yadkin Co., NC).
NC pension records indicate he served in this company (NCT X, 433). James Andrew Winters, b. about 1837, m. Nancy Elizabeth Casstevens, dau. of John and Elizabeth Casstevens on 4-01-1860. Children were: Emily Frances, John Wesley, and William Lafayette Winters (YCMR; *Thomas Casteven: A Genealogical History*, pp. 36–37).

WISE, HENRY A.; CO. G, 4TH REG. (1839–04/09/1865).
Henry A. Wise, a Yadkin Co. resident, e. in Davie Co. at age 22 on 6-4-1861. Reported in confinement as a prisoner of war on 9-27-1862, place and date of capture not reported. Rejoined unit on 5-1-1863, and was present until wounded in the left shoulder at Wilderness, VA, on 5-7-1864. Reported absent-wounded through Aug. 1864. Paroled at Appomattox Court House, VA, on 4-9-1865. Parole indicates he was wounded, but place and date not reported (NCT IV, 84).

WISHON, ISAAC C.; CO. A, 21ST REG.
Isaac C. Wishon e. in Yadkin Co. on 10-1-1863. Present until he deserted on 12-28-1863 (NCT VI, 551). Isaac C. Wishon m. Jane Plowman on 5-21-1854 (YCMR).

WISHON, J. C.; CO. A, 21ST REG.
J. C. Wishon is first listed on company rolls on 2-18-1864 (NCT VI, 551). (This may be a misinterpretation of I. C. Wishon, as I's and J's are sometimes hard to differentiate between.)

WISHON, JAMES A.; CO. B, 44TH REG. (1842–?).
James A. Wishon, a Yadkin Co. resident, e. at age 24 on 11-28-1862. He was reported "under arrest" in Feburary 1863. The reason for his arrest was not stated. He was reported AWOL Nov.-Dec. 1863, and was listed as a deserter and dropped from the company rolls Jan.-Feb. 1864. He went over to the enemy and was confined at Knoxville, TN, on 7-31-1864. He was then transferred to Chattanooga, TN, on 8-2-1864, before being sent to Louisville, KY, where he was confined, but released on 8-10-1864, after taking the Oath of Allegiance (NCT X, 417). James Wishon was the s. of Samuel and Sarah Wishon (1850 Surry).

WISHON, JAMES T.; CO. I, 28TH REG. (1842–10/01/1864).
James T. Wishon e. in Yadkin Co. where he resided at age 19 on 8-13-1861. Captured at New Bern on 3-14-1862, and confined at Ft. Columbus, NY Harbor. Paroled and transferred to Aiken's Landing, James River, VA, on 7-12-1862, and exchanged on 8-5-1862. Returned to duty before 11-1-1862. Hospitalized at Danville, VA, on 6-16-1864 with gunshot wound of the neck, place and date of wound not reported. Returned to duty before 10-1-1864, when he was killed in action at or near Jones' Farm, VA (NCT VIII, 219). J. T. Wishon m. Margaret Beaty on 2-26-1864 (bond date, YCMR).

WISHON, SAMUEL ALEXANDER; CO. I, 28TH REG. (1835–?; Mt. Olive Meth. [tombstone, n.d.]).
Samuel A. Wishon e. in Yadkin Co. at age 27 on 3-8-1862. Captured at Hanover Court House, VA, on 5-27-1862, and confined at Ft. Monroe, VA, then Ft. Columbus, NY Harbor. Paroled and transferred to Aiken's Landing in VA where he was received on 7-12-1862 and exchanged on 8-5-1862. Returned to duty before 11-1-1862. Deserted on 7-15-1863, but returned to duty on an unspecified date. Wounded in the left side and captured near Gravel Hill, VA, on 7-28-1864. Hospitalized at City Point, VA, he was transferred from there to Point Lookout, MD, where he was confined on 12-5-1864. Paroled and transferred to Boulware's Wharf, James River, VA, on 3-18-1865 for exchange. Paroled at Salisbury, NC, April-May 1865 (NCT VIII, 220). There is a tombstone for Samuel Alexander Wishon at Mt. Olive Methodist Church, but no dates were given in Carl Hoots' cemetery book.

WOMACK, ALLEN M.; CO. F, 28TH REG. (1840–07/03/1862).
Allen M. Womack lived in Yadkin Co. and e. at Camp Enon at age 22 on 8-20-1862. He was wounded at Gaines Mill, VA, on 6-27-1862. Hospitalized at Richmond, VA, he d. there July 3-6, 1862, of wounds (NCT VIII, 184).

WOOD, FRANCIS; CO. A, 9TH BAT. HOME GUARD (1818–?).
In 1850, Francis Wood, age 32, was living in a house with wife, Elizabeth V., age 23, and dau. Luvina, age 5 (1850 Surry). Francis Wood m. the widow Martha J. Shore on 4-27-1864 (YCMR).

WOOD, H. R.; CO. B, 21ST REG. SERGEANT.
H. R. Wood e. in Yadkin Co. on 5-21-1861 and was promoted to sergeant on 10-31-1861. Reduced in rank before 4-26-1862, when he transferred to Co. A, 1st Battalion Sharpshooters. After the transfer, Wood was wounded in battle at Second Manassas, VA, on

8-28-1862. He was then detailed as a courier for General Hoke from March through April 1863, and remained on detail through Dec. 1864. Present on muster rolls through that period (NCT III, 76; VI, 554).

WOODHOUSE, FRANCIS M.; CO. I, 28TH REG. (1843–08/04/1862).
Francis M. Woodhouse lived in Yadkin Co. where he e. at age 18 on 3-8-1862. He d. in camp near Richmond, VA, on 8-4-1862 of "fever" (NCT VIII, 220). Francis Woodhouse, at age 7, was living in the household of his parents, Anthony and Mirand(a) Woodhouse (1850 Surry).

WOODHOUSE, M. S.; CO. A, 1ST BAT. SHARPSHOOTERS (1844–?).
M. S. Woodhouse, a Yadkin farmer e. "at camp in Virginia" at age 19 on 11-1-1863. Present on muster rolls through Dec. 1864, and paroled at Appomattox Court House, VA, on 4-9-1865 (NCT III, 76). He is probably the s. of Anthony and Mirand(a) Woodhouse, Motier, age 5 (1850 Surry). There was only one Woodhouse family in the Yadkin Co. area in 1850.

WOODHOUSE, W. A.; CO. B, 21ST REG. (1840–?).
W. A. Woodhouse e. as a private in Yadkin Co. on 5-12-1861 and was present until transferred to Co. A, 1st Battalion Sharpshooters (NCT VI, 554). William A. Woodhouse, age 10, was living in the household of his parents, Anthony and Mirand(a) Woodhouse (1850 Surry).

WOODRUFF, RICHARD W.; CO. B, 21ST REG. 1ST LIEUT. (10/08/1837–07/08/1893; Island Ford Bapt. Ch.).
Richard W. Woodruff e. in Yadkin Co. on 5-12-1861. Mustered in as ordnance sergeant. Elected 2nd lieutenant on 9-11-1861. Present until transferred to Co. A, 1st Battalion, NC Sharpshooters, on 4-16-1862 (NCT VI, 551). Promoted to 1st lieutenant on 6-27-1862. Detailed as acting assistant quartermaster for the battalion from Jan. 1863 to Aug. 1864. Present through Dec. 1864. Paroled at Appomattox Court House, VA, 4-9-1865 (NCT III, 70). Richard W. Woodruff, the s. of Aaron and Charity Cockerham Woodruff, m. on 7-8-1893 Mary E. Gaither, dau. of Ephraim and Sarah H. Gaither (will of Sarah Gaither, Davie Co., NC; 1860 Yadkin). Richard W., at age 22, was listed as a physician in 1860 (1860 Yadkin), and living in Jonesville Township (1850 Surry; 1860 Yadkin).

WOODRUFF, VINCENT; CO. B, 21ST REG. (?–04/19/1863).
Vincent Woodruff e. in Yadkin Co. on 5-12-1861 and was present until transferred to Co. A, 1st Battalion Sharpshooters, on 4-26-1862. After transfer, detailed to General Hospital, Liberty, VA, as a nurse on 5-3-1862. Reported absent on detail until it was reported in March-April 1863 that he had died (NCT III, 76; VI, 555).

WOODRUFF, WILLIAM W.; CO. H, 21ST REG. (1838–05/25/1862).
William W. Woodruff volunteered at Dobson on 6-5-1861 at age 23. He was active until killed on 5-25-1862 at Winchester, VA (NCT III, 611; *Biblical Recorder*, 9-24-1862; Jackson, *Surry County Soldiers in the Civil War*, 200). Woodruff was killed along with two other members of Reece's Church, near Boonville, NC, as reported in the *Biblical Recorder*. They were William Woodhouse and Aaron Caudle. He was the s. of Moses and Charity Cockerham Woodruff, a Yadkin Co. farm family.

WOOTEN, ALVIN; CO. A, 9TH BAT. HOME GUARD (1825–?).
Alvin Wooten, age 35 was living with wife, Janie, and children: Nancy E., Joseph G., Louisa W., Thomas F., Mary M., Alvin L. Alexander, Jane, and Sarah in Yadkin Co. when the 1860 Census was taken. Alvin m. second on 2-20-1867 Lyda Cane (Cain) in Yadkin Co., NC (YCMR).

WOOTEN, LEWIS W.; CO. B, 38TH REG. CORPORAL (1845–?).
Lewis W. Wooten, a Yadkin resident, e. there at age 17 on 4-19-1862 as a substitute. Mustered in as private. Wounded ("shocked") at Mechanicsville, VA, on 6-26-1862. Returned to duty Sept.-Oct. 1862. Wounded at Fredericksburg, VA, about 12-13-1862. Returned to duty Jan.-Feb. 1863 and promoted to corporal in March-April 1863. Present through Oct. 1864 (NCT X, 30). Lewis W. Wooten, s. of Alvin and Jane Wooten, m. E. E. Haynes on 4-20-1862 (YCMR; 1850 Surry).

WOOTEN, THOMAS H.; CO. F, 28TH REG. (1842–?).
Thomas H. Wooten lived in Yadkin Co. where he e. at age 19 on 6-18-1861. He was wounded in the left thigh and captured at Gettysburg, PA, 7-3-1863. Hospitalized at Chester, PA, he was paroled and transferred to City Point, VA, where he was received 9-23-1863 for exchange. Returned to duty on an unspecified date. Reported AWOL from 9-22-1864 through Feb. 1865 (NCT VIII, 184).

WYSONG, ANDREW C.; CO. G, 44TH REG. (1834–?).
Andrew C. Wysong resided in Yadkin Co., but e. at Camp Holmes at age 29 on 10-14-1862. Deserted on 5-9-1863. Returned to duty. Captured at Bristoe Station, VA, on 10-14-1863. Confined at Old Capitol Prison, Washington, DC. Transferred to Point Lookout, MD, on 2-3-1864, and paroled from there about 3-14-1865. Received at Boulware's Wharf for exchange on 3-16-1865 (NCT X, 466). Andrew C. Wysong, the s. of Henry and Jane Wysong, was living with his parents in Yadkin Co. when the 1850 Surry Census was taken. Henry was a blacksmith, and Andrew C. listed his occupation as "farmer."

YARBROUGH, ANDREW J.; CO. F, 28TH REG. (1842–?).

Andrew J. Yarbrough (Yarboro/Yarborough) lived in Yadkin Co. where he e. at age 19 on 6-18-1861. He was captured near Petersburg, VA, on 4-2-1865, and confined at Point Lookout, MD, until released on 6-6-1865 (NCT VIII, 184). Andrew J. Yarbrough (Yarborough) was the s. of Osway and Elizabeth Yarborough. Osway was b. in VA, and Elizabeth in DE (1850 Surry).

YORK, JAMES; CO. A, 54TH REG. (1840–?).
James York, b. ca. 1838 in Surry (Yadkin) Co., where he was a farmer before enlisting at age 22 on 5-3-1862. Reported present through Oct. 1863. Captured at Rappahannock Station, VA, 11-7-1863. Confined at Point Lookout, MD, and paroled there on 3-9-1864. Received at City Point, VA, 3-25-1864 for exchange. Returned to duty and was present Sept.-Oct. 1864 Captured at Ft. Stedman, VA, 3-25-1865 and confined again at Point Lookout, MD, 3-28-1865. He was released there on 6-22-1865, after taking the Oath of Allegiance. NC pension records state that he was wounded by a shell at Petersburg, VA, no date given (NCT XIII, 258).

YORK, LOUIS; 75TH REG., 18TH BRIG. MILITIA (1835–?).
Louis (Lewis) York, the s. of James and Sarah York, m. Wilmouth Joyce (b. 2-19-1839, d. 5-9-1925). Lewis (Louis) York was a doctor. He and Wilmouth had several children. In 1870 the children listed were: Cora (b. 1862), Wallace (b. 1864), Luther (b. 1865, m. Sallie L. Casstevens), Marette, (b. 1864), and Walter (b. 1868, m. Amanda Melissa Prim). Lewis was not listed in the 1880 census, but there are three more children: Lilly (b. 1871), Darbey (b. 1874), and Edward (b. 1878). Both are buried at Deep Creek Friends Church, Yadkin Co., NC (*Thomas Casteven: A Genealogical History*, by William C. Castevens, and Frances H. Casstevens; 1860 Yadkin; 1870 Yadkin Co. Census).

YOUNG, SOLOMON; CO. I, 28TH REG.
Solomon Young's pension records indicate he served in this company (NCT VIII, 220). He may be the same as Woodson S. Young, listed below.

YOUNG, WOODSON S.; CO. I, 28TH REG. (1841–?).
Woodson S. Young e. in Yadkin Co. at age 21 on 3-8-1862. Deserted on 8-1-1862 (NCT VIII, 220). He may be the same as Solomon Young listed above.

YOUNGER, PITTUS P.; CO. B, 44TH REG. (1842–?).
Pittus P. Younger lived in Yadkin Co., where he e. at age 20 on 10-1-1862. He deserted a month later on 11-23-1862 (NCT X, 417).

Bibliography

Primary Sources

Manuscripts and Official Records

Charles Bruce Davis Museum of Art, History, and Science: T. C. Hauser Store Account Books.
Yadkin County Historical & Genealogical Society: Notebook of Alfred "Teen" Blackburn.
Duke University, Durham, North Carolina: Richmond Mumford Pearson Papers.
National Archives, Washington, D. C.: Ninth Census of 1870, Industry, North Carolina, Schedule 4: Products of Industry; Population Schedules of the Eighth Census [1860] of the United States: Yadkin County, North Carolina (microfilm); Population Schedules of the Seventh Census [1850] of the United States: Surry County, North Carolina (microfilm); Record Group 109, Regimental Returns and Field and Staff Muster Rolls; United States Government Pension Records.
North Carolina Department of Archives and History, Raleigh, North Carolina: Adjutant General's Correspondence; Confederate Veteran and Widows Pension Lists 1900–1964 (microfilm); Election Returns; Population Schedules of the Eighth Census [1860] of the United States: North Carolina (microfilm).
Roster of Company A, 9th Battalion, Yadkin County Home Guard, Private possession of Mrs. Anne Arnold Cain, Hamptonville, North Carolina.
Roster of Company F, 28th Regiment, North Carolina Troops: Private possession of Dewey Bowman, East Bend, North Carolina.
University of North Carolina, Chapel Hill, North Carolina: Southern Historical Collection, S. H. Steelman Papers.
United States Department of the Interior, National Park Service.

County Records

Yadkin County, Yadkinville, North Carolina: Court Minutes 1851–1868; Guardian Reports; Marriage Register, Register of Deed's Office; Tax Collector's Office, 1851 Tax List; Wills and Estate Papers.
Surry County, Dobson, North Carolina: Marriage Register.

Public and Official Records

Bradley, Stephen E., Jr., ed. *North Carolina Confederate Militia: Officers Roster as Contained in the Adjutant-General's Officers Roster.* Wilmington, N.C.: Broadfoot, 1992.

_____. *North Carolina Home Guard Examinations 1863–1864.* Privately published, 1993.

_____. *North Carolina Militia and Home Guard Records.* 3 vols. Privately published, 1995.

Brock, R. A. *The Appomattox Roster.* New York: Antiquarian Press, 1962.

Craaybeek, Wanda. *Abstracts from the Minutes of Yadkin County, Board of Commissioner Meetings, 1868–1882, with Additional Abstracts Pertaining to Yadkin County.* Privately published, 1990.

Johnston, Frontis W., ed. *The Papers of Zebulon B. Vance.* 2 vols. Raleigh: N.C. Department of Archives and History, 1963.

Kennedy, J. C. G. *Agriculture in the United States in 1860.* Washington, D.C.: U.S. Government Printing Office, 1884.

_____. *Population of the United States in 1860.* Washington, D.C.: U.S. Government Printing Office, 1864.

McCracken, Anne Whitaker, comp. *1880 Federal Census of Yadkin County, North Carolina.* Privately published, 1991.

Manufacturers of the United States in 1860, Compiled from the Original Returns of the Eighth Census Under the Direction of the Secretary of the Interior. Washington, D.C.: U.S. Government Printing Office, 1865.

Public Laws of North Carolina, 1850–51. Raleigh: Edwards and Broughton, 1851.

Statistics of the United States (Including Mortality, Property, etc.) in 1860, Compiled from the Original Returns and Being the Final Exhibit of the Eighth Census. Washington: U.S. Government Printing Office, 1866.

Tolbert, Noble J., ed. *The Papers of John Willis Ellis.* 2 vols. Raleigh: N.C. Department of Archives and History, 1964.

The War of the Rebellion. A Compilation of the Official Records of the Union and Confederate Armies. 70 vols. 130 parts. Washington, D.C.: United States Government Printing Office, 1880–1905.

Published Diaries and Memoirs

Clark, Walter, ed. *Histories of the Several Regiments and Battalions from North Carolina in the Great War, 1861–1865, Written by Members of the Respective Commands.* 5 vols. Goldsboro, N.C.: Nash Brothers, 1901.

Clingman, Thomas L. *Selections from the Speeches and Writings of Honorable Thomas L. Clingman of North Carolina with Additions and Explanatory Notes.* 2d ed. Raleigh, N.C.: John Nichols, 1878.

Edmondston, Catherine Devereaux. *The Diary of a Secesh Lady: Catherine Devereaux Edmondston 1860–1866.* Beth G. Crabtree and James W. Patton, eds. Raleigh: NC Department of Cultural Resources, 1979.

Kerr, Jane P. "General Thomas Clingman." *Trinity Archive* II (March 1899): 388–396.

"Reuben E. Wilson." *Confederate Veteran* VI (May 1898): 222.

Roman, Alfred. *The Military Operations of General Beauregard in the War Between the States, Including a Brief Personal Sketch and a Narrative of His Services in the War with Mexico, 1846–1848.* 2 vols. New York: Harper & Brothers, 1884.

BIBLIOGRAPHY

Secondary Sources

General Works

Ashe, Samuel A'Court. *History of North Carolina*. 2 vols. Raleigh, N.C.: Edwards and Broughton, 1925.
Barrett, John G. *The Civil War in North Carolina*. Chapel Hill: The University of North Carolina Press, 1963.
Boatner, Mark M. *The Civil War Dictionary*. New York: McKay, 1988.
_____. *The Civil War Dictionary*. Revised ed. New York: Vintage Books, 1991.
Boykin, James H. *North Carolina in 1861*. New York: Bookman Associates, 1961.
Branson's *North Carolina Business Directory for 1867/1868*. Raleigh, N.C.: Branson and Jones, 1867.
Branson's *North Carolina Business Directory for 1869*. Raleigh, N.C.: J. A. Jones, 1869.
Brumfield, Lewis Shore, ed. *Historical Architecture of Yadkin County, North Carolina*. Winston-Salem, N.C.: Winston, 1987.
Canipe, Ruby Bray. *Early Elkin-Jonesville: History and Genealogy*. Jonesville, N.C.: Tarheel Graphics, 1981.
Casstevens, Frances H., ed. *Heritage of Yadkin County, North Carolina*. Winston-Salem, N.C.: Hunter, 1981.
Connor, R. D. W. *History of North Carolina*. 6 vols. Chicago: Lewis, 1919.
Cook, Gerald W. *The Last Tarheel Militia: 1861–1865*. Privately published, 1987.
Corbett, David Leroy. *Formation of the North Carolina Counties*. 2nd ed. Raleigh: N.C. Department of Archives and History, 1969.
Crofts, Daniel W. *Reluctant Confederates*. Chapel Hill: University of North Carolina Press, 1989.
Eaton, Clement. *A History of the Southern Confederacy*. New York: Macmillan, 1954.
Evans, Clement A., ed. *A Confederate Military History*. 12 vols. Atlanta: Confederate Publishing Co., 1899. Vol V: *North Carolina*, by D. H. Hill.
Guide to North Carolina Highway Markers. Raleigh: N.C. Department of Cultural Resources, Division of Archives and History, 1979.
Hamilton, J. G. DeRoulhac. *Reconstruction in North Carolina*. 1914, reprint Glouchester, Mass.: Peter Smith, 1964.
Hoots, Carl, comp. *Cemeteries of Yadkin County, North Carolina*. Spartanburg, S.C.: The Reprint Company, 1985.
Jonathan Hunt Chapter, DAR. *Early Elkin-Jonesville History and Genealogy*. Jonesville, N.C.: Tarheel Graphics, 1981.
Lefler, Hugh Talmage, and Albert Ray Newsome. *The History of a Southern State: North Carolina*. 3d ed. Chapel Hill: University of North Carolina Press, 1975.
Lindsey, Marcellene Blackburn, and Wanda Carter Craaybeek. *People of Color of Yadkin County*. Yadkinville, N.C.: Yadkin County Historical and Genealogical Society, Inc. 1992.
MacDonald, John. *Great Battles of the Civil War*. New York: Macmillan, 1988.
Manarin, Louis H., and Weymouth T. Jordan, eds. *North Carolina Troops 1861–1865: A Roster*. 13 vols. Raleigh: N.C. Department of Archives and History, 1966–1993.
Moore, John W., ed. *Roster of North Carolina Troops in the War Between the States*. 4 vols. Raleigh, N.C.: Ashe and Gatling, 1882.
Nicholson, Claude. *Yadkin County's Centenarian*. Yadkinville, N.C.: The Ripple, 1911.
Ramsey, Robert. *Carolina Cradle*. Chapel Hill: University of North Carolina Press, 1964.
Robert, James Clark. *The Tobacco Kingdom, Plantation, Market and Factory in Virginia and North Carolina 1800–1860*. Glouchester, Mass.: Peter Smith, 1965.
Rutledge, William E. *An Illustrated History of Yadkin County, 1850–1965*. Yadkinville, N.C., privately published, 1965.
Scott, J. L. *36th and 37th Virginia Cavalry*. Lynchburg, Va.: M. E. Howard, 1986.
Sifakis, Stewart. *Compendium of the Confederate Armies: North Carolina*. New York: Facts of File, 1992.

Speer, Allen P. *Voices from Cemetery Hill: The Civil War Diary, Reports, and Letters of Colonel William Henry Asbury (1861–1864)*. Johnson City, Tenn.: The Overthemountain Press, 1997.
Tilley, Nannie May. *The Bright Tobacco Industry 1860–1925*. Chapel Hill: University of North Carolina Press, 1948.
Trotter, William R. *The Civil War in North Carolina: Bushwhackers: The Mountains*. Winston-Salem, N.C.: John F. Blair, 1988.
Tucker, Glenn. *High Tide at Gettysburg* New York: Bobbs-Merrill, 1958; reprint ed., New York: Smithmark, 1995.
Van Noppen, Ina W. *Stoneman's Last Raid*. 2d ed. Raleigh: N.C. State University Press, 1961.
Williams, S. Carter. *Yadkin County Record Book*. Vol. I. Yadkinville, N.C.: Williams, 1939.
Yearns, W. Buck, and John G. Barrett. *North Carolina: Civil War Documents*. Chapel Hill: University of North Carolina Press, 1980.

Genealogies

Absher, Mrs. W. O., ed. *Heritage of Wilkes County, North Carolina*. Vol. I. Winston-Salem, N.C.: Hunter, 1982.
Allgood, Bertie Shore. *Shore Family Records*. Privately published, 1970.
Brumfield, Lewis Shore. *The Brandon, Hudspeth, Reavis and Steelman Book*. Privately published, 1991.
———. *Chief Justice Pearson and His Students*. Privately published, 1992.
———. *Thomas Lanier Clingman and the Shallow Ford Families*. Privately published, 1989.
———. *Timothy Williams Folks*. Privately published, 1990.
———. *The Williams and Hendersons: Descendants of John "The Wealthy Welshman" Williams*. Privately published, 1991.
———. *Wouldn't You Like To Have Known Them?* Privately published, 1992.
Bunn, Maude Davis. *The Genealogy of the Marion-Davis Families*. Raleigh, N.C.: Edwards & Broughton, 1973.
Castevens, William C., and Frances H. Casstevens. *The Descendants of Thomas Casteven: A Genealogical History*. Winston-Salem, N.C.: Hunter, 1977.
Choplin, Curtis D., comp. *An American Tragedy: The Robert Choplin Family in the Civil War 1861–1865*. Privately published, 1995.
Cook, Gerald Wilson. *The Descendants of Claiborne Howard: Soldier of the American Revolution*. Privately published, 1960.
———, comp. *Early Pioneers of Piedmont North Carolina Where Yadkin, Wilkes, & Iredell Meet the Descendants of Isaac Windsor 1753–1821*. Privately published, 1992.
Davis, Earl H., and Marie Davis Wiles. *Descendants of George and Elizabeth Hobson*. 2d ed. Privately published, 1978.
Hinshaw, William Wade. *American Quaker Genealogy*. 3 vols. 1936, reprint Baltimore: Genealogical, 1969.
Jackson, Hester. *Surry County Soldiers in the Civil War*. Charlotte, N.C.: Delmar Printing, 1992.
———, ed. *Heritage of Surry County, North Carolina*. Winston-Salem, N.C.: Hunter, 1983.
Jennings, Carrie M. *Messick Ancestral File 1664–1988*. Huntsville, Ala.: R. S. Jennings, 1989.
Long, Jasper. *Long Family Records*. Winston-Salem, N.C.: Clay, 1965.
Matthews, Irma. *The Matthews Families of Yadkin County*. Winston-Salem, N.C.: Hunter, 1968.
O'Daniel, Julia, and Laura Patton. *Kinfolk of Jacob Conrad*. Privately published, 1970.
Sampson, Nancy W., ed. *Heritage of Wilkes County, North Carolina*. Vol. II. Charlotte, N.C.: Delmar, 1990.
Steelman, Harold. *Descendants of Mathias and Ruth Steelman of Surry County, North Carolina*. Privately published, 1977.
Townsend, Rita H. *Hutchins/Hutchens: Descendants of Strangeman Hutchens*. Vol. I. Baltimore: Gateway Press, 1979.

Wellborn, L. Margaret. *William Holcomb (1650–aft. 1705) of England and New Kent Co., Virginia, and Simon Groce (b. 1711) of Baden Germany, and Rowan Co., North Carolina.* Asheville, N.C.: Ward, 1992.

Whitlock, Doretha Collins. *Whitlock Family of Yadkin County and Descendants.* Privately published, 1978.

Articles in Periodicals

A[ugustus]. H[enry]. J[arratt]. "General Thomas L. Clingman." *University of North Carolina Magazine,* New Series XVIII (April 1901): 169.

Burrus, Elizabeth Reece. "Customs of the Early Days." *Journal of the Yadkin County Historical & Genealogical Society* VI (June 1987): 12–13.

Casstevens, Frances H. "Ante-Bellum Slavery in Yadkin County." *Journal of the Yadkin County Historical Society* V (June 1986): 11–12.

———. "Interview with Mary Lou Howell Foster." *Journal Yadkin County Historical & Genealogical Society* X (September 1991): 16

———. "Lorenzo Dow Whitaker, of Company B, 21st Regiment, CSA." *Journal of the Yadkin County Historical & Genealogical Society* (September 1993): 12–14.

———. "Old Store Account Books." *Journal of the Yadkin County Historical & Genealogical Society* XI (September 1992): 23–24.

———. "Portrait of a 19th-Century Teacher." *Journal of the Yadkin County Historical & Genealogical Society* XIV (June 1995): 26–30.

"Confederate Monument in Cemetery at Philadelphia, Erected by United States." *Confederate Veteran* XIX (1911): 572–573.

Cook, Gerald Wilson. "Some Family Stories About the Madisons of Yadkin County." *Journal of the Yadkin County Historical & Genealogical Society* XIV (December 1995): 15–16.

Edwards, Morgan. *Material Toward a History of the Baptist in the Province of North Carolina.* Vol. VI. Reprinted in *North Carolina Historical Review* VII (March 1930).

"1859 Yadkin County Committees for School Districts." *Journal of the Yadkin County Historical & Genealogical Society* VI (September 1987): 21–24.

Houts, Alice Kinyoun. "Presents for the Yadkin Boys." *Journal of North Carolina Genealogy* IX (Summer 1963): 1113–1135.

Koonts, Russel Scott. "Black North Carolina Confederate Pensioners." *The North Carolina Genealogical Society Journal* (November 1995): 343–352.

"Letter from M. F. Farrington and Iredell Warden to Jesse and William Dobbins, August 28, 1864." *Journal of the Yadkin County Historical & Genealogical Society* IV (December 1986). *Martin Family News* II (July 1, 1986).

Loehr, Walter J., M. D. "Civil War Medicine in North Carolina." *North Carolina Medical Journal* 43 (February 1982): 120.

North Carolina Museum of History. *The Corner Stone* III, no. 3 (December 1995): 1–4.

Robertson, Irma Matthews. "Stories About Yadkin County During the Civil War." *Journal of the Yadkin County Historical & Genealogical Society* IX (June 1990): 21.

Seiders, Victor. "Stoneman's Raid—The Civil War Comes to Yadkin County." *Journal of the Yadkin County Historical & Genealogical Society* XIV (March 1995): 8–10.

Tucker, Glenn. "For Want of a Scribe." *North Carolina Historical Review* XLIII (April 1966).

Newspapers

(Asheville, North Carolina) *Citizen-Times.*
(Greensboro, North Carolina) *Daily News.*

(Raleigh, North Carolina) *Biblical Recorder*.
(Richmond, Virginia) *Times-Dispatch*.
(Salem, North Carolina) *The People's Press*.
(Salisbury, North Carolina) *Daily Carolina Watchman*.
(Winston-Salem, North Carolina) *Journal & Sentinel*.
(Winston-Salem, North Carolina) *Union Republican*.
(Yadkinville, North Carolina) *The Yadkin Ripple*.

Unpublished Works

Casstevens, Frances H. "The Military Career of Brigadier General Thomas L. Clingman." (Master's thesis, University of North Carolina at Greensboro, 1984.)
_____. "The Bovender Genealogy." (Unpublished manuscript.)
_____. "The Harding Family." (Unpublished manuscript.)
_____. "The History of the Kelly Family." (Unpublished manuscript.)
_____. "The Poindexter Family." (Unpublished manuscript.)
_____, and Steve Bradford. "The Ancestors and Descendants of William Paul Speas, Sr." (Unpublished manuscript.)
Doub, Olin. "Doub Family History." (Unpublished manuscript.)
Thomasson, Basil Armstrong. "Book of Remembrance." 2 vols. (Typescript by Jean Harris Thomasson.)
Willard, A. A. "The Bond School House Fight." Tom Willard, ed. (Unpublished manuscript.)

Miscellaneous Sources

Jeff Stepp, North Carolina Confederate Burial Locator Project.
The William Harding Family Bible
The Greenberry Patterson Family Bible
The Peter Shermer Family Bible
The Samuel Speer Family Bible
The W. H. A. Speer Family Papers

Index of Names

Adams, John 19
Adams, John Quincy 19
Adams, Margaret 119
Adams, Thomas 87–88, 90, 91
Adams, William 89
Algood (Allgood), Eck 85, 87–88
Algood (Allgood), John W. 18, 108
Algood, Lum 89
Allgood, Harrison (Horace) 79, 87–90, 94
Allred, Dr. 118
Anderson, A. A. 18
Anglon, Betty 18
Anthony, David 32
Apperson, Capt. Thomas V. 49
Apperson, William H. 32
Armfield, R. F. 20, 23, 33, 79–80, 85, 87, 89
Armfield, R. M. 18
Armstrong, James 111
Arnold, F. A. 50
Arnold, William S. 89
Asbury, Bishop Francis 10

Badger, George E. 20
Baity, Harriet Maynard 8, 63
Baity, Pleasant 63
Baker, H. C. 43
Ball, John H. 19
Ball, William H. 115
Beaty, F. A. 50
Beauregard, Gen P. G. T. 99–100
Bell, John 21
Benbow, Dr. Evan 18, 107
Benham, Dr. B. B. 18, 19
Berk, J. W. 19
Billings, Mrs. 99
Bitting, Joseph A. 11, 19, 21, 67, 116
Bitting, Kate 117
Bitting, Mrs. L. P. 113
Blackburn, A. W. 89

Blackburn, Alfred "Teen" 32, 101, 119–120
Blackburn, John Augustus 119
Blackwell, Selinda 23
Blewbaker, Elexander *see* Brewbaker, Alexander
Bohannon, Col. Caleb 21, 71
Bohannon, Neil 18, 19, 33
Bohannon, Sgt. Simon 47
Bohanon, S. H. 67
Booe, William H. 50
Boone, Daniel 8
Boone, Squire 8
Bovender, Andrew Jackson 42
Bovender, Green 42
Bovender, John 89
Bracken, Thomas 50
Brandon, Joseph 50
Brandon, W. H. 18
Brannon, William H. 108
Breckenridge, John C. 21
Brewbaker, Alexander 75–76
Brewbaker, Ruth Harding 114
Brindle, James Free 33
Brown, B. R. 109
Brown, Cam 42
Brown, Eli 52
Brown, Enoch 87–88, 90, 94–95
Brown, Hugh 89
Brown, J. C. 18, 43
Brown, Jonathan 52
Brown, Brig. Gen. Simeon 99
Brown, William G. 15
Brumfield, Lewis 88
Bryan, Morgan 8
Bryant, William F. 119
Bryant, William Riley 110
Buchanan, James 20
Buchanan, Sgt. 46
Bullock, Lt. W. 94
Burrus, Elizabeth Reece 12, 15, 16
Burrus, George W. 111

Carington, Sarah J. 18
Carson, Lucy 120
Carter, William C. 18
Casstevens, Caren J. 31
Casstevens, Tim 46
Casstevens, William Evan 109
Cast, Sgt. 46
Caudle, Annie 90
Caudle, Early 90
Caudle, Martin 18
Chamberlain, Elizabeth 65, 113
Chamberlain, L. L. 65, 95, 113
Chapman, Mary 76
Chin, Elisha 17
Choplin, John Wesley 105
Choplin, Joseph 43
Choplin, L. 32
Choplin, Robert 43
Choplin, Sidney 18
Choplin brothers 29
Choplin family 7
Clark, Capt. 53
Clay, Henry 19
Clingman, Henry P. 20
Clingman, J. P. 21
Clingman, Jane 35, 65
Clingman, John Jarratt 100
Clingman, Dr. John Patillo 100
Clingman, Brig. Gen. Thomas L. 20, 33, 35, 48, 102, 114–115
Cloer, W. F. 113
Cockerham, D. S. 18
Colvard, J. S. 72
Conelly, Fannie 30
Conelly, Mary Lilly 30
Connally, Lt. Col. John Kerr 33, 47–48, 115–116
Conrad, Capt. 51
Conrad, Elizabeth Ann 115
Conrad, James Dallas 66
Conrad, John Joseph 62
Conrad, John Thomas 32, 36–37, 43, 54, 62, 66, 116
Conrad, Miss E. S. 30
Conrad, Sarah Kinbrough 116
Conrad, Sidney Francis 16, 51, 120
Conrad, Stephen 106
Conrad, William A. 49
Conrad, William Alexander 73
Conrad family 11, 16
Cook, C. L. 18
Cook, Capt. 67
Cook, Gerald Wilson 86
Cook, Thomas J. 32
Cornelius, John H. 32
Cornelius, L. M. 19
Cornelius, Lee 43
Cowles, Col. A. C. 71, 72, 77, 89, 108

Cowles, Andrew C. 19
Cowles, Calvin 107
Cowles, H. C. 89
Cowles, Josiah 67
Cowles, Miles M. 18
Cozzens, B. S. 72
Craig, Burton 23
Cranfill, Dr. M. L. 18, 79, 94
Creson, Abraham 10
Creson, S. D. 43, 72
Critchfield, Richard 19
Crofts, Daniel W. 29
Crumel, Mary M. 18
Cynn, Cope 50

Dalton, Sarah Byrd 17
Daniel, James W. H. S. 32
Daniels, Mrs. Robert 31
Danner, G. M. 43
Danner, J. G. 46
Davis, Alvis Tobias 38
Davis, Horace C. 19
Davis, Isaac 15
Davis, President Jefferson 99, 113
Davis, Lucy 112
Davis, Martin 112
Davis, Mary E. 18
Deafled, David Lenard 32
Dickens, W. A. 19
Dinkins, Pvt. Thomas 44
Dobbins, Jacob 86
Dobbins, Jesse 28, 65, 75, 77, 86–89, 107, 117–118
Dobbins, Sarah Catherine 113, 118
Dobbins, William 65, 75, 87
Dobbins, William T. 77, 90
Dobson, Joseph 18, 79, 89
Dodge, James M. 18
Douglas, Anderson 87–88, 90, 93, 112
Douglas, John "Jackson," Jr. 87–88, 90, 93
Douglas, Sanford 90
Douglas, Stephen A. 21
Dozier, N. B. 19
Dozier, N. C. 47

Eddleman, Frank "Teeter" 76
Eddleman, Horace 53
Eddleman, Prather 76
Eddleman, Samuel 76
Eddleman, Tom 76
Edwards, Arlene 89
Ellis, John W. 21
Evans, Peter G. 50

Farrington, M. F. 65, 94
Featherstone, Brig. Gen. 99

INDEX OF NAMES

Felts, Harrison 108
Felts, Wiley 18
Fleming, J. C. 89
Flinn, J. F. 72
Folger, R. S. 35
Folk, John M. 18
Foote, Henry 17
Forbush, George 10
Foster, Jennie Bryant 110
Foster, Mary Lou Howell 76
Friddle, Peter 18

Gabard, Homer 90
Gabard, Murfe 89
Gabard, Nancy Melinda 114
Gabard, 1st Lt. Richmond Murphy 86, 89
Gabard, William 45
Galoway, Maj. John M. 50
Gee, John 113
Gentry, A. D. 89
Gillem, Brig. Gen. Alvan C. 98
Gilmer, Maj. J. C. 77
Glen, Jeremiah 17
Glen, Louise M. 30, 31
Glen, Mary Elizabeth 30
Glenn, Dudley 32
Glenn, Millie 106
Glenn, Thomas 117
Glenn, Tyre 11, 111, 117
Glenn family 16
Gough, John E. 111
Gough, Lydia 119
Graham, James 20
Graham, William A. 20
Grant, U. S. 65
Gray, Joe 35
Gray, Joseph 17
Gray, Laura 35
Gray, Lou 35
Green, Richard G. 18
Green, Solomon 75
Griffin, Theodore 18
Groce, Henry 77
Gwyn, Richard 63, 111

Haire, Abner S. 43
Haire, Ellan P. 43
Hall, D. C. 46
Hall, L. W. 72
Ham, Col. 88
Hamilton, Alexander 19
Hamlin, Lucy 35
Hampton, E. B. 19
Hampton, H. C. 18
Hampton, J. A. 108
Hampton, J. M. 19

Hampton, John 18
Harbin, Maj. A. A. 78–79
Harding, Betty 47
Harding, Greenberry 29, 100
Harding, Obedience Hutchens 14
Harding, Ruth 16
Harding, Samuel Speer 29, 48, 49, 66
Harding, Thomas R. 114
Harding, William 14, 17, 66, 100
Harding family 16
Harris, Peter Lomax 32
Harrison, John 80
Harvill, John 76
Hauser, Edwin 29
Hauser, John 29
Hauser, John Henry 113, 119
Hauser, T. C. 17, 19, 21, 67, 111, 113
Haynes, Alfred M. 31
Haynes, Elizabeth I. 117
Haynes, J. S. 89
Haynes, Thomas 109
Head, A. E. 43
Headspeth (Hudspeth) 62
Hicks, T. R. 43
Hill, A. P. 43
Hinshaw, Robert 90
Hinshaw, Ruby F. 89, 90
Hinshaw, Solomon 85, 87–88
Hinshaw, Will 89
Hobson, Fred C. 110
Hobson, Stephen 19
Hobson, W. H. 50
Hodges, J. D. 50
Hoke, Gen. J. F. 98
Holcomb, Bloom 48
Holcomb, Calvin M. 53
Holcomb, G. A. 111
Holcomb, George 18, 20
Holcomb, J. L. 51
Holcomb, John D. 108
Holcomb, John G. 46
Holcomb, Jones 46
Holcomb, Thomas Franklin 49
Holcomb brothers 29
Holden, Gov. William W. 53, 107
Holder, John C. 18
Holt, Nancy Reece 52
Hooker, General 44
Hoots, J. A. 112
Horn, Nicholas 111
Howell, N. G. 18
Howell, Sarah Ann Hicks 115
Howell, Thomas 15
Howell, Thomas B. 115
Hughes, John 15
Hunt, Dr. Leander G. 109
Hunt, Col. N. G. 71, 79–80
Hurt, Dicy Ann 114

Hutchens, R. H. 43
Hutchens, Robert E. 87–88, 91

Jackson, Pres. Andrew 19
Jackson, Gen. Thomas J. 44
James, J. H. 112
Jarratt, Isaac 67, 78, 89, 108, 113
Jarvis, J. S. 108
Jester, Lt. 72
Johnson, Alexander 94
Johnson, Alvia H. 18
Johnson, J. M. 19
Johnson, Joseph W. 18
Johnson, Thomas 95
Johnson, Thomas Streeter 32
Johnson, Wiley W. 18
Johnston, Gen. Joseph E. 28, 101–102
Jones, A. S. 108
Jones, C. Hilton 86
Jones, Henry 50
Jones, J. J. 19
Jones, James Monroe 31
Joyce, Lt. Col. William A. 18, 20, 73, 87, 89

Kelly, Effie M. 114
Kelly, John C. 18
Kelly, John O. 32
Kelly, L. D. 18
Kelly, Leonard 86
Kelly, Thomas 32
Kelly, W. D. 18
Kelly, William D. 32
Kenedy, The Rev. Mr. 37
Kerns, J. F. 15
Kerr, John 50
Kimbro, George M. D. 18
Kinyoun, Dr. John H. 16, 18, 32, 33, 37, 62–63, 115
Kinyoung, Letitia 63
Kirk, Col. George W. 94
Kittle, Coston 43

Lakey, Ellis 50
Lakey, Ray 75
Leach, Gen. 22
Lee, Jesse 10
Lee, Gen. Robert E. 7, 33, 49, 54, 99, 102, 105
Lester, Lt. 72
Leventhorp, Gen. Collett 80
Liles, Maj. E. R. 74
Lincoln, President Abraham 27, 102
Lindsay, A. A. 95
Lindsay, Thomas W. 89
Lineberry, Lt. O. A. 72
Livermore, Silas 15

Logan, Martha Doub 65
Long, Frederick 36
Long, Isaac, Sr. 89
Long, Nathan 17
Long, T. 21
Long, Thomas 18
Long, W. W. 21, 89
Long, William 18
Lynch, Larkin 19, 114

McClellan, Gen. George B. 97
Mackie, Benjamin 75
Mackie, Jesse 75
Mackie, Robert 64, 75
McLean, Maj. J. R. 78–79, 94–95
McLean, Wilmer 54
McLeod, Dorothy Shugart 117
McRae, Capt. D. G. 77
Madison, Bertie 100–101
Madison, Charles Andrew 100
Madison, John 101
Madison, William Braxton 19, 100
Mahathey, Findley 77
Mangum, Willie P. 20
Marler, J. G. 108
Marler, John 63
Marler, S. F. 72
Martin, Pvt. Alfred W. 52
Martin, D. A. 111
Martin, James A. 18, 108
Martin, John 13
Martin, John M. 65, 75, 94
Martin, Nancy Elizabeth P. 14
Martin, R. 111
Martin, Reps 14
Martin, T. S. 19, 21
Martin, William 111
Mason, Milas 44–45
Matthews, Shirley Glenn 111
May, Alfred 34, 40
May, Stanley Samuel 114
Melton, Zacharia 51
Miller, Henry 50
Miller, Col. John 99
Miller, P. A. 111
Minesh, George W. 53
Minish, T. R. 6
Minor, Henry 50
Mires, M. C. 18
Mock, John A. 18
Morehead, John M. 20
Murphy, Abe 42
Murrah, Milton 72
Myers, Barnet C. 61
Myers, J. M. 19
Myers, Windford 18

Index of Names

Nance, J. W. 18
Naylor, Joseph L. R. 18
Nicholson, Claude 8
Nicholson, J. G. 18
Nicholson, Moses P. 65
Nicks, George 18, 108
Norman, John 62
Norman, Wm. 72

Palmer, Col. 98
Parks, Dempsey 38
Parks, Ebenezer 38
Parks, Nancy 38
Patterson, R. L. 32
Patterson, W. W. 107–109
Pearson, Richmond, Chief Justice 16, 18, 20, 78, 88
Pendry, Roby 49
Perry, Henry 110
Phillips, B. A. 72
Phillips, Benjamin A. 114
Phillips, R. S. 40
Phillips, Thomas J. 101
Phillips, Dr. William M. 99, 101
Phillips boy 76
Pilcher, Wiley 49
Poindexter, Charlotte M. Pettitt 66
Poindexter, Denson A. 15
Poindexter, Isaac Columbus 43, 44, 47
Poindexter, J. H. 43
Poindexter, R. C. 19, 111
Poindexter, Richard 109
Poindexter, Robert Alexander 66
Poindexter, Thomas C. M. 66
Poindexter, William George 66
Poindexter family 11
Poplin, George C. 31
Potts, Mary E. 18
Puryear, Richard C. 23, 61
Puryear family 1, 16

Reece, Catherine Shugart 98
Reece, Deck 86
Reece, E. H. 46
Reece, Edna Bray 6
Reece, Elizabeth Crutchfield 12
Reed (Yadkin County jail prisoner) 79
Reedy (Reed), James 94
Reeves, William H. 111
Reynolds, J. G. 47
Reynolds, Will 117
Reynolds, William 89
Robertson, Irma Matthews 32, 63, 64, 66, 106, 110
Roby, Elen 18
Roby, Wesley A. 15

Roby, William A. 67
Roughton, E. C. 18, 89, 108
Royall, Isaac 66
Russell, Charles 18
Rutledge, William E., Jr. 6, 88
Rutledge, William W. 31

Salmon, J. F. 18
Schofield, Gen. J. M. 97, 102, 107
Scott, Thomas G. 49
Seiders, Victor 31
Seiders, Wanda Hauser 31
Shepherd, G. W. 72
Sherman, Gen. William T. 28, 101
Shipwash, G. W. 72
Shore, Anderson 76
Shore, "Bridge" Dave 76
Shore, Frederick 76
Shore, Henry 119
Shore, James Henry 116
Shore, John Henry 51
Shore, Wiley F. 107
Shores, David 108
Shugart, Alexander 111
Shugart, Isaac 111
Shugart, James 111
Shugart, James Alexander 102
Shugart, Lafayette Dee 72, 85
Smith, Maj. Gen. E. Kirby 78
Spaugh, E. 108
Speer, Annice 16
Speer, Aquilla 67, 108, 109
Speer, Capt. 67
Speer, Elizabeth Ashby 106, 110
Speer, S. T. 108
Speer, W. A. 72
Speer, Col. William H. Asbury 33, 35, 37, 40, 43, 45, 48–51, 53, 78, 106
Speer family 16
Spicer, Joshua 32
Spillman, William 107
Sprinkle, Hugh 87–88, 90, 93
Sprinkle, John T. 43
Stallings, Henry 61
Starling, Henry 31
Steelman, Alexander 37
Steelman, Joshua 61
Stimpson, Nancy 32
Stoneman, Maj. Gen. George H. 97
Stonemen's men 97–101
Stowe, Lt. Col. G. C. 98
Swaim, David L. 20
Swaim, L. D. 15
Swiney, Anderson E. 32

Tacket, John 43
Tackett, James W. 72

Tapscott, H. C. 17
Taylor, John 18
Thomasson (Thompson), A. H. 19, 108
Thomasson, Basil Armstrong 15
Thomson, Andrew 15
Tiddy, Richard N. 32
Todd, David 50
Tomlin, A. N. 19
Transou, E. L. 112
Transou, Edwin Lafayette 105
Transou, Ephraim 113
Transou, Flora Ann 113
Trimble, Gen. 47
Trotter, William R. 29
Tucker, B. F. 65
Tulbert, Jesse 18
Tulbert, Thomas L. 108
Tyson, The Rev. A. A. 47

Vance, Gov. Zebulon B. 20, 53, 65, 73, 85, 87
Van Eaton, W. L. 18
Vanhoy, Hobert 64
Vanhoy, Nancy 66
Vestal, Bond 61
Vestal, Daniel 86
Vestal, Isaac 108
Vestal, J. N. 108
Vestal, John 61
Vestal, N. H. 61
Vestal, Romulus 94
Vestal, Sandy 65, 94

Wagoner, Jonathan 91
Wall, J. W. 37, 40
Walton, William O. 114
Ward, Benjamin Franklin 38
Warden, I. A. 94
Warden, R. W. 77
Welch, Samuel C. 18
Welfare, Peter W. 19
West, Annie 113
West, James 85–89, 113

Whitaker, Lorenzo Dow 45, 112–113, 119
White, William 114
White, William L. 117
Willard, A. A. 88
Willard, Allen 90
Willard, Benjamin 87–88, 90
Willard, Clarisy 53
Willard, Elkanah 90, 94–95
Willard, Jonathan 52
Willard, Kesiah 52
Willard, Leander 87–88, 90
Willard, Milton F. 52–53, 80, 90
Willard, Nancy 53, 90
Willard, Roscoe 90
Willard, Will R. 90
Willard, William 79, 87–88, 90
Williams, Benjamin 19, 85
Williams, Billy 86
Williams, Franklin 64
Williams, J., Sr. 108
Williams, J. A. 67
Williams, Jesse Frankin 39
Williams, John 39
Williams, John Macintosh 85–89
Williams, Joseph 17, 31
Williams, Lewis A. 49
Williams, Nicholas 109
Williams, Sarah Luzania P. 64
Williams, W. S. 19
Williams, William Sanford 86
Williams family 16
Wilson, Dr. H. C. 18, 21, 23
Wilson, Dr. Henry Clinton 111
Wilson, Reuben E. 33, 39, 113
Wilson, William Henry 65
Womack, Allen 43
Woodhouse, W. L. 112
Woodruff, R. W. 18
Wooten, James Caswell 87–88, 90
Wright, Wilburn 95

York, Lewis 18

www.ingramcontent.com/pod-product-compliance
Lightning Source LLC
Chambersburg PA
CBHW081541300426
44116CB00015B/2711